Central Banking and Monetary Policy in the G20

Paradigms and Challenges

Edited by
İrfan Kalaycı
İnönü University, Malatya, Turkey

Series in Economics
Vernon Press

www.vernonpress.com

In the Americas:
Vernon Press
1000 N West Street, Suite 1200,
Wilmington, Delaware 19801
United States

In the rest of the world:
Vernon Press
C/Sancti Espiritu 17,
Malaga, 29006
Spain

Series in Economics

Library of Congress Control Number: 2024944678

ISBN: 979-8-8819-0082-3

Cover design by Vernon Press with elements by macrovector on Freepik.

Contents

Lists of Tables and Figures

Tables

Figures

Abbreviations

A

AI: artificial intelligence
ALF: alternative liquidity facility
API: application programming interface
APP: asset purchase program
AQR: asset quality review
ARDL: autoregressive distributed lag
ARFIMA: autoregressive fractional integrated moving average
ARMs: adjustable-rate mortgages
ARRA: American Recovery and Reinvestment Act

B

BAT: Banks Association of Turkey
BCB: Banco Central do Brasil
BCRA: Banco Central de la República Argentina
BdF: Banque de France
BdI: Banca d'Italia
BdM: Banco de Mexico
BI: Bank Indonesia
BİST: Borsa Istanbul (İstanbul Stock Market)
BoE: Bank of England
BoJ: Bank of Japan
BoC: Bank of Canada
BoR: Bank of Russia
BRICS: Brazil, Russia, India, China, South Africa
BRL: Brazilian Real
BRSA: Banking Regulation and Supervision Agency
BU: banking union

C

CAD: Canadian Dollar
CADF: *cross-sectional* augmented Dickey Fuller
CBA: Central Bank of Argentina
CBDC: central bank digital currency
CBs: central banks
CBRT: Central Bank of the Republic of Turkey
CCS: carbon capture and storage; cross-currency swaps
CDC: central deposit certificates
CDOs: collateralized debt obligations
CDS: credit default swap
CEPA: closer economic partnership arrangement
CLS: continuous linked settlement
CMB: Capital Markets Board (of Turkey)
CNY: Chinese Yuan (Renminbi)
CRFPI: climate-related financial policy index
CRST: climate-related stress testing
CSPP: corporate sector purchase program

D

DBB: Deutsche Bundesbank
DCR: differentiated capital requirements
DLT: distributed ledger technology

E

EAPs: economic adjustment programs
EBU: European Banking Union
EC: European Commission
ECB: European Central Bank
EDIS: European deposit insurance scheme
EDS: external debt stock
EEC: European Economic Community
EFSF: European Financial Stability Facility
ELA: emergency liquidity assistance
EMDCs: emerging markets and developing countries
EMI: European Monetary Institute
EMU: European Economic and Monetary Union; European Monetary Union
EMS: European monetary system
EONIA: European overnight interest average
ERM: Exchange rate mechanism
ESCB: European system of central banks
ESG: environmental, social and governance
ESM: European stability mechanism
ETFs: exchange-traded funds
EU: European Union
EVs: electric vehicles

F

FBF: Fédération bancaire Francaise
FDI: foreign direct investment
FED: Federal Reserve Bank
FGDR: Fichiers des guichets domiciliataires
FII: Foreign institutional investor
FIT: Financial instability theory
Fintech: financial technology
FOMC: Federal Open Market Committee
FSC: Financial Stability Committee
FSDC: financial stability and development committee
FX: foreign exchange (forex)

G

G7: group of seven
G20: group of twenty
GAR: green asset ratio
GBP: Great Britain Pound
GDP: gross domestic product
GFC: global financial crisis
GFC: Greek financial crisis
G-M-G: goods-money-goods
GNP: gross national product

H

HE: Hanguk Eunhaeng (S. Korean Central bank)
HICP: harmonized index of consumer prices
HKMA: Hong Kong Monetary Authority
HQLA: high-quality liquid assets

I

IBF: Islamic banking and finance
ICR: internal credit rating
IES: Islamic economic system
IISD: International Institute for Sustainable Development
IME: Islamic monetary economics
IMF: International Monetary fund
INR: national currency Rupee

INSPIRE: international network for sustainable financial policy insights, research and exchange
IPBES: intergovernmental science-policy platform on biodiversity and ecosystem services
IPCC: intergovernmental panel on climate change
IPE: international political economy
IPE: Islamic political economy
IRS: interest rate swap
ITL: Italian lira

J

JPY: Japanese Yen

K

KIC: Korea investment corporation
KYC - know your competitor

L

LEED: leadership in energy and environmental design
LER: large exposure restrictions
LPP: loan pledged program
LPR: loan prime rate
LTI: loan-to-income
LTROs: long-term refinancing operations
LTV: loan-to-value

M

m: million
MB: monetary board
MLF: medium-term lending facility
MOC: market operation committee
MoU: memoranda of understanding
MPSC: monetary policy sub-committee
MROs: Main Refinancing Operations

N

NAFTA: North America Free Trade Agreement
NCBs: national central banks
NDFs: non-deliverable forwards
NDOs: non-deliverable options
NFCs: US national finance centres
NFT: non-fungible token
NGFS: network for greening the financial system - Network for greening the finance system
NICs: newly industrialized countries

O

ODI: outbound direct investment
OECD: Organisation for Economic Co-Operation and Development
OII: overseas institutional investor
OMOs: open market operations
OMT: outright monetary transactions

P

PBoC: People's Bank of China
PLS: profit and loss sharing
PSI: private sector involvement
PSL: pledged supplementary lending
PSPP: public sector purchase program

Q

QDII: qualified domestic institutional investor
QE: quant easing

R

R&D: research and development
RBA: Reserve Bank of Australia
RBoE-ALFL): Bank of England Alternative Liquidity Facility Ltd.
RBoI: Reserve Bank of India
REITs: real estate investment trusts
RMB: Renminbi
RQFII: RMB qualified foreign institutional investor
RRR: required reserve ratio
RUB: Russian Ruble

S

SAMA: Saudi Arabian Monetary Authority
SAFE: state administration of foreign exchange
SAR: Saudi riyal
SARB: South African Reserve Bank
SBFN: sustainable banking and finance network
SDR: special drawing right
SDDS: special data dissemination standard
SFTZ: Shanghai free trade zone
SIC: Singapore investment corporation
SLF: standing lending facility
SMP: securities market program
SNB: Swiss National Bank
SRF: single resolution fund
SRM: single resolution mechanism
SSCBs: standing swap line central banks
SSM: single supervision mechanism

T

TARP: Troubled Asset Relief program
TCFD: task force on climate-related financial disclosures
TCFR: TCF risks
TCMB: Türkiye Cumhuriyet Merkez Bankası
TEU: treaty on EU
TFEU: treaty on the functioning of the EU
TMLF: targeted MLF
TN: trillion
TPP: third-party service provider
TRY (TL): Turkish Lira

U

UK: United Kingdom
UN: United Nations
US(A): United States (of America)
USD: US Dollar

Acknowledgements and Remembrance

The editor of this scientific and professional book titled *Central Banking and Monetary Policy in the G20: Paradigms and Challenges* would like to thank all of the chapter authors for their high academic contribution. The great interest and support that the book's publisher, Vernon Press, showed to this modest book project from beginning to end will never be forgotten. The constructive and moderate evaluations of the referee of the publishing house, which is independent of us, who carefully reviewed the book, have been found extremely valuable. Also, the Editor would specially thank John Marangos for helping to find the most suitable author for the Preface, Jeremy Kwork for seriously reviewing Chapter 1 and instilling good ideas in its author, and, of course, Esra Güler for standardizing all the footnotes and bibliographies.

There is no need to state that the language, expression, citation, plagiarism, etc., responsibilities of each chapter contained herein belong to the authors of that chapter. As authors, editor and publisher, we hope that the Book will be useful to all readers and inspire economics researchers interested in monetary-banking issues.

Please allow me to share with you a memory of mass suffering: While I was continuing the preparations for this book, we experienced a devastating twin earthquakes of 7.7 magnitude on February 6, 2023, in the Turkey's Eastern and Southern regions, including Malatya, the city where I live. Our social psychology and working lives have been turned upside down. Our national universities had to switch to online education for another semester after the global Covid-19 crisis. If the publication process of our book was delayed, it was partly because of this. I consider it my duty to commemorate nearly sixty thousand of my citizens who lost their lives in this "disaster of the century" that badly affected 11 of our cities at the same time, and to thank the aid provided at home and abroad.

Editor

İrfan Kalaycı

(December 2023 – June 2024)

About Contributors

Editor / Author

İrfan Kalaycı: Bachelor's degree in economics from Çukurova University; master's and Ph.D. degrees from İnönü University; author of books on the economies of the European Union and Turkey; special interests in global financial crises, monetary economics and agricultural bioeconomy; winner of more than twenty research awards across the country; currently a professor of economics at İnönü University, Malatya, Turkey.

Preface

Louis- Philippe Rochon: Full Professor, Laurentian University, Canada; Editor-in-Chief, Review of Political Economy; founder of the *Review of Keynesian Economics*; Editor, Elgar Series on Central Banking and Monetary Policy; a visiting scholar or professor in Australia, Brazil, France, Italy, Mexico, Poland, South Africa, China, Japan, and the United States.

Authors of Chapters

Aatos Hallipelto: Master's degree in economics from Helsinki School of Economics; investment and finance director in Turku and Helsinki; CEO and partner of FINLIT Partners Oy; EU Erasmus+ supported financial literacy project developer; author of non-fiction books.

Angeliki Nestoroudi: Master in politics and economics of contemporary Eastern and South- Eastern Europe and Master in accounting and finance at the University of Macedonia; Bachelor's degree in economics from the University of Macedonia.

Aukje van Loon: Bachelor's degree in Communication Science (Robert Gordon University Aberdeen), master's degree in European Culture and Economy and Ph.D. in Social Sciences (both Ruhr University Bochum, Germany).

Birol Görmez: Ph.D. in economics, cyber security trainee in Germany; career in banking sector in İstanbul.

Cumhur C. Küçüközmen: Ph.D. in finance from the University of Exeter, UK; full professor of Trade and Finance, Faculty of Business at Izmir University of Economics, Turkey.

Esra Güler: Bachelor's, master's and Ph.D. degrees in economic development and international economics at Uludağ University, Bursa; assistant professor at Uludağ University, Inegol Faculty of Business and Administration.

Fatih Yeter: Bachelor's degree from Cumhuriyet University; master's and Ph.D. degrees from Tokat Gaziosmanpaşa University; working in macroeconomics, monetary economics, and sustainable development as a lecturer at Tokat Gaziosmanpaşa University.

Gökhan Karhan: Graduated from theMathematics Teaching at Cumhuriyet University; Ph.D degree in economics at İnönü University; associate professor in the field of macroeconomics; working in the field of applied economics.

Halil Seyidoğlu: Graduated from Ankara University, Faculty of Political Sciences, department of international relations; PhD in economics at the Faculty of Political Sciences; M.A. in economics at Michigan State University; lectures and seminars at the University of Minnesota; Turkish textbooks copyright prizes by the Turkish Academy of Sciences.

Hatice Özkurt: Lecturer in the foreign trade department at Istanbul University-Cerrahpaşa Vocational School of Social Sciences; master's degree in Business Administration from Okun University.

Hazik Mohamed: Ph.D., Singapore; consultant on project management and operational leadership roles. author of "Belief and Rule Compliance" (Elsevier 2018) on behavioural economics and "Blockchain, Fintech and Islamic Finance" (De|G Press 2019)

H. Mahir Fisunoğlu: Emeritus professor of economics from Cukurova University, Adana; received his degrees from Istanbul University in Istanbul, Hacettepe University in Ankara, Turkey and the University of Michigan in the U.S.A.

İlhan Eroğlu: Bachelor's and master's degrees from Bursa Uludağ University, PhD in economics from Marmara University, İstanbul; professor of economics at Gaziosmanpaşa University; working on economic policies, central banking, crisis economics, inflation, and monetary policy.

Ismail Özsoy: Professor of economics. İstanbul, Turkey; Advisory Board Member, EFC Ethical Funding Co., CA. The main research topics are interest theories, Soviet history, Islamic finance and economics and interest-free banking.

Jeremy Kwok: A doctoral researcher at the University of Westminster, researcher and fellow of the Royal Society for the Encouragement of Arts, Manufactures and Commerce (RSA), United Kingdom; author of the book "Macroeconometric Models for Portfolio Management" published by Vernon Press.

John Marangos: Professor of Comparative Economic Systems at the Department of Balkan, Slavic, and Oriental Studies at the University of Macedonia, Greece; visiting professor of economics at the University of Missouri, Kansas City.

M. Ali Seyidoğlu: Bachelor's degree in Public Administration and PhD in Economics from İnönü University; professional financial advisor.

Mehmet Kaya: Bachelor's degree in business engineering from Istanbul Technical University. Professor of Economics at Dicle University Faculty of Economics and Administration, Diyarbakır, Türkiye.

Metin D. Akyüz: Degrees in economics from Hacettepe and Çukurova Universities, consultant in international private companies in the USA and Turkey, retired.

Muhammad Zulkifly: Ph.D. in Islamic finance at Durham University, UK; a financial supervisor at the Central Bank of Malaysia; teacher of undergraduate courses in econometrics, macroeconomics, and Microeconomics; President of the Durham University Islamic Society.

Mücahit Çayın: Bachelor's and Ph.D. degrees from Atatürk University, Erzurum; started as a research assistant in the Department of Economics at Batman University, working at the same university, Batman, Turkey.

Nalan Kangal: Bachelor's and master's degrees from Selçuk University and PhD in economics from Gaziosmanpaşa University; working at Almus Vocational School, Tokat, Turkey; working in the fields of economic policy, inflation, and monetary policy.

Necati Çoban: Bachelor's degree from Anadolu University; master's and Ph.D degrees from Tokat Gaziosmanpaşa University received the title of associate professor, working in the fields of welfare economics, institutional economics, and silver economy.

Nikos Astroulakis: Ph.D. in Economics from the University of Crete; Economist at the Tax and Customs Academy of the Greek Independent Authority for Public Revenues (IAPR); Adjunct Professor at the Hellenic Open University, Greece.

Paraskevi Kyrilla: Bachelor's degree in Balkan, Slavic & Oriental Studies with a specialization in Business Economics from the University of Macedonia, in Thessaloniki; staff in the finance sector at a cloud company based in Scotland-UK.

Sevgi Ineci: Researcher and Assoc. Professor at Galatasaray University in İstanbul; recent publications focus on the European Banking Union, economic reforms, sustainable development and agriculture.

Themis Anthrakidis: PhD in Economics from the University of Macedonia, Thessaloniki; master's degree in economics from Amsterdam University; special adviser in economy and administration for the Mayor of the Municipality of Pilea-Hortiatis in Panorama, Thessaloniki, Greece.

Preface

Louis-Philippe Rochon

Laurentian University, Canada

The Future of Central Banking and Monetary Policy in a Post-Pandemic World

Central banks have come under considerable scrutiny and criticism post-pandemic. Indeed, with inflation rising to levels not seen in four decades, central banks fell back on the only idea they knew: using interest rates to bring inflation back down to the 2% target, despite the fact there is no empirical support for this target. Indeed, as Benjamin Friedman, from Harvard University – a long-time critic of inflation targeting – once wrote, if central banks focus on an inflation target, "concern for real outcomes will atrophy, or even disappear from policy makers' consideration altogether".[1] More recently, he sharpened his criticism, stating, "there is the arbitrariness surrounding the current 2 percent target. In retrospect, the paucity of serious empirical research underlying the identification of the 2 percent norm, now quite some time back is a professional embarrassment".[2] All this, of course, seems to be of no concern to central bankers.

And so far, central bank policy has been one of the fastest, boldest monetary austerity policies today. Indeed, interest rates have risen the fastest and the highest in decades relative to other inflationary periods – at levels not seen in twenty years. So, in every way, the post-pandemic era is completely different than anything in the last 40 years, during which time a generation of households got accustomed to low levels of both inflation and interest rates, the latter set at near zero.

While output, at least in the United States, does not seem to be affected by the aggressive nature of monetary austerity – indeed growing at 4.9% – it is perhaps a simple question of time before the US economy slows down. Such high growth rates, not seen again in decades, may prove unsustainable.

By the central banks' own admission, the transmission mechanism of these changes in interest rates should be felt some 18 months after the first increase.

---

1 Benjamin M. Friedman, "Why the Federal Reserve Should not Adopt Inflation Targeting", *International Finance* 7, 1 (2004): 135.

2 Benjamin M. Friedman, "The Future of Central Banking," in *The Future of Central Banking: Festschrift in Honour of Vítor Constâncio*, (European Central Bank, 2018), 187.

Since March 2022 until now, there have been eleven increases in the US, and being at the 18-month mark now (November, 2023), we may still yet start feeling the consequences of monetary policy. Indeed, much research shows that while aggregate demand may not react to incremental changes in interest rates, it will eventually react to the cumulative effect of, say, eleven increases. So, the worst, as they say, may still be yet to come.

All of this, of course, must not be surprising. After all, monetary austerity is embedded in New Consensus models by relying precisely on central banks' ability to slow economic activity in the Holy Grail pursuit of a soft landing. In my opening, however, soft landings are virtually impossible to attain. Interest rates are a blunt instrument and it is usually always the same story: too much, too late. Indeed, in his analysis of monetary austerity, David MacDonald concludes that when trying to bring down inflation from such heights, central banks rarely succeed in engineering soft landings.[3]

The story of monetary austerity, however, is flawed from the very start. Underlying the transmission mechanism are a few simple ideas. First, inflation is a monetary phenomenon – or monetary policy phenomenon – and only interest rates can cure it. For this reason, as Abraham Maslow –of the famous Maslow pyramid of needs – has said, "If the only tool you have is a hammer, you tend to see every problem as a nail." In this context, central banks see inflation as being demand-led, and while they do recognize oil and bottlenecks as having played a role (and some even recognize seller's inflation), their rhetoric is all about deflating economic activity – and creating unemployment in the process. There is no discussion of other possible tools, like fiscal policy, to fight inflation.

But what happens if inflation is not the result of demand forces? Recent studies show that demand accounts for only about 25% of overall *post-pandemic*, inflation,[4] while the rest would be attributed to supply-side considerations. In this case, what, then should be the appropriate role of monetary policy?

Second, the transmission mechanism of monetary policy depends on a well-behaved Phillips curve. But the rising consensus seems to be that the Phillips curve has flattened considerably. If this is the case, monetary policy loses its effectiveness. I recognize that some post-pandemic research indicates that this

---

[3] David MacDonald, "Canada's Fight Against Inflation: Bank of Cada Could Induce a Recession," *Canadian Centre for Policy Alternatives, The Monitor* (2022).

[4] Andrea Cerrato and Giulia Gitti, "Inflation Since COVID: Demand or Supply", VOX CEPR, June 12, 2023. https://cepr.org/voxeu/columns/inflation-covid-demand-or-supply

curve has steepened, so there needs to be more research on this important issue.

The overall conclusion is that there needs to be considerable new research on central banking. We cannot rely on outdated assumptions about what monetary policy is and what it does. Everything is an empirical question, and in light of this, policy needs to reflect current research. In other words, as Keynes reminds us, we need a 'vigilant observation' of the world in which we live.

In light of this, the contributions in this book are timely and appropriate. The authors poke and prod the issue of central banking in a post-pandemic world. We need to expand the scope of research, and we must investigate more venues. What about income and wealth distribution? Or the Environment? How about gender issues?

The study of central banking and monetary policy indeed is not done. Despite the popularity of these so-called New Consensus models, there seems to be a lack of consensus post-pandemic. This book contributes to the valuable analysis that is so much required.

Bibliography

Cerrato, Andrea and Giulia Gitti "Inflation Since COVID: Demand or Supply", VOX CEPR, June 12, 2023. https://cepr.org/voxeu/columns/inflation-covid-demand-or-supply

Friedman, Benjamin M. "Why the Federal Reserve Should Not Adopt Inflation Targeting". *International Finance.* 7 (1) (2004): 129–136.

Friedman, Benjamin M. "The Future of Central Banking". *The Future of Central Banking: Festschrift in Honour of Vítor Constâncio.* European Central Bank. 2018, 187-190.

MacDonald, David. "Canada's Fight Against Inflation: Bank of Canada Could Induce a Recession". Canadian Centre for Policy Alternatives. The Monitor. 2022.

[illegible]

Bibliography

[illegible]

INTRODUCTION

Chapter 1

Central Banking and Monetary Policy in the G20: An Introduction

İrfan Kalaycı

İnönü University, Malatya, Turkey

Abstract

The Group of Twenty (G20) is a political economy formation that brings together the twenty largest economies in the world according to gross national product. Consisting of 19 countries (namely; Argentina, Australia, Brazil, Canada, China, France, Germany, India, Indonesia, Italy, Japan, Republic of Korea, Mexico, Russia, Saudi Arabia, South Africa, Turkey, the United Kingdom and the United States) and the European Union, the G20 largely direct and shape global production, trade and finance. There is a need to know the central banks that are behind such a powerful formation. As such, the strategic role of these banks and the effects of their monetary policy practices cannot be denied. This duo is in a dynamic position of lock and key for each other. In this chapter, each of the twenty central banks and their monetary policies are introduced. Thus, all components of the big picture were tried to be shown together. Many central banks within the G20, such as the Fed and the Bundesbank, are famous for their independence and have the power to challenge (or affect) the global economy. The common feature of all of them is to contribute to the sustainability of price and financial stability despite possible global financial crises. In the conclusion, it is suggested that, as a new paradigm (or an alternative), central banks, which have been very helpful to governments in the execution of orthodoxy stabilization programs, should now fight against the actual cost of living as well as inflation and focus on equitable income distribution in a heterodoxy policy scheme.

Keywords: G20, Central Banks, Monetary Policies, Challenges, Paradigms

***

Theme: Key and Lock

To engage the readers right from the beginning of this chapter, I need to craft a thought-provoking and engaging opening. Considering that goal, I pose the following question: "*Did money give birth to the central bank, or did the central bank give birth to money?*" Through a reverse logic lens, I lean towards the former being more plausible, yet the latter might hold its own validity. This proposition resembles the perplexing yet intriguing puzzle of "*the chicken or the egg,*" which not only captivates but also holds relevance to the theme of our book. Central banking and monetary policy are intertwined concepts that exist in symbiosis. Where central banking thrives, discussions on monetary policy arise, and vice versa. These parallel subjects, rather than being distinct and unrelated, are interconnected. It is this very interplay between central banking and monetary policy that has garnered significant attention from researchers and experts, leading to numerous studies and publications. Therefore, in this chapter, we undertake an examination of this dynamic duo from the perspective of the Group of Twenty (G20), recognizing its importance and relevance.

Apart from the traditional functions of money as a means of exchange, calculation, and savings, its modern function as a challenging economic policy tool since Keynes paved the way for the mutual key-lock relationship and, of course, the interaction between central banking and monetary policy that has existed for a long time.

Money and the central bank are each an invention in themselves. There is a general opinion that the inventors of the first coin were the Lydians, who lived in the Aegean region of Turkey thousands of years ago, and that the first modern central bank originated in England, after Sweden. By a historical coincidence, the homelands of these two inventions, Turkey and England, are in the G20, called the Group of Twenty.[1] Indeed, the first Central bank (otherwise known as a reserve bank or monetary authority) was the Bank of Sweden in 1668, followed by the Bank of England and others in 1694. The basic duties and powers of central banks are to print banknotes and put them on the market, to ensure monetary and price stability, to be the last institution that lends money to banks, to keep the foreign exchange reserves of the state, to provide financial consultancy to the treasury, etc. Due to their many duties and powers, it is not a coincidence that they are often the first institutions to be criticized when an economic crisis occurs due to inflation, deflation or stagflation. These criticisms

[1] Deutsche Bundesbank, "The 'Invention' of the Coin – Who, When, Where and Why?" (September 2023), https://www.bundesbank.de/resource/blob/616754/1ae3f2eaadc1dab9a311d4492ff03388/mL/the-invention-of-the-coin-data.pdf.; Britannica, "A Brief (and Fascinating) History of Money," https://www.britannica.com/story/a-brief-and-fascinating-history-of-money; Sveriges Riskbank, "History," https://www.riksbank.se/en-gb/about-the-riksbank/history/#:~:text=In%201668%2C%20the%20Riksdag%2C%20Sweden's,the%20world's%20oldest %20central%20bank.

begin to be made at the global level when the crisis breaks out in major economies such as the G20.

G20, which includes the largest economies by world gross domestic product (GDP), is an intergovernmental forum consisting of 19 countries (in alphabetical order, Argentina, Australia, Brazil, Canada, China, France, Germany, India, Indonesia, Italy, Japan, Republic of Korea, Mexico, Russia, Saudi Arabia, South Africa, Turkey, the United Kingdom, the United States) and the integration of the European Union. Apart from Spain and the Netherlands, some other countries are also represented in the G20 through the African Union. G20 is a strategic economic group and multilateral platform connecting developed and developing economies. As the leading forum for international economic cooperation, the G20, which has a say in shaping and strengthening the global capitalist architecture and governance on all important international economic issues, has an important role in preserving the current free market ideology and ensuring future global economic growth, prosperity and stability.

G20 members represent approximately 85% of world GDP, more than 75% of international trade and 2/3 of the world's population. G20, which started as a meeting attended by finance ministers and central bank governors in 1999 following the 1997-98 Asian financial crisis, has turned into a summit attended by Heads of State and Government every year and has hosted working groups and organized special events throughout the year with various guest states and international organizations.[2]

G20 economies are composed of half the global production and do not act as a single bloc. The members are already politically and economically divided into various blocs or are representative within those blocs. EU, OECD, NAFTA, and Shanghai Cooperation Organisation (SCO) are the most popular blocs. The common features of the countries in the BRICS, MIST and/or MINT groups,[3] which have recently attracted the intense attention of diplomacy, multinational companies, global capital and the academic world, are that they are partially included in the G20 and have high growth potential within the scope of emerging markets. Although central banks in the G20 are based on the universal principles of monetary policy, they generally use monetary instruments at the national or local level in practice. At first glance, this may suggest that each country's central bank is autonomous vis-à-vis another, but it does not change the fact that they interact when it comes to controlling international capital movements. For example, when the US Federal Reserve Bank (Fed) takes a step towards monetary tightening or increasing interest rates to reduce its domestic

---

[2] G20 Members, (September 2023), https://www.g20.org/en/about-g20/#members.

[3] *BRICS:* Brazil, Russia, India, China, S. Africa. *MIST:* Mexico, Indonesia, S. Korea, Turkey. *MINT:* Mexico, Indonesia, Nigeria and Turkey.

inflation, other G20 central banks may take a new step and take a position against this step. A monetary step taken by the European Central Bank (ECB) or the Bank of Japan (BoJ) may also provoke the Fed to take a new position, and this interaction. The national currencies of some G20 economies, like Argentina and Turkey, which experience dollarization and euroization, are quite weak, resulting in their limited influence on the monetary policies of the Fed and the ECB.

Central banks in the G20 use monetary policies following the aims and tools of conventional and modern central banking. Most of these central banks have political, economic and legal independence. Thanks to the independence of goals and means, they fight inflation or deflation more easily and quickly. In addition to protecting the value of money and price stability, they can also have a say with the government on combating global warming, optimal growth, single-digit unemployment and fiscal discipline. This paradigm change, which seems to be in favour of central banks, also reinforces their challenge to global crises. This observation does not change the fact that when a financial crisis breaks out in the G20, especially the USA, Europe, China and Russia, they are the first to unsettle their central banks and become subject to criticism.

It has been observed that not only the central banks and governments but also the economists of countries like Turkey and Argentina, which are both part of the G20 and experiencing high inflation, face uneasiness and criticism regarding their professional reputation. After all, in the eyes of society, the monetary policymaker, the central bank, the political power, the government, and the academic economists who teach the methods of struggle have all been defeated by the inflation they know best. For now, if inflation is still causing pain, it might be because the lock and key were not properly matched or the wrong key was used in the right lock. However, sooner or later, regardless of how high inflation rises, it will eventually fall from its peak. This is similar to how no plane stays in the air indefinitely; even if it is delayed or crashes, it will ultimately land.

Especially since the 1990s, central banks have focused all their attention and efforts on monetary and price stability, and this stability goal has become - in Mishkin's words - a "mantra" (sacred word) for them.[4] However, if central banks, as monetary policy authorities, do not deal with output fluctuations in the context of production and employment, the possibility of being characterized as "*inflation crazy*"[5] - in King's words - becomes stronger. Although central banks

---

[4] Frederic S. Mishkin, *Para Politikası Stratejisi*, çev. Ö. F. Çolak ve A. Zengin (Ankara: Efil Yayınevi, 2014), 78.

[5] Mervyn A. King, "How Should Central Banks Reduce Inflation? - Conceptual Issues," *Economic Review, Federal Reserve Bank of Kansas City* 81, no. Q IV (1996): 25-52, https://www.kansascityfed.org/Jackson %20 Hole/documents/6767/King_JH96.PDF.

would be relieved to leave the forecasts and measures regarding output fluctuations to governments when they resort to a strategy of flexible inflation targeting in a transparent manner, they are concerned with fluctuations in output as well as fluctuations in inflation because central banks are -again in King's words- not inflation crazy.[6] The transparency mentioned here is such a virtue in terms of being a postmodern tool function that it can even remove central banks from being temples of finance behind Mount Qaf.

If today's central banks, with their elite bureaucracies, cannot implement optimal monetary and interest rate policies or achieve inflation stability despite their transparency and open communication strategies, one possible reason could be the "time inconsistency problem" (TIP).[7] TIP, which falls within the scope of the discipline of behavioural economics, means that, in terms of monetary policy, for example, low interest rates that increase economic growth in the short term lead to inflation in the long term. Accordingly, TIP may tie the hands of the central bank, albeit temporarily. In a way, TIP describes the conjuncture in which Turkey, a G20 economy, has been struggling to reduce inflation by insisting on low interest rates in order to maintain high growth for a while in its most current application.

Paradigm changes and challenges may come to the fore for central banks struggling with inflation and/or their derivative problems. In a key-lock context, G20 central banks position themselves according to the conjuncture, the current government and the dominant socioeconomic system, and conduct monetary policy according to New-Keynesian, monetarist or rational-adaptive expectations models. Most CBs are national only and have no mandate to focus on other countries or international markets. They do consider financial stability, but this is often in a national/regional (ECB) context with their policies, which affects the international markets.

Monetary instruments (deposit and loan rates, policy rates, money supply, reserves, bond market operations, liquidity management, emissions, sterilization, exchange rate adjustments, swaps, etc.) may be taken into account, as well as the central bank and monetary policy strategy of any G20 state. Central banks

---

[6] Mervyn A. King, "Changes in UK Monetary Policy: Rules And Discretion in Practice," *Journal of Monetary Economics* 39, 1 (June 1997): 81-97, https://doi.org/10.1016/S0304-3932(97)00009-3

[7] See for TIP: Stefania Albanesi, Varadarajan V. Chari and Lawrence J. Christiano, "How Severe is the Time Inconsistency Problem in Monetary Policy?", NBER Working Paper no. w8139 (February 2001), available at SSRN: https://ssrn.com/abstract=261264; Chengcheng Jia and Jing Cynthia Wu, Average Inflation Targeting: Time Inconsistency and Ambiguous Communication, NBER Working Paper no. 29673 (Jan. 2022, revised May 2023); Stefania Albanesi, Varadarajan V. and Christiano, Lawrence J., "How Severe Is the Time-Inconsistency Problem In Monetary Policy?", *Quarterly Review* 27, no.3 (2003), https://doi.org/10.21034/qr.2732.

are often as concerned, if not more so, about the possibility of deflation or stagflation as they are about inflation. Diagnostic scenarios and treatment prescriptions chase each other. The following projection by Blanchflower and Bryson seems to be a harbinger of the possible stagflation awaiting the G20:

> "Central bankers are raising interest rates on the assumption that wage-push inflation may lead to stagflation. (…) Although unemployment is low, the labour market is not 'tight.' On the contrary, we show that what matters for wage growth are the non-employment rate and the under-employment rate. Both are high and act as brakes on wage growth. By lowering already low levels of consumer confidence, higher interest rates are liable to exacerbate workers' inability to maintain their real wages by reducing labour demand still further. Furthermore, we argue inflationary pressures have been generated by short-term supply side problems, rather than excessive demand in the economy. Under these conditions, just as in the Great Recession,[8] we anticipate deflation in the near future, coupled with rising joblessness and recession." [9]

Independent central banks have great supra-governmental prestige in society when it comes to combating inflation. One of the sources of this is the bias that the central bank can predict inflation better than other economic policy institutions. St. Louis Fed economists Miguel Faria-e-Castro and Fernando Leibovici state that this prediction is not an easy task:

> "Forecasting inflation lies at the heart of economic decision-making, shaping the financial planning of households, guiding strategic investments by firms, and driving monetary policy. It is, however, a difficult task as equilibrium inflation is the outcome of the aggregation of individual actions that depend, among other factors, on the expectations of inflation itself." [10]

Additionally, the same authors who produce inflation forecasts from Google AI PaLM, a state-of-the-art broad-language model, note that the job of forecasting inflation is starting to be delegated to AI models: They found that it provided a correct alternative which the AI model understands the demand for

[8] The old version of the Great Recession dates back to 1929 and the new one dates back to 2008.

[9] David G. Blanchflower and Alex Bryson, "Recession and Deflation?", *Review of Keynesian Economics* 11, 2 (2023): 214-231.

[10] M. Faria e Castro ve Fernando Leibovici, "Artificial Intelligence and Inflation Forecasts," *Federal Reserve Bank of St. Louis Working Paper* (2023-015), https://doi.org/10.20955/wp.2023.015.

inflation forecasts and is cheaper and accurate than traditional forecasts that can also be applied to other types of macroeconomic forecasts.

Scope: Purpose and Structure of the Book

This book aims to highlight the place and importance of the G20 economies in the world system of central banking and monetary policy while opening up to academic discussion the responsibility and creativity of this global economic group for global monetary and financial stability.

If you're curious about the chapters, check the abstracts at the beginning; they act like a store window display. It may be useful to review the full texts to learn more closely the analyses made by the chapter authors and the messages they want to convey. You can imagine this part as if it were products that might interest you on the shelves of that store. As the editor of this book, I would like to remind you which titles[11] I called for from the very beginning. When you look

[11] "The 16 Possible Non-Hierarchical Titles That Were Expected to be Included in This Book Were as Follows," *Vernon Press, Call for Book Chapter Proposals: Central Banking and Monetary Policy in G20: Paradigms and Challenges* (February 2023), https://vernonpress.com/proposal/224/cf1c7d1b73dfe085d2a158a59badbf3e.

- The success of anti-inflationary monetary policy regimes (monetary control-monetary targeting, foreign exchange anchor, currency board, dollarization-euroization, etc.).
- Status quo and independence dilemma in central banking.
- How do central banks view digital currency, fintech, and cryptocurrency democracy?
- The role and effects of the FED and the international reserve currency dollar in the world monetary and financial system.
- Establishment of the European Central Bank (ECB) system as the world's only integration central bank and its functions in the Eurozone.
- History of the FED, Bank of England, and Bundesbank-ECB as the troika of global central banking and their contribution to the universal monetary policy system.
- Situation of Bank of England and Sterling before and after Brexit.
- Current responses of central banks to globalizing problems that recession, negative growth, underemployment-unemployment, climate change, etc., apart from the twin deficits, such as budget deficit or fiscal indiscipline and current account deficit or foreign exchange imbalance.
- The paradigmatic changes created by the Fed's global power and modern central banking after the collapse of the Bretton Woods system.
- The challenges of the world gold-rich Central Bank of China and the Japanese Central Bank, which applies negative interest, to the global financial system on the Asia-Pacific axis.
- Do central banks work against financial crises with Keynesian, monetarist or hybrid tendencies; (which and how much)?

at the content of the book, I would like to point out that some of these titles had the chance to be included in the book, while the rest may be a source of inspiration for other studies, even if they are not included here.

Here, you will find theoretical, political and applied sections that are directly and indirectly related to the theme of the book under the umbrella of monetary macroeconomics and monetary international economics, focusing on the G20 as the subject. It cannot be claimed that these chapters are perfect in terms of quantity and quality, but there is no doubt that their authors have made an enthusiastic effort to create academic interaction and scientific awareness around the discipline of monetary economics.

Introduction: Central Banks and Monetary Policies of the G20

Below, each G20 economy is summarized in alphabetical order in terms of its central bank and the monetary policy it implements. No concepts or theories/ policies regarding central banking and monetary regimes are discussed in detail. When the hypothesis or theory differs in practice, it turns into the policy. For example, the "*impossible trinity rule*" or "*trilemma hypothesis,*" which states that a fixed exchange rate, free capital movement and an independent policy rate cannot be carried out simultaneously in the international political economy, is not applied as a standard by every central bank. For example, the PBoC in China holds a fixed exchange rate and sovereign monetary policy and, therefore does not allow free capital flow. The opposite is true for BoJ / BoE / FED which allow free capital flow and sov monetary policy but does not fix their exchange rates.

1/20. Argentina's central bank and its monetary policy: The Central Bank of the Argentine Republic (Banco Central de la República Argentina, BCRA) was

---

- The position of emerging markets such as BRICS (Brazil, Russia, India, China, South Africa), MIST (Mexico, Indonesia, South Korea, Turkey), MENAT (Middle East and North Africa with Turkey) within the G20, their relations in the context of central banking, their practices of stability programs.
- Do Western central banks approach Islamic or interest-free participation banks, which have developed as a phenomenon and become popular in the world financial system, pragmatically?
- Interactions between the International Monetary Fund (IMF), international credit rating agencies and central banks.
- Before the G20 countries colonize Mars, can their central banks lead the way for a single world currency?
- Scenarios of possible problems that await central banking in the future or Covid-19 era (for example, monetary wars between advanced and emerging central banks, private central bank model, green central banking trend, etc.)

established as a mixed and autarkic institution as a result of the monetary and banking reform in 1935. The national government guarantees the commitments undertaken by the Bank. The purpose of the Bank is to promote economic development with monetary and financial stability, employment and social equity within the framework of its powers and the policies determined by the National Government. The Central Bank, normally subordinate to the Ministry of Economy on policy matters, took on a more prominent role in April 1980 during the Latin American debt crisis. Payments made in suddenly devalued pesos pegged mortgages locally to the value of the U.S. dollar, sending thousands of homeowners and businesses into bankruptcy. This value had increased approximately fifteen times by July 1982, when Central Bank Governor Domingo Cavallo cancelled the policy. During the years of the Cavallo Convertibility Act of April 1991, which established a 1:1 fixed exchange rate between the Argentine peso and the US dollar, the BCRA was primarily responsible for keeping foreign exchange reserves in sync with the monetary base. However, this policy left the BCRA without exchange rate flexibility and resulted in a record economic crisis a decade later. The repeal of the Convertibility Law in January 2002 was accompanied by a 70% devaluation of the peso, after which the role of the Central Bank was to accumulate reserves to maintain some control of the exchange rate. The BCRA buys and sells dollars on the market as needed to absorb large foreign trade surpluses, keep the official exchange rate at internationally competitive levels for Argentine exports and encourage import substitution.[12] The Argentinian economy is now, as in the past, one of the world's and G20's highest inflation and benchmark interest rates (both above 100%), and is mentioned with a weak currency, the peso, excessive dollarization, privatizations to finance debt, and problematic IMF loans operations. Politically, it is observed that BCRA is extremely tired of the solution[13] and has taken on a level of responsibility that it cannot bear.

2/20. Australia's central bank and its monetary policy: The Reserve Bank of Australia (RBA) is the central bank of Australia and derives its functions and powers from the Reserve Bank Act 1959. It was established as a result of the abolition of the central bank functions of the Commonwealth Bank. Its mission

---

[12] Banco Central de la República Argentina (September 2023), https://www.bcra.gob.ar/Institucional/BCRALaw. asp.

[13] Some Argentinian politicians, who think that the central bank has become unable to fulfill its duties and therefore its prestige has been shaken, said that they will close the BCRA when they form a government and implement the "Monetary Board" as a monetary reform instead, which can be considered a radical decision that is not often used on behalf of the G20,. (For news, see Reuters), "Argentina's Milei says shutting central bank 'non-negotiable'", (November 24, 2023), https://www.reuters.com/world/americas/argentinas-milei-says-shutting-central-bank-non-negotiable-2023-11-24/.

is to contribute to the stability of the currency, full employment and the economic well-being and prosperity of the Australian people. It does this by implementing monetary policy to achieve an agreed-upon medium-term inflation target, working to maintain a strong financial system and efficient payments system, and issuing the country's banknotes. The RBA provides certain essential banking services to the Australian Government and its agencies and certain overseas central banks and government agencies. It also manages Australia's gold and foreign exchange reserves. Its official homepage also emphasizes that, as the RBA, it serves the Australian people, conducts monetary policy, determines the payment system, works to maintain a stable financial system, issues the national bank note, the Australian dollar, operates the core of the payments system and provide banking services to the government. The RBA promotes the efficiency and competitiveness of the payments system and regulates the market infrastructure to support financial stability. It works with other regulatory bodies to maintain the stability of the financial system to create favourable conditions that will stimulate economic growth.[14] The Australian economy is considered one of the most stable and prosperous economies in the G20, as evidenced by its balanced macro variables, single-digit inflation and interest rates.

3/20. Brazil's central bank and its monetary policy: The Central Bank of Brazil (Banco Central do Brasil, BCB) was founded in 1964 and became independent in 2020. The BCB issues the national banknote, the Brazilian real (BRL), and is responsible for maintaining its value. Within the scope of the stability program in the country, the famous Real Plan in the history of inflation was implemented: Launched in mid-1993, after six ineffective stabilization plans between 1985 and 1993, 'Plano Real' was a groundbreaking success against the spiral of inflation that had affected Brazil since the mid-80s. The disinflation process was extremely rapid: annual inflation of the Broad National Consumer Price Index (IPCA) measured by the Brazilian Institute fell from 4.922% in June 1994 to 916% in December 1994. A new currency, the Brazilian Real (BRL), came into force on July 1, 1994, marking a major milestone in Brazil. In 1995, the annual inflation rate fell to 22%. Many international and domestic shocks since then have put price stability at risk. However, sustainable long-term price stability was achieved for the first time, thanks to the major disinflation achieved by 'Plano Real' and deep structural and institutional reforms, including the inflation targeting regime adopted in mid-1999. Real replaced Cruzeiro Real in 1994 after the financial crisis. As of April 2019, the real was the twentieth most traded currency. Concretely, elements of the BCB's operational autonomy are built within its formal relationship with the National

[14] Reserve Bank of Australia (September 2023), https://www.rba.gov.au/.

Treasury, while stringent legislation and the Authority's communications strategy strengthen the BCB's accountability and transparency arrangements. The pillar of integrity is reinforced by a comprehensive set of legal provisions, regulations and internal rules. In early 1999, the Brazilian Government established a monetary policy regime based on an inflation-targeting framework. Since then, the inflation target (a midpoint and its tolerance range) has been set by the National Monetary Council (CMN) based on the IPCA's annual increase.[15] In Brazil, which currently displays a stable economy with single-digit inflation, a risky inflation targeting towards deflation is implemented.

4/20. Canada's central bank and its monetary policy: The Bank of Canada (BoC) (Banque du Canada) is the bilingual central bank of Canada, established in 1934. Headquartered in Ottawa, the bank's primary role is to support the economic and financial prosperity of Canada as defined in the Bank of Canada Act. Its primary areas of responsibility are to influence the supply of money circulating in the economy by using the monetary policy framework to keep inflation low and stable and to support safe, sound and efficient financial systems within Canada and internationally. BoC designs, prints and distributes Canada's banknotes. It is the fiscal agent of the Government of Canada, managing its public debt programs and foreign exchange reserves. Although the Bank of Canada Act has been amended several times, the bank is still active in regulating credit and currency in the best interests of the economic life of the nation. Canada's monetary policy framework consists of two key components working together: an inflation control target and a flexible exchange rate. This framework helps monetary policy actions be easily understood and allows the BoC to demonstrate its accountability to Canadians. Every five years, the BoC and the Government of Canada revise the agreement on Canada's monetary policy framework. In 2021, Canada's flexible inflation targeting framework from 2022 to 2026 was renewed.[16] Tho Canada has a stable economy and policies, it is extremely mining heavy (in gold and other metals) and a major non-renewables exporter. Its currency, CAD, is a hard currency linked to the strength of Canadian commodities exports.

5/20. China's central bank and its monetary policy: The People's Bank of China (PBoC) (Chinese: 中国人民银行) is the central bank of China. PBoC was established in 1948 in Shijiazhuang, Hebei Province, by merging the former Huabei Bank, Beihai Bank and Xibei Farmers Bank, and introducing Renminbi (RMB) as the national currency. RMB is the official currency of China, its smaller unit is the Yuan (CNY, "¥"), the latter being the currency most used by

---

[15] Banco Central do Brasil (BCB) (September 2023), https://www.bcb.gov.br/en/monetary policy/realplan, https://www.bcb.gov.br/en/monetarypolicy/Inflationtargeting.

[16] Bank of Canada (September 2023), https://www.bankofcanada.ca/about/.

the public. The last Chinese RMB or CNY series was issued in 2005. The new bank and new currency would become the central bank and legal tender with the founding of the PRoC. Headquartered in Beijing, PBoC is responsible for conducting the country's monetary policy and supervising its financial institutions. With the development of the socialist market economic system, PBoC began to play an even more important role in China's macroeconomic management and integration with capitalist global markets. In 2003, the 10th National People's Congress authorized the PBoC to perform the following functions: formulating and implementing monetary policy in accordance with the law; exporting RMB and managing its circulation; regulating financial markets, including the interbank lending market, the interbank bond market, the foreign exchange market and the gold market; to prevent and reduce systemic financial risks in order to maintain financial stability; adjusting the RMB to exchange rates and keeping it at an equilibrium level; to keep and manage the state's foreign exchange and gold reserves; to manage the state treasury as a financial intermediary.[17] In China, which competes with the USA in terms of wild capitalism in the Asia-Pacific, grows to the point of overgrown and therefore experiences various problems,[18] has a say in global capital traffic and intensifies competition with dumping in global goods markets, the PCoB manages to hold on extremely low rates in critical parameters such as inflation and interest.

6/20. France's central bank and its monetary policy: The Bank of France (Banque de France, BdF), headquartered in Paris, is the central bank of France. Founded by Napoleon Bonaparte in 1800, the company started as a private institution to manage state debts and print bills. BdF is responsible for the accounts of the French government, managing the accounts and facilitating payments of the Treasury and some public companies. When France became the centre of the eurozone[19] by adopting the euro as a common currency on January 1, 1999, the BdF, which until then was responsible for the former national currency, the French franc,[20] became a founding member of the

---

[17] The People's Bank of China (PBoC) (September 2023), http://www.pbc.gov.cn/en/3688066/3688089/index. html.

[18] The Economist, "China's Economy May be Growing Faster, But Big Problems Remain: None Is More Unnerving than the Threat of Deflation," October 18th, 2023, https://www.economist.com/finance-and-economics/2023/10/18/chinas-economy-may-be-growing-faster-but-big-problems-.

[19] The Eurosystem consists of the European Central Bank (ECB) and the national central banks (NCBs) of all European Union (EU) members.

[20] The French Franc (French: franc français, F or F) is the old currency used in France - before the euro. Its use ended with the introduction of the Euro in 2002. Outside of France, F was also used in Andorra, Monaco and French Polynesia. During the transition

Eurosystem with the status of an independent institution. The BdF's mandate is to guide the French monetary strategy, ensure price and financial stability, and provide services to households, small and medium-sized businesses and the French state. The BdF contributes to the design of the euro area's monetary policy (through macroeconomic research and forecasts and by participating in negotiations on ECB decisions) and implements it in France. It prints euro banknotes, of which it is the custodian and largest printer, manages the circulation of banknotes and coins, and prevents the production of counterfeits. It also establishes France's balance of payments and manages part of the ECB's foreign exchange reserves. BdF's printing business faced a major technological and operational challenge, printing a large portion of the new "Europa" series of banknotes introduced in all euro area countries from 2013.[21] In France, one of the largest players in the Eurozone, consumer inflation and interest rates are in single digits in mid-2023, and BdF, which plays an important role in this success, maintains its unshakable prestige in its own society and in international markets.

7/20. Germany's central bank and its monetary policy: Deutsche Bundesbank (DBB) was founded in 1957 as the central bank of the Federal Republic of Germany. Headquartered in Frankfurt and represented in 9 different German cities, DBB provides euro cash to the economy. They offer free and unlimited D-Mark banknote and coin exchange to private customers. DBB, Germany's independent central bank, is famous in the world for its independent central banking. It has been part of the Eurosystem since 1999 and, together with other national central banks and the ECB, is responsible for the common currency, the euro. Its central business area is the monetary policy of the Eurosystem, and its primary goal is to ensure price stability in the Eurozone. This requires comprehensive analysis, a long-term orientation and impartiality towards individual interests. DBB is also dependent on the support of economic, fiscal and wage policy in its stabilization policy. Other tasks include, in particular, the management of Germany's foreign exchange reserves, participation in the national supervision of credit institutions within the framework of uniform European banking supervision, cash and non-cash payment transactions and financial stability. DBB, which specifically supports low-carbon production and employment within the scope of green finance, works in international institutions and committees committed to stabilizing the financial system.

---

to Euro, 1 Euro was converted at a cross rate of 6.55957 F. F, consisting of 100 centimes, ranked 5th in terms of weight in reserve currencies, after the US dollar, German mark, British pound sterling and Japanese yen.

[21] *Banque de France* (September 2023), https://www.banque-france.fr/en/banque-de-france/independent-trusted-institution; https://www.banque-france.fr/en/monetary-strategy/monetary-strategy-mandate.

DBB is independent of the instructions of third parties, including those of the federal government.[22] Germany, which had the world's most terrible hyperinflation experiences during the world wars, has long been taken as a model for monetary and price stability, especially in the EU[23] and throughout the world, thanks to its autonomous central bank.

8/20. India's central bank and its monetary policy: The Reserve Bank of India (RBoI) was established in 1935, with its first head office in Calcutta, in accordance with the Reserve Bank of India Act, 1934. Although the RBoI was initially privately owned, with its head office later moved permanently to Mumbai in 1937, since nationalization in 1949 the Bank has been wholly owned by the Government of India. The main functions of the RBoI are as follows: To formulate, implement and monitor monetary policy aimed at economic growth and price stability; determine the broad parameters of banking transactions operated by the country's banking and financial system; To administer the Foreign Exchange Management Act, 1999 to facilitate foreign trade and payment and promote the orderly development and maintenance of the foreign exchange market in India; To issue, exchange and destroy currency notes of the national currency Rupee (INR) as well as to circulate coins minted by the Government of India.[24] As one of the largest emerging markets in the world, India is closely monitoring innovative financial technology. In India, a former Commonwealth member, the RBoI, which is currently paying more than 100 INR for the UK's 1 pound sterling, appears to have stabilized headline inflation at single digits.

9/20. Indonesia's central bank and its monetary policy: Bank Indonesia (BI) was established in 1953 as the central bank of the Republic of Indonesia. BI's duties were expanded to include commercial banking activities by providing loans, but not limited to money circulation activities. During this period, the Monetary Board (MB) was established to determine monetary policy. While the MB was chaired by the Minister of Finance, the BI governor and the Minister of Trade were also members. During the guided democracy-economy era, BI's governor was a member of the Parliamentary Cabinet. It aimed to consolidate all state-owned banks into single-entity banks under the name Bank Negara

---

[22] Deutsche Bundesbank (September 2023), https://www.bundesbank.de/en; https://www.bundesbank.de/en/bundesbank/green-finance.

[23] As far as I remember, it was claimed that DBB, with its world-famous independent central banking feature, could replace the ECB while it was still in its establishment phase, but this was abandoned due to the reservations of France, the other locomotive of the EU.

[24] Reserve Bank of India (September 2023), https://www.rbi.org.in/Scripts/AboutusDisplay.aspx; https://www. rbi.org.in/Scripts/BS_PressReleaseDisplay.aspx?prid=56750.

Indonesia (BNI) in accordance with the Bank Berjoang Doctrine. Indonesian rupiah (Rp, IDR) is the official currency and is distributed by BI. The subunit of IDR, sen, is not used due to inflation. IDR is also used unofficially in East Timor. BI implements a number of measures, including loan-to-value (LTV) ratios, reserve requirements and capital conservation buffer, within the framework of macroprudential policy against systemic risks and ensures financial stability: BI's monetary policy mix for inflation targeting interest rate, exchange rate, It consists of capital flow management and macroprudential elements.[25] In Indonesia, one of Southeast Asia's largest newly industrialized economies and sensitive about government debt, single-digit inflation and interest rates are considered one of BI's successes.

10/20. Italia's central bank and its monetary policy: Banca d'Italia (BdI), i.e. the (central) Bank of Italy, was founded in 1893 as part of a general restructuring of Italy's issuing banks. In 1926, it became the only institution authorized to issue banknotes. BdI's status as a public institution was expanded by the Banking Law of 1936, granting it banking supervision powers. BdI is the competent national authority on the Single Supervisory Mechanism (SSM) for banks. An important transition in the history of the bank was the stabilization of the Italian Lira / Liret (ITL) in 1947. The post-war rise in inflation was broken, and the monetary conditions for the "economic miracle" of the 1950s were created. The 1948 Constitution enshrined the principle of "protection of savings". The reduction of inflation in Italy following the shocks to the international monetary system and the national currency in the 1970s was supported by stronger legal guarantees for the independence of the BdI. Restoring stability in the currency and initiating regulation of public finances enabled Italy to comply with the standards set by the Maastricht Treaty (1992) and to be among the leading group of countries that adopted the euro as the main currency. BdI became a member of the Eurosystem in 1999, and Euro banknotes and coins came into circulation in Italy in 2002, thus ending ITL, which was in circulation from 1861 to 2002. ITL was used outside Italy in San Marino and part of the Vatican. With the transition to the Euro as the official currency of Italy, 1936.27 ITL began to be exchanged as 1 euro. While BdI stands out in the Eurosystem for not having state ownership, today, the 15 largest shareholders represent more than half of the bank's equity capital.[26] Although

[25] Bank Indonesia (September 2023), https://www.bi.go.id/en/tentang-bi/sejarah-bi/Default.aspx.; Perry Warjiyo, "Indonesia: The Macroprudential Framework and The Central Bank's Policy Mix," *BIS Papers* no. 94 (2017): 189-205.

[26] Banca d'Italia (September 2023), https://www.bancaditalia.it/chi-siamo/storia/index.html; Statute of the Bank of Italy https://www.bancaditalia.it/chi-siamo/funzioni-governance/disposizioni-generali/en-statute.pdf?langua ge_id=1; Shareholders at 17

it challenges the Maastricht criteria from time to time, especially regarding public debt and budget deficit, BdI's commitments and practices on monetary and price stability continue in parallel with the successful monetary policy in the Euro area.

11/20. Japan's central bank and its monetary policy: The Bank of Japan Act of 1882 was published during the first Meiji period, establishing the foundations of the Bank of Japan (BoJ) (Japanese 日本銀行 Nippon Ginkō). Accordingly, the BoJ would have a capital of 10 million Japanese Yen (JPY) and would be given a license to operate for 30 years from the start of business. According to the law of 1942, the BoJ would have a capital of 100 million JPY. The modern BoJ was established in 1953 and became operational in 1956. The bank is responsible for distributing yen notes and coins, ensuring the stability of the financial system, implementing monetary policy and carrying out exchange rate policy. The BoJ is one of the world's three main central banks, along with the Federal Reserve System (FED) and the European Central Bank (ECB). Giving special importance to the principle of institutional transparency and the problem of global climate change, the BoJ implemented measures supporting quantitative and qualitative monetary expansion[27] in 2001 and 2015. In order to fulfil its responsibilities as the central bank of Japan, even in the event of a disaster such as an earthquake, it ensures the smooth operation of banknote distribution and payment systems and continues to improve its business continuity system.[28] It could achieve all this without compromising 2% price stability at the expense of risking deflationary tendencies. Recent BoJ in the last decade has been trying to revive inflation, which didn't happen until 2022~2023. This led to a strong devaluation of the JPY against all currencies. Effectively, the BoJ let the JPY sink to induce inflation. They also employ yield curve control to ensure the JPY stays range-bound. JPY, which has an important share in this success story, is a hard currency and is now used as the most widely used reserve currency after the American Dollar, Euro and British Pound.

12/20. Mexico's central bank and its monetary policy: Founded in 1925 as the country's central bank, Banco de México (BdM) ended a long period of monetary instability and chaotic activity in which a system woven from several large banks operated. This system was largely disrupted by the rise of the Mexican

---

February 2024 https://www.bancaditalia.it/chi-siamo/funzioni-governance/partecipanti-capitale/shareholders_ENG.pdf?language_id=1

[27] Güller Şahin and İrfan Kalaycı, "An Investigation on Quantitative Easing Monetary Policy: Experience of Japan," *Hacettepe University Journal of Economics and Administrative Sciences* 33, no. 3 (2015): 99-130.

[28] Bank of Japan (September 2023), https://www.boj.or.jp/en/about/outline/history/index.htm; https://www.boj. or.jp/en/mopo/outline/qqe.htm.

Revolution in 1910. This accelerated the distrust of banknotes and the collapse of the monetary system in effect at that time. By supplying the national currency, BdM prioritized preserving the constitutional value of this currency. It also supports the healthy development of financial and payment systems. Thanks to its autonomy, BdM is not forced to lend money to the Government and operates with budgetary and management independence. Therefore, it determines its own policies and tools in order to ensure price stability, which is its primary goal, and to realize its performance. Responsibilities such as sending reports to Congress, publishing periodic reports, and being transparent and accountable through rapid dissemination of information to the public accompany the autonomous structure of BdM.[29] Mexico has the potential to easily become part of Latin American debt crises in general, as the ill-historic experiences of the 1980s and 1990s show. In this large economy, the target interest rate is currently set above 10% and annual consumer inflation remains in single digits, demonstrating BdM's determination for price stability.

13/20. Russia's central bank and its monetary policy: Bank of Russia (BoR) (Russian, Центральный банк Российской Федерации) was founded in 1990. The Soviet State Bank, which served as the central banker of the socialist Bolshevik revolution between 1922 and 1992, was liquidated. BoR's predecessor dates back to the State Bank of the Russian Empire, founded in 1860. In 1995, the State Duma adopted the 'Federal Law on the Central Bank of the Russian Federation', which gave the BoR powers and functions such as the monopoly of issuing money, refinancing of commercial banks, banking regulation and supervision, foreign exchange regulation and exchange control. BoR's mission is to ensure the stability of the national currency, the Russian ruble (RUB,), and prices and to contribute to the development of an internationally competitive financial market. Although its authorized capital and other properties are federal property, the BoR has both ownership and financial independence. The State and BoR are not responsible for each other's obligations.[30] Despite Russia's open-ended war economy against Ukraine and its partial isolation by the West, the risk of hyperinflation of the old 1990s does not appear in the shadow of household inflation expectations exceeding 10%. It is noteworthy that BoR's quarter-century liberal central banking experience and controlled attitude are effective here.

14/20. Saudi Arabia's central bank and its monetary policy: Founded in 1952, the Saudi Arabian Monetary Authority (SAMA, Arabic العربي النقد مؤسسة

[29] Banco de México (September 2023), https://www.banxico.org.mx/indexen.html; https://www.banxico.org.mx/tipcamb/main.do?page=inf&idioma=en.

[30] Bank of Russia (September 2023), https://cbr.ru/eng/about_br/history/; https://www.cbr.ru/eng/about_BR/.

السعودي) is the central bank of the Kingdom of Saudi Arabia. When Saudi Hollandia Bank was founded in 1952, it transferred its responsibilities for oil revenues to SAMA and became a model for other foreign banks in the kingdom. The most important functions of SAMA are to deal with the banking affairs of the government, to print and put into circulation the national currency (Saudi Riyal, SAR), to stabilize its internal and external value, to manage the Kingdom's foreign exchange reserves, to implement monetary policy aimed at maintaining price and exchange rate stability, to promote the growth of the financial system, to supervise commercial banks, foreign exchange dealers, cooperative insurance companies and freelance professions related to insurance activity, financial companies and credit information companies. SAMA, the second oldest Central Bank of the Arab World, integrated the national monetary system and first put the Gold SAR into circulation. It was defined as 1 Gold SAR = 40 Silver SAR. SAMA made great efforts to maintain the rate (US$ 1 = Saudi Riyal 3.70) and used all its powers in cooperation with the banking system to achieve this goal.[31] Today, SAMA, which represents the central banking of a rising economy in the Middle East and North Africa (MENA) region and has managed to stabilize single-digit consumer inflation as in the developed West, plays a bridge role in the integration of Gulf capital with Western economies.

15/20. South Korea's central bank and its monetary policy: The Bank of South Korea (Korean: 한국은행 Hanguk Eunhaeng, HE) is the central bank of South Korea. Immediately after the establishment of the government in Korea in 1948, what was needed most was to establish a central bank to establish and implement monetary and credit policies impartially and democratically within a modern financial system. Accordingly, HE was established with a law enacted in May 1950. HE, whose main aim is to ensure price stability, implemented policies that also considered financial stability while trying to restore growth due to the continuation of the low growth and low price trend in the 2010s and the increased risk of financial imbalances such as household debt. A regular monitoring system was established in HE in response to the high level of uncertainty in external conditions. In addition to efforts to improve the robustness of the foreign exchange sector, HE has further strengthened the foundations of financial stability by executing currency swaps with various central banks. It also improved the monetary and credit policy system, including improving the price stability targeting system and strengthening policy communication, in order to increase policy effectiveness and fulfill policy responsibilities. Meanwhile, in the global crisis caused by the Covid-19 epidemic in 2020, it reduced the base

---

[31] Saudi Central Bank (September 2023), https://www.sama.gov.sa/en-US/Currency/Pages/HistoricalInfo.aspx; https://www.sama.gov.sa/en-us/About/Pages/SAMAFunction.aspx; https://www.sama.gov.sa/en-US/Economic Reports/Pages/InflationReport.aspx.

interest rate to an all-time low, provided unlimited won liquidity, and quickly carried out currency swaps with the US Federal Reserve to stabilize the financial situation.[32]

16/20. South Africa's central bank and its monetary policy: The South African Reserve Bank (SARB) is the central bank of South Africa. It was established in 1921 by the "Currency and Banking Act" as a direct result of the abnormal monetary and financial conditions brought about by World War I. The first proposals to establish a Central Bank in South Africa date back to 1879. SARB began offering the first set of banknotes in the national currency, ZAR, to the public in 1922. Unlike the Bank of England, which provided the model for the establishment of the SARB, it is privately owned and performs a variety of functions. For example, establishing and implementing monetary policy, issuing banknotes and coins, supervising the banking system, ensuring the effective functioning of the national payment system (NPS), managing official gold and foreign exchange reserves, acting as the Government's banker (but the bank is not owned by the South African Government), etc. The SARB abandoned the gold standard in 1932, choosing to peg the value of the local currency to the pound sterling as its new monetary policy framework. It then introduced the rand as the new national currency on 14 February 1961, three months before the country left the Commonwealth and became a republic. Between 2000 and 2004, the SARB's mission statement stated that its primary objective in the South African economic system was to "achieve and maintain financial stability". Since 2005, it has been changed to "ensuring and maintaining price stability". In 2000, South Africa became the 13th country to adopt an inflation-targeting monetary policy framework, targeting an inflation band of 3-6% for consumer inflation. This country, which currently implements a real interest policy, has an inflation rate of around 5%.[33] The government's plans include nationalizing the SARB.

17/20. Turkey's Central Bank and its monetary policy: The Central Bank of the Republic of Turkey (Türkiye Cumhuriyet Merkez Bankası, TCMB) is the central bank of Turkey, established in 1930. The first coin was printed in 1326 during the Ottoman Principality. In the Ottoman Empire, of which Turkey is a remnant or continuation, the following three banks started to carry out some activities of the central bank: Bank-ı Dersaadet, founded by Galata bankers in 1847; The Ottoman Bank, established with British capital by the decree of the King of England in 1856; and Bank-ı Osmani-i Şahane, later established in

---

[32] Bank of Korea, (September 2023), https://www.bok.or.kr/portal/main/contents.do?menuNo=200185.

[33] South African Reserve Bank, (September 2023), https://www.resbank.co.za/en/home/about-us/history.

partnership with the British and French. With the establishment of the Republic of Turkey in 1923, an agreement was made with the Ottoman Bank and this bank was authorized to issue banknotes until 1935. Within the scope of financial reforms, the TCMB started monetary and banking activities in 1931 as an independent central bank and as an agent of the Treasury. In 1970, the purpose of the TCMB was expanded to support the development plans and financial policies of the government, and with the liberal stability decisions of January 24, 1980, the TCMB also entered the modernization process and its financial integration with the world was accelerated by removing foreign exchange controls. As a result of the great macroeconomic crisis of 2001 due to high inflation and debts, the TCMB was granted independence, and some of its powers were transferred to the Banking Regulation and Supervision Agency (BDDK) and the Savings Deposit Insurance Fund (TMSF). The ownership structure of the TCMB consists of four different shares: Type A shares can only be owned by the Treasury of the Republic of Turkey, and under no circumstances can the ratio of this share in the capital fall below 51%. (Therefore, the boss of the TCMB is the Treasury.) Class B shares are owned by national banks operating in Turkey. Class C shares are held by foreign banks and privileged companies. Class D is the shares owned by Turkish nationals and commercial organizations.[34] Although its independence is compromised due to government intervention, the TCMB implements a monetary policy based on inflation targeting and floating exchange rate regimes to ensure price stability. In Turkey, which is in the world consumer hyperinflation league and is a big open door for dollarization, the policy rate has been increasing by hundreds of basis points for the last few months in order to ensure the old real value of the Turkish Lira (TL, TRY) within the scope of the anti-inflationary policy.[35]

18/20. The United Kingdom's central bank and its monetary policy: The Bank of England (BoE) is the central bank not just of England but of the United Kingdom (UK) and is the model on which most modern central banks are based. BoE, which was founded in 1694 to operate as the banker of the British Government and is still one of the bankers of the UK Government, is the 8th

---

[34] Türkiye Cumhuriyet Merkez Bankası (TCMB) (September 2023), https://www.tcmb.gov.tr/wps/wcm/connect/TR/TCMB+TR/Main+Menu/Banka+Hakkinda/Tarihce; https://www.tcmb.gov.tr/wps/wcm/connect/TR/TCMB+TR/Main+Menu/Temel+Faaliyetler/Para+Politikasi.

[35] As all independent or non-partisan economists at home and abroad who follow the indicators in the Turkish economy very closely agree, these bold but weak interest-oriented monetary policy steps of the TCMB, despite the government, should be supported by a triple pillar consisting of the rule of law, the fight against corruption and public financial discipline, so that anti-inflationary stability focusing on single-digit consumer inflation could be ensured and sustainable.

oldest bank in the world. Publicly owned and independent since the twentieth century, the BoE has a monopoly on the issuance of banknotes in England and Wales and regulates the issuance of banknotes by commercial banks in Scotland and Northern Ireland. The BoE, which resorted to Keynesian policies against inflation and the weak Pound after 1945, made macroprudential regulations to supervise the UK's financial sector through the Financial Policy Committee established in 2011. The success achieved in inflation targeting is partly attributed to the transparent inflation report submitted by the BoE to the government in 1993. In 1997, during the Labor Party government that came to power for the first time since 1979, it was announced that the BoE would be granted operational independence regarding monetary policy. As a requirement of monetarist independent central banking, if the inflation target exceeds or falls below 1%, the BoE governor was asked to give reasons to the Minister of Finance on behalf of the public and the House of Commons. BoE, which is still a public institution but cannot receive a budget from the UK Treasury, uses a fund created from capital investment, seigniorage revenues and fees collected from the state and private sector institutions to which it provides consultancy services. The BoE, which generates more revenue than it spends and therefore contributes millions of pounds to the UK Treasury each year, manages the British pound (international currency code "GBP"), one of the world's largest and most widespread reserve currencies. The inflation target declared by the BoE, which implements quantitative easing as monetary policy, is 2%, and the current inflation rate is 6.7%.[36] The UK, which joined the European Economic Community in 1973 but definitely left the EU with a referendum in 2020, kept its distance from the European monetary mechanism, relying on its strong currency, and never joined the euro area. After Brexit, the UK continues to navigate the transition process, maintaining alignment with certain EU regulations, customs union protocols, and aspects of the single market.

***19/20. United States's central bank and its monetary policy*:** The Federal Reserve (Fed), or system of central banks, is the central bank of the United States of America (USA), established in 1913. The Currency Act of 1792 came into force and the US dollar (USD) became the official currency of the country. Over time, the Fed's roles and responsibilities have expanded and its structure has changed. Under the Fed Act, each of the 12 Reserve Banks is individually established and has a nine-member board of directors. The Fed Board of Governors guides the operation of the Fed system. All members of the Board serve on the Federal Open Market Committee (FOMC), the body that determines

---

[36] Bank of England (September 2023), https://www.bankofengland.co.uk/about/history; https://www.bankof england.co.uk/about/governance-and-funding; https://www.bankofengland.co.uk/monetary-policy/quantitative-easing.

the Fed's monetary policy. The Fed is not funded by Congressional appropriations. Its operations are financed primarily from interest earned on securities it owns. Fees charged to depository institutions for paid services such as check clearing, funds transfers, and automated clearinghouse transactions are another source of revenue. This revenue is used to cover the cost of those services. After paying expenses and transfers of excess (limited to a total of $10 billion), all net earnings of the Fed banks are transferred to the US Treasury. The country's monetary policy is based on the Fed's goal of maximum employment, stable prices, and moderate long-term interest rates. The US banking system is solid and resilient. Tighter fiscal and credit conditions for households and businesses are likely to put pressure on economic activity, hiring and inflation. The extent of these effects remains unclear. The Board remains highly sensitive to inflation risks with a 2% target.[37] The USA, and therefore the Fed, suffered a loss of credibility with the global financial crisis that began with the bankruptcy of land banks in 2008 and shook almost the entire world. The Fed, due to its undisputed global influence and its dominant structure among the central banks of the G20, has assumed the role of being the central bank not only of the USA but of the entire world. Many countries use USD as official currency; 2/3 of total USD banknotes are in circulation outside the US; economies struggling with high inflation are stuck in dollarization; the US is the founding home of the IMF and the World Bank; USD is directly interactive with global geomonetary and ranks 1st in international reserves; global financial markets react immediately to the interest rates determined by the Fed.

20/20. The European Union's central bank and its monetary policy: The European Central Bank (ECB) was established by the Treaty of Amsterdam in 1999 as the de facto successor to the European Monetary Institute (EMI). Headquartered in Frankfurt, Germany, the ECB is the main component of the Eurosystem and the European System of Central Banks (ESCB), as well as one of the seven institutions of the European Union (EU), established by the Lisbon Treaty in 2009. The ECB, one of the world's most important central banks, sets monetary targets and the key interest rate, manages foreign exchange reserves for both the 27-member EU and the 19-member Eurozone, and operates the TARGET-II or T2 payment system.[38] The ECB, in line with the national central

[37] Federal Reserve System (FED) (September 2023), https://www.federalreserve.gov/aboutthefed/structure-federal-reserve-system.htm; https://www.federalreserve.gov/about_thefed/structure-federal-reserve-board.htm; https://www.federalreserve.gov/newsevents/pressreleases/monetary20231101a.htm

[38] T2, one of the TARGET Services, has now replaced TARGET2 as the Eurosystem's real-time gross settlement (RTGS) system. TARGET2 is RTGS system owned and operated by the Eurosystem. Central banks and commercial banks can submit payment orders in euro to TARGET2, where they are processed and settled in central bank money, i.e. money

banks (NCBs) of full EU member states, has the right to authorize the issuance of Euro banknotes as the common currency and the world's 2nd largest reserve currency from 2002. The ECB went through a process of deep internal transformation as it faced the 2008 global financial crisis and the 2014 Eurozone debt crisis. The ECB made the role of the "Troika"[39] controversial by keeping its distance from the debt-ridden Italian, Spanish, Greek and Irish governments regarding bailout programs. The NCBs of the member states are shareholders of the ECB, whose capital has already exceeded 10 billion euros in proportion to the GNP. In practice, the ECB is dependent on four aspects[40]: personal, financial, political, operational and legal. The EU is the only dynamic integration in the world that does not neglect to deepen its own enlargement[41] to include central banking and monetary policy.

---

held in an account with a central bank. TARGET2 settles payments related to the Eurosystem's monetary policy operations, as well as bank-to-bank and commercial transactions. (See ECB, "What is TARGET2?", https://www.ecb.europa.eu/paym/target/target2/html/index.en.html.

[39] The Troika includes the member state that holds the Presidency of the Council in the EU, the member state that held this duty before it, and the member state that will assume the Presidency after it.

[40] European Central Bank (ECB) (September 2023), https://www.ecb.europa.eu/ecb/html/index.en.html, https://european-union.europa.eu/institutions-law-budget/institutions-and-bodies/search-all-eu-institutions-and-bodies/european-central-bank-ecb_en. https://www.ecb.europa.eu/stats/html/index.en.html.

[41] When it comes to the most difficult enlargement expected for the EU, Turkey comes to mind as the only country that is almost stooped because of carrying the candidate member status on its back. As an academician who enthusiastically wrote several books on this subject, I find it necessary to make a footnote in history: Those who see harm in the EU's continued expansion with Turkey are none other than European and Turkish "*hawks*" and tertiary actors. I think it would be useful to listen to the "*pigeons*" as well: First of all, Turkey wants to become a full member of the EU, with which it has carried out almost half of its foreign trade since 1959 and which it helps with its position as a *superimmigrant* country. However, Turkey, which has the second most populous market in Europe, is not still accepted as 28th full member of the EU, despite becoming a member of the Customs Union in 1996, being deemed a candidate member in 1999, starting the negotiation process since 2005, and its always high geoeconomic-political value. It is thought that Turkey's failure to comply with EU norms sufficiently and not being as excited about this integration as before, as well as the EU's stalling attitude and systematic rigid behavior, play a role in this. Turkey is not expected to protest the EU by leaving the Customs Union ("TRexit"), but it can be argued that if full membership is achieved, it even has the potential to join the Eurozone and the ECB can achieve a more dynamic structure with the TCMB. If the conjuncture does not change, even Ukraine, whose application for NATO membership was blocked by Russia through war, may become a surprise member of the EU family before Turkey.

Conclusion: Challenges Are Expected, but What About Adopting a New Paradigm?

Please allow me to bring these two individual notes to your attention here: First, contrary to popular belief, the world economy is not limited to the G20, and global finance is much broader than just these twenty countries. Don't get fixated on the numbers; instead, question and look beyond the statistics. Second, monetary policy is not a cure-all and cannot work miracles on its own. If it could, the capitalist G20 would not continually face crises, or at least the fear of them, despite long economic cycles. It is known that liberal capitalist, anarcho-capitalist or mixed capitalist G20 economies have grown despite crises and that success stories have emerged here. However, despite this success, mass and cross-border impoverishment, unemployment, income and wealth distribution injustice, and high cost of living do not disappear, and the system will not disappear due to its nature. Is it necessary to say that pseudo and artificial success emerged from this dramatic picture? With such a record of reel unsuccess, how can capitalism, whose developed central banks (CBs) and brilliant monetary policies, be a good model for the world? Relative improvements are exceptions and are details that do not change the main framework.

We have the idea that the CBs and monetary policies play both the key and lock role for each other. The source of this idea is the types, functions and effects of the monetary object and the powers, duties and responsibilities of the central bank subject.

The narrow-sense purchasing power competition observed between the currencies of the world countries is shifting towards a broad-sense competition for independence and prestige between the CBs of those countries. It can be observed that this situation is stronger for the G20 because the countries in this group are the largest in the world in terms of GNP and, with this basic feature, they continue to give direction and shape to the world economy, which consists of more than two hundred countries, large and small. We know that as GNP grows in terms of income or expenditure, the risk of instability and the performance of exiting the crisis increases. When you look at the history of crises around the world, how quickly they spread, and how they were resolved, you'll see the globalized macro economies of the G20 in action.

Price instability alone, such as inflation and its opposite, deflation, is enough to alarm CBs. If governments do not have any obstacles, such as the electoral economy or war economy, CBs are technically capable of solving the problems of price and financial instability.

I would prefer to leave the debate to the reader whether the G20 is challenging the world or the world is challenging the G20, depending on the GNP ranking. It should not be forgotten that the countries that make up the G20 are not standardized among themselves and experience various contradictions and conflicts. GNP is not a simple indicator as the economy is fertilized and born there.

Significantıy, the G20 derives its subjective power from the size of GNP before the level of development.[42] So much so that central banks objectively design many nominal variables and indicators, from money supply to interest rates, from foreign exchange reserves to current account deficit, taking GNP into account.

Why is the necessary sensitivity for equitable income and wealth distribution, which falls within the scope of the state's political economy, not demonstrated by central banks, which are overly concerned with money and price stability and the natural rate of unemployment? It would be a pleasant surprise if this concern were shown, indicating a bold paradigm shift. When will it be realized that it is not the increase in GNP that causes society to become psychopathic, but rather the unequal and unfair distribution of the increasing GNP?

Contemporary and enlightened expert bureaucrats or technocrats of CBs can lead their governors and monetary boards to see this fact and develop policies. To do this, they need to turn their heads away from technical reports and bloated individual portfolios and towards society and its demands for monetary justice. In this new paradigm, CBs stand out that the cost of living, rather than inflation, is the most destructive. My individual suggestion is that CBs should not give up the fight against inflation, which changes the amount of GNP, but they should also start addressing the cost of living problem, which changes the quality of GNP depending on income distribution, as soon as possible.

As alternatives, the central banks of the G20 could also support the implementation of heterodox stabilization policies, which are associated with government income policies and have the potential to address the limitations

[42] Because while some of the G20 consists of developed-industrialized economies (Australia, Canada, France, Germany, Italy, Japan, UK, USA, EU), the other part consists of developing-industrializing economies (Argentina, Brazil, China, India, Indonesia, Mexico, Russia, S.Arabia, S.Korea, S.Africa, Turkey). Have you noticed that if it were a football match, it would be an lopsided matchup of 9 versus 11? I think it is an unbalanced but natural situation, that is, without intervention. Moreover, if you pay attention, the developed ones within the G20 are geographically located in the Northern hemisphere, most of the developing ones are located in the Southern hemisphere, and geopolitically, the first ones are located in the Center and the second ones are located in the Periphery. This means that G20, in addition to the famous West-East opposition, also contains the Center-Periphery opposition. It is not a coincidence that central banks also take positions according to this structure.

of conventional monetary and fiscal policies in tackling monetary macro problems. This approach might offer a more effective and quicker solution.

Bibliography

Albanesi, Stefania, Varadarajan V. Chari, and Lawrence J. Christiano. "How Severe is the Time Inconsistency Problem in Monetary Policy?". NBER Working Paper no. w8139. February 2001. SSRN: https://ssrn.com/abstract=261264.

Albanesi, Stefania, Varadarajan V. Chari, and Lawrence J. Christiano. "How Severe is the Time-Inconsistency Problem in Monetary Policy?". *Quarterly Review* 27, no. 3 (2003). https://doi.org/10.21034/qr.2732.

Banca D'Italia. September 2023. https://www.bancaditalia.it/chi-siamo/storia/index.html.

Banco de México. September 2023. https://www.banxico.org.mx/indexen.html; https://www.banxico.org.mx/tipcamb/main.do?page=inf&idioma=en.

Bank Indonesia. September 2023. https://www.bi.go.id/en/tentang-bi/sejarah-bi/Default.aspx.

Bank of England. September 2023. https://www.bankofengland.co.uk/about/history, https://www.bankofengland.co.uk/about/governance-and-funding, https://www.bankofengland.co.uk/monetary-policy/quantitative-easing.

Bank of Japan. September 2023. https://www.boj.or.jp/en/about/outline/history/index.htm; https://www.boj.or.jp/en/mopo/outline/qqe.htm.

Bank of Korea. September 2023. https://www.bok.or.kr/portal/main/contents.do?menuNo=200185.

Bank of Russia. September 2023. https://cbr.ru/eng/about_br/history/; https://www.cbr.ru/eng/about_BR/.

Banque de France. September 2023. https://www.banque-france.fr/en/banque-de-france/independent-trusted-institution; https://www.banque-france.fr/en/monetary-strategy/monetary-strategy-mandate.

Blanchflower, David G. and Alex Bryson. "Recession and Deflation?". *Review of Keynesian Economics* 11, 2 (2023): 214-231, accessed Sep 1, 2023, https://doi.org/10.4337/roke.2023.02.06.

Britannica. "A Brief (and Fascinating) History of Money". September 2023. https://www.britannica.com/story/a-brief-and-fascinating-history-of-money.

Castro, Faria-e-Miguel and Fernado Leibovici. "Artificial Intelligence and Inflation Forecasts. Federal Reserve Bank of St. Louis". Working Paper (2023-015). URL https://doi.org/10.20955/wp.2023.015.

Deutsche Bundesbank. September 2023. https://www.bundesbank.de/en; https://www.bundesbank.de/en/bundesbank/green-finance.

Deutsche Bundesbank. "The 'invention' of the coin – who, when, where and why?". September 2023. https://www.bundesbank.de/resource/blob/616754/1ae3f2eaadc1dab9a311d4492ff03388/mL/the-invention-of-the-coin-data.pdf.

ECB. "What is TARGET2?". September 2023. https://www.ecb.europa.eu/paym/target/target2/html/index.en.html.

European Central Bank (ECB). September 2023. https://www.ecb.europa.eu/ecb/html/index.en.html, https://european-union.europa.eu/institutions-law-budget/institutions-and-bodies/search-all-eu-institutions-and-bodies/

european-central-bank-ecb_en, https://www.ecb.europa.eu/stats/html/index.en.html.

Federal Reserve System (FED). September 2023. https://www.federalreserve.gov/aboutthefed/structure-federal-reserve-system.htm, https://www.federalreserve.gov/aboutthefed/structure-federal-reserve-board.htm, https://www.federalreserve.gov/newsevents/pressreleases/monetary20231101a.htm

G20 Members. September 2023. https://www.g20.org/en/about-g20/#members

Jia, Chengcheng Jia and Jing Cynthia Wu. "Average Inflation Targeting: Time Inconsistency and Ambiguous Communication". NBER Working Paper no. 2967.3 (Jan. 2022). Revised May 2023.

King, Mervyn A. "Changes in UK Monetary Policy: Rules and Discretion in Practice." *Journal of Monetary Economics*, Elsevier 39, no. 1 (June 1997): 81-97. https://doi.org/10.1016/S0304-3932(97)00009-3.

King, Mervyn A. "How Should Central Banks Reduce Inflation? - Conceptual issues". *Economic Review.* 81(Q IV) (Federal Reserve Bank of Kansas City, 1996): 25-52. https://www.kansascityfed.org/Jackson%20Hole/documents/6767/King_JH96.PDF.

Mishkin, Frederic S. *Para Politikası Stratejisi.* Trans. ed. Ö. F. Çolak ve A. Zengin. Ankara: Efil Yayınevi, 2014.

Reserve Bank of India. September 2023. https://www.rbi.org.in/Scripts/AboutusDisplay.aspx; https://www.rbi.org.in/Scripts/BS_PressReleaseDisplay.aspx?prid=56750

Reuters. "Argentina's Milei Says Shutting Central Bank 'Non-Negotiable". Nov. 24, 2023. https://www. reuters.com/world/americas/argentinas-milei-says-shutting-central-bank-non-negotiable-2023-11-24/

Saudi Central Bank. September 2023. https://www.sama.gov.sa/en-US/Currency/Pages/HistoricalInfo.aspx, https://www.sama.gov.sa/en-us/About/Pages/SAMAFunction.aspx, https://www.sama.gov.sa/en-US/Economic Reports/Pages/InflationReport.aspx

South African Reserve Bank. September 2023. https://www.resbank.co.za/en/home/about-us/history.

Sveriges Riksbank. "History". https://www.riksbank.se/en-gb/about-the-riksbank/history/#:~:text=In% 201668%2C%20the %20Riksdag%2C%20Sweden's, the%20world's%20oldest%20central%20bank.

Şahin, Güller and Kalaycı, İrfan. "An Investigation on Quantitative Easing Monetary Policy: Experience of Japan". *Hacettepe University Journal of Economics and Administrative Sciences* 33 (3) (2015): 99-130.

The Economist. "China's Economy may be Growing Faster, But Big Problems Remain: None is More Unnerving than the Threat of Deflation". October 18, 2023. https://www.economist.com/finance-and-economics/2023/10/18/chinas-economy-may-be-growing-faster-but-big-problems-remain?utm_medium=cpc.adword.pd&utmsource= google&ppccampaignID=18151738051&ppcadID=&utm_campaign=a.22brand_pmax&utm_content=conversion.direct-response.anonymous&gad_source=1&gclid=Cj0KCQjw-ai0BhDPARIsAB6hmP7vzzOrwCmDgtQw2 DL3WDYdAKbSypulMBlAFwFWO5JVKmbmajMlRdoaAqrUEALw_wcB&gclsrc=aw.ds

Türkiye Cumhuriyet Merkez Bankası. September 2023. https://www.tcmb.gov.tr/wps/wcm/connect/TR/TCMB+TR/Main+Menu/Banka+Hakkinda/Tarihce; https://www.tcmb.gov.tr/wps/wcm/connect/TR/TCMB+TR/Main+Menu/Temel+Faaliyetler/Para+Politikasi.

Vernon Press. Call for Book Chapter Proposals: *Central Banking and Monetary Policy in G20: Paradigms and Challenges.* February 2023. https://vernonpress.com/proposal/224/cf1c7d1b73dfe085d2a158a59badbf3e.

Warjiyo, Perry. "Indonesia: The Macroprudential Framework and The Central Bank's Policy Mix". BIS Papers no 94 (2017): 189-205.

Chapter 2

The Global Power of the FED After the Collapse of the Bretton Woods System and the Paradigmatic Shifts Created by Modern Central Banking

İlhan Eroğlu

Gaziosmanpaşa University, Turkey

Nalan Kangal

Gaziosmanpaşa University, Turkey

Fatih Yeter

Gaziosmanpaşa University, Turkey

Necati Çoban

Gaziosmanpaşa University, Turkey

Abstract

Purpose- With the deterioration of the global monetary discipline that emerged with the collapse of the Bretton Woods system, the hegemonic power of the US dollar started to be questioned again. At the end of these processes, a different approach to central banking came to the agenda. This study aims to analyze this process and reveal the new central banking paradigm shifts. Design/methodology/approach- Qualitative research techniques are used. Information about monetary policy practices and central banking from the Bretton Woods System to the present day will be given with a descriptive approach. Findings- As a result of the research, it has been determined that after the collapse of the monetary policy system based on the fixed exchange rate regime that emerged with the implementation of the Bretton Woods system, a different monetary policy process started and a transformation to independent central banking, which has become an indispensable element of modern central banking, has been experienced. Research limitations/implications-

It is planned to limit the research within the framework of the following topics. Practical implications- After 1970, the oil crises and the subsequent unemployment caused the exchange relationship between inflation and unemployment to lose its validity, and 'stagflation' was experienced in the economy. This situation revealed the necessity of pursuing an independent monetary policy in the fight against high inflation. This situation into which countries fell was the beginning of the foundations of modern central banking. Such a development was pioneered by the Monetarist view pioneered by Milton Friedman in the 1970s with the approach that "inflation is always and everywhere a monetary phenomenon." The foundations of this view are based on Milton Friedman's 1962 article "Should There Be an Independent Monetary Authority?". In his article, Friedman emphasized the importance of price stability and pointed out the importance of independent central banking in the fight against inflation. Originality/value- This study reveals that central banking should be handled with a dynamic structure to establish macroeconomic stability according to the conditions in which the economy is and that the paradigm shift should be constructed to keep pace with the development of economic events and phenomena.

Keywords: Bretton Woods System, FED, Modern Central Banking, Paradigmatic Shift

***

There have been three great inventions since the beginning of time:
fire, the wheel, and central banking.
(Will Rogers, American humourist and actor)

Introduction

In the stagflation process that emerged with the collapse of the Bretton Woods system, the fight against high inflation was seen as a priority problem of economic policies. Central banks have assumed an active role in the fight against inflation based on the acceptance that the inflation encountered is monetary, and the fundamental dynamics of modern central banking have started to be established for the construction of an independent monetary policy.

In this context, the main objectives of central banks are considered to be maintaining monetary stability, thereby ensuring price stability and monitoring financial stability. In line with this objective, central banks have assumed many functions such as payment systems, printing banknotes, performing clearing and settlement transactions for banks through banks' accounts at the central bank, managing gold and foreign exchange reserves, on the one hand, to ensure monetary stability and on the other hand to oversee the financial system by cooperating with other decision-making institutions. In addition to the functions shaped around this primary objective, central banks also undertake banking activities, asset and debt management services for the government, and, occasionally, advise on economic and development policies.

The *first and most important of* these is the declaration that price stability is the most crucial objective of monetary policy and that this objective is the ultimate goal. *Secondly,* to ensure the authorized and effective conduct of monetary policy, decision-making processes should be legally guaranteed, and formal independence from the sphere of influence of the executive branch should be ensured. The *third is* to make transparent policy decisions as a requirement of authority and responsibility in implementing monetary policy determined by the law and to ensure the operation of the accountability mechanism in terms of compliance with the target.

After the 2008 Global Financial Crisis, compared to the pre-crisis period, the structure of central banks has undergone significant changes in paradigms regarding the management, prevention, and resolution of the crisis process. Governance problems related to the crisis have been concentrated on specific issues.[1] *The first of* these issues is related to the role of the central bank in financial stability. Regarding this role, it is stated by many circles that central banks should assume a position that should consider systematic risks related to the financial system. The *second* problem concerns how the decision-making mechanism for financial stability will function. In this context, while monetary policy decisions require a decision-making mechanism with a well-established and experienced procedure, decisions related to financial stability require a decision-making process that requires more knowledge and expertise. Thirdly, how to protect against the financial and reputational risks arising from financial stability-related operations. When these issues are considered, expanding the scope and scale of central bank operations for monetary and financial stability would entail the risk of banks being exposed to losses. Realizing these risks or the failure of policy actions to achieve their objectives would involve a trust and reputational problem.

This study aims to reveal the changes and transformations that have occurred in modern central banking after the collapse of the Bretton Woods System, taking into account the 2008 Global Financial Crisis. In line with this purpose, this study will cover the following topics: the global economic outlook before the Bretton Woods System, monetary policies and central banking until the Bretton Woods System, the Bretton Woods System and its fundamental dynamics, the dead ends of the Bretton Woods System and the story of the collapse of the

---

[1] David Archer ve Gavin Bingham, "The Main Tendencies in Modern Central Banking," in *Issues in the Governance of Central Banks - A Report From the Central Bank Governance Group,* (Chair) Guillermo Ortiz- Governor of the Bank of Mexico, BIS, 2009, 5.

system, new searches after the Bretton Woods System and the foundations of modern central banking and paradigmatic changes after modern central banking. Finally, the study will include a conclusion and evaluation section.

Before the Bretton Woods System Historical Process in Monetary Policy and Central Banking

Although today, central banking and its monetary policy as a method of influencing the economic order are complex and multifaceted, the first examples of central banking in the world emerged in the seventeenth century. The oldest central banks are the Swedish Riksbank and the Bank of England, established in 1668 and 1694, respectively. Despite the historical origins of central banking spanning nearly four centuries, today's central banks should be seen as a product of the twentieth century, when institutional developments such as the modern state and democracy took place.[2] The historical evolution of central banks is not the result of brilliant ideas that sprang from the mind of a clever man but rather the development of existing practices influenced by the changing economic and political environment.[3] Therefore, the intricate networks in today's financial system have given central banks a vital role, not only for the banking system but also as a result of the economic system as a whole and foreign economic relations that depend on the degree of integration into the global financial system.

When the first banks mentioned above were established in the historical development of central banking, they did not have the objectives and fundamental principles central to banks today, such as the bank of banks or the "lender of last resort." The privileged position of these banks compared to other banks - whether private or state banks - stemmed from the fact that the government generally supported them through legislation. These banks, which have monopoly power, have undertaken the role of meeting financial needs and providing war financing as an extraordinary condition. In the nineteenth century, central banks underwent an evolutionary process in which they were centralized around other banks in the growing economic relations in economies. In principle, there is no technical difference between government-backed banks and other banks regarding the convertibility of banknotes into precious metals. However, in the centralization process of these banks, the government-backed concessions led to a degree of accumulation/centralization of gold and silver

---

[2] Susanne Lohmann, "Central Banks," in *The Encyclopedia of Public Choice* (Boston: MA Springer, 2003), 70.

[3] Stefano Ugolini, *The Evolution of Central Banking: Theory And History* (London, England: Palgrave Macmillan, 2017), 271.

reserves in these banks.[4] believes this may have weakened the early development of other commercial banks in countries such as England and France.[5] Therefore, the issue at the centre of the debate on central banking and monetary policy in the nineteenth century was "free banking," in other words, banking free from the presence of a central bank. Accordingly, the debate centred mainly around the question of whether the market discipline imposed by a well-functioning clearing house would be sufficient to keep the banking system in order. Free bank advocates argued that the central bank, as a market maker and regulator institution over the self-balancing market mechanism as the dominant economic paradigm of the period, would disrupt market efficiency and be a source of unnecessary interventionist inflationary processes. However, historical processes related to central banking show that central banks have developed to fulfil essential roles and functions in the financial system .[6]

The central countries in Europe and the Bank of England played a leading role in the formation of the understanding of central banking and monetary policy during the classical gold standard period. The first striking situation in the classical gold standard period was that central banks were restricted in using interest rates and money supply instruments to stabilize the economy. These restrictive rules were based on the requirement to strictly ensure the convertibility of the national currency to gold at a fixed rate. When the classical gold standard was applied in the decades roughly between 1880 and 1914, monetary stability was surprisingly successful [7].

The success of the classical gold standard was influenced by factors such as price stability, international trade, confidence, and limited government intervention. These are [8];

- *Price stabilization:* Since the gold standard pegs the value of the national currency to a certain amount of gold, governments are restricted from printing more money to finance their expenditures. The restrictive gold standard has helped to support price stability by preventing government inflationary interventions.

---

[4] Charles Goodhart, "Central Banking," in *The New Palgrave Dictionary of Economics*, 3. ed., ed. G. Jones (Palgrave Macmillan, 2018), 1471-1474.

[5] Goodhart, "Central Banking", 1471.

[6] Charles Goodhart, *The Evolution of Central Banks*, (MIT press,1998).

[7] Michael D. Bordo, *The Gold Standard and Related Regimes*, (Cambridge University Press, 1999).

[8] Pierre L Siklos, *The Changing Face of Central Banking: Evolutionary Trends Since World War II*, (Cambridge University Press, 2002).

- *International trade:* The strict convertibility of each national currency into gold also ensures exchange rate stability, which indicates the relative value of national currencies. Stable exchange rates help economic agents, firms, and investors to predict the future value of money and facilitate international trade and investment.
- *Confidence:* By providing a tangible asset (gold) that can be used to support the value of currencies, the gold standard helps to increase confidence in the monetary system and prevents the realization of risks to the financial system in extraordinary circumstances, such as bank runs.
- *Limited state intervention:* The gold standard was based on limited state intervention in the economy. Using the gold standard as a nominal framework, the adherence of monetary policy to a specific rule, fiscal discipline, and the compliance of the major economic powers, the UK, the USA, and France, with the gold standard increased the system's reliability.

Although the gold standard was eventually abandoned due to its limitations, there are views on the success of the gold standard and the failures of the gold standard due to the restrictions of monetary policy. Accordingly, if the rate of economic growth is faster than the increase in money supply, the national money supply may become insufficient, leading to a fall in prices and the danger of the economy being dragged into deflation. Deflationary stagnation under the gold standard means that central banks cannot increase the money supply and lower interest rates, which may worsen economic stagnation. If countries' economic structures tend to be inflationary, the gold standard is an appropriate monetary method to ensure price stability. However, it is also seen that it cannot provide flexibility in terms of producing anti-recession policies.[9]

The classical gold standard era ended when many countries suspended the convertibility of national currencies into gold and devalued their money to finance war expenditures during the First World War. While the exit from the gold standard helped countries to pay off their war debts, it also created significant uncertainty in international trade and financial markets. The war had a profound impact on the global monetary system as it led to the disruption of international trade and capital flows and the suspension of the convertibility of gold by most belligerents. After the war, the global monetary system tried stabilizing exchange rates and re-establish the gold standard. The desire to return to the gold standard after the war was because it was a financial system that was "knave-proof" against governments' desire for uncontrolled monetary expansion. The reasons for the failure to re-establish the financial system are

---

[9] Bordo, *The Gold Standard*, 349.

based on the loss of coordination between countries whose economic integration was linked by exchange rate anchors in the interwar period, economic and political instability, followed by the Great Depression and a series of financial crises and competitive devaluation. [10]

The failure of the efforts to return to the classical gold standard in the aftermath of the First World War was influenced by the decline of the British hegemonic power over the gold standard and the reduction of international clout after the war. And the British economy had difficulty recovering from the war's devastating effects. The Bank of England, which played a central role in the pre-war gold standard, was weakened by the war and needed help to maintain its dominant position in the international monetary system. Many central banks were established or restructured between the two wars. After the war, the United States emerged as the world's dominant economic and financial power. Founded in 1913, the Federal Reserve played a key role, especially during the Great Depression. On the other hand, the leading "hegemon" in the interwar period was the Bank of France, which accumulated large amounts of gold reserves and used them to stabilize the franc and support the international gold standard. The decline of the British hegemonic power over the gold standard was reflected in the failure to achieve monetary stability and the inability of the devalued sterling to maintain its pre-war parity during the Great Depression. [11]

Paradigm Shift in Central Banking Before the Bretton Woods System

The interwar period represents a significant period in the historical development of central banking and monetary policy experiences. First, there was a debate on the need for central banks to be given more functions to ensure internal stability rather than the external stability of the currency, which had been attributed to central banks under the gold standard. This shift towards internal stability was reflected in changes in the structure and governance of central banks, which became more independent from political authorities and were given greater responsibility for maintaining price stability and promoting full employment. To overcome the devastating economic consequences of the war, Keynesian thinking and the welfare state, which challenged the classical economic doctrine, began to rise. Accordingly, it was argued that more than the self-balancing mechanism of the market economy was needed to achieve economic stability and that monetary policy should be actively used to achieve economic stability and full employment. The Keynesian paradigm started to take its place as the new orthodoxy in using flexible exchange rate regimes and active monetary and fiscal policy instead of the straitjacket monetary policy

---

[10] Siklos, *The Gold Standard and Related Regimes*, 193.

[11] Lawrence Broz, "The Domestic Politics of International Monetary Order: The Gold Standard," in *International Political Economy*, (Routledge, 2002), 208-209.

approach of the gold standard in times of crisis. This paradigm shift, the first seeds of which were sown in the interwar period, became the dominant paradigm after the Second World War. [12]

The First World War brought about an increase in monetary policy and central banking instability, and the increase in the monetary base, which led to the rise in monetary illusion due to arbitrary practices, brought the restoration of monetary and financial structures to the agenda after the war. The wartime experiences and the economic difficulties in continental Europe led central banks to demand more independence. In this process, Montagu Norman, the Governor of the Bank of England, and Benjamin Strong, the Chairman of the Federal Reserve, demanded more independence. Developments such as the increasing power of central banking research departments, the intensification of experience feedback in the conduct of monetary policy due to increased cooperation between central banks, and institutionalization efforts in their internal functioning have brought central banks to a more technical level. Norman explicitly challenged the legitimacy of political intervention in monetary affairs, arguing that central banks should be independent of governments. Moreover, at the conference held in Genoa in 1922, it was decided that central banks should be established in all member countries to re-establish the international monetary system and that central banks and monetary policies should be independent of the political struggles of governments. In response to the desire for greater independence of central banks in continental Europe, the problem of high public deficits, which emerged in the victorious states to eliminate the ravages of war and in the defeated states after high war reparations, forced general budget policies to give a kind of direction to monetary policy. Some central banks had to implement monetary policies that led to hyperinflationary processes (Germany, Poland, Austria, Hungary) and devaluations in the UK, France, Belgium, and Italy[13]. Overall, the two world wars and the Great Depression led to a significant change in the understanding of monetary strategies and the role of central banking, leading to the adoption of new policies and practices aimed at promoting domestic stability and preventing and mitigating economic crises.

Bretton Woods System and Basic Dynamics

The Great Depression of 1929 paved the way for changing the international monetary system based on the gold standard. The decline in production and

[12] Michael D. Bordo, "A Brief History of Central Banks", *Federal Reserve Bank of Cleveland, Economic Commentary,* (2007): 1-4, https://www.clevelandfed.org/publications/economic-commentary/2007/ec-20071201 -a-brief-history-of-central-banks.

[13] Bertrand Blancheton, "Central Bank Independence in A Historical Perspective. Myth, Lessons and a New Model," *Economic Modelling* 52 (2016): 102.

employment levels led countries to devalue their currencies to gain a competitive advantage in international trade. This practice adversely affected the world economy, and a new international monetary system, the Bretton Woods Monetary System, was developed to establish a properly functioning payment system between countries by reviving the world economy, which collapsed with the additional burdens of World War II on the economies of countries.[14] Bretton Woods is a fundamental element, a building block and also a symbol that forms the basis of the second post-war sharing process and the new international division of labor.[15] The system was created to ensure monetary and financial stability to support international trade in addition to global economic growth by avoiding unfavourable conditions such as protectionism, currency wars, hot money flows, and unstable exchange rates in the world economy between the two world wars.[16] Among the objectives of the system is to prevent the foreign trade barriers and devaluations and foreign exchange surplus policy of the countries applied in the period between the two world wars.[17]

The Bretton Woods Monetary System was established under the leadership of the United States in 1944 at the International Monetary and Financial Conference held in Bretton Woods, New Hampshire, at the height of World War II, where representatives of 45 countries came together to design a new international monetary order for the post-war period. With the compromise reached, an adjustable system based on the US dollar, which can be converted into gold at $ 35 per ounce, was established with capital controls.[18] In the Bretton Woods System, all IMF member countries except the US defined the value of their national currencies as the official exchange rate in dollars. Therefore, the currencies of the member countries were also linked to gold. With this practice, the system was based on the dollar-based gold standard, also seen as the basis of today's dollarisation. With this practice, the foundation of today's dollarisation

---

[14] Halil Seyidoğlu, *İktisat Biliminin Temelleri,* (İstanbul: Güzem Can Yayınları, 2016):792; Fatma Doğruel and A.Suut Doğruel, *Bıçak Sırtı Büyüme ve İstikrar: Küreselleşmenin Yükselişi ve Düşüşü,* (İstanbul: İstanbul Bilgi Üniversitesi Yayınları, 2018):49.

[15] Sinan Sönmez, "Bretton Woods, Fordizm ve Hegemonya," *Hacettepe Üniversitesi İktisadi ve İdari Bilimler Fakültesi Dergisi* 34, no.1 (2016): 43-62.

[16] Michael D. Bordo, "The Operation and Demise of The Bretton Woods System; 1958 to 1971," *National Bureau of Economic Research Working Paper* 23189 (2017), 3.

[17] Michael D. Bordo "The Bretton Woods International Monetary System: A Historical Overview", in *A Reprospective on the Bretton Woods System,* ed. M. Bordo and B. Eichegreen (Chicago: University of Chicago Press, 1993), 3.

[18] Bordo, "The Operation and Demise", 2.

was laid.[19] With the Bretton Woods System, the power of the US dollar was institutionalized and became a reserve. The currencies of the member countries were also indexed to gold, making it possible for countries with more dollars than they could spend to convert these savings into gold.[20]

The system is a compromise between the fixed exchange rates of the gold standard, seen as favourable for the reconstruction of the global trade and financial network, and the excellent flexibility countries resorted to in the 1930s to restore and maintain domestic economic and financial stability. It was designed to combine the advantages of the fixed exchange rates of the pre-World War I gold standard with some flexibility against large shocks.[21]

Unlike the fixed exchange rate system based on the gold standard, the new monetary system, called the Bretton Woods Monetary System, was shaped around the understanding that the exchange rates would fluctuate within limits set by the central banks of the member countries and that the exchange rates would be adjusted (adjustable exchange rate) if certain conditions were met.[22] In the system, the US must purchase the dollar in the reserves of the central banks of the member countries at a fixed price. In contrast, the member countries must keep the fluctuation in the official exchange rate within the lower upper limit of ± 1% margin. Thus, the value of the currencies of the member countries, which were indexed to the dollar and, therefore, to gold, was targeted within these limits.[23]

The agreement also obliged member countries to lift restrictions on the current account while allowing them to maintain controls on transactions on the capital account (to limit destabilizing capital flows). Capital controls and the ability to adjust parties in response to shocks gave members the flexibility to use domestic monetary and fiscal policy to mitigate business cycle shocks. Still, the commitment to pegged likenesses limited the extent of these policy actions. The IMF provided relief to members for temporary current account deficits, based on the principle of a credit union in which members could withdraw more than their original gold quota.[24] In addition to the ability of

---

[19] Ece C. Akdoğan, "Uluslararası Para Sisteminin Geçmişi, Bugünü ve Geleceği," *Çankaya Üniversitesi Hukuk Fakültesi Dergisi* 5, no. 1 (2020): 97.

[20] Allan H. Meltzer, "US Policy in the Bretton Woods Era," *Federal Reserve Bank of St. Louis Review* 73 (1991): 62.

[21] Bordo, "The Operation And Demise", 3.

[22] İlhan Eroğlu, "Türkiye'de Kriz Yönetimi ve IMF Politikaları", in *Türkiye'nin İktisadi Görünümü*, ed. İlhan Eroğlu (Bursa: Ekin Yayınevi, 2021), 423.

[23] Jane D'Arista, "The Evolving International Monetary System," *Cambridge Journal of Economics* 33 (2009): 639.; Akdoğan, "Uluslararası Para Sisteminin Geçmişi," s. 98.

[24] Bordo, "The Operation and Demise", 4.

member countries to finance their short-term external deficits with loans from the IMF, they also have the option of using their gold and foreign exchange reserves but resorting to devaluation as a last resort.[25] However, the depreciation to be made at a rate higher than 10% required the approval of the IMF, and for the support of the IMF, the existence of a 'fundamental imbalance' in the balance of payments was required.[26] Because of this practice, the Bretton Woods System is also known as the IMF or Adjustable Fixed Exchange Rate System.[27]

The Bretton Woods negotiations resulted in the establishment of the monetary system to be implemented after World War II and the establishment of the International Monetary Fund (IMF) and the World Bank, the so-called Bretton Woods twins. The World Bank was tasked with providing financial resources for the reconstruction and development of European countries damaged after the war. In contrast, the IMF was charged with the establishment of a stable exchange rate regime, the financing of countries with deficit balance of payments, and the regular functioning of the international financial system.[28] The International Monetary Fund (IMF) is an essential institutional innovation that distinguishes the post-World War I exchange rate regime from previous international monetary arrangements. The IMF contributed to the initial smooth functioning of the Bretton Woods system.[29]

The Bretton Woods System gave members exchange rate stability and independence for monetary authorities to maintain full employment. The system lasted from 1944 to 1971 and led to a remarkable economic performance.[30] The Bretton Woods System was short-lived, and although it had some shortcomings, it showed the world economy to have a higher and more stable growth rate in the last 150 years, except for the Great Moderation Period (1983-2006). In this respect, the Bretton Woods System can succeed more than all regimes except the classical gold standard and the Great Moderation Period.[31] At this point, the question of which features of the Bretton Woods System help

---

[25] Akdoğan, "Uluslararası Para Sisteminin Geçmişi", 96 97.

[26] Seyidoğlu, *İktisat Biliminin Temelleri*, 545.

[27] Hasan Bardakçı, "Uluslararası Para Sistemlerinin Gelişimi," *Avrasya Dosyası Dergisi* 13, no.1 (2022):11.

[28] Akdoğan, "Uluslararası Para Sisteminin Geçmişi", 62.; Melzter, "US Policy", 62.

[29] Barry Eichengreen, "Epilogue: Three Perspectives on the Bretton Woods System", in *A Retrospective on the Bretton Woods System: Lessons for International Monetary Reform*, ed. Michael D. Bordo and Barry Eichengreen, (Chicago: University of Chicago Press, 1991), 623.

[30] Bordo, "The Operation and Demise", 2.

[31] Luca Benati and Charles Goodhart. "Monetary Policy Regimes and Economic Performance: The Historical Record 1979-2008", in *Handbook of Monetary Economics*, ed. Benjamin Friedman and Michael Woodford, vol 3., (New York: New York North Holland Press, 2010), 1165.

economic stability comes to the fore. Two hypotheses have been developed to answer this question.

i- *The* Bretton Woods institutions provide rules that discipline policymakers and solve the problem of time inconsistency they typically face.

ii- Bretton Woods's arrangements deter behaviour inconsistent with international cooperation and stabilize the international system.[32]

The Dilemmas of the Bretton Woods System and the Story of the Collapse of the System

The Bretton Woods System functioned quite smoothly until the early 1970s. However, Bretton Woods brought temporary solutions to the problems of capitalist accumulation at a time when specific historical conditions came together. Still, ultimately, the collapse was inevitable.[33] There is no consensus on the reasons for the destruction of Bretton Woods. Differences between US and foreign monetary policies, differences between US and foreign fiscal policies, the inability of deficit countries to devalue, failure of surplus countries to revalue, and decline in international competition. Flaws in the system's structure are among the reasons put forward for the plan's collapse.[34]

The Bretton Woods System became a gold dollar standard linked to US monetary authorities pursuing sound low inflation policies. As the system evolved, it faced severe problems of adjustment, confidence, and liquidity, as with the interwar gold swap standard. The adjustment problem meant that member countries with balance of payments deficits struggled between currency crises and recessions in the face of nominal rigidities. With its great flexibility for the USA, the system fuelled irresponsibility in this country and led to the spread of rising inflation rates to other member countries through the dollar. Surplus countries had to sterilize dollar inflows to prevent inflation.[35]

Firstly, the devaluation of the UK in 1949 was followed by devaluations in 23 other member countries due to the misalignment of their currencies. Second, as the system converted to the gold dollar standard, the three major problems

---

[32] Barry Eichengreen, "Epilogue: Three Perspectives on the Bretton Woods System", in *A Retrospective on the Bretton Woods System: Lessons for International Monetary Reform*, ed. Michael D. Bordo and Barry Eichengreen, (Chicago: University of Chicago Press, 1991), 624.

[33] Sönmez, "Bretton Woods", 45.

[34] Eichengreen, "Epilogue: Three Perspectives", 625.

[35] Bordo, "The Operation and Demise", 2.; Yalçın Acar, "70 Sonrası Uluslararası Enflasyona Bretton - Woods Sisteminin Etkileri", *Bursa İktisadi ve Ticari İlimler Akademisi İktisat Fakültesi Dergisi*, 2, no.1 (1981): 165.

of the interwar gold exchange standard, such as harmonization, confidence, and liquidity, re-emerged.[36]

Increasing private and official demand for the dollar was fuelled by personal and official long-term capital outflows over the current account surplus. This led to official balance of payments deficits beginning as early as 1950.[37]

In the first years of the Bretton Woods System, member countries with a surplus balance of payments preferred to hold foreign exchange instead of gold. For this reason, US treasury bonds were in demand, and countries earned interest income and converted their foreign exchange into gold when necessary. In addition to these, the continuous foreign trade surplus of the USA led to the need for dollars to meet the demands of the member countries for American goods. The system functioned smoothly until the end of the 1960s, but problems started in the design from the beginning of the 1970s. With the US exporting large amounts of dollars to finance the Vietnam War, the external deficit and inflation started to rise.[38] Due to these developments, the dollar became overvalued. A group of countries led by France and the UK started to buy gold by selling dollars. In 1971, the dollar's value against gold was redetermined as 38 dollars instead of 1 ounce of gold 35 dollars. With the new arrangement called the Smithsonian Accords, new exchange values were determined for national currencies, and the problems of the Bretton Woods System were solved, albeit temporarily. With the new arrangement, the fluctuation margin of national currencies against the dollar was revised as ±2.5 per cent. With these arrangements, there is an idea to ensure the stable structure of the dollar again. However, despite these steps, the US foreign trade deficit continued to increase, leading the German and Japanese central banks to buy dollars. By 1973, the second devaluation had to be made in the system, and 1 ounce of gold was set at 42.3 dollars. These steps and exchange rate adjustments were not enough to slow down the process of flight from the dollar by failing to stabilize prices in international financial markets, and the dollar could not be supported in the system. In March 1973, Japan, Canada, the Scandinavian countries, and then the European Economic Community (EEC), among the Bretton Woods System member countries, broke the link between their national currencies and gold and left their exchange rates floating. In 1976, with the conference

---

[36] Bordo, "The Operation and Demise", 12.

[37] Michael D. Bordo, "The Bretton Woods International Monetary System: A Historical Overview", in *A Reprospective on the Bretton Woods System,* ed. M. Bordo and B. Eichegreen, (Chicago: University of Chicago Press, 1993), 47.

[38] Bordo, "The Operation and Demise", 25.

held in Jamaica, the free-floating exchange rate was legalized, and the Bretton Woods System officially ended.[39]

In 1971, the Bretton Woods System collapsed due to some reasons such as reactions to the emission gains of the USA, Triffin's Dilemma (security-liquidity problem), an asymmetric structure that puts the burden of maintaining external balance on the country with the external deficit, the mixed effect of the formation of a rigid fixed exchange rate system, liquidity problem, insecurity, emission gains problem and development problems of less developed countries.[40] German financier Hjalmar Schacht's following observations about the Bretton Woods System reveal the defective aspects of the system:[41]

> "An artificial system, even if it is skilfully constructed, cannot ensure the stability of international payments. An international monetary system cannot be established according to the arbitrary discretion of governments, erroneous decisions, and agreements to be drawn up according to the day's needs. The international stability of money, its ability to have a standard that can be accepted everywhere and at all times, will be possible not through gold exchange but through the binding of gold to itself."

The collapse of the Bretton Woods System is the natural and inevitable result of the capitalist accumulation and development process and dynamics. In the Bretton Woods system, national economies were mainly focused on local/national growth dynamics, but the development laws of capitalism were ignored because it was impossible to control them. The Bretton Woods system has fallen far from responding to the needs of globalizing capitalism.[42]

The Bretton Woods System, designed as a fixed exchange rate system, was implemented in 1944 and remained in practice until 1973. It ended with the developed countries leaving their currencies to float. Especially in the 1960s, with the good functioning of the system, it supported the excellent progress of two countries such as Germany and Japan. In 1973, with the collapse of the Bretton Woods System and the subsequent amendment of the Articles of Association of the IMF in 1978, a new order was introduced for the world economy. In the new order, a new practice was adopted between the floating exchange rate practice, in which state intervention would be at a minimum

---

[39] Oktay Salih Akbay, "Küresel Finansal Krizin Kökenleri Üzerine Bir Değerlendirme", *Sosyal Bilimler Metinleri Dergisi* 6 (2010): 1-12.; Akdoğan, "Uluslararası Para Sisteminin Geçmii", 100.

[40] Yusuf Bayraktutan, "Küreselleşme Kriz ve IMF", *Liberal Düşünce* 5, no.19 (2000): 16.

[41] Acar, "70 Sonrası Uluslararası", 166.

[42] Sönmez, "Bretton Woods, Fordizm", 56.

level, and the fixed exchange rate practice, which links the country's currency to a basket of foreign currencies.[43]

New Searches after the Bretton Woods System and the Foundations of Modern Central Banking

The role of money in economic activity has brought about a continuous process of change and transformation since the discovery of money. This change and transformation has taken place widely, from money as a medium of exchange to the financial sector as a lending fund. The development of information and communication technologies has brought about significant changes, especially in financial markets. Cecchetti et al. (2006: 3) summarised the framework of this change and transformation under six headings. These are money, financial markets, financial institutions, financial instruments, government regulatory and supervisory institutions, and central banks.

The main elements in these headings are money and the central bank, essential arguments in shaping economic activity. Central banks have assumed an essential role in realizing the economic activity targeted by money. In the early periods of central banking, central banks, which were in operation to meet the financial fund needs of the state and to finance wars, later turned into modern institutions that make decisions and produce policies related to money with the effect of developing world trade and economic events, and prepare the ground for the formation of a stable financial structure with decisions to regulate the financial system in the light of leading indicators.

The establishment of the International Monetary Fund (IMF) and the World Bank and the decisions taken on the international monetary system (Bretton Woods System) at the "International Monetary and Financial Conference" held by the United Nations Organisation in the town of Bretton Woods in New Hampshire, USA on 1-22 July 1944 was influential in the formation of modern central banking. At the Bretton Wood Conference, the IMF was assigned the role of being an economic and financial organization responsible for the functioning of the international monetary system, while the part of the World Bank was determined as providing funds for long-term development projects.[44] In particular, the international monetary systems shaped after the Second World War were shaped under the hegemony of the US Dollar, and the currencies of the IMF member countries were linked to the US Dollar at a fixed exchange rate, thus preventing a change in the axis of international trade in favour of a

---

[43] Bardakçı, "Uluslararası Para Sistemlerinin Gelişimi", 18.

[44] Timothy Lane, "Tensions in the Role of the IMF and Directions for Reform," *World Economics* 6, no. 2 (2005): 47-66.; Il-Hyun Yoon, "The Changing Role of The IMF: Evidence From Korea's Crisis," *Asian Perspective* 29, no. 2 (2005): 182.

country through devaluation. The possibility of governments implementing an independent monetary policy was conditioned by the fixed exchange rate regime and capital controls, the two main pillars of the Bretton Woods system. In this context, policymakers in open economies aimed to achieve three macroeconomic objectives. These are stabilizing the exchange rate, benefiting from free international capital mobility, and conducting monetary policy towards domestic goals. However, since only two of these three objectives can be consistent with each other (the impossible trinity), policymakers have had to abandon one. On the other hand, it isn't easy to agree on measuring these three objectives. Although central banks such as the German Bundesbank, the Federal Reserve, and the Bank of England used the quantity of money as a measure of monetary policy independence for a while after 1970, financial innovations and instability in demand for money in recent years have made the quantity of cash inapplicable and short-term interest rates have been adopted as a policy instrument instead.[45]

Especially with the end of the Bretton Woods system, a new era was entered in which capital mobility, the other two pillars of the impossible trinity, was free, and an independent monetary policy could function. This situation necessitated the abandonment of the fixed exchange rate regime and the floating of exchange rates. In this context, separate monetary policy is defined as the capacity of central banks to use the interest rate instrument at their disposal independently of foreign interest rates.[46]

When the Bretton Woods system was actively functioning, central banks necessarily preferred the fixed exchange rate regime in their monetary policy implementations, and freedom of capital movements was not allowed. In this situation, the interest rate instrument in the hands of traditional central banking was used independently from the world interest rate, and the monetary policy was expected to function effectively by implementing expansionary and contractionary monetary policy. In this case, provided that the two pillars of the impossible trilemma, the exchange rate and capital movements, were fixed, the active role of money in economic policies was ensured.

On the other hand, when capital movement is liberalized, interest rates, which are monetary policy instruments, become fixed by being equalized to the world interest rates determined by the central countries, and exchange rates are kept constant. Under these conditions, if central banks raise domestic

---

[45] Maurice Obstfeld et al.,"The Trilemma in History: Tradeoffs among Exchange Rates, Monetary Policies, and Capital Mobility," *NBER Working Paper* no. 10396 (2005): 1-2.

[46] Joshua Aizenman et al., "Assessing the Emerging Global Financial Architecture: Measuring the Trilemma's Configurations Over Time", *National Bureau of Economic Research* no. w14533 (2008):1-38.

interest rates to pursue a contractionary monetary policy for price stability in the face of high inflation, there is no change in other conditions since the return on financial assets will be more attractive in the country where interest rates are increased compared to other countries, capital inflows to the government will increase, and foreign exchange inflows to the country will increase, as a result of the increase in foreign exchange supply, exchange rates will tend to decrease. Since the central banks are committed to fixing the Exchange rate, they will not allow it to fall by purchasing foreign exchange against the national currency. As a result, the tight monetary policy implemented for price stability against high inflation will not work effectively. Under these circumstances, the success of the monetary policy in controlling high inflation depends on either giving up the freedom of capital movement or abandoning the fixed exchange rate.

The functioning of this system, which constitutes the essence of the Bretton Woods system, depends on specific economic conditions. In particular, with the increase in structural fragility, the removal of barriers to capital movements, and the rise in the importance of financial markets, it won't be easy to talk about successful central banking using traditionalist methods in this system. In this case, instead of the fixed exchange rate regime applied in the Bretton Woods system and monetary policy independence in the absence of capital mobility, it is suggested that either independent monetary policy should be abandoned or the fixed exchange rate regime should be abandoned. As the conditions summarised in the fourth heading began to emerge that the Bretton Woods system would no longer work efficiently, the fixed exchange rate regime was abandoned in the US and replaced by a floating exchange rate regime (the US dollar maintained its reserve currency position even in the post-Bretton Woods period), followed by developed countries. The European Union (EU) followed a more cautious path and took a new step towards independent monetary policy in central banking by establishing the European Monetary System in 1979. In the following period, the European Union followed this move by establishing the Eurozone in 2002, launching a new currency for this region, the Euro, and letting it float against other currencies.

The transition to the floating exchange rate regime following the Bretton Woods System, the financial liberalization after 1980, and the new conditions created by the liberalized capital movements, first in developed countries and then in developing countries, have revealed the necessity of redesigning monetary policies in central banking. This situation has shown that the impossible trinity can no longer explain the conditions for effective monetary policy implementation and that new searches for monetary policy are inevitable.

The new searches of central banks after Bretton Woods can be associated with the fact that the exchange relationship between inflation and unemployment lost its validity with the 'stagflation' phenomenon experienced after 1970 due to the oil crises and the increase in unemployment and rising inflation. In the face of this situation, policymakers started to consider the necessity of pursuing an independent monetary policy in the fight against high inflation. This process was the beginning of the foundations of modern central banking. Such a development was pioneered by the Monetarist view pioneered by Milton Friedman in the 1970s with the approach that "*inflation is always and everywhere a monetary phenomenon.*" The foundations of this view can be traced back to Milton Friedman's 1962 article "*Should there be an Independent Monetary Authority?*".[47] In his article, Friedman emphasized the importance of price stability and pointed out the importance of independent central banking in the fight against inflation. This understanding was reflected in central banking after the collapse of the Bretton Woods system. According to this understanding, monetary aggregates have been used as a policy instrument within the framework of monetary targeting (monetary aggregates) strategy in the fight against inflation for price stability under the leadership of monetarist economic theory. However, problems in the determination of monetary aggregates weakened the effectiveness of this instrument, and short-term interest rates were used as a policy tool. The introduction of short-term interest rates as a monetary policy tool has changed objectives, and price stability has become the main objective in monetary policy implementations, with central banks targeting a specific inflation rate. In this context, the importance of the independent structure of central banks has come to the fore, and the necessity of making decisions with a transparent perspective to overcome the crisis of confidence caused by the time inconsistency problem has come to the fore (Woodford, 2003: 861-886).

In parallel with these developments, in the post-1990 period, the inflation targeting strategy constituted the basic framework of the monetary policies of the central banks of developed countries with the primary objective of price stability. In addition to this, the importance of financial markets has increased. With the development of new financial instruments, the financial system in developed countries has transformed into an institutional structure in the light of legal regulations, and a process that will set an example for developing countries has been experienced. As a result, the developments in the post-Bretton Woods period showed that developed countries were affected by the developments in national and international markets. In contrast, in developing countries, fundamental macroeconomic indicators were shaped by external

---

[47] Milton Friedman, "Should There be an Independent Monetary Authority?", in *Search of A Monetary Constitution*, ed. *Leland* B. Yeager, (Cambridge, MA: Harvard University Press, 1962), 219-243.

influences.[48] This situation has revealed the necessity of considering a more complex structure in the work of central banks under the influence of national and international financial developments.[49] Especially the economic conditions that emerged with the 2008 Global Financial Crisis revealed that short-term interest rates, which are seen as an effective policy tool in preventing financial instability, which is seen as an economic risk according to new developments in addition to the price stability target, will not be sufficient and new policy instruments must be developed.

In this context, capital movements and financial developments are considered to significantly limit the ability of central banks to implement effective monetary policy, regardless of the exchange rate regime. Under these conditions, it is assumed that being open to financial innovations will increase efficiency. Accordingly, it has been preferred to limit the impact of regulations on financial markets by either abolishing or softening the rules. These developments are due to the lack of depth in financial markets; it has been observed that essential macroeconomic variables in developing countries are more affected by capital movements, whereas in developed countries, internal processes in financial markets are more determinant in fundamental macroeconomic indicators. The most obvious example is the decline in the interaction between asset prices and central bank policies in advanced economies due to capital flows. The most obvious example is the decline in the relationship between the US Federal Reserve's policy rates and market long-term interest rates.[50]

As a result, During the implementation of the Bretton Woods system, the monetary policy effectiveness of central banks was possible with the realization of the impossible trinity under the assumption of control of capital movements and fixed exchange rate. However, with the abandonment of the Bretton Woods System, monetary policy objectives were tried to be achieved through short-term interest rate policies as a result of the liberalization of capital movements and the relaxation of the rules regarding financial markets. Still, with this preference, monetary policy effectiveness was overshadowed mainly by capital movements and financial market dynamics. These developments finally brought

---

[48] Hasan Cömert, *Central Banks and Financial Markets: The Declining Power of US Monetary Policy*, (Cheltenham: Edward Elgar Publishing, 2013).

[49] Ben S. Bernanke, "Globalization and Monetary Policy", Remarks by the Chairman of the Board of Governors of the US Federal Reserve System, at the Fourth Economic Summit, Stanford Institute for Economic Policy Research, Stanford, California, March 2, 2007, https://www.federalreserve.gov/newsevents/speech/bernanke200 70302a.htm.

[50] Hasan Cömert, "From Trilemma to Dilemma: Monetary Policy During and After The Bretton Woods System", *Hacettepe University Journal of Economics and Administrative Sciences* 34, no.1 (2016):127.

along new searches with central banks' new central banking approach after the 2008 Crisis.

Modern Central Banking and Basic Dynamics

After 1970, the collapse of the Bretton Woods system paved the way for independent monetary policy implementations, which also constituted the beginning of a new structuring process in central banking, and the first steps of modern central banking began to be taken. This situation made it necessary to examine central banking in terms of the role it has assumed and the objectives it wants to achieve. In this context, it was considered to set targets for macroeconomic stability by defining the duties of central banking and the necessity to construct public policy to meet the needs of the government, the financial system and the market. The related structures can be summarised as follows:[51]

*1- **Monetary policy governance:*** central banks should aim for macroeconomic stability when determining monetary policy management and establish accountable governance concerning their decisions and actions. Regarding this issue:

- ***Independence:*** By isolating the central bank's powers from political pressures, an independent central bank is institutionally established, and the functioning of the accountability mechanism is ensured.
- ***Objectives: central banks may aim to achieve many objectives*** in their monetary policy implementations. However, price stability, widely agreed upon due to the importance of macroeconomic stability and sustainable growth, has become the primary objective in recent years. Setting such a target makes it possible for central banks to focus on the mark on the one hand and to isolate themselves from political pressures through accountability on the other. In addition, shaping central bank policies around the target may require flexibility in different economic conditions. In these cases, a policy strategy can be formulated to incorporate flexibility.
- ***Exchange Rate Regime:*** The exchange rate regime has particular importance in monetary policy management. The central bank's role in monetary policy and its role and authority in determining the exchange rate assume an influential role in the choice of the exchange rate to prevent the inconsistency that may arise in ensuring macroeconomic stability. However, it is not common for the official authority to

[51] Archer and Bingham, "The Main Tendencies", 5-16.

determine the exchange rate regime alone. In addition, within the framework of its powers, central banks, as an institution that closely monitors financial markets, manage exchange rate policy and foreign exchange assets to prevent instability in foreign exchange markets.

2- Governance of Financial Stability: Although financial stability is among the main objectives of central banks, it is less prominent in the legislation than the price stability objective. For the financial stability function, central banks assume the role of a lender of last resort when liquidity assistance is required by maintaining the stability of reserves in the banking system. In addition, functions such as stability of the payment system, regulation and supervision of institutions and markets, development of prudential policies, and encouragement of the development of the financial system can be considered within this scope. Ensuring stability in the financial system is of public importance. Considering that there is no other institutional structure to ensure financial stability, it has been accepted in recent years that central banks are responsible for the financial system's stability.

Other governance arrangements include the provision of banking services to commercial banks, fiscal agencies to the government, provision and development of financial sector infrastructure, protection of consumers based on individual financial contracts, price stability, and financial stability as monetary policy objectives of central banks.

Overall, these functions focus on three aspects of central bank governance. *First,* the state banking activity involves central banks' transactions with governments. In particular, governments' debt issuance and investment activities will impact financial markets and prices in which monetary policy actions take place. In this case, central banks are involved in short-term and long-term government funding. However, in this funding, the government's desire to borrow at low cost and the central banks' willingness to keep short-term interest rates at a certain level in line with the monetary policy they pursue may bring about a conflict. *Secondly,* encouraging financial sector development is an essential function of central banks. Financial depth is an important factor that increases the effectiveness of monetary policy. However, although central banks' role in promoting financial development is often explicitly stated in the laws, its boundaries must be clearly defined. In other words, a concrete target measure has yet to be set for this function. *Thirdly,* consumer protection is also seen as an essential central banking function. Financial services, consumer protection, and access to information should be considered within this scope.

3- Legal Status and Guarantees: Central bank laws outline the general framework of the role and responsibility of central banks. However, this is not above constitutional provisions and may also be influenced by other laws.

Central banks determine their relationship with the government within the framework of the laws they are subject to, and the framework of their autonomous structure is drawn. *Firstly,* harmonized macroeconomic policy arrangements can be seen as an essential issue. In this respect, the exchange rate regime of monetary policies and harmonizing fiscal and monetary policy are essential elements. *Secondly,* constraints on the government's monetary financing are essential regulations. In this framework, some legal arrangements either restrict the central bank's direct lending to the government or impose limits or quantitative restrictions in exceptional cases. *Thirdly,* the autonomy of decision-making is considered an essential indicator of independence. Decision-making independence, as guaranteed by legal provisions, includes provisions to prevent government pressure on the central bank by making it a criminal offence to seek or receive instructions from other state institutions or government officials in the performance of central bank functions. *Fourth,* appointment procedures are also seen as an essential legal safeguard for the activities of central banks. Important factors affecting autonomy are how central bank officials are selected, to whom they are accountable, for what reasons, and by whom they can be dismissed. *Fifthly,* the security of tenure also draws attention as an essential factor in autonomy. In particular, the fact that decision-makers make decisions within the security of tenure can be seen as a protective arrangement against unwarranted and external influences. For this reason, it is generally preferred that the terms of office of governors and other decision-makers in an autonomous central bank structure are longer than the election periods.

4- Decision-making structures and the relationship between the government and the legislature: In modern central banking, central bank policy decisions are made through the group decision mechanism rather than by senior management. The supervisory board also supervises the management. The legitimacy and credibility of decisions are enhanced by the fact that they are based on expertise and diversity of opinion. This allows decision-makers to decide without the government or other pressure factors. On the other hand, given that central banks are public institutions, central banks are in communication with the government and legislative bodies. This communication may take the form of a meeting between the central bank governor and the finance minister, especially in developed countries, or it may take the form of government representatives attending the central bank board of directors (as in emerging market economies). On the other hand, central banks regularly contact the legislature through reporting to or scrutiny by elected representatives as a requirement of accountability arrangements.

5- Transparency, oversight, and accountability: Transparency protects against hidden pressures. Building transparency through oversight mechanisms emphasizes trust in policy implementation. In this regard, legislative committees, audit committees, judicial reviews, and exceptional reviews by panels of experts and international financial institutions fulfil the function of oversight mechanisms. The oversight of legislative committees generally refers to the oversight of boards involved in supervising administrative matters. Audit committees oversee the bank's operational budget, accounts review, and audit process. Judicial oversight comes into play in audits where accountability mechanisms are challenging to implement and provides oversight of the process by which decisions are made and actions are taken. On the other hand, as the powers of central banks expand, the accountability mechanism also expands and develops. The general framework for accountability should consider identifying clear measurable and non-contradictory objectives, the lagged results of policy implementation, the influence of non-policy forces on these results, and unobservable individual effects when formulating policy options.

Paradigmatic Changes After Modern Central Banking

When the Bretton Woods system was implemented, monetary policy was adequate under the assumption of control of capital movements and fixed exchange rates, referred to as the impossible trinity. However, economic developments after 1970 led to a process in which the monetary policy effectiveness of the central bank of the Bretton Woods system depended on more than just the control of capital movements and exchange rates. After 1970, the stagflation phenomenon that emerged with the oil crisis changed the understanding of implementing a monetary policy under the impossible trilemma in central banking. By the monetarist acceptance that inflation is a monetary phenomenon, it has been generally accepted that the primary objective of central banking is to fight inflation, which can be achieved by controlling the monetary volume.

In the monetary policy approach in which the monetary targeting strategy is widely used, monetary volume is taken as a monetary policy instrument. However, the uncertainty in the measurement of monetary volume and the unstable structure of money demand brought about the search for a new paradigm, and the new economic conditions created by the liberalized capital movements as a result of the financial liberalization after 1980 increased the importance of financial markets and institutions in central banking. The new paradigm of central banking is observed in the balance sheets of deposit-taking banks, where deposits constitute passive assets and loans constitute active assets, and loans, regarded as active assets, are considered assets with low liquidity levels. In this situation, a search for a new paradigm has emerged, considering that if banks fall into a liquidity crisis for any reason, there will be a problem of trust, and it is possible for banks to fall into a liquidity crisis at any time. In this quest, central banks assumed the role of the lender of last resort to prevent banking panic. They aimed to prevent instability in financial markets by funding banks at the lending interest rate on the condition that they provide qualified collateral. As the lender of last resort, central banks aimed to restore confidence in financial markets. In the lender of last resort function, characteristics such as incurring an interest fee in return for providing liquid funds to the whole system, requiring collateral, and being solvent but illiquid institutions are sought.[52] However, the role of 'lender of last resort' given to central banks with the post-1980 financial liberalization has caused the capital mobility brought about by financialization to turn towards the financial sector due to the lack of expected profitability in the real sector. Especially the 2008 financial crisis has been a crucial turning point in the change of this process. Depending on a rapid change in the functioning or structure of financial markets, the role of central banks as the lender of last resort will also change. According to Minsky's[53] approach, changes in the functioning of money markets and financial institutions make this change inevitable. These changes may occur in financial institutions, financial markets, financial instruments, and regulations related to the financial system.

Financial liberalization and globalization, which started in the late 1970s, led to the formation and development of financial markets based on neoliberal policies and a transformation from traditional commercial banking to investment banking.[54] This transformation in banks rendered the lending role insufficient. In case of unquantifiable and incalculable risks, the trading volume in financial markets decreased due to fear and panic. Dissipating the panic atmosphere in financial markets and creating a climate of confidence were considered necessary for financial stability. With this transformation, liquidity, which has become the most critical problem faced by financial intermediaries and indirect financing in the financial system, has been placed on the agenda of financial markets with new problems of different types and dimensions. It is now considered that these problems cannot be overcome with the central banks as the lender of last resort. Central banks have assumed a new function to prevent other existing and potential problems in financial markets. With the "role of the last market

[52] Gayane Oganesyan, "The Changed Role of the Lender of Last Resort: Crisis Responses of the Federal Reserve", European Central Bank and Bank of England, Institute for International Political Economy, Berlin, *Working Paper* no. 19 (2013): 2-3.

[53] Hyman P. Minsky, "Central Banking and Money Market Changes", *The Quarterly Journal of Economics* 71 no.2 (1957): 172.

[54] Costas Lapavitsas, "Finansallaşmış Kapitalizm: Kriz ve Finansal Müsadere", in *Finansallaşma ve Kapitalizmin Krizi*, ed. C. Lapavitsas (İstanbul: Yordam Kitap, 2009), 25.

maker", it aims to mediate the formation of healthy pricing so that financial instruments can be traded reliably.

This role is reflected in the direct purchase and sale of various private sector securities and the acceptance of various private sector securities as collateral for repos, collateralized debt, and rediscount window advances. This role aims to establish a price at which financial instruments can be traded, rather than a liquidity regulating role as in open market operations. Thus, by accepting poor-quality assets as collateral under crisis conditions, the functioning of the market was intended to be secured by trading financial instruments that are unlikely to make a profit.[55] The last market-making function emerged as a substitute policy to solve the problems faced, especially after the 2008 Financial Crisis, and the last lending function could not deal with that. In this policy setting, unconventional monetary policy instruments such as quantitative easing, credit expansion, expanding the list of assets eligible as collateral, direct purchases of mortgaged assets, and interest rate corridor were preferred as new policy instruments because monetary policies could not have the desired effect and caused high costs as a result of the fall in interest rates to zero level and the deterioration of monetary transmission mechanisms in the central banks of developed countries, especially the US central bank Fed.[56]

Since the financial institutions holding mortgage-backed securities were faced with the problem of the fall in the prices of these securities and the problem of devaluation, the US Federal Reserve Fed primarily aimed to prevent devaluation and the fall in security prices and managed this process by trying to recover the financial structure of private sector financial institutions by taking the losses incurred in private sector institutions. In this context, this new policy move, which started with the Fed as the last market maker to be put into practice, especially after the 2008 Crisis, and continued with the central banks of developed countries, has shown the practice of protecting against the crises of the capitalist system without giving up neo-liberal policies. In doing so, it trivialized inflation targeting and focused monetary policy attention on asset prices rather than inflation, making a policy strategy such as inflation targeting controversial.[57]

---

[55] Borko Krstić ve Mirjana Jemović, "The Impact of Global Financial Crisis on Changing The Central Bank Role in The Market Positioning of Financial Institutions," *Facta Universitatis Series: Economics and Organization* 6, no. 3 (2009): 231.

[56] Aleksandra Szunke, "A New Paradigm of Modern Central Banking", International Conference, Governance & Control in Finance & Banking: A New Paradigm for Risk & Performance, (Paris: France, April 18-19, 2013), 75-78.

[57] Özgür Balmumcu, "Küresel Finans Krizi Ekseninde Para Politikası Tartışmaları," *Ege Stratejik Araştırmalar Dergisi* 14, no.2 (2013), 33.

When the functions of central banks are reconsidered, it has become expected to assume a different function beyond being a bank of banks, a state bank, and an emission bank. This expectation of a different function is broader than the traditional monetary policy strategy's objectives. Still, it has been met with central banking, where financial stability has become the main objective. In such central banking, the role of the lender of last resort has changed, and the "buyer of last resort role" has come to the fore with special asset purchase programs. As part of this role, central banks became the ultimate purchaser of toxic assets that deteriorated banks' balance sheets. In this way, it was envisaged to increase banks' liquidity and create a basis for more efficient capital investments.[58]

The impossibility of achieving price stability on the one hand and financial stability on the other with the policy rate, which is the only policy instrument focusing only on price stability, has been the determining factor in the emergence of this situation. However, the risks inherent in the new paradigm created in this process should also be taken into consideration: In this context, the transformation of central banks from lenders of last resort to market makers of last resort was aimed at affecting long-term interest rates by increasing or decreasing the prices of securities through quantitative easing and credit expansion without creating an inflationary process through the role of central banks as net buyers in securities markets. In such a policy choice, the liability of central banks will increase, and the inability to fulfil the increased liability may cause a trust problem.[59]

Conclusion

In the nearly four hundred years of central banking history, institutional development has maintained its vitality as a continuous dynamic structure, and the current structure of central banking has emerged. This change and transformation will continue to parallel economic events and phenomena. In this process, central banks have not only produced economic policy within the intricate networks within the economic system but also assumed a 'playmaker role' as a close follower of the economic system as a whole and the global economic system and foreign economic relations.

The role of central banks in economic life has changed from time to time. As a matter of fact, in the nineteenth century, central banking and monetary

[58] Szunke, "A New Paradigm of Modern", 76.

[59] Demophanes Papadatos, "Günümüz Kapitalizminde Merkez Bankacılığı: Enflasyon Hedeflemesi ve Krizler", in *Finansallaşma ve Kapitalizmin Krizi,* ed. Costas Lapavitsas (İstanbul: Yordam Kitap, 2009), 196-198.

policy debates were centred on the principle of "free banking," which implies a banking approach that is free from the presence of a central bank. At the same time, the dominant economic paradigm of the period the understanding of the self-balancing market mechanism as the dominant economic paradigm of the period was effective in this positioning. It was thought that central banks, as market makers and regulators, could disrupt market efficiency, which would be a source of inflationary processes.

Between the two world wars before the Bretton Woods system, new ideas were put forward that central banks should be given more functions to ensure internal stability instead of the currency's external stability, attributed to central banks under the gold standard. Over time, these ideas were reflected in a central banking system that became more independent from political authorities and assumed more responsibility for maintaining price stability and promoting full employment.

After 1970, following the collapse of the Bretton Woods system, the monetary policy, which was based on the assumption of control of capital movements and fixed exchange rates, expressed as the impossible trinity in the period when the Bretton Woods system was implemented, transformed as a result of the economic developments after 1970, in which the effectiveness of monetary policy did not depend only on the control of capital movements and exchange rates. Accordingly, paving the way for independent monetary policy implementations constituted the beginning of a new structuring in central banking, and the first steps of modern central banking were taken. In this structural change, *monetary policy governance*, which includes issues such as independence, objectives, and exchange rate regime; *financial* stability *governance, in* which central banks assume the role of a lender of last resort when liquidity assistance is required for the financial stability function, by maintaining the stability of reserves in the banking system; *legal status and assurance*, which outline the general framework of the role and responsibility of central banks; *decision-making structures, the relationship between the government and the legislature*, and *transparency, oversight and accountability*.

Especially after the 2008 Global Financial Crisis, there have been significant paradigm shifts in the structure of central banks in terms of the management, prevention, and resolution of the crisis process compared to the pre-crisis period. Problems such as the role of the central bank in financial stability, how the decision-making mechanism on financial stability will function, and how to protect against the financial and reputational risks arising from financial stability-related operations have formed the building blocks of new paradigms. Undoubtedly, confrontation with these problems and the realization of the banks' concern about making losses may distort their political objectives and bring along a problem of trust and reputation.

In the aftermath of the 2008 Global Crisis, the paradigm shift in central banking is associated with central banking that is wider than the objectives set by the traditional monetary policy strategy and where financial stability has become the main objective. In this context, the role of the central bank as "lender of last resort" has changed, and a paradigm shift has taken place in the "buyer of last resort role," as it is the ultimate buyer of toxic assets that worsen the balance sheets of banks through special asset purchase programs. The primary rationale for this paradigm shift is that achieving financial stability with the policy rate focusing only on price stability is considered impossible. The net buyer role assumed by central banks in securities markets aims to affect long-term interest rates by increasing and decreasing the prices of securities through quantitative easing and credit expansion without creating an inflationary process. With this practice, it was possible to achieve price stability on the one hand and financial stability on the other.

Bibliography

Acar, Yalçın. "70 Sonrası Uluslararası Enflasyona Bretton - Woods Sisteminin Etkileri". *Bursa İktisadi ve Ticari İlimler Akademisi İktisat Fakültesi Dergisi 2*, no.1 (1981): 162-167.

Aizenman, Joshua, Menzie D. Chinn, and Hiro Ito. "Assessing the Emerging Global Financial Architecture: Measuring the Trilemma's Configurations Over Time." *National Bureau of Economic Research Working Paper* no. w14533 (2008).

Akbay, Oktay Salih. "Küresel Finansal Krizin Kökenleri Üzerine Bir Değerlendirme". *Sosyal Bilimler Metinleri Dergisi* 6 (2010): 1-12.

Akdoğan, Ece C., "Uluslararası Para Sisteminin Geçmişi, Bugünü ve Geleceği." *Çankaya Üniversitesi Hukuk Fakültesi Dergisi* 5, no. 1 (2020): 91-120.

Archer, David, and Gavin Bingham. "The Main Tendencies in Modern Central Banking." In *Issues in the Governance of Central Banks - A Report from the Central Bank Governance Group*, edited by Guillermo Ortiz, 2009.

Balmumcu, Özgür. "Küresel Finans Krizi Ekseninde Para Politikası Tartışmaları". *Ege Stratejik Araştırmalar Dergisi* vol.4, no.2 (2013):32-55.

Bayraktutan, Yusuf. "Küreselleşme Kriz ve IMF". *Liberal Düşünce* 5, no.19 (2000): 14-18.

Bardakçı, Hasan. "Uluslararası Para Sistemlerinin Gelişimi." *Avrasya Dosyası Dergisi* vol. 13, no. 1 (2022): 30-59.

Benati, Luca and Charles Goodhart. "Monetary Policy Regimes and Economic Performance: The Historical Record 1979-2008". In *Handbook of Monetary* Economics, ed. Benjamin Friedman and Michael Woodford. New York: New York North Holland Press,2010.

Bernanke, Ben S. "Globalization and Monetary Policy." Remarks by the Chairman of the Board of Governors of the US Federal Reserve System at the Fourth Economic Summit. Stanford Institute for Economic Policy Research. Stanford, California. March 2, 2007. https://www.federalreserve.gov/news-events/speech/bernanke20070302a.htm. Erişim tarihi: 22 Temmuz 2023.

Blancheton, Bertrand. "Central Bank Independence in A Historical Perspective. Myth, Lessons and A New Model". *Economic Modelling 52* (2016): 101-107.

Bordo, Michael D. "The Bretton Woods International Monetary System: A Historical Overview." In *A Retrospective on the Bretton Woods System*, edited by M. Bordo and B. Eichengreen, Chicago: University of Chicago Press, 1993.

Bordo, Michael D. *The Gold Standard and Related Regimes.* Cambridge University Press, 1999.

Bordo, Michael D. "A Brief History of Central Banks". *Economic Commentary* 12, no.1 (2007). https://www.clevelandfed.org/publications/economic-commentary/2007/ec-20071201-a-brief-history-of-central-banks (22.07.2023).

Bordo, Michael D., "The Operation and Demise of The Bretton Woods System; 1958 to 1971". *National Bureau of Economic Research, Working Paper* 23189 (2017):1-37.

Broz, Lawrence. "The Domestic Politics of International Monetary Order: The Gold Standard". *International Political Economy* (2002):199-219.

Cecchetti, Stephen G., Kermit Schoenholtz and J. Fackler. *Money, Banking, And Financial Markets.* McGraw-Hill/Irwin, 2006.

Cömert, Hasan. *Central Banks and Financial Markets: The Declining Power of US Monetary Policy.* Cheltenham: Edward Elgar Publishing, 2013.

Cömert, Hasan., "From Trilemma to Dilemma: Monetary Policy During and After The Bretton Woods System". *Hacettepe University Journal of Economics and Administrative Sciences* 34, Issue 1(2016):115-136.

D'Arista, Jane. "The Evolving International Monetary System". *Cambridge Journal of Economics* 33, (2009): 633-652.

Doğruel, Fatma. Ve A.Suut Doğruel. *Bıçak Sırtı Büyüme ve İstikrar: Küreselleşmenin Yükselişi ve Düşüşü.* İstanbul: İstanbul Bilgi Üniversitesi Yayınları, 2018.

Eichengreen, Barry. Epilogue: "Three Perspectives on the Bretton Woods System". In *A Retrospective on the Bretton Woods System: Lessons for International Monetary Reform.* Ed. Michael D. Bordo and Barry Eichengreen. Chicago: University of Chicago Press, 1991.

Eroğlu, İlhan, "Türkiye'de Kriz Yönetimi ve IMF Politikaları." In *Türkiye'nin İktisadi Görünümü,* ed. İlhan Eroğlu. Bursa: Ekin Yayınevi, 2021.

Friedman, Milton, "Should There be an Independent Monetary Authority?". In *Search of A Monetary Constitution.* Ed. Leland B. Yeager. Cambridge MA: Harvard University Press, 1962.

Goodhart, Charles. *The Evolution of Central Banks.* MIT Press, 1988.

Goodhart, Charles. "Central Banking." In *The New Palgrave Dictionary of Economics,* edited by G. Jones, 3rd ed. Palgrave Macmillan, 2018.

Krstić, Borko, and Mirjana Jemović. "The Impact of Global Financial Crisis on Changing The Central Bank Role in the Market Positioning of Financial Institutions." *Facta Universitatis Series: Economics and Organization* 6, no. 3 (2009): 221-236.

Lane, Timothy. "Tensions in the Role of the IMF and Directions for Reform". *World Economics* 6, no.2 (2005): 47-66.

Lapavitsas, Costas. "Finansallaşmış Kapitalizm: Kriz ve Finansal Müsadere". In *Finansallaşma ve Kapitalizmin Krizi*, ed. C. Lapavitsas. İstanbul: Yordam Kitap, 2009.

Lohmann, Susanne. "Central Banks". In *The Encyclopedia of Public Choice*. Boston, MA: Springer US, 2003.

Meltzer, Allan H. "US Policy in the Bretton Woods Era." *Federal Reserve Bank of St. Louis Review* 73 (1991): 54-83.

Minsky, Hyman P. "Central Banking and Money Market Changes". *The Quarterly Journal of Economics* 71, no. 2 (1957): 171-187.

Obstfeld, Maurice, Jay C. Shambaugh and Alan M. Taylor. "The Trilemma in History: Tradeoffs among Exchange Rates, Monetary Policies, and Capital Mobility". NBER Working Paper no.10396, 2005.

Oganesyan, Gayane. "The Changed Role of the Lender of Last Resort: Crisis Responses of the Federal Reserve". European Central Bank and Bank of England, Institute for International Political Economy Berlin, Working Paper no.19 2013.

Papadatos, Demophanes. "Günümüz Kapitalizminde Merkez Bankacılığı: Enflasyon Hedeflemesi ve Krizler", In *Finansallaşma ve Kapitalizmin Krizi*, ed.Costas Lapavitsas. İstanbul: Yordam Kitap, 2009.

Seyidoğlu, Halil. *İktisat Biliminin Temelleri*. İstanbul: Güzem Can Yayınları, 2016.

Siklos, Pierre L. *The Changing Face of Central Banking: Evolutionary Trends Since World War II*. Cambridge University Press, 2002.

Sönmez, Sinan. "Bretton Woods, Fordizm ve Hegemonya". *Hacettepe Üniversitesi İktisadi ve İdari Bilimler Fakültesi Dergisi* 34, no.1 (2016): 43-62.

Szunke, Aleksandra. "A New Paradigm of Modern Central Banking." International Conference "Governance & Control in Finance & Banking: A New Paradigm for Risk & Performance." Paris, France, April 18-19, 2013.

Ugolini, Stefano. *The Evolution of Central Banking: Theory and History*. London: Palgrave Macmillan, 2017.

Woodford, Michael. "Optimal Interest-Rate Smoothing". *The Review of Economic Studies* 70, no.4 (2003): 861-886.

Yoon, Il-Hyun. "The Changing Role of The IMF: Evidence From Korea's Crisis". *Asian Perspective* 29, no. 2 (2005):179-201.

PART I:
EUROPEAN CENTRAL BANKING AND FINANCIAL STABILITY

Chapter 3

The Role of the European Central Bank During the Greek Financial Crisis

John Marangos

University of Macedonia, Greece; University of Missouri Kansas City, USA

Nikos Astroulakis

Tax and Customs Academy IAPR and Hellenic Open University, Greece

Themis Anthrakidis

University of Macedonia, Thessaloniki, Greece

Angeliki Nestoroudi

University of Macedonia, Thessaloniki, Greece

Paraskevi Kyrilla

University of Macedonia, Thessaloniki, Greece

Abstract

The Greek Financial Crisis (GFC) of the years 2010-2018 was one of the largest sovereign financial crises in the global financial history of advanced economies, assisted by the largest financial package in economic history. At the same time, the Greek economy and society were "invaded" by the Troika's crisis management and its imposed policies. In turn, the European Central Bank (ECB), as a member of the Troika, played a decisive role in that process of crisis management. In this chapter, we unfold the role of ECB during the GFC by investigating the landscape and the characteristics of the GFC, the institutional features of ECB, its involvement in the GFC and its pivotal role during that tumultuous period. In addition, we examine the alternative measures that the ECB should have taken during the GFC to achieve better economic and social outcomes.

Keywords: European Central Banking, Greek Financial Crisis

***

Introduction

This chapter unfolds the crucial role of the European Central Bank (ECB) during the Greek financial crisis (GFC). The GFC extended from 2010, when the credit line to service Greek debt was effectively cut by international markets, until 2018, when the country officially ended the Economic Adjustment Programs (EAPs). During the years 2010-2018, "the Troika," consisting of the European Commission (EC), the ECB, and the International Monetary Fund (IMF), imposed and supervised the implementation of three Memoranda of Understanding (MoU).

The rescue package for the Greek economy by the Troika was around €290 bn, the largest financial assistance package in the economic history[1]. The ECB, through its institutional role and as a member of the Troika, was responsible for contributing to the formation and implementation of the three EAPs. However, the ECB's stance towards the GFC, reflecting the provision of article 125 of the Lisbon Treaty for the "no bail-out" clause, did not facilitate an early resolution of the crisis[2]. This delayed intervention increased the cost of the Greek rescue package. In turn, beyond its institutional role as the central bank of the eurozone economies, the ECB's monetary policy has been heavily influenced by the Bundesbank's ordoliberalism and low-inflation policy doctrine[3]. The ECB's main policy of low inflation constrained aggregate demand and the growth process. As well, the lack of a "lender of a last resort" policy increased the financial and social costs in the case of GFC.

The purpose of the chapter is to assess the decisive role played by the ECB in the GFC in the context dictated by its founding principles, its constitutional imperatives, and the ECB's political and ideological stances. The chapter investigates the ECB's policy decisions with respect to the GFC. For instance, its role in stabilizing market conditions and avoiding the risk of *moral hazard* and the repercussions of its policies. It also presents an alternative to the ECB policy during the Greek EAPs where the ECB would act as the "lender of last

---

[1] Vassiliki Dimakopoulou, George Economides, and Apostolis Philippopoulos, "The Greek Great Depression 2009-2016 and the Role Played by the ECB," in *Greece and The Euro From Crisis to Recovery*, ed. George Alogoskoufis and Kevin Featherstone (Hellenic Observatory and the Fletcher School, Tufts University, 2021), 118–137.

[2] Carlo Panico and Francesco Purificato, "The Debt Crisis and the European Central Bank's Role of Lender of Last Resort," Working Paper Series (Amherst, 2013), 8.

[3] Thorsten Beck and Hans-helmut Kotz, *Ordoliberalism: A German Oddity?*, (London: CEPR Press, 2017), 9; Thomas Biebricher, "The Return of Ordoliberalism in Europe - Notes on a Research Agenda,", *I-Lex* 21, no. March (2014): 16.

resort"[4] in this case, providing excess liquidity to the Greek banks to boost aggregate demand, increase consumption and recover the growth prospects while increasing employment and output[5].

To our knowledge, no such research endeavour on the role and the imposed policies of the ECB during the GFC has been attempted before. Students and scholars of economics, economics and international development may benefit from assessing the apparent role of the ECB in one of the largest sovereign financial crises in the global financial history of advanced economies.

The structure of the paper is as follows: section 2 provides information regarding the GFC; section 3 determines the institutional foundation of the ECB; section 4 delves into the ECB's involvement in the GFC and uncovers its pivotal role during that tumultuous period; section 5 offers recommendations concerning the actions that the ECB could have taken; and section 6 concludes.

The Greek Financial Crisis

The GFC refers to the financial and economic difficulties faced by Greece due to the global financial crisis of 2008. The GFC was characterized by a high level of public debt, low economic growth, and a high level of unemployment.[6] Greece joined the European Union in 1981 and adopted the euro as its currency in 2001. In the following years, the Greek economy experienced strong rates of GDP from 4.13% of GDP in 2001 to 5.65% in 2006, fueled mainly by low interest rates and foreign investment.[7] However, the global financial crisis of 2008 and the subsequent eurozone crisis had a profound impact on the Greek economy. This revealed structural weaknesses such as a high level of public debt, low

---

[4] John Marangos, "The Neoclassical and Keynesian Standpoint and Policy Implications Regarding the Greek Financial Crisis," *International Journal of Social Economics* 49, no. 3 (2022): 48, https://doi.org/10.1108/IJSE-07-2021-0376.

[5] Alberto Botta, "Conflicting Claims in the Eurozone? Austerity's Myopia and the Need for a European Federal Union in a Post-Keynesian Eurozone Center–Periphery Model," *Review of Keynesian Economics* 2, no. 1 (2014): 46,62; Eckhard Hein, Achim Truger, and Till Working van Treeck, "The European Financial and Economic Crisis: Alternative Solutions from a (Post-) Keynesian Perspective," IMK Working Paper (Düsseldorf, 2011), 27; Hansjörg Herr, "An Analytical Framework for the Post-Keynesian Macroeconomic Paradigm" (Berlin, 2013), 9.

[6] Ada Cristina Albu and Lucian Liviu Albu, "Public Debt and Economic Growth in Euro Area Countries. A Wavelet Approach", *Technological and Economic Development of Economy* 27, no. 3 (2021): 611,616, https://doi.org/10.3846/tede.2021.14241; Georgios Maris, Pantelis Sklias, and Napoleon Maravegias, "The Political Economy of the Greek Economic Crisis in 2020," *European Politics and Society* 23, no. 4 (2022): 144, https://doi.org/10.1080/23745118.2021.1895552.

[7] Dimakopoulou, Economides, and Philippopoulos, "The Greek Great Depression", 119.

competitiveness, and weak institutions[8] and a solvency crisis due to fiscal "indiscipline" in Maastricht rules.[9]

The GFC was caused by a combination of factors, such as macroeconomic imbalances, unsustainable public finances, and the structural weaknesses of the Greek economy. In the years leading up to the crisis, the Greek government borrowed heavily to finance its budget deficits, which led to a significant increase in the country's debt-to-GDP ratio. An additional factor that contributed to the crisis was the lack of competitiveness in the Greek economy. Greek labour costs were high, productivity was low compared to other European countries, and corruption was high in an environment of weak rule of law.[10] These chronic political and economic imbalances had the effect of blocking the competitiveness of Greek businesses for the provision of goods and services in the international markets, consequently limiting the country's economic development potential. Thus, the cost of borrowing increased, making it difficult for the Greek government to finance its fiscal deficits.

The aforementioned factors led to the implementation of the 2010, 2012 and 2016 MoUs between the Greek government and the Troika. The first Memorandum in 2010 of 110 billion euros was deemed necessary due to Greece's inability to gain access to international markets in order to meet its financial needs. The second MoU in 2012 was 172.6 billion euros, and the third in 2015 was 86 billion euros and attempted to correct "implementation errors" of the preceded programs in order to address the serious, protracted financial crisis and the derailment of unemployment.[11]

The MoUs were aimed at addressing the country's high public debt and fiscal deficits, but their implementation had significant implications for both the economy and society. The measures imposed by the EAPs were widely criticized for adversely affecting key Greek macroeconomic figures, contributing to a further

---

[8] Pierre Olivier Gourinchas, Thomas Philippon, and Dimitri Vayanos, "The Analytics of the Greek Crisis," *NBER Macroeconomics Annual* 31, no. 1 (2016): 1–3, https://doi.org/10.1086/690239.

[9] Stella Michopoulou, "Developmental and Social Impacts of IMF Stability Policies (in Greek)", (Athens, 2012): 47.

[10] Panagiotis Mitropoulos et al., "The Impact of Economic Crisis on the Greek Hospitals' Productivity," *International Journal of Health Planning and Management* 1, no. 14 (2017): 173, https://doi.org/10.1002/hpm.2410.

[11] Charalampos K. Arachovas and Manolis M. Manioudis, "Attempting an Assessment of the MoUs' Role in Confronting the Greek Crisis," in *Bridging Microeconomics and Macroeconomics and the Effects on Economic Development and Growth*, ed. Pantelis C. Kostis (Hershey, Pennsylvania, USA: IGI Global, 2020), 260, https://doi.org/10.4018/978-1-7998-4933-9.

deterioration of the Greek economy and society, and increasing the magnitude of the initial repercussions of the 2009 crisis.[12] It is worth noting, however, that the largest percentage of the funds disbursed through the Greek bailout programs was used to repay the debt and interest of foreign banks (mainly German and French), which were the most important investors in Greek public debt.[13] The first MoU in May 2010 aimed at stabilizing Greece's public finances. The EAP that was implemented required the government to implement a series of structural reforms and austerity measures including cuts to public sector wages and pensions, tax increases, and reductions in public spending.

Although the first memorandum succeeded in stabilizing Greece's public finances, it led to a severe recession, with GDP falling by 17% between 2008 and 2013.[14] The unemployment rate increased significantly, reaching its peak of 27.8% in 2013, with a parallel increase in poverty and inequality rates that negatively impacted the country's social welfare system. The second MoU in February 2012 aimed to build on the reforms implemented under the first memorandum and address the underlying structural weaknesses of the Greek economy.[15]

The second memorandum's demands for austerity included cuts in wages and pensions in the public sector, and further tax increases coupled with reductions in public spending produced recession, poverty, and inequality and negatively affected public health and education.[16] The country's GDP fell by more than 25% between 2008 and 2016, and the unemployment rate increased, reaching 27.8% in 2013. Ultimately, austerity measures, which included tax increases and spending cuts, had a significant impact on the Greek population, leading to a decline in living standards. Indicative is the fact that the percentage of people at risk of poverty or social exclusion in Greece increased from 29.4%

---

[12] John Marangos, "The Travels of the Washington Consensus : From the Global Financial Crisis to the Greek Financial Crisis The Travels of the Washington Consensus : From the Global Financial Crisis to the Greek Financial Crisis," *Forum for Social Economics* 0, no. 0 (2023): 1–20,

https://doi.org/10.1080/07360932.2023.2245977; Stavros P. Migkos et al., "Analyzing Greece 2010 Memorandum's Impact on Macroeconomic and Financial Figures through FCM", *Economies* 10, no. 178 (2022): 16, https://doi.org/10.3390/economies10080178.

[13] Judith Clifton, Daniel Diaz-Fuentes, and Ana Lara Gómez, "The Crisis as Opportunity? On the Role of the Troika in Constructing the European Consolidation State, "*Cambridge Journal of Regions, Economy and Society* 11, no. 3 (2018): 605, https://doi.org/10.1093/cjres/rsy021.

[14] "The Chronicle of the Great Crisis: The Bank of Greece 2008-2013" (Athens, 2013).

[15] Gourinchas, Philippon, and Vayanos, "The Analytics of the Greek Crisis," 65–66.

[16] Marangos, "The Neoclassical and Keynesian Standpoint", 227.

in 2005 to 35.6% in 2016.[17] In March 2012, private government bonds received a cut of 53.5% of their nominal value under a procedure called the Private Sector Involvement (PSI) and corresponded to a reduction of €106 bn in Greek debt.[18] Following the completion of the third EAP in August 2018, Greece was placed under enhanced surveillance until August 2022, when it committed to continue implementing reforms to restructure and create a competitive economy.[19]

The MoUs, in response to the country's debt crisis, have been heavily criticized for adhering to the principles of the Washington Consensus, which emphasizes the importance of market-oriented policies, including fiscal austerity, privatization, deregulation and trade liberalization.[20] Such policy measures incorporated in the EAPs are fiscal austerity, reductions in public spending, wage cuts and tax increases. They also include measures aimed at improving the competitiveness of the Greek economy, such as labour market reforms, measures to improve the business environment, and provisions for privatization and deregulation, also in line with the principles of the Washington Consensus.[21] There are some differences between these two frameworks, with the main difference being that the MoUs also include measures aimed at addressing the social consequences of the crisis, such as measures to protect vulnerable groups and support social welfare. Another difference is that the MoUs were implemented as part of a rescue program rather than in response to a crisis facing a developing country. In conclusion, the relationship between the Memoranda and the Washington Consensus highlights the ongoing debate about the appropriate role of market-oriented policies in promoting both economic growth and broader development.

---

[17] Hellenic Statistical Authority, *Living Conditions in Greece*, ed. Hellenic Statistical Authority, (2017).

[18] Dimakopoulou, Economides, and Philippopoulos, "The Greek Great Depression", 121-22; George Pagoulatos, "Greece After the Bailouts: Assessment of a Qualified Failure", *GreeSE Paper* no.130, *Hellenic Observatory Papers on Greece and Southeast Europe* no. 130 (2018): 9–10.

[19] John Marangos, "The Post-Keynesian Perspective and Policy Recommendations for the Greek Financial Crisis", *Review of Radical Political Economics* (2023): 8-10, https://doi.org/10.1177/04866134221142057.

[20] Marangos, "The Post Keynesian Perspectives", 12; Georgios Maris, Pantelis Sklias, and Napoleon Maravegias, "The Political Economy of the Greek Economic Crisis in 2020," *European Politics and Society* 0, no. 0 (2021): 461–62, https://doi.org/10.1080/23745118.2021.1895552.

[21] IMF, "2016 Article IV Consultation—Press Release; Staff Report; and Statement by The Executive Director For Greece", *IMF Staff Country Reports* (February 2, 2017): 2-15, https://doi.org/10.5089/9781484335918.002.

Furthermore, responses and policies regarding the crisis depend not only on economic analysis but also on the perception of social reality and moral issues. The neoclassical paradigm, according to the Washington Consensus, advocates market-oriented incentives and macroeconomic stability, which requires austerity measures such as minimizing fiscal deficits, minimizing inflation, and maximizing privatization. The neoclassical paradigm justifies austerity measures, while the Keynesian paradigm considers austerity measures as degrading the lives of millions of people. The insistence on the full repayment of the debt in the case of Greece is neither realistic nor ethical.[22] In this context, Nikiforos et al.,[23] argue that Greece needs a major write-off and restructuring of its public debt since its repayment cannot be realized on realistic and moral grounds.

The GFC is multifaceted because of a series of events that stemmed from global financial liberalization, the construction of the eurozone, and the collapse of the US subprime mortgage system. The causes of the crisis are due to the poor institutional structure of the eurozone, combined with the uneven economic development among the eurozone members. Although the introduction of the euro stabilized exchange rates, Greece and other southern European countries lacked competitiveness and small export sectors, making them vulnerable to economic shocks. It is emphasized that the loss of competitiveness is not attributed to the very high relative nominal labour cost per unit of production but to the fact that Greece is limited to lower and medium levels of technology, resulting in the transfer of value during international trade with high productivity countries.[24] It is also mentioned that the Troika's assessment of the Greek fiscal multiplier was inaccurate.[25]

The Institutional Foundation of the ECB and *Ordoliberalism*

When the ECB was founded, the tasks covered by the Monetary Policy Sub-Committee (MPSC) were split between the Eurosystem Monetary Policy Committee (MPC) and the Market Operation Committee (MOC). The Monetary policy in the Eurosystem is based on a collective decision-making system. This rule applies to the top decision-making groups of the ECB, such as the Governing Council and the Executive Board. It also applies to the committees and subgroups of the Eurosystem. The Governing Council is made up of 15

[22] Marangos, "The Neoclassical and Keynesian Standpoint", 470-477,481-482.

[23] Michalis Nikiforos, Laura Carvalho, and Christian Schoder, "'Twin Deficits' in Greece: In Search of Causality", *Journal of Post Keynesian Economics* 38, no. 2 (2015): 800, https://doi.org/10.1080/01603477.2015.1065675.

[24] Marangos, "The Post-Keynesian Perspective", 1–4.

[25] Costas Lapavitsas, "Political Economy of the Greek Crisis", *Review of Radical Political Economics* 51, no. 1 (2019): 32, https://doi.org/10.1177/0486613417730363.

governors from the euro area National Central Banks (NCBs) and six members from the Executive Board. The main responsibility of the European Central Bank is determining the utilization of money within the eurozone. In addition, they ensure that the Eurosystem is functioning effectively. However, it is also the group that makes choices for the other tasks of the ESCB. In simple terms, when the Governing Council is deciding on monetary policy, they make decisions based on what most of the council members agree on. This is stated in Article 129 of the Treaty on the Functioning of the European Union is an agreement that outlines how the European Union works.

In defining the institutional structure for a central banking system, there are important a priori trade-offs to be considered between the benefits of decentralization and the speed of decision-making-decisiveness. The decentralized set-up of the Eurosystem does not imply that the ECB's monetary policy decision-making process focuses on regional aspects or is subordinated to regional interest groups. To ensure the singleness of monetary policy, monetary policy decisions are made centrally by the Governing Council of the ECB. The Executive Board of the ECB, with the help of ECB staff, is in charge of preparing the meetings of the Governing Council to ensure an efficient process. The involvement of the NCBs boosts the efficiency of the process, as several Eurosystem tasks require the existence of a national infrastructure, which the NCBs contribute to the Eurosystem-wide infrastructure. Bonzom and Barontini[26] point out that the NCBs are not only in charge of the implementation of monetary policy but are also involved in the process of monetary policy preparation in the Eurosystem staff macroeconomic projections.

Being a prime illustration of effective ideas and knowledge, the Bundesbank was considered a suitable reference for both the ECB and ESCB, which constituted the restructured national central banking system. Until the end of 1998, the Deutsche Bundesbank was solely responsible for preserving German price stability. This role was handed to the Eurosystem with the launch of the European monetary union and the introduction of the euro in early 1999. Since then, the Eurosystem has been comprised of the ECB and the national central banks of the EU member states that have embraced the euro.

The design of the ECB was the confluence and product of a decades-long evolution of ideas and an accumulation of real-world experience. As for real-world experience, the Deutsche Bundesbank and its foundational "stability culture" were the role model and major source of inspiration for the ECB. Lorenzo Bini Smaghi[27], a former member of the Executive Board of the ECB,

---

[26] Philippe Bonzom and Christian Barontini, *A National Central Bank within a Federal System* (na, 2005).

[27] Lorenzo Bini Smaghi, "Central Bank Independence in the EU: From Theory to Practice", *European Law Journal* 14, no. 4 (2008): 446–60.

pointed out that economists and politicians have debated the usefulness of different frameworks for expressing central banks' institutional mandates since the ECB's establishment. These debates and the frameworks that were created have shown how the economics profession's ideas about money have changed over time and how they realized that previous theories were not effective. These principles can be stated as follows.

The first principle of central bank behaviour can be expressed in three words: independence, delegation, and accountability. By the start of the 1990s, it was broadly acknowledged that it was ideal to outsource the financial approach to a de-politicized institution instead of being a mere of short-term political contemplations and bearings. The assignment to a central bank run by proficient financial specialists is one way of ensuring that the imposing business model of control is not manhandled to the point where the socially appealing capacities of cash, as a solid metric and store of value, are corrupted or misplaced. It also corresponds to the basic fact that one needs specialized competencies in this highly technical domain. According to Tucker,[28] under fiat money, independence for the monetary authority is a corollary of the higher-level separation of powers between the fiscal authority of the legislature and the elected executive government. If the elected executive were to control the monetary levers, it would have the power to tax through unexpected bursts of inflation. Central bank independence is, therefore, grounded in the values of constitutional government. As expressed by Fischer[29], a central bank may not be able to resort to the necessary devices utilized to address the challenges without its autonomy in accomplishing its objective. On the other hand, the asset to exceptional measures may have expanded the dangers to its notoriety, authenticity, and freedom.[30] Besides, according to Goodhart and Lastra[31] the central banks' expanded inclusion and organization shields from monetary solidness.

Second, the costs of inflation offer another viewpoint from which to see central banks' inflation-stabilization mission. High inflation is exceptionally exorbitant for society. It could be a backward charge that falls excessively on

---

[28] Paul Tucker, "How the European Central Bank and Other Independent Agencies Reveal a Gap in Constitutionalism: A Spectrum of Institutions for Commitment", *German Law Journal* 22, no. 6 (2021): 999–1027.

[29] Stanley Fischer, "Central-Bank Independence Revisited", *The American Economic Review* 85, no. 2 (1995): 201–6.

[30] Jaime Caruana and Adrian Van Rixtel, "International Financial Markets and Bank Funding in the Euro Area: Dynamics and Participants", *Bank for International Settlements* (2013).

[31] Charles Goodhart and Rosa Lastra, "Populism and Central Bank Independence", *Open Economies Review* 29 (2018): 49–68.

individuals who have restricted accessibility of substitutes to cash when choosing to set aside their investment funds. A further reason for giving price stability privileged status in a central bank's founding charter is that in the medium to long run, stable inflation and sustained growth are not substitutes but they are complements.

Third, an articulation of goals is not sufficient. The discipline and clarity of a mandate provide too tenuous an anchor for the economy unless they are embedded in a broader strategy describing how the central bank intends to go about enforcing its mandated objective(s), including its approach to disclosing judgments to the public about the economic outlook and resulting monetary policy stance. This is due to two factors. The economy is constantly subjected to disruptions. A strategy embodies the high-level operating modalities that the central bank commits to following to offset the destabilizing shocks and bring the economy back to the desired path. Knowledge of the strategy and of the resolve with which the central bank is prepared to defend and enforce its objective in the face of adverse shocks is as important as the objective itself in anchoring the public's expectations. In addition, shocks may present central banks with complicated alternatives in the day-to-day conduct of policy.

Ordoliberalism is deeply interwoven with the tumultuous economic history of Germany in the twentieth century. It developed in the 1920s and 1930s in response to the economic crises of the Weimar Republic. Its foundational thinkers were Walter Eucken, Wilhelm Röpke, Franz Böhm, and Alfred-Müller Armack. Its original intellectual epicentre was Freiburg, where legal (i.e. Böhm) and economic (i.e. Eucken) scholars worked together to develop what became known as the "Freiburg School of Law and Economics", also known as ordoliberalism. For monetary policy, ordoliberalism translates into an emphasis on a powerful central bank that is deeply committed to price stability. Given their inherent distrust of market power, ordoliberalists are also concerned with insulating central banks from the pressures of interest groups and politics. The same year, 1948, also witnessed the birth of postwar German central banking with the establishment of the Bank Deutscher Lander, the precursor to the Bundesbank.

This approach suggests that the government should ensure the efficient functioning of the free market while not supporting the concept of a welfare state. The influence of ordoliberalism is most evident in the German position on price stability and its defence of the independence of the ECB. Both the Maastricht Agreement and the accompanying Stability and Growth Treaty bear the handwriting of the Germans ordoliberalism school of thought. This is not new; it is the legacy of the Deutsche Bundesbank, which the Freiburgers argued exemplified the primacy of Ordoliberalism. This contention argues that the Bundesbank's monetary arrangement is characterized by a solid anti-inflationary predisposition established within the ordoliberal convention, a perspective shared by Biebricher[32] as well as Bonefeld.[33]

Since the 1960s, new ideas have dominated the political agenda and economic thought. The neoclassical synthesis provided the theoretical background for the emerging policy concept of "Globalsteuerung." Karl Schiller coined the phrase "global control" to describe an economic policy notion influenced mostly by the theoretical views of economist John Maynard Keynes. It was enshrined by the Stability and Growth Act of 1967, and Europe's leaders have spent many years having to contend with it, beginning with the 1980s and the nascent plan to build monetary union. In the early and mid-1990s, the founding architects of European Monetary Union (EMU) incorporated fiscal constraints into the Maastricht Treaty and the Stability and Growth Pact.[34] Specifically, the central bank was expected to foster economic growth by keeping interest rates low.

The idea of adopting a formal quantitative target for money growth, which would provide a nominal anchor for inflation and inflation expectations, rapidly gained ground. As it happened, this period coincided with the "monetarist counterrevolution." The leading monetarists Milton Friedman, Karl Brunner, and Alan Meltzer argued that central banks should avoid any attempt to fine-tune the economy and instead pursue a monetary targeting strategy.[35] In general, such ideas were well received in Germany.[36] In 1974, the German central bank announced a money supply target for the first time – and continued to do so even after several central banks adopted inflation targeting in the 1990s. Thus, from the mid-seventies onwards, the Bundesbank followed a monetary policy rule reflecting the ideas of Milton Friedman. Also, the main feature of Bundesbank policy – monetary targeting – is also a monetarist concept.

Today, Ordnungspolitik is perceived as the conviction that the principal means by which economic policy can seek to improve 'the economy' is by improving the institutional framework within which economic activities take place. The Ordnungspolitik perspective justifies the rationale for EMU. A common

---

[32] Biebricher, "The Return of Ordoliberalism in Europe", 8–9.

[33] Werner Bonefeld, "On the Strong Liberal State: Beyond Berghahn and Young", *New Political Economy* 18, no. 5 (2013): 782.

[34] Fischer, "Central-Bank Independence Revisited".

[35] David F Hendry and Neil R Ericsson, "An Econometric Analysis of UK Money Demand in Monetary Trends in the United States and the United Kingdom by Milton Friedman and Anna J. Schwartz", *The American Economic Review* (1991): 8–38.

[36] Jürgen Von Hagen, "Money Growth Targeting by the Bundesbank", *Journal of Monetary Economics* 43, no. 3 (1999): 681–701.

currency in Europe provides money that governments cannot create, i.e., money that is removed from the political influence of the individual member states. This can readily be seen from the institutional design of EMU: The Maastricht Treaty and the Treaty of Lisbon commit the ECB to the goal of price stability. At the same time, it obtains a large degree of independence. Thus, the institutional design of the ECB is more similar to that of the Bundesbank than to any other central bank of the Eurozone. According to the former president of the ECB, Mario Draghi,[37] "It is worth recalling that the monetary constitution of the ECB is firmly grounded in the principles of 'Ordoliberalism,' particularly two of its central tenets: first, a clear separation of power and objectives between authorities; and second, adherence to the principles of an open market economy with free competition, favoring an efficient allocation of resources."

The ECB was unwilling to respond and intervene in the bond markets. The ECB has rules that limit the purchasing of government bonds, as stated in Article 123 stands for the Treaty on the Functioning of the European Union. Furthermore, the ECB decided in 2005 that the lowest credit rating of BBB- is a requirement for all Eurozone bonds to be qualified as collateral for the ECB's open market operations. This meant that if private rating agencies were to downgrade a sovereign bond below that threshold, many banks would suddenly become illiquid because they would lose access to the ECB's main policy of low inflation-constrained aggregate demand and the growth process refinancing operations. While some technical features of the strategy (e.g., the exact definition of the target variable) were changed over time, its major elements – the explicit derivation of the annual money growth targets from medium-term macroeconomic benchmark figures, the flexible implementation, which included temporary departures from the medium-term rule, and the two-stage implementation procedure – stayed intact. In this respect, the Bundesbank's approach certainly stands out by reason of its consistency and remarkable continuity. Orphanides[38] and Kilponen and Leitemo[39] have discussed the implications of targeting money growth for a central bank that sets the short-term interest rate.

---

[37] ECB, "Speech by Mario Draghi, President of the European Central Bank at the Global Investment Conference in London 26 July 2012", 2012, 1–2, https://www.ecb.europa.eu/press/key/date/2009/html/sp090428.en.html.

[38] Athanasios Orphanides, "12 Monetary Policy and Fiscal Discipline: How the ECB Planted the Seeds of the Euro Area Crisis," *Hawks and Doves: Deeds and Words*, 2018, 115.

[39] Juha Kilponen and Kai Leitemo, "Model Uncertainty and Delegation: A Case for Friedman's K-Percent Money Growth Rule?", *Journal of Money, Credit and Banking* 40, no. 2-3 (2008): 547–56.

Moreover, in 2010, the ECB, led by Jean-Claude Trichet, was unsure about taking action to make the financial markets stable. Before May 6, 2010, Trichet said in a few press conferences that the ECB probably would not buy any government bonds, even though Greece, Portugal, Spain, and Italy were having trouble paying back their debts and their interest rates were increasing. Until 2007, the ECB had exceptionally effectively overseen the preservation of inflation near but below 2%.[40]

The Greek Financial Crisis and the ECB

The GFC that emerged in the late 2000s shook the foundations of the European Union, challenging the stability of the Eurozone and raising questions about the efficacy of the EMU. Central to handling the GFC was the role ECB, the institution responsible for monetary policy and maintaining financial stability within the eurozone. In this subsection we investigate the multifaceted role of the ECB during the Greek financial crisis, examining its decisions, actions, and their impact on the development of the financial crisis and subsequent recovery efforts.

To understand the ECB's role during the GFC, it is crucial to examine this role within the context of its responsibilities and objectives. The ECB faced a formidable challenge when the GFC unfolded. As the central monetary authority responsible for the stability of the eurozone, the ECB had to navigate a delicate balancing act between its mandate of maintaining price stability, conducting monetary policy, safeguarding the financial system[41], stabilising financial markets and preserving the integrity of the Eurozone. To maintain the viability of the Greek banking system, the ECB decided four times to waive the quality threshold for accepting Greek debt securities as collateral in refinancing operations.[42] The ECB provided crucial liquidity to prevent a likely default due to the increasing deposit withdrawals and the reduction of the deposit base of Greek banks during the Greek financial crisis, thus preventing an escalation of instability.[43]

---

[40] Michael Ioannidis, Sarah Jane Hlásková, and Chiara Zilioli, "The Mandate of the ECB: Legal Considerations in the ECB's Monetary Policy Strategy Review", *ECB Occasional Paper* (Frankfurt a. M., 2021): 3–9, https://doi.org/10.2139/ssrn.3928298.

[41] Ioannidis, Hlásková, and Zilioli, 3,9.

[42] Nikolaos Petrakis et al., "Greek Banking Sector Stock Reaction to ECB's Monetary Policy Interventions", *Journal of Risk and Financial Management* 15, no. 448 (2022): 2, https://doi.org/10.3390/jrfm15100448.

[43] Helen Louri and Petros Migiakis, "Economic Activity and Sources of Finance in Greece: The Predominant Role of Banks," in *Greece and The Euro From Crisis to Recovery*, ed.

The initial response of the ECB to the GFC was characterized by a cautious approach aimed at preventing a complete collapse of the Greek banking system. The ECB accepted Greek public debt as collateral regardless of its credit rating to avoid a complete collapse of the Greek banking system. It also purchased public debt to facilitate the proper function of financial markets that funded the Greek government. In the aforementioned context, the ECB undertook "conventional" measures as a sharp reduction of policy interest rates and also "unconventional" or quantitative measures.[44] Conventional monetary policy was implemented by the ECB by setting a target for the overnight rate in the interbank money market and adjusting the central bank's money supply to this target through open market operations. ECB operations that provide liquidity to the European banking system by steering the key interest rates are carried out against acceptable collateral with the aim of fulfilling the target of price stability.[45] The open market operations are also conducted by the ECB in the form of Main Refinancing Operations (MROs) or Long-Term Refinancing Operations (LTROs) coordinated by the ECB but conducted decentralized by each of the national central banks.[46]

In times of crisis, conventional monetary policy tools may prove insufficient to achieve the central bank's objective. In general, unconventional measures can be defined as those policies that directly target the cost and availability of external finance to banks, households, and non-financial companies. These sources of finance can be in the form of central bank liquidity, loans, fixed-income securities, or equity.[47] The unconventional monetary policy of the ECB incorporated a policy of loans with a full distribution of fixed interest rates, the extension of maturity provision, the issuance of Emergency Liquidity Assistance (ELA) and the limited purchase of collateral themselves[48] The aforesaid decisions of the ECB were nevertheless inadequate, as they were not supplemented

---

George Alogoskoufis and Kevin Featherstone (Hellenic Observatory and the Fletcher School, Tufts University, 2021), 114.

[44] Petrakis et al., "Greek Banking Sector", 3.

[45] Lorenzo Bini Smaghi, "Conventional and Unconventional Monetary Policy," Keynote Lecture at the International Center for Monetary and Banking Studies (ICMB), 2009, 2, https://doi.org/10.4337/9781788972345.00014.

[46] Carolina Tuckwell and António Mendonça, "The Global Crisis and Unconventional Monetary Policy: ECB versus Fed", Working Paper (Lisbon, 2016), 9, http://pascal.iseg.utl.pt/~cesa/index.php/menupublicacoes/working-papershttp://pascal.iseg.utl.pt~cesa/index.php/menupublicacoes/working-papers.

[47] Smaghi, "Conventional and Unconventional Monetary Policy," 3.

[48] Dimakopoulou, Economides, and Philippopoulos, "The Greek Great Depression", 123.

by the responsibilities as lender of last resort in the government bond markets.[49] The Greek experience marked the ineffectiveness of the ECB's role as the "lender of last resort" to governments and pointed the need to re-examine its fundamental principles and its policy paradigm.[50]

The first of a series of unconventional measures utilized to deal with the GFC was the Securities Market Program (SMP), aimed at supporting the monetary transmission mechanism.[51] In this context, the ECB intervened in the secondary bond market, claiming preferred status for the public debt bonds it acquired to calm down the markets.[52] The SMP was launched in May 2010 following a deepening of the eurozone debt crisis with widening yield spreads for Greece. The announcement of the SMP followed that of the Greek rescue package, as at the time, the country had large bond repayments and access to the markets was essentially prohibited due to very high interest rates.[53] However, this measure did not address Greece's problems. It had a limited impact on the bond market as market participants were unconvinced that the crisis would not spread further.[54] The SMP of the ECB may have temporarily "bought time" for the Eurozone, but it did not manage to stop the progress of the sovereign debt crisis. Its purpose was mainly to shield the European banks that were holding Greek government bonds rather than to directly tackle the GFC.[55]

Due to the PSI, the sovereign crisis began to turn into a banking crisis when the markets diagnosed the potential impact of the rescheduling and the restructuring of the Greek sovereign debt. At the same time, the impending banking crisis underestimated the assessment of the government's solvency due to the expectation of further support of the banking system from the state budget. Despite the ECB's policy of facilitating the funding requirements of banks by lowering the minimum reserve requirements from 2% to 1% and the introduction of two 'very-long-term' refinancing operations, the tensions of

[49] Paul De Grauwe, "Only a More Active ECB Can Solve the Euro Crisis", *CEPS Policy Brief* no. 250 (2011): 5.

[50] Marica Frangakis, "The ECB's Non-Standard Monetary Policy Measures and the Greek Financial Crisis," in *The Internal Impact and External Influence of the Greek Financial Crisis*, ed. John Marangos (Palgrave Macmillan, Cham, 2017), 68.

[51] Frangakis, "The ECB's Non-Standard Monetary Policy", 61.

[52] Petrakis et al., "Greek Banking Sector Stock Reaction", 2.

[53] Christoph Trebesch and Jeromin Zettelmeyer, "ECB Interventions in Distressed Sovereign Debt Markets : The Case of Greek Bonds," Working Paper (Washington, D.C, 2018), 6.

[54] Margarita Katsimi and Thomas Moutos, "EMU and the Greek Crisis: Are There Lessons to Be Learnt?", *European Journal of Political Economy* 26, no. 4 (2010): 2.

[55] Frangakis, "The ECB's Non-Standard Monetary Policy", 62.

distress and mutual mistrust within the banking system continued to build up in the first half of 2012.[56]

In light of the adverse developments and to address growing fears of a possible worsening of the crisis, the then-ECB President Mario Draghi declared in August 2012 that the ECB "do whatever it takes – within our mandate – to have a single monetary policy in the euro area, to maintain price stability in the euro area and to preserve the euro".[57] In line with this announcement, the ECB's Governing Council announced in September 2012 the creation of a new policy tool, the Outright Monetary Transactions (OMT). Under this second set of the series of unconventional measures, the ECB would acquire sovereign bonds of one- to three-year maturity, provided the issuing country has agreed to a fiscal adjustment program with either the European Financial Stability Facility (EFSF) or its successor, the European Stability Mechanism, the ESM. Although this new program abandoned the restrictions of its predecessor, its strict conditionality concerning the country's commitment to a program excluded Greece from its benefits, as did its successor, the Asset Purchase Program (APP). The aforementioned program covered both private Corporate Sector Purchase Program (CSPP) and public sector securities Public Sector Purchase Program (PSPP). All 18 Eurozone members participated in the most radical unconventional monetary policy measure, the PSPP, also named "quantitative easing", excluding Greece because it did not meet the quality criteria set by the ECB.[58]

To combat the GFC, the ECB applied a pack of unconventional measures that included a series of unorthodox monetary-policy measures, namely quantitative easing, forward guidance, full-allotment of funds at a fixed rate, expansion of banks' eligible collateral, and negative interest rates.[59] Apart from those measures, the ECB addressed solvent banks' liquidity issues by implementing the provision of emergency liquidity assistance or ELA. However, as the crisis deepened, the national central banks of the eurozone members also resorted to ELA due to the liquidity deficit of the member states, as was the case for Greece.[60] The ECB

---

[56] Stefano Micossi, "The Monetary Policy of the European Central Bank (2002-2015)," CEPS Special Report (Brussels, 2015), 14–15, https://www.ceps.eu/system/files/SR 109 SM Monetary Policy of the ECB_0.pdf.

[57] ECB, "Speech by Mario Draghi", President of the European Central Bank at the Global Investment Conference in London 26 July 2012," 1–2.

[58] Frangakis, "The ECB's Non-Standard Monetary Policy", 65.

[59] ECB, "The Transmission of the ECB's Recent Non-Standard Monetary Policy Measures," ECB Economic Bulletin (Frankfurt, 2015), 1–2.

[60] Heather D. Gibson et al., "The Effect of Emergency Liquidity Assistance (ELA) on Bank Lending During the Euro Area Crisis", *Journal of International Money and Finance*, Working Paper (Athens, 2020), 3, https://doi.org/10.1016/j.jimonfin.2020.102154.

provided the ELA to prevent the Greek banking system from collapsing, allowing the national central bank of Greece to provide emergency funds to Greek banks when they were cut off from other sources of financing. This lifeline helped to prevent a disorderly bank run and provided temporary stability to the Greek financial sector. As the PSI eroded the value of the Greek government bonds that could be held as collateral to guarantee monetary policy operations, Greek banks rapidly resorted to the ELA, which was more expensive.[61]

In June 2015, Greece introduced controls on capital outflows in order to stabilize the banking system after a period of intense political and economic turbulence and a massive bank run. The Greek government's decision to bring a referendum on the terms of a new agreement on an adjustment program with the Troika and the ECB's reaction to cap its ELA limit to Greek banks led to the implementation of a range of measures to stabilize the banking system. The ECB declared that it would not facilitate a further deposit outflow from Greek banks, eventually leading to capital controls. The Troika decided not to stabilize the Greek banking system while the Greek government was negotiating with its lenders about the possibility of not continuing its bailout program.[62] The ELA provision was constantly reviewed by the ECB Governing Council, which had the authority to cancel the program directly depending on the negotiations for the extension of the adjustment program. Eventually, the ECB terminated the ELA facility for the Greek banks and stopped accepting Greek government bonds as collateral for additional liquidity to cover the outflow of deposits. Since the ECB is a member of the Troika, the conditionality of its programs was a pressure tool to force the country to comply with the austerity measures of the adjustment program.

The ECB's role during the GFC remains a subject of critique and debate. Within an alternative proposed policy framework, the role of the ECB could be re-examined, and its policy guidelines could be reprogrammed, especially regarding its dogmatic position against assuming the role of "lender of last resort."

ECB: What Actions Ought to Have Been Taken During the Greek Financial Crisis?

Previous analysis has shown that the role played by the ECB in the GFC was dictated by its founding principles, its constitutional imperatives, and

[61] Louri and Migiakis," Economic Activity and Sources of Finance in Greece", 146.

[62] Karl Whelan, "Banking Union and the ECB as Lender of Last Resort," UCD Centre for Economic Research Working Paper Series (Dublin, 2016), 10–11, http://hdl.handle.net/10197/7860.

particularly the political and ideological stances within the Troika. Simply put, the ECB's policies followed the Troika's applied policy framework implemented during the GFC. In this part, we answer the question of what the ECB should have done to respond to the GFC. We investigate a lattice of normative issues for the handling of the GFC in the angle of Post Keynesian analysis as an alternative to the applied dominant neoclassical doctrine of Troika.

The Troika's policy framework was in line with the dominant applied neoliberal policies.[63] This policy framework created dubious results in the Greek economy and society. In macroeconomic terms, at the end of the three consecutive EAPs in 2018, Greece's debt-to-GDP ratio was nearly 180%, while in 2009, before the crisis and the adjustment programs, Greece's debt-to-GDP ratio was approximately 130%.

As we mentioned, the ECB, through its institutional role and as a member of the Troika, was responsible for contributing to the formation and implementation of the EAPs. The EAPs were accompanied by strict conditionality on certain agreed policy measures, such as fiscal consolidation, structural reforms, and austerity measures, which Greece had to fulfil in order to receive the disbursements. Within the Troika's policy framework, the ECB's stance towards the GFC, reflecting the "non-bail-out" clause in Article 125 of the Lisbon Treaty, did not facilitate an early resolution of the crisis. The ECB's lack of a "lender of a last resort" policy at the beginning of the crisis increased the overall bailout and social costs of the GFC. In any case, the delayed intervention also increased the cost of the Greek rescue package.

Post-Keynesians argue that Troika's and ECB's policies exacerbated the crisis instead of solving it.[64] The main critics focus on the Troika's imposed rapid fiscal consolidation, wage cuts, and neoliberal structural reforms. The Troika's policy framework deepened the recession, increased unemployment, and widened income inequality. For the role of the Central Bank, the Post Keynesian alternative to the neoliberal paradigm proposes a strategy of expansionary monetary policy and a shift from austerity to stimulus measures for the Greek

---

[63] Ben Behrend, "The Supranational Governmentality of Neoliberalism : An Analysis of the Governing Principles of Troika Programs for Greece", *The IAPSS Journal of Political Science* 26 (2015): 34; Geoff Kennedy, "Embedding Neoliberalism in Greece: The Transformation of Collective Bargaining and Labour Market Policy in Greece during the Eurozone Crisis," in *Annual Conference of the Western Political Science Association 24-26 March, San Diego*, 2016, 12, https://doi.org/10.1080/07078552.2016.1249129.

[64] Manos Matsaganis, "The Greek Crisis : Social Impact and Policy Responses", *Friedrich-Ebert-Stiftung* (Berlin, 2013), 5; Edward Seyler and John Levendis, "What Was the Role of Monetary Policy in the Greek Financial Crisis," *South-Eastern Europe Journal of Economics* 11, no. 2 (2013): 117.

economy and exit from the GFC. At the heart of the debate about the role of the central bank is the position that "central banks were put on this earth to be lenders of last resort".[65] Essentially, the Post Keynesian critique focuses on the ECB's avoidance of exercising the role of the lender of last resort in the case of the GFC, particularly at the beginning of the crisis. It is important to consider that timing plays an important role in the effective results and consequences of an implemented policy. The lattice of Post-Keynesian alternative proposals for what the ECB should have done during and especially at the beginning of GFC is below-mentioned.

a) Typical lender of last resort

Proponents of the Troika's policy framework argue that the central bank had to balance its role in addressing the negative effects while maintaining financial stability and adhering to its mandate of price stability. The neoliberal theoretical base of the ECB asserts that prohibiting unlimited liquidity of any form with preferential conditions to the public sector by financial institutions without the impositions of conditions undermines the credibility and sustainability of the Eurozone.[66] In line with this belief, the ECB's response to the crisis has been characterized by a delicate balancing act between providing liquidity and imposing austerity conditions in the context of the three memoranda signed by Greece with the Troika. In the Post Keynesian framework, the financial system is inherently unsustainable. Thus, the lender of last resort function of the ECB can guarantee confidence in the financial system. "Without a lender of last resort, financial stability is not possible, and systemic financial crises get out of control".[67]

Post-Keynesians contend that the ECB's insistence on austerity measures, rather than focusing on providing liquidity, exacerbated the economic downturn and deepened the economic and social effects of the crisis in Greece. The ECB's strict collateral requirements limited the availability of liquidity for Greek banks and further strained the financial system. At the beginning of the crisis, Greece faced severe liquidity constraints, with its banks experiencing significant deposit outflows. As Greek banks relied heavily on ECB funding, there were expectations that the ECB would act as a typical lender of last resort to support the Greek banking system and prevent a collapse. As the lender of last resort, the ECB should have provided liquidity to Greek banks, ensuring the stability

[65] Whelan, "Banking Union and the ECB", 11.

[66] ECB, "The Monetary Policy of the ECB" (Frankfurt, 2011), 35.

[67] Hansjörg Herr, "The European Central Bank and the US Federal Reserve as Lender of Last Resort", *Panoeconomicus* 61, no. 1 1 Spec. Issue (2014): 59, https://doi.org/10.2298/PAN1401059H.

of the financial system and facilitating credit availability to support the economic recovery from the very beginning of the crisis. This liquidity assistance should have been provided to the Greek government in order to halt the progression of the crisis in its initial stages.[68]

For the Post Keynesians, the conditions imposed on the Greek banking system by the ECB moved beyond the limits of a typical role of the central bank. For instance, in 2015, in the midst of the newly-elected Greek government's negotiations with the Troika, the ECB declared that it would not facilitate further deposit outflows from the Greek banks. This verdict was not based on purely central banking criteria. In the question, "why did this happen?".[69] Whelan commentates that "Politics is the most likely answer". It was rather a punitive and ideologically charged decision that led to the imposition of capital controls. In fact, the ECB's policy has been harmonized with the policy motivations of its counterparts in the Troika. For Post Keynesians, the provision of liquidity and solvency support to the Greek banks, a typical lender of last resort policy, would help to avoid the imposition of capital controls on the Greek economy.

b) Debt Restructuring for Sustainable Recovery

The "one-size-fits-all" monetary policy conducted by the ECB was ill-suited for countries with differing economic structures and productivity levels. In the context of the Greek financial crisis, the Troika implemented the Washington Consensus agenda, which follows the doctrine of the "one-size-fits-all" approach[70] without taking into account the distinct features of the Greek economy.

The Post Keynesians, in contrast, advocate a path-dependence strategy[71], as the reform process is always path-dependent.[72] Implementing a more flexible monetary policy that recognized and accommodated these differences could

[68] Engelbert Stockhammer, Collin Constantine, and Severin Reissl, "Explaining the Euro Crisis: Current Account Imbalances, Credit Booms and Economic Policy in Different Economic Paradigms", *Journal of Post Keynesian Economics* 43, no. 2 (2020): 19,22, https://doi.org/10.1080/01603477.2020.1734464.

[69] Whelan, "Banking Union and the ECB", 1.

[70] Marangos, "The Neoclassical and Keynesian Standpoint", 12.

[71] Engelbert Stockhammer, "Post-Keynesian Macroeconomic Foundations for Comparative Political Economy", *Politics and Society* (2021): 14, https://doi.org/10.1177/003232922 11006562.

[72] John Marangos, "Developing a Civilised Society in Transition Economies: The Post Keynesian Paradigm", *Journal of Socio-Economics* 35, no. 4 (2006): 666, https://doi.org/ 10.1016/j.socec.2005.11.009.

have mitigated the impact of the crisis in Greece. Post Keynesian theory suggests that "one size does not fit all" as the appropriate retort to the financial crisis is strongly determined by the country's particularities.[73]

Post-Keynesians emphasize the importance of debt restructuring as an imperative step towards sustainable recovery. Debt restructuring becomes particularly decisive when traditional fiscal and monetary measures are no longer effective or lead to prolonged recessionary periods. The ECB should have actively supported comprehensive debt relief measures for Greece, reducing the debt burden through write-downs, maturity extensions, and lowered interest rates. Further, the ECB, in a post-Keynesian framework, should intervene towards facilitating a common sovereign asset backed by the rest of the eurosystem economies.[74] In this vein, the ECB would bail out the commercial banks along with the issuing of a common government bond, the so-called "Eurobond", to provide extra liquidity to the Greek government.[75] The Greek banks that would be recapitalized and bailed out by the ECB, as well as with public funds, should be subject to public scrutiny to ensure state control and intervention in their policy towards the objectives of the national political economy.[76] In light of the international market turmoil over Greek government assets, the ECB, unconstrained by profit maximization criteria, should replace the usual markets and remove a critical amount of distressed assets, acting as a "market maker of last resort".[77] Greece, as a peripheral European country, under the function of the ECB acting as a lender of last resort issuing Eurobonds and restoring financial tranquillity, would carry out an expansionary fiscal policy to counter the effects of the deep recession.[78]

---

[73] Agustín S. Bénétrix and Philip R. Lane, "International Differences in Fiscal Outcomes During the Global Crisis," *Fiscal Studies* 36, no. 1 (2015): 2–3, https://doi.org/10.1111/j.1475-5890.2015.12043.x.

[74] Engelbert Stockhammer and Syed Mohib Ali, "Varieties of Capitalism and Post-Keynesian Economics on Eurocrisis", Working Paper, 2018, 14.

[75] Marangos, "The Neoclassical and Keynesian Standpoint", 10.

[76] Engelbert Stockhammer, "Neoliberal Growth Models, Monetary Union and the Euro Crisis. A Post-Keynesian Perspective", *New Political Economy* 21, no. 4 (2016): 369–70, https://doi.org/10.1080/13563467.2016.1115826.

[77] Laurent Le maux and Laurence Scialom, "Central Banks and Financial Stability: Rediscovering the Lender-of-Last-Resort Practice in a Finance Economy", *Cambridge Journal of Economics* 37, no. 1 (2013): 10, https://doi.org/10.1093/cje/bes040.

[78] Alberto Botta, "The Short- and Long-Run Inconsistency of the Expansionary Austerity Theory: A Post-Keynesian/Evolutionist Critique", Working Paper (Annandale-on-Hudson, NY, 2016), 61.

By addressing solvency issues and reducing debt overhang, the ECB could have fostered an environment conducive to sustainable economic growth. The appropriate retort to the crisis requires international cooperation at the European level, i.e., a "pan-European solidarity".[79] Post Keynesians would propose, for the case of the GFC, a debt restructuring to address Greece's unsustainable levels of public debt. The aforementioned Greece's debt burden reduction would take place through outright debt forgiveness, debt swaps, or longer repayment periods.[80] This would provide Greece with greater fiscal space to stimulate the economy and prioritize social welfare. Debt restructuring can be perceived as a kind of reciprocity within the monetary union member states. A Post Keynesian approach emphasizes the importance of international cooperation and debt relief in addressing the debt sustainability challenges faced by countries in crisis. It recognizes that unsustainable debt burdens cannot be resolved solely through fiscal consolidation measures and that external support and debt restructuring may be necessary. A complex financial crisis as the one that hit the Greek economy and society requires responses "based on European solidarity and cohesion".[81] This approach encourages dialogue and collaboration between creditors, debtors, and international institutions to negotiate fair and sustainable debt restructuring agreements that consider the long-term economic prospects and social well-being of the debtor country.

c) Expansionary Fiscal Policy and Targeted Investments

The post-Keynesian theory emphasizes the need for expansionary fiscal policy during times of crisis financed by the state budget to stimulate aggregate demand.[82] The ECB should have indirectly supported the Greek government's efforts to implement countercyclical measures that prioritize public investment, job creation, and social welfare in the times of the GFC. Anti-cyclical policy should be delivered within an interventionist policy framework facilitating employment benefits, progressive income tax and social allowances[83] along with the provision of public education and health, housing, water and sanitation,

---

[79] Kathleen Lynch and Manolis Kalaitzake, "Affective and Calculative Solidarity: The Impact of Individualism and Neoliberal Capitalism", *European Journal of Social Theory* 23, no. 2 (2018): 4, https://doi.org/10.1177/1368431018786379.

[80] Marangos, "The Neoclassical and Keynesian Standpoint", 13.

[81] Konstantinos J. Hazakis, "The Political Economy of Economic Adjustment Programs in the Eurozone: A Detailed Policy Analysis", *Politics and Policy* 43, no. 6 (2015): 843, https://doi.org/10.1111/polp.12141.

[82] Robert Skidelsky, *Keynes: The Return of the Master* (New York: Public Affairs, 2009), 179.

[83] Stockhammer, "Neoliberal Growth Models", 28.

public transportation, training and public amenities.[84] By providing efficient monetary support to the banking system and facilitating an increase in government spending, the ECB could have played a crucial role in stimulating aggregate demand and promoting speedy economic recovery.

In this context, the ECB, using the banking sector, could have actively promoted targeted investment in productive sectors of the Greek economy to foster sustainable growth. Crucial public investments directed to specific areas in which the country has a comparative advantage can stabilize and stimulate the investment climate and create new jobs.[85] By directing funds towards areas such as renewable energy, healthcare, education, and infrastructure development, the central bank policy could have facilitated job creation, enhanced productivity, and improved the country's long-term economic prospects. The provision of financial support for targeted investments would have contributed to economic diversification and reduced Greece's vulnerability to external shocks. The above anti-cyclical policies in preferential sectors would motivate national industry with increased competence to enhance its international comparative position. Full employment is the key to eliminating uncertainty.[86]

d) Enhanced regulation of financial sector

With the aim of stabilizing the system and providing credibility within a fundamentally unstable system, the ECB should modify and adapt its banking policy against the novel conditions and guarantee financial stability in order to prevent such banking crises in the future.[87] An overall restructuring of the financial sector accompanied by enhanced regulation, strong financial supervision, restriction of destabilizing international capital flows and innovative financial products would be beneficial to stabilize the whole system.[88] In the Post Keynesian framework, a more prudent regulation and supervision of the financial system should be accompanied by a countercyclical direction of

---

[84] Alfredo Saad-Filho, "Life beyond the Washington Consensus: An Introduction to pro-Poor Macroeconomic Policies", *Review of Political Economy* 19, no. 4 (2007): 130, https://doi.org/10.1080/09538250701622352.

[85] Herr, "An Analytical Framework", 33.

[86] Hyman P. Minsky, "Uncertainty and the Insitutional Structure of Capitalist Economies", *Journal of Economic Issues* XXX, n. 3, (1996): 366.

[87] Stockhammer, Constantine, and Reissl, "Explaining the Euro Crisis", 19,22.

[88] Marc Lavoie and Engelbert Stockhammer, "Wage-Led Growth: Concept, Theories and Policies", in *Regulating for Decent Work (RDW) Conference* (Geneva, Switzerland: International Labour Office, 2012), 37.

credit.[89] Moreover, this policy should be supported by a relatively closed capital account, capital controls, autonomous rate of interest and the establishment of development banks to provide long-term finance.[90]

Conclusion

The Greek financial crisis of the late 2000s presented a significant challenge to the ECB and the stability of the eurozone. At the centre of managing this crisis was the ECB, tasked with monetary policy and financial stability within the Eurozone. The ECB's multifaceted role during the crisis included accepting Greek debt as collateral, implementing conventional and unconventional measures, such as the SMP, and providing ELA to prevent a collapse of the Greek banking system. The ECB's actions were influenced by its mandate, including maintaining price stability and safeguarding the financial system. However, the ECB's measures, such as collateral waivers and the SMP, were mainly aimed at protecting European banks holding Greek bonds rather than directly addressing the Greek crisis. The ECB's provision of ELA and its role within the Troika, alongside the IMF and EC, also raised concerns about the conditionalities and the impact on Greece's austerity measures. The crisis ultimately led to the introduction of capital controls in Greece, with the ECB playing a destabilizing role in the banking system but also restricting further deposit outflows. The termination of ELA and refusal to accept Greek government bonds as collateral further strained the situation.

The Post Keynesian perspective presents alternative proposals for the ECB's response to the GFC. Firstly, Post Keynesians argue that the ECB should have acted as a typical lender of last resort, providing liquidity to Greek banks early on to stabilize the financial system and facilitate economic recovery. Instead of pursuing austerity measures, which worsened the crisis, a focus on liquidity provision could have mitigated its impact. Secondly, the Post Keynesian approach advocates for debt restructuring as a means to achieve sustainable recovery. Recognizing the necessity of tailored monetary policies based on each country's economic structure, this approach suggests that Greece should have been offered flexibility in managing its debt burden. A third set of actions prioritizes expansionary fiscal policy and targeted investments to stimulate aggregate demand, create jobs, and improve long-term economic prospects. By

---

[89] José Antonio Ocampo, "Rethinking the Development Agenda", *Cambridge Journal of Economics* 26, no. 3 (2002): 399, https://doi.org/10.1093/cje/26.3.393.

[90] John Marangos, "The Troika's Conditionalities during the Greek Financial Crisis of 2010–2014: The Washington Consensus Is Alive, Well, and Here to Stay", *European Journal of Economics and Economic Policies: Intervention* November 2019 (2021): 154, https://doi.org/10.4337/ejeep.2021.0075.

adopting expansionary fiscal measures, Greece could have regained economic momentum and strengthened its prospects for the future. Fourthly, Post Keynesians call for enhanced regulation of the financial sector to prevent excessive risk-taking along with future crises and to ensure financial stability.

Bibliography

Albu, Ada Cristina and Lucian Liviu Albu. "Public Debt and Economic Growth in Euro Area Countries. A Wavelet Approach". *Technological and Economic Development of Economy* 27, no. 3 (2021): 602–25. https://doi.org/10.3846/tede.2021.14241.

Arachovas, Charalampos K. and Manolis M. Manioudis. "Attempting an Assessment of the MoUs' Role in Confronting the Greek Crisis", in *Bridging Microeconomics and Macroeconomics and the Effects on Economic Development and Growth*, edited by Pantelis C. Kostis, 259–75. Hershey, Pennsylvania, USA: IGI Global, 2020. https://doi.org/10.4018/978-1-7998-4933-9.

Beck, Thorsten and Hans-helmut Kotz. *Ordoliberalism: A German Oddity?*. London: CEPR Press, 2017.

Behrend, Ben. "The Supranational Governmentality of Neoliberalism: An Analysis of the Governing Principles of Troika Programs for Greece". *The IAPSS Journal of Political Science* 26 (2015): 33–47.

Bénétrix, Agustín S. and Philip R. Lane. "International Differences in Fiscal Outcomes during the Global Crisis". *Fiscal Studies* 36, no. 1 (2015): 1–27. https://doi.org/10.1111/j.1475-5890.2015.12043.x.

Biebricher, Thomas. "The Return of Ordoliberalism in Europe - Notes on a Research Agenda". *I-Lex* 21, no. March (2014): 1–24.

Bini Smaghi, Lorenzo. "Central Bank Independence in the EU: From Theory to Practice". *European Law Journal* 14, no. 4 (2008): 446–60.

Bonefeld, Werner. "On the Strong Liberal State: Beyond Berghahn and Young". *New Political Economy* 18, no. 5 (2013): 779–83.

Bonzom, Philippe and Christian Barontini. *A National Central Bank within a Federal System*. na, 2005.

Botta, Alberto. "Conflicting Claims in the Eurozone? Austerity's Myopia and the Need for a European Federal Union in a Post-Keynesian Eurozone Center–Periphery Model". *Review of Keynesian Economics* 2, no. 1 (2014): 45–70.

Botta, Alberto. "The Short- and Long-Run Inconsistency of the Expansionary Austerity Theory : A Post-Keynesian/Evolutionist Critique". Working Paper. Annandale-on-Hudson, NY, 2016.

Caruana, Jaime and Adrian Van Rixtel. "International Financial Markets and Bank Funding in the Euro Area: Dynamics and Participants". *Bank for International Settlements*, 2013.

Clifton, Judith, Daniel Diaz-Fuentes and Ana Lara Gómez. "The Crisis as Opportunity? On the Role of the Troika in Constructing the European Consolidation State". *Cambridge Journal of Regions, Economy and Society* 11, no. 3 (2018): 587–608. https://doi.org/10.1093/cjres/rsy021.

Dimakopoulou, Vassiliki, George Economides and Apostolis Philippopoulos. "The Greek Great Depression 2009-2016 and the Role Played by the ECB". In

Greece and The Euro From Crisis to Recovery. Edited by George Alogoskoufis and Kevin Featherstone, 118–37. Hellenic Observatory and the Fletcher School, Tufts University, 2021.

ECB. "Speech by Mario Draghi, President of the European Central Bank at the Global Investment Conference in London 26 July 2012". 2012. https://www.ecb.uropa.eu/press/key/date/2009/html/sp090428.en.html.

ECB. "The Monetary Policy of the ECB." Frankfurt, 2011.

ECB. "The Transmission of the ECB's Recent Non-Standard Monetary Policy Measures." ECB Economic Bulletin. Frankfurt, 2015.

Fischer, Stanley. "Central-Bank Independence Revisited". *The American Economic Review* 85, no. 2 (1995): 201–6.

Frangakis, Marica. "The ECB's Non-Standard Monetary Policy Measures and the Greek Financial Crisis". In *The Internal Impact and External Influence of the Greek Financial Crisis.* Edited by John Marangos, 47–70. Palgrave Macmillan, Cham, 2017.

Gibson, Heather D., Stephen G. Hall, Pavlos Petroulas, Vassilis Spiliotopoulos and George S. Tavlas. "The Effect of Emergency Liquidity Assistance (ELA) on Bank Lending during the Euro Area Crisis". *Journal of International Money and Finance.* Working Paper. Athens, 2020. https://doi.org/10.1016/j.jimonfin.2020.102154.

Goodhart, Charles and Rosa Lastra. "Populism and Central Bank Independence". *Open Economies Review* 29 (2018): 49–68.

Gourinchas, Pierre Olivier, Thomas Philippon and Dimitri Vayanos. "The Analytics of the Greek Crisis." *NBER Macroeconomics Annual* 31, no. 1 (2016): 1–81. https://doi.org/10.1086/690239.

Grauwe, Paul De. "Only a More Active ECB Can Solve the Euro Crisis". CEPS Policy Brief no. 250 (2011): 1–8.

Hagen, Jürgen Von. "Money Growth Targeting by the Bundesbank". *Journal of Monetary Economics* 43, no. 3 (1999): 681–701.

Hazakis, Konstantinos J. "The Political Economy of Economic Adjustment Programs in the Eurozone: A Detailed Policy Analysis". *Politics and Policy* 43, no. 6 (2015): 822–54. https://doi.org/10.1111/polp.12141.

Hein, Eckhard, Achim Truger and Till Working van Treeck. "The European Financial and Economic Crisis: Alternative Solutions from a (Post-) Keynesian Perspective". IMK Working Paper. Düsseldorf, 2011.

Hellenic Statistical Authority. *Living Conditions in Greece.* Edited by Hellenic Statistical Authority, 2017.

Hendry, David F, and Neil R Ericsson. "An Econometric Analysis of UK Money Demand in Monetary Trends in the United States and the United Kingdom by Milton Friedman and Anna J. Schwartz". *The American Economic Review,* 1991, 8–38.

Herr, Hansjörg. "An Analytical Framework for the Post-Keynesian Macroeconomic Paradigm". Berlin, 2013.

Herr, Hansjörg. "The European Central Bank and the US Federal Reserve as Lender of Last Resort." *Panoeconomicus* 61, no. 1 1 spec. Issue (2014): 59–78. https://doi.org/10.2298/PAN1401059H.

IMF. "2016 Article Iv Consultation—Press Release; Staff Report; and Statement by the Executive Director for Greece. *IMF Staff Country Reports.* February 2. Washington, D.C., 2017. https://doi.org/10.5089/9781484335918.002.

Ioannidis, Michael, Sarah Jane Hlásková and Chiara Zilioli. "The Mandate of the ECB: Legal Considerations in the ECB's Monetary Policy Strategy Review". ECB Occasional Paper. Frankfurt a. M., 2021. https://doi.org/10.2139/ssrn.3928298.

Katsimi, Margarita and Thomas Moutos. "EMU and the Greek Crisis: Are There Lessons to be Learnt?" *European Journal of Political Economy* 26, no. 4 (2010): 1–17.

Kennedy, Geoff. "Embedding Neoliberalism in Greece: The Transformation of Collective Bargaining and Labour Market Policy in Greece during the Eurozone Crisis", in *Annual Conference of the Western Political Science Association 24-26 March, San Diego,* 1–14, 2016. https://doi.org/10.1080/07078552.2016.1249129.

Kilponen, Juha and Kai Leitemo. "Model Uncertainty and Delegation: A Case for Friedman's K-Percent Money Growth Rule?". *Journal of Money, Credit and Banking* 40, no. 2-3 (2008): 547–56.

Lapavitsas, Costas. "Political Economy of the Greek Crisis". *Review of Radical Political Economics* 51, no. 1 (2019): 31–51. https://doi.org/10.1177/0486613417730363.

Lavoie, Marc and Engelbert Stockhammer. "Wage-Led Growth: Concept, Theories and Policies". In *Regulating for Decent Work (RDW) Conference,* 1–43. Geneva, Switzerland: International Labour Office, 2012.

Louri, Helen, and Petros Migiakis. "Economic Activity and Sources of Finance in Greece: The Predominant Role of Banks", in *Greece and the Euro From Crisis to Recovery.* Edited by George Alogoskoufis and Kevin Featherstone. 138–69. Hellenic Observatory and the Fletcher School, Tufts University, 2021.

Lynch, Kathleen, and Manolis Kalaitzake. "Affective and Calculative Solidarity: The Impact of Individualism and Neoliberal Capitalism". *European Journal of Social Theory* 23, no. 2 (2018): 1–33. https://doi.org/10.1177/1368431018786379.

Marangos, John. "Developing a Civilised Society in Transition Economies: The Post Keynesian Paradigm". *Journal of Socio-Economics* 35, no. 4 (2006): 660–81. https://doi.org/10.1016/j.socec.2005.11.009.

Marangos, John. "The Neoclassical and Keynesian Standpoint and Policy Implications Regarding the Greek Financial Crisis". *International Journal of Social Economics* 49, no. 3 (2022): 470–85. https://doi.org/10.1108/IJSE-07-2021-0376.

Marangos, John. "The Post-Keynesian Perspective and Policy Recommendations for the Greek Financial Crisis". *Review of Radical Political Economics* 2023, 1–25. https://doi.org/10.1177/04866134221142057.

Marangos, John. "The Travels of the Washington Consensus: From the Global Financial Crisis to the Greek Financial Crisis The Travels of the Washington Consensus : From the Global Financial Crisis to the Greek Financial Crisis". *Forum for Social Economics* 0, no. 0 (2023): 1–20. https://doi.org/10.1080/07360932 .2023.2245977.

Marangos, John. "The Troika's Conditionalities during the Greek Financial Crisis of 2010–2014: The Washington Consensus Is Alive, Well, and Here to

Stay". *European Journal of Economics and Economic Policies: Intervention* November 2019 (2021): 470–85. https://doi.org/10.4337/ejeep.2021.0075.

Maris, Georgios, Pantelis Sklias and Napoleon Maravegias. "The Political Economy of the Greek Economic Crisis in 2020". *European Politics and Society* 0, no. 0 (2021): 1–21. https://doi.org/10.1080/23745118.2021.1895552.

Maris, Georgios. "The Political Economy of the Greek Economic Crisis in 2020". *European Politics and Society* 23, no. 4 (2022): 447–67. https://doi.org/10.1080/23745118.2021.1895552.

Matsaganis, Manos. "The Greek Crisis : Social Impact and Policy Responses". *Friedrich-Ebert-Stiftung*. Berlin, 2013.

Maux, Laurent Le and Laurence Scialom. "Central Banks and Financial Stability: Rediscovering the Lender-of-Last-Resort Practice in a Finance Economy" *Cambridge Journal of Economics* 37, no. 1 (2013): 1–18. https://doi.org/10.1093/cje/bes040.

Michopoulou, Stella. "Developmental and Social Impacts of IMF Stability Policies (in Greek)". Athens, 2012.

Micossi, Stefano. "The Monetary Policy of the European Central Bank (2002-2015)". CEPS Special Report. Brussels, 2015. https://www.ceps.eu/system/files/SR 109 SM Monetary Policy of the ECB_0.pdf.

Migkos, Stavros P., Damianos P. Sakas, Nikolaos T. Giannakopoulos, Georgios Konteos and Anastasia Metsiou. "Analyzing Greece 2010 Memorandum's Impact on Macroeconomic and Financial Figures through FCM". *Economies* 10, no. 178 (2022): 1–19. https://doi.org/10.3390/economies10080178.

Minsky, Hyman P. "Uncertainty and the Institutional Structure of Capitalist Economies". *Journal of Economic Issues* XXX, n. 3, (1996): 357–68.

Mitropoulos, Panagiotis, Ioannis Mitropoulos, Haralampos Karanikas, and Nikolaos Polyzos. "The Impact of Economic Crisis on the Greek Hospitals' Productivity". *International Journal of Health Planning and Management* 1, no. 14 (2017): 1–15. https://doi.org/10.1002/hpm.2410.

Nikiforos, Michalis, Laura Carvalho, and Christian Schoder. "'Twin Deficits' in Greece: In Search of Causality". *Journal of Post Keynesian Economics* 38, no. 2 (2015): 302–30. https://doi.org/10.1080/01603477.2015.1065675.

Ocampo, José Antonio. "Rethinking the Development Agenda". *Cambridge Journal of Economics* 26, no. 3 (2002): 393–407. https://doi.org/10.1093/cje/26.3.393.

Orphanides, Athanasios. "12 Monetary Policy and Fiscal Discipline: How the ECB Planted the Seeds of the Euro Area Crisis." *Hawks and Doves: Deeds and Words*, 2018, 115.

Pagoulatos, George. "Greece after the Bailouts: Assessment of a Qualified Failure". *Hellenic Observatory Papers on Greece and Southeast Europe* no. 130 (2018): 1–130.

Panico, Carlo, and Francesco Purificato. "The Debt Crisis and the European Central Bank's Role of Lender of Last Resort". Working Paper Series. Amherst, 2013.

Petrakis, Nikolaos, Christos Lemonakis, Christos Floros and Constantin Zopounidis. "Greek Banking Sector Stock Reaction to ECB's Monetary Policy

Interventions". *Journal of Risk and Financial Management* 15, no. 448 (2022): 1–19. https://doi.org/10.3390/jrfm15100448.

Saad-Filho, Alfredo. "Life Beyond the Washington Consensus: An Introduction to pro-Poor Macroeconomic Policies". *Review of Political Economy* 19, no. 4 (2007): 513–37. https://doi.org/10.1080/09538250701622352.

Seyler, Edward,and John Levendis. "What Was the Role of Monetary Policy in the Greek Financial Crisis". *South-Eastern Europe Journal of Economics* 11, no. 2 (2013): 117–37.

Skidelsky, Robert. *Keynes: The Return of the Master*. New York: Public Affairs, 2009.

Smaghi, Lorenzo Bini. "Conventional and Unconventional Monetary Policy". Keynote Lecture at The International Center for Monetary and Banking Studies (ICMB), 2009, 1–17. https://doi.org/10.4337/9781788972 345.00014.

Stockhammer, Engelbert. "Neoliberal Growth Models, Monetary Union and the Euro Crisis. A Post-Keynesian Perspective". *New Political Economy* 21, no. 4 (2016): 1–36. https://doi.org/DOI: 10.1080/13563467. 2016.1115826.

Stockhammer, Engelbert. "Post-Keynesian Macroeconomic Foundations for Comparative Political Economy". *Politics and Society*, 2021. https://doi.org/10.1177/00323292211006562.

Stockhammer, Engelbert, Collin Constantine and Severin Reissl. "Explaining the Euro Crisis: Current Account Imbalances, Credit Booms and Economic Policy in Different Economic Paradigms". *Journal of Post Keynesian Economics* 43, no. 2 (2020): 1–36. https://doi.org/10.1080/01603477.2020.1734464.

Stockhammer, Engelbert and Syed Mohib Ali. "Varieties of Capitalism and Post-Keynesian Economics on Eurocrisis". Workıng Paper, 2018.

"The Chronicle of the Great Crisis: The Bank of Greece 2008-2013". Athens, 2013.

Trebesch, Christoph and Jeromin Zettelmeyer. "ECB Interventions in Distressed Sovereign Debt Markets : The Case of Greek Bonds". Working Paper. Washington, D.C, 2018.

Tucker, Paul. "How the European Central Bank and Other Independent Agencies Reveal a Gap in Constitutionalism: A Spectrum of Institutions for Commitment". *German Law Journal* 22, no. 6 (2021): 999–1027.

Tuckwell, Carolina and António Mendonça. "The Global Crisis and Unconventional Monetary Policy: ECB versus Fed" Working Paper. Lisbon, 2016. http://pascal.iseg.utl.pt/~cesa/index.php/menupublicacoes/working-papers, http://pascal.iseg.utl.pt/~cesa/index.php/menupublicacoes/working-papers.

Whelan, Karl. "Banking Union and the ECB as Lender of Last Resort". UCD Centre for Economic Research Working Paper Series. Dublin, 2016. http://hdl.handle.net/10197/7860.

Chapter 4

Financial Market Turmoil and Financial Stability in the European Banking Union

Sevgi İneci

Galatasaray University, İstanbul, Turkey

Abstract

The 2008 financial crisis resulted in the formation of enormous bank-support programs in the euro area and revealed three essential problems. The first was the need for banking market integration. The second was high exposure to risk concerning loss or debt in the banking system. Finally, the third problem pertained to structural weaknesses in financial stability. The European Banking Union was created as a response to those problems. The share of small and medium-sized enterprises was high (99%) in the real economy, and the European economy was dependent on financing from banks. The euro's introduction as a single currency of the Monetary Union was expected to create better opportunities for savers and borrowers in a well-integrated European capital market. This study starts with a brief overview of the origin of the recent financial collapse and its global contagion. The first section explains the complex mechanism of euro area monetary policy conducted by the European Central Bank (ECB) on behalf of all EU members. The second section discusses issues arising from governments' debt in an economic and monetary union as they are expected to keep their debt within union-defined limits. The third section highlights the importance of the creation of the Banking Union in the euro area after the 2008 global financial turmoil. The European Monetary Union (EMU) imposed a series of strict rules called convergence criteria on euro area candidate countries before becoming full members. The Banking Union was formed in 2012 with the goal of solving this issue of bank sovereign co-dependency. The first two pillars of the Banking Union, the Single Supervision Mechanism (SSM) and the Single Resolution Mechanism (SRM), improved the euro area's financial stability by harmonizing rules, reducing fragmentation and ensuring a common fund. This section concludes that fundamental weaknesses like sovereign debt pressures, growing inflation risk, unemployment risk, recession risk, weak fiscal harmonization and finally, asymmetric growth rate among members remain a threat to financial stability in the European Union and the euro area.

Keywords: Financial Turmoil, Financial Stability, European Banking Union, European Central Bank, European Monetary Union, Stability and Growth Pact

***

Introduction: Origin of the Recent Financial Collapse and its Global Contagion

In the United States (US), the period after World War II until the end of 1990 was the longest period of economic expansion, where economic growth and productivity burgeoned and inflation and unemployment declined continually. In the mid-1990s, a worldwide development in technology and communication sectors incentivized investors to purchase over-the-counter equities with anticipation of higher future sell prices. Meanwhile, in this growing market, internet startups were not generating sufficient revenue or profit in spite of large market capitalizations. Yet, investors encouraged by financial analysts continued to believe in their potential profitability. A financial bubble formed. As called *dot com bubble*, this revolutionary internet sector started to collapse in 1999. The dot com bubble crash was a market shock, and investors saw a massive stock sell-off.[1]

During the first half of the 2000s, the Federal Reserve Bank kept interest rates low, and their stance on monetary policy was accommodative. Lower borrowing costs encouraged households to incur debt to become homeowners. After the collapse, capital flowed towards the real estate sector in the United States. Encouraged by public and private financial bodies, this highly profitable and rapidly expanding market attracted new investors. As prices rose, investment and speculation increased rapidly. A bubble gradually formed in the real estate market. Many investors purchased real estate with the expectation to sell at a gain in the near future. However, a growing number of banking clients applying for mortgages were lower-quality borrowers. Some banks offered attractive financing terms without adequate inspection of borrowers' credit risk. Lenders and their mortgage agreements with borrowers carried a higher debt service obligation with lower cash flow capability. High-risk borrowers increased as housing prices rose. Subprime mortgage lenders declared bankruptcy as millions of housing loans could not be repaid by borrowers.

In September 2008, Lehman Brothers, one of the most prestigious investment banks in the world, filed for bankruptcy. After the filing, the bank's share price fell to 13 cents compared to 80 dollars a year before. A sharp fall in their stock price triggered the subprime mortgage crisis in the United States.

---

[1] Eli Ofek and Matthew Richardson, "Dotcom Mania: The Rise and Fall of Internet Stock Prices", *The Journal of Finance* 58, no.3 (June 2003): 2-25.

Rising inflation began to threaten the economy beginning in 2004 and the Federal Funds Effective Rate gradually increased. Household borrowers began to fall behind on their debt payments. During this time, banks were also securitizing subprime mortgage loans, which involved repackaging mortgages into new financial instruments such as mortgage-backed securities (MBS) and collateralized debt obligations (CDOs). This played a role in the increase of subprime lending. Since banks resold these securitized subprime loans to other banks and hedge funds both in the United States and globally, it was extremely difficult to assess the individual risk exposure in global real estate markets after the crisis.

When the bubble burst, several funds exposed to subprime loans were forced to shut down. With declines in housing prices and high household debt, household spending decreased. The US government intervened with the Troubled Asset Relief Program (TARP) and the American Recovery and Reinvestment Act (ARRA) to stabilize the financial system.

Central banks in Europe made similar interventions like the liquidity injection program to the banking sector. The financial crisis became more visible between 2007 and 2008 as several major financial institutions collapsed and credit constraints were imposed on businesses and consumers. The Great Financial Crisis was the first major crisis since the Great Depression of 1929.

The first bank affected by the crisis was the *Northern Rock Bank* in the United Kingdom (UK). It was nationalized by the British Government in 2008. The bank received liquidity support from the Bank of England (the central bank of the UK) due to its exposure to credit markets.[2] In 2012, *Virgin Money*, a banking and financial service brand in the UK, purchased the *Northern Rock Bank*.

Bear Stearns, the American investment bank founded in 1923, also failed during the 2008 crisis. The firm was heavily involved in the subprime mortgage crisis. After its closure, it was sold to JP Morgan Chase. The collapse of Bear Stearns was the start of the meltdown in the investment banking sector in the United States.

Fannie Mae and Freddie Mac, government-sponsored entities that finance home mortgages in the US through bond issuance, became illiquid during the subprime mortgage crisis. They were both placed under the supervision of the US Treasury. Naturally, a debate arose during this period: should we save all these companies?

---

[2] Sebastian Paulo, "Europe and Global Financial Crisis: Taking Stock of the EU's Policy Response", Foundation Robert Schuman. April 2011, 3-8, https://old.robert-schuman.eu/en/doc/questions-d-europe/qe-200-en.pdf.

In each case, authorities must tradeoff between short-term stability and long-term moral hazard. Lehman Brothers, 158 years old holding company, filed for bankruptcy in September 2008. Bank of America had offered to take over but gave up because it did not obtain the support of the American federal authorities.

The banking sector rescue lasted several months. Governments announced programs of recapitalization to halt the systemic crisis, primarily through the nationalization of defaulted banks. Stock markets lost half of their value, and the economic crisis spread to western economies.

Financial Turmoil and European Monetary Policy

When the financial market turmoil started in 2007 in the US, the illiquidity problem spread across Europe through to the European banking sector, turning into a financial crisis and then a sovereign debt crisis.

European economies had encountered several economic and monetary stresses before 2007, particularly between the 70's and 80's. In 1970, the European Economic Community (EEC) attempted to establish its own monetary union, taking into account the contagion risk of exchange rate crises experienced by the international monetary system. This plan was put forward as the Verner Plan of the European Monetary Union (EMU) in 1970 but was established in 1999, almost 30 years later.

While the euro was introduced as a common currency for a unique monetary policy in a common market in January 1999, the European Central Bank (ECB) officially assumed responsibility for this policy on behalf of the Eurozone's first eleven eligible members.

The greatest advantage of a common currency is the reduction in the transaction cost of doing business across national boundaries within the European Union. The primary mandate of the ECB was to maintain price stability, as set by Article 105(1) of the Treaty on the European Union.

The political independence of the ECB was deemed essential and was guaranteed in two ways. First, the Treaty required each member country's national central bank to be formally independent of their national governments. Second, the Treaty ensured the decision-making authority of the Governing Council of the ECB to be formally independent from the European Union.

As mentioned before, the objective of the ECB's monetary policy is price stability. The ECB supports general economic policies in the Community, such as sustainable and non-inflationary growth and a high level of employment, contingent upon the presence of price stability. So, this primary objective of the ECB aims to ensure that the growth of money supply or a reduction of interest rates will not threaten price stability.

How Does the ECB Accomplish its Mission of Ensuring Price Stability Within a Multi-Country Monetary Union Zone?

First of all, the ECB monitors the economic and monetary well-being of the euro area economies by conducting analyses of economic indicators of sectors and regions. These analyses inform the ECB on measures it should take to offset potential economic shocks. This responsibility was assigned to the ECB by the Maastricht Treaty. The Maastricht Convergence Criteria defines four target indicators and each member of the Eurozone must adhere to the criteria put in place by the Treaty. These indicators are price stability, sound public finance, exchange rate stability, and long-term interest rates.[3] The target rate of inflation is set at 2% annual inflation rate for the goal of price stability. The "debt/GDP" and deficit/GDP ratios are set to 60% and 3%, respectively. Finally, candidates are required to participate in the exchange rate mechanism (ERM II) for at least two years without the local currency devaluing against the euro and with the absence of severe tensions. These criteria were set for the eurozone as a whole.

According to the first indent of Article 140(1) of the Treaty, "The achievement of a high degree of price stability; this will be apparent from a rate of inflation which is close to that of, at most, the three best performing Member States in terms of price stability".[4]

This article requires that for sustainable price performance in a country, the average rate of inflation observed over a period of one year before the examination must not exceed by more than 1.5 percentage points that of, at most, the three best-performing member states in terms of price stability.

The average rate of inflation is calculated using the change in the latest available 12-month average of the Harmonized Index of Consumer Prices (HICP) over the previous 12-month average. An HICP has been constructed by the European Monetary Institute (EMI) since 1993 for each member state.[5]

The reference rate of inflation is a value which tracks the three best-performing member states in terms of price stability. The rate is calculated by taking the unweighted arithmetic average of the rate of inflation of the three member states with the lowest inflation rate.

---

[3] Dominick Lasok, "The Maastricht Treaty on European Union", *Marmara Journal of European Studies* (1993).

[4] "Official Journal of the European Union, Consolidates version of the Treaty on European Union and the Treaty on the Functioning of the European Union, Information and Notices", 2016/C 202/01, 59 (7 June 2016), 1-412, https://eur-lex.europa.eu/legal-content/EN/TXT/PDF/?uri=OJ:C:2016:202:FULL

[5] Vitor Gaspar, "Eurostat's HCIP and the European Central Bank's Definition of Price Stability", *Defining and Measuring the Target*, (International Monetary Fund, 2001), 138-156.

According to the second indent of Article 140(1) of the Treaty, the sustainability of the financial position of the member countries' governments depends on the absence of an excessive deficit in the budgetary position. The limit rate of budgetary deficit/GDP is 3%. This is a reference value.

Another reference rate is defined by the Maastricht Convergence Criteria for government debt ratio. A country's government's "debt/GDP" reference ratio is 60%. Article 140(1) refers to article 126(6) for excessive deficit procedure.[6] Article 126 sets out that, in case of excessive government budgetary deficit, related countries should be under examination by the European Commission.

According to the Convergence criteria of the Maastricht Treaty, the Commission and the ECB assess the progress made by the eurozone members at least once every two years or at the request of a member state with a derogation.

Table 4.1 Four Convergence Criteria of the Maastricht Treaty

	Price stability	**Sound public finance**	**Durability of convergence**	**Exchange rate stability**
Convergence criteria	A price performance is sustainable if average inflation rate is no more than 1.5% points above the rate of the three best performing member states.	Not under excessive deficit procedure at the time of examination.	Not more than 2% points above the rate of three best performing member states in terms of price stability.	Participation in ERM II at least two years without devaluing against euro and absence of severe tensions.*
Measure methodology	Harmonized consumer price inflation	Government deficit and debt	Long-term interest rate	Exchange-rate performance in ERM I

Source: Author.

*Severe tensions are calculated by examining the extent to which exchange rates deviate from the central rates against the euro in ERM II.

As the observation authority, the European Commission prepares a report about the country under investigation, indicating that it does not fulfil the fiscal requirements.[7] Moreover, the Maastricht Treaty requires EU member countries to meet several macroeconomic convergence criteria before joining the EMU. These additional factors include the integration of markets and the development of the balance of payments.

[6] Official Journal of the European Union, 2016/C 202/01:108-110.

[7] Official Journal of the European Union, 2016/C 202/01:99.

The Two Pillar Strategy of the ECB and Monetary Policy Coordination

The target inflation rate is the first pillar of the monetary policy coordination in the Eurozone. Each national central bank has to maintain the growth rate of the money supply at a steady rate to reach a target rate of inflation in a currency area, assuming that the growth rate of real GDP and the rate of decline of money velocity are independently driven.

The second pillar of the Two Pillar Strategy sets the standard for the money supply growth rate determined by the ECB. The euro is the only circulating currency (M1) of the Eurozone, and its supply is directly controlled by the ECB. However, bank deposits and time deposits (M2) in the banking system are not directly controlled by the ECB policy instruments. Similarly, the ECB does not directly control repurchase agreements, money market fund shares/units, and debt securities with a maturity of up to two years (M3). The control of the M2 and M3 are under the control of member states.

EMI, which existed between 1993 and 1997, managed inflation control within the Eurozone and passed on this responsibility to the ECB, which cooperated with all central banks in the Eurozone. EMI was a temporary body established on January 1, 1994, to strengthen cooperation among member country central banks and enhance monetary policy coordination to establish the European System of Central Banks (ESCB) to execute a single monetary policy. During this period, the inflation rates of the member states converged to the annual target of 2% set by the ECB. EMI was replaced by the ECB on June 1, 1998.

After the introduction of the euro as a single currency, there was inflation rate dispersion among member states of the euro area. While high inflation rates were observed in Ireland, Spain, Greece and Portugal, Germany, France, Belgium, and the Netherlands remained low-inflation rate countries. Per capita income differences between these two groups of countries make it difficult for inflation rates to converge.

Let's now refer to the Balassa-Samuelson effect, which has major implications for the interpretation of inflation and exchange rate criteria: Under a fixed exchange rate regime, the Balassa-Samuelson effect will result in CPI and real exchange rate appreciation. This is due to the differences in productivity growth rates between trade partners. In the Eurozone, the productivity growth rate differentiation between low-inflation and high-inflation countries resulted in income per capita differences among countries. Finally, low productivity and low per capita income countries experienced high inflation rates.[8]

[8] Mihaljec Dubravko and Marc Klau. "Catching up Inflation in Transition Economies: The Balassa Samuelson Effect Revisited", Bank for International Settlements, 2008, 2-26.

The Policy Actions of the ECB

ECB conducts its monetary policy actions using the discount rate and open market operations. The discount rate is the lending rate of the ECB to banks of the euro area. When banks need liquidity overnight or over the short term, they can borrow funds from the ECB at the lending rate. The European Overnight Interest Average (EONIA) is the daily rate of interbank lending within the euro area. This is the rate at which the ECB offers liquidity to member countries' banks. Open market operations are the ECB's second tool for monetary policy action. The ECB offers a fixed amount of euros at a set interest rate to member country banks. The ECB holds government debt offered by member banks as eligible assets and earns the average rate of interest bid on bonds it holds. As such, the ECB provides a fresh infusion of euros to the euro area banking sector. The ECB determines interest rates that banks use as part of interbank operations.[9]

Table 4.2 ECB Key Interest Rates

Lending rate	Banks short-term borrowing rate
Marginal lending rate	Banks may use it for overnight credit from the Eurosystem
MRO rate	Main refinancing operation rate provides bulk liquidity to the banking system
EONIA rate	Euro Overnight Index Average Rate Closing rate for the overnight maturity is calculated by collecting data on unsecured overnight lending in the euro area provided by banks
Deposit rate	Banks may use it to make overnight deposits with the Eurosystem

Source: Author. Information collected from the ECB website https://www.ecb.europa.eu/stats/policy_and_exchange_rates/key_ecb_interest_rates/html/index.en.html

The average rate of EONIA fluctuates daily around the refinancing rate, and the ECB sets it weekly. The lending rate is set at one percentage point above the refinancing rate, while the deposit rate is set one percentage point below with the objective of creating a two-percentage point spread.

Cooperation with National Central Banks

The ECB cooperates with central banks of member countries to ensure full compliance with the monetary policy under changing international money market conditions and strictly follows the Maastricht Criteria while using the monetary policy tools within its jurisdiction. National central banks cannot

[9] Philippine Cour-Thimann, and Jung C. Alexander, "Interest Rate Setting and Communication at the ECB in its First Twenty Years", *European Journal of Political* Economy (2021): 3-11.

conduct separate monetary policies as a single monetary union should have a single monetary policy.

The execution and supervision responsibilities of the single monetary policy are under the full authority of the European Central Bank. National central banks are responsible for keeping macroeconomic indicators under control to prevent an adverse effect on the external value of the euro as a common currency.[10]

Article 130 of the Maastricht Treaty guarantees the political independence of the ECB in order to carry out the tasks assigned to itself. This desire for independence is justified by arguments from macroeconomic theory. "ECB independence is conducive to maintaining price stability, as shown by a wealth of theoretical studies and empirical data on central bank independence". There are several studies on this subject, and researchers have developed indices of independence in empirical studies.[11] As explained before, the first objective of the ECB and the ESCB is attaining price stability in the Eurozone. This is a priority over all other considerations.

The Tools of European Monetary Policy

Similar to a national central bank, the ECB has several tools at its disposal to manage the money supply in circulation and curb inflationary pressures when necessary. The ECB uses two pillars to anticipate the level of future inflation:

- Monetary Pillar
- Economic Pillar

The Monetary Pillar is a direct application of the quantity theory of money, which establishes a direct link between the money supply in circulation and the changes in prices. According to economist Irving Fisher, the relationship between money supply and the value of goods purchased can be expressed by the equation below.[12]

Fisher's equation: $M \times V = P \times Y$

---

[10] Official Journal of the European Union, 2016/C 202/01: 99 108-110.

[11] Lazarus Angbazo, "Commercial Bank Net Interest Margins, Default Risk, Interest-rate Risk and Off-Balance Sheet Banking", *Finance* 21 (1997): 55-87; Harold James, *Making the European Monetary Union,* (Cambridge MA: Belknap, Harward University Press, 2012); José Fernandez-Albertos, "The Politics of Central Bank Independence", *Annual Review of Political Sciences* 4,(2015): 4-23; Alesina, Alberto F. and Andrea, Stella. "The Politics of the Monetary Policy", NBER Working Paper, 15856, 2010, 40-42.

[12] Frederic S. Mishkin, *The Economics of Money, Banking and Financial Markets,* (Pearson, 2004), 71.

M represents the money supply in circulation in the national economy. The ECB tries to assess the quantity of money in circulation based on the monetary aggregate M3 and sets a growth target for this aggregate for the upcoming months. However, economist Paul de Grauwe claims that the growth of the monetary aggregate M3 has not been an adequate tool for anticipating inflation in the Eurozone.[13] Several phenomena can explain why this first pillar is less linked to inflation and why it can be difficult to control its fluctuation. One explanation would be that interconnections of financial markets generate international movements of liquidity, which reduces central banks' ability to influence a monetary aggregate such as M3.

In 2003, the ECB decided to rely more on the Economic Pillar to set objectives of its monetary policies, considering the difficulty of anticipating inflation in the Eurozone and the limits of the Monetary Pillar.[14]

The Economic Pillar consists of an analysis of several economic indicators which help evaluate the state of overheating of the economy, meaning the presence of inflationary pressures. The ECB examines economic activity by price and cost indicators in the Eurozone at the geographical and sectoral levels. The central bank tries to anticipate the probable development of prices from the perspective of the confrontation of supply and demand for goods and services and short-term factors. The ECB also observes other indicators, including the growth of aggregate supply and demand in the Eurozone, the level of unemployment, changes in wages, price changes of energy factors, the price of financial assets, changes in exchange rates, the balance of payments and the evolution of the world economy. To manage the money supply, the ECB uses three tools:

- Open Market Operations,
- Standing Facilities
- Reserve Requirements.

The ECB is a liquidity provider and lender of last resort for private banks in the area. The central bank lends over periods of one week (main refinancing operations) or three months (longer-term financing operations) by executing open market operations. Banks borrow funds from the ECB for one week contingent upon providing collateral. The main refinancing operations rate is the interest rate banks pay to borrow from the central bank and is a key rate for

---

[13] Paul De Grauwe, "The Governance of Fragile Eurozone", *The Australian Economic Review* 45, no.3 (2012): 194.

[14] Jacques Pelksman, "European Industrial Policy", *Bruges Policy Paper Briefing* no.15 (2006).

all banks in the Eurozone as it indicates the cost at which banks can obtain liquidity.

Banks can also obtain short-term loan facilities from the ECB. These are called marginal loan facilities, and their rate is higher than the main refinancing operations rate.

Finally, the ECB sets reserve requirements for credit institutions in the euro area. The ECB mandates credit institutions to deposit part of their reserves in their national central banks, and the amount held is determined on average over a maintenance period of about six weeks.

Liberalization of Capital and the Impossible Trilemma

The removal of capital controls by member country central banks, also known as liberalization of capital, had positive and negative consequences. A positive aspect of the liberalization of capital is the easy access to financing, which may result in a reduction in the cost of financing and an increase in investments.

However, member countries' financing needs are not all the same. These differences impact the expected return on investments. As a result, the cost of financing differs among countries and affects investors' expectations of the rate of return on investments. The cost of financing increases in countries that need more financing. The increasing cost of financing causes an increase in public and budget debts (negative impact).

Capital market liberalization and its impact on monetary policy and the real economy have attracted the attention of many researchers. A framework was developed by economists Robert Mundell and Marcus Fleming during the 60s and denoted the impossibility of simultaneously pursuing three macroeconomic policy objectives within a group of countries.[15] According to the Impossible Trilemma framework, countries may choose from three possible choices as they make fundamental decisions on managing their international monetary policy. The Trilemma defines the three choices as follows:

- Setting a fixed exchange regime,
- Allowing free flow of the capital
- Autonomous monetary policy

However, these three policies are in conflict with each other due to mutual exclusivity. As a result, only two of the three options can be pursued at the same time. The example below illustrates this framework:

---

[15] Jacob A. Frenkel and Assaf Razin, "The Mundell-Fleming Model: A Quarter Century Later", NBER Working Paper Series, *National Bureau of Economic Research*, 1987, 2-68.

Let's consider two countries, A and B, which provide full freedom in capital movements between each other. They decide to implement a fixed exchange rate regime. The most important condition for maintaining the rate fixed is to employ a similar monetary policy. Let's now assume that country A tries to fight inflation by cutting the money supply and allowing interest rates to rise while country B makes no changes to its monetary policy. As nominal interest rates in country A rise, interest rates between the two countries begin to differ. Investors in country B who want to evaluate this interest rate difference as an increase in income will cause capital flow to country A, thanks to the freedom provided in capital movements.

Assets held in terms of country B's currency will now move to the banking and financial system of country A in the currency of country A. The currency of country A will appreciate relative to that of B, and the initial fixed exchange rate parity will change against country B. The domestic currency of country A will appreciate as the currency of country B depreciates, leading to a change in the fixed parity between the two countries.

Mundell and Fleming showed that in a fixed exchange rate regime, currencies have some cost to maintain under the full freedom of capital movements and that it is almost impossible for the Central Bank to follow an independent monetary policy.

The monetary authority has two primary intervention tools against the interest rate differential, which causes capital flight from one country to another.

- Restriction of capital movements and control of the freely convertible currency,
- Increase nominal interest rates enough to eliminate the interest rate difference.

The monetary policy authority that resorts to these methods is unable to follow an independent monetary policy under the pressure of capital and foreign exchange market movements. This demonstrates that it is not possible to meet the three policy choices simultaneously.

Countries in the European Monetary System experienced similar problems between 1990 and 1999, and eventually, the strong currency of the period, the Deutsch Mark, became the reference currency of the system. Central Banks of countries with weaker currencies had to abandon the fixed exchange rate regime by giving up their foreign exchange reserves. Efforts to establish a new monetary union after the collapse of the system led to the emergence of the euro as a single currency.

Sovereign Debts of the Member States and Economic and Monetary Union

According to the Maastricht Treaty, the execution of budgetary policy is exclusively controlled by member states. Therefore, there could be free rider behaviour. They could also engage in unwise public spending, thereby generating inflation and driving up interest rates across the Eurozone. Other states of the Eurozone would suffer the diluted effects of this inflation rate, even though they would have properly controlled their own public expenditure.

This risk was identified by several members of the Delors Committee, including the Jacques de Larosière and Alexander Lamfalussy objections.[16] To counter this risk, Jacques de Larosière proposed the Stability and Growth Pact. The pact set monetary penalties for Eurozone member states with lasting government deficits of more than 3% of their gross domestic product. No matter the size of the deficit, the penalty could not exceed 0.5% of the country's GDP. This penalty was imposed on member countries in the form of a forced deposit with the ECB. The pact stated that the deposit could be levied if the member country does not take measures to correct the deficit within two years.

Member countries of the euro area agreed on a Stability and Growth Pact at the Amsterdam summit in 1997. As per the pact, each member pledged to keep future government deficits below 3% of gross domestic product.

However, the pact had less authority than a treaty. For example, it was violated by France and Germany, two countries that supported its creation. After three years of continued violations, the Council of Ministers revised and reinterpreted the pact in 2005[17]. Germany stated that the reunification expenses of *the two lands* on infrastructure were high. This period had spanned fifteen years, and Germany had managed a self-imposed expenditure. Other countries explained that expenditures such as disaster relief and the construction of large infrastructure projects, such as Olympic facilities constructed by Greece for the 2004 games, contributed to the violations.

Sustainability of Public Expenditure

This section discusses major difficulties encountered by member countries as they tried to manage their public expenditures.

First, countries exhibited differing levels of socio-economic development at the beginning of the formation of the European Community. This made it

---

[16] Ivo Maes, *Alexander Lamfaloussy Selected Essays*, ed. Ivo Maes, (Magyar Nemzeti Bank, 2017), 283.

[17] Philip R. Lane, "The Real Effects of European Monetary Union", *Journal of Economic Perspectives* 20, 4 (2006): 63.

difficult to put in place a common macroeconomic policy as these national differences made it necessary to meet different needs in terms of monetary policy. Since governments' investment objectives were different from each other, their budgetary spending was also different.

Second, Eurozone economies were not synchronized in terms of business cycles. Peripheral economies sought to catch up and synchronize with the business cycle of founding countries. The degree of trade openness and production differentiation differed meaningfully between centre and periphery countries. According to McKinnon, an economy that diversifies its pattern of products is less likely to be affected by an asymmetric shock.[18] The risk of asymmetric shock is always present for some member countries.

Third, the Stability and Growth Pact provided for economic sanctions in the event of a public deficit above 3%, but this criterion is not rigorously applied. The Commission failed to apply the sanction mechanism because of the blocking of the Council. Finally, the Pact criteria are reformed and defined in a less rigorous way. Thus, Italy, Greece, Portugal, Malta and Germany experienced a public deficit above 3% in 2006 or 2007.[19]

The average "debt/GDP" ratio for the Eurozone as a whole was around 69.1% in 2001 and rose to 91.6% in 2022. Regarding the Eurozone public deficit criterion, despite large disparities between the Member States, this ratio is around -3.6 % in 2022.

Stability and Growth Pact and the Maastricht criteria imposed macroeconomic criteria, but these criteria were not affordable measures against a large-scale systemic crisis such as the 2008 crisis. Countries such as Italy and Greece, which already had high levels of public debt before the 2008 financial crisis, failed to manage the crisis. It was expected that by meeting the criteria of the Maastricht Treaty and the Growth and Stability Pact, member states would not face a budget deficit and be able to manage a cyclically balanced budget. The criteria were supposed to ensure the improvement of certain member states' public finances, especially those prone to deficits and heavy public debts. Unfortunately, as the American great financial crisis hit the European economy in 2010, some member states were not able to follow the criteria in a strict manner.

In the end, the Stability and Growth Pact did not work well in practice and was criticized in academic and institutional circles. The ECB objected to the

---

[18] Ronald I. McKinnon, "Optimum Currency Areas", *American Economic Review* 53, no. 41963, 717.

[19] Eurostat, "Euro indicators, News Release 170/2010," European Commission, November 15, 2010.

pact's revision, but the objection was unsuccessful. The Stability and Growth Pact was ultimately revised with more flexible mandates, as proposed by member countries.

Table 4.3 Euro Zone and European Union Government Deficit and Debt

		1998	2001	2006	2009	2015	2020	2022
Eurozone*	million euro							
GDP market prices		5 883 044	6 813 825	8 561831	8 977 933	10 413 302	11 464 342	13 334 915
Gov.def (-) / (+)		-127 888	-86 295	-116 763	-565 111	-215 238	-809 582	-484 115
	% of GDP	-2.2	-1.3	-1.4	-6.3	-2,1	-7.1	-3.6
Gov. dept		4 324 582	4 707 756	5 865 245	7 062 625	9 440 246	11 144 783	12 214 492
	% of GDP	73.5	69.1	68.5	78.7	90.7	97.2	91.6
EU **	million euro							
GDP market prices		7 630 870	9 349 470	11 700 493	11 804 734	14 641 508	13 469 027	15 810 123
Gov.def (-) / (+)		-119 596	-123 077	-173 319	-801 866	-351 561	-908 176	-532 558
	% of GDP	-1.6	-1.3	-1.5	-6.8	-2.4	-6.7	-3.4
Gov. dept		5 248 575	5 790 648	7 292 373	8 690 304	12 477 670	12 118 750	13 272 709
	% of GDP	68.8	62.0	58.8	73.6	85.2	90.0	84.0

Source: Table prepared by the author using data collected from Eurostat, European Union Statistical Office.

*: in 2001 Eurozone12; in 2006 Eurozone 16; in 2009 Eurozone 19; In 2022 Eurozone 20.
**: EU: European Union: in 1998, EU 15; in 2001, EU 15; in 2006, EU 25; in 2009, EU 27; in 2015, EU 28; since 2020, EU: 27.

Is the Eurozone Monetary Policy Appropriate for All Members of the Eurozone?

As stated earlier, Eurozone economies have imperfect business cycle synchronization. Governments employ different monetary policies across the euro area due to weaker trade openness and differentiation of goods in certain economies, as well as different domestic market investment needs. For example, the economy overheated in Ireland, Greece and Spain in the 2000s amid the rise in construction and real estate values, and a bubble formed in the real estate sector. These bubbles could have been controlled by employing restrictive monetary policies that aimed to reduce liquidity in circulation and raise interest rates to curb demand for real estate.

The example above attempts to explain the difference in public and private sector investment needs in member countries of the monetary union. Considering Taylor's rule, Taylor proposes that a central bank's choice of key interest rate will depend essentially on two factors: the anticipation of inflation and the output gap (the level of capacity utilization in the economy compared to the full employment of the factors of production.[20] According to some analysts, this rule allows us to measure the difference between the rate set by the ECB and the rates expected from member states of the Eurozone.[21]

The Fragility of Peripheral Economies

Peripheral economies of southern and eastern Europe experiencing structural weaknesses reinforced the effects of the crisis on their economies compared to the rest of the Union.[22] These countries' economic growth was characterized by trade deficits financed by capital inflows in the form of bank loans or foreign direct investment.[23] As the financial crisis hit the real economy, capital flows declined. The Eurozone protected member states with more fragile economies for a couple of months, but peripheral countries in central and eastern Europe outside the Eurozone (Romania, Latvia, Poland, and Hungary) requested financial assistance from the IMF.

The Problem of Sovereign Debts

EU banks increased investments in other member states, particularly in government bonds, driven by the liberalization of capital movements and the elimination of exchange rate risk with the adoption of the euro. As a result, the share of sovereign debt held by European foreign banks suddenly increased

---

[20] Michael Artis and Frederic Nixson, *Economics of the European Union,* (OUP Oxford, 2007), 272.

[21] Carlo Bastasin, "Saving Europe: How National Politics Nearly Destroyed the Euro", (Brookings, Washinton DC, 2012),115; Michel Aglietta and Thomas Brand, *UN New Deal pour l'Europe,* French Edition, (Paris: Odile Jacob, 2013), 154-70; Maes, *"Alexander Lamfaloussy Selected Essay", 304-20.*

[22] Sevgi Ineci and Yeşim Gürbüz, "The Effect of the European Banking Union on Banking Performance of the Central and Eastern European Countries-Avrupa Bankacılık Birliği'nin Orta ve Doğu Avrupa Bankacılık Performansına Etkileri", *Marmara Journal of European Studies* 28, no.1 (2020):81-107.

[23] Claudiu T. Albulescu, "Banks' Profitability and Financial Soundness Indicators: A Macro-Level Investigation in Emerging Countries." *Procedia Economics and Finance,* 23 (2014): 203-209.

between 1999 and 2008. In 2009, private banks were able to access financing from the ECB at low rates and massively bought back sovereign debt securities from their states, which offered them better rates.[24] These triggered bankruptcies in the banking system for banks that were overexposed to the bond market. It also caused the interbank lending to dry up, which led to liquidity problems and bank failures. This phenomenon first occurred in Greek banks that were exposed to Greek government bonds of around 55 billion euros. During the crisis, the share of public debts of the Eurozone member states went from an average of 70% in 2008 to 85,7% in 2010 and 90,7% at the end of 2010[25]. As a result, borrowing rates increased for member states, which aggravated their risk of default and the risk of a banking system collapse in the Eurozone. "The Security Markets Program was introduced to address malfunctioning sovereign bond markets following the outbreak of the sovereign debt crisis in particular in Greece, Portugal and Ireland which suffered from illiquidity".[26]

Member states with no public deficits have pushed their partners to adopt a new stability and growth program to better control budget deficits. This new budget pact, the Treaty on Stability, Coordination and Governance within the Economic and Monetary Union, was established on January 1, 2013.[27]

The new treaty requires that the national budgets of member states be in balance or in surplus. This objective is met if the annual structural general government deficit does not exceed 0,5% of the nominal GDP. However, countries are given some leeway to deviate from the rule in the event of an exceptionally severe economic recession. If the public debt is significantly lower than the reference value of 60% of GDP, the limit for the deficit can be set at 1% of GDP. In 2012, 21 states out of 27 were at risk of excessive deficits.

Why Was it Important to Set Up a Banking Union in the Euro Area Just After the 2008 Global Financial Turmoil?

The 2008 financial crisis exposed structural weaknesses of the European banking and financial system. There was an urgent need to strengthen the

---

[24] Bastasin, "Saving Europe", 110; Aglietta and Brand, "UN New Deal", 176.

[25] ECB, "Monthly Bulletin, June 2013," European Central Bank, https://www.ecb.europa.eu/pub/mopo/html/index.en.html.

[26] Philipp Hartmann and Frank Smetts, "The First Twenty Years of Central Bank of the European Central Bank: Monetary Policy," ECB Working Paper Series, no. 2219 (European Central Bank, Eurosystem, December 2018), 48, [https://www.ecb.europa.eu/pub/pdf/scpwps/ecb.wp2219.en.pdf].

[27] Council of the European Union, "Treaty on Stability Coordination and Governance in the Economic and Monetary Union", 2013, https://www.consilium.europa.eu/media/20399/st00tscg26_en12.pdf.

banking system after the crisis, especially in the Eurozone. While the Basel Banking Regulations had existed since the 70s, the rationale behind the need for a new restructuring reform in the Eurozone can be explained as follows. Previous regulations (Basel I and Basel II) generally focused on improving the performance of the banking system but lacked mechanisms and institutional arrangements that could hold together a multi-country economic integration system using a common currency.

After overcoming the first years of the crisis, the institutional structure was strengthened, and the European Supervisory Authority and the European Systemic Risk Board were established. The ECB initiates and coordinates close cooperation between national central banks and financial institutions. The European Systemic Risk Managers identify systemic risks, develop early warning systems and convey suggestions to institutions to facilitate risk management.

The public debt crisis in Europe showed how high public deficits in a monetary union can damage a banking system. There have been debates in academic and institutional circles since 2008 to develop an efficient solution for a sustainable banking system in the Eurozone.

As a result of these debates, the ECB's powers were strengthened under a single structure and a single supervision mechanism (SSM) in the European Banking Union. Similarly, efforts towards capital markets integration were accelerated within the action plans in 2015 under the chairmanship of EU Commission President Jean-Claude Junker.[28] The formation of the Banking Union is an important stage in the completion of the Economic and Monetary Union, which assumes a transparent and secure banking market under a single structure.

The Capital Markets Union aims to reduce EU companies' cost to access financing. A strong Capital Markets Union will complement the Banking Union and increase the efficiency of the Economic and Monetary Union as a whole. The ECB's institutional regulatory and supervisory role is very important for supporting member countries' ability to overcome financial crises and gain resilience. Therefore, the creation of laws to improve the asset quality of banks and their implementation by member states will be ensured through the bank and capital market union.[29]

---

[28] Cristina S.P. Dias and Kristina Grigaitė. "A Road Map to Completing the Banking Union", in *Depth Analysis*, IPOL Economic Governance Support Unit, Directorate General for Internal Policies, European Parliament, June 2020, PE 645.707: 3-24.

[29] Council of the European Union, "Report of the FSC Subgroup on Non-Performing Loans", Ecofin 481, 9854/17 (31 May 2017): 46-48, https://data.consilium.europa.eu/doc/document/ST-9854-2017-INIT/en/pdf

European Central Bank and Financial Stability

Ensuring price stability depends on having a good monetary transmission mechanism. However, achieving price stability may not always guarantee financial stability, which requires additional measures to be taken and fulfilled. Changes in the policy interest rate of the European Central Bank are reflected in the markets as a monetary transmission mechanism through changes in bank lending rates and affect credit conditions, aggregate demand, and investments. This monetary transmission mechanism is provided through three markets.

- Interbank Money Market (Interbank),
- Covered Bond Market,
- Sovereign Bond Market.

Unexpected confusion in financial markets drags banks and capital markets into a crisis in the absence of guidance on what additional measures should be taken to ensure financial stability.[30] The lack of national central bank liquidity during the European financial and debt crisis urged policymakers to strengthen the ECB's powers, which resulted in a single institutional guiding and supervisory delegation in banks and capital markets in the Eurozone. EU banking system financial ratios improved as a reflection of the adoption of this supranational structure and related improvements in the decision-making mechanism.

Basel III does not completely change the philosophy of the capital requirement calculation method previously regulated in Basel II but improves it quantitatively and qualitatively such that banks and financial institutions can be more institutionally resilient to crises. The 2008 crisis exposed weaknesses in the balance sheets of these institutions. It revealed that amounts that appear as capital on a bank's balance sheets are not actually functionally capable of fulfilling the role of capital. Therefore, improving liquidity and leverage ratios both qualitatively and quantitatively was a necessary measure.[31]

Improvements in Basel III

Capital Conservation Buffer: Basel III introduces the capital contribution buffer regulation. This regulation aims to put safeguards in place to conserve the bank's capital when losses are incurred during stress periods. The capital conservation buffer is above the minimum capital requirement and is applied

---

[30] Ugo Albertazzi and Leonardo Gambacorta. "Bank Profitability and the Business Cycle." *Journal of Financial Stability* 5 (2009):393–409.

[31] ECB, European Central Bank. "Basel III", Special Features, *Financial Stability Review* (Dec 2010): 125-132, https://www.ecb.europa.eu/pub/pdf/fsr/art/ecb.fsrart201012_02.en.pdf

to Common Equity Tier 1 capital, which is the bank's core capital. If the bank's capital level fails to meet the buffer and falls in the range between the buffer level and the minimum requirements, the bank would be able to continue its operations but would be subject to constraints on capital distribution. As in Basel II, core capital includes elements with high loss coverage potential. Core capital includes paid-in capital, retained earnings (loss), other comprehensive income statement items, and values to be deducted from this total. The minimum core capital ratio is standardized. This ratio is calculated as Core Equity/Risk Weighted Assets (RAV).

Circular Capital Buffer: Another important improvement introduced in Basel III is the circular capital buffer. The buffer ranges between 0% and 2,5% based on the country's economic condition and the growth rate of the economy.

Improvements to the Leverage Ratio: The leverage ratio is defined as a transparent, simple and non-risk-based ratio. It was announced in the First Structural Block on January 1, 2018. The ratio is calculated as Tier I Capital/Assets + Off-Balance Sheet Items.

Liquidity Coverage Ratio: Basel III introduces new liquidity ratios. The regulation requires the liquidity coverage ratio and the bank's cash inflows and outflows to be monitored over 30 days. The liquidity coverage ratio is calculated by dividing the bank's liquid assets by the net cash outflows that will occur within 30 days and must be at least 100%. Net cash outflow is defined as the difference between cash outflows within 30 days and cash inflows within 30 days.

Net Stable Funding Ratio: The net stable funding ratio was introduced to strengthen banks funding structures over the medium and long term. The ratio is calculated by dividing the available stable funding amount by the required stable funding amount and must be at least 100%. The available stable funding amount is comprised of Tier 1 and Tier 2 capital in the bank's capital and liabilities. The required stable funding amount consists of the items in the bank's assets. These should be taken into account at varying rates according to the assets and liabilities' maturity and quality characteristics.[32]

---

[32] Bank for International Settlements (BIS), "High Level of Summary of Basel III Reforms," Basel Committee on Banking Supervision (2017), 5-12. https://www.bis.org/bcbs/publ/d424_hlsummary.pdf

Table 4.4 European Banking Sector Performance

	Jun 2011	Jun 2012	Jun 2013	Jun 2014	Jun 2015	Jun 2016	Jun 2017	Jun 2018	Jun 2019
Common Equity Tier 1 Capital	5.3%	7.8%	9.0%	11.4%	11.8%	12.8%	13.8%	14.3%	14.3%
CET1 Shortfall (Euro bn) at 4.5%	29	9	15	0.0	0	0	0	0	0
CET1 Shortfall (Euro bn) at 7 %	277	130	65	1.68	1	1	0	0	0.2
Tier1 Capital	6.8%	8.1%	9.2%	12.1%	12.3%	13.4%	14.7%	15.7%	15.6%
Total Capital	8.1%	9.1%	10.9%	14.3%	14.7%	16.1%	17.4%	18.5%	18.9%
Tier1 Capital shortfall (Euro bn)	411	249	120	4.54	8	4	0	1	0.8
Total Capital shortfall (Euro bn)	544	383	190	16.42	18	6	0	1	0
Leverage Ratio (3%)	2.8%	3.1%	3.1%	4.0%	4.4%	4.7%	5.0%	5.2%	5.1%
Leverage shortfall (Euro bn)	N/A	N/A	64	2.10	9	3	2	0	2.5
Liquidity Coverage Ratio	71%	N/A	110%	115.8%	128%	135%	143%	147%	147%
LCR shortfall (Euro bn)	1 200	N/A	262	36.10	33	3	0	21	4.7
Net Stable Funding Ratio	89%	95%	N/A	103%	105%	108%	112%	114%	113%
NSFR shortfall (Euro bn)	1 800	1 200	N/A	0.0	341	159	51	33	33.7

Source: https://www.ebf.eu/facts-and-figures/banking-sector-performance/

Table 4.4 shows the European banking sector performance between 2011 and 2019. After the recovery and stability efforts made since 2010 in the European Banking Union, European banks started to build a solid capital position and strong balance sheets. With the recapitalization effort, European banks became more resilient and robust. Common Equity Tier 1 Capital, which includes only capital of the highest quality, reached from 5.3% in June 2011 to 14.30% in 2019. Total Capital Shortfall was 544 billion euros in 2011 and successfully decreased and reached zero in 2017. in 2019, all banks met the liquidity coverage ratio above the minimum.

The Return on Equity (ROE), as a key indicator to assess banking sector attractiveness for investors, measures the share of net profit of the bank on the shareholders' equity. In 2008, due to the global financial crisis, the ROE reached a sharp decrease of -2.78 %. However, it took a hit until the first year of the Covid-19 pandemic through the several institutional improvement efforts made for the formation of a European Banking.

Table 4.5 Key Performance Indicators 2021

Indicator (%)	Q1 2021	Q2 2021	Q3 2021	Q4 2021
Return on Equity(ROE)	7.21	6.92	7.19	6.71
Return on Assets (ROA)	0.45	0.43	0.45	0.43
Cost to Income Ratio (CIR)	64.66	64.82	63.57	64.29
Cost of risk (COR)	0.64	0.57	0.53	0.50

Source: ECB, Supervisory Banking Statistics, First Quarter 2022, July 2022, p.11.

As a result, the ROE of the European banking sector improved in 2021. It was 2.31 % in 2020 and 6.71% in quarter 4 of 2021.

The Return on Assets (ROA) is also a key indicator. Due to the poor economic conditions during Covid 19 Pandemic, there was a significant decrease in the average return on assets (ROA) of the European banking sector. In 2021, the ROA remained relatively high at 0.44% compared to -0.11% in the 2008 financial crisis and 0.16% in 2020 just after the pandemic.

European Banking Union and Three Structural Blocks

As stated before, the European Banking Union (EBU) defines the Single Control Mechanism, the Single Solution Mechanism and the Single Deposit Insurance system with a single law.

Pillar One: Single Supervisory Mechanism

The Single Control Mechanism, the first structural block of the EBU, covers the ECB and the national supervisory administrations of member countries. Their duties include improving and supervising the asset quality of banks of member countries in the Eurozone and members of the EU that are not part of the Eurozone.

Pillar Two: Single Resolution Mechanism: The Single Resolution Mechanism (SRM) aims to minimize the cost of liquidation of banks that are on the verge of bankruptcy, specifically trying to minimize the time and cost to taxpayers and the real sector. The ECB plays an important role in deciding on a bankruptcy decision or monitoring banks that have reached the point of bankruptcy.

Pillar Three: European Deposit Insurance Scheme: In 2015, the European Commission (EC) proposed the creation of a deposit insurance system for banks operating in the euro area. This important measure was accepted and enacted as an indispensable step towards the completion of the Economic and

Monetary Union (EMU).[33] According to this regulation, the deposit guarantee limit is 100 thousand Euros for member countries of the EU.

Conclusion

The spread of the 2008 financial crisis to Europe and the pursuing period of recovery highlighted the need for a stronger banking system in the European Union. The Banking system had to be resilient to shocks to ensure the Economic and Monetary Union's (EMU) sustainability. The formation of enormous bank-support programs in the euro area revealed three important problems. The first was the need for banking market integration. The second was high exposure to risk concerning loss or debt in the banking system. Finally, the third problem pertained to structural weaknesses in financial stability. The European Banking Union was created as a response to those problems.

The European Banking Union and Single Supervisory Mechanism envisioned supervision under a single structure in order to strengthen the Economic and Monetary Union and increase its resiliency to financial crises.

The ECB was assigned to monitor and supervise this system. While the European Banking Union and Single Supervisory Mechanism are meant to cover the Eurozone only, peripheral members' inclusion is also expected in the future due to capital movements' multilateral and complex nature.

The objective of the ECB's monetary policy is price stability. The ECB supports general economic policies in the Community, such as sustainable and non-inflationary growth and a high level of employment, contingent upon the presence of price stability. So, the ECB monitors the economic and monetary well-being of the euro area economies.

EU member countries have to meet several macroeconomic convergence criteria before joining the EMU. These criteria are defined in the 1992 Maastricht Treaty. The Maastricht Convergence Criteria defines four target indicators, and each member of the Eurozone must adhere to the criteria put in place by the Treaty. These indicators are price stability, sound public finance, exchange rate stability, and long-term interest rates. The target rate of inflation is set at a 2% annual inflation rate. The debt/GDP and deficit/GDP ratios are set to 60% and 3%, respectively. Finally, candidates are required to participate in ERM II for at least two years without the local currency devaluing against the euro and with the absence of severe tensions. These criteria were set for the eurozone as a whole.

---

[33] See, Commission of the European Union, 2015; Directive 2014/49; EU Regulation, 1024/2013; European Parliament and of the Council Directive, 2014; On the deposit Guarantee Schemes, OJ L 173, 12.6.2014, 149-178.

To ensure price stability in the Eurozone, the ECB coordinates all member countries' central banks by utilizing several tools and methodologies. The two pillars strategy, comprised of the monetary pillar and the economic pillar, is the main tool to coordinate monetary policy among member countries. However, financial globalization complicates the ECB's ability to manage these two pillars. As mentioned earlier during the explanation of the Impossible Trilemma, the ECB is unable to follow an independent monetary policy under the pressure of capital and foreign exchange market movements.

The Banking Union's success depends on Eurozone economies' ability to bring their public expenditures and budget deficits in line with the convergence criteria. I observe that public expenditures have risen recently amid the Covid 19 pandemic.

The Stability and Growth Pact and the Maastricht criteria imposed macroeconomic criteria, but these criteria were not affordable measures against a large-scale systemic crisis such as the 2008 crisis. Countries such as Italy and Greece, which already had high levels of public debt before the 2008 financial crisis, failed to manage the crisis effectively. It was expected that by meeting the criteria of the Maastricht Treaty and the Growth and Stability Pact, member states would not face a budget deficit and be able to manage a cyclically balanced budget.

The criteria were supposed to ensure the improvement of certain member states' public finances, especially those prone to deficits and heavy public debts. Unfortunately, as the American great financial crisis hit the European economy in 2010, some member states were not able to follow the criteria in a strict manner. In the end, the Stability and Growth Pact did not work well in practice and was criticized in academic and institutional circles. The ECB objected to the pact's revision, but the objection was unsuccessful. The Stability and Growth Pact was ultimately revised with more flexible mandates, as proposed by member countries.

The public debt crisis in Europe showed how high public deficits in a monetary union can damage a banking system. There have been debates in academic and institutional circles since 2008 to develop an efficient solution for a sustainable banking system in the Eurozone.

As a result of these debates, the ECB's powers were strengthened under a single structure and a single supervision mechanism in the European Banking Union. The formation of the Banking Union is an important stage in the completion of the EMU, which assumes a transparent and secure banking market under a single structure.

The Capital Markets Union aims to reduce EU companies' cost to access financing. A strong Capital Markets Union will complement the Banking Union and increase the efficiency of the Economic and Monetary Union as a whole. The ECB's institutional regulatory and supervisory role is very important for supporting member countries' ability to overcome financial crises and gain resilience.

Generally speaking, global recession risk increased due to international political tension, which heightened financial stability risk in the Euro area due to weak macro-financial conditions. Eurozone economies' dependence on energy and natural gas, along with public expenditures made to address the recession triggered by Covid 19 pandemic, were among the macro-financial weaknesses. As a result of these challenging economic conditions, monetary policy priorities diverged among European Union members. The low growth rate and high inflation rate are worsening the vulnerabilities of the indebted economy. Similarly, the rise in food and energy prices is eroding the real income of households in low-income countries. As it is mentioned before rising interest rates support bank profit but decrease asset quality.

Eurozone banking sector strengthened supervision regulation through the European Banking Union, which defines the Single Control Mechanism, the Single Solution Mechanism and the Single Deposit Insurance system with a single law.

After the recovery and stability efforts made since 2010 in the European Banking Union, European banks started to build a solid capital position and strong balance sheets. With the recapitalization effort, European banks became more resilient and robust. Common Equity Tier 1 Capital, which includes only capital of the highest quality, reached from 5.3% in June 2011 to 14.30% in 2019. Total Capital Shortfall was 544 billion euros in 2011 and successfully decreased and reached zero in 2017. So, in 2019, all banks met the liquidity coverage ratio above the minimum.

Bibliography

Aglietta, Michel and Thomas Brand. *Un New Deal pour l'Europe*, French Edition, (Paris, Odile Jacob, 2013).

Albertazzi, Ugo and Leonardo Gambacorta. "Bank Profitability and the Business Cycle". *Journal of Financial Stability* 5 (2009): 393–409.

Albulescu, Claudiu T. "Banks' Profitability and Financial Soundness Indicators: A Macro-Level Investigation in Emerging Countries". *Procedia Economics and Finance* 23 (2014): 203-209.

Alesina, Alberto F. and Andrea Stella. "The Politics of the Monetary Policy". NBER Working Paper, 15856, 2010.

Angbazo, Lazarus. "Commercial Bank Net Interest Margins, Default Risk, Interest-rate Risk and Off-balance Sheet Banking". *Finance* 21 (1997): 55-87.

Artis, Michael and Frederic Nixson. *Economics of the European Union*, OUP Oxford, 2007.

Berger, Allen N. “The Relationship Between Capital and Earnings in Banking”. *Journal of Money Credit Bank* 27 (1995): 432-456.

Bastasin, Carlo. “Saving Europe: How National Politics Nearly Destroyed the Euro”. Brookings, Washinton DC, 2012.

Bank for International Settlement (BIS). “High Level of Summary of Basel III Reforms.” Basel Committee on Banking Supervision, 2017. https://www.bis.org/bcbs/publ/d424_hlsummary.pdf.

Bank for International Settlements (BIS). “Evaluation of the Impact and Efficacy of Basel III Reform.” Basel Committee on Banking Supervision, 2022. https://www.bis.org/bcbs/publ/d544.pdf

Council of the European Union. *Treaty on Stability Coordination and Governance in the Economic and Monetary Union.* 2013. https://www.consilium.europa.eu/media/20399/st00tscg26_en12.pdf

Council of the European Union. *Report of the FSC Subgroup on Non-Performing Loans.* Ecofin 481, 9854/17, May 31 2017. https://data.consilium.europa.eu/doc/document/ST-9854-2017-INIT/en/pdf

Cour-Thimann, P and Alexander C. Jung. “Interest Rate Setting and Communication at the ECB in Its First Twenty Years”. *European Journal of Political Economy* (2021): 1-23.

De Grauwe, Paul. “The Governance of Fragile Eurozone”. *The Australian Economic Review.* Melbourne Institute 45, no.3 (2012): 255-68.

Dias, Cristina S.P. and Kristina Grigaité. *A Road Map to Completing the Banking Union.* In-Depth Analysis, IPOL Economic Governance Support Unit, Directorate General for Internal Policies, European Parliament, June 2020, PE 645.707.

Dubravko, Mihaljec and Marc Klau. “Catching up Inflation in Transition Economies: The Balassa Samuelson Effect Revisited”. Bank for International Settlements, 2008, 2-26.

Eurostat. *Annual Report 2000.* Statistical Reports, European Commission, 2000.

Eurostat. *Euro Indicators, News Release 170/2010.* European Commission, 15 November 2010.

ECB. European Central Bank. *Monthly Bulletin.* June 2013.

ECB. European Central Bank. “*Basel III”, Special Features, Financial Stability Review.* Dec. 2010. https://www.ecb.europa.eu/pub/pdf/fsr/art/ecb.fsrart201012_02.en.pdf

ECB. European Central Bank. *Supervisory Banking Statistics.* (First Quarter 2022), July 2022.

European Parliament and of the Council Directive. *On the Deposit Guarantee Schemes.* OJ L 173, 12.6.2014, 2014. https://eur-lex.europa.eu/legal-content/EN/TXT/PDF/?uri=CELEX:52023PC0228

Eurostat. *Euro Indicators, News Release 170/2010.* European Commission, 15 November 2010.

Fernandez-Albertos, José. “The Politics of Central Bank Independence”. *Annual Review of Political Sciences* 4 (2015).

Frenkel Jacob A. and Assaf Razin. “The Mundell-Fleming Model: A Quarter Century Later”. NBER Working Paper Series, National Bureau of Economic Research (1987): 2-68.

Gaspar, Vitor. "Eurostat's HCIP and the European Central Bank's Definition of Price Stability". *Defining and Measuring the Target*, International Monetary Fund, 2001, 138-156.

Hartmann, Philipp and Frank Smetts. "The First Twenty Years of Central Bank of the European Central Bank: Monetary Policy". ECB Working Paper Series no.2219, December 2018.

European Central Bank: "Monetary Policy". ECB Working Paper Series, European Central Bank, Eurosystem, no.2219, December 2018.

Ineci, Sevgi and Yeşim Gürbüz. "The Effect of the European Banking Union on Banking Performance of the Central and Eastern European Countries-Avrupa Bankacılık Birliği'nin Orta ve Doğu Avrupa Bankacılık Performansına Etkileri". *Marmara Journal of European Studies* 28, no.1 (2020):81-107.

James, Harold. *Making the European Monetary Union*. Cambridge MA: Belknap, Harward University Press, 2012.

Lane, Philip, R. "The Real Effects of European Monetary Union". *Journal of Economic Perspectives* 20 (4) (2006): 47-66.

Lasok, Dominick. "The Maastricht Treaty on European Union". *Marmara Journal of European Studies*. Marmara University, 1993.

Maes, Ivo (ed.). *Alexander Lamfaloussy Selected Essays*, Magyar Nemzeti Bank, 2017.

McKinnon, Ronald I. "Optimum Currency Areas". *American Economic Review* 53, no.4 (1963): 717-725.

Mishkin, Frederic S. *The Economics of Money, Banking and Financial Markets*, Pearson, 2004.

Ofek, Eli. and Matthew Richardson. "Dotcom Mania: The Rise and Fall of Internet Stock Prices". *The Journal of Finance* 58, no.3 (June 2003): 2-25.

Official Journal of the European Union. "Directives, 2014/49 of the Parliament and of the Council on Deposit Guarantee Schemes", 16 April 2014. https://eur-lex.europa.eu/legal-content/EN/TXT/PDF/?uri=CELEX :32014L0049

Official Journal of the European Union. "Council Regulation on Conferring Specific Tasks on the European Central Bank Concerning Policies Relating to the Prudential Supervision on Credit Institutions" no.1024/2013, L/287/63, 29.10.2013. https://eur-lex.europa.eu/LexUriServ/LexUriServ. do?uri=OJ:L: 2013:287:0063:0089: EN:PDF

Official Journal of the European Union. "Consolidated Version of the Treaty on European Union and the Treaty on the Functioning of the European Union, Information and Notices" 2016/C 202/01, 59, (7 June 2016): 1-412. https://eur-lex.europa.eu/legal-content/EN/TXT/PDF/?uri=OJ:C:2016:202:FULL

Paulo, Sebastian. *"Europe and Global Financial Crisis, Taking Stock of the EU's Policy Response"*, Foundation Robert Schuman. 2011.

Pelksman, Jacques. "European Industrial Policy", Bruges Policy Paper Briefing no.15, College of Europe, Bruges, 2006.

Chapter 5

The Governments' Positions of Germany and France in Banking Union: Defending Diversity?

Aukje van Loon

University of Applied Sciences Bochum, Germany

Abstract

This book chapter is concerned with the creation of the Banking Union (BU), a significant step in ensuring the stability of the euro area financial system and strengthening the Economic and Monetary Union (EMU) framework. The global financial crisis and sovereign debt crisis highlighted the need to make faster progress towards completing EMU. The first pillar, the Single Supervisory Mechanism (SSM), is an authority responsible for ensuring the safety and soundness of the European banking system, thereby promoting financial integration, and ensuring consistent supervision by fostering harmonised practices. The second pillar, the Single Resolution Mechanism (SRM), continues to be strengthened, both through the creation of the Single Resolution Fund (SRF), reaching its target by the end of 2023, and through the agreement on a backstop by the European Stability Mechanism (ESM). The implementation of these two pillars highlights a milestone in European integration and European financial stability. In completing BU, the final pillar, the European Deposit Insurance Scheme (EDIS), proposed in 2015, still finds itself at the national level, and there has been little enthusiasm to change this. As the level of confidence in the safety of bank deposits diverges between member governments, this is problematic with deposit insurance and the link between a bank and its home sovereign remaining on the national level. The political will to implement this third pillar is missing from the member states. Building on this general information and descriptive section of the book chapter, a case study will be presented focusing on the completed pillars—SSM, SRM, and SRF—as well as the incomplete EDIS. This case study will analyze the positions of the German and French governments. Employing a domestic politics approach, the independent variables, material interests, value-based ideas and national institutions, will be applied to provide an answer to the question of defending diversity: *why the governments' positions of Germany and France diverged towards SSM, SRM and SRF and still vary with regard to EDIS?* Applying a qualitative, in-depth case study, focus on which domestic actors were more able to shape their respective governments' EDIS positions and why will be highlighted, and a correlation between governments' responsiveness and responsibility in times of crisis will be investigated.

Keywords: European Deposit Insurance Scheme, Defending Diversity

***

Introduction

The global financial, followed by the banking and sovereign debt crises, led to a massive leap of reforms in the European Union (EU) in terms of economic integration within the Economic and Monetary Union (EMU) framework.[1] Euro and bank bailouts were coordinated through emergency mechanisms, and new structures were subsequently created to prevent a new crisis in the future. Banking Union (BU) was one of these and resulted in diverging positions of EU governments, especially between 2011 and 2015.[2] The aim of BU is to create centralised banking supervision at the European level and carried out by the European Central Bank (ECB) within the framework of three pillars, with a uniform European set of rules (Single Supervisory Mechanism (SSM), Pillar I entered into force in 2013) it intends to prevent future banking crises and the resulting expensive rescue operations (European Council 2023). Furthermore, a Single Resolution Mechanism (SRM) facilitates the resolution of insolvent banks through a bank-financed Single Resolution Fund (SRF, both Pillar II entered into force in 2014) without burdening investors and taxpayers (European Council 2023). A uniform European Deposit Insurance Scheme (EDIS) secures the deposits of European private customers, optimises existing national deposit insurance systems and creates confidence in the banks (Pillar III not completed).

In sum, BU is expected to stabilise the European financial system by reducing market fragmentation. The reform negotiations particularly strained Franco-German relations. Although both governments were in favour of the idea of BU in principle, the question of design and content resulted in protracted negotiations. To date, Pillar III of BU, EDIS remains incomplete. The focus of this chapter is, therefore, on the question of defending diversity: *why did the governments' positions of Germany and France diverge towards SSM, SRM and*

---

[1] Aukje van Loon, "European Financial Governance: FTT Reform, Controversies and Governments' Responsiveness," *Politics and Governance* 9, no. 2 (2021).

[2] David Howarth and Lucia Quaglia, "Die Bankenunion als Krönung der Wirtschafts- und Währungsunion?", *Integration* 38, no. 1 (2015); Joachim Schild, "Germany and France at Cross Purposes: the Case of the Banking Union", *Journal of Economic Policy Reform* 21, no. 2 (2018).

SRF and still vary with regard to EDIS? Using the societal approach to governmental preference formation,[3], this question is answered within the framework of a theory-guided empirical analysis, thus expanding the state of research on the BU.

The advantage of the societal approach is its inclusiveness of three independent domestic variables (material interests, value-based ideas and national institutions), enabling it to merge different theoretical streams of liberal-domestic politics theories of International Political Economy (IPE). It examines which domestic variables are decisive in shaping the German and French governments' positions in the case under investigation and how these relate to each other. In other words, under what conditions do certain domestic variables prevail over others and thus dominate national preference formation?[4] Since much of the existing literature on national preference formation in the case of BU either only deals with a single pillar or primarily uses one domestic variable, either interests or ideas or institutions as an explanation for shaping governments' positions, a deeper understanding of national preference formation in the case of BU is to be achieved by applying said approach.

Empirical Puzzle: BU Governments' Positions in Germany and France

At the beginning of the debate, then-German Finance Minister Wolfgang Schäuble was critical of the EU Commission's plans regarding the design and content of BU. Schäuble argued that only systemically important banks should be supervised by the ECB instead of all 6000 banks in the EU.[5] He justified this with doubts about the capacities of the ECB and the feasibility of such a scope of supervision. He advocated for alternative uniform rules that could be implemented by the national supervisory authorities and, in an emergency, be enforced by the ECB with a right of intervention.[6] The German government's resistance to monitoring of all 6000 EU banks was finally clearly communicated: "ECB's supervision should initially focus on systemically important banks and cover banks that pose systemic risks or receive state support. Non-systemically

---

[3] Stefan Schirm, "Refining Domestic Politics Theories of IPE: A Societal Approach to Governmental Preferences", *Politics* 40, no. 4 (2020).

[4] Schirm "Refining Domestic Politics," 400.

[5] "Staatsschulden Dürfen Nicht Durch Geldpolitik Finanziert Werden", Deutschlandfunk, September 9, 2012, https://www.deutschlandfunk.de/staatsschulden-duerfen-nicht-durch-geldpolitik-finanziert-100.html.

[6] "Staatsschulden Dürfen Nicht Durch Geldpolitik Finanziert Werden".

relevant banks should in principle continue to be supervised by the national supervisory authorities".[7]

French Finance Minister Moscovici demanded, however, that "[t]he ECB should supervise all banks with a European passport."[8] The German BU position was thus clearly at odds with the French government's proposals as they diverged with regard to the financing of the SRF and the question of which banks should be involved with which sums.[9] Regarding EDIS, Germany has been strongly opposed since the beginning of the debate: "The Federal Government rejects a uniform European deposit guarantee scheme, at least for the foreseeable future. But we are very vehemently in favour of finally coming to terms with the harmonisation of European deposit systems", said Angela Merkel.[10]

Tümmler illustrates that the EDIS discussion dynamics at the European level have changed since 2016. The question was no longer whether an EDIS was sensible, but instead, the focus was now on a potential design.[11] In the implementation drafts, there was a shift from a "full-fledged EDIS" - i.e. a full communitarisation - to an "EDIS reinsurance system".[12] The German government equally proposed an EDIS reinsurance system in 2019.[13] This corresponds to the position of the Minister of Finance, Christian Linder, who in 2022 assured that Germany "[...] would be prepared to make some kind of reinsurance one day. A complete European deposit guarantee is not part of the political

---

[7] Michael Kaczmarek, "Euro Banking Supervision: German Criticism of EU Proposal," *Euractiv*, September 13, 2012, https://www.euractiv.de/section/finanzen-und-wirtschaft/news/euro-bankenaufsicht-deutsche-kritik-am-eu-vorschlag/.

[8] "Franco-German Dispute over EU Banking Supervision", *Euractiv*, December 4, 2012, https://www.euractiv.de/section/finanzen-und-wirtschaft/news/deutsch-franzosischer-streit-um-eu-bankenaufsicht/.

[9] Schild, "Germany and France," 112.

[10] Federal Government, "Speech by Federal Chancellor Dr Angela Merkel at the 24th German Savings Banks Day in Dresden", *Bulletin* 48, no 3, April 25, 2013, https://www.bundesregierung.de/breg-de/service/bulletin/rede-von-bundeskanzlerin-dr-angela-merkel-808646.

[11] Mario Tümmler, "Completing Banking Union? The Role of National Deposit Guarantee Schemes in Shifting Member States' Preferences on the European Deposit Insurance Scheme", *Journal of Common Market Studies* 60 no 6 (2022): 1557.

[12] Tümmler, "Completing Banking Union?", 1559-1561.

[13] Federal Ministry of Finance, "BMF Non-Paper: Position Paper on the Goals of the Banking Union", 6, 2019, http://prod-upp-image-read.ft.com/b750c7e4-ffba-11e9-b7bc-f3fa4e77dd47.

intentions of the Federal Government."[14] Since the new proposal of the German government stipulates the harmonisation of national deposit insurance as a condition for a reinsurance fund[15] and, according to Lindner, a full European deposit insurance is still rejected, the position of the German government has remained relatively constant.[16]

Table 5.1 Overview of the Diverging BU Governments' Positions of Germany and France

Banking Union		Position Germany	Position France
Pillar I	SSM	Only large systemically important banks Monitoring of small credit institutions continue to be national	All banks
Pillar II	SRM SRF	Small banks (and only banks under direct observation of the ECB) Higher contributions for system-relevant banks	Large banks (all 6000) Contributions dependent on risk profiles of banks
Pillar III	EDIS	Rejection of full EDIS, since 2014 advocacy of reinsurance system	Approval EDIS, no institutional preference

Source: Schild (2018, p. 112), Lindner (2022) and Federal Ministry of Finance (2019, p. 6).

France clearly supported EDIS[17], and statements have repeatedly emerged from government circles according to which the completion of BU is in France's interest.[18] In an Ecofin Q&A, French Finance Minister Bruno Le Maire expressed clear support for the completion of the BU: "We must take ambitious actions to complete a truly integrated European banking market, while ensuring that we design strong crisis management and depositor insurance frameworks".[19]

---

14 Christian Lindner, "Banking Union deepened: Statement by Christian Lindner after the June meeting of the Eurogroup," *Federal Ministry of Finance*, June 16, 2022, https://www.bundesfinanzministerium.de/Content/DE/Video/2022/2022-06-16-eurogruppe-bankenunion/2022-06-16-eurogruppe-bankenunion.html.

15 Federal Ministry of Finance, "BMF Non-Paper".

16 Lindner, "Banking Union Deepened".

17 Schild, "Germany and France," 112.

18 Élysée, "Déclaration: Meseberg Declaration - Renewing Europe's Promises of Security and Prosperity," July 19, 2018, https://www.elysee.fr/en/emmanuel-macron/2018/06/19/meseberg-declaration-renewing-europes-promises-of-security-and-prosperity.

19 Bruno Le Maire, "Q&A Bruno Le Maire, Europe's sovereignty is a core object for the French Presidency of the EU", *EUROFI Views Magazine*, February, 2022, https://www.eurofi.net/wp-content/uploads/2022/05/eurofi_bruno-le-maire_europe-sovereignty-is-a-core-objective-for-the-french-presidency-of-the-eu_paris_february-2022.pdf

A fully integrated European banking sector is decisive for the profitable development of the European financial sector, whereby EDIS plays a special role alongside the further development of the SRM[20]. Thus, the fact that the French government - unlike its German counterpart - does not signal a clear rejection of full communitarisation and does not formulate any conditions indicates that France is in favour of EDIS. This summarises that Germany is very critical regarding a deeper integration of the banking sector, whereas France is not, and both governments are strongly defending diversity.

Societal Approach to Governmental Preference Formation

Regarding the literature on the financial and euro crises, some scholarly studies have focused on the national preferences of EU member states and the subsequent economic integration process, including negotiations, through liberal-domestic and intergovernmental theories. A quantitative study by Tarlea et al. analysed the domestic origins of national preferences in general.[21] The study also includes BU as one of the many EMU reforms. Tarlea et al. conclude that institutions and ideas were of little relevance for the formation of national preferences and that instead the crisis impact on the national financial sectors was significant for member states' positions.[22] Accordingly, states with heavily affected financial sectors were more willing to integrate than states with more crisis-resistant financial sectors. Interestingly, other academic literature on the origins of diverging national preferences contradicts these findings. For instance, Ferber[23], Howarth and Quaglia[24] and Tümmler[25] argue that in the case of BU, institutions are more influential during the process of national preference formation. Interestingly, all authors consider domestic ideas – for example, moral hazard or Euroscepticism – as inadequate for explaining governments' positions regarding BU or EMU reforms. Tümmler suggests an interaction of institutional structures and sectoral interests.[26] The

[20] Le Maire, "Q&A Bruno Le Maire".

[21] Silvana Tarlea et al., "Explaining Governmental Preferences on Economic and Monetary Union Reform", *European Union Politics* 20, no 1 (2019).

[22] Silvana Tarlea et al., "Explaining Governmental Preferences", 39-40.

[23] Tim Ferber, "European Banking Regulation after the Financial Crisis: Franco-German conflict of Interest During the Negotiations on a Single Resolution Fund", Papers on International Economy Working Papers no. 27 (2016).

[24] David Howarth and Lucia Quaglia, "The Difficult Construction of a European Deposit Insurance Scheme: a Step Too Far in Banking Union", *Journal of Economic Policy Reform* 21, no. 3 (2018): 190-209 (preprint).

[25] Tümmler, "Completing Banking Union?".

[26] Tümmler, "Completing Banking Union?", 1561-1564.

aim of this chapter is, therefore, to complement the state of research on national preference formation in the case of the BU.

As explained, scholarly literature primarily focuses on one of the three domestic independent variables, interests, ideas or institutions. The societal approach to governmental preferences aims to fill this research gap and create a deeper understanding of the national preference formation process. It belongs to the tradition of domestic politics theories of IPE, which, due to elected politicians' desire to stay in office or to be elected and therefore are responsive to society, view the primary origins of national preference formation in domestic factors.[27] In this respect, it represents a more inclusive approach that includes all three possible domestic factors shaping national preference formation – material interests, value-based ideas and national institutions – as independent variables on an equal footing in its empirical analysis. Starting point of the societal approach is that these independent variables can shape national preference formation and can interact, - i.e. compete with each other, strengthen or weaken each other.[28]

In addition, the societal approach, through its specific hypothesis formulation, enables a consideration of the conditions under which one independent variable prevails over the other.[29] Interests are defined as "[...] material considerations of domestic sectors or groups that can react rapidly to changing circumstances, that is, according to the benefits and costs induced by national, regional, or global economic developments and politics".[30] It is thus assumed that sectors articulate their cost-and-benefit-based interests in the face of potential new policies and attempt to promote or defend these through lobbying. This can be observed in an empirical analysis of position papers and statements by important associations, lobby groups and sector representatives. Ideas are defined as "[...] fundamental, path-dependent, and value-based individual and collective expectations about appropriate governmental positions".[31] Empirically, value-based guiding principles or demands that the population places on its government can be found in public opinion surveys. Institutions are defined as "[...] formal regulations which structure domestic political and

[27] Schirm, "Refining Domestic Politics", 397.

[28] Schirm, "Refining Domestic Politics", 404.

[29] Schirm, "Refining Domestic Politics", 405.

[30] Schirm, "Refining Domestic Politics", 402.

[31] Schirm, "Refining Domestic Politics," 402.

socio-economic coordination".[32] Based on Varieties of Capitalism[33] and Historical Institutionalism[34], it is assumed that governments' positions usually seek to protect domestic institutional structures to do justice to their socio-traditional legitimacy and to protect domestic sectors from disadvantages. Institutions are described as "[...] codification of previously existing sets of ideas and interests [...]",[35] thus implying that national institutions are closely connected to interests and ideas.

It is important to note that the dependent variable here is the varying BU positions of the German and French governments. The focus is not on the actual outcome of the reform negotiations but on the BU positions the governments represented prior to entering the negotiations. The societal approach cannot do justice to an analysis of the negotiation outcome. This would require other theories as analytical tools, such as Andrew Moravcsik's Liberal Intergovernmentalism.[36] Regarding the analysis of negotiations, the societal approach allows itself the assumption that interest-led diverging positions are easier to resolve than idea-led ones. This is justified with the assumption that short-term interest-based opinions can be solved more easily through distributional compromises regarding costs and benefits, while long-term value-based ideas cannot usually be changed rapidly.[37]

Within the context of the case study on the BU, if in the national preference formation process any of the three independent variables vary, then it is to be expected that the dependent variable equally diverges. This does not imply that within this process any of the independent variables matters more. The focal point here is on the conditions under which an independent variable becomes more significant in actually shaping the governments' BU positions. Based on the standardised hypotheses of the societal approach,[38] these conditions are as follows: (1) banking sectors' potential high concentrated costs or benefits (H1); (2) electorate's long-term and shared societal expectations towards governments' steering of economic governance (H2); or a combination of both of these

---

[32] Schirm, "Refining Domestic Politics," 403.

[33] Peter A. Hall and David Soskice, "An Introduction to Varieties of Capitalism," in *Varieties of Capitalism. The Institutional Foundations of Comparative Advantages*, ed. Peter A. Hall and David Soskice (Oxford: Oxford University Press, 2001).

[34] Orfeo Fioretos, "Historical Institutionalism in International Relations," *International Organization* 65, no. 2 (2011).

[35] Schirm, "Refining Domestic Politics," 403.

[36] Andrew Moravcsik, *The Choice for Europe: Social Purpose & State Power from Messina to Maastricht*, (Cornell: Cornell University, 1998).

[37] Schirm, "Refining Domestic Politics," 404-405.

[38] Schirm, "Refining Domestic Politics," 404-405.

conditions (H3) and (3), national institutions' reflection of domestic regulations in the form of socio-economic and political coordination (H4). These conditions enable testing the following four hypotheses:

H1) If the creation of BU concerns directly affected banking sectors in the form of potential high concentrated costs or benefits, material interests, through substantial lobbying efforts, will predominantly shape the German and French governments' positions.

H2) If the creation of BU concerns long-term and shared societal expectations of the electorate towards governments' steering of economic governance and material interests' distributional consequences are diffusely affected, value-based ideas will predominantly shape the German and French governments' positions.

H3) If the creation of BU concerns banking sectors' potential high concentrated costs and benefits as well as long-term societal expectations of the electorate towards governments' steering of economic governance, both material interests and value-based ideas will either reinforce each other or compete in shaping the German and French governments' positions.

H4) If the creation of BU concerns domestic regulations in the form of socio-economic and political coordination, national institutions, in reflecting these regulations, will shape the German and French governments' positions.

Methodology & Operationalisation

The empirical analysis focuses on the governments' positions of Germany and France regarding the creation of BU. In this chapter, this dependent variable is based on Schild having investigated and summarised both BU positions in great detail.[39] Based on the assumption of governments' aim to enter or remain in office, thereby inducing responsivity, the dependent variable is supported mainly by governmental documents and statements. Briefly put, evidence is sought for a qualitative correlation between the stated concerns of supporters and opponents and the respective governments' responsiveness to these concerns during the national preference formation process.

The case selection of Germany and France represents the division of EU member states regarding the crisis management of the euro crisis, While France took the side of the indebted GIIPS countries (Greece, Ireland, Italy, Portugal, Spain) regarding the creation of BU and thus acted as the representative of the "demandeurs",[40] Germany opposed it. In addition, Germany and France

[39] Schild, "Germany and France".

[40] Schild, "Germany and France", 105-106.

are considered the most influential EU member states and are known for jointly driving the integration processes, particularly within the EMU framework.[41]

The time frame of the empirical analysis for the pillars I and II of the BU – SSM and SRM – covers the years 2011 until their entry into force in 2013 and 2014. For pillar III – EDIS – which is still incomplete, the scope of the analysis extends to date. In terms of operationalisation, this chapter analyzes the rhetorical logic of the discourse between the domestic stakeholders and responsible elected politicians in Germany and France during national preference formation. Regarding operationalisation of the independent variable material interests, the following applies: since a shift in banking supervision from the national to the European level primarily affected banking sectors, statements of banking associations and bank representatives communicating sector preferences as well as affectedness by the potential reforms are used as indicators. For Germany, statements of the German Banking Industry (DK), the Association of German Cooperative Banks (BVR), the German Savings Banks and Giro Association (DSGV), the Federal Association of Public Banks (VÖB) and the Federal Association of German Banks (BDB) are used. The French banking sector, due to its different institutional structure, is represented based on statements by the Fédération Bancaire Francaise (FBF).

The independent variable value-based ideas are determined on the basis of representative public opinion survey results. Eurobarometer data is used with a focus on the idea of solidarity in German and French society, as well as expectations on future economic governance. The presentation of the relevant national institutions is based on previous studies mentioned above, which identified the structures of the national banking sectors and the national deposit guarantee schemes as relevant domestic institutions.[42] In addition, the empirical analysis includes scholarly literature for all independent variables, as this contributes to in-depth and relevant insights into the different variables (as is the case with the independent variable national institutions).

Material Interests, Value-Based Ideas and National Institutions in the German and French BU Positions

German and French Material Interests

Regarding the creation of BU, a clear division of sectoral interests can be seen in Germany depending on the affiliation to the respective banking pillars. While the private commercial banks were clearly in favour of BU, savings banks

---

[41] Schild, "Germany and France", 102.

[42] Ferber, "European Banking Regulation"; David Howarth and Lucia Quaglia. "The Difficult Construction"; Tümmler, "Completing Banking Union?".

and cooperative banks did not reject the idea, but were critical of the inclusion of their institutions and called for proportionate banking regulation mechanisms taking subsidiarity into account. The German private banks, represented by the German Banking Association (BDB), supported the idea of BU, according to Michael Kemmer, then Managing Director of the German Banking Association: "We see the Banking Union very positively and consider it to be the right and important step on the way to a common internal market in Europe. The same banking business requires the same supervision. This also leads to a level playing field in supervisory matters within Europe. We welcome this".[43]

Cooperative banks and savings banks were critical of a uniform European banking supervisory apparatus and demanded their institutions be excluded from the regulatory framework. They pushed for compliance with the principles of regionality, subsidiarity and proportionality and referred to the functionality and crisis resilience of their institutions.[44] Both associations, therefore, jointly called for the protection of small and medium-sized banks and warned against standardised and centralised European banking regulation measures. Instead, they called for regulatory measures "[...] in an appropriate relationship to the importance of the institution for the financial system, the type and scope and complexity of the transactions, the risk situation and the quality of the risk management".[45] The EU is expected to ensure that future regulations "[...] support the functioning and successful structures of national banking markets [...]",[46] and in particular preserves and promotes small and medium-sized banks. In their argument, the banking associations pointed out that "[...] regionally active and anchored institutions, unlike large international banks, do not pose a threat to the stability of the financial system",[47] which is why the existing national banking supervision apparatus is sufficient. It is therefore necessary that "[...] diversity and heterogeneity of structures in banking markets [...]" [48] are promoted.

In contrast to the divided German banking sector, the French banking sector was unitedly in favour of the introduction of BU. BNP-Paribas CEO Jean-

---

[43] Liechtenstein Bankers Association, "Bankenunion - Interview with BdB Managing Director Michael Kemmer", *Bankenmagazin*, Winter 2013/2014. https://www.bankenverband.li/application/files/8315/4408/7515/Bankenmagazin_201_4_issue_29_directory.pdf

[44] BVR and DSGV, *Declaration of the Cooperative Banks and Savings Banks on the European Elections: Securing Stability, Strengthening Subsidiarity - For the Creation of a Middle-Class Banking Policy In Europe*, (2014), 1-3.

[45] BVR and DSGV, *Declaration of the Cooperative Banks*, 1.

[46] BVR and DSGV, *Declaration of the Cooperative Banks*, 1.

[47] BVR and DSGV, *Declaration of the Cooperative Banks*, 2.

[48] BVR and DSGV, *Declaration of the Cooperative Banks*, 2.

Laurent Bonnafé emphasised the positive expectations of the internationally active and system-relevant private banks for BU: "Once the banking union is complete, we will have additional efficiency, more transparency and a better understanding of the global and regional economy".[49]

Single Supervisory Mechanism (SSM)

Regarding the first pillar of BU, the Single Supervisory Mechanism, the German private banks were in favour of a complete transfer of banking supervision to the ECB.[50] They called for a broad supervisory framework that includes all 6000 banks in the eurozone, regardless of their legal form. "There must be no differentiation between supposedly systemically important institutions and non-systemically important institutions", said Andreas Schmitz, then President of the BDB.[51]

French banks were also consistently in favour of transferring banking supervision to the European level: "French banks have always called for greater supervision at European level, adapted to the size of cross-border banking groups, as this will ensure better transaction security. The new supervisory framework will ensure greater stability and will consolidate the monetary union. The application of the same standards across Europe will reinforce the single market".[52]

The three banking associations of the German savings banks, cooperative banks and public banks insisted on the exclusion of their institutions with regard to the SSM and strictly rejected supervision by the ECB.[53] With reference to the subsidiarity principle, only the largest systemically important banks should be supervised by the SSM in addition to the institutions already

---

[49] Toby Fildes, "Banking Union Could Trigger Consolidation", *Global Markets – Emerging Markets* (October 11, 2013), https://www.globalcapital.com/globalmarkets/article/28myg1zat9wedl0g21qtc/emerging-markets/banking-union-could-trigger-consolidation.

[50] Markus Frühauf and Manfred Schäfers, "Banks Want Supervision Without Schäuble", *Frankfurter Allgemeine Zeitung*, August 12, 2012, https://www.faz.net/aktuell/wirtschaft/wirtschaftspolitik/bankenaufsicht-banken-want-supervision-without-schaeuble-11863609.html.

[51] "Verband will Ministerium Bei EU-Bankenaufsicht Entmachten", *Handelsblatt*, August 8, 2012, https://www.handelsblatt.com/dpa/economy-business-und-finance-verband-will-ministerium-bei-eu-bankenaufsicht-entmachten/7038236.html.

[52] FBF, *The Banking Sector in 2012 Management Report*, (February 2013), 28.

[53] BVR, VÖB, DSGV, *Joint Position Paper on a Single Supervisory Mechanism For Credit Institutions In Line with The Summit Declaration of The Euro Area Members of 29 June*, (August 2012), 1-2.

recapitalised by the European Stability Mechanism (ESM).[54] Instead of the planned 6000 banks, only the 200 largest institutions should be subject to ECB supervision (BVR 2012).

Single Resolution Mechanism (SRM) & Single Resolution Fund (SRF)

Regarding the second pillar of BU, the SRM and SRF, German private banks were clearly in favour of SRF participation for all banks, regardless of their legal form. Managing Director of the BDB, Michael Kemmer, was clearly against a "two-tier resolution right".[55] It becomes very clear that the private banks - in contrast to the savings banks and cooperative banks - had no need for individual regulations based on the subsidiarity principle and did not demand any consideration of the European regulatory apparatus for special institutional national-specific sector structures: "The institutional framework for the national financing mechanisms as well as for the assessment of contributions should also leave little room for special national approaches. This is the only way to avoid distortions of competition".[56]

French banks did not comment on whether small institutions should also participate in the SRF. Instead, they pleaded for SRF financing including a risk factor adjustment instead of only accepting the size of the institution/systemic relevance as a criterion for the amount of the contribution payments.[57] After the SRM came into force, the FBF resisted the costs incurred and complained about unfair financing of the SRF: "The contribution of French banks is estimated at 15.4 billion euros, representing 28% of the target amount of the fund. This amount does not appear to be in line with the level of risk represented by the French banking sector".[58]

This is because the French banking sector was dominated by five large, internationally active banks and naturally has to pay higher contribution amounts if only the size of the bank is taken into account as a contribution criterion. Interestingly, the preferences of the French banks are closer to those of the German cooperative and savings banks than to the German private banks. Both demand a kind of proportionality of the SRF, which is due to their institution size. Indeed, BVR and DSGV opposed the co-financing of the resolution fund by cooperative and savings banks and demanded, reflecting

---

[54] BVR, VÖB, DSGV, *Joint Position Paper*, 1-2.

[55] Ifo Institute, "Single Resolution Mechanism (SRM) for Europe's Banks: How to Assess the EU Commission's Proposal?", *Ifo Schnelldienst* no. 17, (2013): 18.

[56] Ifo Institute, "Single Resolution Mechanism", 19.

[57] FBF, *The Banking Sector in 2013 Management Report*, (February 2014).

[58] FBF, *The Banking Sector 2014 Management Report*, (April 2015), 19.

the preferences of French banks, a "[…] risk-adjusted calculation in strict compliance with the agreed principle of proportionality […]"[59]. It was unacceptable that small banks had to pay for the rescue of bankrupt, systemically important banks.[60]

European Deposit Insurance Scheme (EDIS)

Regarding the rejection of an EDIS as the third pillar of the BU, there was unanimity between private, public and cooperative banks, at least at the beginning of the debate.[61] In a joint statement by the German banking industry, the public and private umbrella organisations unanimously opposed the introduction of the EDIS and announced their moral hazard fears that this would only lead to "[…] a communitarisation of risks, in particular at the expense of German credit institutions […]".[62] Instead, the EU should push for the harmonisation of national deposit guarantee guidelines.[63] The associations of the savings and cooperative banks have continuously emphasised the proportionality of the regulations regarding SSM and SRM. While they seem to be in favour of EDIS in principle and consensually, they opposed the Commission's proposal "[…] with all their might".[64] Thus, the willingness to compromise regarding the third BU pillar on the part of the cooperative and savings banks seemed to be non-existent. The position of these banks remained unchanged: "Communitarisation of liability for existing risks increases systemic dangers within the Banking Union. The German government should, therefore, take a clear stance against EDIS, as the preconditions for such a far-reaching step are not in place", said Marija Kolak, BVR President.[65]

The opposition of private banks to EDIS in principle weakened in 2014, and a future introduction of the EDIS under certain conditions has been promised by the private banks. According to Michael Kemmer (BDB), a deposit guarantee could be considered in the very distant future, but first, the SSM and SRM would have to prove their worth.[66] According to recent statements by former

---

[59] BVR and DSGV, *Declaration of the Cooperative Banks*, 2.

[60] BVR and DSGV, *Declaration of the Cooperative Banks*, 2.

[61] Uwe Fröhlich, "Press Conference of the German Banking Industry: Statement Uwe Fröhlich", *Deutsche Kreditwirtschaft*, July 25, 2012, 3.

[62] Fröhlich, "Press Conference", 3.

[63] Fröhlich, "Press Conference", 3.

[64] BVR and DSGV, *Declaration of the Cooperative Banks*, 2.

[65] BVR, *Press Release: Cooperative Banks Remain Reliable and Successful Even In Difficult Times / Kolak: "German Government Needs To Adopt A Firm Anti-EDIS Stance*, (March 16, 2021).

[66] Liechtenstein Bankers Association, "Bankenunion - Interview with BdB Managing Director Michael Kemmer", *Bankenmagazin Winter*, 26.

BDB Managing Director Christian Ossig, however, the German private banks seem more optimistic. According to Ossig, "[t]he completion of the banking union [...] is important for a strong Europe".[67]

The first steps towards a liquidity support system, i.e. a kind of reinsurance system, were supported, but a full communitarisation of risks in the second phase was still unrealistic. However, Ossig emphasised that EDIS "[...] should not fail because of the institutional protection systems of the associations [of savings banks and cooperative banks]" and that special national regulation for savings and cooperative banks would not only damage competition and the harmonised internal market but also the European idea.[68] While in other statements by the BDB, the financial advantages of the private banks were rarely discussed, Ossig mentioned that, from the BDB's point of view, BU ultimately only exists for the overriding goal of" [...] creating a single, European internal market [...]", which, based on estimates, could result in cost advantages of around 95 billion euros in the European banking sector.[69]

French banks were also striving for a uniform European internal market as BU was viewed as an important step towards a uniform European legal framework.[70] Regarding EDIS, they also advocated a reinsurance system with certain conditions: "For banks, in order to prevent moral hazard, it is essential that the status of this European fund is limited to reinsurance. In addition, it must be preceded by an asset quality review (AQR), and only institutions subject to banking regulations should be allowed to benefit from the system. It is also important to ensure that the cost of the Banking Union observes the political commitments made".[71]

In sum, the position of the German government coincided with the interest of the German cooperative and savings banks, as well as those of the German private banks. Especially regarding the scope of the SSM and SRM and the contribution scheme of the SRF are not taken up by the German government. Regarding France, there was no division in the banking sector, which is why it communicated its interests unitedly via the FBF. It turned out that the interests of the FBF largely coincided with the positions of the French government.

---

[67] Christian Ossig, "Ossig: "Advancing Europe - Especially in Uncertain Times", Press Statement, Federal Association of German Banks, June 1, 2022.

[68] Ossig, "Ossig: "Advancing Europe".

[69] Ossig, "Ossig: "Advancing Europe".

[70] FBF, *2019-2025 For a Well-Financed Society in Sovereign Europe,* (April 2019), 12-13.

[71] FBF, *The Banking Industry in 2017. Management Report,* (May 2018), 37.

German and French Value-Based Ideas

Schieder has shown in his publication on Germany's leadership role during the euro crisis that the German population falls short of the EU average in terms of solidarity and scores poorly in comparison.[72] Looking at Eurobarometer data willingness to help without economic self-interest sets stemming from this period and comparing the German and French respondents' results (Table 5.2), the value-based idea of solidarity and the is above the EU average in France and significantly more pronounced than in Germany (Table 5.2, QC10, QC11). France also shows greater agreement than Germany regarding debt sharing (Table 5.2, QA11).

Table 5.2 Value-Based Ideas: Solidarity

Period	Questions	EU-27	G	FR
Aug/Sep 2010	QC10: Giving financial help to another EU Member State facing severe economic and financial difficulties in times of crisis is desirable.	49%	46%	51%
	QC11: Main reason why helping is desirable? Own economic interests: Solidarity:	44% 51%	53% 43%	36% 60%
Sep 2011	QA11: Setting aside a share of the public debt of all Member states to be held jointly would be necessary in the name of the European Union of solidarity.	61%	56%	60%
Sep/Oct 2021	QA22: Greater solidarity between EU member states is most helpful for the future of Europe.	21%	26%	28%

Source: TNS Opinion & Social (2010, pp.65, 69); TNS Opinion & Social (2012, p. 77); EU (2021, p. 101).

Since the third pillar of the Banking Union (EDIS) has not yet been realised, it is also worth taking a look at more recent Eurobarometer data on solidarity. Here, almost ten years on, it is illustrated that solidarity seems more important to the French population (Table 5.2, QA22).

Regarding expectations for future economic governance within the framework of the EMU (Table 5.3), correspondence between value-based ideas and governments' positions was less clear. On the one hand, Eurobarometer data in 2010 and 2011 showed a clear convergence in both countries regarding support for increased regulatory measures and a greater role for the EU in this regard (Table 5.3, QC14a; QC5). However, a general deepening of the coordination of European economic governance received comparatively less support from both countries (Table 5.3, QC14b). In addition, in both countries, half of the

[72] Siegfried Schieder, "Zwischen Führungsanspruch und Wirklichkeit: Deutschlands Rolle der Eurozone" *Leviathan* 42, no 3, (2014): 384-385.

respondents (54%) prefer coordinated EU measures to national efforts when it comes to successful protection against the financial crisis (Table 5.3, QC6).

Table 5.3 Value-Based Ideas: Attitudes of European Economic Governance

Period	Questions	EU-27	G	FR
Aug/Sep 2010	QC6: In the face of the current crisis, I would be better protected if my country adopted measures and applied them in a coordinated way with other EU countries.	52%	54%	54%
	QC14a: Stricter regulation and supervision of financial market players would be effective in preventing and avoiding future crises.	70%	81%	75%
	QC14b: Establishing European economic governance, ensuring the coordination of the economic, budgetary and financial policies of all EU Member States would be effective in preventing and avoiding future crisis	63%	59%	64%
Sep 2011	QC5: A more important role for the EU in regulating financial services is effective	71%	73%	72%
Sep/Oct 2021	QA22: Stronger economic integration is most helpful for the future of Europe.	16%	11%	7%

Source: TNS Opinion & Social (2010, p. 45, 89); TNS Opinion & Social (2011, p. 134); EU (2021, p. 101).

This can be interpreted as a sign of a lack of trust in the EU and, thus, Euroscepticism. Although this value is even slightly above the EU average, it must be said that this does not represent a particularly strong commitment to trust in the EU but rather an almost 50/50 split in society regarding trust in coordinated EU measures to combat the crisis. To classify these values for the still unfinished EDIS, the approval ratings for stronger economic integration for the year 2021 were added (Table 5.3, QA22). Interestingly, this shows an extreme drop in approval ratings and, thus, a rejection of further European economic integration. Regarding the value-based idea of solidarity, Schieder[73] and Schild[74] have pointed to Euroscepticism as a value-based idea with significant influence on the national preference formation process.

German and French National Institutions

As mentioned above, Ferber[75], Howarth & Quaglia[76] and Tümmler[77] have shaped the state of research on the role of institutions in national preference

[73] Schieder, "Zwischen Führungsanspruch und Wirklichkeit", 381.

[74] Schild, "Germany and France", 105.

[75] Ferber, "European Banking Regulation".

[76] Howarth and Quaglia, "The Difficult Construction".

[77] Tümmler, "Completing Banking Union?".

formation within the context of BU. The authors identify the following as influential for governments' national preference formation: 1) the structure of national banking sectors[78] and 2) the design and status of harmonisation of existing national deposit insurance schemes.[79]

Regarding the former, Ferber views the origins of divergent governments' positions of France and Germany towards the SRF mainly in the different structures of the banking sectors and financing systems in Germany and France. He concludes that the governments tried to protect their national institutions.[80] Similar to the societal approach, Ferber included the Varieties of Capitalism approach in his analysis, and these theoretical assumptions regarding the importance of institutions coincide with the employed approach in this chapter, as well as with H4.[81] Regarding Germany and France, Ferber identifies the following divergent institutional structures as decisive for national preference formation in the case of the SRF:

Ferber argues that the German government's efforts to keep participation in the SRF as small as possible for small banks or even to exclude them altogether, as well as a strict risk factor adjustment, are a clear sign that the German government is trying to protect the institutional structures of its banking sector and financial system: Small and medium-sized credit institutions such as savings and cooperative banks should be protected because of their stabilising and crisis-resistant effect on the economy and their ability to finance companies and grant loans should be preserved.[82] Instead, the French position was based on the interest in keeping the costs for the five large, systemically relevant national champions relatively small and involving as many banks as possible (including small and medium-sized credit institutions) in the financing of the SRF in order to distribute the costs among as many actors as possible.[83]

Regarding the third pillar of BU, Howarth and Quaglia attribute the diverging governments' positions of Germany and France to the differently developed and harmonised national deposit insurance systems.[84] They argue the debate and incompletion of EDIS stems from the fact that the existing national deposit insurance systems grew out of the specific structure of the banking sectors,

---

78 Ferber, "European Banking Regulation", 16.

79 Howarth and Quaglia, "The Difficult Construction", 31-33.

80 Ferber, "European Banking Regulation", 16.

81 Ferber, "European Banking Regulation", 12.

82 Ferber, "European Banking Regulation", 12-14.

83 Ferber, "European Banking Regulation", 16.

84 Howarth and Quaglia, "The Difficult Construction", 1-2.

resulting in respective governments aiming to protect their specific national institutions.[85]

Table 5.4 Institutional Differences of Banking Sectors in Germany and France

Germany	France
Fragmented banking sector (3-pillar model) with high bank density Mainly bank-based financing	Banking sector with low bank density: five large systemically important national banks with an internationally-oriented business model Largely market-based financing
Only private institutions hit hard by banking crisis due to foreign business transactions Savings banks & cooperative banks continue to function due to their domestic business models Small and medium-sized enterprises as well as private households can continue to benefit with be supplied with credit.	All banks equally affected by crisis, no stabilising pillar available in the banking sector Financing companies & private households is difficult

Source: Ferber (2016, p. 4-12).

In Germany, a far-reaching national deposit insurance system already existed before the EU's push, which had largely grown out of the special structure of the German banking sector (3-pillar model).[86] While the savings and cooperative banks organised their own deposit protection through national statutory deposit guarantee schemes, they were covered by their own institution-specific private-law guarantee schemes, which are largely financed ex-ante and have a particularly high overall coverage compared to other countries. They are normally not subject to the statutory deposit guarantee schemes. According to Howarth & Quagila, the German rejection of EDIS is motivated by the need to protect the functioning system of specifically sectoral, stable and functioning private-law deposit guarantee schemes of the savings and cooperative banks and to protect them from standardisation in a European general deposit guarantee scheme.[87]

The "Fichiers des Guichets Domiciliataires" (FGDR) deposit guarantee scheme was created in France as a product of the highly concentrated French banking sector of the five "national champions", and the private deposit guarantee and

---

[85] Howarth and Quaglia, "The Difficult Construction", 32.

[86] Howarth and Quaglia, "The Difficult Construction", 15.

[87] Howarth and Quaglia, "The Difficult Construction", 32.

resolution fund FGDR was financed by annual contributions from the banks.[88] According to Tümmler, a switch to EDIS would be unproblematic for the French banking sector due to its low banking density and uniform structure (mainly internationally active and large banks) and would result in a reduction of compliance costs.[89]

Conclusion

The aim of this chapter was to extend the state of research on the creation of the BU by an empirical analysis employing the societal approach and to answer the research question of defending diversity: *why did the governments' positions of Germany and France diverge towards SSM, SRM and SRF and still vary with regard to EDIS?* The German government continuously argued for a limited version of BU, tried to prevent the integration of small, non-systemically relevant credit institutions into the SSM and SRM, and strictly opposed the idea of EDIS in the sense of full communitarisation. The German government presented a reinsurance system as an alternative that complements the harmonised national deposit guarantee systems with a deposit guarantee fund. In contrast, France pushed for a BU with a broad supervisory and resolution framework (including all credit institutions) and an SRF contribution based on risk assessment and has not objected to the proposals for EDIS. In order to answer the research question, the relevant domestic material interests, value-based ideas and national institutions regarding the creation of BU were empirically analysed on the basis of the societal approach and tested for a correlation with the dependent variable diverging German and French governments' positions. The analysis of the three domestic factors, illustrated an interaction of material interests, value-based ideas and national institutions having shaped the national preference formation of both Germany and France, whereby national institutions and material interests clearly prevailed and were mostly strengthened by value-based ideas.

Regarding SSM and SRM, the German government's BU position included both reflections of the interests of the cooperative and savings banks while strongly advocating the exclusion of small and medium-sized credit institutions (H1) as well as the preservation of the German fragmented banking sector (H4). In addition, the rather critical BU position of the German government coincided with the relatively low solidarity values of German respondents (H2). These low solidarity values also go hand in hand with the positions of the cooperative and savings banks, which criticised the fact that small and stable institutions lose their privileges or have to pay to save large and foreign institutions (H3). All

[88] Howarth and Quaglia, "The Difficult Construction", 18.

[89] Tümmler, "Completing Banking Union?, 1563.

three variables thus seem to interact and reinforce each other. This could also explain why the sectoral interests of the German private banks regarding the SSM and SRM could not prevail against the interests of the cooperative banks and savings banks. However, since BU was in the interest of the private banks, the German government's position seemed to accommodate the private banks and their business models through its support of BU in principle, but only to the extent that this was compatible with securing the existence of the cooperative and savings banks.

Regarding the French government's position on the SSM and SRM, a similar interaction of domestic factors became apparent. The government's intention to include as many credit institutions as possible in the SRM and SSM and thus to achieve greater economic integration, yet at the same time to link SRF contribution payments to risk factors, was in line with the interests of the French banking sector (H1). As the French banking sector largely consisted of five internationally oriented national champions, there was no necessity to consider small banks with their own business models (H4). In addition, French respondents showed comparatively higher solidarity values than their German counterparts, and respondents' support for stronger EU regulation of financial services was high (H2). In addition, the French banking sector - unlike Germany's banking sector - was united (which in turn relates to the structure of the French banking sector (H4); it is assumed that domestic support from all three independent variables (H3 and H4) to a fully integrated BU was stronger than in Germany.

The EDIS case illustrates a strong interaction and reinforcement of material interests, value-based ideas and national institutions. The German government's position on EDIS seemed to represent a compromise between the divided material interests of the German banking sector. On the one hand, the German government rejected a full European deposit guarantee in line with the interests of the savings banks and cooperative banks (H1). This is consistent with the fact that solidarity among the German population is low in 2021 (H2). Furthermore, it is consistent with the strong rejection of increased economic integration in 2021 (H2). These independent variables, material interests and value-based ideas thus reinforced each other in resisting EDIS (H3). On the other hand, the German government was willing to make compromises in this area if the national deposit insurance schemes were untouched and only complemented these with an EDIS fund, as the position towards a reinsurance EDIS reveals. This is advocated by the German private banks and supports their overriding goal of a single domestic market. However, the fact that the German government is conflicted between two associations in its banking sector, it ultimately tries to support both in some way, reflecting the institutional structure of the banking sector on the government's position (H4).

The French government favours the completion of BU through EDIS and does not have a preference in terms of institutional design. French banks clearly express their approval of a reinsurance EDIS. This is based on the findings regarding material interests (H1) and national institutions (H4). Eurobarometer data showed that identical to German respondents, support for solidarity and stronger economic EU integration was low in France in 2021 (H2). This illustrates that although the independent variables, material interests and value-based ideas, interacted (H3), they did not weaken each other in changing the French positive BU position, mainly due to the strong reinforcement of material interests and national institutions (H4).

In sum, this theory-guided empirical analysis based on the societal approach was able to illustrate that the governments' positions of Germany and France regarding BU were shaped by a strong interaction of the three independent variables. Thus, by analysing all three pillars of BU through the employment of three independent variables, this chapter has complemented the state of research and has provided a deeper understanding of national preference formation in examining why and under which conditions the German and French governments' positions diverged towards SSM, SRM and SRF and still vary with regard to EDIS.

Bibliography

BVR. "BVR on the Annual Report of the German Council of Economic Experts: ECB supervision of large Internet Banks". 7 November, 2021. https://www.bvr.de/Presse/Pressemitteilungen/BVR_zum_Jahresgutachten_des_Sachverstaendigenrates_EZB_Aufsicht_auf_grosse_Banken_konzentrieren

BVR, VÖB, DSGV. "Joint Position Paper on a Single Supervisory Mechanism for Credit Institutions in Line With The Summit Declaration of The Euro Area Members of 29 June". 31 August, 2012. https://www. bvr.de/p.nsf/20C0CEB3DD976153C1257D25004867D7/$FILE/Positionspapier-AufsichtBVR_DSGV_VOEB_20120822.pdf

BVR. "BVR on the Results of the Euro Summit". 19 October 2012. https://www.bvr.de/Presse/Pressemitteilungen/BVR_zu_den_Ergebnissen_des_Eurogipfels

BVR and DSGV. "Declaration of the Cooperative Banks and Savings Banks on the European Elections: Securing Stability, Strengthening Subsidiarity - For the Creation of a Middle-Class Banking Policy in Europe". 2014. https://www.bvr.de/p.nsf/6292A0070EE13234C1257CD300444EA3/$FILE/140324_Gemeinsame_Erklaerung_DSGV-BVR.pdf

BVR. "Press Release: Cooperative Banks Remain Reliable and Successful Even in Difficult Times / Kolak: "German Government Needs to Adopt a Firm Anti-EDIS Stance". 16 March 2021. https://www.bvr.de/Press/Press_releases/Cooperative_banks_remain_reliable_and_successful_during_difficult_periods_Kolak_German_government_needs_to_adopt_a_firm_anti_EDIS_stance

Élysée. "Déclaration: Meseberg Declaration - Renewing Europe's Promises of Security and Prosperity". 19 July 2018. https://www.elysee.fr/en/emmanuel-macron/2018/06/19/meseberg-declaration-renewing-europes-promises-of-security-and-prosperity

EU. "The Future of Europe, Special Eurobarometer 517 Report (Survey September-October 2021)". January 2022. https://europa.eu/eurobarometer/surveys/detail/2554

European Council. Banking Union. 2023. https://www.consilium.europa.eu/en/policies/banking-union/

FBF. "The Banking Sector in 2012 Management Report". February 2013. https://www.fbf.fr/uploads/2022/05/FBF-management-report-2012.pdf

FBF. "The Banking Sector in 2013 Management Report". February 2013. https://www.fbf.fr/uploads/2022/05/Management-report-FBF-E2%80%93-The-banking-sector-in-2013.pdf

FBF. "The Banking Sector 2014 Management Report". April 2015. https://www.fbf.fr/uploads/2021/07/Management-report-FBF-2014.pdf

FBF. "The Banking Industry in 2017 Management Report". May 2018. https://www.fbf.fr/uploads/2021/09/FBF_Annee-de-la-banque-2017_ENGLISH-WEB.pdf

FBF. "2019-2025 For a Well-Financed Society In Sovereign Europe". April 2019. https://www.fbf.fr/uploads/2021/09/2019-2014-For-a-well-financed-society-in-a-sovereign-Europe.pdf

Federal Government. "Speech by Federal Chancellor Dr Angela Merkel at the 24th German Savings Banks Day in Dresden". *Bulletin* 48, no 3, April 25, 2013. https://www.bundesregierung.de/breg-de/service/bulletin/rede-von-bundes kanzlerin- dr-angela-merkel-808646

Federal Ministry of Finance. "BMF Non-Paper: Position Paper on the Goals of the Banking Union". 2019. http://prod-upp-image-read.ft.com/b750c7e4-ffba-11e9-b7bc-f3fa4e 77dd47

Ferber, Tim. "European Banking Regulation After the Financial Crisis: Franco-German Conflict of Interest During the Negotiations on a Single Resolution Fund". Papers on International Economy (PIPE) Working Papers no. 27 (2016).

Fildes, Toby. "Banking Union Could Trigger Consolidation". *Global Markets – Emerging Markets.* 11 October 2013. https://www.globalcapital.com/global markets/article/28myg1zat9wedl0g21qtc/emerging-markets/banking-union-could-trigger-consolidation

Fioretos, Orfeo. "Historical Institutionalism in International Relations". *International Organization* 65, no 2 (2011): 365-399.

"Franco-German Dispute Over EU Banking Supervision". *Euractiv.* 4 December 2012. https://www.euractiv.de/section/finanzen-und-wirtschaft/news/deutsch-franzosischer-streit-um-eu-bankenaufsicht/

Fröhlich, Uwe. "Press Conference of The German Banking Industry: Statement Uwe Fröhlich. Deutsche Kreditwirtschaft". 25 July, 2012. https://die-dk.de/media/files/Statement_UweFroehlichDK-PK_250712.pdf

Frühauf, Markus and Manfred Schäfers."Banks Want Supervision Without Schäuble". *Frankfurter Allgemeine Zeitung.* 12 August 2012. https://www.faz.net/aktuell/wirtschaft/wirtschaftspolitik/bankenaufsicht-banken-want-supervision-without-schaeuble-11863609.html

German Banking Industry. "No support of German Banks and Savings Banks for a European Deposit Guarantee Scheme". 1 July, 2012. https://die-dk.de/themen/pressemitteilungen/keineunterstutzung-der-deutschen-banken-und-sparkassen fur-eine-europaische-einlagensicherung-8def40/

Howarth, David and Lucia Quaglia. "Die Bankenunion als Krönung der Wirtschafts- und Währungsunion?" *Integration* 38, no, 1 (2015): 44-59.

Howarth, David and Lucia Quaglia. "The Difficult Construction of a European Deposit Insurance Scheme: a Step Too far in Banking Union". *Journal of Economic Policy Reform* 21, no. 3. (2018): 190-209. https://orbilu.uni.lu/bitstream/10993/36423/1/Howarth%20and%20Quaglia%20The%20Difficult%20Construction%20of%20a%20European%20Deposit%20Insurance%20Scheme.pdf.

Ifo Institute. "Single Resolution Mechanism (SRM) for Europe's Banks: How to Assess the EU Commission's Proposal?" *Ifo Schnelldienst* no. 17 (2013): 3-19. https://www.ifo.de/publikationen/2013/zeitschrift-einzelheft/ifo-schnelldienst-172013.

Kaczmarek, Michael. "Euro Banking Supervision: German Criticism of EU Proposal". *Euractiv.* 13 September, 2012. https://www.euractiv.de/section/finanzen-und-wirtschaft/news/euro-bankenaufsicht-deutsche-kritik-am-eu-vorschlag/.

Le Maire, Bruno. "Q&A Bruno Le Maire, Europe's Sovereignty is a Core Object for the French Presidency of the EU". *EUROFI Views Magazine.* February, 2022. https://www.eurofi.net/wp-content/uploads/2022/05/eurofi_bruno-le-maire_europe-sovereignty-is-a-core-objective-for-the-french-presidency-of-the-eu_paris_february-2022.pdf.

Liechtenstein Bankers Association. "Bankenunion - Interview with BdB Managing Director Michael Kemmer". *Bankenmagazin.* Winter 2013/2014. https://www.Bankenverband.li/application/files/8315/4408/7515/Bankenmagazi_201_4_issue_29_directory.pdf

Lindner, Christian. "Banking Union Deepened: Statement by Christian Lindner After the June Meeting of the Eurogroup". Federal Ministry of Finance. 16 June, 2022. https://www.bundesfinanzministerium.de/Content/DE/Video/2022/2022-06-16-eurogruppe-bankenunion/2022-06-16-eurogruppe-bankenunion.html.

Moravcsik, Andrew. *The Choice for Europe: Social Purpose & State Power from Messina to Maastricht.* Cornell: Cornell University, 1998.

Ossig, Christian. "Ossig: "Advancing Europe - Especially in Uncertain Times". Federal Association of German Banks. 1 June 2022. https://bankenverband.de/bankenaufsicht/ossig-europa-voranbringen-gerade-unsicheren-zeiten/

Peter A. Hall and David Soskice, "An Introduction to Varieties of Capitalism", in *Varieties of Capitalism. The Institutional Foundations of Comparative Advantages.* Edited by Peter A. Hall and David Soskice. Oxford: Oxford University Press, 2001.

Schieder, Siegfried. "Zwischen Führungsanspruch und Wirklichkeit: Deutschlands Rolle der Eurozone". *Leviathan* 42, no. 3 (2014): 363-397.

Schild, Joachim. "Germany and France at Cross Purposes: the Case of the Banking Union". *Journal of Economic Policy Reform* 21, no. 2 (2018): 102-117.

Schirm, Stefan. "Refining Domestic Politics Theories of IPE: A Societal an Approach to Governmental Preferences". *Politics* 40 no. 40 (2020):396-412.

"Staatsschulden Dürfen Nicht Durch Geldpolitik Finanziert Werden". Deutschlandfunk. 9 September, 2012. https://www.deutschlandfunk.de/staatsschulden-duerfen-nicht-durch-geldpolitik-finanziert-100.html.

TNS Opinion and Social. "Public Opinion in the European Union". Standard Eurobarometer 76. Autumn 2011.

TNS Opinion and Social. "Crisis Report". Special Eurobarometer Wave 76.1. Fieldwork September 2011. Published January 2012. https://www.europarl.europa.eu/at-your-service/files/be-heard/eurobarometer/2011/europeans-and-the-crisis-iv/aggregate-report/en-aggregate-report-europeans-and-the-crisis-iv-201201.pdf.

TNS Opinion & Social. "Europeans and the Crisis – Report". Special Eurobarometer Wave 74.3. Fieldwork August-September 2010. Published November 2010. https://www.europarl.europa.eu/at-your-service/files/be-heard/eurobarometer/2010/europeans-and-the-crisis-ii/aggregate-report/en-aggregate-report-europeans-and-the-crisis-ii-201011.pdf

Tarlea, Silvana, Stefane Bailer, Hanno Degner, Lisa M. Dellmuth, Dirk Leuffen, Magnus Lundgren, Jonas Tallberg and Fabio Wasserfallen."Explaining Governmental Preferences on Economic and Monetary Union Reform". *European Union Politics* 20, no. 1, (2019): 24-44.

Tümmler, Mario. "Completing Banking Union? The Role of National Deposit Guarantee Schemes in Shifting Member States' Preferences on the European Deposit Insurance Scheme". *Journal of Common Market Studies* 60, no. 6 (2022): 1556-1572.

"Verband Will Ministerium Bei EU-Bankenaufsicht Entmachten". *Handelsblatt*, August 8, 2012. https://www.handelsblatt.com/dpa/economy-business-und-finance-verband-will-ministerium-bei-eu-bankenaufsicht-entmachten/7038236.html

Van Loon, Aukje. "European Financial Governance: FTT Reform, Controversies and Governments' Responsiveness". *Politics and Governance* 9, no. 2 (2021): 208-218.

Wissenschaftliche Dienste Deutscher Bundestag. "Banking System and Banking Supervision in Germany". 2 July 2009. https://www.bundestag.de/resource/blob/409624/7592c651aef84a826a8e2251d4d676ff/WD-4-094-09-pdf-data.pdf.

PART II:
GREEN CENTRAL BANKING AND DIGITAL CURRENCY PARADIGMS

Chapter 6
Central Banks and Policy Development for Decarbonization in the G20

Hazik Mohamed

Independent Consultant on projects, Singapore

Abstract

The G20 countries are among the world's largest producers and exporters of oil and gas. However, the G20 countries are also vulnerable to the impacts of climate change, including rising sea levels, extreme weather events, and water scarcity. The role of their central banks is crucial to the assurance of financial stability, as well as shaping the regulatory landscape of financial services. In this paper, we explore how central banks and financial regulators in the G20 can coordinate regulatory approaches to tackle climate risk, overcome sustainability challenges and ensure human security. The financial system faces very significant risks posed by climate change, as well as the transition to a low-carbon economy. The need to achieve sustainable economic development in the G20 and its transition to a low-carbon economy requires strong policies and regulatory implementation to drive green and sustainable finance for the purpose of achieving public policy objectives effectively. Central banks play vital roles in ensuring financial stability and in shaping the regulatory landscape of financial services. In light of their implicit or explicit responsibility for financial and macroeconomic stability, central banks should address climate-related and other environmental risks in a systematic way. In addition, by overseeing money, credit, and the financial system, central banks can ensure that financial institutions adequately price environmental and carbon risks. As part of their monetary and financial policy mandates, central banks should develop capacity, set regulatory frameworks, encourage green loans and products, and consider climate change. It is possible for central banks to persuade the distribution of credit and investment of financial firms through a variety of powerful tools. The legal mandate of a central bank and its ability to rectify certain types of market failures that lead to green transformation determine whether it should utilize its powers and engage actively in greening the financial system and economy. For global climate targets to be met, the financial sector in the G20 must finance sustainable and green investments as well as limit funding for harmful activities. In the absence of regulations, banks and other financial institutions may allocate their resources to activities that are environmentally and socially harmful. In order to improve efficiency, government intervention is needed to improve environmental and social returns, which differ from private returns. It is imperative that GCC central banks play a role in developing policies and regulations to support decarbonization efforts, including carbon pricing mechanisms, renewable energy standards, and energy efficiency regulations. As such it is necessary for them to develop a sustainable finance toolkit that consists of a range of policy measures and tools that they can use to promote sustainability and address environmental and social risks within the financial system. These tools, both at the macro and micro-level, can help central banks to ensure that financial institutions take into account environmental and social factors when making lending and investment decisions, and can help to mitigate risks associated with climate change and other environmental challenges.

Keywords: Decarbonization, G20, Policy Development

***

Introduction

Ensuring financial stability and influencing the financial services regulatory environment are key responsibilities of central banks. Central banks should approach climate-related and other environmental risks in a systematic manner because they are either implicitly or explicitly responsible for the stability of the financial and macroeconomic systems. Additionally, central banks can make sure that financial institutions appropriately price environmental and carbon risks by regulating money, credit, and the financial system.[1] As part of their monetary and financial policy mandates, central banks should develop capacity, set regulatory frameworks, encourage green loans and products, and consider climate change.[2]

Through a variety of effective tools, central banks can influence how financial firms distribute credit and invest. Whether a central bank should exercise its authority and take an active role in greening the financial system and economy depends on the legal mandate of the institution and its capacity to address specific types of market failures that contribute to the transition to a green economy.

---

[1] Ulrich Volz, "On the Role of Central Banks in Enhancing Green Finance. Geneva: UN Environment Inquiry into the Design of a Sustainable Financial System", 2017, 14.

[2] Aziz Durrani, Ulrich Volz and Masyitah Rosmin, "The Role of Central Banks in Scaling up Sustainable Finance: What Do Monetary Authorities in Asia and the Pacific Think?" ADBI Working Paper Series, (2020), 1099.

Central banks must examine climate and environmental risks in addition to maintaining price and financial stability, but due to their limited mandates, they are not obligated to take additional actions to promote sustainability and green finance. Central banks should be required to pursue social, economic, and environmental goals, like many developing and emerging economies.

For global climate targets to be met, the financial sector in the G20 must finance sustainable and green investments as well as limit capital for detrimental actions. The absence of regulations may result in banks and other financial institutions allocating their resources to activities that are harmful to the environment and society.[3] Government intervention is required to increase environmental and social returns, which are different from private returns, so as to increase efficiency. It is essential that G20 central banks take part in creating policies and rules to support decarbonization efforts, such as carbon pricing mechanisms, requirements for renewable energy sources, and rules governing energy efficiency. In order to promote sustainability and address ecological and shared collective risks within the financial system, they must, therefore, create a sustainable finance toolkit, which should include a variety of policy measures and tools. These resources, both macro and micro, can assist central banks in ensuring that financial institutions consider environmental and social factors when making lending and investment decisions and can help to reduce risks.

Monetary Policy and Sustainability

As they become more frequent and severe, extreme weather events and human-caused climate change may have an impact on prices and price variability. First off, agricultural production could be negatively impacted by climate change both domestically and abroad, which would raise food prices, a major driver of consumer inflation.

Droughts and floods resulting from climate change, for instance, can lead to inflation and price increases, particularly if the economic systems depend on agricultural production. Climate change mitigation policies in this context are likely to have a negative impact on energy production and prices.[4] There are several reasons for concern, the primary one being the impact that climate change-related hazards may have on prices directly, while the secondary one is the impact that its mitigation policies may have on inflation directly.[5]

---

[3] Simon Dikau and Ulrich Volz, "Central Banking, Climate Change and Green Finance." ADBI Working Paper (2018), 867.

[4] Volz, "On the Role of Central Banks", 21.

[5] Dikau and Volz, "Central Banking, Climate Change", 869.

Theoretically, various climate change policies, such as carbon taxes, permit trading systems, and other governing mechanisms could have an impact on monetary policy regimes. A carbon tax would result in higher inflation and lower output, and if central banks did nothing, there would be a permanent decline in output and stagnant long-term growth rates. A strict inflation-targeting strategy would result in higher interest rates, a further slowdown of the economy, and an appreciation of the currency when inflation spikes. Monetary policy should consider these climate-related effects since climate mitigation measures may have significant effects on core inflation.

Macroprudential Policy and Tools to Promote Sustainability

Systemic risks that pose a threat to financial stability are intended to be reduced by regulatory macroprudential policies. Such policy instruments accomplish this by preventing the unwarranted accumulation of systemic risk that results from events like asset price bubbles or unwarranted bank risk-taking. Examples of macroprudential policies include limits on particular lending practices or higher capital requirements for particular asset classes. Climate and environmental risks should be included in regulatory frameworks to cover for shortcomings in macroeconomic and microprudential policy.

Stress Testing Climate Factors

Financial institutions can use climate-related stress testing (CRST) to assess the potential financial impact of climate-related risks, changes in regulations, and changes in consumer behaviour. When it comes to green finance, CRST can be used to assess the potential financial effects of funding various kinds of green projects and to pinpoint the most reliable and lucrative bets.

In order to assess how the potential effects of climate change might affect banks' loan portfolios and balance sheets, regulators can mandate that banks conduct stress tests that take climate risk scenarios into account.[6] The CRST could be used by a bank, for instance, to assess the potential financial effects of a severe drought on a portfolio of solar power projects in a specific area.

The potential financial impact of various policy and regulatory changes on green projects can also be assessed using CRST. To assess the potential financial effects of a carbon tax on a portfolio of wind power projects, for instance, a bank could use CRST.

---

[6] Mercy Berman DeMenno, "Environmental Sustainability and Financial Stability: Can Macroprudential Stress Testing Measure and Mitigate Climate-Related Systemic Financial Risk?" *Journal of Banking Regulation* (2022).

Additionally, CRST can be used to assess the potential financial effects of consumer behaviour changes, such as a sharp rise in demand for electric vehicles or a decline in demand for products derived from fossil fuels.

Cyclical Green Capital Buffers

In order to support the development of green finance, the concept can be applied to banks by mandating that they hold a higher capital "cushion" during times of rapid economic growth and then release the buffer during times of economic stress.

This could be accomplished by establishing a minimum capital requirement in green finance for banks and by giving banks incentives to invest in green projects, such as lowered capital requirements or other regulatory relief. A "green cushion" that is distinct from the counter-cyclical buffer and is only used to support green finance initiatives could also be established by regulatory authorities.

By applying cyclical green capital cushions to green finance, authorities can ensure that there is a stable flow of funding available for green projects during both good and bad economic times, which will help to stimulate the shift to the goal of a low-carbon economy.

Differentiated Capital Requirements

Regulatory authorities can set different capital requirements for various types of assets or activities based on their level of risk using differentiated capital requirements (DCR). Differential capital requirements must be used to properly price carbon risks.[7] For green investments, DCR can encourage financial institutions to lend money by lowering the capital requirements.

Setting lower capital requirements for banks that invest a portion of their investable assets in green ventures is one way to apply DCR to green finance. An institution that invests at least 10% of its assets in green projects, for instance, might be required to hold less capital than a bank that does the same.

Setting different capital requirements for various green project types based on their level of risk is another way to apply DCR to green finance. For investments in established technologies like solar and wind power, a bank might be required to hold less capital than for investments in more experimental ones.

---

[7] Dirk Schoenmaker, and Rens Van Tilburg, "What Role for Financial Supervisors in Addressing Environmental Risks?" *Comparative Economic Studies* 58, 3 (2016): 317–334.

Additionally, DCR could be used to increase capital requirements and deter funding for environmentally destructive activities.

Loan-To-Value and Loan-To-Income Ratio Limits

An asset's value or the borrower's income is used to determine the loan-to-value (LTV) or loan-to-income (LTI) cap, which limits how much debt a borrower can take on. These caps can be used in the context of green finance to promote the construction of energy-efficient structures and other kinds of green projects.

Setting higher caps for loans used to finance energy-efficient structures and other kinds of green projects is one way to apply LTV and LTI caps to green finance. In the case of energy-efficient buildings, a borrower might be able to borrow up to 90% of the property's value as opposed to 80% for conventional buildings.

Offering lower interest rates for loans used to finance green projects like energy-efficient buildings is another way to apply LTV and LTI caps to green finance. In order to reduce the risk of defaults and financial instability, authorities may also use LTV and LTI caps to restrict the amount of debt that developers and investors in green projects may incur.

Large Exposure Controls

Applying exposure restrictions by counterparty, sector, or region prevents financial institutions from investing in assets with high risks or, in the case of green finance, assets with high carbon footprints. Although LER can be used to encourage financial institutions to diversify their investments across different kinds of green projects and lessen their exposure to particular sectors or regions, its primary goal may be to safeguard financial institutions from the risk of credit concentration (carbon bubble).

Setting lower limits on the amount of credit that a financial institution can extend to a single borrower or network of connected borrowers involved in green projects is one way to apply LER to the field of green finance. For instance, a bank might be prohibited from lending a single borrower involved in a renewable energy project more than 10% of the total amount of loans in its portfolio.

Another strategy is to set various restrictions based on the risk involved in various green project types. A bank might be prohibited from lending a single borrower involved in a cutting-edge, experimental green technology more than 5% of its entire loan portfolio, but it could lend up to 10% for a more established technology like solar or wind power.

LER could also be used to restrict credit concentration in particular industries or areas, such as restricting the amount of credit that a bank can extend to a single borrower involved in a specific type of green project in a certain region, in order to reduce the risk of regional or sectoral imbalances.

Microprudential Regulation and Financial Supervision

Microprudential regulation refers to the oversight of specific financial institutions in order to ensure that they are operating in a safe and sound manner, are resilient to shocks from the outside world and changes in the economy and have enough capital and liquidity to stay afloat. Regulators and central banks can assist in directing capital toward sustainable development and aid in the shift to a low-carbon economy by incorporating environmental risk assessments, stress testing, disclosures, and capital requirements. To encourage the consideration of environmental and ecological hazards in loan origination processes or financial stability concerns, a wide range of financial regulation tools can be adapted. Banks may be required to comply with ESG risk-management standards by order of their central banks and other financial regulatory bodies, and risks related to climate change may need to be evaluated and disclosed, or reserve holdings may have to be adjusted.[8]

Disclosure Requirements and Transparency

The assessment of the climate risk in a bank's loan portfolio and investment portfolio, as well as the disclosure of the results, may be mandated by central banks. By doing this, investors and regulators would have transparency into how banks are managing their exposure to climate-related risks. Financial institutions may be required by regulators to disclose both their exposure to environmental risks and their risk management plans. This could lead to improved sustainability practices by giving investors and stakeholders greater visibility into a financial institution's sustainability performance.

According to Volz,[9] regulation of green macro-prudentially necessitates improved clarity and appropriate pricing of environmental risks. Financial institutions can ensure that climate-related and ecological risks are appropriately priced by requiring financial institutions to disclose climate change-related risks. Before implementing the pricing mechanisms, investors who are concerned about the environment and/or climate risk must have all the information

---

[8] Simon Dikau. and Volz, "Central Banking, Climate Change", 867.

[9] Volz, "On the Role of Central Banks", 27.

required to evaluate a firm's environmental performance.[10] Investors would be unsure of how to adjust their asset valuations without this information. Disclosure mandates are based on the premise that there is information asymmetry between investors and businesses interested in green investments, which calls for regulation.[11]

ESG Risk Management

Mandatory ESG risk-management standards require financial institutions to disclose ESG factors in their governance frameworks in the same ways that disclosure requirements do. Beyond disclosure, these standards will align lending practices with risk management related to the environment. New financial services and products may have potentially negative environmental effects in addition to assessing these risks. Furthermore, banks that offer loans based on mandatory green risk management standards may take into account ESG risks in the loan origination process. Reduced funding for traditional brown businesses and increased funding for greener businesses would be the allocative results. Every company deals with ESG-related issues, some of which may have an effect on the company's finances or reputation. An organization is also more likely to experience a controversy or incident involving these issues if it ignores social, environmental, and governance issues. ESG risk management should be a part of a company's standard risk reduction procedures because it essentially is a business risk.

Financial institutions may be required by central banks to disclose their ESG opportunities and risks as well as their risk management plans. This could lead to improved ESG practices by giving investors and stakeholders greater visibility into a financial institution's ESG performance. To promote comparisons between financial institutions and ensure consistency across jurisdictions, common ESG metrics and reporting standards can be created. To enforce such rules, central banks could implement rewards and sanctions to persuade financial institutions to give ESG risk management. For example, banks that perform well on ESG metrics could receive regulatory benefits or reduced capital requirements, while banks that perform poorly could face higher regulatory scrutiny or penalties.

---

[10] Sebastian Steuer and Tobias H. Tröger, "The Role of Disclosure in Green Finance", *Journal of Financial Regulation* 8, 1 (April 2022): 1–50.

[11] Tobias H.Tröger and Sebastian Steuer, "The Role of Disclosure in Green Finance", European Corporate Governance Institute – Law, Working Paper (2021), 604/2021; SAFE Working Paper (2021), 320; LawFin Working Paper (2021), 24.

Reserve Requirements

Different reserve requirements can lead to different reserve rates, which can then affect credit allocation and encourage green investments for portfolios with a skewed balance towards greener, less carbon-intensive assets. This depends on the composition of banks' portfolios. The market for carbon certificates may grow if commercial banks accept carbon certificates as legal reserves. Carbon certificates are used to promote green investment by giving them out in exchange for loan concessions for low-carbon projects.[12]

Then, central banks could use their reserves to buy green bonds, which fund green projects. This could boost interest in green bonds by demonstrating to the market that the central bank is committed to promoting sustainable development.

Green Asset Ratio (GAR)

A Green Asset Ratio (GAR), which would require banks to hold a specific proportion of their assets in green investments like renewable energy initiatives or environmentally friendly infrastructure, could also be established by central banks. Banks would be encouraged to increase their lending to green projects as a result, assisting in the flow of funding for sustainable development.

According to Brühl[13], the GAR calculates the percentage of a bank's assets that are deemed "green" or environmentally sustainable. It provides banks with a means of measuring how much they have contributed to the creation of sustainable solutions and the transition to a low-carbon economy. By dividing a bank's green assets by its total assets, the GAR can be calculated. Loans and investments in sustainable transportation, green buildings, renewable energy, and energy efficiency are examples of green assets, and other environmentally sustainable projects. The GAR can be expressed as a percentage or a ratio.

The green asset ratio is designed to persuade financial institutions to align their operations with more sustainable ones. Financial institutions would be encouraged to shift their lending and investment activities towards sustainable development and decrease their exposure to environmentally harmful projects by mandating that a minimum percentage of assets be held in green investments. A crucial performance indicator for gauging the sustainability of financial institutions, GAR has been adopted by some central banks. It is

[12] J.Rozenberg at al., "Funding Low-Carbon Investments in the Absence of a Carbon Tax", *Climate Policy*, 13, 1 (2013): 134–141.

[13] Volker Brühl, "The Green Asset Ratio (GAR) - A New KPI for Credit Institutions", CFS Working Paper Series no. 683, Goethe University Frankfurt, Center for Financial Studies (CFS), (Frankfurt, 2023).

important to keep in mind that different institutions and jurisdictions may have different definitions of what exactly qualifies as a "green" asset. Additionally, standardized reporting methodologies and frameworks are required to ensure comparability among various banks and geographical areas.

The green asset ratio is still a relatively new concept and has not yet been widely adopted by central banks or financial regulators, although it is gaining popularity as a tool for measuring and tracking the progress of banks and financial institutions in promoting sustainability and reducing their carbon footprint.

Developing Green Finance and Sustainability Guidelines and Frameworks

Due to their role in the international and domestic financial systems, central banks are in a strong position to promote sustainability through their advocacy, research, involvement in, and support of international and national initiatives to create standards, frameworks, and guidelines. They consist of, but are not limited to:

- The Task Force on Climate-related Financial Disclosures (TCFD)
- The Task Force on Climate-related Financial Risks (TCFR)
- The Network for Greening the Financial System (NGFS) which develops climate scenarios for use by central banks and other financial institutions for scenario analysis
- The Green Bond Principles (and national green bond guidelines and frameworks)
- The Green and Sustainability-Linked Loan Principles
- Initiatives to harmonise sustainability standards (such as that led by the IFRS Foundation)

In many countries, national central bank-led green and sustainable finance guidelines have begun to emerge, developed by central banks and financial regulators themselves or often in co-operation with finance sector bodies and other stakeholders.

Green finance principles, guidelines, or roadmaps have been published by the IFC's Sustainable Banking Network, which focuses on sustainable banking. These documents are not mandated. This network for knowledge exchange includes banking associations and financial regulators with the goal of advancing ESG risk management procedures and green lending. In order to create the NGFS, a number of central banks and financial supervisors came together in December 2017. These institutions include the Bank of England, Banque de France, Bank of Spain, Deutsche Bundesbank, European Central

Bank, National Bank of Belgium, Nederlandsche Bank, Oesterreichische Nationalbank, and People's Bank of China. It represents one of the most significant and effective efforts to date to unite the biggest and most significant monetary, economic, and regulatory institutions in the world.

Policy and Regulatory Improvements for Decarbonization

Policies and regulations must be improved in order to ensure that the necessary investments are made in low-carbon technologies and to create an environment that encourages the adoption of cleaner energy sources by businesses and households. Greening initiatives should concentrate on technologies to lower CO_2 emissions from fossil fuels and coal-fired industrial facilities in addition to renewable energies for the generation of electricity. Various technologies with high impact and readiness for decarbonization for various G20 countries should be the subject of studies. In some nations, including those in the G20, efforts to reduce CO_2 emissions have not given much attention to Carbon Capture and Storage (CCS) technologies because the primary focus has been on substituting renewable energy for fossil fuels.

The following are some examples of policy and regulatory improvements that can be implemented to support the shift to a greener economy and to foster decarbonization. Intuitively, the most effective policies should be suited to the specificities of each territory or region and will likely involve a combination of different policy and regulatory measures.

Carbon Pricing, Carbon Tax and the Cap-and-Trade System

By instituting a carbon price, businesses and households can be encouraged to lower their greenhouse gas emissions. In a cap-and-trade system, businesses can exchange emission permits for a price that caps emissions and levies taxes on them in accordance with that limit. Carbon pricing is a method of valuing greenhouse gas emissions. As a result, there is a financial incentive for people and companies to cut back on emissions. There are numerous ways to charge for carbon, including carbon taxes and cap-and-trade programs.

A carbon tax directly taxes an organization for the greenhouse gas emissions it produces. In order to provide financial incentives for emissions reduction, taxes are calculated based on emission volume. The amount of greenhouse gases released determines the taxes that are levied. Oil, natural gas, and coal can all be subject to carbon taxes.

Emissions of greenhouse gases are "capped" by covered entities under a cap-and-trade system. Then, a specific number of permits are given to these organizations, allowing them to emit greenhouse gases. If they require additional allowances, they can buy them from other organizations whose emissions have fallen below the permitted levels. The price of emission allowances is then determined by supply and demand when they are traded on the market.

The advantages of carbon pricing include:

I. *Economic efficiency:* Carbon pricing allows the market to determine the most cost-effective way to reduce emissions, which can lead to more efficient solutions.

II. *Revenue generation:* Governments can fund other programs for the environment by generating revenue from carbon pricing or be returned to citizens through rebates or other means.

III. *Predictability:* Carbon pricing provides a clear and predictable signal to the market about the cost of emitting greenhouse gases, which can encourage investment in low-carbon alternatives.

IV. *International cooperation:* Carbon pricing can provide a common framework for international cooperation on climate change by providing a consistent mechanism for countries to reduce emissions.

However, some potential disadvantages of carbon pricing include:

I. *Equity:* Carbon pricing can disproportionately impact low-income households, who may not have the resources to transition to low-carbon alternatives.

II. *Competitiveness:* Carbon pricing can put domestic industries at a disadvantage compared to foreign competitors that do not face the same carbon pricing.

III. *Political feasibility:* Carbon pricing can be politically challenging to implement, particularly in countries or regions with strong opposition to taxes or regulation.

The carbon footprint of the global power, transportation, and industrial sectors can be significantly reduced by using Carbon Capture and Storage (CCS) technology. Despite its potential, CCS has not been widely adopted in the G20, where no nation lacks a carbon tax. A reliable carbon tax imposed by national governments can promote the use of CCS. A further accelerator would be regional carbon trading, in which a nation's carbon credit could be sold to a third party. Companies and individuals can be given a financial incentive to cut back on carbon emissions by implementing carbon pricing mechanisms, such as carbon taxes or cap-and-trade programs.

Cross-border Carbon Capture and Storage (CCS)

Costs can be reduced, and performance can be increased by funding R&D for low-carbon technologies like carbon capture and storage or energy storage.

This may reduce the competitiveness of fossil fuels and hasten the deployment of CCS.

Carbon dioxide emissions from industrial processes or power plants may be captured and stored for future use using carbon capture and storage (CCS). The potential for CCS projects to move captured carbon dioxide across international borders for storage is referred to as cross-border CCS.

Cross-border CCS can offer several benefits, including:

I. *Lower costs:* Cross-border CCS projects can potentially achieve economies of scale, reducing the cost of capturing and storing carbon dioxide.

II. *Access to storage sites:* Some countries may have limited storage capacity for carbon dioxide, while others may have abundant geological formations that are suitable for storage. Cross-border CCS can allow countries to access these storage sites and reduce the need to store carbon dioxide domestically.

III. *International cooperation*: Climate change cooperation can be promoted through cross-border CCS, by providing a mechanism for countries to work together to reduce greenhouse gas emissions.

However, there are also several challenges associated with cross-border CCS, including:

I. *Regulatory issues:* Cross-border CCS projects may need to navigate different regulatory frameworks and standards for carbon capture and storage in different countries.

II. *Liability issues:* Cross-border CCS projects may need to address issues related to liability for carbon dioxide storage, particularly in cases where the storage site crosses international borders.

III. *Technical challenges:* Cross-border CCS projects may face technical challenges related to transporting carbon dioxide across long distances, including issues related to pipeline integrity and safety.

Despite these difficulties, cross-border CCS has the potential to aid in the global reduction of greenhouse gas emissions. Cross-border CCS allows nations to collaborate to deploy CCS technology at scale, thereby accelerating the shift to a low-carbon economy and mitigating climate change. Government coordination is required to make cross-border CCS projects possible. Laws, rules, and permits must be in place to control the movement of CO_2 across international borders.[14] A regional coordinating body might be the most

---

[14] Hon Chung Lau et al., "A Review of the Status of Fossil and Renewable Energies in Southeast Asia and Its Implications on the Decarbonization of ASEAN", *Energies* 15, 6 (2022): 2152.

effective way to carry out these negotiations. Furthermore, a public-private partnership that includes project management can be used to transfer technology and money internationally.

Capacity-Building and Development of the Green Ecosystem

Investments in both core and emerging technologies, talent development, capacity building, and improved policy environments for creative start-ups driven by the ESG agenda will ultimately define the ecosystem. By forming alliances with numerous organizations and stakeholders in the green ecosystem, businesses can strengthen their current efforts or address weak points and deficiencies.

As part of an investment package that can help to improve project preparation, planning, and management, as well as improve the prospect of achieving the desired project outcomes, MDBs and their partners frequently provide technical assistance and other advisory services. An investment can be made stronger economically and technically by offering support and expertise, which will encourage funding and participation from the private sector. Furthermore, it can help build expertise and know-how that can be used to support future projects designed to promote climate change mitigation and adaptation.

Additionally, creating market awareness and providing complex projects with specialized technical support can promote the creation of environments that are supportive of such complexity and aid in the successful development of subsequent projects. Technical assistance facilitates knowledge exchange and the dissemination of experience and best practices, but it should be ensured that there is a transfer of knowledge and experience to local professionals to improve national capital markets and institutions' capacity and capability in relation to green and sustainable finance, rather than merely a demonstration effect that has no lasting impact.

- *Green Procurement Policies:* The development of green technologies and the rise in demand for sustainable products can both be aided by encouraging government agencies and other organizations to buy goods and services that are environmentally friendly and sustainable. By offering subsidies and tax breaks, the government can foster favourable conditions for private investments in green projects.
- *Decarbonization Subsidies and Incentives:* Financial incentives, such as subsidies and incentives for the purchase of electric vehicles (EVs), can help to increase the adoption of EVs and lower emissions from the transportation sector. These incentives can be used to encourage the development of low-carbon technologies and the transition away from

fossil fuels. To promote the purchase and use of environmentally friendly goods and services, such as EVs, solar-powered generators, and other alternatives, a variety of incentives can be put in place for both individuals and businesses. These financial incentives may come in the form of tax credits, rebates, grants, and financial aid for the installation of equipment like EV charging stations, solar panels, wind turbines, and geothermal systems.

- *Education and Training:* The provision of education and training programs for individuals and organizations in order to assist them in understanding the importance of sustainability and the ways in which they can implement eco-friendly practices.
- *Research and Development (R&D):* Conducting research and development to produce novel solutions that support environmental protection and sustainability. Additionally, funding R&D for low-carbon technologies like carbon capture and storage or energy storage can aid in lowering costs and enhancing performance. This could increase these technologies' parity with fossil fuels and hasten their adoption.

Crediting and Certifying Green Business Practices

Sector-specific green certifications and eco-labelling programs, such as "100% recycled" for products made from recycled materials or timber certification from organizations like the Rainforest Alliance Certification, have an impact on the rising demand for green business practices. The cost of obtaining certification and the amount of staff time required to comply with their requirements should be balanced out by the business advantages of going green and complying with their requirements. To be recognized, the certification or eco-label needs to be promoted to a large audience right away. Chambers of commerce and trade associations should create marketing and advertising materials to showcase a company's "green credentials" to its clients.

Examining a company's environmentally friendly operations and policies in order to confirm that the company is putting them into practice is a necessary step in the process of crediting and certifying green business practices. To accomplish this, a variety of initiatives and certification programs can be used, such as ISO 14001 for environmental management systems and Leadership in Energy and Environmental Design (LEED) for buildings. By obtaining these certifications, businesses demonstrate their dedication to sustainability and let customers and other stakeholders know that they are doing their part to protect the environment while also benefiting their bottom line. Typically, companies must undergo a rigorous assessment process to obtain these certifications, which is followed by ongoing audits and assessments so as to ensure their green business practices are maintained.

Environmental management system implementation is frequently hampered by a lack of technical expertise, financial resources, and knowledge.[15] Other challenges include a lack of resources, low public awareness, and high upfront costs. Environmental management systems (EMS) for businesses must be customized to their needs in terms of both content and delivery. When enhancing business management procedures, it is crucial to prioritize easy-to-implement changes. A small business may choose an EMS with varying levels of complexity and little paperwork as opposed to becoming ISO 14001 certified, which is a time-consuming and expensive process.

There are numerous types of green business certifications available that can be helpful for preventing green washing and demonstrating a company's commitment. The fundamental policy and procedure sets that are assessed by all of these certification programs have striking similarities at their core. Some checklists that cover the actions and initiatives that assess businesses are:

- Building and Maintenance Checklist
- Community and Employee Checklist
- Energy Savings Checklist
- Food Consumption and Management Checklist
- Product & Packaging Checklist
- Supply Chain and Procurement Checklist
- Transportation Checklist
- Waste Management Checklist
- Water Conservation Checklist

The business areas that each initiative will affect, such as buildings, food service, transportation, or office supplies, are categorized along with the effort, expense, and environmental impact that each initiative will have on that particular business area as part of the initiative listing. An organization will be able to identify and implement the efforts that are best suited to meet the needs and opportunities of the organization by using a structure that is simple yet flexible quickly and effectively. The Green Business certification can become a platform through which member companies can communicate, differentiate

[15] OECD, *Facilitating the Green Transition for ASEAN SMEs: A Toolkit for Policymakers*, (Paris, France: OECD Publishing, 2021).

themselves from the competition, and be recognized for their environmental commitment, in addition to offering a variety of tools and opportunities.

Green Innovation and Entrepreneurship Programs

Supporting start-ups and entrepreneurs working on low-carbon technologies can hasten the creation and implementation of fresh ideas. This may involve financial support, programs for incubation and acceleration, and access to networks and knowledge. The development and adoption of low-carbon technologies can be sped up with the aid of green innovation and entrepreneurship programs, which can also result in new business ventures and employment opportunities in the green economy. Here are some potential initiatives to encourage green entrepreneurship and innovation:

- *Incubation and acceleration programs:* These programs provide support for entrepreneurs and start-ups to develop their green business ideas. This can include mentorship, access to funding and networks, and business development support.
- *Grant programs:* Government and private sector organizations can provide grants to fund research and development of low-carbon technologies. This can help entrepreneurs and start-ups develop and commercialize new solutions without the burden of paying back a loan.
- *Competitions and challenges:* Competitions and challenges can provide incentives for entrepreneurs and start-ups to develop innovative green solutions. This can include cash prizes, access to funding and networks, and public recognition for their ideas.
- *Public-private partnerships:* Public-private partnerships can bring together government, industry, and academia to collaborate on green innovation projects. This can help pool resources and expertise and accelerate the development and deployment of new technologies.
- *Training and education programs:* Training and education programs can provide entrepreneurs and start-ups with the skills and knowledge they need to develop and commercialize green technologies. This can include courses on green finance, sustainability, and entrepreneurship.

Governments and private sector organizations can speed up the transition to a low-carbon economy by supporting entrepreneurs and start-ups while also generating new business opportunities and jobs in the green economy.

Conclusion

G20 central banks have developed new instruments in some cases to advance green and sustainable finance, and they should recalibrate conventional central banking tools with a green and sustainable focus. These include tools for determining credit allocation policy, risk weightings, research and advocacy, and the creation of standards and frameworks. In order to unlock capital from the private sector through co-financing and deploying their own capital, public actors in the green and sustainable finance sector must play an important role.

By offering specialized technical assistance and developing capacity and capability in sustainable finance more generally, one can aid in creating an environment that is supportive of complex projects, raise customer awareness of the market, and aid in the successful growth of upcoming projects. In fact, policy and regulatory changes are essential to decarbonization because they can help households and businesses switch to low-carbon energy options while also promoting innovation and financial investment in clean technologies.

Bibliography

Böttcher, Jörg. *Green Banking: Realizing Renewable Energy Projects.* Berlin, Boston: De Gruyter Oldenbourg, 2020.

Brühl, Volker. "The Green Asset Ratio (GAR) - A New KPI for Credit Institutions". *CFS Working Paper Series* no. 683, Goethe University Frankfurt, Center for Financial Studies (CFS), (Frankfurt, 2023).

Campiglio, Emanuele, Yannis Dafermos, Pierre Monnin, Josh Ryan-Collins, Guido Schotten, and Misa Tanaka. "Finance and Climate Change: What Role for Central Banks and Financial Regulators?". *Nature Climate Change* 8, (2018): 462–468.

Dikau, Simon, and Ulrich Volz. "Central Bank Mandates, Sustainability Objectives and the Promotion of Green Finance". *Ecol. Econ.* 184, (2021): 107022.

Dikau, Simon, and Josh Ryan-Collins. *Green Central Banking in Emerging Market and Developing Country Economies.* London: New Economics Foundation, 2017.

DeMenno, Mercy Berman. "Environmental Sustainability and Financial Stability: Can Macroprudential Stress Testing Measure and Mitigate Climate-Related Systemic Financial Risk?" *Journal of Banking Regulation* (2022).

McKibbin, Warwick, Adele Morris, Augustus Panton, and Peter Wilcoxen. *Climate Change and Monetary Policy: Dealing with Disruption.* Rochester, NY: Social Science Research Network. 2017.

Network for Greening the Financial System (NGFS). *A Call for Action. Climate Change as a Source of Financial Risk.* Paris: Network for Greening the Financial System. 2019.

Rizzello, Alessandro. "What's in a Name? Mapping the Galaxy of Green Finance". İn *Green Investing. Palgrave Studies in Impact Finance.* Palgrave Macmillan: Cham, 2022.

Schoenmaker, Dirk and Rens Van Tilburg. "What Role for Financial Supervisors in Addressing Environmental Risks?" *Comparative Economic Studies* 58, 3 (2016): 317–334.

Tröger, Tobias H. and Sebastian Steuer. "The Role of Disclosure in Green Finance". European Corporate Governance Institute – Law, *Working Paper* (2021), 604/2021; SAFE *Working Paper* (2021), 320; LawFin *Working Paper* (2021), 24.

Chapter 7

Discussions on Green Central Banking and the 'Green' Performance of the Central Bank of Turkey: Comparison with G20 Countries

Esra Güler

Uludağ University, Bursa, Turkey

Halil Seyidoğlu

Yalova University, Turkey

Abstract

The systemic effects of anthropogenic climate change and, more broadly, biodiversity loss and environmental degradation on price stability and the financial system are becoming increasingly evident, and actual and potential losses point to a climate crisis. Since Turkey is located in the Mediterranean Basin, which will be most affected by climate change, it is one of the countries that should take an active role in this process. The aim of our study is to examine the situation of the Central Bank of the Republic of Turkey (CBRT) as one of the central banks that is expected to be most exposed to possible price shocks and financial problems due to macroeconomic climate risks. For the analysis, the recently announced 2022 results of The Green Central Banking Scorecard, which evaluates the performance of central banks at the scale of G20 countries, are used. The scores obtained from the data collected by qualitative research methods in different categories show the performance ranking among the central banks of G20 countries. In the study, the policy practices assessed by the Scorecard in the Financial Regulation category are also supported by an analysis of reports from the Sustainable Banking and Finance Network (SBFN). As Türkiye belongs to the group of emerging economies, it was considered appropriate to make a comparison with countries in the same group within the G20. The focus of our review is to investigate the CBRT's performance results, which are also presented in the reports, in detail. By taking into account the details of policy implementations based on country scores, it has been tried to trace the developments in the green transformation process. Comparative results show that there are significant performance differences between central banks and financial regulatory authorities despite similar levels of economic development. The results of the analysis show that the CBRT and the financial system have a rather weak outlook in terms of implementing long-term effective policies in the green transformation. The CBRT has not yet implemented any green monetary policy. In the area of financial regulation, the Banking Regulation and Supervision Agency (BRSA), despite its considerable efforts, has performed rather inadequately. The emerging economies that have made relatively more progress in both areas are China, Brazil and Indonesia. In the post-pandemic period, the CBRT has diverged negatively from many countries in a similar group in the efforts to tackle inflation, which has become a global problem. The most important reason for this failure is that it has been subjected to intense political interference in monetary policy implementation and has lost its independence to a great extent. Contrary to global practices, the preferred monetary policy prioritises growth over disinflation. The government preference, which plays a significant role in this choice, also ignores the structural causes of inflation. In our opinion, this situation makes it more difficult for the CBRT to focus on the green transformation process while at the same time making its effectiveness in this process more dependent on the government's preferences towards climate change. Therefore, the role of both the central bank and the financial system in green transformation is determined by the central authority's voluntary efforts and decisive practices in this field. By making the CBRT's green central banking performance more visible, our review hopes to provide a basis for future studies.

Keywords: Green Central Banking, Turkey's Central Bank, Emerging Economies

***

Introduction

Global warming and climate change have become almost "existential" threats all over the world with their effects that have manifested themselves noticeably especially in the last decade. The Paris Climate Agreement and, most recently, the Covid-19 Pandemic have been the beginning of moving this phenomenon, which has been on the agenda for a long time, from the level of "discussion" to the level of "action". Considering the socio-economic impacts of climate change and environmental problems, "greening" almost every aspect of life has become the number one issue on the world agenda.

In the context of climate change, there are two decisive factors in the field of economy. One of these is to increase the resilience of economies against the physical shocks caused by climate change, and the other is to realise the ultimate goal of reducing greenhouse gas emissions, also called "net zero" in all sectors, through a transparent and fair transition process. Price and financial stability, which is a prerequisite for long-term sustainable growth, naturally places both central banks and regulatory authorities at the centre of the "green economy" agenda. The responsibilities of central banks to maintain overall financial stability, in particular price stability, imply that they should take an active role not only in identifying climate-related risks but also in accelerating the transition to a net-zero economy. The adverse effects of climate change on key macroeconomic components such as production, consumption, investment, employment, wages, international trade, exchange rates and inflation also challenge the traditional structure of central banks as an indispensable element of economic stability. Central banking, which has been shaped by changing needs and conditions in different periods of history, is now being forced to change again and again in the new conditions emerging from global climate and environmental risks. Green central banking, which is the expression of this transformation, is the subject of intense debates on how to adapt central banks' institutional structures and monetary policy strategies to the green transformation. The scope of these debates is mainly centred on the legal mandates of central banks and macroprudential governance arrangements. Given the diversity of central banks' monetary policy regimes, legislated objectives defined sustainability goals and green central banking activities across countries, this discussion is about how to incorporate a net-zero target into the objective function of central banks on the basis of existing differences rather than trying to establish a uniform approach that can be applied globally.

The hot agenda of green central banking also closely concerns the Central Bank of the Republic of Türkiye (CBRT), both due to its location in the geography under the impact of climate-related risks and its approval of the Paris Climate Agreement. Moreover, Türkiye's inclusion in the G20, which represents the leading global economies and is also a major contributor to global carbon emissions, makes its participation in climate policy implementation at the international level even more important. While the CBRT law sets price stability as the main objective, it is among the central banks with an indirect sustainability mandate due to its mandate to support the government's growth and employment policies, provided that this objective is not contradictory. The aim of our study is to examine the situation of the CBRT as one of the central banks that are expected to be most exposed to possible price shocks and financial problems due to macroeconomic climate risks. For the analysis, the recently announced 2022 results of The Green Central Banking Scorecard, which evaluates the performance of central banks at the scale of G20 countries, are used. In the study, the policy practices assessed by the Scorecard in the Financial Regulation category are also supported by an analysis of reports from the Sustainable Banking and Finance Network (SBFN). As Türkiye belongs to the group of emerging economies, it was considered appropriate to make a comparison with countries in the same group within the G20.

The study consists of 3 sections. In the first section, the macroeconomic risk types of environmental problems related to climate change and, more broadly, biodiversity loss, are explained, and the importance of central banks in the green transformation process is emphasized. The second section focuses on the green central banking debate in the literature. The nature of the debates and the arguments put forward shed light on the role of central banks in the green transformation process. The last section of the paper focuses on the green performance of the CBRT. This section analyzes the performance of the CBRT as a central bank with an implicit sustainability objective in comparison with emerging economies in the G20. The aim is to make visible the CBRT-specific developments that affect the results of the reports and to evaluate the performance results. Thus, it is hoped that it will provide motivation for future studies.

Climate Change and Macroeconomic Risks

Climate change is defined by the United Nations (UN) Framework Convention on Climate Change as "a change in climate resulting from human activities that directly or indirectly alters the composition of the global atmosphere, in addition to natural climate variability observed over comparable time periods".[1] The emphasis on "human activities" in the definition points to the source of the climate change we are experiencing in the current period. Throughout the 4.6 billion years of the geological history of the earth, changes (cooling-warming) have been experienced in the climate system at all time scales, depending on internal and external factors and processes. However, since the Industrial Revolution, a new era has dawned in which anthropogenic external forces have been added to these natural factors for the first time. This new era is changing and redefining both the environment in which we live and our living conditions in dimensions ranging from social geography to physical geography.[2]

With the Industrial Revolution, anthropocentric activities such as the burning of fossil fuels, land changes, deforestation, agricultural and livestock activities and various industrial processes have led to a rapid increase in greenhouse gas emissions. Among these gases, CO2, which is ubiquitous in the

---

[1] United Nations (UN), *United Nations Framework Convention on Climate Change,* (New York: 1992), 23. https://unfccc.int/resource/docs/convkp/conveng.pdf.

[2] Murat Türkeş, "Küresel İklim Değişikliği Nedir? Temel Kavramlar, Nedenleri, Gözlenen ve Öngörülen Değişiklikler", *İklim Değişikliği ve Çevre* 1, no.1 (2008): 28, https://dergipark.org.tr/tr/download/article-file/518059.

atmosphere and has a lifetime of 50-200 years, is recognised as a greenhouse gas under the direct influence of human activity and can effectively absorb the thermal energy released by the Earth.[3] In the UN Intergovernmental Panel on Climate Change (IPCC) 2018 Special Report on Global Warming of 1.5°C, it was stated that most of the detected global warming is due to human-induced (anthropogenic) forcing.[4]

Climate change and global warming are only one aspect of human-induced environmental problems. Biodiversity loss is another environmental impact and is closely linked to climate change. For example, biodiversity loss due to deforestation or loss of forest cover is one of the largest sources of greenhouse gas emissions. Similarly, the oceans are an important store of CO2 and play a crucial role in climate regulation.[5] As a result, biodiversity loss exacerbates climate change and global warming, while climate change and global warming cause biodiversity loss. The holistic impacts of environmental problems mean that risks to the human and natural systems are increasing. According to the report by the Intergovernmental Science-Policy Platform on Biodiversity and Ecosystem Services (IPBES), the most comprehensive global biodiversity assessment to date, changes in nature, which have accelerated since the 1970s, are due to five main factors: changing land and sea use, climate change, natural resource use, pollution and invasive alien species. According to the report, these impacts are underpinned by social values and behaviours, including existing patterns of production and consumption, population dynamics, trade, technological innovation and governance models.[6]

The tackling of climate change is based on two pillars: mitigation of climate change and adaptation by increasing the readiness and resilience of economies and societies.[7] Mitigation-based efforts are primarily possible through the transition to a low-carbon economy. Limiting climate change requires a significant and sustained reduction in greenhouse gas emissions, together with

---

[3] Murat Türkeş, "Sera Gazları, Kuvvetlenen Sera Etkisi ve Küresel İklim Değişikliği", *İktisat ve Toplum* no.129 (July 2021): 7

[4] IPCC, *Special Report: Global Warming of 1,5 °C: Summary for Policymakers,* (Switzerland: 2018), 6, https://www.ipcc.ch/site/assets/uploads/2018/11/SR1.5_SPM_Low_Res.pdf.

[5] NGFS, "Biodiversity and Financial Stability: Exploring The Case For Action", NGFS Occasional Paper (2021):6, https://www.ngfs.net/sites/default/files/medias/documents/biodiversity_and_financial_stability_explor ing_the_case_for_action.pdf.

[6] IPBES, *The Global Assessment Report on Biodiversity And Ecosystem Services: Summary for Policymakers,* (Bonn: 2019), 12, https://zenodo.org/record/3553579.

[7] Jeffry D. Sachs, *Sürdürülebilir Kalkınma Çağı,* trans. Barış Gönülşen (İstanbul: Yeditepe Üniversitesi Yayınevi, 2019), 369.

adaptation.[8] Otherwise, long-term changes in all components of the climate system will increase the likelihood of irreversible impacts on humans and ecosystems.[9] Indeed, as the embodiment of a global policy response, the Paris Climate Agreement explicitly declared the responsibilities of governments to take action against climate change and recognized that they have a wide range of policies.[10] Practices that fall short of the Paris Agreement commitments to tackle climate change will make it very difficult to keep global warming between 1.5°C and 2°C.

The main objective of economic policies at the national level is to ensure stable economic growth without high levels of inflation and unemployment.[11] In particular, price stability is a necessary precondition for sustainable growth and development.[12] Considering the current economic consequences and possible future impacts of environmental problems such as climate change and biodiversity loss, it can be said that the current period is a kind of "climate crisis". Therefore, after the 2017-2018 Global Financial Crisis and the Covid-19 Pandemic, the world is now facing a major and long-term threat to macroeconomic stability, this time from the environment.

The impacts of climate change risk on macroeconomic stability have to be considered together with biodiversity and nature loss. Considering biodiversity loss as a secondary and separate risk brings about the danger of underestimating existing and potential risks.[13] In a joint study, the International Network for Sustainable Financial Policy Insights, Research and Exchange (INSPIRE) and the Network for Greening the Finance (NGFS) have shown that climate change

---

[8] IPCC, *Climate Change 2014: Synthesis Report,* (Geneva, Switzerland: 2014), 20, https://www.ipcc.ch/site/assets/uploads/2018/02/SYR_AR5_FINAL_full.pdf.

[9] Mark Carney, "Breaking the Tragedy of The Horizon–Climate Change and Financial Stability", BIS Central Bankers' Speeches, London, 2015, https://www.bis.org/review/r151009a.pdf.

[10] Lena Boneva, Gianluigi Ferrucci, and Paolo Mongelli, "Climate Change and Central Banks: What Role For Monetary Policy?", *Climate Policy* 22 no.6 (May 2022): 771, doi: 10.1080/14693062.2022.2070119.

[11] Halil Seyidoğlu, *İktisat Biliminin Temelleri,* Geliş. 2. Baskı (İstanbul: Güzem Can Yayınları, 2011), 661.

[12] Simon Dikau and Ulrich Volz, "Central Bank Mandates, Sustainability Objectives and The Promotion of Green Finance", *Ecological Economics* 184 (2021): 16, https://doi.org/10.1016/j.ecolecon.2021.107022.

[13] Elena Almeida et al., "Beyond Climate: Addressing Financial Risks From Nature And Biodiversity Loss", The INSPIRE Sustainable Central Banking Toolbox Policy Briefing Paper 09, December 2022, 2, https://www.inspiregreenfinance.org/wp-content/uploads/2022/12/INSPIRE-Sustainable-Central-Banking-Toolbox-Policy-Briefing-Paper-9.pdf.

and biodiversity loss are inextricably linked.[14] Climate change is the third main driver of biodiversity loss on a global scale, after land use change and over-exploitation of natural resources. However, as climate change intensifies, it is possible that this factor will move to the first place. This implies that the scope of nature-related risk is wider, first and foremost, due to the diversity of nature resources and ecosystem services available. Biodiversity loss or nature loss may not be possible to measure with a single metric, such as greenhouse gas emissions used in climate change. Financial risks from biodiversity and nature loss can come from many sources and can be diverse.[15] This makes it very difficult to identify the financial risks associated with biodiversity loss.

The risk categories of climate change and biodiversity loss to price stability and the financial system are similar and can be categorized under three headings: Physical Risks, Transition Risks and Liability Risks.[16]

Physical risks can be "chronic", such as crop and productivity losses due to loss of biodiversity with climate change, or "acute", such as widespread diseases due to reduced natural resilience. Sometimes, this impact can be both chronic and acute, such as deforestation that disrupts the water cycle. Reductions in the nature or quality of ecosystem services due to such risks could damage physical assets, such as infrastructure, while also disrupting supply chains and business operations. These physical risks tend to be "local", although they may be becoming functional according to resource dependence, scarcity or quality. But because they can spread across multiple sectors and fields of activity, they can quickly become globalized. Risks of a physical nature may expose financial institutions to losses due to price increases due to reduced product yields and/or declining performance of economic activities or assets. In his classification of climate change-related price shocks, Schnabel[17], a member of the Executive Board of the European Central Bank (ECB), refers to price increases due to shocks brought about by natural disasters and severe

---

[14] NGFS, "Central Banking and Supervision in The Biosphere: An Agenda for Action on Biodiversity Loss, Financial Risk and System Stability", NGFS Occasional Paper, 2022, 2-3, https://www.ngfs.net/sites/default/files/medias/documents/central_banking_and_supervision_in_the_biosphere.pdf.

[15] Almedia et al., "Beyond Climate", 1-5.

[16] Carney, "Breaking The Tragedy of The Horizon", 4.

[17] Isabel Schnabel, "A New Age of Energy İnflation: Climateflation, Fossilflation and Greenflation", (speeches at a panel on "Monetary Policy and Climate change" at The ECB and its Watchers XXII Conference, Frankfurt: March 17, 2022) May 10, 2023, https://www.bis.org/review/r220317b.pdf.

weather events as "climateflation". In addition to all these effects, physical risks have the potential to be a source of geopolitical instability or conflict.[18]

Transition risks arise from government policies, regulations, technology and changes in consumer and investor preferences to halt or reverse nature loss. Transition risks emerge when financial institutions are directly or indirectly exposed to these factors.[19] In Schnabel's classification, price shocks that he calls "fossilflation" and "greenflation" are also in this group. According to Schnabel, in tackling climate change, fossil fuels should be made more expensive, and their use should be discouraged. In addition, the need for metals and minerals required for technologies to tackle climate change will cause price increases due to limited supply.[20] Unfortunately, the fact that fossil energy sources have not been sufficiently reduced over the past decades increases the cost of such an intervention. On the other hand, limiting the increase in global temperature to 1.5°C or 2°C would turn a significant portion of assets, especially those based on existing fossil resources, into "stranded assets". In this case, the disposal of such depreciating assets has the potential to cause mass sales with systemic impacts.[21] On the other hand, measures to mitigate biodiversity loss also pose transitional risks. For example, the expansion of protected areas will reduce the supply of inputs for businesses that exploit them and fuel price increases.[22]

One of the financial risk categories of climate change and biodiversity loss is "liability risks" that may arise from legal situations. Although this category of risk is considered as "transition" risk in some sources, it is mostly treated separately. Where parties who have suffered or are suffering damage from the effects of climate change seek compensation from those they hold responsible, these include payments, penalties, insurance costs, financing costs and reputational costs.[23]

These risks can increase price volatility for goods and services and can also destabilize financial markets. It is transmitted into the financial system through the declining value of assets or collateral, reduced corporate profitability,

---

[18] NGFS, "Biodiversity and Financial Stability", 9; Patrick Bolton et al., "Green Swans: Central Banks in the Age of Climate-Related Risks", *Bulletin de la Banque de France* 229, 8 (May-June 2020): 2, https://publications.banque-france.fr/sites/default/files/medias/documents/820154_bdf229-8_green_swans_vfinale.pdf.

[19] NGFS, "Biodiversity and Financial Stability", 9.

[20] Schanabel, "A New Age of Energy Inflation".

[21] Bolton et al., "Green Swans", 2.

[22] NGFS, "Biodiversity and Financial Stability", 10.

[23] Carney, "Breaking the Tragedy of the Horizon", 4.

financial risks realized as credit, business liquidity and market risks.[24] The broad risk and transmission channels include country-level risks that could impair the ability of countries to manage their financial operations, including long-term debt servicing, and to operate the monetary system.[25]

When assessing the risks of climate change and environmental factors on financial stability, it should not be overlooked that the financial system also contributes to climate change and biodiversity loss. The function of the financial system to mitigate environmental risks and support ecosystem protection while contributing to climate change and biodiversity loss is referred to as "dual materiality".[26] The double materiality is particularly relevant in the context of the policy practices of banks, institutional investors and international financial institutions, as well as central banks and financial regulatory authorities, which are driving the development of "green finance". This is because green finance has two main functions; one is to internalize environmental externalities and the other is to reduce the perception of risk in order to encourage investments that will create environmental benefits.[27] However, according to the International Institute for Sustainable Development (IISD), global subsidies for fossil fuels are 4 times higher than subsidies for renewable energy sources and exceed $650 billion annually.[28] Since the Paris Agreement, fossil fuel financing by the world's 60 largest banks has reached $4.6 trillion.[29] While the share of assets that contribute to sustainability has increased in recent years, they still represent less than 5% of financial assets.[30] Double materiality is, therefore, extremely important in greening the financial system as a whole.

[24] Almedia et al., "Beyond Climate", 4.

[25] NGFS, "Biodiversity and Fnancial Stability", 13.

[26] NGFS, "Biodiversity and Financial Stability", 9.

[27] Kathrin Berensmann and Nannette Lindenberg, "Green Finance: Actors, Challenges and Policy Recommendations", German Development Institute Briefing Paper, 23, 2016, https://www.idos-research.de/ uploads/media/BP_23.2016.pdf.

[28] Erinç Yeldan, "Paris Sözleşmesi'nin Beşinci Yılı", *İktisat ve Toplum Dergisi,* no.123, (Ocak 2021): 30.

[29] Nikki Eames, "Green Central Banking Goes Mainstream, But Words Aren't Yet Matched by Actions", Green Centralbanking News, November 24, 2022, https://greencentral banking.com/2022/11/24/green-central-banking-goes-mainstream/.

[30] SFWG, "Presidency and Co-Chairs Note on Agenda Priorities", G20 First Sustainable Finance Working Group Meeting, 2-3 February, 2023, 2, https://g20sfwg.org/wp-content/ uploads/2023/03/SFWG-Presidency-and-Co-Chairs-Note-on-Agenda-Priorities.pdf.

Climate Change and Discussions on Green Central Banking

The macroeconomic impacts of climate-related risks have led to a redefinition of central banking as "green central banking", emphasizing the need for monetary policy to be "green" along with finance. Green central banking is defined as "central banking that takes into account environmental risks, including risks arising from climate change, that could have a significant impact on the short- and long-term stability and development of the financial sector and the macroeconomy".[31] Central banks' financial supervision over money and credit flows, on the one hand, and their explicit or implicit responsibilities for financial and macroeconomic stability, on the other, pave the way for central banking that addresses environmental risks at a systemic level.[32]

The literature on green central banking has identified 3 main rationales to explain central banks' actions in assessing the impacts of climate change on the economy and financial markets, incorporating climate-related factors into their policy structures, and supporting their governments' carbon emission targets. One of these is the effects of physical and transition risks on money and financial markets, as mentioned earlier. A second rationale is that climate change could lead to depreciation in the value of assets held by central banks on their balance sheets, which could cause financial losses. Finally, many central banks have a legal mandate to support government policies without undermining the objective of price stability.[33]

The first step in turning the projections towards central banks was a speech by Mark Carney, former governor of the Bank of England, entitled "breaking the tragedy of the horizon".[34] In his speech, Carney underlined that climate change will seriously affect financial stability and that there is a mismatch between current central bank policies and climate change. Thus, for the first time, central banks turned their attention to the systemic implications of climate risks for financial institutions and their mispricing in financial markets.[35]

---

[31] Simon Dikau and Ulrich Volz, "Central Banking, Climate Change and Green Finance", ADBI Working Paper Series no. 867, September 2018, 1, https://www.adb.org/sites/default/files/publication/452676/adbi-wp867.pdf.

[32] Paola D'Orazio and Lilit Popoyan, "Realising Central Banks' Climate Ambitions Through Financial Stability Mandates", *Intereconomics* 57, 2 (2022): 103, https://www.intereconomics.eu/contents/year/2022/number/2/article/realising-central-banks-climate-ambitions-through-financial-stability-mandates.html.

[33] Lena Boneva, Gianluigi Ferrucci, and Paolo Mongelli, "Climate Change and Central Banks: what Role for Monetary Policy?", *Climate Policy* 22 no.6 (2022): 772, doi: 10.1080/14693062.2022.2070119.

[34] Carney, "Breaking The Tragedy of The Horizon", 4.

[35] Boneva, Ferrucci and Mongelli, "Climate Change and Central Banks" , 772.

The international political commitments embodied in the Paris Climate Agreement of the same year have also led to an intense debate on the role of central banks in addressing climate-related risks and contributing to the development of green finance.[36]

Many central banks and regulators around the world seem to agree on the need to acknowledge and address the risks to macroeconomic stability posed by climate change and other environmental challenges. As a matter of fact, in 2021, the commitment of central banks and regulatory authorities to include climate factors in their decision-making processes was confirmed in the Glasgow Declaration of the 26th Conference of the Parties (COP26) together with the NGFS.[37] But this consensus does not mean "one-size-fits-all".[38] In addition to the many structural and institutional differences across countries, the nature of climate and environmental risks poses significant challenges in how to address them. Although many central banks seek to achieve their climate goals through their financial stability mandates, concerns about market neutrality and overreaching of their mandates, violations of the "as many tools as goals" rule (Tinbergen Principle) and threats to independence, and the adequacy of traditional monetary policy tools are among the most debated issues in the green central banking literature.[39] Central banks, scientists and policymakers agree that climate change-related risks and long-term uncertainties pose a serious threat to monetary policy and financial stability. The debate centres on whether central banks should take an active position against climate impacts, take on auxiliary functions or ignore the issue. A key concern is also how to align climate targets with their operational imperatives should they take action. Although there are historical differences in the institutional political traditions of central banks, a common feature is that all central banks generally have a price stability objective.[40]

For the debate on the extent to which climate change and environmental risk mitigation and adaptation policies are consistent with the current legal mandate and objectives of central banks, Dikau and Volz's empirical analysis[41]

---

[36] Simon Dikau and Ulrich Volz, "Central Bank Mandates, Sustainability Objectives and The Promotion of Green Finance", *Ecological Economics* 184 (2021): 1, https://doi.org/10.1016/j.ecolecon.2021.107022.

[37] D'Orazio and Popoyan, "Realising Central Banks' Climate Ambitions", 103.

[38] Paola D'Orazio and Lilit Popoyan, "Do Monetary Policy Mandates and Financial Stability Governance Structures Matter for the Adoption of Climate-Related Financial Policies?", *International Economics* no. 173 (January 2023): 285, https://doi.org/10.1016/j.inteco.2023.01.004.

[39] D'Orazio and Popoyan,"Realising Central Banks' Climate Ambitions", 103.

[40] D'Orazio and Popoyan, "Realising Central Banks' Climate Ambitions", 104.

[41] Dikau and Volz, "Central Bank Mandates, Sustainability Objectives".

provides a comprehensive overview. Using the IMF Central Bank Legislation Database (April 2017 version), the study uses data from 135 central banks. According to the results of this study, 70 central banks out of these 135 central banks have sustainability objectives either directly or indirectly. Of these, only 15 central banks have a direct mandate to promote, encourage and support sustainability or sustainable development. Although these mandates were written at a time when the problems of climate change and the environment were not so severe, since the concept of sustainability in the Brundtland Report explicitly refers to environmental aspects, these 15 central banks are considered to have a "direct" mandate. The 54 central banks out of 135 central banks are considered to have an indirect sustainability mandate based on their purpose of supporting government policies or economic objectives without directly using the term "sustainability". In the same study, the number of countries participating in green central banking activities without direct or indirect mandates was found to be 33.

Dikau and Volz's work also points to two aspects of green central banking, one "passive" and the other "active". The inclusion of these risks in their traditional policies by taking into account climate and environmental risks, as well as the primary objectives of central banks, which consist of price stability and, in most cases, financial stability, points to the "passive" side. No obligation for central banks, as it is not legally within their mandate. However, "active" central banking requires a proactive central bank that not only addresses climate and environmental risks, but also takes them forward. This requires an explicit mandate defined in the legal framework. This requirement stems from the potential for central bank actions to undermine the market-neutral character of the central bank, as mentioned earlier. It is noteworthy that central banks in developing and emerging economies have taken on a relatively more active role. As in the cases of Bangladesh, Brazil, China, India and Indonesia.[42]

On the other hand, it is also pointed out that in a market structure where markets are not carbon-neutral, the monetary policies implemented will naturally not be market-neutral. This is because central banks' monetary policy decisions will affect asset prices through the monetary transmission mechanism, and thus, central banks will increase the liquidity of bonds of carbon-neutral companies, thereby reducing their high carbon-intensive costs.[43] At this point, existing collateral structures are one of the most debated issues. This is because the central bank collateral system is generally accepted to play a strong role in

---

[42] Simon Dikau and Josh Ryan-Collins, "Green Central Banking in Emerging Market and Developing Country Economies", *New Economics Foundation* (July 2017): 2, https://neweconomics.org/uploads/files/Green-Central-Banking.pdf.

[43] Dirk Schoenmaker, "Greening Monetary Policy", *Climate Policy* 21, no.4 (January 2021): 581, doi: 10.1080/14693062.2020.1868392.

today's market-based financial systems. Collateral rules and practices, which form the core of the liquidity operations of many central banks around the world, affect the demand of financial institutions for financial assets, which in turn affects credit conditions and the real economy. In existing collateral structures, marketable assets (with lower interest rates and higher prices) are more popular and, therefore, more demand. Therefore, central banks' decisions and practices regarding the collateral structure have non-neutral effects on credit conditions and the real economy.[44]

The current debate on "green central banking" is, in fact, consistent with the history of this institution. Indeed, the history of central banking shows that these institutions were established on the basis of the needs of the time and that the objectives of many of them have constantly changed since their inception.[45] The historical progression has been from central banks that were mainly responsible for financing wars and carrying out government directives to central banks that are independent, transparent, accountable and responsible for price and financial stability. Today, central banks are crucial elements of economic stability. In this process of change and transformation, the effects of the post-1980 neoliberal era and the global financial crisis of 2007-2008 are particularly decisive. The financial crises that increased in parallel with financial liberalization in the 1980s forced central banks responsible for price stability and financial stability to develop new approaches in both their institutional structures and monetary policy strategies.[46] However, prior to the recent global financial crisis, the belief that price stability alone is a sufficient objective for central banks was reinforced. In line with this acceptance, policy implementation for the financial sector has been implemented in the form of "microprudential" policies, which are decided outside the monetary authorities and mostly applied to troubled financial institutions since systemic risk is not foreseen.[47] After the crisis, it was realized that price stability and microprudential policies alone were not sufficient. First of all, in advanced economies, the monetary policy objectives of central banks have come under intense debate, and

---

[44] Yannis Dafermos at al., "Greening Collateral Frameworks", The INSPIRE Sustainable Central Banking Toolbox Policy Briefing Paper 07, August 2022, 2, https://www.lse.ac.uk/granthaminstitute/wp-content/uploads/2022/08/INSPIRE-Sustainable-Central-Banking-Toolbox-Policy-Briefing-Paper-7.pdf.

[45] Nazire Nergis Dinçer, "Merkez Bankaları Değişiyor mu?", *İktisat ve Toplum Dergisi* no. 127 (Mayıs 2021): 4.

[46] Suat Oktar, Erkan Tokucu ve Zekayi Kaya, *Finansal Küreselleşme Sürecinde Merkez Bankacılığı ve Para Politikaları*, 2. Basım (Ankara: Nobel Yayınları, 2013), 100-134.

[47] Z. Yeşim Gürbüz, Gilbert Koenig ve İrem Zeyneloğlu, *Para Politikası, Makro İhtiyati Politikalar ve Finansal İstikrar*, (İstanbul: Kriter Yayıncılık, 2020), 5-6.

macroprudential policies have been introduced while financial stability has been included in the objectives of central banks.[48] Between 2007 and 2017, central banks in advanced economies created unprecedented amounts of money and more than tripled the size of their balance sheets to stabilize the financial system and boost economic growth.[49] In 2000, the proportion of central banks with financial stability objectives increased from 16% to 58% in 2020. While developed countries, with their focus on price stability, have incorporated economic stability into their hierarchy, developing countries have generally compensated for this with the objective of economic growth and development. For this reason, the power and responsibilities of central banks, as well as supervisory authorities responsible for macroprudential policies, have recently been at the centre of the debate.[50]

Macroprudential policies are policies that support monetary and fiscal policies and are applied to the entire financial system. The focus of these debates is rather on the governance of macroprudential policies. When practices are taken into account, it is possible to talk about three types of governance. One of them is the "central bank model", in which prudential policy is included in the central bank's legal mandate, and monetary and prudential policies are unified under one roof. In this model, the central bank is the "prudential" authority responsible for financial stability. However, such a model requires significant changes in the institutional structure of central banks. This is because it is quite difficult and complex to achieve financial stability with different qualities through traditional monetary policy structures and instruments.[51]

The second model is classified as the "separate committee model". While prudential regulation is still within the legal authority of the central bank, the central bank is not responsible for the implementation of financial policies. There is partial institutional integration of the central bank and supervisory agencies. The third type of governance model is the "separate structure model", in which there is no partial and institutional integration between the central bank and supervisory agencies, and monetary and prudential policies are separated. In this arrangement, prudential authority is delegated to institutions such as ministries, banking associations, the government or capital market

[48] Dinçer,"Merkez Bankaları Değişiyor mu?", 4-7; Gürbüz, Koenig ve Zeyneloğlu, *Para Politikası, Makro İhtiyati Politikalar*, 6-9.

[49] Pierre Monnin, "Central Banks and the Transition to a Low-Carbon Economy", CEP Discussion Note, 1, (2018), 1.

[50] D'Orazio and Popoyan, "Realising Central Banks' Climate Ambitions", 105.

[51] Oktar, Tokucu ve Kaya, *Finansal Küreselleşme Sürecinde Merkez Bankacılığı*, 128-129.

regulators.[52] Although there has been a tendency since the 1990s to delegate responsibility for financial stability to private financial supervisory authorities, the fact that central banks are the authorities of last resort gives them the ability to directly influence financial stability.[53] Therefore, the interaction between monetary policy and macroprudential policies makes coordination inevitable in separate structure models. After all, as a state body with the authority to regulate and/or supervise a country's monetary issuance and monetary as well as macroprudential policies,[54]central banks are in a very powerful position to support the development of green finance models through money, credit and the financial system and to guide financial institutions against climate and nature risks.[55]

In the aftermath of the 2007-2008 crisis, the addition of financial stability to the objective caused intense debates, drawing attention to its different characteristics from price stability and emphasizing that it could undermine central bank independence. In the aftermath of the financial crisis, unconventional quantitative easing (QE) policies implemented by central banks in advanced economies have been severely criticized on the grounds that they are outside the objectives of the institution and affect income distribution.[56] Similar debates can be observed in the field of green central banking. First of all, the incorporation of climate change into monetary policy operations requires the adoption of unconventional measures, just like the "unconventional" instruments introduced after the crisis. This is because traditional monetary policy tools may be insufficient for climate policies. Critics argue that this would undermine central bank independence and market neutrality. The survey for G20 countries shows that the People's Bank of China and Bank of Japan prefer unconventional monetary policies. It is also observed that the ECB is increasingly inclined towards such policies.[57]

The prevailing view in the green central banking mandate debate is that, at least for the time being, there is no need to modify existing legal powers for net-

---

[52] D'Orazio ve Popoyan, "Do Monetary Policy Mandates and Financial Stability", 290.

[53] Gürbüz, Koenig ve Zeyneloğlu, *Para Politikası, Makro İhtiyati Politikalar*, 24-25.

[54] Radu Şimandan, Cristian Valeriu and Bogdan Glăvan, "Post Pandemic Greenness? How Central Banks Use Narratives to Become Green", *Sustainability* 15, 1630 (2023):1 https://doi.org/10,3390/su 15021630.

[55] Dikau ve Volz, "Central Banking, Climate Change", 1.

[56] Dinçer,"Merkez Bankaları Değişiyor mu?", 4-7; Gürbüz, Koenig ve Zeyneloğlu, *Para Politikası, Makro İhtiyati Politikalar*, 6-9.

[57] D'Orazio and Popoyan, "Realising Central Banks' Climate Ambitions", 103.

zero central banking.[58] In the Eurozone, where debates are frequent, Benoit Coeuré[59], a member of the Governing Council of the ECB, acknowledged that climate change will inevitably have an impact on monetary policy but pointed out that failure to control climate change will make it difficult for central banks to accurately forecast shocks to the medium-term inflation outlook. He also noted that the increased likelihood of extreme events related to climate change could further strain the traditional policy space of central banks, forcing them to prioritize price stability over growth and, hence, employment. Coeuré, therefore, argued that central banks have room to play a supportive role in climate change mitigation policies by remaining within their designated mandates.

Central Bank of the Republic of Turkey's Green Scorecard Performance Analysis: a Comparison With the Emerging Economies in G20

This section of the study evaluates the performance of the Central Bank of the Republic of Türkiye (CBRT) in addressing climate and environmental risks and supporting green finance. The assessment is based on the categories in "The Green Central Banking Scorecard" issued by Positive Money and Green Central Banking[60] in 2022, and attempts to analyze the results in these categories. The Scorecard is an assessment that scores and ranks all green policies and initiatives adopted by G20 central banks. As a member of the G20, Türkiye is

---

[58] Nick Robins, Simon Dikau and Ulrich Volz, "Net-Zero Central Banking: A New Phase in Greening The Financial System", *Grantham Research Institute on Climate Change and the Environment Policy Report* (March 2021):5, https://www.lse.ac.uk/granthaminstitute/wp-content/uploads/2021/03/Net-zero-central-banking.pdf.; Signe Krogstrup and William Oman, "Macroeconomic and Financial Policies for Climate Change Mitigation: A Review of the Literature", IMF Working Paper, 19, 185, (September 2019), 30; https://www.imf.org/en/Publications/WP/Issues/2019/09/04/Macroeconomic-and-Financial-Policies-for-Climate-Change-Mitigation-A-Review-of-the-Lite.; Simon Dikau and Ulrich Volz "Central Bank Mandates, Sustainability Objectives and the Promotion of Green Finance", SOAS Department of Economics, Working Paper, no. 222, March 2019, 16, https://www.soas.ac.uk/sites/default/files/2022-10/economics-wp222.pdf.

[59] Benoît Cœuré, "Monetary Policy and Climate Change", speech at a conference on "Scaling up Green Finance: The Role of Central Banks", organised by the Network for Greening the Financial System, the Deutsche Bundesbank and the Council on Economic Policies, Berlin, 8 November 2018, https://www.bis.org/review/r181109f.pdf.

[60] Nikki Eames and David Barmes, *The Green Central Banking Scorecard 2022* Edition (Surry Hills: November 2022).

also included in the Scorecard. The scorecard is based on literature, expert opinions and interviews with central banks and regulatory authorities.[61]

The G20 is an important representative of the global economy in terms of population, economic size, international trade and growth parameters. On the one hand, it accounts for the largest share of global wealth, while on the other, it is responsible for around 75-80% of global greenhouse gas emissions. Therefore, the G20 has a leading and decisive role in tackling global climate change and environmental problems. However, 8 countries in the G20 (Argentina, Brazil, China, Indonesia, Mexico, Russia, South Africa and Türkiye) are emerging economies in the upper-middle income group in the World Bank's classification of income groups. India is among the emerging economies of the lower-middle income group, while the remaining 10 G20 countries belong to the upper-income group of developed countries. The economic and financial challenges faced by central banks and financial regulatory authorities in G20 countries that are classified as emerging economies or developing countries are, therefore, very different from those faced by advanced economies. Similarly, financial markets and market forces are less widespread in these country groups.[62] These differences also apply to exposure to, and potential to tackle, climate change and environmental risks. Therefore, even though the CBRT is a member of the G20, it would be more appropriate to compare the green performance of the CBRT with countries in a similar class due to its unique circumstances.

The Green Central Banking Scorecard consists of 4 main categories: Research and Advocacy, Monetary Policy, Financial Regulation, and Leading by Example. In each of these four categories, green policies are re-evaluated according to high, medium and low impact levels.

The G20's score in all categories is shown in Table 7.1. The numbers in parentheses in the "rank" column of the table indicate the rankings of the central banks of the respective country for the previous year. Accordingly, Italy, Germany, Japan, Canada, Canada, Russia and Türkiye have increased their total score in 2022 compared to 2021, while Brazil, China, Indonesia, India, South Korea, Australia, the United States, South Africa and Saudi Arabia have decreased their score.

---

[61] Green Central Banking, *The Green Central Banking Scorecard 2022 Edition* (Surry Hills: November 2022):13, https://positivemoney.org/publications/green-central-banking-scorecard-2022/.

[62] NGFS, "Central Banking and Supervision in The Biosphere", 65.

Table 7.1 Green Central Banking Scorecard, 2022

Rank		Country	Research and Advocacy *(out of 10)*	Monetary Policy *(out of 50)*	Financial Policy *(out of 50)*	Leading by Example *(out of 20)*	Aggregate Score (out of 130)	Grade (A+ to F)
1	-	France	10	12	31	17	70	B-
2	↑	Italy	10	12	31	[illegible]	61	C+
3	↑	Germany	10	12	30	8	60	C+
4	-	European Union	10	12	28	[illegible]	58	C
5	-	United Kingdom	10	10	27		56	C
6=	↓	Brazil	10	[illegible]	[illegible]	[illegible]	53	C
6=	↓	China	10	12	31	0	53	C
8	↑	Japan	10	6	14	5	35 (25)	D+
9	↓	Indonesia	10	1	14	5	30 (20)	D+
10	↑	Canada	10	2	14	2	28 (15)	D
11	-	Mexico	10	4	4	5	23 (17)	D
12	↓	India	10	0	10	1	21 (18)	D
13	↓	South Korea	10	1	6	2	19 (17)	D-
14	↑	Russia		0	8	2	18 (12)	D-
15	↓	Australia	10	0	4	3	17 (16)	D-
16	↓	United States	10	0	6	0	16 (15)	D-
17	↑	Turkey	10	0	2	2	14 (4)	D-
18	↓	South Africa	10	0	2	1	13 (10)	D-
19	-	Argentina		0	0	0	6 (0)	F
20	↓	Saudi Arabia	0	0	0	0	0 (0)	F

Source: Green Central Banking, *Scorecard*, 8.

The assessment in the Research and Advocacy category takes into account central banks' membership in the NGFS and whether central banks have published articles, speeches and research reports on climate change and environmental issues. The maximum score in the relevant category is 10, with a maximum score of 5 for low-impact policies. In this category, all countries except Russia, Argentina and Saudi Arabia achieved full points for 2022. Scoring "0", the Saudi Arabian Monetary Authority is the only G20 country that is not a member of the NGFS and has not committed to multilateral action.

The importance of policy actions for research and disclosure is that they can be used as a green microprudential policy tool, enabling central banks and regulators to empower the financial sector to identify and accept green assets.[63] In this category, Türkiye, along with Argentina, is the only country to improve its score. Banque de France, which ranks first in the Scorecard's overall score ranking, is the only central bank that has produced the most progressive research on framing environmental risks. With the exception of Russia and Argentina, all emerging economy countries perform similarly in this category. The CBRT's policies in this category are shown in Table 7.2.

Table 7.2 Research&Advocacy Performance of CBRT

Category	Implemented Policies
Research & Advocacy	• Membership of the Central Bank of the Republic of Türkiye (CBRT) and the Banking Regulation and Supervision Agency (BRSA) in the 2021 NGFS (medium impact) • BRSA's Turkish Banking Sector Sustainability Report • BRSA's membership in the Sustainable Banking and Finance Network (SBFN) in 2015 • CBRT's 2021 press release declaring that it recognizes climate as an inflationary pressure • 2021 Makroeconomic Outlook (climate-related risk emphasis in inflation)

Source: Author's own edit from, The Green Central Banking Scorecard 2022.

As seen in Table 7.2, the fact that NGFS membership started in 2021 is remarkable in terms of Türkiye's green policy actions. Although Türkiye was one of the first signatories of the 2015 Paris Agreement, it was only in 2021 that the agreement was approved by its parliament, declaring 2053 as its net-zero target. In the same year, the Ministry of Trade published the "Green Deal Action Plan". For Türkiye, this process was inspired by the EU's "European Green Deal", which redefined the framework of growth and employment policies and was announced to the world public in 2019. In 2021, the EU's announcement of the Fit for 55 program, which increased the carbon emission reduction target from 40% to 55% in the action plan announced within the framework of the Paris Agreement, raised Türkiye's awareness of the global adaptation process.[64] Therefore, Türkiye, as an important part of the global economy, especially with its close economic ties with the EU, has put the process of cooperation and adaptation with international institutions and organizations regarding climate and environmental risks on its agenda since 2021.

The CBRT adopted macroprudential policies in 2010. The expansionary monetary policies implemented by the US and EU central banks in response to the 2007-2008 global financial crisis led to massive capital inflows to emerging economies, while Türkiye also experienced massive capital inflows. Accordingly,

[63] Dikau ve Collins, "Green Central Banking in Emerging Market", 2.

[64] Güven Sak, "İklim Değişimi", *İktisat ve Toplum Dergisi* no. 139 (Mayıs 2022): 38.

the increase in financial fragilities has created a need for macroprudential policies in addition to micro-prudential policies that are insufficient against systemic risks. In the discussions on which institution or institutions should design and implement these policies, it was decided to assign this task to the Banking Regulation and Supervision Agency (BRSA), which was established in 1999 in view of its role in the banking sector. Since macroprudential policies also imply financial stability-oriented policies of more than one institution, the Financial Stability Committee (FSC) was established in 2011.[65] However, the FSC was abolished by an omnibus law published in the Official Gazette on January 8, 2019, and replaced by the Financial Stability and Development Committee (FSDC).[66] The new regulation changes some of the provisions and wording of the previous regulation.

As a result, macroprudential policies in Türkiye are implemented by the CBRT and the BRSA, and the coordination between these policies is planned to be ensured by the FSDC. As a regulatory body, it is important that the BRSA became a member of the "Sustainable Banking and Finance Network" (SBFN) in 2015. This is because SBFN member institutions make a formal commitment on two important points; one is to incorporate environmental, social and governance (ESG) criteria into the financial sector and the other is to direct capital flows to activities with positive environmental and social impacts. SBFN membership, therefore, represents a commitment to these commitments.[67]

Monetary policy, the second category of the Green Central Banking Scorecard, is one of the key performance indicators with a maximum impact rating of 50 points. The monetary policy assessment takes into account central banks' monetary policy instruments for green finance, such as asset purchases, money reserves, collateral structures, funding and refinancing schemes, reserve requirements, interest rates, and direct lending. Coordination of central banks with other financial authorities is another element subject to evaluation.[68] The policy actions of Türkiye and other emerging economies on green monetary policy are summarized in Table 7.3.

---

[65] Gürbüz, Koenig ve Zeyneloğlu, *Para Politikası, Makro İhtiyati Politikalar*, 129-131.

[66] Resmi Gazete, "Sigortacılık İle Diğer Bazı Alanlara İlişkin Kanunlarda ve Bir Kanun Hükmünde Kararnamede Değişiklik Yapılmasına Dair Kanun", 31491, (20.05.2021), Kanun no. 7319/3. md. https://www.resmigazete.gov.tr/eskiler/2021/05/20210525-12.htm.

[67] SBFN, *Turkey Country Progress Report: Supplement To The 2021 Global Progress Report of The Sustainable Banking and Finance Network*, March 2022, https://sbfnetwork.org/wp-content/uploads/pdfs/2021_Global_Progress_Report_Downloads/2021_Country_Progress_Report_Turkey.pdf.

[68] Green Central Banking, *Scorecard*, 13.

Table 7.3 Green Monetary Policies of Emerging Economies (EM) in the G20

COUNTRIES (Central Bank/ Supervisor)	GREEN MONETARY POLICIES
Brazil: Banco Central do Brasil (BCB)	• Ban on financing for sugar cane crop expansion in the Amazon, Pantanal and other zones (medium impact) • Condition on rural credit in the Amazon whereby borrowers must show proof of environmental compliance (study on the impact on deforestation – criteria have recently been expanded and strengthened) (medium impact) • Green liquidity facility (formal commitment) (medium impact) • Green Bureau of Rural Credit and incentives for green rural credit (formal commitment – latest BCB report refers to this as the Sustainable Rural Credit Bureau) • Sustainability criteria in the management of international reserves and monitoring of CO2 emissions to assess portfolio's carbon profile. (low impact) • Public consultation on sustainability criteria applicable to rural credit operations (low impact)
China: People's Bank of China (PBoC) and China Banking & Insurance Regulatory Commission	• Carbon emission reduction facility –banks must offer reduced interest rates for loans to pollution control facilities, environmental protection and infrastructure, renewable energy, etc. (fully implemented); scorecard points suspended due to credit guidance towards coal under the "special central bank lending to support the clean and efficient use of coal" (medium impact) • PBoC's notice regarding promoting credit assets and collateral in central bank evaluation established green bonds, loans and securities; ratings of AA and above accepted as collateral in the medium-term lending facility and green loans accepted as part of the standing lending facility (fully implemented) (medium impact) • Interest rate provided to banks on required reserves may be increased if the bank is assessed to be greener in the PBoC's macroprudential assessments (medium impact) • PBoC issued notice on issues relating to improving environmental protection in credit policy, which provided guidance for banks on "how to better include environmental variables in credit decisions (low impact) • PBoC is increasing the allocation of green bonds in the country's foreign exchange reserves (low impact)
Indonesia: Bank Indonesia (BI) and Otoritas Jasa Keuangan	• Acceptance of non-governmental green bonds as collateral in market operations (under discussion, referred to in bilateral interactions) (low impact) • BI issued voluntary green lending model guidelines for mini-hydro power plant projects (low impact)
Mexico: Banco de Mexico (BdM) and Comision National Bancaria y de Valores	• Inclusion of data on individuals and businesses sanctioned by the Federal Environmental Protection Agency in credit analysis (under discussion) (medium impact) • Banco de Mexico is considering expanding the exclusion criteria for investment in international reserves to environmental considerations (under discussion) (medium impact) • BdM is assessing ESG data and rating providers' methodologies, seeking to expand the universe of eligible green bonds in their international reserves

	• Banco de Mexico is including ESG evaluation in the risk management framework of international reserves
Russia: Bank of Russia	
South Africa: South African Reserve Bank (SARB)	• Sarb to develop guidelines for monetary policy to respond to physical and transition risk (formal commitment) (low impact)
Türkiye: Central Bank of the Republic of Türkiye and Banking Regulation and Supervision Agency	
Argentina: Central Bank of Argentina	

Source: Author's own edit from, The Green Central Banking Scorecard 2022.

Among the countries listed in Table 7.3, the country with the highest score in this category is Brazil, with 18 points. China ranked second with 12 points, while Mexico ranked third with 4 points. Along with Türkiye, Russia, South Africa, and Argentina have a score of 0. Given that the maximum score in this category is 50, emerging economies generally perform poorly in the area of monetary policy. In fact, it is not a very good result for developed countries either. This is because, apart from France, Italy, Germany and the UK, no country has yet reached even half of the maximum score. It is noteworthy that none of the countries in the table has a "high impact" score for existing green monetary policies. This implies that central banks have not yet actively contributed to diverting financial flows away from the responsible activities that caused the climate crisis. Nevertheless, it can be said that in the group of emerging economies and developing countries in general, central banks and/or regulatory authorities have started to play an important role in addressing climate change risks.[69] On the other hand, when the G20 as a whole is taken into consideration, it is seen that sustainable finance and climate change have moved from a limited area to mainstreaming. The fact that 19 out of 20 countries are members of the NGFS is considered positive.[70]

When assessing the performance of emerging markets (economies) and developing countries (EMDCs), one of the arguments that can be used is that the risk of exposure to climate change is much higher for many of the countries

[69] Dikau ve Collins, "Green Central Banking in Emerging Market", 2.

[70] Green Central Banking, *Scorecard*, 6.

in this category. In particular, the physical risks associated with extreme weather events, which have become increasingly evident in the period we are living in, are one of the driving factors for these economies to move towards a sustainable green growth path.[71] In addition, these groups of countries are known to be more vulnerable not only to climate change risks but also to biodiversity loss. This vulnerability and the threat of economic risk due to biodiversity loss make it all the more imperative for these countries to address the implications of these risks for financial and economic stability.[72] As mentioned earlier, EMDCs have less prevalent financial markets and market forces compared to developed countries. Moreover, central banks and financial supervisory authorities in these countries face very different financial and economic challenges compared to developed countries. First of all, underdeveloped capital markets may lead to greater financial risk and price volatility due to climate change and environment, depending on credit concentration. This is even more the case for natural resource-based economies. Another distinctive challenge for monetary and financial authorities in EMDCs is that resource and capacity pressures limit the focus on environmental issues. Another problem is that the economic deterioration associated with the impacts of biodiversity loss will require the expertise and resources of a central bank. Finally, financial systems are marred by institutional deficiencies, market failures, uncompetitive banking systems, artificially low interest rates and administrative resource allocation deficiencies, which are more common in these countries.[73]

Despite these challenges, in contrast to advanced economies, the mandate of central banks is interpreted more flexibly in most EMDCs. Many of the central banks in these countries are also implicitly considered to have a sustainability mandate, as they are also tasked with supporting development and government economic policy. Moreover, since central bank independence is not as sanctified[74] as in developed countries, these institutions play an important role in supporting their governments' economic and industrial policies through closer cooperation with the finance ministry and other government agencies. This indirect mandate also allows central banks to be more proactive in tackling climate and environmental risks. However, since central banks in developed countries have a high degree of institutional and operational independence, they are reluctant to take an active role in long-term sustainability. The climate and environmental actions of central banks in these countries are considered

[71] Dikau ve Collins, "Green Central Banking in Emerging Market", 2.

[72] NGFS, "Central Banking and Supervision in The Biosphere", 65.

[73] NGFS, "Central Banking and Supervision in The Biosphere", 65.

[74] Dikau and Collins, "Green Central Banking in Emerging Market", 8.

"second-best" interventions, as they prioritize market-based policy actions such as taxing carbon emissions and carbon trading at the border.[75] The theoretical underpinning behind this stance is the belief that the design of monetary policy should be market-neutral. Hence, the reluctance of central banks across advanced economies is due to concerns that a more active climate intervention would politicize monetary policy.[76] Eames[77] emphasized that this market-neutrality fanaticism, which applies mostly to developed countries, leads to a narrow interpretation of the powers of central banks, resulting in the prioritization of exploratory analysis (such as scenario analysis) over action in financial regulation. In developing countries, central banks have a relatively broader mandate to address climate and environmental issues. In their empirical study, D'Orazio and Popoyan[78] show that there is a statistically significant relationship between broader monetary policy authority and the adoption of climate-related financial policies. This means that in countries where mandates are interpreted more loosely, such as India, Brazil and China, central banks are able to act more flexibly.

In addition to different interpretations of central bank mandates, central banks in developed and developing countries have different institutional structures and financial governance models due to their different path dependencies. Naturally, these differences also differentiate central bank policies. For instance, the monetary policy instruments often preferred in EMDCs are green credit allocation instruments. Credit allocation or orientation policies are, in fact, instruments that have played an important role in the past in orienting credit to priority sectors in developing economies. More recently, similar instruments have been designed, this time for green investments. In other words, many countries direct the process by adding new categories within the scope of tackling climate change. They are the most common among green credit allocation instruments: the creation of refinancing facilities for commercial banks to encourage green investments, the setting of different reserve requirements for green loans, the implementation of maximum and minimum loan quotas for bank portfolios, and the support of development banks by central banks.[79] Brazil, which ranks first in the monetary policy category among the countries in Table 3, has implemented a green liquidity

---

[75] D'Orazio and Popoyan, "Realising Central Banks' Climate Ambitions", 106.

[76] Jens Van't Klooster and Clément Fontan, "The Myth of Market Neutrality: A Comparative Study of the European Central Bank's and the Swiss National Bank's Corporate Security Purchases", *New Political Economy* 25, no.23 (August 2019): 1-2, doi: 10.1080/13563467.2019.1657077.

[77] Eames, "Green Central Banking Goes Mainstream".

[78] D'Orazion and Popoyan, "Do Monetary Policy Mandates and Financial Stability", 292.

[79] Dikau and Collins, "Green Central Banking in Emerging Market", 13-15.

committed credit policy with the "Green Bureau of Rural Credit ".It has also set policies in the management of international reserves and carbon assessment of portfolios, such as monitoring CO2 emissions and public consultation in rural credit operations. China, in second place, has launched initiatives to provide financing to support areas such as clean energy, energy conservation, environmental protection, and carbon reduction technology, with credit facilities for companies that reduce carbon emissions. Although China is seen as an "innovative leader" with these practices, its support for the use of coal with the characterization of "green and efficient" caused its success score in 2021 to drop in 2022.

The fact that the CBRT failed to score any points in this category means that the CBRT is not yet active in green monetary policy practices. The Bank's actions in this category were monitored by analysing the content of its annual reports. Accordingly, it is seen that the CBRT Annual Report for 2022 includes the heading "Activities for Green Economy and Climate Change". Under this heading, it was pointed out that the "Green Economy and Climate Change Directorate", which was established in 2021, has started the infrastructure work for the inclusion of climate change in the Bank's policies. In the same report, the Central Bank declared its support by participating in various workshops and meetings organized by the Ministry of Environment, Urbanization and Climate Change, the Ministry of Trade and the Ministry of Energy and Natural Resources as other institutions involved in tackling climate change in Türkiye. He also stated that he participated in the NGFS General Assembly and sub-group activities, answered NGFS questionnaires and followed international developments in this field. Moreover, it was also stated that various seminars have started to be organized within the bank to enhance awareness of climate change. Meanwhile, the CBRT's collateral structure has not been subject to any new arrangements or changes regarding the green transformation.[80]

Meanwhile, the CBRT's collateral structure has not been subject to any new arrangements or changes regarding the green transformation. An analysis of all texts under the heading "Factors and Risks Affecting Inflation" in the "Summaries of the Monetary Policy Committee Meetings" available on the CBRT's website since the year the CBRT became a member of the NGFS reveals that only the texts of September, October and November 2021 include the concept of "climatic conditions". Only in the January 2022 inflation report, the term "agricultural drought" was used.[81] The current situation suggests that, for the time being, the CBRT plans to follow international developments and initiate

---

80 TCMB, *Yıllık Faaliyet Raporu*, Ankara, 2022, 50, https://www3.tcmb.gov.tr/yillikrapor/2022/tr/index.html.

81 TCMB, *Enflasyon Raporu*, Ankara, (2021, 2022), https://www.tcmb.gov.tr/wps/wcm/connect/tr/tcmb+tr/search+results?search-

the necessary actions. The current situation indicates that, for the time being, the CBRT is content to follow the developments at the international level.

When the comparative analysis of the CBRT's Scorecard performance is supported by empirical studies that consider the factors affecting the adoption of climate-related financial policies, meaningful conclusions can be drawn. First of all, as a country in the emerging economies group, Türkiye faces constraints and challenges that apply to these countries in general and are specific to them. Many of the factors mentioned earlier, such as institutional deficiencies, market failures, an uncompetitive banking system, artificially low interest rates, and deficiencies in administrative resource allocation, as well as resource and capacity constraints, are also valid for Türkiye. However, D'Orazio's study for G20 countries shows that economic and financial characteristics do not affect the adoption of climate-related financial policies.[82] The climate-related financial policy index (CRFPI), developed by D'Orazio and Thole[83] and used to assess global engagement in climate-related financial policies, allows for an objective and comprehensive comparison both across and within country groups. This new composite index categorizes climate-related financial policy space into 5 categories: Green prudential regulations, green credit distribution policies, green financial principles, disclosure requirements and green bond issuance and taxonomy. The results of D'Orazio's analysis for developed, developing and emerging economy groups show that emerging economies have the highest level of participation in green financial policymaking.[84] However, these countries also have the highest intra-group variability. Therefore, there is no standard or general approach to greening the financial system. The findings of the study show that the countries with the highest index values are in Asia Pacific and Northern Europe (Brazil, China, France, Indonesia, and South Korea). Türkiye has an index value below the average.[85]

Another empirical finding is that developed countries are leading the adoption of climate-related financial policies. Emerging economies joined the green financial policy formation process in the "second" wave. Although Türkiye is

---

[82] Paola D'Orazio, "Mapping the Emergence and Diffusion of Climate-Related Financial Policies: Evidence From A Cluster Analysis on G20 Countries", *International Economics* 169 (December 2022): 136, https://doi.org/10.1016/j.inteco.2021.11.005.

[83] Paola D'Orazio, "Measuring the Engagement in Climate-Related Financial Policymaking: The Climate-Related Financial Policy Index", SUERF Policy Brief, no. 383, 2022, https://www.suerf.org/docx/f_abe147752c8bd fa42ffb9a4aef3df1af_49871_suerf.pdf.

[84] D'Orazio, "Measuring the Engagement in Climate-Related", 1-5.

[85] Paola D'Orazio and Steffen Thole, "Climate-Related Financial Policy Index: A composite Index to Compare the Engagement in Green Financial Policymaking at the Global Level", *Ecological Indicators* 141 (2022): 13, https://doi.org/10.1016/j.ecolind.2022.109065.

also in the second wave of emerging economies, it is in the "latecomers" class when the policy-making process is taken into account.[86]

It has been empirically shown that central bank independence has a significant and positive contribution to the CRFPI index.[87] Masciandaro and Russo[88] have also stated that the ability of central banks to achieve a reduction in emissions is confirmed only for independent central banks that have the capacity to directly monitor the productive and polluting sectors. The CBRT's performance in green monetary policy is consistent with these empirical findings. This is because, although the CBRT has instrument independence as defined by law, its independence has become highly controversial due to the political interference it has been subjected to for a long time. Moreover, in a country like Türkiye with a high level of currency substitution, central bank independence is highly problematic from both a political and exchange rate perspective. Politically, the government directly intervenes in the central bank, while the central bank constantly needs to control the exchange rate for price stability.[89]

One of the most obvious indicators of political interference is that the central bank governor has been changed 7 times since 2006. This situation, which has severely damaged central bank independence in de facto terms, seems to be reflected in the monetary policy implemented within the so-called "Turkish Economic Model" specific to the country in the last few years. For a long time, Turkey's priority has been growth rather than disinflation. The monetary policy preferred in the struggle against inflation, which has become a global problem after the pandemic, partly due to the increase in demand and partly due to supply shocks, is a result of this preference and the intervention of the government that uses its preference in this direction. Despite interest rate rises in line with tight monetary policy in much of the world, from December 2020 to June 2023, the CBRT continuously reduced its policy rate. Far from controlling inflation, this policy exacerbated the problem. Indeed, in July 2023, Türkiye ranked second among G20 countries, after Argentina, with an inflation rate of 47.83%. Currently, Türkiye and Argentina are the only countries in the G20 with double-digit inflation.

---

[86] D'Orazio, "Mapping the Emergence and Diffusion", 143.

[87] D'Orazio ve Popoyan, "Do Monetary Policy Mandates and Financial Stability", 292.

[88] Donato Masciandaro and Riccardo Russo, "Central Banking and Climate Change Policies: It is not Always a Positive Sum Game", SUERF Policy Brief, no. 398, August 2022, 6, https://www.suerf.org/docx/f3ebfdb36a 1c7 82dd12d9780e51881a2c_51055_suerf.pdf.

[89] Mahfi Eğilmez, "Merkez Bankalarının Değişen Rolü ve Para Politikası", *İktisat ve Toplum Dergisi* no. 127 (Mayıs 2021): 31.

Table 7.4 CBRT Inflation Target And Realised Inflation (2006-2023)

Years	Inflation Target (%)	Realised Inflation (%)
2006	5	9,7
2007	4	8,4
2008	4	10,1
2009	**7,5**	**6,5**
2010	**6,5**	**6,4**
2011	5,5	10,4
2012	5	6,2
2013	5	7,4
2014	5	8,2
2015	5	8,8
2016	5	8,5
2017	5	11,92
2018	5	20,30
2019	5	11,84
2020	5	14,60
2021	5	36,08
2022	5	64,27
2023	5	58 (forecast)
2024	5	33 (forecast)

Source: CBRT.

As seen in Table 7.4, although the CBRT adopted the explicit inflation targeting regime in 2006, inflation has been above the target except for 2009 and 2010. Inflation has been in the double digits since 2017, when the new system of government, the Presidential Government System, was adopted. This period is also interesting in that it represents the period when the Central Bank was subjected to much more intense political interference. Despite the change in interest rate policy with the change of president in June 2023, inflation is expected to remain a headache for a long time to come. Forasmuch, in the most recent inflation report[90], the year-end inflation forecast for 2023 was raised from 22,3 per cent to 58 per cent. The end-2024 inflation forecast was revised upwards from 8,8 per cent to 33 per cent.

The most important reason for this is that the structural character of inflation, which cannot be solved by conventional interest rate policy, is ignored. Türkiye has a growth model with low domestic savings and constant dependence on

---

[90] TCMB, *Enflasyon Raporu,* Ankara, 2023-III, 59, https://www.tcmb.gov.tr/wps/wcm/connect/d2e5a80e-e1d4-44cb-9825-ab60782970b9/enf23_iii_tam.pdf?MOD=AJPERES&CACHEID=ROOTWORKSPACE-d2e5a.

external resources.[91] This implies an increase in domestic and external vulnerabilities due to international capital inflows and, hence, a frequent deterioration in price stability. One of the most important sources of current inflation in Türkiye is food inflation. The root cause of this is the bottlenecks in the agricultural sector. Excessive use of fertilizers in production, production declines due to global warming and low productivity, high input costs[92] and the decreasing area of agricultural land every year are among the major structural problems. In addition, other bottlenecks, such as the excessive import dependence of fossil fuel-dependent industries and the increasing need for foreign capital in domestic industry[93], prevent the inflation problem from being solved permanently without structural reforms.

Although there is empirical evidence suggesting that central banks can also achieve their price and financial stability objectives if they address climate-related risks,[94] The CBRT's exposure to a high level of political intervention, the failure to address the structural problems underlying inflation and macroeconomic instability in general adversely affect the price stability performance of the central bank. The CBRT has been slow to take necessary and timely steps in the struggle against inflation, and its traditional monetary policy is likely to undermine the green transition's central bank initiatives. Moreover, price shocks (climateflation, fossilflation and greenflation) that are likely to emerge due to climate change may also affect Türkiye. Therefore, the CBRT needs to green its operations by developing green monetary policy tools as soon as possible. In fact, according to Yeldan, the CBRT's adoption of a green monetary policy would also improve its ability to achieve its price stability target.[95]

At least for now, the CBRT's performance in both price stability and green central banking seems to be much more dependent on the government's policies in this direction. However, progress in government policies seems to be rather weak and insufficient for the time being. In fact, in the Climate Change Performance Index (CCPI), which has been tracking the climate protection performance of 59 countries and the EU since 2005, Türkiye dropped 6 points to 47th place in 2023 compared to the previous year. Although Türkiye announced an update to its Paris Agreement Nationally Determined

---

[91] Özgür Orhangazi, "Türkiye Modeli'nin Bir Senesi", *İktisat ve Toplum Dergisi* no. 144 (Ekim 2022): 56.

[92] Erinç Yeldan, "Green Central Banking is a Necessity: Economist Erinç Yeldan Discusses Prospects and Opputunities in Turkey", *Green Central Banking News*, July 5, 2023, https://greencentralbanking.com/2023/07/05/green-central-banking-erinc-yeldan-turkey/.

[93] Erinç Yeldan , "Green Central Banking is a Necessity".

[94] Masciandaro and Russo, "Central Banking and Climate Change Policies", 6.

[95] Erinç Yeldan, "Green Central Banking is a Necessity".

Contribution (NDC) before the last Conference of the Parties (COP 27), it has not yet submitted its new target.[96] CCPI experts say that Türkiye has not been transparent in its NDC target discussion and climate action. They also criticize the fact that while some ministries are working towards a 2053 net-zero vision in the tackling climate change, there are no declarations, milestones or pathways towards this goal.[97]

However, most of Türkiye is located in the Mediterranean climate zone, one of the most vulnerable regions to the impacts of climate change. This means that the country is among the medium-high risk countries in terms of both current climate, climate change and variability, and future climate. Further, the physical impacts of climate change are being felt in tangible ways, with warmer winters, drier and hotter summers, changes in biodiversity and the retreat of mountain glaciers. Disasters caused by extreme weather events due to climate change and the social and economic losses caused by these disasters are increasing every year.[98] Despite high per capita emissions[99] and high climate change exposure, low governance performance also negatively affects the CRFPI. In these circumstances, the government's policy and its commitment to its international commitments will determine the green performance of the central bank, which depends on the country and the relevant institutional structures.

Another important category of the Scorecard is financial regulation. In the emerging economies group of the G20, China ranked first this time with 31 points, while Brazil ranked second with 18 points. With a score of 14 points, Indonesia is followed by the other EMs in the lower ranks with scores below 10 points (see Table 7.1). With a score of 2, Türkiye has made little progress relative to its performance in monetary policy. Nevertheless, considering that the maximum score is 50, it can be stated that the success in this category is still very limited for all EMs.

Policies in the Financial Regulation category can be evaluated by taking into account the proposed 4 basic approaches. One of them is to prevent the

---

[96] UN Environment Programme, *The Closing Window: Climate Crisis Calls for Rapid Transformation of Societies,* UN Emissions Gap Report, (New York: 2022): 16, https://www.unep.org/resources/emissions-gap-report.

[97] Climate Change Performnace Index (CCPI), *CCPI 2023-Country Scorecard,* 2023, https://ccpi.org/country/tur/.

[98] T.C. Çevre ve Şehircilik Bakanlığı, *Türkiye'nin Yedinci Ulusal Bildirimi,* (2018), 22, https://webdosya.csb.gov.tr/db/cygm/icerikler/yed-nc—ulusal-b-ld-r-m-20190909092640.pdf.

[99] Renita D'Souza and Debosmita Sarkar, "Climate Performance Index: A Study of the Performance of G20 Countries in Mitigation Observer", ORF Occasional Paper, no. 391 (February 2023): 24, https://policycommons.net/artifacts/3453254/climate-performance-index/4253575/fragments/on13Aug2023.CID:20.500.12592/kj976m.

underpricing of climate risks and to correct non-transparent risks. In line with this approach, it is suggested to capture climate-related financial data, make risk disclosures, classify green assets (taxonomy), conduct climate-related stress tests, and use macroprudential tools. The second policy approach is to undertake prudential and corporate governance reforms to reduce short-term carbon bias and improve the governance frameworks of financial institutions. Another suggested policy is to support the development of green financial securities. For this, instruments such as a standardized taxonomy of green assets, the preparation of low carbon indices and the issuance of active green bonds are recommended. The fourth policy is to actively promote climate finance using financial regulatory instruments. Instruments such as determining factors that support green investments and penalize brown investments, the minimum amount of assets on balance sheets and nominal carbon prices are tools that can be used within the scope of this policy.[100] The details of the green financial regulation policies of EMs in the G20 are shown in Table 7.5, ranked from the highest to the lowest score in this category in the Scorecard.

To achieve a medium impact score in this category of the Scorecard assessment, central banks and financial regulators should include in their scenario analysis banks and insurers that collectively hold a majority of assets. In addition, these scenario analyses should use the global warming scenarios developed by the NGFS of 1.5°C (best case scenario) and 4-5°C (worst case scenario), referred to as Hothouse World. In this context, central banks and/or regulators in countries that have performed relatively better in this category have begun piloting scenario analyses, particularly in line with the NGFS.[101] Among EMs, Brazil, China, Indonesia, Russia, Indonesia, Russia and Mexico do not have high impact scores but have medium impact scores. Türkiye and South Africa, which have the same score, do not score at the high or medium impact level. This means that the relevant policies should be seen as small but positive steps rather than having tangible long-term effects on the financial system. In Türkiye, BRSA has made a formal commitment to implement stress testing and scenario analysis that include climate risks by 2025.

In the aftermath of the global financial crisis of 2007-2008, macroprudential policies had an important role in green central banking actions as macroprudential policies were introduced, and financial stability was added to the objectives of central banks in addition to price stability. Again, as mentioned in the previous section, although there are different prudential governance models, coordination between the central bank and regulatory agencies is inevitable in models where central banks are supervisors. Green macroprudential regulations can be in various forms, such as climate-related scenario analyses, stress tests, capital

---

[100] Krogstrup and Oman, "Macroeconomic and Financial Policies",18.

[101] Green Central Banking, *Scorecard*, 18-19.

buffers, differentiated capital requirements, identification of systemically important financial institutions and additional capital charges.[102] In addition to these tools, central banks and financial regulators should incorporate climate-related risks into their risk management processes and implement explicit transition plans with clear criteria for financial institutions to be considered as policy instruments in this area.[103]

Table 7.5 Financial Regulation Policies of Emerging Economies in the G20

COUNTRIES (Central Bank / Supervisor)	FINANCIAL POLICY
Brazil: Banco Central do Brasil	• Financial institutions are required to disclose social, environmental and climate risks (medium impact) • Financial institutions are required to implement a policy for socio-environmental responsibility "consisting of a set of principles and guidelines involving social, environmental and climate-related aspects that orientate business conduct, company activities and relations with stakeholders" (updated regulation including climate) (medium impact) • Financial institutions are required to incorporate socio-environmental risks into their risk management and governance structures (updated regulation including climate risks) (medium impact) • Inclusion of climate risk scenarios in new and improved system-wide stress tests (formal commitment) (low impact) • BCB surveying financial institutions on the incorporation of climate risks into the risk management process, including exposure assessments, climate scenarios, stress testing and internal governance • CMN Resolution No. 4,968: financial institutions are required to integrate ESG into their internal control systems (referred to in bilateral interactions) (low impact) • Creation of new indicators to monitor social, environmental, and climate risk (formal commitment) • Public consultation on regulation of risk management and social, environmental and climate responsibility (low impact)
China: People's Bank of China and China Banking & Insurance Regulatory Commission	• Banks and insurance institutions are required to gradually reduce the carbon intensity of asset portfolios in an orderly manner and finally realise the carbon neutrality of asset portfolios (as per green finance guidelines) (medium impact) • Banks are required to incorporate environmental risks into risk management and governance processes (medium impact) • Banks are required to shift lending towards environmentally friendly projects (medium impact) • Banks are required to shift lending away from unsustainable projects (medium impact) • Mandatory climate risk disclosure for all financial firms (formal commitment) (medium impact) • Lower risk weights for green assets (under discussion) (medium impact)

[102] Dikau and Collins, "Green Central Banking in Emerging Market", 15-17.

[103] Green Central Banking, *Scorecard*, 19-20.

	• PBoC conducted stress tests of 21 commercial banks and two development banks; only focused on the effects of increased emissions costs on asset quality and capital adequacy levels; results published (low impact) • PBoC guidelines on environmental information disclosure for financial institutions: information on voluntary disclosures, which are encouraged to happen at least once a year (low impact) • CBIRC issued opinions on energy efficiency and emission reductions in credit extension, which provided "specific guidance on how banks can contribute to national environmental goals" (low impact) • CBIRC's Notice of Submission of Green Credit Statistics requires that the 21 main banks report green credit statistics (low impact) • CBIRC's Notice of the Key Performance Indicators of Green Credit Implementation, which established "quantitative and qualitative indicators for assessing performance" (low impact) • CBIRC issued guidelines on incorporating ESG requirements into the entire credit granting process (low impact) • Banks and insurance institutions are required to establish green finance organisation and coordination mechanisms and are encouraged to carry out innovation in green finance (under green finance guidance) (low impact) • Banks and insurance institutions are encouraged to incorporate ESG requirements into management processes, disclosures and interaction with stakeholders (under green finance guidance) (low impact) • CBIRC issued guidelines on environmental risk management systems (low impact) • Inclusion of green bonds in the green finance evaluation plan, which will assess the share of green bonds in financial institutions' total assets (low impact) • Banks and insurance institutions are guided to actively support the green and low-carbon development efforts under the Belt and Road initiative (under green finance guidelines) (low impact) • PBoC has said it will "not build coal-fired power plants abroad" (as the statement was vague and details are yet to be provided, this is a 'low impact' policy)
Indonesia: Bank Indonesia and Otoritas Jasa Keuangan	• BI has implemented borrower-based prudential measures for incentivising financing of green automotives and housing (medium impact) • BI, OJK and LPS are developing a climate-related stress test for the banking sector (formal commitment, referred to in bilateral interactions) (low impact) • BI accepts sustainable bonds within the macroprudential inclusive financing ratio (low impact) • BI is working in coordination with government departments to develop a carbon calculator to promote climate-related disclosures (formal commitment, referred to in bilateral interactions) (low impact) • BI is working in coordination with government departments to conduct a climate-related transition risks assessment of the Indonesian economy (formal commitment, referred to in bilateral interactions) (low impact) • BI is developing a green data centre to capture and record emissions of banks and debtors (formal commitment, referred to in bilateral interactions) (low impact)

	• BI is developing a framework for the regulatory and development direction of the green money market in Indonesia (formal commitment, implementation in 2024) (low impact) • OJK issued a clean energy handbook for financial institutions (low impact) • Integrated environmental factors into risk management (low impact) • Sustainable finance targets and submission of an annual sustainable finance action plan, as well as a sustainability report to OJK (low impact) • Checking if borrowers have a valid environmental license (low impact) • Development of sustainable finance products and/or services and building the human resources necessary to run sustainable finance programmes (low impact) • Allocation of a portion of corporate social responsibility funds to support sustainable finance implementation (low impact) • Integration of sustainable finance into vision, mission, governance, etc (low impact) • Engagement in external education on sustainable finance (low impact)
Russia: Bank of Russia	• Bank of Russia is considering raising capital requirements for lending to firms with insufficient climate disclosures (under discussion) (medium impact) • Bank of Russia considering reducing capital requirements for lending to green projects (under discussion) (medium impact) • Mandatory ESG disclosures (formal commitment) (medium impact) • Regulatory incentives for ESG financing (under discussion), including differentiated criteria for banks depending on exposure to climate-related financial risks (under discussion) (medium impact) • Bank of Russia to run stress tests on the impact of climate-related transition risks on major Russian exporters and the financial sector (formal commitment) (low impact) • Development of recommendations for financial intermediaries on the integration of climate-related risks into investment activities (formal commitment) (low impact) • Creation of a database on the occurrence and impact of natural disasters for insurance firms (formal commitment) (low impact) • Ran a consultation on the impact of climate change on the financial sector (low impact) • Developed guidelines for institutional investors on responsible investment principles (low impact)
Mexico: Banco de Mexico and Comision National Bancaria y de Valores	• Measures related to climate and environmental disclosure (under discussion) (medium impact) • Mandatory incorporation of climate into risk management practices of commercial and development banks (under discussion) (medium impact) • Climate scenario analysis of the financial system (formal commitment) (low impact) • Banking sustainability protocol: voluntary commitment to sustainable development by the members of the Asociación de Bancos de México (low impact)

	• Sustainable finance committee created a group on ISSB draft standards to promote the implementation of financial disclosure standards (low impact)
South Africa: South African Reserve Bank	• Integration of climate risks into Sarb's common scenario stress test of six systemically important banks (low impact) • Incorporation of climate change risks into supervisory framework (formal commitment) (low impact) • Incorporation of climate change risks into macroprudential monitoring framework (formal commitment) (low impact) • Incorporation of climate change risks into regulatory framework (formal commitment) (low impact) • Prudential communication to financial institutions on climate-related risks (low impact)
Türkiye: Central Bank of the Republic of Turkey and Banking Regulation and Supervision Agency	• BRSA stress test and scenario analysis, which incorporates climate risk (formal commitment, implementation in December 2025) (low impact) • BRSA to standardise ESG practices within regulatory infrastructure (formal commitment, implementation in December 2025) (low impact) • BRSA to encourage sustainable loans through incentive mechanisms within the microprudential regulatory framework (vague how this will be done, formal commitment, implementation in 2025) (low impact) • BRSA to increase of bank's climate risk management capacity through corporate structuring, risk analysis, risk management plans, reporting and elimination of data gaps (formal commitment, implementation in December 2023) (low impact) • BRSA creation of data infrastructure at sector, sub-sector, location and firm levels to analyse climate-related financial risks (formal commitment, implementation in December 2022) (low impact) • BRSA (2021) guidelines on loan origination and monitoring processes set expectations for banks on the development of policies on climate risks and environmentally sustainable lending (low impact) • BRSA raised the LTV ratio from 80% to 90% for housing with class A energy performance certificate and 85% for housing with class B (this measure was only in place for a few months before all LTV ratios were raised in response to Covid-19) (low impact)
Argentina:	-

Source: Author's own edit from, The Green Central Banking Scorecard 2022.

As one of the green macroprudential regulation tools, scenario analysis has an important place in the agenda of central banks as it is effective in identifying the risks posed by environmental degradation and shaping financial strategies and policies accordingly. However, scenario analysis to date has not reflected changes in capital requirements. The lack of historical evidence for scenario analysis based on historical data is a major limitation that prevents accurate measurement. For this reason, the Federal Reserve has stated that these analyses are different from stress tests and are exploratory in nature. However, the fact that climate-related risks have begun to have an impact on their inclusion in the Basel II[104] supervisory process is considered an important development.[105]

As clearly stated in its law, the CBRT is responsible for ensuring financial stability in addition to its main objective of price stability.[106] As mentioned earlier, macroprudential policies in Türkiye are implemented by the CBRT and the BRSA, and the coordination between these policies is planned to be ensured by the FSDC. In addition to the BRSA and the CBRT, institutions related to sustainable finance are the Banks Association of Türkiye (BAT), the Capital Markets Board (CMB), the Ministry of Trade, the Ministry of Treasury and Finance, and Borsa Istan

We can use the SBFN Türkiye Progress Report to analyze Türkiye's progress in financial regulation. SBFN's Türkiye Progress Report for 2022 reports the latest developments in the field of sustainable finance and reveals Türkiye's performance in the relevant field. The SBFN assessment is based on 3 pillars: ESG Integration, Climate Risk Management and Financial Sustainability. Each of these pillars is divided into preparation, implementation and maturation sub-stages, respectively. Each stage is further divided into two sub-stages: the preparation stage consists of commitment and formulation; the implementation stage consists of developing and progressing; and the maturation stage consists of consolidation and mainstreaming behavioural changes. Table 7.6 shows a matrix of the results of the SBFN Türkiye Progress Report.

Türkiye is at the "advancing" level of the "implementation" sub-stage in the area of ESG Integration. According to the SBFN report, Türkiye has a national framework addressing ESG risk integration and performance assessments. There are also continuing activities, implementation tools and initiatives to raise awareness and build capacity. In addition, financial institutions consistently report on their ESG practices, guidelines and templates. The main source of these advances is the strategic alignment activities of institutions promoting sustainable finance.

---

[104] The rapid growth of the global financial system and new financial instruments, as well as the use of different instruments and legal entities by financial institutions to escape regulation and supervision, have rendered Basel I inadequate in risk assessment. In response, the Basel Committee on Banking Supervision developed new rules called Basel II. Built on three pillars, Basel II is a risk-based integrated regulation. These pillars are minimum capital requirement, effective supervisory process and market discipline.

[105] Green Central Banking, *Scorecard*, 6.

[106] TCMB, *Türkiye Cumhuriyet Merkez Bankası Kanunu*, (14.01.1970), kanun no. 1211, 1-2, https://www.tcmb.gov.tr/wps/wcm/connect/4b4d0592-f3e1-46d2-9814-11e0ad94ab7c/Turkiye_Cumhuriyet_Merkez_Bankasi_Kanunu.pdf?MOD=AJPERES.

Table 7.6 Results of the SBFN Turkey Progress Report

	Preparation		Implementation		Maturing	
TÜRK YE	Commitment	Formulating	Developing	Advancing	Consolidating	Mainstreaming Behavioral Changes
ESG Integration				X		
Climate Risk Management		X				
Financing Sustainability			X			

Source: Author's own edit from SBFN, *Turkey Country Progress Report 2022.*

In 2014, BAT published the "Sustainability Guidelines for the Banking Sector" and updated it in 2021. BIST established the "BIST Sustainability Index" in 2014. The CMB issued the "Sustainability Principles Compliance Framework" in 2020. The BRSA prepared a "Turkish Banking Sector Sustainability Survey & Sustainability Report" and published "Sustainability Principles for the Banking Sector". In 2021, the same institution issued "Guidelines on Loan Origination and Monitoring Processes".[107] "Economic Reform Action Plan" was prepared by the Presidency of Strategy and Budget and the Ministry of Treasury and Finance, and the "Green Deal Action Plan" was also prepared by the Ministry of Trade. A working group is created in The Green Deal Action Plan, including the BRSA, the Ministry of Finance, the Central Bank and the CMB, to coordinate activities related to information exchange and green finance. In addition, 5 banks have joined the Task Force on Climate-related Financial Disclosure (TCFD) supporters since 2017. In 2017, the "Global Compact Turkey Sustainable Financing Declaration" was signed by 8 UN Global Compact member banks. In 2021, an independent "Climate Risks Report" was published in line with TCFD recommendations, and in the same year, banks issued sustainable subordinated sukuk and partnership-based green sukuk for the first time. The first green bond issuance at international standards was also made in 2016.[108]

According to the progress report, Turkey has started to implement a sustainable finance structure, accompanied by a range of tools such as guidance, principles, reporting, training, online tools and audit guidance. A number of 26 banks (representing 87% of Turkish banking assets) have an internal sustainable ESG strategy and policy established by the board of directors. A number of 15 banks (70% of the sector) report on all climate risks and/or climate risk management approaches. A number of 10 banks (50% of

---

[107] BDDK, *Sustainable Banking in Turkey,* May 2022, https://www.bddk.org.tr/Kurum Hakkinda/EkGetir/19?ekId=145.

[108] BDDK, *Sustainable Banking in Turkey.*

the sector) conduct environmental/climate risk-based scenario analyses and/or stress tests. A number of 4 banks (21% of the sector) have reported in line with the TCFD standards. Finally, approximately 13% of outstanding cash loans went through the environmental and social risk assessment process.[109]

In the field of Climate Risk Management, Turkey has passed the commitment stage, which is a sub-stage of the "preparation" stage, and has reached the "formulating" stage, which is the second stage. In this area, it has been evaluated that the BRSA, BAT and CMB have published principles and principles that include climate risk in risk management in the banking sector and capital markets. The preparation and activities undertaken include research, review and/or multi-stakeholder engagement and raising awareness of expectations in climate risk management.[110]

According to the SBFN Progress Report, Turkey is in the "developing" stage of the "implementation" phase in the Financial Sustainability pillar. The assessment found that there is a national framework in place to direct financial flows towards sustainability-related projects and sectors while at the same time building capacity to finance such activities and promoting awareness raising.[111]

The comparison between Turkey and emerging economies, which are also included in the G20, is shown in the matrix in Table 7.7. Table 7.7 shows that all emerging economies in sustainable banking and finance have passed the commitment stage in all three pillars but have not reached the "maturing" stage in any area except China and Indonesia. These results are also consistent with the overall scores in the "financial regulation" category of the scorecard, although the macroprudential governance structure varies across countries.

Governance models of prudential policies are an important variable in the adoption of climate-related financial policies. In the "central bank model", where the central bank has climate-related macroprudential regulatory authority, monetary and macroprudential policies are so intertwined that a clear distinction between the two policy objectives is ineffective and impossible. For instance, macroprudential measures to reduce carbon-intensive credits and redirect resources to sustainable sectors may conflict with the price stability objective of monetary policy. However, the "separate structure model" would benefit from central banks' expertise in analyzing systemic risk and coordination between the two policy decision-making processes while avoiding short-term political pressure. The research for G20 countries shows

[109] SBFN, *Turkey Country Progress Report*, 3.

[110] SBFN, *Turkey Country Progress Report*, 7.

[111] SBFN, *Turkey Country Progress Report*, 9.

that central banks that do not have explicit financial stability mandates or are at the bottom of the hierarchy use the "separate structure model".

Table 7.7 Comparative Results of SBFN Progress Report

	Preparation		Implementation		Maturing	
Developing Countries in G20	Commitment	Formulating	Developing	Advancing	Consolidating	Mainstreaming Behavioral Changes
ESG Integration			Argentina	Turkey Brazil Mexico S. Africa	China Indonesia	
Climate Risk Management		Turkey Argentina Indonesia Mexico S. Africa	Brazil China			
Financing Sustainability			Turkey Argentina	Brazil Mexico S. Africa	China Indonesia	

Source: Author's own edit from SBFN, *Country Reports, 2021, 2022.*

Central banks, where financial stability is characterized by the decisive role of the monetary authority, prefer the "central bank" or "separate committee" model. Accordingly, Turkey, Indonesia and Mexico use the "separate structure" model, South Africa and China use the "separate committee" model, and Russia, Brazil and Argentina use the "central bank" model.[112]

Since the CBRT is also in charge of supporting the Government's growth and employment policies, provided that they do not jeopardize the objective of price stability, it indirectly has a sustainability objective, similar to other G20 countries except Russia. In this case, the CBRT does not have any mandate obstacle in tackling climate and environmental risks, and it seems to have an advantage in adopting climate-related financial policies with its prudential governance model preference for a "separate structure" model. This is because a multi-part (complex) financial governance structure based on less integrated regulations has been empirically shown to be more successful in the adoption of climate-related financial policies.[113]

This is because when macroprudential policy authority is shared among institutions, each with technical expertise in its field, it makes decision-making on the implementation of new climate-related instruments much easier and more specialized.

---

[112] D'Orazio and Popoyan, "Realising Central Banks' Climate Ambitions", 109.

[113] D'Orazio and Popoyan, "Do Monetary Policy Mandates", 293.

Along with membership in climate-related international organizations, the establishment of a climate change department within the CBRT and the progress made by the financial sector are important but insufficient. In addition to research and exploratory analysis, the formulation of appropriate monetary policy instruments that can be used in the fight against climate change and close coordination with financial regulators is necessary and imperative. Apart from technical initiatives, it is also possible for central banks to increase the acceptance, knowledge and implementation of green finance by putting climate change and environmental issues more broadly on their agenda and signalling their importance to market participants. The use of reputable and powerful departments by central banks for these initiatives, which can also be called "soft power", will ensure effective results. Similarly, capacity building activities for investors and banks are also very effective methods.[114] The institutional capacity of the CBRT is sufficient and valuable in this respect. However, Turkey's unique macroeconomic stability issues naturally affect the performance of the CBRT and financial regulatory authorities in the field of green finance. One of these is the long-standing failure of the CBRT to achieve price stability. This has led to a decline in institutional confidence while creating an uncertain environment for the financial sector.

The BRSA's findings on the barriers to sustainable finance are also important. Many of these findings are in line with those expressed by Green Central Banking. Accordingly, there are problems that need to be overcome for sustainable finance in Turkey, one in the structural category and the other in the institutional category. Structural problems include macroeconomic uncertainties, low domestic savings rates and the short-term funding structure of the banking sector.[115] The last point, in particular, is a frequently mentioned problem in the context of risk assessments in the financial sector, focusing more on the short term.[116] The main problems in the institutional category are listed as follows:[117]

---

[114] Dikau and Volz, "Central Banking, Climate Change", 5.

[115] BDDK, *Sustainable Banking in Turkey.*

[116] David King et all., *Climate Change: A Risk Assessment,* ed. James Hynard and Tom Rodger, Simon Sharpe, (University of Cambridge: Centre for Science and Policy: 2015), 25; Ulrich Volz and Peter Knaack, "Inclusive Green Finance: A New Agenda for Central Banks and Financial Supervisors", The INSPIRE Sustainable Central Banking Toolbox Policy Briefing Paper, no.12, June 2023, 7, https://www.lse.ac.uk/granthaminstitute/wp-content/uploads/2023/06/INSPIRE-Sustainable-Central-Banking-Toolbox-Policy-Briefing-12.pdf.

[117] BDDK, *Sustainable Banking in Turkey.*

- The lack of a green taxonomy of economic activities,
- Lack of a standardized reporting practice in the real sector, particularly in SMEs,
- Lack of a system to verify reports with a second-party opinion,
- Lack of a carbon market for carbon pricing,
- Difficulties in following and internalizing emerging approaches and methods in risk management,
- Lack of a regulatory and supervisory framework for sustainability.

These problems also prevent the production of consistent, reliable and comparable data and the creation of institutional capacity, which are crucial for the financial sector and, in particular, for international transparency. These shortcomings also pave the way for greenwashing[118] behaviours that are increasingly becoming a global problem.[119] According to a report by the London School of Economics, the number of cases of this kind increased from less than 10 in 2020 to 26 in 2022.[120] Financial regulators see this as one of the key risks of green transform

Besides all these concrete problems, one of the most serious shortcomings of green central banking, not only for Turkey but in general, is that biodiversity loss is often overlooked. The exclusion of biodiversity loss as a secondary problem ultimately leads to an incomplete assessment of risks. EMDCs are particularly vulnerable to biodiversity loss.[121] The biodiversity-related macroeconomic risks discussed in the first part of our study make the job of central banks even more difficult. Potential supply shocks, especially in regions with large ecological services-dependent sectors, would put central banks in a dilemma between maintaining price stability and stimulating economic activity.[122] Moreover, the difficulty of measuring biodiversity loss, its non-

---

[118] Also called "climatewash", is defined as situations that challenge companies and sometimes governments due to misinformation or misleading green information or claims. It concerns misleading information or claims that products or services are more climate-friendly than they actually are.

[119] BDDK, *Sustainable Banking in Turkey.*

[120] Joana Setzer and Catherine Higham, "Global Trends in Climate Change Litigation: 2023 Snapshot", LSE Home, 2023, https://www.lse.ac.uk/granthaminstitute/wp-content/uploads/2023/06/Global_trends_in_climate_change_litigation_2023_snapshot.pdf.

[121] NGFS, "Central Banking and Supervision in the Biosphere", 65.

[122] Almedia et al., "Beyond Climate", 13.

linearity and forecasting difficulties cause a kind of "green swans"[123] for central banks.[124] It is therefore urgent and necessary to include not only climate change but also biodiversity loss in risk assessments. Central banks will be able to incorporate the risks associated with biodiversity loss into their monetary policy operations through both protective and proactive measures within their legal mandate. In other words, central banks should aim to mitigate the impact of biodiversity loss on their balance sheets through protective measures on the one hand and to reduce the impact of monetary policy on biodiversity through proactive measures on the other.[125] While it is accepted that central banks and financial regulators cannot address climate change on their own, they have the potential to make significant contributions with their competencies in areas such as prudential rules, disclosure, risk monitoring, appropriate accounting standards, stress testing, etc.[126] Therefore, central banks and regulatory authorities are expected to develop analytical methods that include biodiversity and incorporate all types of environmental risks into monetary and macroprudential policies.

The last category of the Green Central Banking Scorecard, "Example by Leadership", consists of policies such as the use and promotion of taxonomies and standards by central banks, greening non-monetary policy portfolios, providing training on environmental risk and green finance, and incorporating environmental principles into daily operations.[127] In this category, where the maximum score is 20, the countries with high scores are advanced countries. As mentioned earlier, advanced economies have a leading role in green central banking. The emerging economies with the highest scores in this category are Brazil, Indonesia and Mexico. The central banks of Indonesia, Mexico, and South Africa have so far committed to implementing "Socially Responsible Investment Principles".[128] The CBRT, on the other hand, was only able to score

[123] The term green swan is inspired by Nassim Nicholas Taleb's book "Black Swan". Black swan refers to rare, unexpected, extreme and unpredictable events. Green swan is also used to emphasize the similar nature of biodiversity loss and climate risks.

[124] Partha Dasgupta, "The Economics of Biodiversity: The Dasgupta Review", 2021, 425, https://assets.publishing.service.gov.uk/government/uploads/system/uploads/attachment_data/file/962785/The_Economics_of_Biodiversity_The_Dasgupta.

[125] NGFS, "Central Banking and Supervision in the Biosphere", 65.

[126] Minouche Shafik, "Opening Panel – How in Practice Can the Financial Sector Take Immediate Action Against Climate Change-Related Risks?", (Green Swan 2021: Coordinating Finance on Climate, Conference Volume, 2–4 June 2021), 6, https://www.bis.org/publ/othp31.pdf.

[127] Green Central Banking, *Scorecard*, 13.

[128] Green Central Banking, *Scorecard*, 20.

2 points as its policies in this area are still in their infancy. This result is consistent with its performance in monetary policy and financial regulation.

Conclusion

The current and future macroeconomic impacts of climate change and, more broadly, biodiversity loss inevitably make central banks and regulatory authorities one of the main actors in the green transformation. Of course, central banks are not the "only game in town" but the physical and transition risks of environmental problems, particularly climate change, target price and financial stability, which are essential conditions for macroeconomic stability. Although there are differences in institutional structures and practices across countries, the primary objective of almost all central banks is to achieve price stability. Particularly after the global financial crisis of 2007-2008, financial stability has generally been included in the objectives of central banks. According to different financial governance structures, central banks are institutions responsible for both price stability and, directly or indirectly, financial stability. Since macroeconomic stability is a prerequisite for sustainable growth and development, central banks cannot be expected to stay out of the green transformation process.

The involvement of central banks in the green transformation process has given rise to the field of "green central banking", which has been the subject of much debate. The nature of these debates has moved beyond the question of whether central banks should be involved in the process to the question of how they should be involved. The debate in advanced economies is rather on whether central banks have the legal authority to achieve sustainability objectives or how these objectives can be achieved with the existing authority. It is seen that the importance attributed to the principles of institutional independence, accountability and transparency is at the heart of the authorisation debate. However, it is recognised that many central banks around the world have sustainability mandates, if not directly, then indirectly through supporting government policies. As a result, it is widely accepted that central banks do not need a separate mandate for green policies. Empirical studies to date suggest that developing or emerging economies are able to interpret their mandates more broadly and act more flexibly than developed countries. Indeed, in emerging economies or developing countries, the need for institutional independence or market neutrality is not much debated, often in line with the political form of governance. In a sense, this allows central banks to act more flexibly in line with the policy decisions of the country concerned and without prejudice to the price stability objective.

This study aims to analyse the CBRT's performance in monetary policy and macroprudential policies during the green transformation process, taking into account the debates on green central banking. Since the CBRT is responsible for ensuring financial stability together with the BRSA, the green practices of the BRSA are also included in the assessment. For this purpose, the results of the Green Central Banking Scorecard, which is based on the green monetary policy and financial regulation practices of the central banks and financial regulatory authorities of G20 countries so far, are used. Scorecard collects the data that constitute the basis for the scores it gives in 4 different categories from the literature, expert opinions and institutions in the relevant countries. The study attempts to contribute to the understanding of the CBRT's current performance by evaluating the CBRT's scores for each category in comparison with the emerging economy group within the G20.

The scores on the Scorecard indicate that the CBRT has so far failed in two categories, monetary policy and financial regulation, with a total of 2 points out of a total of 100 points. Even though the aggregate scores show that for the G20 as a whole, green central banking has moved from a limited area to the mainstream, differences across countries are striking. Within the group of emerging economies, the best performers in all categories are Brazil, China and Indonesia in terms of total score. The divergence within similar country groups is thought to be due to countries' government policies towards green transformation and different macroeconomic conditions rather than different interpretations of central banks' mandates. At this point, it is believed that the CBRT's performance has been affected by inflation and stability issues, which have been a long-standing problem and have been negatively differentiated within the G20 with Argentina. Turkey's failure to control inflation in the aftermath of the pandemic and the negative expectations for price stability at this point take away the comfort that would allow the central bank to focus on green transformation in the first place. On the other hand, a failure to control inflation will ultimately damage growth, thus greatly weakening the potential to realise the green transformation.

Although the CBRT indirectly aims at sustainability through its mandate, which allows it to support the government's growth and employment policies, it has de facto lost its instrumental independence due to both the structural problems of the economy and political interference. Moreover, since the structural causes of inflation have been ignored for a long time, it seems to have reached a point that cannot be resolved by conventional monetary policy. In our opinion, an independent monetary policy that takes into account the structural character of inflation will not only help to achieve price stability but will also pave the way for the central bank to play a more effective role in the green transformation process. This would also relax the central bank's hand by making it easier to mitigate the expected negative risks of climate change. But this alone is not enough. Since the central bank has no direct sustainability mandate, it must be supported by government policies. Moreover, in a situation where independence is de facto abolished, the policies to be pursued by the government will also determine the role of the CBRT in the green transformation. Our observations within the scope of the study show that, unfortunately, government policies remain also weak in terms of green transformation. As it is known, although Turkey is one of the first signatories of the Paris Climate Agreement, it took a long time for the agreement to be approved by parliament. In setting 2053 as its net-zero target, Turkey is thought to be motivated by the 'Green Deal' due to its close economic ties with the EU. Especially the fact that the steps taken after 2021 are more is an indication of this. It is clear that the efforts that have been made, both at the level of governments and at the level of central banks and the financial sector, have been meaningful but quite inadequate. These efforts are rather limited to participation in international initiatives and official declarations. The most recent international assessments also emphasise that Turkey has not been sufficiently willing and transparent.

The fact that Turkey does not have a "high impact" score in any category of the Scorecard shows that long-term and result-oriented policies are not yet in place. Moreover, Turkey is geographically located in the Mediterranean Basin, one of the regions that will be most affected by climate change. Therefore, we believe that Turkey, and therefore the central bank and the financial sector, should take decisive and concrete steps not only with EU motivation but also independently. As the accumulated burden of structural problems grows, the cost to the country is likely to be very high, as it will not be able to focus sufficiently on the opportunities as well as the threats of climate change. Climate change is a global problem and the challenge must also be global. In this respect, it is also crucial for Turkey to remain faithful to its international commitments, to act transparently and to access international financial support to manage the transition process. It is equally important for the central bank to provide leadership to the financial sector by further strengthening its existing institutional capacity and tools in order to ensure that the process is conducted properly and effectively. It is, therefore, not an option but a necessity to implement highly effective monetary and macroprudential policies as soon as possible.

Bibliography

Almeida, Elena, Simon Dikau, Nick Robins, Jeanne Stampe, Romain Svartzman, Thomas Viegas and Ulrich Volz. "Beyond Climate: Addressing Financial Risks From Nature and Biodiversity Loss". The INSPIRE Sustainable Central Banking Toolbox Policy Briefing Paper 09, December 2022. Accessed 10 June 2023 https://www.inspiregreenfinance.org/wp-content/uploads/2022/12/INSPIRE-Sustainable-Central-Banking-Toolbox-Policy-Briefing-Paper-9.pdf.

BDDK. *Sustainable Banking in Turkey.* May 2022. Access 05 June 2023. https://www.bddk.org.tr/KurumHakkinda/EkGetir/19?ekId=145.

Berensmann, Kathrin and Nannette Lindenberg. "Green Finance: Actors, Challenges and Policy Recommendations". *German Development Institute Briefing Paper* 23 (2016). Access 08 May 2023 https://www.idos-research.de/uploads/media/BP_23.2016.pdf

Bolton, Patrick, Morgan Després, Luiz Awazu Pereira Da Silva, Frédéric Samama, Romain Svartzman. "Green Swans: Central Banks in the Age of Climate-Related Risks". *Bulletin de la Banque de France* 229, 8 (May-June 2020). Access 05 May 2023. https://Publications.Banque-France.Fr/Sites/Default/Files/Medias/Documents/82 0154_Bdf229-8_Green_Swans_Vfinale.Pdf.

Boneva, Lena, Gianluigi Ferrucci and Paolo Mongelli. "Climate Change and Central Banks: What Role For Monetary Policy?". *Climate Policy* 22, no.6 (May 2022): 770-787. Accessed 03 May 2023 doi: 10.1080/14693062.2022.2070119.

Carney, Mark. "Breaking The Tragedy of The Horizon – Climate Change and Financial Stability". BIS Central Bankers' Speeches, London, 2015. Accessed 02 July 2023 https://www.bis.org/review/r151009a.pdf.

Climate Change Performance Index (CCPI). *CCPI 2023-Country Scorecard.* https://ccpi.org/country/tur/.

Cœuré, Benoît. "Monetary Policy and Climate Change". Speech at a conference on "Scaling up Green Finance: The Role of Central Banks", organised by the Network for Greening the Financial System, the Deutsche Bundesbank and the Council on Economic Policies, Berlin, 8 November 2018. Accessed 03 May 2023 https://www.bis.org/review/r181109f.pdf.

Costa, Moriah. "BaFin to Reign in Greenwashing as Part of New Sustainability Strategy ". The Green Central Bank News. 17 July 2023. Access 30 July 2023 https://greencentralbanking.com/2023/07/17/bafin-greenwashing-strategy/.

D'Orazio, Paola and Lilit Popoyan. "Do Monetary Policy Mandates and Financial Stability Governance Structures Matter for The Adoption of Climate-Related Financial Policies?". *International Economics* no. 173 (January 2023): 284-295. Accessed 03 May 2023 https://doi.org/10.1016/j.inteco.2023.01.004.

D'Orazio, Paola and Lilit Popoyan. "Realising Central Banks' Climate Ambitions Through Financial Stability Mandates", *Intereconomics* 57, 2 (2022): 103-111. Access 01 July 2023. https://www.intereconomics.eu/contents/year/2022/number/2/article/realising-central-banks-climate-ambitions-through-financial-stability-mandates.html.

D'Orazio, Paola and Steffen Thole. "Climate-related Financial Policy Index: A Composite Index to Compare The Engagement in Green Financial Policymaking at the Global Level". *Ecological Indicators* 141 (2022): 1-17. Accessed 03 June 2023 https://doi.org/10.1016/j.ecolind.2022.109065.

D'Orazio, Paola. "Mapping The Emergence and Diffusion of Climate-Related Financial Policies: Evidence From a Cluster Analysis on G20 Countries". *International Economics* 169 (December 2022): 135-147. Accessed 10 June 2023 https://doi.org/10.1016/j.inteco.2021.11.005.

D'Orazio, Paola. "Measuring The Engagement in Climate-Related Financial Policymaking: The Climate-Related Financial Policy Index". SUERF Policy

Brief no. 383 (2022). Access 10 May 2023. https://www.suerf.org/docx/f_abe147752c8bdfa42ffb9a4aef3df1af_49871_suerf.pdf.

D'Souza, Renita and Debosmita Sarkar. "Climate Performance Index: A Study of the Performance of G20 Countries in Mitigation Observer. ORF Occasional Paper no. 391 (February 2023).

Dafermos, Yannis, Daniela Gabor, Maria Nikolaidi, Frank van Lerven. "Greening Collateral Frameworks". The INSPIRE Sustainable Central Banking Toolbox Briefing Paper 07 (August 2022). Access 20 July 2023 https://www.lse.ac.uk/granthaminstitute/wp-content/uploads/2022/08/INSPIRE-Sustainable-Central-Banking-Toolbox-Policy-Briefing-Paper-7.pdf.

Dasgupta, Partha. "The Economics of Biodiversity: The Dasgupta Review". 2021. Access 15 June 2023 https://assets.publishing.service.gov.uk/government/uploads/system/uploads/attachment_data/file/962785/The_Economics_of_Biodiversity_The_Dasgupta.

Dikau, Simon and Josh Ryan-Collins. "Green Central Banking in Emerging Market And Developing Country Economies". *New Economics Foundation* (July 2017). Accessed 20 July 2023 https://neweconomics.org/uploads/files/Green-Central-Banking.pdf.

Dikau, Simon and Ulrich Volz. "Central Bank Mandates, Sustainability Objectives and the Promotion of Green Finance". *Ecological Economics* 184, (2021): 103-111. Access 05 July 2023. Access 03 May 2023. https://doi.org/10.1016/j.ecolecon.2021.107022.

Dikau, Simon and Ulrich Volz. "Central Bank Mandates, Sustainability Objectives and the Promotion of Green Finance". SOAS Department of Economics, Working Paper no. 222 (March 2019). Accessed 10 June 2023 https://www.soas.ac.uk/sites/default/files/2022-10/economics-wp222.pdf.

Dikau, Simon and Ulrich Volz. "Central Banking, Climate Change and Green Finance". ADBI Working Paper Series no. 867 (September 2018). Access 03 June 2023. https://www.adb.org/sites/default/files/publication/452676/adbi-wp867.pdf.

Dinçer, Nazire Nergis. "Merkez Bankaları Değişiyor mu?". *İktisat ve Toplum Dergisi* no. 127 (Mayıs 2021): 4-11.

Eames, Nikki. "Green Central Banking Goes Mainstream, But Words Aren't Yet Matched by Actions". Green Centralbanking News 24 November 2022. Access 30 July 202 https://greencentralbanking.com/2022/11/24/green-central-banking-goes-mainstream/.

Eğilmez, Mahfi. "Merkez Bankalarının Değişen Rolü ve Para Politikası". *İktisat ve Toplum Dergisi* no. 127 (Mayıs 2021): 29-31.

Green Central Banking. *The Green Central Banking Scorecard 2022 Edition.* Surry Hills: November 2022. https://positivemoney.org/publications/green-central-banking-scorecard-2022/

Gürbüz, Z., Yeşim, Gilbert Koenig ve İrem Zeyneloğlu. *Para Politikası, Makro İhtiyati Politikalar ve Finansal İstikrar.* İstanbul: Kriter Yayıncılık, 2020.

IPBES. *The Global Assessment Report on Biodiversity and Ecosystem Services: Summary for Policymakers.* Bonn, 2019. Accessed 11 July 2023. https://zenodo.org/record/3553579

IPCC. *Special Report: Global Warming of 1,5 °C: Summary for Policymakers.* Switzerland, 2018. Access 05 June 2023. https://www.ipcc.ch/site/assets/uploads/2018/11/SR1.5_SPM_Low_Res.pdf

IPCC. *Climate Change 2014: Synthesis Report.* Geneva, Switzerland, 2014. Access 05 May 2023. https://www.ipcc.ch/site/assets/uploads/2018/02/SYR_AR5_FINAL_full.pdf.

King, David, Daniel Schrag, Zhou Dadi, Qi Ye and Arunabha Ghosh. "Climate Change: A Risk Assessment". 2015. https://www.csap.cam.ac.uk/media/uploads/files/1/climate-change—a-risk-assessment-v11.pdf.

Klooster, Jens Van't and Clément Fontan. "The Myth of Market Neutrality: A Comparative Study of the European Central Bank's and the Swiss National Bank's Corporate Security Purchases". *New Political Economy* 25, no.23 (August 2019). Access 10 May 2023 doi: 10.1080/13563467.2019.1657077

Krogstrup, Signe and William Oman. "Macroeconomic and Financial Policies for Climate Change Mitigation: A Review of the Literature". IMF Working Paper 19, 185, (September 2019). Access 10 June 2023 https://www.imf.org/en/Publications/WP/Issues/2019/09/04/Macroeconomic-and-Financial-Policies-for-Climate-Change-Mitigation-A-Review-of-the-Lite.

Masciandaro, Donato and Riccardo Russo. "Central Banking and Climate Change Policies: It is not Always a Positive Sum Game". SUERF Policy Brief no. 398 (August 2022). Access 10 June 2023 https://www.suerf.org/wp-content/uploads/2023/12/f_3ebfdb36a1c782dd12d9780e51881a2c_51055_suerf.pdf.

Monnin, Pierre. "Central Banks and the Transition to a Low-Carbon Economy". CEP Discussion Note, 1 (2018).

NGFS. "Biodiversity And Financial Stability: Exploring the Case for Action". NGFS Occasional Paper, 2021. Access 03 July 2023. https://www.ngfs.net/sites/default/files/medias/documents/biodiversity_and_financial_stability_exploring_the_case_for_action.pdf.

NGFS. "Central Banking and Supervision in the Biosphere: An Agenda for Action on Biodiversity Loss, Financial Risk And System Stability". NGFS Occasional Paper, 2022. Access 03 July 2023. https://www.ngfs.net/sites/default/files/medias/documents/central_banking_and_supervision_in_the_biosphere.pdf.

Oktar, Suat, Erkan Tokucu ve Zekayi Kaya. *Finansal Küreselleşme Sürecinde Merkez Bankacılığı ve Para Politikaları.* 2. Basım. Ankara: Nobel Yayınları, 2013.

Orhangazi, Özgür. "Türkiye Modeli'nin Bir Senesi". *İktisat ve Toplum Dergisi* no. 144 (Ekim 2022): 54-60.

Resmi, Gazete. 31491, (20.05.2021), Kanun no. 7319/3. Md. Access 30 July 2023 https://www.resmigazete. gov.tr/eskiler/2021/05/20210525-12.htm.

Resmi Gazete. "Sigortacılık İle Diğer Bazı Alanlara İlişkin Kanunlarda ve Bir Kanun Hükmünde Kararnamede Değişiklik Yapılmasına Dair Kanun", 31491, (20.05.2021), Kanun no. 7319/3. Md. https://www.resmigazete.gov.tr/eskiler/2021/05/20210525-12.htm.

Robins, Nick, Simon Dikau and Ulrich Volz. "Net-zero Central Banking: A New Phase in Greening the Financial System". Grantham Research Institute on

Climate Change and the Environment Policy Report. (March 2021). Accessed 10 June 2023 https://www.lse.ac.uk/granthaminstitute/wp-content/uploads/2021/03/Net-zero-central-banking.pdf.

Sachs D, Jeffry. *Sürdürülebilir Kalkınma Çağı,* trans. Barış Gönülşen. İstanbul: Yeditepe Üniversitesi Yayınevi, 2019.

Sak, Güven. "İklim Değişimi". *İktisat ve Toplum Dergisi* no. 139 (Mayıs 2022): 36-48.

SBFN. "Turkey Country Progress Report: Supplement to the 2021 Global Progress Report of The Sustainable Banking and Finance Network". March 2022. Access 10 July 2023 https://sbfnetwork.org/wp-content/uploads/pdfs/2021_Global_Progress_Report_Downloads/2021_Country_Progress_Report_Turkey.pdf.

Schnabel, Isabel. "A New Age of Energy Inflation: Climateflation, Fossilflation and Greenflation". Speeches at a panel on "Monetary Policy and Climate Change" at The ECB and its Watchers XXII Conference, Frankfurt, March 17, 2022. Access 10 June 2023. https://www.bis.org/review/r220317b.pdf.

Schoenmaker, Dirk. "Greening Monetary Policy". *Climate Policy* 21, no.4 (January 2021): 581-592 doi: 10.1080/14693062.2020.1868392.

Setzer, Joana and Catherine Higham. *Global Trends in Climate Change Litigation: 2023 Snapshot.* London, 2023. Access 31 July 2023 https://www.lse.ac.uk/granthaminstitute/wp-content/uploads/2023/06/Global_trends_in_climate_change_litigation_2023_snapshot.pdf.

Seyidoğlu, Halil. *İktisat Biliminin Temelleri.* 2. Baskı. İstanbul: Güzem Can Yayınları, 2011.

SFWG. "Presidency and Co-Chairs Note on Agenda Priorities". G20 First Sustainable Finance Working Group Meeting: 2-3 February, 2023. Access 30 July 2023. https://g20sfwg.org/wp-content/uploads/2023/03/SFWG-Presidency-and-Co-Chairs-Note-on-Agenda-Priorities.pdf.

Shafik, Minouche. "Opening Panel–How in Practice Can The Financial Sector Take Immediate Action Against Climate Change-Related Risks?". Green Swan 2021: Coordinating Finance on Climate, Conference, Volume, 2–4 June 2021. Accessed 14 June 2023 https://www.bis.org/events/green_swan_2021/overview.htm.

Şimandan, Radu, Cristian Valeriu and Bogdan Glăvan. "Post Pandemic Greenness? How Central Banks Use Narratives to Become Green". *Sustainability* 15, 1630 (2023): 1-28. https://doi.org/10.3390/su 15021630.

T.C. Çevre ve Şehircilik Bakanlığı. *Türkiye'nin Yedinci Ulusal Bildirimi.* 2018. Access 30 July 2023 https://webdosya.csb.gov.tr/db/cygm/icerikler/yed-nc—ulusal-b-ld-r-m-20190909092640.pdf.

TCMB. *Enflasyon Raporu.* 2021, 2022. Access 30 July 2023 https://www.tcmb.gov.tr/wps/wcm/connect/tr/tcmb+tr/search+results?search-

TCMB. *Enflasyon Raporu.* 2023, III. Access 30 July 2023 https://www.tcmb.gov.tr/wps/wcm/connect/d2e5a80e-e1d4-44cb-9825-ab60782970b9/enf23_iii_tam.pdf?MOD=AJPERES&CACHEID=ROOTWORKSPACE-d2e5a

TCMB. *Yıllık Faaliyet Raporu.* 2022. Access 30 July 2023. https://www3.tcmb.gov.tr/yillikrapor/2022/tr/index .html.

TCMB. "Türkiye Cumhuriyet Merkez Bankası Kanunu," Kanun No. 1211 (1970). Access 30 July 2023 https://www.tcmb.gov.tr/wps/wcm/connect/4b4d0592-f3e1-46d2-9814-11e0ad94ab7c/Turkiye_Cumhuriyet_Merkez_Bankasi_Kanunu.pdf?MOD=AJPERES.

Türkeş, Murat. "Küresel İklim Değişikliği Nedir? Temel kavramlar, Nedenleri, Gözlenen ve Öngörülen Değişiklikler". *İklim Değişikliği ve Çevre* 1, no.1 (2008): 26-37, https://dergipark.org.tr/tr/download/article-file/518059.

Türkeş, Murat. "Sera Gazları, Kuvvetlenen Sera Etkisi ve Küresel İklim Değişikliği". *İktisat ve Toplum* no.129 (July 2021): 4-17.

UN Environment Programme. *The Closing Window: Climate Crisis Calls for Rapid Transformation of Societies Emissions Gap Report.* New York, 2022. Access 30 July 2023 https://www.unep.org/resources/emissions-gap-report.

UN Environment Programme. *United Nations Framework Convention on Climate Change.* New York, 1992. https://unfccc.int/resource/docs/convkp/conveng.pdf.

Volz, Ulrich and Peter Knaack. "Inclusive Green Finance: A New Agenda for Central Banks and Financial Supervisors". The INSPIRE Sustainable Central Banking Toolbox Policy Briefing Paper no.12. June 2023. Accessed 05 June 2023 https://www.lse.ac.uk/granthaminstitute/wp-content/uploads/2023/06/INSPIRE-Sustainable-Central-Banking-Toolbox-Policy-Briefing-12.pdf.

Yeldan, Erinç. "Green Central Banking is a Necessity: Economist Erinç Yeldan Discusses Prospects and Opportunities in Turkey". Written by Scott Speer. *Green Central Banking: News*, 5 July 2023. Access 30 July 2023https://greencentralbanking.com/2023/07/05/green-central-banking-erinc-yeldan-turkey/.

Yeldan, Erinç. "Paris Sözleşmesi'nin Beşinci Yılı". *İktisat ve Toplum Dergisi* no.123 (Ocak 2021): 28-31.

Chapter 8

Central Bank Digital Currency: Redefining the Concept of Money in a Digital Context

Aatos Hallipelto

Helsinki School of Economics, CEO, Finland

Cumhur C. Küçüközmen

Izmir University of Economics, Turkey

Abstract

Money is an ancient subject, as the history of money shows. We have been talking about money and its effects for millennia. Today, money is still relevant because the digital revolution is changing the role and nature of money perhaps more radically than ever before. Digitalisation shows money can take many forms. It can be in your pocket or wallet as physical money, i.e. notes and coins, or increasingly on a card with a chip or in a smartphone in a digital wallet. Among all these different manifestations of money, the physical form of money, i.e. cash, is a unique group. Cash possesses certain 'essential' properties that define it as both cash and money. Today, we can ask whether cash can exist in a digital form. Only a few decades ago, cash, or its paper equivalents, was almost the only way to make payments. This era is slowly coming to an end. Due to digitalization, the increase in contactless payments and online shopping has led to an even greater shift away from cash payments. However, the rate of change varies from country to country. The endpoint of the growth of cashless payment options would be a completely cashless society. It means that financial transactions are no longer conducted with physical notes or coins, but only with digital information and associated payment methods. The development towards a cashless society has both disadvantages and benefits. From the point of view of an individual, a consumer, we can evaluate and analyse the benefits and disadvantages of a cashless society, inter alia, with the help of the basic properties of cash. The conclusion of the evaluation and analysis is obvious: a situation where a person does not have access to cash, or it is only limited, has a great impact on the realisation of equality and the development of inequality, as well as the realisation of financial inclusion. Some scientists and other experts predict that physical cash has come to its end stop. And the driving force behind this change is not cell phones or credit cards but central banks. In addition to the increase in cashless payments, the emergence of cryptocurrencies encourages central banks to develop their own more stable digital currencies. These have a common established designation: Central Bank Digital Currency (CBDC). A Central Bank Digital Currency is the digital form of a country's fiat currency that is also a claim on the central bank. Instead of printing money, the central bank issues electronic coins or accounts backed by the full faith and credit of the government. However, it is unlikely that the endpoint of cash transformation could lead to a totally cashless society, and that this would be based on legislation, which would remove all physical money from circulation after the introduction of CBDC. Strong indications from the direction of the ECB, the EU Commission, and the FED say that CBDC will not displace cash but will come alongside it and complement it. At the same time, various cryptocurrencies are challenging the so-called fiat money created by central banks. These financial products based often on blockchain technology have many creative solutions that can lead the way to an increasingly efficient and fair way of making various financial contracts, but their ability to retain their value is largely based only on the faith of their owners. More research, analysis and pilot testing of the impact of CBDC implementation on both retail and international financial markets is needed. At the same time, the competition for the future of money increases when the concept of money has to be redefined in a digital context because the monetary system is increasingly diversified according to the purpose of use. Some forms of money can be convenient, specifically as a medium of exchange, another in international trade and a third in the sense of preserving value.

Keywords: Digitalization, Central Bank Digital Currency, Future of Money

***

Introduction

Today, money can take many forms due to digitalisation. Multiple forms of money include the following:

- Central bank money is a liability of the central bank to the bearer of money. Today central bank money appears in the form of physical currency to the general public, issued by the central bank, and digital balances held by commercial banks at the central bank.
- Commercial bank money is the digital form of money that is most commonly used by the public. Commercial bank money is held in accounts at commercial banks.
- Nonbank money is digital money held as balances at nonbank financial service providers. These private firms typically conduct balance transfers on their own books using a range of technologies, including mobile apps.

Money available to the public can take different forms. It can be in your pocket or wallet as physical money, i.e. notes and coins, or increasingly on a card with a chip or in a smartphone in a digital wallet. However, among all these different manifestations of money, the physical form of money, i.e. cash, is a unique group. Today, we can raise a question: can cash take a digital form? In order to assess what digital cash would be like, we first need to understand the basic principles that make cash unique. These are also essential aspects when evaluating and illustrating issues related to digital central bank money and digital private money (nonbank money). The essence of cash consists of those properties that make cash what it is essentially and which properties it must necessarily have in order to exist. We can call these properties "essentials", indicating that cash must have them in order to be both cash and money.

These essential properties of cash are: 1) cash is a bearer instrument, 2) the counterparty of cash is a central bank, and it is the only method of payment offered by a central bank to the general public, 3) cash has the status of legal tender, 4) all payment transactions made in cash are private peer-to-peer payments and 5) payments made in cash are real-time and secure.

Traditionally functions of money are listed as follows: money serves as a means of payment, a store of value, and a unit of account. Unique features of cash, i.e. properties listed above, emphasise that among payment instruments, cash is more than a means of payment. Anyone can make money transfers anytime, anywhere and without third parties. It follows the fact that cash has a strong protection of privacy and autonomy, as no external service providers are required. A cash-based peer-to-peer payment also does not require electricity, a network connection, or external intermediaries or equipment. The identities of the payer and recipient are not recorded in the registers, like when paying by card, bank transfer or mobile payment. There are also no records of other information about the payment transaction, such as the time, amount, and basis of the payment. This anonymous payment method does not collect data on, for example, personal consumption behaviour or location.[1]

However, the anonymous payment method also has its downside, as it allows cash to be used for criminal purposes such as money laundering and terrorism finance. However, in addition to cash, crimes can also be committed with digital assets. For example, the EU, in addition to existing AML/CTF regulation, aims to prevent criminals and terrorists from circumventing AML regulation by using cryptocurrencies.[2]

---

[1] Heike Mai, "Cash Empowers the Individual Through Data Protection", *Deutsche Bank Research,* (2 July 2019), Frankfurt am Main.

[2] European Parliament, "New EU Measures Against Money Laundering and Terrorist Financing", News, European Parliament, Press Releases ECON, (28 March 2023).

Cash also has other societal dimensions. Cash is available to all citizens, which is why it enables everyone to participate in society. This is important in terms of financial inclusion. Understanding the nature of cash and using it in a planned way also makes it easier to monitor a person's own income and expenses and can thus improve personal money management as part of financial literacy.

The concrete meaning of cash becomes especially clear in a bank-run situation. It is often based on the fear that a bank will become insolvent and will not be able to pay back depositors' funds. The concrete meaning of cash becomes particularly clear in banking situations. It is often based on the fear that the bank will become insolvent and will not be able to pay back depositors' funds. Deposit guarantee systems in different countries are a way for governments to protect deposits and secure their exchange into cash (1:1) in all situations up to the ceiling defined by law. The deposit guarantee system is especially important in uncertain situations to prevent a possible banking crisis.

The Challenges

The properties listed above are related to the essence of cash; in other words, without these properties, any material item is not cash or, more strictly interpreted, money at all. By analysing these properties, it is logically notified that converting cash into digital form is not a simple issue if all the properties of cash are wanted to be preserved.

Payment behaviour is influenced by several factors, such as payment habits, the availability of payment instruments intended for consumers, the acceptance of merchants and the amount of money in people's wallets. Demographic factors also influence behaviour but also preferences.

Only a few decades ago, cash or its paper equivalents (e.g. checks) were almost the only way to make payments. This era is slowly coming to an end. Even before COVID-19, many countries were on their way to a future of cashless (non-cash) payment. The increase in contactless payments and online shopping boosted by the coronavirus pandemic led to an even greater shift away from cash payments - but not at the same speed in all countries.

According to the ECB's SPACE study published in 2020, cash was still the dominant retail payment method in the euro area at points of sale and person-to-person payments, with a transaction share of 73 per cent. According to a study conducted three years earlier, the share was still 79 per cent of payments. However, in different types of payment situations, the use of cash varied considerably depending on the place of payment, the commodity to be purchased and the size of the payment.[3]

Looking at the countries of the euro area, the fewest cash payments, or about 0.5 payments per day per person, were made in the Netherlands, Estonia, and Finland, while the most, or about 1.6 per day per person, were made in Greece, Italy, and Portugal.[4]

The endpoint of the growth of cashless payment options would be a completely cashless society. It means that financial transactions are no longer conducted with physical notes or coins, but only with digital information (a common, widely used electronic money presentation) and associated payment methods. The final death blow to cash in this dystopian development path would be to outlaw all cash use by legislation and remove physical money from circulation. Although digital cashless payment methods bring advantages, the end result of development, i.e. a cashless society, is not ideal according to many.

The Development Towards a Cashless Society – Disadvantages

The development towards a cashless society has both disadvantages and benefits. The following aspects of disadvantages can be taken into consideration.

One is related to the abstract content of cash: the counterparty of cash is the central bank, and cash is currently the only means of payment offered by the central bank to the general public. The existence of cash secures the possibility of withdrawing notes and coins from a personal bank account. If it is assumed that cash would disappear completely, the guarantors of the value of money would be private commercial banks, which, in principle, are also at risk of going bankrupt. This could undermine people's confidence in the entire monetary system if there is a fear that they would lose the ability to exchange the digital assets in their bank accounts for cash, especially in the case of a bank run. Under these circumstances, most people would probably put more faith in the central bank's promise. "*We cannot be 100% certain the state will redeem our claims and maintain a stable currency—as we have seen throughout history—but I would definitely argue that a claim on the state of Sweden is better than a claim on a commercial bank. And most will agree.*"[5]

In an unpredictable world, there is always concern about the vulnerability of the (financial) system. How sustainable is the technology supporting a cashless society? Natural disasters or even large-scale cyber-attacks can render entire

---

[3] European Central Bank (ECB), "Study on the Payment Attitudes of Consumers in the Euro Area (SPACE) – 2022", (December 2022).

[4] European Central Bank (ECB), "Study on the Payment Attitudes".

[5] Niklas Arvidsson, *Building a Cashless Society, The Swedish Route to the Future of Cash Payments*, (Stockholm, Sweden: Royal Institute of Technology, 2019), 79.

financial systems useless and prevent people from accessing their money or buying what they need. In this scenario, the old-fashioned, physical quality of cash seems reassuring.

Another point of view is related to the nature of cash as central bank money. If the general public's access to central bank money were to disappear, the access to payment systems that use cash would also disappear for those people who do not have an account in the bank (unbanked). Although this is not a major disadvantage, for example, in many eurozone countries, however, there are differences within Europe. Globally it is estimated that there are around 1.7 billion adults in the world who are unbanked. Thus, they have no access to smooth and reliable payment or deposit systems either.

In addition, vulnerable groups must be considered. Elderly people may not be as used to using the latest technology and may have a weaker ability to change physical forms of money and payment methods to new ones. Rural areas can also remain vulnerable due to weak broadband and mobile connections. People on low incomes or in debt also tend to find it easier to manage cash.

According to the Access to Cash report published before the COVID pandemic in 2019, up to one in five British citizens may be left behind in the transition to digital-only payment transactions.[6] Global poll made by EY (2019) on digital and cash payments indicates that while all respondents believe the end of cash is near, there are concerns over financial inclusion, data security and privacy that need to be ironed out.[7]

The conclusion is obvious: a situation where a person does not have access to cash, or it is only limited, has a great impact on the realisation of equality and the development of inequality, as well as the realisation of financial inclusion.

The third aspect related to disadvantages is the issues involved in *information security* [8] and privacy protection. During the pandemic, people made a lot of

---

[6] UK Finance, "Access to Cash Review", UK Payment Market Report 2018, Final Report (March 2019). (Note: UK Finance is a trade association for the UK banking and financial services sector, formed on 1 July 2017. It represents over 300 firms in the UK providing credit, banking, markets and payment-related services.)

[7] Ernst & Young (EY), "Cashless Society Benefits Financial Crime Prevention but Raises Concerns with Inclusion and Data Privacy," EY Press Release, (19 November 2019), London, GB.

[8] Information security is a broad concept. It means maintaining the availability, confidentiality, and integrity of information. Data security includes the protection of the confidentiality, integrity, availability, authenticity, and non-repudiation of user data. The

online and mobile purchases, and data breaches increased accordingly. According to the opposite view, giving up cash helps reduce theft and fraud.

The threats posed by organised cybercriminals are very real, and they often find new ways to breach established security systems. In addition to criminal activity, unauthorized use of personal data and weakening privacy protection are growing concerns closely related to security. Identity theft and compromised personal information are potential dangers in a cashless society, although privacy can also be compromised in other ways. In a digital environment, the customer must log in to the digital information system and payment intermediaries, i.e. third parties, will conduct all payment transactions. These transactions generally require that the user's personal information be stored in different registers. This is how a cashless society, digital payment transactions and digital assets will require you to leave a *digital footprint.*[9] Consumers are understandably concerned that big companies, including financial institutions, are collecting and tracking their personal data, money spending, and consumption habits.

The Development Towards a Cashless Society – Benefits

The following aspects can be considered. Many studies and articles show that digital cashless payment methods bring advantages to consumers in terms of speed, reliability, transaction costs, and ease. According to a Global poll made by EY, digitizing all financial transactions could lead to greater accountability and reduce the occurrence of black-market transactions. Respondents cite the top benefits of a cashless economy as being convenience (39%) and financial crime prevention (36%).[10] Some other studies also support the view that policies and technologies that enable the spread of cashless transactions have the desired effect on crime prevention. [11]

---

data to be protected can appear in several different forms. These include, for example, digital and physical records and the knowledge of people such as employees.

[9] A digital footprint is a set of data that has been created, for example, from online activities and communication (e.g. blogs, photos, videos, tweets, messages, forums, comments, clicks) and that can be traced back to an individual. Digital footprints can be used to find which device has downloaded or used the website, for example via phone or computer. It includes all digital traces left on the internet and social media networks. It can provide information about individuals or groups by calculating and deriving from the collected information what they like or are interested in, what they are looking for, where they are, what is their appearance, character, gender, etc. A digital footprint can also tell about a person's income, spending habits and money transfers.

[10] Ernst & Young (EY), "Cashless Society Benefits Financial Crime".

[11] Laura E Armey, Jonathan Lipow and Natalie Webb, "The Impact of Electronic Financial Payments on Crime", Information Economics and Policy 29 (December 2014).

Cash is often blamed for illicit financial transactions, such as money laundering, counterfeiting, bribery, corruption, finance of terrorism, tax evasion, etc. Because cash is virtually untraceable, it is a useful tool for criminals. Instead, digital currency is less easily exploited for criminal purposes and can be shut down quickly if it falls into the wrong hands. Therefore, when people use less cash or no cash at all, these crimes will decrease.

In addition, digital money is more difficult for criminals to launder. Cashless payments leave a digital trail that can be used to track down perpetrators. Finally, without access to a physical form of money, criminals are less able to finance their operations. There is a wide belief that all these factors together make it harder for crime to take place on a large scale.

The question is, with the recent decrease in cash transactions, have these deterred financial crimes? Is it safer to pay in cash or in other ways ultimately depends on the risk of physical theft and fraud on the one hand and cyber-related crime on the other in any given situation or location. In addition, it is also a question of whether the consumer has the ability to use available payment methods safely and whether he usually knows how to pay attention to security issues. It should also be noted that no current situation is permanent, and criminal activity is preferably carried out where the money is. Therefore, it is impossible to give a general, unequivocal answer to questions about the security of paying in cash or other ways and the security of different payment methods.[12]

Observing the publications and discussions related to the cashless society, it is - on a quite general level - noticeable that the banking sector and FinTech companies are the ones who advocate most often development towards a cashless society. On the other hand, some more critical comments are presented by researchers, mainly social scientists, but also consumer associations. The official statements (directed to citizens) of central banks, such as the ECB and other authorities, are mainly technocratic and rather narrow in their perspectives. However, positive views and explanations in favour of the development have also been presented.[13]

---

[12] Heike Mai, "Cash, Freedom and Crime, Use and Impact of Cash in a World Going Digital", *Deutsche Bank Research* (23 November 2016).

[13] Michelle Faverio, "More Americans Are Joining the 'Cashless' Economy", Pew Research Center, (5 October 2022); Sam Gazeley, "Are There Any Benefits to a Cashless Economy?" ABI Research, 2022; ABI Research, "Mobile Payments Market: Innovation Strategies for Future Success", Research Report, October 27, 2022; Digital Mahbub, "How Does a Cashless Society Reduce Crime?", (20 January 2023).

Cashless or cash less Society?

According to Eswar Prasad, these various financial innovations are small miracles compared to the huge experiments currently underway around the world. Large companies (such as tech giants known as the "Big Tech", consisting of companies Alphabet, Amazon, Meta (formerly Facebook), Apple and Microsoft and governments, including the EU, are competing to benefit from the possibilities of new financial technology. In this race for the future of money, the global financial players are on the edge of a major disruption affecting businesses, bankers, governments, and, finally, all of us. Digital transformation of money means redefining the concept of money in a digital context and separating its traditional functions as a unit of account, medium of exchange and store of value. A promise of the future is increased efficiency and flexibility, increased sensitivity to the needs of different consumers and better market access for the unbanked. The risk is instability, lack of responsibility and loss of privacy. [14]

But above all, Prasad foresees the end of physical cash. The driving force for this transformation will not be mobile phones or credit cards but rather central banks, spurred by the emergence of cryptocurrencies to develop their own, more stable digital currencies. Meanwhile, cryptocurrencies themselves will evolve continuously and unpredictably. The changes will be accompanied by snowballing innovations that are reshaping finance and have already begun to revolutionise how we invest, trade, insure, and manage risk.[15]

It is unlikely that Prasad's argument about the "end of physical cash" would be based on legislation and remove all physical money from circulation after the introduction of a digital central bank currency, at least if we look at developments in the Eurozone. In fact, the development in the Eurozone (countries using the euro) is the opposite. In connection with the CBDC development phase, the ECB has announced that the digital euro will not replace cash but will come alongside it.[16] A similar message has also been given by the U.S. Federal Reserve System (FED).[17]

---

[14] Eswar S Prasad, *The Future of Money - How the Digital Revolution Is Transforming Currencies and Finance*, Harvard University Press, (2021).

[15] Prasad, *The Future of Money.*

[16] European Central Bank ECB, "Digital Euro - FAQ on a Digital Euro", https://www.ecb,europa,eu/paym/digital_euro/faqs/html/ecb,faq_digital_euro,en,html; ECB, "The Eurosystem Cash Strategy - The role of Cash", https://www.ecb.europa,eu/euro/cash_strategy/cash_role/html/index,en,html.

[17] Federal Reserve Board (FED), "Frequently Asked Questions / Central Bank Digital Currency (CBDC)", (11 April 2023) https://www,federalreserve,gov/cbdc-faqs.htm.

The Eurosystem [18] is also committed to the principle that every individual in the Eurozone should be able to decide how to make day-to-day payments, regardless of their individual payment preference, geographical location, or technological savviness.[19]

Cryptocurrencies, such as bitcoin or stablecoins, have proven to be an unreliable store of value, and their use as a means of payment has not developed favourably either. It is also quite unlikely that cryptocurrencies, which are a form of private money, would gain a significant position on the agenda of central banks and governments, other than perhaps in the regulatory mind.

Official currencies, like the euro, consist of a monetary system designed and controlled by a state or, as regards the euro, by supranational structures. The euro is the single currency shared by a number of European Union countries that have adopted the euro. A total of 20 of the 27 EU Member States have introduced a common currency, the euro. Within the Eurozone, only the euro has the status of *legal tender*.[20] Article 128 (1) TFEU[21] lays down the legal tender status of euro banknotes, and Article 11 of Regulation EC/974/98 does so with regard to euro coins.

The status of legal tender means that the creditor is obliged, in principle, to accept a payment made in euros, which subsequently discharges the debtor from his payment obligation. There can be exceptions to this principle of mandatory acceptance, for instance, where the parties to a contract agree on another means of payment or where a refusal of cash is made in good faith. Limits to cash payments are also possible, for example, to combat tax evasion and money laundering.

In June 2023, the European Commission adopted a legislative proposal on the legal tender of euro banknotes and coins to safeguard the role of Euro cash, which must be accepted as a means of payment everywhere in the EU and

---

[18] The Eurosystem, which comprises the European Central Bank and the national central banks of the Member States whose currency is the euro, is the monetary authority of the Eurozone.

[19] Alejandro Zamora-Pérez, "Guaranteeing Freedom of Payment Choice: Access to Cash in The Euro Area", *ECB Economic Bulletin* 5 (2022): 91-106; ECB," Digital Euro".

[20] European Commission (EC), "Commission Recommendation of 22 March 2010 on the Scope and Effects of Legal Tender of Euro Banknotes and Coins (2010/191/EU)," EC L 83/70, Official Journal of the European Union, (30 March 2010).

[21] The Treaty on the Functioning of the European Union (TFEU) is one of 2 primary treaties of the EU, alongside the Treaty on European Union (TEU). It forms the detailed basis of EU law by defining the principles and objectives of the EU and the scope for action within its policy areas. It also sets out organisational and functional details of the EU institutions.

accessible for citizens and businesses. This proposal codifies and clarifies the judgment by the European Court of Justice in January 2021, which sets out the principles of legal tender.[22] The main objective of the proposal is to safeguard euro cash as a means of payment so that people will continue to be able to use it for their payments if they so wish. To achieve this goal, the proposal clarifies what legal tender means and sets out the rules for the mandatory acceptance of euro cash and possible exceptions to it. In addition, it also sets out what Member States need to do in order to ensure that cash is widely accepted and that it can be easily accessed by its users.[23]

In addition, in view of the establishment and potential issuance by the ECB of a digital euro (CBDC) with legal tender status, it is also important to regulate the meaning of legal tender for the existing physical form of the euro. In this way, it is possible to ensure consistency among the two forms (physical and digital) of the euro. In addition, the Commission's proposal seeks to address issues concerning the acceptance of cash that have emerged, which can lead to difficulties for citizens wanting to pay in cash.[24]

The Race to Define the Money of the Future

Money is about to undergo essential changes in the ways it is created, stored, transferred, and used. The changing nature of money will fundamentally affect how we understand money in the future. The background driving force is financial technology, which enables new ways of creating and using digital forms of money. These new forms of digital money have the huge potential to make payments faster, cheaper, and more secure and enable new economic activity and business models. These are changes that even could potentially transform the whole financial system both locally and globally.

The effects of digitisation can be seen in almost all of our activities: in the content of work and working methods, in managing social relationships, interaction and in the use of time (like social media), and in financial issues (like online banking and crypto assets). Digitalisation has changed our consumption habits, our thinking, and our culture. It has changed the way we live — in the light of human history in a very short time period. No wonder these effects are also visible in all tasks, products and services related to money.

---

[22] Court of Justice of the European Union, "Judgment of the Court (Grand Chamber) of 26 January 2021" (ECLI:EU:C: 2021:63).

[23] European Commission, "Proposal for a Regulation of the European Parliament and of the Council on the Legal Tender of Euro Banknotes and Coins", Brussels, (28 June 2023).

[24] European Commission, "Proposal for a Regulation", https://ec,europa,eu/eurostat/web/products-eurostat-news/-/DDN-20180115-1.

Digital forms of money creation, storage, transfer, and payment systems are already here.

At the heart of innovations is money. New innovative payment methods and instruments are already on the market and still emerging. Not long ago, cash was pretty much the only way to pay for purchases. Today, instead of cash, we are already accustomed to fluently using different forms of private digital money, such as online bank transfers, payment cards and applications on our smartphones or watches. These are changes that directly affect everyone operating in the financial markets, including central banks that are looking for a new role for themselves.

A new industry has emerged: financial technology (fintech). The term refers to technology, mainly information technology, which is included in the production, storage, transmission and use of banking, insurance, financial, investment or payment services. The term fintech companies is used to refer to growth companies that develop new financial technology or new services that utilise financial technology. Examples of fintech innovations and products are digital wallets, peer-to-peer money transfer and lending apps, robotic asset managers, crypto assets, and smart contracts.[25] And AI is also penetrating the online customer contacts of financial services.

Digital technology is also changing the shape of financial services and markets. When transaction and ownership information can be presented in one shared ledger, participants can transact with each other without the involvement of traditional financial intermediaries. At the same time, the automation and coordination of transaction processes among several stakeholders becomes possible. This, in turn, changes the costs and distribution options of financial products. The result could be the emergence of new private networks that would displace current intermediaries and enable greater automation and integration across borders and asset classes. On the other hand, this fast technological development could also create new opportunities for traditional banks, stock exchanges, custodians, and other financial market institutions if they embrace the opportunities of new technology without prejudice and adapt their business models accordingly.

State-of-the-art digital technology and advanced cryptography methods are the driving force for these changes. These enable consumers, investors, companies, and others to make money transactions directly using e.g. smart contracts, without going through banks, brokers, and custodians. Digital solutions

---

[25] Smart contracts are digital contracts (programs) stored on a blockchain that are automatically executed when predetermined terms and conditions are met. In this way all participants can be immediately certain of the outcome, without any involvement of intermediaries, or time loss.

by using blockchain technology, DLT (distributed ledger technology)[26] and NTF (non-fungible token)[27] are enabling the creation of a broad array of assets and offer novel ways to transfer value. It can cover from traditional financial instruments, such as stocks and bonds, to digitized versions of historically illiquid assets, such as art, real estate, and intellectual property. These new forms of assets have the potential to attract a large number of entities and investors and transform their participation by fuelling the rise of new financial products and business models.

The race for the future of money is on; the formation lap is over. The nature of this competition is extensive: all against all. Competitors include traditional banks, central banks, digital intermediaries as well as Big Tech companies. We can already see that developments are changing our perception of money and changing the way we buy, sell and invest. And it will probably shake up the current financial systems of various countries. Therefore, not only the aforementioned competitors but also the "audience", i.e. companies and consumers, must pay attention to these changes and adapt to them.

Challenge for Traditional Banks: KYC - Know Your Competitor

The first group of competitors consists of *traditional banks.*[28] The main task of the traditional banks has been to receive deposits and grant credit to both personal and business customers. In this way, the savings of households and other operators are directed to investments and partly also to consumption. In addition, banks' tasks include payment services and investment and asset management services. Banks also operate actively in the money and capital markets, i.e. they buy, sell and broker various financial instruments or securities.

Banks may face stiff competition from payment service providers or new digital intermediaries. If banks manage to maintain strong trust in banking and the banking sector, they can gain a competitive advantage based on this trust,

---

[26] Distributed ledger technology (DLT) is a database of information that's shared and duplicated across a network of computers in different locations. In contrast to a centralized ledger, it's a flexible system of recording information.

[27] Non-fungible tokens (NFTs) are assets that have been tokenized via a blockchain. They are assigned unique identification codes and metadata that distinguish them from other tokens.

[28] Here, the term "traditional banks" is used to mean commercial and saving banks, and other established financial institutions, as distinguished, inter alia, from online lenders, which are non-traditional players and new loan providers challenging established banking (usually "banks" for short).

which banks have the opportunity to exploit and perhaps even strengthen the share of traditional banking in money and payment transactions.

Today, banking business is extensively regulated. Regulation, like solvency requirements, competition, and changes in the operating environment, such as digitisation, will significantly affect banks' business models today and in the next few years. The rapid development of technology creates challenges but, at the same time, enables the creation of new kinds of customer experiences.

The Nordic countries are the most digital societies in Europe, which is also reflected in the Nordic banking sector's already made and future investments in digital business models. Traditional banks in the Nordic countries have moved quickly to digital financial services in recent years. A significant number of bank branches have been partially or completely closed, and personal banking service is more difficult to obtain. In addition to the number of bank branches, the availability of services is weakened by their limited service hours and appointment booking practices. Banking services are moving more and more online and to mobile devices that move with people. According to statistics, the Nordic banks are the pioneers of digitisation.[29]

This rationalisation is taking place in the whole EU banking sector as well. It continued to target bank branches, the number of which was further reduced in 2021. Compared to the previous year, the total number of branches in the EU-27 decreased by approximately 5.5%. [30]

It is reasonable to assume that, e.g. in Europe, customers increasingly demand better banking service and clear personal added value, which leads to the need to offer more customer-oriented innovations and new types of services. In this way, banks will have to compete more with each other in the future. But consumers' expectations regarding banking services are no longer compared exclusively to the customer experience offered by other banks, but also to the customer experience of other digital services available in the financial sector. In this way, the competition and pressure for change experienced by the banking sector also partly come from outside the industry when new players enter the industry (for example, so-called fintech players).

Due to the competition and the development of technology, traditional banks have adapted their service concepts and moved to digital financial services at speed. In order to cope with the challenges of traditional banking and maintain their competitive advantage, traditional banks must totally move their operations

[29] Eurostat, "Internet Banking on the Rise", (15 January 2018), https://ec.europa.eu/eurostat/web/products-eurostat-news/-/DDN-20180115-1

[30] European Banking Federation (EBF), "Banking in Europe: EBF Facts & Figures 2022 - 2021 Banking Statistics", (2022).

into the 2020s. Changes in banking may lead to the need to make difficult choices regarding what kind of customers to serve, which products and services to offer, and how to create a successful business. Therefore, banks must rebuild their organisation around the customer and simplify and reduce structural costs. In addition, banks must learn to be agile, innovative, and adaptive in order to operate effectively – and to be able to deal with the uncertainty of the future.[31] This means that traditional banks must not only comply with the requirements of the present but also radically innovate and change their structure and operations for the future.

In the digitalising financial environment, in addition to banks, many other players are also interested in offering consumers and businesses money management and payment transfer services. Traditional banks and other incumbents are exploring ways of using state-of-the-art technology to turn deposits, bonds, stocks, and other assets into tokens and transfer and trade these assets on their own platforms.

But not everything needs to be competition, cooperation can also be done. For traditional banks, one option to meet the challenges of competition created by fintech companies is to follow the principle "if you can't beat them, join them". In the financial environment, this principle has been replaced by the term "Open banking". It means giving a safe way to a third-party service provider (TPP) access to a customer's money-related bank information using an application programming interface (API). Open banking enables the networking of accounts and data between operators for use by consumers, financial institutions and an authorised third party, or TPP. The third-party status offers new opportunities for many fintech companies, but especially for those that are already involved in the provision or development of some kind of financial services. These include, for example, fintech and Big Tech companies (incl. telecom companies), digital intermediaries, and insurance companies.

A New Player in the Market: Sovereign Digital Money Issuer

The second group of competitors consists of *central banks*. These are participating in the race for the future of money with their efforts to develop their own sovereign digital cash, better known as CBDC. Today, most of the world's central banks are exploring or testing CBDCs to preserve fiat money as the anchor of the global economy and to secure their independence in monetary policy and other central banking functions.

---

[31] PwC, "Retail Banking 2020, Evolution or Revolution?", (2020).

According to the Central Bank Digital Currency Tracker website maintained by the Atlantic Council's Geoeconomics Center, a think tank, in June 2023 total of 130 countries, representing 98 percent of global GDP, are exploring a CBDC. (In May 2020, only 35 countries were considering a CBDC). And 19 of the G20 countries are now in the advanced stage of CBDC exploration (development, pilot, or launch). Of those, 9 countries are already in the pilot stage. Nearly every G20 country has made significant progress and invested new resources in these projects over the past six months since the beginning of 2023.[32]

Furthermore, according to the mentioned CBDC tracker, 11 mainly small countries have fully launched their own digital currency. The ECB will probably start a digital euro pilot project in October 2023 after finalising the development stage. Other G7 banks, excluding FED, are developing CBDC prototypes and consulting the public and private sectors on privacy and financial stability issues.[33]

China is likely to be the first major economy to issue CBDC. China's CBDC is also known as e-CNY, DC/EP, or digital yuan. China's pilot reaches today 260 million people and is being tested in more than 200 scenarios. The e-CNY is a centralized, cash-like digital currency that is expected to be primarily used, at least at the beginning, for retail payments in China. The People's Bank of China (PBOC), the central bank, and e-CNY operating institutions have conducted large-scale e-CNY pilot programs in multiple cities since 2022.

According to Deutsche Bank's research,[34] the introduction of e-CNY serves two different but related goals. The first one, the immediate goal, is a "retail CBDC"[35], i.e. to change China's current payment system by providing a cash-like digital payment method that is accessible to everyone, affordable, anonymous (to some extent) and facilitates competition between payment service providers. Another longer-term goal is a cross-border CBDC, i.e. to create a digital currency that can compete with other digital currencies, such as those issued by other central banks, but also with certain private virtual currencies such as

[32] Atlantic Council, "Central Bank Digital Currency Tracker", Geoeconomics Center, (15 February 2022).

[33] Atlantic Council, "Central Bank Digital Currency".

[34] Deutsche Bank, "Digital Yuan: What Is It and How Does It Work?", Deutsche Bank Research, News (2021).

[35] "Retail CBDC" is generally designed as a central bank liability universally accessible to individuals and businesses within a jurisdiction's financial system. Instead "wholesale CBDC" refers to a digitised central bank liability designed for sizable (generally interbank) transactions, and for which access is limited to certain financial institutions.

bitcoin and stablecoins, ensuring that the renminbi remains the dominant currency in China.

At least for now, the U.S. has lagged behind the rest of the world in CBDC development. Partly because, as the holder of the global reserve currency, it has less to gain from changes in the international monetary system status quo. The situation has also not been improved by the fact that the idea of CBDC (mainly retail CBDC) has met, especially lately, with populist opposition in the U.S., where opponents and sceptics, even authoritative ones, have speculated that CBDC could be used, inter alia, as a restrictive social credit system or it even could become a financial surveillance tool against citizens by the federal government. [36]

The Federal Reserve published Money and Payments: The U.S. Dollar in the Age of Digital Transformation as a first step to fostering a broad and transparent public dialogue about CBDCs in general and the potential benefits and risks of US CBDCs. The document defines a CBDC as a digital liability of a central bank that is widely accessible to the public. In this respect, it is analogous to the digital form of paper money. According to the document, it is not intended to promote any particular political outcome, and the Federal Reserve has not decided to issue CBDC.[37]

The FED is still evaluating the potential impact of a digital dollar. It currently has several studies, pilot tests and experiments underway to determine the technology's opportunities and limitations. In particular, attention has focused on wholesale CBDC development, perhaps because it faces less resistance compared to retail CBDC. However, it is unlikely FED, and other U.S. stakeholders will form a consensus for or against a digital dollar until they get a sense of the structure of a U.S. CBDC and how much of an impact, if any, it would have on the average American. By then, the rest of the world may already be behind the digital horizon of finance.

In this regard, on the one hand, the race for the future of money focuses on the reserve currency issue related to the geoeconomy, where major central banks, like ECB, FED and PBOC, fight for global currency dominance in world trade. On the other hand, the issue is the use of public and private money

[36] Wayne Duggan & Benjamin Curry, "Will The U,S, Launch A Digital Dollar?", Forbes Advisor, Updated: July 7, 2023, https://www,forbes,com/advisor/investing/digital-dollar/; Marcel de Graaff, Michiel Hoogeveen and Jörg Meuthen, "Verbatim Session Reports 16, The Digital Euro (Debate)", European Parliament, (19 April 2023), Strasbourg, Final Version.

[37] "Federal Reserve, Money and Payments: The US Dollar in the Age of Digital Transformation", *Research & Analysis*, (January 2022).

domestically and internationally in connection with, for example, monetary policy, financial stability, and payment transfers.

Depending on the way the CBDC is implemented and the benefits it brings to different stakeholders or users, central banks can gain a central position in the transfer of payments, thus emphasising their autonomy and the importance of their national own currency as the only legal means of payment. This potential shift in payment flows from private to public money could have a significant impact on banks' business models. Banks should adapt their business models to consider the potential transformations in these payment flows, especially in terms of revenue sources, balance sheets and funding models.

If CBDC plays a bigger role in the economy, central banks can have more tools to regulate and manage the money supply, as well as more real-time data. This scenario may lead to greater financial stability as central banks gain more visibility and control over the money supply. On the other hand, it may create the potential for unintended consequences and new risks both at national and international levels.

The role of fintech companies as providers of payment services and payment infrastructure may increase, depending on how central bank money is integrated into mainstream payment systems. Central banks can also partner with private sector fintech companies to share and maintain access to money. This may open new opportunities and business models that focus on the distribution and allocation of public funds.

Global Players and Niche Service Providers

The third group is digital *intermediaries* and *Big Tech companies,* which are also orienting their business to this rapidly changing financial environment. New innovations are emerging that will cause significant changes that undercut traditional banks in speed and cost. Market dynamics that open new opportunities create space for these new digital newcomers to build new kinds of innovative financial services and instruments and gain economies of scale.

In order for digital assets to grow to large dimensions on a large scale, it would require some reliable digital money solution. Additionally, it would require an increase in reliability, regulation, and size of stablecoin issuers. Or the emergence of some other efficient and compliant market infrastructure solutions, such as liquidity-focused cryptocurrency exchanges. It also requires digital intermediaries will need regulatory acceptance of their business models.

Notwithstanding recent failures, many cryptocurrencies have rebounded, more or less. They still exist and continue to re-evolve. For example, the use of stablecoins in payment transactions, one of the traditional functions of money, namely acting as a means of exchange, illustrates a stage of profound change. Stablecoins are crypto assets whose value is tied to other assets.

As one indication of this profound change, the US giant PayPal issued its own stablecoin. The value of PayPal's stablecoin has been tied to exactly one dollar.[38] PayPal is, inter alia, an Internet-based payment processing system designed to replace traditional payment methods. The fact that this giant has offered its own stablecoin was also raised by Fabio Panetta, a member of the ECB's Executive Board, when he spoke in 2023 in the European Parliament. Panetta is worried that large technology companies will reach a monopoly position in the European payment market. This could have negative effects on, for example, information security and financial stability. That's why the ECB is starting to get busy developing and promoting its own digital euro, Panetta pointed out.[39]

In this context, especially from a European financial system and digital euro perspective, it is worth noting as an additional observation that the European payment cards market is currently dominated by two U.S. companies: Visa and Mastercard. Electronic payments are heavily concentrated in these two companies, and they also have enormous pricing power. Therefore, their dominant market position is problematic, although in Europe, perhaps for a different reason than in China, for example. However, in severe financial market crises, even these giants could sink into big problems because they operate much in the same way as banks.

As a short summary, we can state that the solid profitability of digital intermediaries would enable them to launch compelling new services. These could include innovative financial services, including lending and liquidity provision. Competition between financial services providers would start to move from control of operating accounts to custody as money increasingly moves into stablecoins, or some other digital money, held in digital wallets. Beyond banks, competition between digital intermediaries and other similar players could also accelerate. It would also likely include the entry of big tech players to the field.

Many, but not all, new innovations in financial technology can bring both advantages and disadvantages to consumers and businesses. The essential

---

[38] "News: PayPal Launches US, Dollar Stablecoin" *Newsroom Paypal-Corp*, https://news room,paypal-corp,com/2023-08-07-PayPal-Launches-U-S-Dollar-Stablecoin.

[39] Fabio Panetta, "Shaping Europe's Digital Future: The Path Towards a Digital Euro," introductory statement at the Committee on Economic and Monetary Affairs of the European Parliament, Brussels, September 4, 2023; DL News, "PayPal's New Stablecoin Threatens the European Union's Financial Stability, Warns ECB Executive," DL News / Preiss, Inbar, (4 September 2023).

issue is that, at the same time, these innovations are shaping the future of money. Future money is safer and easier to use than what we have today, and that can make near-instant payments anywhere in a country or around the world at a fraction of the current cost. But the race has just begun. Therefore, the leadership in this struggle of the giants is far from clear, and the conditions of the race can change quickly and significantly.

Synthesis - Money Has No Homeland

The future of money and the related payment infrastructure can lead to different outcomes, depending on, for example, the scale differences of different forms of money, the business and technology models and use cases chosen by issuers, the incentive opportunities included in different options, and whether the regulatory and political environment is prioritizing a solution.

The synthesis of different options can be the emergence of several open networks, which would give different parties, borrowers and lenders, issuers and investors and other market participants the opportunity to trade directly without payment transaction intermediaries, i.e. third parties. Transactions would be made with digital money, which could be a CBDC, a tokenised deposit,[40], a fiat-packaged stablecoin,[41] or a decentralized stablecoin,[42] or perhaps some other yet unknown form of digital money that has acquired sufficient reliability and general acceptance as a means of payment. In addition, transactions would be done with smart contracts and institutional decentralized financial protocols.

Scenario, which Oliwer Forum writers call a "Universal Networks", would mean greater participation of players and expansion of capital markets. If users and investors are connected to each other by automation, i.e. universal networks, instead of intermediaries, participation models could change dramatically from the present models. New financial services can speed up if users can control their own data and their digital wallets. This, in turn could blur the lines between banking and commerce further. At the same time, the growth and expansion of market-based financing require both investors and companies to improve their risk management. [43]

---

[40] A digital form of a bank deposit issued by a regulated institution.

[41] Digital assets designed to maintain a stable value against a national currency, such as the US dollar.

[42] Private sector-issued digital assets designed to maintain a stable value while backed by other digital assets.

[43] Larissa de Lima, Jason Ekberg and Douglas J Elliott, "Four Visions For The Future of Digital Money", Oliver Wyman Forum, May 25, 2023, 12.

If credits were created and allocated algorithmically through highly integrated networks, it would accelerate the trend towards capital market-based financing. On the other hand, this kind of development could disrupt the business models of traditional banks and digital brokers. For this reason, it is also the most radical scenario, which one would strongly transform the present financial system. It would include a lot of risky elements.[44]

This scenario created on the basis of the synthesis could strongly change the financial system. Therefore, the change would require great support at the national and international levels. Policymakers could be more receptive if financial networks had reliable solutions that meet compliance and safeguards. Alternatively, transnational organizations could enable cooperation between countries on new platforms, such as the Bank for International Settlements (BIS) vision of a single global ledger (unified ledger)[45] or the International Monetary Fund (IMF) proposal for a multi-currency market, a suggested global marketplace to trade tokenized money directly across borders.[46]

It is also possible that trust is built over time by trying out new policy instruments. Truly universal networks also depend on the convergence of common standards and the continuous development of technology that enables both scale and trust.

Conclusions

Cash covers all traditional functions of money: a means of payment, a store of value, and a unit of account. However, closer analysis reveals unique features (properties) of cash, emphasising the fact that among payment instruments, cash is more than a means of payment. Cash also has other dimensions, like societal and political dimensions. But looking at only own properties of cash, the conclusion is converting cash into digital form is not a simple issue, if all the properties of cash are wanted to be preserved.

Cryptocurrencies, such as bitcoin or stablecoins, have proven to be an unreliable store of value, and their use as a means of payment has not developed favourably either. It is also quite unlikely that cryptocurrencies, which are a

---

[44] Lima, Ekberg and Elliott, "Four Visions For".

[45] Bank for International Settlements (BIS), "III. Blueprint for the Future Monetary System: Improving the Old, Enabling the New," *BIS Annual Economic Report* (June 20, 2023): 86-88.

[46] Tobias Adrian, Rodney Garratt, Dong He and Tommaso Mancini-Griffoli, "Trust Bridges and Money Flows: A Digital Marketplace to Improve Cross-Border Payments," *IMF Fintech Note* 2023/001, Washington, DC (2023): 19-26.

form of private money, would gain a significant position on the agenda of central banks and governments, other than perhaps in the regulatory mind.

Despite technological, legal, and political problems, a great deal of the world's central banks are studying and planning a central bank digital currency, i.e. CBDC, which could replace cash, depending on its technological implementation, the content of new legislation and ultimately people's faith in the digital currency in question. CBDC, which, if implemented, could bring drastic changes to different levels of society as well as to international money and currency markets.

The endpoint of the growth of cashless payment options would be a cashless society. The final death blow to cash in this dystopian development path would be to outlaw all cash use by legislation and remove physical money from circulation. Therefore cashless society is not ideal according to many. The conclusion is as follows: in a society where a person does not have access to cash, or it is only limited, has a great impact on the realisation of equality and the development of inequality, as well as the realisation of financial inclusion.

A cashless society has both disadvantages and benefits. It could bring benefits to consumers in terms of payment speed, reliability, transaction costs, and convenience. On the other hand, the disadvantages are privacy concerns. Privacy is a basic value of EU citizens and a key promoter of acceptability and trust in money. The emphasis between privacy and, e.g. the authorities' right to access and control information about citizens varies in different countries. Privacy conflicts with other, equally valid political goals: combating money laundering, terrorist financing and tax evasion. This conflict also will definitely be reflected in the CBDCs that may be issued, as can be observed already today.

We will probably see solutions according to the synthetic scenario and some, if not all, forms of money according to it will co-exist. They can play a growing role depending on whether they are used for retail payments in a brick-and-mortar store or to finance multi-billion euro cross-border trade agreements or investments. The prerequisites are, of course, reliability and general acceptability - the fundamental parameters of money regardless of its external or visible form.

Bibliography

ABI Research. "Mobile Payments Market: Innovation Strategies for Future Success". Research Report 2022. Publish Date 27 Oct 2022.

Adrian, Tobias, Garratt, Rodney, He, Dong and Mancini-Griffoli, Tommaso. "Trust Bridges and Money Flows: A Digital Marketplace to Improve Cross-Border Payments". IMF Fintech Note (2023/001), Washington, DC.

Armey, Laura E., Lipow, Jonathan and Webb, Natalie. "The Impact of Electronic Financial Payments on Crime". *Naval Postgraduate School.* Information Economics and Policy, Monterey, CA. (Dec. 2014).

Arvidsson, Niklas. "Building a Cashless Society. The Swedish Route to the Future of Cash Payments". Royal Institute of Technology. Stockholm, Sweden, (2019).

Atlantic Council. "Central Bank Digital Currency Tracker". *Atlantic Council. Geoeconomics Center.* (February 15, 2022). Retrieved 27.9.2023. https://www.atlanticcouncil.org/cbdctracker/ Last updated: May 2024.

Bank for International Settlements (BIS). "III. Blueprint for the Future Monetary System: Improving the Old, Enabling the New." BIS Annual Economic Report 2023. (June 20, 2023).

Court of Justice of the European Union. "Judgment of the Court (Grand Chamber) of 26 Jan. 2021" (ECLI:EU:C: 2021:63). *Court of Justice of the European Union.* https://curia.europa.eu/juris/document/document.jsf?mode=lst&pageIndex=0&docid=236962&part=1&doclang=EN&text=&dir=&occ=first&cid=2502469.

De Graaff, Marcel, Michiel Hoogeveen, and Jörg Meuthen. "Verbatim Session Reports 16, The Digital Euro (Debate)." European Parliament, (April 19, 2023), Strasbourg, Final Version.

De Lima, Larissa, Jason Ekberg, and Douglas J. Elliott. "Four Visions For The Future of Digital Money." Oliver Wyman Forum, (May 25, 2023).

Deutsche Bank. "Digital Yuan: What Is It and How Does It Work?" *Deutsche Bank Research,* News, (2021). https://www.db.com/news/detail/20210714-digital-yuan-what-is-it-and-how-does-it-work.

Digital Mahbub. "How Does a Cashless Society Reduce Crime?" (January 20, 2023). https://digitalmahbub. com/cashless-society-reduce-crime/

DL News. "Paypal's New Stablecoin Threatens the European Union's Financial Stability, Warns ECB Executive". DL News / Preiss, Inbar. (September. 4, 2023). https://www.dlnews.com/articles/regulation/paypal-stablecoin-may-threaten-eu-warns-ecb-executive/

Duggan, Wayne & Curry, Benjamin. "Will The U.S. Launch A Digital Dollar?" *Forbes Advisor.* Updated (July 7, 2023). https://www.forbes.com/advisor/investing/digital-dollar/.

Ernst & Young (EY). "Cashless Society Benefits Financial Crime Prevention but Raises Concerns with Inclusion and Data Privacy". *E&Y Global Ltd.* EY Press Release. (November 19, 2019) London, GB. https://www.ey.com/en_gl/news/2019/11/cashless-society-benefits-financial-crime-prevention-but-raises-concerns-with-inclusion-and-data-privacy.

European Banking Federation (EBF). "Banking in Europe: Facts & Figures 2022-2021 Banking Statistics". (2022).

European Central Bank "Study on the Payment Attitudes of Consumers in the Euro Area (SPACE) – 2022". (December 2022).

European Central Bank. "Digital Euro - FAQ on a Digital Euro". https://www.ecb.europa.eu/paym/digital_euro/faqs/html/ecb.faq_digital_euro.en.html Updated (13 June 2024).

European Central Bank. "The Eurosystem Cash Strategy - The Role of Cash". (2022). https://www.ecb.europa.eu/euro/cash_strategy/cash_role/html/index.en.html.

European Commission (EC). "Commission Recommendation of 22 March 2010 on the Scope and Effects of Legal Tender of Euro Banknotes and Coins

(2010/191/EU)". *EC* L 83/70. Official Journal of the European Union (March 30, 2010).

European Commission (EC). "Proposal for a Regulation of The European Parliament and of The Council on the Legal Tender of Euro Banknotes and Coins". Brussels (June 28, 2023).

European Parliament. "New EU Measures Against Money Laundering and Terrorist Financing." European Parliament, News. Press Releases ECON (March 28, 2023). https://www.europarl.europa.eu/news/en/press-room/20230327IPR78511/new-eu-measures-against-money-laundering-and-terrorist-financing

Eurostat. "Internet Banking On the Rise". Eurostat, News (January 15, 2018). https://ec.europa.eu/eurostat/web/products-eurostat-news/-/DDN-20180115-1.

Faverio, Michelle. "More Americans Are Joining the 'Cashless' Economy". Pew Research Center (October. 5, 2022). https://www.pewresearch.org/short-reads/2022/10/05/more-americans-are-joining-the-cashless-econo my/

Federal Reserve Board (FED) "Money and Payments: The U.S. Dollar in the Age of Digital Transformation". *FED Board* Research & Analysis. Jan. 2022.

Federal Reserve Board (FED). "Central Bank Digital Currency (CBDC)". Frequently Asked Questions. *Board of Governors of The Federal Reserve System.* Last Update (April 11, 2023). Available at: https://www. federalreserve.gov/cbdc-faqs.htm

Gazeley, Sam. "Are There Any Benefits to a Cashless Economy?" *ABI Research* (2022). https://www.abiresearch.com/blogs/2022/11/29/cashless-economy/

Mai, Heike. "Cash Empowers The Individual Through Data Protection". German Translation."Bargeld sorgt für besseren Datenschutz – und stärkt so den Einzelnen" *Deutsche Bank Research.* (July 2, 2019), Frankfurt am Main.

Mai, Heike. "Cash, Freedom and Crime: Use and Impact of Cash in a World Going Digital". *Deutsche Bank Research. EU Monitor.* Global Financial Markets (November 23, 2016).

Panetta, Fabio. "Shaping Europe's Digital Future: The Path towards a Digital Euro". Introductory statement at the Committee on Economic and Monetary Affairs of the European Parliament. Brussels (September 4, 2023). https://www.ecb.europa.eu/press/key/date/2023/html/ecb.sp230904~8f5dff1e57.en.html

PayPal. "PayPal Launches U.S. Dollar Stablecoin". PayPal Corp, Newsroom (2023). https://newsroom.paypalcorp.com/2023-08-07-PayPal-Launches-U-S-Dollar-Stablecoin

Prasad, Eswar S. *The Future of Money - How the Digital Revolution Is Transforming Currencies and Finance.* Harvard University Press (2021).

PwC. "Retail Banking 2020. Evolution or Revolution?". *PwC* Retail Banking (2020). https://www.pwc.com/gx/en/banking-capital-markets/banking-2020/assets/pwc-retail-banking2020-evolution-or-revolution.pdf

UK Finance. "Access to Cash Review". UK Finance, UK Payment Market Report 2018. Final Report. March 2019.

Zamora-Pérez, Alejandro. "Guaranteeing Freedom of Payment Choice: Access to Cash In The Euro Area". *ECB Economic Bulletin* 5/2022.

PART III: CENTRAL BANKING AND MONETARY RISKS IN EMERGING MARKETS AND G20

Chapter 9
Financial Risks and Central Bank Reserves in G20 Countries

Mahir Fisunoğlu
Çukurova University, Adana, Turkey

Metin Akyüz
Consultant in international private companies in the Turkey and USA

Abstract

During the last 40 years, several financial crises, some of which have had a significant effect on economies, forced the central banks' reserves. This is true not only for developing countries but also for the developed economies. Indeed, the central banks have used the reserves as a shield against the financial crises. G20 countries have stayed at the centre of these crises. It is quite a common policy tool that central banks create international reserves in their balance sheets in order to achieve price stability and provide sustainable growth and employment as well as financial stability. Needless to say, this policy causes problems on macroeconomic equilibriums. This policy, therefore, demands a clear definition of the central bank's monetary policy, monetary policy tools, operating targets and intermediate targets. This chapter will search for answers to the following questions for G20 countries: Do reserves cause risks in the economy? What is the optimal level of reserves in order to prevent the exchange rate risks during the short-term and sudden outflow of foreign capital? The important question is, how could countries be avoided from such an outflow of foreign capital? How should macroeconomic balances be maintained and the monetary policy be guided during this process?

Keywords: Financial Risk, Central Bank Reserves, G20

***

Introduction

The G20 was established on September 26, 1999, after the 7 largest countries in the world formed the G7 and it consists of the 19 economically largest countries and the EU. It has a looser structure than the G7 as the member nations are very different economically: some are advanced industrialized countries (G7: Italy, France, Germany, The United Kingdom, Canada, The United States, and Japan, EU, S. Korea and Australia), some are BRICs (Brazil, The Russian Federation, India and The People's Republic of China) and some are developing countries and/or "emerging market" countries (Argentina, Indonesia, The Republic of South Africa, Mexico, Saudi Arabia, and Turkey). The member countries have meetings and working groups with government ministers and central bank governors to discuss issues in economics, finance, foreign trade, agriculture, health, medicine, technology and energy. Beginning in 2008, meetings have been held with different groups twice a year in 2009 and 2010, and then once a year thereafter. These include business meetings under the B20, civil society meetings under the C20, labour union meetings under the L20, academic and NGO meetings under the S20, think tank meetings under the T20, city meetings under the U20, women's meetings under the W20 (organized for the first time by German Chancellor Merkel), and youth meetings under the Y20. The role of president is held for one year, on a rotating basis by each country. As of 2022, G20 countries produce 85 per cent of the world's GDP, comprise 65 per cent of the world's total population, account for 75 per cent of the world's total trade, and 80 per cent of the world's total investments.

Central banks of G20 countries, and especially those other than developed countries and BRIC countries, will be examined, specifically the reserve-holding behaviour of those banks and the measures they take against financial risks. This chapter covers three subtopics: central banks and money markets, central bank behavior patterns, and the monetary rules choices of central banks and will include examples from G20 countries. In the second sub-section, the motivation of central banks to accumulate international reserves, developments in international reserve accumulation, reserve adequacy, and appropriate foreign trade regimes are discussed. The "Conclusion" section of the third chapter is organized under three subheadings which discuss whether central banks can maintain their independence, the comparison of the recent crisis with the 1970 crisis, and the possible new roles of central banks.

Central Banks and Money Markets

Money markets are the result of historical development; unlike a country's possession of natural resources, they are formed when the country voluntarily sacrifices from their consumption and saves for long periods of time. Low-income countries (such as Turkey in the G20) have a low savings capacity for investment and must use their capital domestically. Developed/wealthy countries, on the other hand, have higher savings and hence investment capacity. Additionally, there are some "newly industrialized countries (NICs)" (such as

S. Korea), which, like developed countries, have a significant share of the world's private sector capital and thus are able to export capital.

Central bank reserves are a tool that they use in the difficult task of controlling their balance sheets in parallel with the increase in capital flows. The optimization approach requires capital markets to ensure the efficient allocation of money and capital around the world. However, it should be recognized that there are obstacles to this optimal approach, the main ones being the personal preference of investors, the behaviour of investment banks, and the existence of government controls. These obstacles can prevent the optimal flow of money and capital to the areas where it is needed most.

Just as capital has globalized, so has the banking sector. International banks have existed as early as the Medici and Rothschild, financing firms, governments, the Age of Exploration, and operations in the colonies. While the internationalization of British and French banks and their presence in other countries became common in the 16th and 17th centuries, the internationalization of American, Japanese and other European banks came much later (in the 1960s and 1970s). Banks that became internationalized earned high profits and initially went to other countries to conduct banking transactions for their own firms and citizens in other countries, but later began to serve foreign customers and governments as well.

In the process, some financial instruments were developed to avoid the strict banking rules imposed by countries. 'Eurocurrencies' is the general name given to these financial instruments, and these are held in legal accounts 'offshore', outside the country(ies) the bank(s) serves. They financed much of the growth in world trade after the 1960s and provided loans to borrowers with very few strings attached as well as providing investors with higher interest rates than they could earn in their own countries. These were initially characterized as "eurodollar" markets because they started with U.S. dollar accounts in Europe. Although the dollar still has a significant share in these markets, currencies such as the euro and yen are also used.

The U.S., the largest economy among the G20 countries, has been running a foreign trade deficit since the early 1970s. The main reasons for this are the cheapening of imports by the overvalued dollar, the relatively high cost of labour in the U.S., which makes export products more expensive than other countries' export products, the demand of American consumers for imported products and their ability to buy these products by borrowing, and the ability of some countries to increase their exports by undervaluing their national currencies.

The important consequences of the U.S. economy's persistent foreign trade deficit can be summarized as follows: An increase in the volume of imports depresses the prices of domestic products that compete with these products, leading to a downward movement, and while this is a positive development for American consumers, it is a decidedly negative development for American producers as it leads to lower profit margins for them. The foreign trade deficit makes the U.S. a net debtor nation; this debt is held by foreigners, including the U.S. Treasury and the private sector from Asia, Wester Europe and the Middle East. In 2009 this debt amounted to $14 trillion and 90 percent of the GDP. This debt means that he amount of goods and services coming into the US is greater than the number of goods and services leaving the US. The opposite is true for some countries, such as China. Because of the high trade deficit and high federal government indebtedness, 26 per cent of U.S. assets were owned by foreigners in 2008.

The power of central banks derives from their ability to create reserves and thus to buy or lend assets. The balance sheets of central banks can, therefore, answer the following questions: How much of which asset should be purchased? Meanwhile, central banks strive to meet their inflation targets and reduce risks to the financial system, which can have large-scale repercussions such as the bankruptcies in the U.S. during the 2007-2009 crisis and the European Central Bank's (ECB) slowness to play the role of lender of last resort for heavily indebted countries such as Italy, Greece and Spain. Indeed, Italy's public debt/GDP rose from 125% in 2019 to 150% in 2021. The same ratios were 100 per cent and 120 per cent for Spain (not a G20 member), 100 per cent and 115 per cent for France, and 60 per cent and 70 per cent for Germany.

Many countries, including G20 countries, are known for their budget deficits; thus, central banks hold reserves in both Treasury bills and foreign currency.

When the central bank engages in open market operations, the increase in money supply will lower interest rates below world interest rates. Financial investors would then sell low-yielding sovereign bonds and buy higher-yielding foreign bonds. To do so, they will buy foreign currency and hence, there will be capital flows out of the country. If there is a flexible exchange rate policy, capital outflow will lead to devaluation of the national currency.

If a fixed exchange rate policy is followed in an effort by the central bank to defend the national currency, as citizens of the country try to exchange their national currency for foreign currency and buy foreign assets, they will sell their national currency to the central bank and buy foreign currency. The central bank will then sell foreign currency to the market to fulfil its fixed exchange rate obligation. If the cycle continues, the central bank will have reduced its reserves while, at the same time, the domestic money supply will decrease.

The loss in foreign exchange reserves should equal the open market transaction, a process that leads to an increase in the money supply and a fall in domestic interest rates. Only in the case of this equality will the money supply rise to its original level and domestic interest rates rise to the level of world interest rates, resulting in further reserve losses.

Central banks may occasionally fail to achieve this balance and end up with increased treasury bonds on their balance sheets and lower foreign exchange reserves. In the case of fixed exchange rates and free capital movements, central banks do not have the ability to control the money supply. In a fixed exchange rate regime, there is no monetary autonomy; that is, the central bank has no independence in determining the money supply and interest rates. Therefore, any attempt to increase the money supply through open market operations will lead to further loss of foreign exchange reserves and have no effect on the money supply. However, this does not mean that the money supply will be constant. Shocks to the demand for money (shocks to the domestic price level, shocks to domestic output, or changes in world interest rates) will lead to changes in the domestic money supply.

The extreme of the fixed exchange rate regime is the 'currency board', which Argentina has had since 1991, before the establishment of the G20. A currency board requires both a legal obligation through a law passed by parliament and automatic intervention rules to guarantee a fixed exchange rate. The main reason for countries to adopt a fixed exchange rate regime is that if inflation is caused by exchange rate depreciation, the prices of imported goods will rise with depreciation and the country's inflation rate will be close to the world average. Indeed, with purchasing power parity, domestic inflation will be the average of international inflation plus the percentage of the national currency's depreciation. Under a fixed exchange rate regime, the national currency would be protected against depreciation and remain at around zero.

A fixed exchange rate does not mean that exchange rate parities will not change. For example, if the central bank depletes its reserves to defend the national currency, a devaluation would be inevitable, and the credibility of the fixed exchange rate would thus be suspect. Changes in expectations about the future value of the exchange rate can also occur under a fixed exchange rate regime from high inflation, high budget deficits, political risks, and 'irrational' changes in investors' behaviour. In reaction to these variables, when the future exchange rate is expected to be higher than the current exchange rate, the central bank has to prevent capital flows abroad by allowing interest rates to rise above world interest rates.

To restore balance in the money market, central banks can reduce the equilibrium money supply not only by selling foreign exchange but also by selling treasury bills through open market operations. Both transactions would reduce the money supply and raise interest rates to the level of world interest rates. An increase in world interest rates would prompt central banks to reduce domestic money supply (either by selling foreign exchange reserves or by open market operations), thereby reducing liquidity in the market, and so on, until domestic interest rates equalize with world interest rates.

Central banks can sterilize their interventions in exchange rates to prevent changes in the money supply and interest rates. Sterilization interventions also have some negative aspects; if the national currency is under devaluation pressure, sterilization intervention will prevent the interest rate from rising or remove the cause of the pressure on exchange rates. In that situation, a 'non-sterilization intervention' would be required to reduce the money supply and raise interest rates to prevent excessive selling of domestic assets.

Fixed exchange rate regimes are prone to collapse because there are situations in which the rate at which the exchange rate is fixed may not be in line with the fundamentals of the economy. When such a situation arises, if investors' expectation that the fixed exchange rate is sustainable is replaced by the expectation of a devaluation, it leads to central bank intervention in foreign exchange markets and, thus, to a loss of reserves. At any point in time, if the market demand for foreign exchange is higher than the market supply of foreign exchange, the central bank will continue to lose reserves. If central bank intervention is sterilized, the loss of reserves will continue because interest rates will not rise, and foreign exchange will flow out of the country. Since central bank reserves are limited, the fixed exchange rate will be different from the fundamental equilibrium rate of the economy, and reserves will fall to zero. In this case, the central bank would have to switch to a flexible exchange rate regime with a large devaluation.

There are some reasons why a fixed exchange rate regime is inconsistent with the fundamentals: i) If the country's inflation rate is higher than the world inflation rate, it leads to a real appreciation of the country's currency. ii) Likewise, when the government runs a budget deficit and plans to cover this deficit with seigniorage, the money supply will not increase because the money supply of the country is pegged to world interest rates; this monetary increase will end up in a decrease in foreign exchange reserves. Under a flexible exchange rate, the increase in money supply would end in a depreciation of the domestic currency at the exchange rate.

On the other hand, under flexible exchange rate regimes, central banks face a series of problems. First, the exchange rate can be affected by speculative factors that are not related to fundamental economic conditions, and these factors can lead to excessive volatility in exchange rates, deviations from the equilibrium level of nominal and real exchange rates, and adverse consequences for output, investment and foreign trade. Second, in particular, high volatility can increase risks on asset prices and investments in the country and reduce trade in goods and services. This can result in 'beggar thy neighbour' policies and thus lead to disputes between countries, triggering protectionist policies in response to exchange rate devaluation. Finally, a flexible exchange rate can lead to high domestic inflation, while a fixed exchange rate might lead to a quicker 'convergence' to low international inflation.

Apart from the fixed exchange rate regime, another regime that countries can use is the 'crawling peg', but some countries reject this regime because they claim that the crawling peg regime does not reduce the inflation differential between the country and the rest of the world and domestic inflation does not fully 'converge' to world inflation. Therefore, they prefer to remain in a fixed exchange rate regime and converge to world inflation quickly and rapidly. However, if such an inflation and exchange rate regime is caused by economic structural factors (persistent wage-price inertia), the inflation rate will not fully converge to the world inflation rate, the real appreciation of the domestic currency will increase, and the country will experience a negative impact on foreign trade.

In a variant of the crawling peg regime where the exchange rate crawls below the inflation rate, even if it does not fully converge to the world inflation rate, domestic firms and workers will engage in a struggle over wages versus inflation, leading to a real appreciation of the exchange rate and a negative impact on foreign trade. However, the real appreciation of the exchange rate would not be as large as under a fixed exchange rate. Nevertheless, Mexico and the European countries in the European Monetary System faced high real appreciation of their currencies in the 1990s by insisting on fixed exchange rates.

Therefore, the fixed exchange rate regime, which most G20 countries preferred at the time, leads to a real appreciation of the domestic currency and a widening of the current account deficit over time, making the sustainability of the regime increasingly difficult. As a result, the current account deficit has to be financed by external borrowing or capital flows. Especially in the early stages of the process, when the exchange rate has not yet stabilized and there is no risk of devaluation, capital flows are more aggressive, with the domestic currency appreciating as a result of high-rate capital flows. As the appreciation of the domestic currency is sustained over time, the current account deficit becomes persistent and becomes more dependent on capital flows to finance the current account deficit. In the later stages of this process, investors' expectations of devaluation increase, leading to an increase in the expected return on foreign assets and capital outflows from the country. The central bank's interventions to defend the domestic currency would end with the depletion of reserves. If these interventions are not sterilized, high domestic interest rates will only stabilize exchange rates for a while. If sterilization is implemented, the pressure on the exchange rate will continue, and the central bank will continue to deplete its reserves. Thus, both the current account deficit and capital outflows would hasten the day of disaster. Once all reserves are exhausted, the exchange rate will collapse, and a flexible exchange rate regime will have to be adopted. Speculative runs on the country's currency would lead to a high and sharp devaluation of the exchange rate.

This is precisely what happened to the Mexican Peso in the 1990s and resulted in the Peso's collapse in December 1994. The 1997 Asian Crisis was also a consequence of the issue described here. In addition, Argentina and Turkey (early 2000s) went through this painful experience.

Patterns of Central Bank Behavior

It is a common practice for central banks to send 'signals' to the market before making important decisions. The Reserve Bank of New Zealand, which first implemented inflation targeting in 1990, also used this practice. This provides market actors with the necessary time to take positions. Careful scrutiny of central bank meeting notes provides a source of information for future decisions. These notes and information reflect the central bank's economic forecasts. If the central bank's forecasts and economic results are consistent, confidence in the central bank increases; otherwise, the central bank starts to make policy changes. However, it is important to distinguish between the central bank's forecasts and the central bank's promises/commitments about the future.

A central bank promise/commitment aims to change public expectations about the future. For example, in a recession or near recession, the central bank does not have much room to manoeuvre to lower short-term interest rates; consequently, interest rates cannot be expected to fall below zero easily. In this case, the central bank is expected to announce that it will keep interest rates low for a long period of time. If economic agents believe the central bank, inflation expectations will rise, and real borrowing rates will fall without the central bank touching policy rates.

Two recent examples of this policy include the Bank of Canada when it announced that it would leave interest rates unchanged for 14 months during the 2007-2009 financial crisis, and in 2016, the Bank of Japan announced quantity easing until the inflation rate reached its target of 2 per cent. Many central banks made the same promises during the pandemic. When interest rates are close to zero, the expectation from the central bank is to announce what they will do.

Some more liberal central banks may not bind themselves to a promise/ commitment, especially in cases where tight monetary policies have to be pursued. When we look at the rate at which central banks change interest rates, generally, changes are made in small intervals (except for Turkey and Argentina), and these small rate changes signal more of the same will continue in the future. However, if investors perceive these signals correctly, they will price in long-term interest rates.

If the central bank fails to fulfil a promise, markets react harshly. This would not only increase volatility but also undermine the credibility of the central bank, undermining belief in future promises (such as the CBRT's failure to meet its inflation targets). Given the difficulty of keeping promises/commitments, central banks are reluctant to overpromise.

Central Banks' Choice of Monetary Rules

One of the two long debates on central bank monetary rules was Milton Friedman's rule, valid between the 1960s and 1980s, that central banks should increase the money supply by a certain amount every year. With the breakdown of the relationship between GDP and money supply, this rule has lost its relevance. The second rule was put forth by John Taylor when he published a paper known as 'Taylor's rule'. This rule is a formulation that carries the deviation from the inflation rate and the GDP growth rate, and when applied to observed data in the 1980s and 1990s, it often yielded rates close to the correct overnight lending rates.

Having found a 'magic' formula for obtaining the right interest rates for the future, by the end of the 1990s, the rates calculated with Taylor's rule started to be lower than those of the Federal Reserve. Thus, the search for a new and alternative rule formulation based on the Taylor rule with some giving more weight to the GDP gap, others developed formulas based on 'inertia', while still others emphasized future inflation expectations.

If these rules to be followed by central banks are expressed in terms of a 'central bank objective function', it is necessary to first develop assumptions (long-run unemployment rates and theoretical interest rates - the interest rate that would support full GDP), decide on the variables to be used in this function, and then decide on the weights of these variables, all of which are not easy for a simple formula.

If international trade is one of the issues that central banks need to look at carefully when choosing a monetary rule, others are international money and capital markets. These include stock exchanges, 'future exchanges' markets and 'tax havens'. The growth of the global financial system is driven by the globalization of money, banking, and capital markets. In 1973, with the introduction of floating exchange rates and the growth of liquid assets held by the private sector, international money markets developed and, together with capital mobility, led to the expansion of 'international currency markets'.

Capital flows take two main forms: borrowing and lending and financial investments in corporate assets. Borrowing and lending can be done by public and private institutions, and some international institutions (such as the World Bank and various agencies of the United Nations) can also borrow and lend. The latter can take the form of 'portfolio investment', which is short-term and does not involve corporate governance, or 'direct investment', which also involves corporate governance.

Capital flows have increased as a result of national and international financial liberalization, and in the 1980s and 1990s (when the G20 had not yet been established, but future developing members had already seen the benefits). Likewise, the likelihood of financial crises increased.[1] It is therefore worth examining the causes and effects of financial crises for those members of the G20 countries that have experienced financial crises (Mexico, Turkey, Argentina) to see how central banks reacted. The Mexican peso crisis (December 1994) and the Brazilian real crisis (January 1999), the Argentine and Turkish crises before the establishment of the G20 will be analyzed as cases.

Exchange rate crises are explained by three factors: inconsistencies in monetary, fiscal and exchange rate policies that lead to speculative episodes, inconsistencies in the exchange rate system despite consistent macroeconomic policies and stable market conditions, and the existence of a weak financial sector and credit markets, where first and second generation models act together.

The Mexican peso crisis. Economic reforms in Mexico between 1988 and 1993, disinflation and an improvement in the public sector budget deficit. To reduce inflation, the peso/dollar rate was pegged between 1987 and 1989, and after January 1989 a crawling peg was implemented with a small margin and with prior announcement. The floor of the peg was kept constant, while the ceiling was set to depreciate relative to the US dollar. Between January 1990 and December 1993, the peso depreciated by 17 per cent against the dollar and continued to depreciate at smaller rates between January and December 1994. Against this depreciation in current (nominal) rates, the real effective exchange rate appreciated by 35 per cent according to the calculation based on the consumer price index and by 35 per cent according to the index of unit labour

---

[1] Graciela L. Kaminsky and Carmen M. Reinhart, "The Twin Crises: The Causes of Banking and Balance-of-Payments Problems," *American Economic Review* 89, no. 3 (1999): 473–500, https://doi.org/10.1257/AER.89.3.473; Reuven Glick and Michael Hutchinson, "Capital Controls and Exchange Rate Instability in Developing Economies," *Journal of International Money and Finance* 24, no. 3 (April 2005): 387–412, https://doi.org/10.1016/j.jimonfin.2004.11.004.

wage costs. The current account deficit rose from 3.2 per cent of GDP in 1990 to 6.6 per cent in 1993, but in contrast, capital flows partially compensated for the current account deficit and short-term treasury bills were issued to sterilize capital flows. When the U.S. Congress ratified the North America Free Trade Agreement (NAFTA) in November 1993, capital flows to Mexico continued, and 'currency risk' and 'default risk' emerged as the spread between short-term bonds issued and U.S. interest rates widened. In addition to this, in 1994, the government loosened its fiscal policy, adopted an expansionary fiscal policy, and expanded the volume of credit extended by state-owned banks. This expansion was thought to be related to the upcoming elections. In the Bank of Mexico, net foreign assets decreased, and base money increased in response to the credit expansion. Thus, the peso came under pressure, which increased after the second half of 1994. On December 20, 1994, the Mexican authorities announced that they would widen the band by 15.3 per cent, making 4 pesos equal to 1 dollar. However, the Bank of Mexico failed to achieve this ratio and collapsed with a 30 per cent depreciation between December 20 and January 3.

Brazil Crisis. Brazil, another member of the G20, was experiencing triple-digit inflation in the 1990s and launched the ambitious stabilization program 'the Real Plan' in 1994. The successful plan led to a rapid decline in inflation, which led to an expansion of domestic demand and real exchange rate appreciation. This led central bank authorities to keep real interest rates high. Fiscal policy deteriorated due to debt repayments. The public budget deficit/GDP ratio rose from 6 per cent in 1994 to 10 per cent in 1998. While the stock of public domestic debt increased between 1995 and 1998, the appreciation of the real exchange rate compared to the early years of the plan also increased the current account deficit. This twin deficit threat encouraged speculative attacks in 1997 (the year of the Asian Crisis). Central bank authorities adopted a tight monetary policy, interest rates rose, and capital flows began. The government planned to reduce the budget deficit to 2 per cent of GDP in 1998. Capital flows started to increase central bank reserves from 1998 onwards. The plan to reduce the budget deficit to 2 per cent of GDP had to be approved by the Brazilian Parliament, and the reform of the civil service, which was part of this program, was rejected by the Parliament in December 1997. Fiscal weakness, the failure of foreign markets and the economic collapse of the Russian Federation in August 1998 exacerbated exchange rate pressures in Brazil, as in all developing countries. The central bank raised interest rates and intervened in the foreign exchange market. After the January 1998 presidential election, the IMF prepared a $44.5 billion package but with the condition that fiscal policy should be corrected. The IMF program was not very effective at the beginning; interest rate spreads on Brazil's international debt remained high, and capital flows continued. Meanwhile, the crisis began when the Parliament rejected a number of fiscal policy reforms on the grounds of their effectiveness and the doubts of the government authorities to implement them. Of the total debt, 28 per cent was denominated in U.S. dollars or dollar-indexed debt. In early 1999, the Central Bank continued to lose reserves and the Governor of the Central Bank resigned. When the government's attempt at a small and controlled devaluation failed, the real was floated on January 15, 1999. In two months, it lost 40 per cent of its value.

Although Argentina, Mexico and Turkey are in the G20, unlike other member countries, another currency (the U.S. dollar) is circulated alongside the domestic currency. When the economic problems of these three countries are considered together, it is seen that this issue has been going on since they became G20 members. When Argentina made its most recent agreements with the IMF in 2018 and 2020, it also kept in mind the negative effects of these agreements in the past. The austerity program put into effect to receive a loan in the 2001 agreement ended in an $82 billion default.[2] As a result, Argentina saw widespread unemployment, rising poverty and a one-year government freeze on bank accounts. By 2018, the peso's depreciation against the dollar continued, and the Argentine Central Bank's efforts to stop it were insufficient. The government's tightening of the budget and sales from reserves also failed. Argentina's problem stemmed from the strengthening of the US dollar and high interest rates in the US. Among the G20 countries, Turkey and Mexico are also affected by the U.S. dollar and interest rate problems. Argentina (like Turkey) has problems such as high inflation and the central bank's failure to meet inflation targeting, foreign currency debt rising to 40 per cent of GDP, budget deficit, and current account deficit. Due to its underdeveloped capital market, it is also unable to provide the necessary financing for its development and frequently resorts to central bank resources (seignorage) and uses reserves. This situation deflects foreign investors from investing in Argentina.

Between 2015 and 2017, Argentina's economy saw a partial recovery: The lifting of currency controls, lower export taxes, and an agreement with creditors gave the economy a breathing space. Low international borrowing rates also allowed the budget deficit to be resolved at a low cost. Foreign investors also started to return to Argentina. In 2017, the Argentine Central Bank raised its inflation target for 2018 from 12 per cent to 15 per cent. Thus, it tried to reduce the impact of high interest rates on growth. As inflation expectations rose, the policy interest rate was lowered, and investors began to doubt the independence of the central bank and its ability to reduce inflation. Investor unease increased when the government introduced a capital-gain tax on Argentine bonds in April 2018. As credit became harder to come by, Argentina again sought a deal with the IMF and announced that it would accept the IMF's conditions.

---

[2] "Argentina's Economic Woes, The Crisis of Macrinomics", *The Economist*, May 12, 2018.

Turkey. Crises. During its time as a member of the G20, Turkey has been exposed to intense capital flows; the value of the lira makes exports more difficult and imports easier; the foreign trade deficit, and increasingly the current account deficit, have become a major problem. This process continued during the 2007-2009 crisis; growth weakened with the weakening of capital flows after 2015, and exchange rates started to rise in 2018. Economic growth and monetary policy showed similar practices during the pandemic. Thus, Turkey entered the process of 'early deindustrialization'. As of 2021, the government announced that it would adopt policies to transform the current account deficit into a current account surplus and started to pursue a low interest rate policy against inflation (a method to reduce inflation caused by the output gap in economies without a chronic current account deficit and with a single currency system). For Turkey, in the short term, the plan was to close the chronic current account deficit through a contraction in the domestic market and an increase in exports as a result of a depreciation of the lira, higher inflation and lower-than-inflationary income growth. Thus, as exchange prices stabilized and the domestic market contracted, inflation was expected to decline, and with price and financial stability in place, growth and higher income levels could be achieved using a new strategy.

However, measures to tighten the domestic market were kept loose. The Central Bank of the Republic of Turkey (CBRT) cut policy rates from 18 per cent in October 2021 to 8.5 per cent in April 2022. When economic actors turned to foreign currency, support from reserves started to keep exchange rates stable; $165 billion has been sold since 2019, and reserves decreased and fell to negative numbers. In the process, various macroprudential measures and capital controls were introduced. For example, companies holding 15 million liras worth of foreign currency, or with annual sales exceeding this figure, or holding more than 10% of their asset value in foreign currency could not receive loans in lira; banks with a foreign currency weight in savings deposits could additionally receive treasury bills, first 20% and then 40% of export revenues would be converted into lira at CBRT exchange rates; and finally KGM, a special accounting method that compensates for the depreciation of the lira against the dollar, was implemented at the end of 2021. This last method (KGM) has reached 2.5 trillion liras according to government statements (bank deposits are known to consist of half TL and half foreign currency). The government's decisions to encourage firms to hold less foreign currency weakened their capacity to protect their savings against inflation and, thus, their sense of security, and, given the dependence of exports on imports, reduced their import capacity. Turkey began to experience an exchange rate-inflation-price-wage spiral. The uncertainty for Turkey is whether the above-mentioned planning to close the current account deficit (or equalize foreign exchange income and expenditure) continues or a 'manageable current account deficit' policy is adopted instead.

Motivations of Central Banks to Accumulate International Reserves

The economic infrastructures and monetary policies of developing countries, together with financial globalization, have led to economic imbalances and severe financial crises. The 1982 debt crisis, which covered all Latin American countries, can be considered as the milestone of financial imbalances and crises. These fluctuations led to serious economic collapses in Mexico in 1995, East Asia in 1997, Russia in 1998, Turkey in 1994 and 2001, and Argentina in 1999 and 2002. Moreover, when the commodity price bubbles that began to emerge in 2003 burst in the US in 2007, the crisis started to affect the whole world and turned into a major recession for various reasons and in different places. The most noteworthy point in the crises that emerged at that time was that the crises of some countries affected other countries, and the crises followed each other. For example, the crisis in Turkey in 1994 was followed by the crisis in Mexico in 1995; the crisis in East Asia in 1997 was followed by the crisis in Russia in 1998 and in Argentina in 1999; the crisis in Turkey in 2001 was followed by the crisis in Argentina in 2002; the crisis in the US in 2007 was followed by the crisis in the Far East and the BRIC countries (Brazil, the Russian Federation, India and the People's Republic of China) from 2010 onwards. The causes and effects of these crises may be different in each country.

This has led to a substantial body of literature on the causes of these crises and the measures to be taken. Although international capital flows had become the easiest way for emerging economies to obtain the capital they needed to achieve growth in the 1980s and post-1990s, this extraordinarily sensitive and highly volatile capital caught emerging economies unprepared and exposed them to greater risks. As a result, the liquidity that had been expanding in the world since 2004 became attractive to emerging economies until 2007-2008, at which time the financial crisis that had started in developed countries caused capital to shift more from developed countries to emerging economies.

The question of capital flows during the crisis and the recovery process remains a controversial issue. Some have emphasized the importance of 'push' factors, particularly monetary and fiscal policies in advanced economies, as the main culprits behind this surge in capital flows. On the contrary, others have emphasized "pull" factors, such as the real divergences between developing countries (GEOs) and advanced economies (GEs), as the main drivers of the current pattern of capital flows. In fact, this debate has become one of the main topics of discussion in international capital markets.[3]

During the crisis, the behaviour of the different players in global capital flows, their reactions according to geographical distribution, and central bank behaviour

---

[3] Marcel Fratzscher, "Capital Flows, Push Versus Pull Factors and the Global Financial Crisis," European Central Bank Working Paper no. 1364 (2011), http://www.ecb.europa.eu.

have once again brought to the fore the necessity to analyze them very well. Martin Feldstein's conclusion after the Asian financial crisis of 1999 was that developing countries cannot rely on the International Monetary Fund or reforms of the 'international financial architecture' to protect them from such crises. Is it enough to rely on sound macroeconomic policies, knowing, as Feldstein reasoned, that crises elsewhere may threaten contagion even to well-governed countries? Feldstein argues that countries with higher (net) levels of liquid foreign assets are better able to withstand panic in financial markets and sudden reversals in capital flows.

They can, therefore, not only reduce the costs of financial crises but also make such crises less likely. Liquidity can be provided through three strategies, respectively: reducing short-term debt, establishing a collateralized credit facility, and increasing the foreign exchange reserves of the central bank.[4] For developing countries, the most popular option among the three strategies has been to increase foreign reserves. Today, foreign exchange reserves held by developing countries have always been held at high levels, several times the amount (in relation to their income or trade) that is held by advanced countries. But as Feldstein and others have pointed out, accumulating reserves is also costly. Central banks hold foreign exchange reserves mostly in the form of low-yielding short-term US Treasury (and other) securities, and each amount of reserves that a country invests in these assets imposes an opportunity cost on that economy (or, alternatively, on the social rate of return on investment in that economy) equal to the cost of external borrowing. The difference between the return on liquid reserve assets and the external cost of funds - a difference of a few percentage points in normal times - represents the social cost of self-insurance.

Many central banks - notably Japan and emerging Asian countries - hold foreign currency assets, known as foreign exchange reserves, which can help countries stabilize their currencies, but they can also lead to investment losses for central banks. The large share of dollar assets among reserve assets has made foreign financial centres important players in US financial markets. In recent years, central banks' holdings of foreign currency assets, especially securities of foreign governments, have risen sharply. This value, which was approximately Special Drawing Rights (SDR) 100 billion in the 1970s, reached SDR 1.5 trillion in the early 2000s, SDR 4 trillion in 2005, SDR 8.4 trillion in 2014 and SDR 11.4 trillion in 2021. (IMF's data) This development is even more striking when we look at the details of the figures. Approximately one-third of

---

[4] Martin Feldstein, "Self-Protection for Emerging Market Economies", National Bureau of Economic Research Working Paper, no. 6907 (1999), http://www.nber.org/papers/w6907.

this value is accumulated in developed countries, while the rest is in developing countries.

Another striking point is that more than half of the reserves accumulated in developing countries are in developing countries in Asia. While these developments are taking place, the world has been growing at a rate of approximately 3-3.5% from 1970 to 2008, so it does not seem logical to explain this development solely in terms of global growth. Especially after the 1960s, inflation and price instability have been seen as the most fundamental economic problem in all economies, first in developed countries and in general. Among these, the most important and primary task of central banks is to ensure price stability in the long run. The measures taken in monetary policy to stabilize the real economy should in no way disrupt price stability; that is, actual inflation should not contradict target expectations.[5]

The real economy and the economic performance of the country, in general, can be seen as the results of the economic policies implemented by the central bank. According to Mishkin, "The behavior of central banks affects interest rates, the amount of credit, and the money supply, all of which have an impact not only on financial markets but also on aggregate output and inflation".[6]

The accumulation of international reserves has shown a rather unusual pattern of development over the past years. In particular, conventional indicators for 'reserve adequacy' show that the stock of international reserves is excessive in a number of emerging markets, particularly in Asia. This suggests the possibility that other factors may be driving the rapid accumulation of foreign exchange reserves. A number of studies have focused on the extent to which this development can continue.[7] In order to assess the sustainability of the factors behind the accumulation of reserves, we will assess the main factors for developed and emerging markets in the accumulation of reserves (i.e. not only the volatility reduction of more official targets but also a floating exchange rate target).

---

[5] Michael Woodford, "Inflation Targeting and Financial Stability", National Bureau of Economic Research Working Paper, no. 17967 (2012), http://www.nber.org/papers/w17967.

[6] Frederic S Mishkin, "Is Monetary Policy Effective During Financial Crises?", National Bureau of Economic Research, no. 14678 (2009), http://www.nber.org/papers/w14678.

[7] M. Bahmani-Oskooee and F. Brown, "Demand for International Reserves: A Review Article", *Applied Economics* 34, no. 10 (2002): 1209–26, https://doi.org/10.1080/00036840110096129; Roland Beck and Ebrahim Rahbari, "Optimal Reserve Composition in the Presence of Sudden Stops: The Euro and the Dollar as Safe Haven Currencies", European Central Bank Working Paper, no. 916 (2008), http://www.ecb.europa.eu; David K Backus et al., "Monetary Policy and the Uncovered Interest Rate Parity Puzzle", NBER Working Paper, no. 16218 (2012).

In general, we have tried to distinguish the following points: First, international reserves in emerging markets are usually based on coping with 'volatile capital flows', while in advanced economies, they are based on transferring liquidity surpluses generated by trade surpluses to future periods. In such cases, higher uncertainty (for developing countries) implies a higher optimal level of reserves. Second, international developments, such as, for example, financial globalization, or country-specific factors, such as, for example, demographic issues or temporarily high income from oil exports, can contribute to accumulation. However, these factors are still not sufficient to explain accumulation: fluctuating freely beyond a certain minimum level, the continuous accumulation of foreign exchange reserves is unnecessary and potentially costly.

Thus, when the accumulation of foreign exchange reserves occurs very quickly, and there are strong indications that the stock of reserves is too high, it can lead to exchange rate management. For example, if countries keep their exchange rates appreciated as part of an export-led growth strategy, the exchange rate will drive the accumulation of foreign exchange reserves up to the level required by economic fundamentals. It is important to recognize that there may be clear differences in policy choices, especially between the objectives of private and public sector investors. For private investors, the objective is to maximize expected returns relative to perceived risks. In contrast, central banks' buying and selling of foreign assets for policy purposes may go beyond seeking to maximize risk-adjusted returns. It is important to recognize the distinct difference between public and private investors, where the medium- and long-term sustainability of a given policy should be intact, if not completely economically optimal. For example, central banks may be eager to increase foreign reserves for political reasons, even if economic reasons predict slow reserve accumulation, as in the case of a depressed reserve currency value.

Central banks are equipped with some special powers and functions, which vary from country to country. These are as follows: to determine the monetary policy of the country and be responsible for the implementation of this policy, to regulate and supervise the banking sector, to be the lender of last resort for both the government and other financial institutions, to control the money supply, and to manage the country's foreign exchange and gold reserves.

The monetary policy instruments of a central bank equipped with these functions can be classically defined as rediscount interest rates, open market operations (OMOs), foreign exchange and gold trading, direct trading and reserve requirement ratios[8] These instruments can also be called monetary

---

[8] Alvaro Cencini, *Monetary Theory: National and* International, (Routledge, Taylor & Francis e-Library, 2003).

policy instruments. Monetary policy implementation consists of three elements. The first is the choice of the operational target of monetary policy (for example, an overnight market interest rate). The second is the establishment of an operational framework that allows the central bank to control the chosen operational objectives (e.g., identifying the instruments to be used, determining the relationships between these instruments, and defining the appropriate list of collateral for instrument use). The third is to use the instruments on a daily basis to achieve the operational objective.

Reserve holding can be explained as 'insurance' to be used in case of 'sudden stop' situations that arise in times of crisis, and the management of the exchange rate, in particular, is a tool to boost exports. Foreign reserves are largely accumulated to provide liquidity and to eliminate fluctuations in the exchange rate.[9] However, studies also show that saving glut, commodity price increases, wealth bequeathed to future generations, and capital additions to banks are also used to strengthen their financing power and the Monetary Board.

It is noteworthy that global crises and the subsequent cessation of capital flows in emerging economies occur immediately after periods when gross foreign capital inflows, foreign direct investments and short-term capital flows increase.

One of the traditional motivations of central banks to accumulate international reserves is the need for foreign exchange against possible turmoil in money markets. In the face of a balance of payments deficit, countries have several options (the use of one or more non-mutually exclusive policies). First, they can adopt expenditure-altering policies, such as accepting a low exchange rate or imposing tariffs or import quotas. Second, it could impose expenditure-reducing policies that would lower economic growth. Third, it may engage in export promotion policies. And finally, in the short run, it can finance payment imbalances through the use of reserves.

The pace of accumulation and the size of world foreign exchange reserves have shown important unexpected features since 2002 in terms of the degree of concentration and geographical distribution of ownership. First, the rate of change: while the world foreign exchange reseres have more than tripled in the past decade, they have doubled at a dramatically accelerating rate in only the last four years. From $1.2 trillion in January 1995 to $11.4 trillion by the end of 2021, the pace of world reserves has changed dramatically. Between 1995 and 2001, in the context of increasingly liberalized capital flows, reserves were

[9] Ben S Bernanke, "The Global Saving Glut and the U.S. Current Account Deficit", (ElischolarLibrary, 2005, https://elischolar.library.yale.edu/ypfs-documents/4221.

important factors in the financial crises that affected a number of 'emerging market economies' (EMDEs), and as insurance against future crises, to be used and replenished if needed. It is worth noting that even after the 2007 global crisis, this increase has not slowed down. This contradicts the notion that post-World War II reserve accumulations were funded mainly from widely used exchange rate-indexed regimes and renders explanations and studies conducted after 2005 inadequate.

The exchange rate-indexed regime declined substantially until the 1970s and almost completely disappeared in the second half of the 1990s. In the last decade, in particular, one-third of all currencies moved independently and freely according to the IMF classification. Although this figure is declining, many countries are freeing their currencies by anchoring them to either the dollar or the euro. Second, the degree of concentration of reserve accumulation has also been increasing over time. This means that officially, at least until 2004, the US current account deficit was financed more by a smaller number of central banks with current account surpluses. After 2007, this changed to a completely different structure. The top 5 reserve accumulating central banks account for 68.4% of reserve accumulation over the 1995-2023 period.

Only two countries, the People's Republic of China and Japan, have accumulated more than half of the world's reserves since 2007 and currently hold 40% of the world's reserves. Third, in terms of geographical distribution, Asian economies are the most important region in terms of both reserve accumulation and the volume of reserve stocks. Oil exporters such as the Russian Federation, Algeria and Norway accumulate significant amounts of foreign assets. This feature is actually related to oil prices, which have become more pronounced since 2004. This is despite the fact that oil funds are not included in the IMF reserve statistics, which is where most countries' oil revenues are concentrated. In this case, we should not forget to mention Venezuela, Kuwait, Oman, Norway and, again, the Russian Federation.

Developments in International Reserve Accumulation

In addition to the recent surge in oil prices, there are three main reasons for this unprecedented accumulation of foreign assets, which stems from monetary policy. Firstly, in response to the financial crises of the 1990s and early 2000s, many GPEs (Emerging Market Economies) felt the need to prepare for future financial crises.[10] Secondly, at the beginning of the post-crisis recovery after the strong erosion of the national currency, crisis-stricken Asian economies followed

[10] Age F.P. Bakker and Ingmar R.Y. van Herpt, *Central Bank Reserve Management: New Trend, From Liquidity to Return* (Edward Elgar Publishing, 2007), https://EconPapers.repec.org/RePEc:elg:eebook:12513.

an export-led growth strategy supported by an exchange rate regime anchored to the US dollar.[11] Thirdly, the characteristics of local financial systems in GPEs, especially in Asia, probably played a special role in this increase. These characteristics are due to the fact that in underdeveloped local financial systems, high-cost or inefficient 'hedge' markets lack appropriate channels to channel private savings into investment.

A certain proportion of creditor GPEs have a tendency to 'dollarize' official and/or cross-border assets. From a macro perspective, the ratio of excess investment to savings is high, driven either by excess savings (as in the case of the People's Republic of China) or underinvestment (as in other emerging market economies in Asia).

Another apparent common feature of reserve accumulation is the role played by the accumulation of official foreign assets as an instrument of concern and as a result of moves by GPEs in global financial markets.[12] While a few developing countries, especially those in Asia, are major players in international trade, they are still financially underdeveloped. It is this asymmetry that leads GPEs to hold a third of the world's reserves.

As highlighted in the literature, the persistence of reserve accumulation raises issues of risk and cost: inflationary pressures, overinvestment, asset bubbles, confusion/inconsistencies in the conduct of monetary policy, measurable capital losses on the monetary authority's balance sheet, sterilization costs, public debt market segmentation, and misallocation of domestic bank borrowing.[13]

---

[11] Heung Sik Choo, "Dealing with Reserve Accumulation: The Case of Korea", in *Central Bank Reserve Management:New Trends, From Liquidity to Return*, ed. Age F.P. Bakker and Ingmar R.Y. van Herpt (Edward Elgar Publishing, 2007); Hidehiko Sogano, "Foreign Reserve Adequacy from the Asian Perspective", in *Central Bank Reserve Management: New Trend, from Liquidity to Return*, ed. Age F. P. Bakker and Ingmar R.Y. van Herpt (Edward Elger Publishing, 2007).

[12] Robert N Mccauley, "Assessing the Benefits And Costs of Official Foreign Exchange Reserves", in *Central Bank Reserve Management: New Trend, from Liquidity to Return*, ed. Age F.P. Bakker and Ingmar R.Y. van Herpt (Edward Elgar Publishing, 2007), 19–36.

[13] Esteban Jadresic, "The Cost-Benefit Approach to Reserve Adequacy: The Case of Chile", in *Central Bank Reserve Management: New Trend, from Liquidity to Return*, ed. Age F.P. Bakker and Ingmar R.Y. van Herpt (Edward Elgar Publishing, 2007); Amy Yip, "Implications of Growing Reserves of Central Banks for Asset Allocation", in *Central Bank Reserve Management: New Trend, from Liquidity to Return*, ed. Age F.P. Bakker and Ingmar R.Y. van Herpt (Edward Elgar Publishing, 2007); Ludek Niedermayer, "Central Bank Risk Management: The Case of the Czech National Bank", in *Central Bank Reserve Management: New Trend, from Liquidity to Return*, ed. Age F.P. Bakker and Ingmar R.Y. van Herpt (Edward Elgar Publishing, 2007).

Not only have world reserves increased significantly in recent years, but the way in which these foreign reserves are managed has also evolved over time. The management framework can vary considerably across countries, with the People's Republic of China and Japan - the two major reserve holders - having different management trends given their management styles. The main features of the reserve policies of these two countries are summarized below.

In Japan, reserve management is still considered strictly a policy instrument and is managed by the Ministry of Finance through a passive guideline of limited risk/return sensitivity. In recent years, there have been reports in the business press that the Bank of Japan will hire professional managers for reserve management. This can be interpreted as a shift to more active reserve management in Japan rather than passive management of reserves in areas with low risk and low return. Little information is available on reserve management in the People's Republic of China. In relation to other Asian economies, reserve management is used as an important development tool. Moreover, so-called Singapore heritage funds and S. Korean investment companies have been established with long-term return-oriented objectives.

New investment instruments have become an important feature of reserve management in some Asian countries. In S. Korea, foreign reserve assets with an initial value of USD 20 billion began to be managed by the Korea Investment Corporation (KIC) as an independent entity in 2005 in order to seek higher yields. The funds are composed of USD 17 billion from the reserves of the Bank of Korea and USD 3 billion from the Foreign Exchange Stabilization Fund of the Ministry of Finance. The Bank of Korea, however, retains the option to call its own assets in an emergency. In other words, even if the management of the funds is entrusted to the KIC, they still retain their international reserve character. The KIC is partly similar to Singapore's fastest-growing foreign reserves model, the Singapore Investment Corporation (SIC), established in May 1981, but with some minor differences. While the KIC manages a portion of reserves, the SIC manages the entire reserves of the Central Bank of Singapore for anti-intervention purposes in international markets. In other words, the reserve managed by the KIC is the released portion of the country's total foreign reserves. The main purpose of this move is to generate high long-term returns and preserve the value of assets for future generations (hence, the funds are sometimes referred to as 'next generation' or 'legacy' funds). These funds, which draw from a pool of investment-eligible instruments, often differ significantly from those used by traditional reserve managers and include, for example, equities, corporate bonds and investment private funds.[14] In addition, such institutions often have other objectives, such as promoting the domestic

[14] Mccauley, "Assessing the Benefits".

asset management industry (S. Korea) and the domestic capital market (Singapore and Hong Kong SAR).

Although the pace of this diversification into new instrument types has been impressive, the picture has not changed significantly. According to McCauley[15], given security and liquidity constraints, the vast majority of reserve assets are still in government or government-guaranteed bonds, while the percentage of foreign exchange reserves not invested in interest rate products is still negligible. Thus, while there have been significant changes in the management of foreign reserves, these changes do not appear to have kept pace with the pace of reserve accumulation.

The US dollar is still by far the dominant reserve currency, especially in Asia. In fact, there are several common reasons, tightly linked to asset management, that appear to play an important role in the US dollar's dominance: how US fixed-income markets (and US financial markets in general) compare with the Eurozone and Japan in terms of breadth, depth and liquidity; the expectation that all major reserve accumulators, public or private, will continue to use the US dollar as a tool for intervention; increased use of derivatives by central bank portfolio managers, allowing greater flexibility than in the past (i.e., for example, while bearing interest rate risk in one market, one can invest in another currency using currency swaps).

Relative to the data released by individual central banks, such as the Bank of Japan, the aggregate data released by the US Treasury can be distinguished by four types of investment. First of all, a large share of foreign exchange reserves went into treasury bills and US Treasury securities. The amount used here represents almost a quarter of the net securities issued by the country. Secondly, foreign official investors also bought high-yielding FED bonds. Thirdly, a significant portion of reserves was held in time deposits in the periods following large foreign exchange purchases. Information on this third component can be used for Japan, which held 15% of total foreign exchange reserves in time deposits. Fourthly, only a small part of reserves accounted for investment in corporate bonds and equities. However, the relative importance of these instruments is that they will grow over time. For example, the Central Bank of S. Korea noted this trend in a report submitted to the Finance and Economy Committee of the National Assembly of S. Korea on February 24, 2005.

In the Russian Federation, the devaluation of the ruble in 1998 and rising commodity prices led to current account surpluses that reached 10% of GDP in

---

[15] Robert N Mccauley and Jean-François Rigaudy, "Managing Foreign Exchange Reserves in the Crisis and After", in *Bank of International Settlements (BIS)*, vol. 58 (Bank for International Settlements, 2011), 19–47.

2004. On the other hand, the decline in crude oil prices following the 2007 global crisis brought current account deficits back to the agenda. In 2015, the ruble was devalued again, but this time, commodity prices started to fall instead of rising. The consequence of this was another increase in current account deficits. The main reason for not using the reserves transferred to the fund to cover current account deficits is to prevent further crises if capital outflows become too large to prevent them. Significant outflows prevented the reserves from growing, but between 2003 and 2008, rising oil revenues and more stable capital flows led to a significant accumulation of reserve assets. However, the war, first over Crimea and then directly with Ukraine, led to a serious financial crisis in the Russian Federation and, together with the sanctions imposed by Western countries, to a social and economic crisis. In Latin America, reserves rose from USD 95 billion (January 1995) to USD 239 billion (August 2005). Mexico and Brazil are the region's two major reserve holders.

International Reserve Adequacy and the Foreign Trade Regime

Foreign reserve adequacy and exchange rate regimes or foreign exchange controls may not provide a complete understanding of the reserve accumulation phenomenon. Firstly, the presence or absence of controls on capital flows is not a factor that explains the differences between reserve-accumulating economies and other economies. Secondly, even a free exchange rate regime can involve sustained interventions, thus de facto confirming the management inherent in such regimes. This may be partly due to the expectations of exchange rate appreciation generated by short-term capital inflows in combination with the pressure on exchange rates in the economy, which would alert the authorities to intervene in order to smooth volatility and/or prevent excessive exchange rate appreciation. Thirdly, the concepts of 'sufficient' and 'excessive' for foreign reserves, which have been used in the literature at least since 2002, do not capture the basic concepts of the accumulation process. Indeed, in the main reserve-accumulating economies, the ratio of reserve assets to imports is well above 3-4 months. Similarly, the ratio of reserves to external debt, which, according to the Greenspan-Guidotti rule, should be 1 year, but way above 1, for example, around 10 in the People's Republic of China. The ratio of reserves to broad money - which can also be seen as a domestic currency shield - indicates the potential for capital flight from the domestic currency. This indicator has risen significantly above the threshold, reaching around 90% in India and Singapore. Finally, an alternative indicator could be the country's reserve assets and IMF quotas. In many reserve-accumulating countries, this ratio is well above 100%.

When looking at the ratios of foreign reserves to imports across country groups, two important points should be noted. First, as a world average, reserves held in all countries since 1992, which amounted to about 2 months of imports, increased to 3 months of imports after 1996[16], to 4 months of imports in 2007, and to 5 months of imports from 2009 to 2014. It is possible to argue that the impact of the contraction in world trade during the 2008 global crisis was also a factor. As a result, the underlying arguments here suggest that most countries that have accumulated reserves have far exceeded their traditional indicators, suggesting the existence of other factors affecting these accumulations. The second is the recent rise in oil prices.

There are 3 main reasons for increasing reserves, all related in the same direction as financial globalization. First, the desire to provide self-insurance against financial crises. Second, at least for the purpose of following the export-led, de facto or de jure exchange rate-supported growth anchored to the US dollar followed by many Asian economies in the aftermath of the financial crises. Third, the combined effect of some of the features associated with the financial structures of several GPEs, including the concentration of foreign assets and underdeveloped domestic financial systems in major net lending Asian economies.

Looking at the variables and sources of monetary crises, a number of studies have shown that reserve adequacy is an important variable. Reserves can be accumulated either for potential turbulence in foreign exchange markets and/or balance of payments shocks. The literature suggests that this may be particularly characteristic of GPEs, which are defined by high capital mobility paired with underdeveloped domestic financial systems. This vulnerability to financial risks is, in fact, mainly associated with developments such as the impressive expansion of assets and liabilities held across borders and the increased vulnerabilities that come with a sudden stop in capital inflows in the context of financial liberalization. While the accumulation of reserves may not be commensurate with the real risks faced by some countries, this is not yet the case for most indebted emerging Latin American economies. At least until recently, these economies have not been able to borrow abroad in their own currency. Even today, in Asia, accumulating reserves remains an important motive to alleviate external risk concerns. Maintaining reserve accumulation independently of the IMF's potential sources of finance constitutes an important form of independence and substitutes for the financing of contingent borrowing sources.

Studies on the monetary crisis and the variables that these studies deal with have significant results. Here, the most significant variable seems to be the international reserve. Reserve accumulation is sustained when the current account

---

[16] Guillermo Calvo, "Capital Flows and Capital-Market Crises: The Simple Economics of Sudden Stops", *Journal of Applied Economics* 1 (1998): 35–54.

is in deficit or close to balance, along with net foreign direct investment (FDI) inflows and financial inflows from other advanced economies. GPEs provide net resources to the rest of the world, and especially to the United States, from current account surpluses. Although this is a result of the investment and saving trends that economies are interested in, it shows that, as a rule, all large reserve accumulators have domestic savings in excess of investment. Moreover, some economies have not only lost current account surpluses but have also faced increased exchange rate pressure from net financial inflows. Reserve accumulating countries can be distinguished on the basis of their saving-investment balance and balance of payments trends. Moreover, when re-differentiated into emerging economies with current account surpluses and developing economies with higher domestic savings than investments, it is easy to see that reserve accumulating countries have different economic indicators. However, this alone is not enough to explain the reason for reserve accumulation.

For example, in the People's Republic of China, the depreciation of the current exchange rate caused by the exchange rate reform in 2005 to provide a price-competitive advantage for exports was partially reversed in the following year. In addition, the unemployed labour force of the rural population, which accounts for two-thirds of the population but less than 30% of GDP, has been the main support for economic growth (unemployed cheap labour in rural areas contributes to growth as cheap labour for the industrial sector), while at the same time, together with low labour costs, it has provided significant support to the price competitiveness of exports of the People's Republic of China.[17]

In addition to the developments described above, another reason for reserve accumulation should be analyzed in relation to certain features of the financial structure of the GPEs, namely the net savings surplus. Given the inadequacy of financial markets in the private savings channel for domestic or foreign investment, the public sector of some countries may turn to savings from abroad. This can lead to reserve accumulations. This seems to be the case for the People's Republic of China, given its exchange controls and the role of the public sector in the economy. Indirect confirmation of this interpretation is probably associated with a significant part of the increase in the share of foreign assets held by the private sector, probably due to the postponement of intervention in operations since mid-March 2004.[18]

---

[17] Georges Pineau et al., "The Accumulation of Foreign Reserves by an International Relations Committee Task Force", European Central Bank Occational Paper Series, no. 43 (February 2006), http://www.ecb.int.

[18] Pineau et al., "The Accumulation of Foreign Reserves".

Looking in the direction of the few reserve accumulating countries becoming net international creditors, in some of these countries, foreign assets are largely or entirely denominated in foreign currency, with either only limited amounts of domestic currency borrowing (as in Japan) or domestic currency lending prevented by asymmetric foreign exchange control (as in the People's Republic of China). The large amount of liquid assets denominated predominantly in US dollars, which is not offset by the liability side of the balance sheet, leads to fundamental mismatches in national balance sheets. Asset dollarization, especially in Asia, has led to attempts at 'socialization of currency risk' (used in the sense that people convert even their daily needs into foreign currency and transact in foreign currency), i.e. reserve assets have been used as a means of transfer from the private to the public sector, although this has not diminished for the economy as a whole. In some countries, even in the absence of restrictions on private capital outflows, hedging can be more difficult and expensive through one-way purchases. In contrast to Asia, there has been little socialization of currency risk in Latin America. The currency mismatch of the corporate and banking sectors has been transferred to the public sector through a series of measures, including the issuance of US dollar-linked Treasury securities. The exception was Brazil in 1997-1999. Treasury bonds sold to the public were indexed to the dollar so that exchange rate fluctuations did not cause a significant change in the overall risks of the economy. As a result, since 1999, the Brazilian private sector has protected itself from exchange rate risk in this way.

In general, the latter factors leading to reserve accumulation seem to have one thing in common: the integration of GPEs with global financial markets seems to have played a role in the accumulation of official foreign assets, both as a tool and as a consequence. It is possible to conclude that many developing countries, especially in Asia, have, in fact, become major players in international trade, but they are still underdeveloped financially.

Sudden private capital inflows threaten to bring about undesirable changes in a country's exchange rate and create turbulence in money markets. If private capital outflows threaten to weaken the currency, the central bank may sell reserves and buy domestic assets. If speculators suddenly put upward pressure on the currency by buying domestic currency-denominated assets, the central bank tries to mitigate this pressure by selling domestic currency and accumulating foreign reserves.[19]

When the currency is overvalued, holding foreign exchange reserves is particularly important as insurance against a currency crisis. For example, Mexico, South Korea and the Russian Federation have recently experienced the

[19] Backus et al., "Monetary Policy and the Uncovered Interest Rate".

destabilization of their currencies during financial crises. Against this backdrop, it should come as no surprise that these countries' high foreign exchange reserves provide protection. This argument is not relevant for most such Asian countries, where the currency is undervalued (it is not always clear whether a currency is overvalued or undervalued, as evidenced by the large variation across models in estimates of 'equilibrium exchange rates').

In a narrow sense, the role that international reserves act as a buffer to smooth the balance of payments shocks has not changed. However, the economic operating environment of emerging market economies has undergone a significant transformation in recent years: The capital account of emerging market economies is often highly volatile, and countries have different exchange rates and monetary policy rules, which can affect the country's ability to respond to sudden capital inflows or outflows and thus the desired stock of foreign exchange reserves. In addition, the rapid development of financial globalization provides countries with new possibilities that were not possible a few years ago, such as risk diversification or geographical savings. And finally, other factors, such as demographic developments (structural), can exert downward pressure on a country's exchange rate.[20]

Will Central Banks Maintain Their Independence?

Central banks have adopted low inflation targeting since the 1990s. Indeed, the effects of globalization, technological advances, productivity gains stemming from the Chinese economy, and the political environment contributed to low inflation. However, after the 2008 Crisis, many G20 countries were faced with rising inflation. Thus, central bank bureaucracy and technocrats started to lose public confidence. During the ensuing Covid 19 pandemic, especially in 2020, the majority of G20 governments quickly introduced wage payment programs while the supply chain disintegrated. In the aftermath of the Covid 19 pandemic, the Federal Reserve and the European Central Bank, in particular, aimed to reduce inflation by raising interest rates at a rate unprecedented in the last 30 years. The rise in inflation worldwide was driven by increases in food, raw material and energy prices. While it is possible to compare post-2015 inflation with the rise in energy (oil) prices in the 1970s, the key question is how central banks today understand and interpret their role in the face of high inflation. In the 1970s, central banks (today's G20 countries) were unsure of their position and ability to slow down price increases. But over the last 30 years, many G20 governments have given central banks autonomy in policymaking, institutionally known as 'central bank independence'. European central banks (and the European Central Bank), notably the Federal Reserve,

[20] Mccauley and Rigaudy, "Managing Foreign Exchange Reserves".

have set low inflation targets and made them publicly available (Turkey, Mexico and Argentina are dual currency economies where the dollar 'circulates' alongside the national currency).

The basic understanding of central bank independence was that an apolitical approach to monetary policy would yield better economic results. It is not politically desirable to raise interest rates and slow down economic activity, and politicians prefer to leave such actions to the central bank (Turkey and Argentina also wrote them into their development plans, but they did not achieve the goal). The Federal Reserve has accepted high employment/low unemployment as well as low inflation.

However, after 2015, central banks in almost all G20 countries started to receive serious reactions from the public on inflation. While inflation should have been predicted to rise and necessary measures should have been taken, some of the G20 central banks failed to do so. Among them, the performance of the central banks of Canada, the UK, the US and Australia has been questioned and is being reviewed by governments and parliaments. The 'trade-offs' between high inflation or low growth rates and high unemployment are difficult for the whole society, especially elected politicians, to accept, and this increases the backlash against central banks.

Another policy problem for central banks is that the amount of money they lose as they pay more interest on reserves is greater than the money they gain from the 'bond purchase programs' they buy to boost economic growth and regulate the credit market. Central banks can show this loss on their balance sheets as a 'deferred asset' item, but they cannot escape criticism.

Politicians and central banks pursued policies that restricted public spending and money supply as economies slowed down during the 2008 Crisis. During the Covid 19 pandemic, the opposite policies were pursued. Meanwhile, G20 governments faced the following situations. Labour markets were misinterpreted because many workers withdrew from the labour market during the pandemic, and returns to the labour market were slow. Based on their experience of the last 20 years central bank technocrats focused on the fact that the most important risk to economic growth would come from low demand from consumers and businesses. Due to government aid and spending restraints during the pandemic, they failed to anticipate strong demand after the pandemic, and high demand occurred in a disrupted supply chain environment. Finally, looking at the low growth rates in the Japanese economy caused by Japan's zero or even negative interest rates for the last 20 years, the G20 central banks preferred to avoid the pressure of low growth rates and low inflation that would prevent economies from moving on a high growth path.

Yet a danger remains for central banks; the impact on consumers and businesses due to expectations of high and prolonged inflation. If both groups perceive that inflation will be persistent, it will create self-reinforcing inflation, which will require higher interest rates to return to low inflation rates. Central banks thus have to trade-off between achieving low inflation rates and the threat of unemployment or even recession.

Moreover, governments will try to support central banks' efforts to lower inflation and reduce the risk of a financial crisis by cutting public spending and/or raising taxes. When inflation is high, and interest rates are rising, governments need to determine how loose they can leave fiscal policy and at what limit they have to stop. Fiscal consolidation is an important support tool in the fight against inflation, reducing the need for interest rates to remain high for longer and the risk of financial instability.

Athanasios Orphanides, in 2018, asked the question, "What are the consequences if an independent central bank adopts a price stability policy but has to use an unconventional monetary policy?". Unconventional monetary policies, with a high rate of asset purchases and a zero current (nominal) interest rate, create fiscal policy problems, worsen income distribution and increase risks on the central bank's balance sheet. The lack of agreement on the precise definition of price stability brings certain contradictions with large increases in the balance sheet. In such a situation, it would be more favourable for the central bank to adopt quantity easing rather than low inflation. The zero lower-bound inflation policy adopted by the Bank of Japan in 2013 was a clearer definition of price stability. For Japan, Friedman proposed monetary easing and Krugman's high inflation rate targeting.[21]

Comparison of the New Crisis with the 1970 Crisis and Central Banks

The oil embargo imposed by OPEC in the 1970s transformed the moderate inflation in the G20 countries into high inflation and stagflation. Rising inflation and insufficient economic activity (GDP) in the 2020s raise the question: "Are we going back to the 1970s?". Stagflation, which is the combination of high inflation and low growth rates, is a significant problem, as it is normally very rare to see these two economic indicators together. Covid 19 caused factory closures, especially in Southeast Asia, which affected industrial production worldwide. Inflation in the G20 countries has exceeded central bank targets, with inflation rates above 3 per cent in the G20 countries in Europe and above 5 per cent in the United States. Yet, with the exception of Argentina and Turkey,

---

[21] Milton Friedman, "Rx for Japan: Back to the Future", *The Wall Street Journal*, December 17, 1997; Paul Krugman, "It's Baaack: Japan's Slump and the Return of the Liquidity Trap", *Brookings Papers on Economic Activity* 29, no. 2 (1998): 137–206.

which are experiencing high double-digit inflation, the rest of the G20 countries are experiencing inflation of around 5 per cent.

The starting point for those worried about stagflation is that energy prices are rising, as they did in the 1970s, and this time, food prices are also rising. Higher energy prices, in particular, lead to higher inflation, and central banks do not have much room for manoeuvre in this regard. Rising energy prices also increase transportation costs. Consumer demand, which was suppressed and started to increase after Covid 19, increases the demand for labour, and the bargaining power of workers increases as firms compete for labour. Proponents of the idea of stagflation also argue that macroeconomic thinking opens the door to stubborn inflation, almost like regression analysis. Indeed, the prevailing policy of the 1960s and 1970s was for governments and central banks to prioritize low unemployment in the inflation-employment trade-off, leaving price stability in the background. However, the experience of stagflation led central bankers to change their thinking and taught them to pay attention to inflation. The global financial crisis of 2007-2009 and the period of low demand that followed brought a shift in focus to rising unemployment: Central bankers looked either at price stability or employment. Low interest rates weakened fiscal discipline. This raised the possibility that, as in the 1970s, central banks and governments could adopt policies to solve supply-side problems, which would involve a combination of inflation and slow growth.

Nevertheless, the parallels with what happened in the 1970s do not provide much of a clue to current economic developments. The increases in energy and food prices concern economists in several ways. First, they will lead to wage bargaining and inflation expectations, creating a wage-price spiral. (In this case, central banks are expected to keep inflation expectations stable and low. If they can do this, they can control inflation). Today, the strong bargaining power of the labour unions of the 1970s has been weakened. (The proportion of unionized workers in the OECD has fallen from 38 per cent in the 1970s to 16 per cent today.[22] Second, the automatic pass-through of inflation to wages is not the case today in G20 countries, except for Turkey and Argentina, which have high inflation. Third, while productivity declines were observed in the G7 countries in the 1970s, today, many G20 countries have post-pandemic productivity gains, and investment increases that show that they are sustainable. Fourth, unlike in the 1970s, G20 central banks are much better prepared and have more tools at their disposal to deal with inflation and price stability. Finally, there is a more integrated international trading and financial system than in the 1970s, particularly in the G20 countries. This integration can create both advantages and disadvantages.

---

[22] "The World Economy: Stagflation Sensations", *The Economist*, October 9, 2021.

Possible New Roles of Central Banks

As the determinants of monetary policy, central banks are among the most important institutions of the capitalist system. The decisions taken/to be taken by central banks directly concern economic actors. Especially during the financial panics in the nineteenth century, central banks supported the banking system against crisis as "lenders of last resort".

In the 1980s and 1990s, when inflation reached double digits in developed countries (G7), central banks focused on 'price stability'. 'Central bank independence' gained importance in this period and many central banks developed strict rules on price stability. In addition, the Maastricht Criteria of inflation, growth rates and debt/GDP ratios became an important anchor for the G7. After the average annual inflation rate of 8 per cent in the 1970s caused by the oil crises, the US, the UK, Japan and Germany experienced an average annual inflation rate of 2 per cent between 1990 and 2007. After the 2007-2009 financial crisis, there were even complaints that inflation was too low until the Covid-19 pandemic.

After the pandemic, high inflation became the main problem for all G20 countries. Just like in the 1970s, energy prices have been driven up again, this time by rising wages and supply chain problems. International organizations such as the IMF and BIS stated that the world was on the brink of a new period of high inflation. The central banks of the G20 countries played active roles during the Covid 19 pandemic: intervening in asset markets, buying treasury bonds, and lending directly to firms and governments. Thus, as institutions that have been able to achieve and sustain low inflation except for a few members of the G20, especially the G7 countries, with the pandemic, they have assumed a full policymaker position, pursuing policies that put the steps taken in areas such as income inequality and climate change at risk. Rising inflation has the potential to put these issues on the back burner for some time to come.

The role of central banks has reached a new level. One reason is the resurgence of inflation in the aftermath of the financial crisis (2007-2009), despite a sustained fall in interest rates. The fact that central banks are raising interest rates has to convince investors. As inflation rises, central banks use all the instruments at their disposal. Especially in the G7 countries, purchases of treasury bonds are being made to lower long-term interest rates. The European Central Bank has been known to buy corporate paper and fund consumers and businesses through banks. The Bank of Japan has announced that it will keep the yield on 10-year Treasury securities at 0.25%.

Another reason for the increasing importance of central banks is the growing importance of financial stability. As governments and regulators (such as the SEC in the U.S. and the BRSA in Turkey) tightly regulated banks, non-bank intermediaries emerged in the credit market. With the onset of the crisis, central banks made efforts to stabilize these markets. In 2020, due to the full closures, central banks turned to credit allocations. Developments in technology and the emergence of virtual money markets also began to reduce the interest in paper money issued by central banks. Therefore, central banks have started to consider whether the banknotes they supply will be virtual.

Central banks played an important role in absorbing the financial shocks that occurred when countries shut down in spring 2020 (during the pandemic). Investors sold even the safest treasury securities to meet their cash needs. Credit markets virtually dried up. Central bank assets in the G7 countries increased by $10 trillion during the pandemic.[23] Central banks in South Africa, Indonesia and India, other key G20 countries, also bought treasury bonds.

There are several problems created by large-scale bond buying. These interventions by central banks create the danger of 'moral hazard'. This practice increases the risks to investors and raises the expectation that central banks will continue to intervene in the future. Central banks have to break these expectations. Even if the policy of providing liquidity is reduced rapidly, quant easing (QE) will continue for some time to hold assets. The Bank of Japan holds 44 per cent of government paper, the ECB holds 40 per cent of German, Finnish and Dutch bonds, the Federal Reserve holds 40 per cent, and the Bank of England holds 30 per cent and these ratios started in 2020.

In effect, QE means replacing long-term bonds with central bank reserves. These reserves are used for public financing. The fact that central banks hold large amounts of bonds significantly constrains the structure of public debt, which means that governments pay more when interest rates rise. Instead of low and long-term interest rates, governments may prefer to increase short-term interest rates for public financing and may raise interest rates more slowly or even not at all, especially if central bank independence comes into question. In this case, fiscal policy is expected to step in when monetary policy reaches its limits. But fiscal policy is an area where political decisions need to be taken. To exit a recession, the textbooks say that monetary and fiscal policies should be coordinated and used together, but past experience shows that central banks have been left alone at the end of parliamentary debates.

Political issues have become another key issue. One of the reasons why governments and environmental activists have brought issues such as income inequality and climate change to the forefront has been the demand to transfer resources from central bank balance sheets to these areas. The pandemic and

[23] Rachana Shanbhogue, "Special Reports: Central Banks", *The Economist*, April 23, 2022, https://www.economist.com/special-report/2022-04-23.

the growth in central bank balance sheets have further increased this demand. Central banks inevitably became interested in these issues.

The functions of central banks are changing in G20 countries, particularly in the G7. Historically (and classically), central banks have been seen as institutions in regular contact with governments, preventing financial crises and recessions. Central bank bureaucrats have worked out an optimum situation of low inflation, a stable financial system, high employment and the credibility of the national currency. As mentioned above, during the pandemic, central banks were working on many issues: buying government securities, rescuing firms, etc. In the aftermath of the pandemic, G7 central banks, in particular, preferred monetary tightening to bring down the rising inflation to the targeted 'magic' 2 per cent or close to it. Meanwhile, the reduction in inflation while protecting labour markets should be seen as an indicator of the resilience of these countries' economies. Central banks are now being asked to be more effective in financing climate change, being partners in solving social problems such as income inequality, digital money and even credit allocation. In emerging members of the G20, this demand is on the rise, while the PBOC has been tasked with multi-tasking, managing its balance sheet and allocating credit. Central banks in the G7 (and the ECB) have been asked to use their balance sheets according to their stated objectives. Beyond the issue of interest rates, new instruments need to be experimented with. They cannot be expected to ignore increasing risks and technologies. Governments' demands and directives on digital currency will increase. It will also be necessary to work on how climate change will affect the economy and the financial system.

Bibliography

Backus, David K, Federico Gavazzoni, Chris Telmer, and Stanley E Zin. "Monetary Policy and the Uncovered Interest Rate Parity Puzzle." *NBER Working Paper*, no. 16218 (2012).

Bahmani-Oskooee, M., and F. Brown. "Demand for International Reserves: A Review Article." *Applied Economics* 34, no. 10 (2002): 1209–26. https://doi.org/10.1080/00036840110096129.

Bakker, Age F.P., and Ingmar R.Y. van Herpt. *Central Bank Reserve Management: New Trend, from Liquidity to Return*. Edward Elgar Publishing, 2007. https://EconPapers.repec.org/RePEc:elg:eebook:12513.

Beck, Roland, and Ebrahim Rahbari. "Optimal Reserve Composition in the Presence of Sudden Stops: The Euro and the Dollar as Safe Haven Currencies." *European Central Bank Working Paper*, no. 916 (2008). http://www.ecb.europa.eu.

Bernanke, Ben S. "The Global Saving Glut and the U.S. Current Account Deficit." Elischolar. library.yale.edu, 2005. https://elischolar.library.yale.edu/ypfs-documents/4221.

Calvo, Guillermo. "Capital Flows and Capital-Market Crises: The Simple Economics of Sudden Stops." *Journal of Applied Economics* 1 (1998): 35–54.

Cencini, Alvaro. *Monetary Theory: National and International.* Routledge, Taylor & Francis e-Library, 2003.

Choo, Heung Sik. "Dealing with Reserve Accumulation: The Case of Korea." In *Central Bank Reserve Management: New Trends, from Liquidity to Return,* edited by Age F.P. Bakker and Ingmar R.Y. van Herpt. Edward Elgar Publishing, 2007.

Feldstein, Martin. "Self-Protection For Emerging Market Economies." *National Bureau of Economic Research Working Paper,* no. 6907 (1999). http://www.nber.org/papers/w6907.

Fratzscher, Marcel. "Capital Flows, Push Versus Pull Factors And The Global Financial Crisis." *European Central Bank Working Paper,* no. 1364 (2011). http://www.ecb.europa.eu.

Friedman, Milton. "Rx for Japan: Back to the Future." *The Wall Street Journal,* December 17, 1997.

Glick, Reuven, and Michael Hutchinson. "Capital Controls and Exchange Rate Instability in Developing Economies." *Journal of International Money and Finance* 24, no. 3 (April 2005): 387–412. https://doi.org/10.1016/j.jimonfin.2004.11.004.

Jadresic, Esteban. "The Cost-Benefit Approach to Reserve Adequacy: The Case of Chile." In *Central Bank Reserve Management: New Trend, from Liquidity to Return,* edited by Age F.P. Bakker and İngmar R.Y. van Herpt. Edward Elgar Publishing, 2007.

Kaminsky, Graciela L., and Carmen M. Reinhart. "The Twin Crises: The Causes of Banking and Balance-of-Payments Problems." *American Economic Review* 89, no. 3 (1999): 473–500. https://doi.org/10.1257/AER.89.3.473.

Krugman, Paul. "It's Baaack: Japan's Slump and the Return of the Liquidity Trap." *Brookings Papers on Economic Activity* 29, no. 2 (1998): 137–206.

Mccauley, Robert N. "Assessing the Benefits And Costs of Official Foreign Exchange Reserves." In *Central Bank Reserve Management: New Trend, from Liquidity to Return,* edited by Age F.P. Bakker and Ingmar R.Y. van Herpt, 19–36. Edward Elgar Publishing, 2007.

Mccauley, Robert N, and Jean-François Rigaudy. "Managing Foreign Exchange Reserves in the Crisis and After." In *Bank of International Settlements (BIS),* 58:19–47. Bank for International Settlements, 2011.

Mishkin, Frederic S. "Is Monetary Policy Effective During Financial Crises?" *National Bureau of Economic Research,* no. 14678 (2009). http://www.nber.org/papers/w14678.

Niedermayer, Ludek. "Central Bank Risk Management: The Case of the Czech National Bank." In *Central Bank Reserve Management: New Trend, from Liquidity to Return,* edited by Age F.P. Bakker and Ingmar R.Y. van Herpt. Edward Elgar Publishing, 2007.

Pineau, Georges, Ettore Dorrucci, Fabio Comelli, and Angelika Lagerblom. "The Accumulation Of Foreign Reserves by an International Relations Committee Task Force." *European Central Bank* Occasional Paper Series, no. 43 (February 2006). http://www.ecb.int.

Shanbhogue, Rachana. "Special Reports: Central Banks." *The Economist,* April 23, 2022. https://www.economist.com/special-report/2022-04-23.

Sogano, Hidehiko. "Foreign Reserve Adequacy from the Asian Perspective." In *Central Bank Reserve Management: New Trend, from Liquidity to Return*, edited by Age F. P. Bakker and Ingmar R.Y. van Herpt. Edward Elger Publishing, 2007.

The Economist. "Argentina's Economic Woes, The Crisis of Macrinomics." May 12, 2018.

The Economist. "The World Economy. Stagflation Sensations." October 9, 2021.

Woodford, Michael. "Inflation Targeting And Financial Stability." *National Bureau of Economic Research* Working Paper, no. 17967 (2012). http://www.nber.org/papers/w17967.

Yip, Amy. "Implications of Growing Reserves of Central Banks for Asset Allocation." In *Central Bank Reserve Management: New Trend, from Liquidity to Return*, edited by Age F.P. Bakker and Ingmar R.Y. van Herpt. Edward Elgar Publishing, 2007.

Chapter 10
China's Central Banking System, Monetary Policy and Currency Markets

Jeremy Kwok
University of Exeter, England

Abstract

This chapter explores the central banking system, foreign exchange market, and related topics in China, focusing on the role of the People's Bank of China (PBoC) and its implications for the country's economic growth, stability, and global influence. As the second-largest economy in the world, China's monetary policies and decisions have far-reaching consequences for the global economy and financial markets. Understanding the PBoC's approach to digital currency, fintech, and cryptocurrency provides valuable insights into the future of money and the financial system. The chapter begins by providing a historical overview of the PBoC, tracing its roots back to the Second Sino-Japanese War and its subsequent establishment as the central bank of the newly founded People's Republic of China. It explores the PBoC's role in issuing and regulating the Renminbi, managing currency supply, and promoting financial stability. Additionally, the PBoC's responsibilities extend to overseeing the financial system, commercial banks, non-bank financial institutions, and the payment system while addressing risks to maintain stability. The implementation of monetary policy by the PBoC is crucial in controlling inflation, stabilizing the economy, and promoting financial stability. The bank utilizes tools such as setting interest rates and reserve requirement ratios to achieve these objectives. The chapter also delves into the foreign exchange rate policy in China, highlighting the PBoC's efforts to balance a stable exchange rate with the promotion of an export-oriented economy. Examining the onshore and offshore Renminbi markets, the chapter discusses the PBoC's role in promoting economic development through financial inclusion and supporting the growth of small and medium-sized enterprises (SMEs). It explores the PBoC's collaboration with government agencies and international organizations to foster global financial stability and cooperation. The chapter also touches upon offshore market dynamics, including the role of offshore RMB centres, such as Hong Kong, and the issuance of Dim Sum bonds.

Keywords: China's Central Bank, Foreign Exchange Market and Products

***

Introduction

The PBoC plays a crucial role in China's economic development by implementing monetary policies that support growth and stability. The bank sets interest rates, reserve requirement ratios, and other monetary policy tools to control inflation, stabilize the economy, and promote financial stability. Additionally, the PBoC is responsible for issuing and regulating the supply of money, and maintaining financial stability. The bank also plays a significant role in promoting financial inclusion and supporting the growth of small and medium-sized enterprises (SMEs) through financial services. Furthermore, the PBoC works closely with other government agencies and international organizations to promote financial stability and cooperation at the global level, which helps China to maintain its position as a major player in the global economy.

The PBoC has faced several challenges recently in light of the economic impact of the coronavirus pandemic, and the reopening of the economy in 2023.[1] One of the main challenges is balancing the need to control inflation and stabilize the economy while supporting economic growth. The PBoC has been implementing monetary policies such as lowering interest rates and cutting reserve requirement ratios to support growth, but at the same time, it has to be mindful of the potential inflationary pressures. Additionally, managing the exchange rate of the Renminbi (RMB) has been a challenge as the PBoC has to balance the need for a stable exchange rate with the need to promote China's export-oriented economy.

Brief History of the PBoC

The historical roots of the People's Bank of China (PBoC) can be traced back to the period of the Second Sino-Japanese War. On November 7, 1931, during the "First National Soviet Congress" held in Ruijin, Jiangxi, the "Central Soviet Republic State Bank" (commonly known as the Soviet State Bank) was established through a resolution, and the currency was issued.[2] From the Land Revolution to the eve of the founding of the People's Republic of China, the political power was fragmented into disconnected regions. Each base area established relatively independent and decentralized base area banks, each issuing its own currency circulated within its respective territory.[3]

---

[1] PBoC, *MPC Meeting Notes*, 2023, http://www.pbc.gov.cn/en/3688229/3688311/3688329/index.html.

[2] PBoC, *History*, 2023, http://www.pbc.gov.cn/en/3688066/3688089/index.html.

[3] Peter Drysdale, Adam Triggs and Jiao Wang, "China's New Role in The International Financial Architecture", *Asian Economic Policy Review* 12, no. 2 (2017): 258-277.

Initial Establishment - The Establishment of the People's Bank of China and the National Banking System (1948-1952)

The establishment of the PBoC on December 1, 1948, marked its transformation into the central bank and legal tender issuer of the newly founded PBoC. It was formed in Shijiazhuang, Hebei, through the merger of the North China Bank, North Sea Bank, and Northwest Farmers' Bank. Shortly after its establishment, the PBoC's currency was declared the unified circulation currency in North China, East China, and the Northwest regions.[4]

In February 1949, the PBoC relocated to Beijing and was included as a directly affiliated unit of the Central People's Government according to the "Organic Law of the Central People's Government of the People's Republic of China." Under the guidance of the Finance and Economic Commission and in close cooperation with the Ministry of Finance, the PBoC was entrusted with crucial functions, including issuing the national currency, managing the national treasury, overseeing national finance, stabilizing the financial market, and supporting economic recovery and reconstruction.

During the period of national economic recovery, the PBoC took significant steps to establish a unified national banking system. It introduced an independent and unified currency system, with the Renminbi becoming the domestic circulating currency. The bank also collaborated with various economic sectors to control inflation and established branches nationwide to form a comprehensive banking system. It restructured private financial industries, managed foreign capital, and unified foreign exchange management, abolishing the circulation of foreign currencies.

By the end of the national economic recovery period in 1952, the PBoC had established a nationwide organizational structure, unified the issuance of the Renminbi, and successfully made it the unified national currency. The bank effectively utilized currency issuance and monetary policies to regulate the currency supply and demand, resolving the hyperinflation issues inherited from the previous Kuomintang government. It also played a vital role in supporting the rapid growth of state-owned and private economies, facilitating the exchange of goods between urban and rural areas, stabilizing the Renminbi's value, and contributing to the stability, recovery, and development of the national economy.

---

[4] Greg Lewis, "Financial Warfare in Revolutionary China, 1949–1950: Chen Yun, Nan Hanchen, and the People's Bank", *Twentieth-Century China* 29, no. 1 (2003): 105-119.

Planned Economy- The National Bank During the Planned Economy Period (1953 to 1978)

During the Planned Economy period from 1953 to 1978, China operated under a centralized economic system, with the PBoC as the central bank overseeing financial activities. All credit funds were under the unified control of the PBoC, and it played a crucial role in implementing monetary policies and credit planning. However, after the economic reform in 1978, China shifted away from the Planned Economy system and embraced market-oriented reforms. This change led to the introduction of various economic liberalization measures, opening up to foreign investments, and transitioning to a more market-driven economy, reducing the central planning role of the PBoC.

In the context of the centralized planned economic system, the PBoC functioned as a crucial institution for the state to absorb, mobilize, concentrate, and allocate credit funds in a top-down manner. As China underwent a socialist transformation, private financial sectors were integrated into public-private joint ventures, establishing a centralized and unified financial system. The PBoC assumed a dual role as the state agency overseeing financial management and as the national bank conducting comprehensive banking operations.

To complement the highly centralized banking structure, a centralized and unified comprehensive credit planning and management system was instituted in 1953. This system brought all credit funds in the country under the unified control of the PBoC's head office, regardless of their origins or purposes. The "unified deposit and unified loan" management approach incorporated bank credit plans into the national economic plan, becoming a pivotal tool for state economic management. This centralized national banking system facilitated comprehensive financial supervision and services to support the extensive economic construction carried out by the state.[5]

The PBoC's responsibilities encompassed currency circulation organization, various credit operations, and playing a comprehensive role in reflecting economic conditions and exercising monetary supervision during the implementation of national plans. The bank offered various loans, including over-quota working capital loans, seasonal loans, and limited major repair loans to state-owned enterprises. Additionally, it provided production working capital loans to collective and individual economies in both urban and rural areas, as well as to private enterprises. For impoverished rural farmers, the bank offered production loans, food loans, and other living expense loans. This system, wherein long-term funds belonged to the treasury, and short-term funds belonged to the

---

[5] Lin Jianhao et al.,"Is the People's Bank of China consistent in Words and Deeds?", *China Economic Review* 78 (2023): 101919.

bank, persisted until 1978, with certain modifications while maintaining its fundamental structure.

Transition From National Bank to Central Bank System (1979 to 1992)

In January 1979, the China Agricultural Bank was reinstated to provide support for rural economies, while in March of the same year, the Bank of China underwent structural reform, designated as the state-designated foreign exchange specialized bank, along with the establishment of the State Administration of Foreign Exchange. This period also witnessed the revival of domestic insurance operations, leading to the re-establishment of the China People's Insurance Company and the establishment of trust and investment companies and urban credit cooperatives in various regions, contributing to the diversification of financial institutions and services.[6]

As the economy and the number of financial institutions expanded, the need for strengthened unified management and comprehensive coordination of the financial sector became apparent. In response to this, the PBoC's specific role as the central bank was emphasized in a report endorsed by the State Council in July 1982. It was designated as China's central bank and the state institution responsible for the unified management of the national financial system under the leadership of the State Council. This marked the initiation of preparations for the establishment of a specialized central bank system.

On September 17, 1983, the State Council decided to entrust the specific functions of the central bank to the PBoC, defining ten specific responsibilities for the bank. From January 1, 1984, the PBoC exclusively exercised the functions of the central bank, focusing on macroeconomic decision-making in the financial sector, enhancing control over credit volumes, and regulating the funding of financial institutions to maintain currency stability. During this period, the Industrial and Commercial Bank of China was established to handle the commercial credit and savings business previously managed by the PBoC. Thc bank's branches were placed under vertical leadership, and the China People's Bank Council was established as a coordinating decision-making body. The introduction of reserve requirements and central bank lending to specialized banks laid the initial foundation for the central bank system.

In the early phase of exclusively exercising central bank functions, the PBoC underwent continuous reform to adapt to the evolving national economic system and rapid economic development. In response to diverse financial institutions,

---

[6] Knut Benjamin Pißler, "History and Legal Framework of the People's Bank of China", in *Central Banking and Financial Stability in East Asia,* (Cham: Springer International Publishing, 2015), 11-24.

financing channels, and credit instruments, the bank continuously reformed its mechanisms to stimulate and develop the financial sector, promoting financial market innovation. The PBoC explored and improved methods for macroeconomic regulation, gradually incorporating interest rates, reserve requirements, and central bank lending into its toolkit to control credit and monetary supply. The aim was to achieve a balance between macro-level control and micro-level vitality, fostering the bank's capacity to regulate the economy through monetary policy. This process aimed to curtail credit expansion, address economic overheating, and facilitate economic structural adjustments, establishing the bank's ability to impact the economy through monetary policy.

The Establishment of the New Financial System - (1993 to the Present)

In 1993, as part of the financial system reform, the PBoC underwent changes in its roles and responsibilities. Subsequently, in 1995, the PBoC was officially established as the central bank of China through the "Law of the People's Republic of China on the People's Bank of China," signifying a crucial milestone in the formalization and standardization of the central bank system. Further management system reforms occurred in 1998, abolishing provincial branches and introducing cross-provincial branches, along with the establishment of the PBoC System Party Committee for party affairs management.

In 2003, the PBoC's regulatory responsibilities for various financial institutions were separated and integrated with the Central Financial Work Commission to form the China Banking Regulatory Commission. The PBoC's newly defined functions focused on formulating and implementing monetary policies, maintaining financial stability, and providing financial services. This included enhancing the capacity for formulating and implementing monetary policies, monitoring financial markets, and improving risk control mechanisms between the currency market and other financial sectors.[7]

Moreover, the PBoC transformed its approach to financial macro-regulation and systemic risk prevention, moving from a focus on approval and regulation of financial institutions to monitoring overall risks and formulating industry reform and development strategies. The PBoC also assumed additional responsibilities in anti-money laundering efforts and credit information management.

---

[7] Stephen Bell and Hui Feng, "How Proximate and 'Meta-Institutional' Contexts Shape Institutional Change: Explaining the Rise of The People's Bank Of China", *Political Studies* 62, no. 1 (2014): 197-215.

These changes have reinforced the PBoC's role as China's central bank, emphasizing financial macro-control, currency stability, sustainable economic growth, and systemic risk prevention. As China's market economy continues to develop, the PBoC's role as the central bank in the macroeconomic control system is set to become even more prominent.

In recent years, the PBoC has taken steps towards internationalization, adopting the Special Data Dissemination Standard (SDDS) of the International Monetary Fund in 2015 and establishing the Financial Technology Committee in 2017 to strengthen research and coordination in financial technology. The PBoC also collaborated with the Hong Kong Monetary Authority in 2018 to facilitate the issuance of central bank bills in Hong Kong and enhance RMB financial products.

In 2023, the PBoC underwent further reforms with the establishment of the China Banking and Insurance Regulatory Commission, assuming daily regulatory responsibilities for financial holding companies and other financial groups. The PBoC's branch institutions were restructured, with provincial branches set up in 31 provinces and planned municipal branches established in select cities. The PBoC's roles and functions have been standardized, with personnel regulated under the national civil service system.

These developments demonstrate the continuous evolution of the PBoC's functions and responsibilities, adapting to China's changing economic landscape and contributing to the stability and growth of the nation's financial system.

China's Monetary Policy Institutional Framework and Implementation

The institutional framework governing China's monetary policy is established by the Law of the People's Republic of China on the People's Bank of China. Article 2 of this law outlines the role of the PBoC as the central bank responsible for formulating and implementing monetary policy under the leadership of the State Council. The primary objective of this policy is to maintain the stability of the currency's value, which, in turn, promotes economic growth in the country.

To achieve its monetary policy objectives, Article 23 of the law grants the PBoC the authority to utilize various monetary policy instruments. These instruments include requiring banking financial institutions to maintain deposit reserves at a prescribed ratio, deciding on the benchmark interest rates of the central bank, and providing discount services to banks that have accounts with the PBoC. Additionally, the PBoC is empowered to offer loans to commercial banks and engage in the purchase and sale of central government bonds, other government securities, financial bonds, and foreign exchange in the open market.

Overall, the PBoC has a comprehensive set of tools to influence the money supply and interest rates in the economy, allowing it to adjust its monetary policy to address changing economic conditions and achieve its objectives of currency stability and economic growth. The State Council also has the authority to introduce other monetary policy instruments, as deemed necessary, to support the country's economic goals and ensure a well-functioning financial system. The PBoC's role as the central bank and its ability to use a diverse range of monetary policy instruments provide the foundation for maintaining the stability and growth of the Chinese economy.

Implementation of Monetary Policy

This section presents a review of the institutional arrangements governing the implementation of monetary policy in China. The study focuses on the regulation of interest rates for deposits, retail lending, and window guidance, which differ from those used in advanced economies. The development of the interbank market, which has grown in significance for monetary policy in China, is also discussed.[8]

The PBoC employs a series of monetary policy instruments, including Open Market Operations (OMO), Required Reserve Ratio (RRR), Medium-term Lending Facility (MLF), and Standing Lending Facility (SLF), to manage liquidity in the banking system.[9]

With recent reforms, the PBoC introduced a new RRR framework with "three tranches of reserve requirements and two additional preferential treatments" to guide small and medium-sized banks in supporting local enterprises and the real economy. The three tranches categorize banks based on their systemic importance and service positioning. The first tranche applies to large banks, the second tranche to medium-sized banks, and the third tranche to small banks operating in counties. The two additional preferential treatments offer further RRR cuts for banks meeting inclusive finance criteria.

In terms of the interest-rate system, the PBoC introduced the Loan Prime Rate (LPR) to improve the formation mechanism among commercial banks. The LPR, based on the MLF rate, guides the determination of real interest rates for financing enterprises. The LPR now covers longer maturities, serving as a pricing reference for long-term loans.

---

[8] Jonathan Anderson, "The China Monetary Policy Handbook", *China's Emerging Financial Markets: Challenges and Opportunities* (2009): 167-265.

[9] Weibo Xiong, "Measuring the Monetary Policy Stance of The People's Bank Of China: An Ordered Probit Analysis", *China Economic Review* 23, no. 3 (2012): 512-533.

The PBoC also utilizes various tools, such as targeted RRR reductions, central-bank lending, rediscounts, Pledged Supplementary Lending (PSL), and Targeted MLF (TMLF), to encourage financial institutions to support key sectors and weak areas in the economy, including Micro and Small Businesses (MSBs) and private firms.[10]

Regarding exchange-rate regime reform, the PBoC has made significant progress in increasing the flexibility of the RMB exchange rate. The RMB's exchange rate now fluctuates based on market supply and demand, referencing a basket of currencies, and is maintained at a reasonable and equilibrium level.

Furthermore, the PBoC places great emphasis on communication with the public through various channels, such as press conferences, monetary policy reports, statements on the PBoC website, newspapers, and official social media accounts like WeChat and Weibo. This approach enhances transparency and ensures that the public is well-informed about the central bank's policies and actions.

The PBoC operates under the leadership of the State Council, and its objective, as stated in the Central Bank Law, is to maintain currency stability and promote economic growth. To achieve this, the PBoC sets intermediate targets for various economic indicators and utilizes a mix of monetary policy instruments to influence liquidity and interest rates in the interbank money market. The PBoC also employs window guidance to influence lending behaviour by commercial banks, although its effectiveness has diminished over time. The regulations of retail lending and deposit rates have undergone liberalization, but ceilings on deposit rates and floors on lending rates are still in place to maintain financial stability and bank profitability. The interbank money market in China is composed of the money market, bond market, and foreign exchange market, with various short-term and long-term interest rates that are influenced by the PBoC's policy actions. Overall, the PBoC's monetary policy approach has evolved to be more market-based, promoting stability and growth in the Chinese economy.

The PBoC employs various communication channels to convey its monetary policy decisions. These channels include quarterly press briefings on financial statistics, the publication of the Monetary Policy Report, and regular meetings of the Monetary Policy Committee. The PBoC also disseminates statements through its official website, as well as newspapers and online social media platforms like WeChat and Weibo.

---

[10] Wenzhe Li, "Does Targeted Monetary Policy Matter? A Perspective From China", *Economic Affairs* 38, no. 1 (2018): 106-124.

In terms of liquidity management, the PBoC utilizes required reserves with 10-day maintenance periods and reserve ratios ranging from 5% to 9.5% for domestic currency and 6% for foreign currency. The actual reserves amount to CNY 20 trillion, which accounts for 17% of the country's GDP.

Open Market Operations are conducted by the PBoC through repos and reverse repos with varying maturities ranging from 7 days to 1 year. These operations take place on a daily basis, and the pricing method is based on auctions, limited to Primary Dealers. Additionally, the PBoC employs the MLF and PSL as tools for liquidity management.[11]

Since 2005, the PBoC has operated a Real-Time Gross Settlement (RTGS) system and provides intra-day liquidity facilities through collateral loans and overdrafts. The bank has also established foreign currency settlement systems and allows banks to participate in the Continuous Linked Settlement (CLS) system.

The PBoC accepts eligible collateral for its standing facilities and open market operations, which include high-quality bonds and loans. To enhance collateral availability, the PBoC has expanded programs such as the Loan Pledged Program (LPP) and Internal Credit Rating (ICR).

While operational information on liquidity forecasts is not publicly disclosed, details regarding open market operations, including volume and price, are disseminated through the PBoC website, China Bond website, and China Money website. Monthly reports on the usage of standing facilities can be found on the PBoC website, and the China Monetary Policy Report, offering insights into policy developments, is released quarterly on the PBoC website.

China's monetary policy trilemma refers to the challenge faced by the country in managing its exchange rate, monetary policy, and capital flows simultaneously. According to the trilemma, a country can only choose two out of these three objectives, making it difficult to achieve all of them simultaneously.[12]

China, like many other countries, desires a fixed exchange rate to promote stability and facilitate international trade. A fixed exchange rate ensures that the value of the country's currency remains constant relative to another currency, usually the U.S. dollar. This stability provides certainty for businesses and investors engaged in cross-border transactions. At the same time, China also seeks to maintain an independent monetary policy. This means having

---

[11] Chaoying Lin and Lerong He, "Targeted Monetary Policy and Agriculture Business Loans", *The North American Journal of Economics and Finance* 54 (2020): 101290.

[12] John G. Fernald, Mark M. Spiegel and Eric T. Swanson, "Monetary Policy Effectiveness in China: Evidence From a FAVAR Model", *Journal of International Money and Finance* 49 (2014): 83-103.

control over interest rates, money supply, and other monetary tools to manage inflation, economic growth, and financial stability within the country. Independent monetary policy allows the central bank to respond to domestic economic conditions and adjust interest rates accordingly.

However, pursuing a fixed exchange rate and an independent monetary policy can create conflicts when it comes to managing capital flows. Capital flows refer to the movement of funds in and out of a country for investment purposes. In an open economy, unrestricted capital flows can result in significant inflows or outflows of funds, which can impact a country's exchange rate and monetary policy.

China faces challenges in managing capital flows due to its large and growing economy.[13] As the country implements monetary easing measures or lowers interest rates to stimulate economic growth, it can attract foreign investors seeking higher returns. However, this can lead to capital inflows, which put upward pressure on the currency's value. To counteract this, the central bank may need to intervene by selling its own currency and buying foreign currencies, resulting in an increase in foreign exchange reserves. On the other hand, if China tries to maintain a fixed exchange rate while pursuing an independent monetary policy, it may face difficulties in managing capital outflows. If investors perceive higher risks or better investment opportunities abroad, they may move their funds out of China, leading to a depletion of foreign exchange reserves and potential currency depreciation.

To address the monetary policy trilemma, China has implemented various measures over the years. It has made efforts to gradually liberalize its capital account, allowing more freedom for capital flows in and out of the country. China has also been moving toward a more flexible exchange rate regime, allowing the yuan to appreciate or depreciate within certain limits.

In an article titled "China's Trilemma—and a Possible Solution", Bernanke discusses the economic challenges faced by China and proposes a potential solution. The author, Ben S. Bernanke, explains that China confronts a classic policy trilemma in international economics. This trilemma states that a country cannot simultaneously have all three of the following: a fixed exchange rate, independent monetary policy, and free international capital flows.

Bernanke highlights four key premises about China's current situation and objectives. First, China is undergoing a necessary transition from a growth model focused on heavy industry, construction, and exports to one that emphasizes services and domestic consumer demand. Second, China's growth

---

[13] Rongrong Sun, "Does Monetary Policy Matter in China? A Narrative Approach." *China Economic Review* 26 (2013): 56-74.s

has slowed more than expected, which is concerning for the government due to its impact on job creation and income growth. Third, China has implemented monetary easing measures to support economic growth during the transition. Fourth, China has been opening up its capital markets, allowing citizens to invest abroad.

These last two points contribute to China's trilemma. As China eases monetary policy and offers lower returns to domestic savers, there is an outflow of capital seeking higher returns abroad. This capital flight puts downward pressure on China's exchange rate. In the short run, the PBoC can defend the exchange rate by selling its dollar-denominated securities and buying yuan. However, this depletes China's reserves, and if no changes occur, the currency will eventually fall. The risk of future devaluation can further accelerate the decline in reserves.[14]

To resolve this trilemma, Bernanke suggests a potential solution. He proposes that China should adopt a flexible exchange rate regime that allows the yuan to depreciate gradually over time. This would help rebalance the economy, support the transition toward services and domestic demand, and alleviate the pressure on reserves. Additionally, Bernanke recommends implementing structural reforms to increase the productivity of the service sector and promote domestic investment.

China's Foreign Exchange Rate Policy

China's Foreign Exchange Rate Policy has been a subject of intense scrutiny and debate both domestically and internationally. For decades, China maintained a fixed exchange rate regime, pegging its currency, the Renminbi (RMB), to the U.S. dollar. This policy allowed the Chinese government to stabilize the RMB's value, which supported export-oriented industries and facilitated foreign investment inflows. However, it also faced accusations of currency manipulation and unfair trade advantages from other countries, especially the United States.[15]

In response to growing international pressure and domestic economic changes, China began to gradually liberalize its exchange rate policy in the early 2000s. In 2005, Beijing discontinued the RMB's dollar peg and introduced a managed floating exchange rate system, allowing the currency to fluctuate within a limited band against a basket of currencies. This move aimed to

---

[14] Richard CK. Burdekin and Pierre L. Siklos, "What Has Driven Chinese Monetary Policy Since 1990? Investigating the People's Bank's Policy Rule", *Journal of International Money and Finance* 27, no. 5 (2008): 847-859.

[15] Aaron Mehrotra and José R. Sánchez-Fung, "China's monetary policy and the exchange rate", *Comparative Economic Studies* 52 (2010): 497-514.

increase the RMB's flexibility and demonstrate China's commitment to market-oriented reforms.

Since then, China has allowed the RMB to appreciate moderately against major currencies, although critics argue that the currency remains undervalued. The PBoC continues to intervene in the foreign exchange market to influence the RMB's value and maintain stability. China's exchange rate policy is a crucial aspect of its economic strategy, impacting its trade relationships, foreign investments, and global economic dynamics. The ongoing evolution of China's foreign exchange rate policy reflects the country's efforts to strike a delicate balance between its domestic economic priorities and international expectations.[16]

In 1998, Beijing's decision not to devalue the RMB received praise and compliments from various countries for avoiding further destabilization of the international economy during the pandemic crisis. However, as China's trade and global influence grew rapidly in the new century, its exchange rate policy faced criticism from Western countries, including the United States, and some emerging and developing nations. China's rise to become a major player in global trade and the largest recipient of foreign direct investment (FDI) among developing countries put its currency, the RMB, under intense international scrutiny.

China's rapid economic growth led to an explosive increase in trade, with its share of world merchandise imports and exports more than doubling. The country became the largest exporter and second-largest importer in the world. The massive inflow of FDI and surging trade surpluses resulted in a significant increase in China's foreign reserves, making it the largest holder of foreign reserves in the world. This accumulation of reserves and the perceived undervaluation of the RMB fueled international debate over the currency's exchange rate.[17]

Numerous studies attempted to estimate China's real "equilibrium" exchange rate with varying results. Despite different estimates, there was a general consensus that the RMB was undervalued, which fueled tensions with trading partners who argued that the undervaluation gave Chinese exporters unfair advantages. The undervaluation also contributed to global imbalances, affecting international savings and investment flows. The United States, in particular, raised serious concerns about China's exchange rate policy due to its large trade

---

[16] Qing He et al., "Factor-Augmented VAR Analysis of the Monetary Policy in China", *China Economic Review* 25 (2013): 88-104.

[17] Bernard Laurens and Rodolfo Maino, "China: Strengthening Monetary Policy Implementation", IMF Working Papers, January 1, 2007.

deficits with China. The U.S. government exerted pressure on China to revalue its currency and adopt a more flexible exchange rate system. The debate over RMB revaluation became a contentious issue in U.S. politics, with various stakeholders expressing differing opinions.

Internally, the Chinese leadership faced conflicting preferences in exchange rate policymaking. On the one hand, a revaluation of the RMB could negatively impact agricultural and export-oriented sectors, potentially leading to unemployment and social instability. On the other hand, a more balanced development model, focusing on domestic demand and consumption, called for a more flexible exchange rate regime. Moreover, China's monetary authorities faced the "impossible trinity" dilemma, where they had to choose between a fixed exchange rate, free capital movement, and independent monetary policy. As China's capital account became more porous, the PBC's ability to conduct independent monetary policy was restricted.

Amid these dynamics, the Chinese leadership was hesitant to make significant moves on the RMB exchange rate. The international pressure did not help, as the leadership did not want to be seen as capitulating to foreign demands on a critical policy issue. Instead, they emphasized maintaining an "independent initiative, controllability, and gradual progress" in exchange rate policymaking.

Various economic ministries had divergent views on RMB revaluation.[18] The National Development and Reform Commission (NDRC) was concerned about the potential negative impact on poverty reduction efforts, while the Ministry of Finance (MOF) worried about the repayment of loans to local governments and fiscal burdens. The Ministry of Commerce (MOFCOM) supported exports and was against a large appreciation but could tolerate a gradual move to a more flexible exchange rate.

Despite these internal dynamics, the PBoC pushed for exchange rate liberalization to gain greater monetary policy discretion. The PBoC faced the challenge of balancing a fixed exchange rate with independent monetary policy, given the increasing supply of foreign exchange, which led to a substantial increase in the domestic money supply.

China's Foreign Exchange Rate Policy is closely related to the concept of the "impossible trilemma," also known as the "trilemma of international finance." The trilemma posits that in an open economy, a country can only achieve two out of three policy objectives simultaneously: a fixed exchange rate, free capital movement, and an independent monetary policy.

---

[18] James Xiaohe Zhang, "The Impact of The RMB Revaluation on China and The World Economy", *China's Integration with the Global Economy* (2009): 141-160.

In the context of China, the trilemma becomes evident in its efforts to balance its exchange rate regime with monetary policy autonomy and capital mobility. Before China's exchange rate reform in 2005, the country had a fixed exchange rate system, pegging the RMB to the U.S. dollar. By pegging the RMB, China sacrificed its monetary policy independence since it needed to maintain large foreign exchange reserves to stabilize the currency's value. This massive accumulation of foreign reserves led to a substantial increase in the domestic money supply, impacting domestic monetary policy.

As China's economy grew and integrated further into the global economy, the pressures to achieve monetary policy autonomy and allow capital mobility intensified. The PBoC faced a dilemma: either maintain a fixed exchange rate and sacrifice monetary policy independence or move towards a more flexible exchange rate system and gain greater control over domestic monetary policy.

With the 2005 exchange rate reform,[19] China partially moved away from the fixed exchange rate system, introducing a managed floating exchange rate system. This allowed the RMB to appreciate moderately and gain some degree of flexibility. However, the PBoC still intervenes in the foreign exchange market to influence the RMB's value and maintain stability, reflecting the country's struggle to fully relinquish control over its exchange rate.[20]

Cash/FX restrictions in China involve certain limitations on the convertibility of the Chinese yuan (RMB). The RMB is not freely convertible and cannot be taken or remitted out of China. It is pegged to a basket of foreign currencies, including USD, EUR, JPY, KRW, and other major currencies. The PBoC has lifted the restriction on RMB/USD transactions, allowing banks to set their own exchange rates for RMB against USD based on market conditions. The daily fluctuation range for RMB against USD in the interbank market is set at 2%, while other non-USD currencies have different trading bands. Sale proceeds and income from B shares can be repatriated, but foreign exchange controls are still in place, and approval from the State Administration of Foreign Exchange (SAFE) is required for funds converted from RMB and other currencies with exchange controls.

Foreign institutional investors (FIIs) in the interbank bond market have certain FX risk management rules to follow. Eligible FIIs include commercial banks, insurance companies, securities companies, and other asset management institutions. They are required to fulfil information reporting obligations,

---

[19] Zhaohui Wang, "The Faltering RMB Exchange Rate Reform, 2005–2007", *The International Political Economy of China's Exchange Rate Policy Making* (2021): 81-101.

[20] Goldstein Morris and Nicholas Lardy, "China's Exchange Rate Policy Dilemma", *American Economic Review* 96, no. 2 (2006): 422-426.

including transaction details, trade date, country/region, purpose or source, and transaction type. FIIs can access the market directly or through prime brokerage, and daily information reporting is done through the CFETS PostTrade Processing Platform.

Overseas institutional investors (OIIs) investing in the China bond market must comply with the Measures for Cash Management issued jointly by the PBoC and SAFE. OIIs can conduct spot FX with onshore qualified financial institutions, and there are no restrictions on the number of counterparties for FX derivatives. OIIs have repatriation ratios based on the duration of the PBoC Filing Notice, and they are allowed to hedge their CIBM FX risk exposure using either RMB or foreign currency.

On-shore Chinese Renminbi (CNY) Market and Products

Markets

The PBoC serves as the central bank of mainland China and is responsible for managing the country's currency, the Renminbi (RMB), within a market-based, managed float system. The RMB's exchange rate is determined with reference to a basket of currencies, allowing for flexibility and adjustment based on international market conditions. The RMB is partially convertible, meaning that it can be exchanged for other currencies to a certain extent. Additionally, there are two separate offshore markets for the RMB: the deliverable CNH market and the non-deliverable CNY market. This dual-market system facilitates international transactions and investment activities involving the Chinese currency.[21] Moreover, the foreign exchange (FX) regime in China has experienced notable liberalization in recent years, indicating a gradual shift towards increased openness and flexibility in managing the country's currency and exchange rate policies. These developments have been aimed at enhancing China's integration into the global financial system and promoting further internationalization of the RMB.[22]

The liberalization of the FX regime in China signifies significant progress in the country's efforts to embrace international economic interactions and financial market reforms. By allowing the RMB to float within a managed framework and referencing a basket of currencies, the PBoC seeks to maintain stability in the exchange rate while simultaneously enabling the currency to

[21] Chang Shu et al., "One Currency, Two Markets: The Renminbi's Growing Influence in Asia-Pacific", *China Economic Review* 33 (2015): 163-178.

[22] Yin-Wong Cheung and Dagfinn Rime, "The Offshore Renminbi Exchange Rate: Microstructure and Links To The Onshore Market", *Journal of International Money and Finance* 49 (2014): 170-189.

respond to market forces and global economic dynamics. The existence of both deliverable (CNH) and non-deliverable (CNY) offshore markets for the RMB facilitates cross-border trade and investment, offering greater flexibility for international businesses and investors to conduct transactions with China. These reforms reflect China's commitment to becoming an increasingly open and transparent player in the global financial landscape, fostering confidence in its currency and promoting its acceptance on the international stage. As China continues to move towards greater financial liberalization, the PBoC's ongoing efforts to reform and develop its FX regime demonstrate its dedication to fostering a more inclusive and interconnected global financial system.

The On-shore Chinese renminbi (CNY) market offers a wide range of CNY-linked products, catering to various financial needs and risk management strategies for market participants. These products are designed to facilitate currency exchange, hedging, and investment activities in the on-shore CNY market, which is the domestic market within mainland China.

One of the fundamental products available in the on-shore CNY market is the Onshore spot FX, which involves the immediate exchange of CNY for another currency at the prevailing market rate. This product facilitates cross-border trade and financial transactions, allowing businesses and individuals to conduct real-time currency conversions. In addition to spot FX, the market also offers deliverable and non-deliverable forwards (cash settled in CNY) and FX swaps with varying maturities, including up to five years. These forward contracts enable market participants to lock in future exchange rates, providing them with protection against potential currency fluctuations and associated risks.

The on-shore CNY market also provides deliverable FX options, cross-currency swaps, and interest rate swaps. Deliverable FX options give investors the right but not the obligation to buy or sell CNY at a specified exchange rate at a future date, offering flexibility in managing currency risk. Cross-currency swaps allow entities to exchange cash flows denominated in different currencies, reducing currency exposure and ensuring stable financing costs. Interest rate swaps, on the other hand, enable parties to exchange interest payments on loans or bonds, mitigating interest rate risk.[23]

In addition to on-shore products, the market also involves offshore non-deliverable forwards (NDFs), non-deliverable FX options, cross-currency swaps, and interest rate swaps. Offshore NDFs, in particular, are essential in situations where the CNY is not fully convertible or deliverable outside of

---

[23] Yongqi Feng and Tianshu Zhang, "Interest Rate Linkages Between Offshore and Onshore Renminbi Markets", *Australian Economic Papers* 55, no. 4 (2016): 434-450.

China. These contracts settle in a major freely traded currency, such as the USD, but their rates are based on the expected future value of the CNY. Offshore NDFs play a crucial role in managing currency risk for businesses and investors engaged in cross-border transactions with China, where the use of deliverable CNY products may be restricted.[24]

Products

The On-shore Chinese renminbi (CNY) market offers a diverse range of CNY-linked products, providing various financial instruments for currency exchange, hedging, and investment purposes. Among the available products are the Onshore spot FX transactions, which require documentary proof of underlying transactions, except for individual spot FX transactions under the USD50,000 per annum quota, where supporting documents are not necessary. Spot FX transactions play a crucial role in facilitating real-time currency conversions for businesses engaged in international trade. By allowing for immediate settlement of currency trades at prevailing exchange rates, these transactions enable companies to manage their foreign currency exposures and optimize their cash flow management effectively.

Additionally, the market offers deliverable and non-deliverable forwards and FX swaps, with maturities of up to five years, providing onshore institutions the ability to hedge FX exposure. These forward contracts and swaps allow businesses to protect themselves from adverse currency movements, especially when they have future payment or receipt obligations in foreign currencies. By locking in the exchange rate today for a future currency transaction, companies can mitigate the risk of currency fluctuations and ensure predictability in their financial planning and budgeting.

Furthermore, the Onshore CNY market offers deliverable FX options with tenors out to three years, and further tenors on a case-by-case basis. These options enable market participants to buy or sell CNY against foreign currencies based on real needs. FX options provide businesses and investors with greater flexibility in managing currency risk, as they offer the right but not the obligation to exchange currencies at pre-determined rates on or before a specified future date. By utilizing FX options, companies can hedge against potential currency losses while maintaining the opportunity to benefit from favourable exchange rate movements, striking a balance between risk management and profit potential.

---

[24] Jing.Qin, "Relationship Between Onshore And Offshore Renminbi Exchange Markets: Evidence From Multiscale Cross-Correlation and Nonlinear Causal Effect Analyses", *Physica A: Statistical Mechanics and Its Applications* 527 (2019): 121183.

The offshore market also provides USD-settled non-deliverable options (NDOs) on CNY with tenors of up to five years and further tenors available on a case-by-case basis. Similar to onshore FX options, NDOs allow market participants to hedge their currency exposure, particularly for offshore businesses that engage in cross-border trade and financial activities. These options are particularly valuable for those who operate in markets where the CNY is not fully convertible, as they provide a means to manage currency risk without requiring actual delivery of the underlying currency.

Interest rate options in the Onshore market include LPR (Loan Prime Rate) interest rate options trading, where European LPR caps/floors and LPR IRS swaptions are tradable. LPR interest rate options serve as valuable tools for managing interest rate risk. By utilizing these options, businesses can hedge against potential interest rate fluctuations, ensuring stability in their borrowing and lending costs. This is particularly crucial for businesses that rely heavily on debt financing or have exposure to interest rate-sensitive assets and liabilities.

On the other hand, Cross-currency swaps (CCS) allow institutions to trade CNY currency swaps against currencies such as USD, HKD, EUR, JPY, AUD, GBP, and IDR, with tenors up to 10 years and the best liquidity within three years. These swaps can be tailored to match underlying assets/liabilities, making them suitable for corporate needs and investment purposes. Cross-currency swaps enable businesses to manage their exposure to foreign currencies and interest rates effectively. They allow companies to convert their liabilities from one currency to another, mitigating foreign exchange risk and interest rate risk simultaneously.

In the realm of CNY interest rate swaps (IRS), financial institutions in the national interbank market can conduct transactions with other market participants, and all standard interbank IRS transactions are cleared at Shanghai Clearing House (SCH). CNY interest rate swaps play a vital role in managing interest rate risk for businesses and financial institutions. By exchanging fixed-rate and floating-rate cash flows, parties can effectively hedge against interest rate fluctuations, ensuring a predictable interest expense or income stream. This is particularly important for businesses with floating-rate debt or investments, as interest rate movements can significantly impact their financial positions.

The On-shore CNY market provides a comprehensive array of products, allowing participants to manage risks, conduct real-time currency conversions, and engage in various financial activities within the framework of the Chinese economy's evolving financial system. These products cater to the diverse needs of businesses and investors operating in the Chinese market, offering them sophisticated tools to protect against market volatility, enhance financial planning, and optimize their overall risk-return profile.

Individuals' Foreign Exchange (FX) Conversion

In mainland China, individuals' foreign exchange (FX) conversion rules vary depending on residency status and the purpose of the transactions. For residents engaging in current account transactions, there is an annual quota of USD 50,000 for currency conversion in both directions. This means they can convert up to USD 50,000 worth of foreign currency into RMB or vice versa within a year. Additionally, there is a daily limit of USD 50,000 for remitting foreign currency out of mainland China. Any conversion or remittance that exceeds this daily limit requires supporting documents to be provided.[25]

Non-residents, including those from Hong Kong, Macau, and Taiwan, have their own set of rules. They are also allowed an annual quota of USD 50,000 for converting foreign currency into RMB, but any conversion beyond this limit must be supported by relevant documents. Conversely, when non-residents want to convert RMB back into foreign currency, they are required to provide supporting documents regardless of the amount. Interestingly, there is no daily limit for foreign currency remittances out of mainland China for non-residents. This allows them to freely transfer funds in foreign currency without restrictions on a daily basis.

For residents of Hong Kong, Macau, and Taiwan under the Closer Economic Partnership Arrangement (CEPA), specific daily transfer limits apply for current account purposes. Hong Kong and Taiwan residents are allowed to transfer up to RMB 80,000 daily, while Macau residents have a daily transfer limit of RMB 50,000. Furthermore, both the principal and interest can be repatriated to Hong Kong, Macau, and Taiwan, allowing for greater ease in conducting cross-border financial activities.[26]

These FX conversion rules are designed to strike a balance between promoting international financial transactions and maintaining the stability of the domestic economy. By implementing annual quotas and daily limits, the authorities can manage the flow of foreign currency and prevent excessive capital outflows that could potentially destabilize the financial system. The requirement for supporting documents ensures transparency and compliance with regulations, reducing the risk of illegal or illicit activities.

The differences in rules based on residency status and economic partnerships are aimed at accommodating various needs and economic ties between mainland

---

[25] Lin Guijun and Ronald M. Schramm, "China's Foreign Exchange Policies Since 1979: A Review of Developments and An Assessment", *China Economic Review* 14, no. 3 (2003): 246-280.

[26] Song Shi and Xunpeng Shi, "The Impact of Chinese Regulation of Limitation on Currency Transactions (LCT) on Sydney Housing Prices", *Housing Studies* (2023): 1-22.

China and other regions. These measures contribute to enhancing financial connectivity and cooperation while safeguarding the integrity of China's financial system. As the global economic landscape evolves, these FX conversion rules may continue to be adapted to respond to changing market conditions and promote further internationalization of the Chinese currency.

Offshore Chinese Renminbi (CNH) – Market and Products

Market

The introduction of the Chinese renminbi (RMB) as a deliverable currency in offshore markets, particularly in Hong Kong, marked a significant development in the global financial landscape. The offshore RMB, known as CNH (Chinese renminbi offshore), became available for trading in July 2010. This move was part of China's efforts to internationalize its currency and promote its use in cross-border trade and investment.[27]

The CNH market, also known as the offshore Chinese renminbi market, emerged as a significant development in the global financial landscape in the early 2010s. The history of the CNH market can be traced back to July 2010, when the Chinese government allowed the Chinese renminbi (RMB) to be delivered offshore in Hong Kong. This move was part of China's efforts to internationalize its currency and promote its use in cross-border trade and investment.

The historical background of the offshore Chinese renminbi (CNH) market in Hong Kong traces back to the early 2000s when efforts to internationalize the Chinese currency gained momentum. In late 2003, the PBoC and the Hong Kong Monetary Authority (HKMA) collaborated, allowing Hong Kong banks to conduct personal RMB business on a trial basis. Bank of China (Hong Kong) was designated as the RMB clearing bank in Hong Kong, playing a crucial role in facilitating RMB transactions and settlements in the territory.

The market continued to evolve in subsequent years. In 2004, the RMB clearing bank began providing services for participating banks to offset RMB open positions resulting from permitted RMB exchange business. In 2008, the PBoC and HKMA signed an agreement to establish a currency swap line, providing further support to the growing offshore RMB market. The size of the currency swap line doubled to RMB 400 billion in 2011, signalling the increasing importance of the offshore CNH market.

---

[27] Yin-Wong Cheung, "The Role of Offshore Financial Centers in The Process of Renminbi Internationalization", Asian Development Bank Institute, ADBI Working Paper Series, April, 2014.

The breakthrough for the offshore CNH market came in July 2010 when the PBoC and Bank of China (Hong Kong) signed an agreement lifting the last restrictions on Hong Kong's RMB interbank market. This allowed banks in Hong Kong to establish RMB accounts and offer related services to corporations and individuals. Non-bank financial institutions were also granted the ability to open RMB accounts held at different Hong Kong banks for any purpose, further boosting the accessibility and appeal of the offshore CNH market.[28]

Subsequent milestones included the launch of the spot USD-CNH fixing by the Treasury Market Association of Hong Kong in June 2011, providing a reference rate for offshore RMB products. In September 2012, the Stock Exchange of Hong Kong (SEHK) started trading the first deliverable RMB futures, providing investors with hedging and investment opportunities. To enhance market transparency and efficiency, the Treasury Market Association of Hong Kong launched the CNH Hong Kong Interbank Offered Rate fixing in June 2013, serving as a benchmark for loan facilities and RMB interest rate products.[29]

The historical journey of the offshore CNH market in Hong Kong demonstrates the collaborative efforts of Chinese and Hong Kong authorities to promote the use of RMB in international trade and investment. The market's continuous development has transformed Hong Kong into a vital global hub for RMB-denominated transactions, contributing significantly to the currency's internationalization and integration into the global financial system. One of the key advantages of CNH is its free transferability between offshore accounts. This means that individuals and businesses can move CNH freely without the restrictions imposed on the onshore RMB (CNY). The liberalization of CNH allows for smoother cross-border transactions and provides businesses with increased flexibility in managing their international financial activities.

Moreover, offshore banks can create and sell investment products denominated in CNH, adding to the financial products and services available in the offshore RMB market. This development has attracted global investors looking to diversify their portfolios and access investment opportunities denominated in RMB.

The increasing interaction between the onshore and offshore markets also reflects China's broader push to integrate its financial system with the global economy. As China continues to open up its financial markets and gradually

---

[28] Yinghua Ren et al., "The Onshore–Offshore Exchange Rate Differential, Interest Rate Spreads, and Internationalization: Evidence From The Hong Kong Offshore Renminbi Market", *Emerging Markets Finance and Trade* 54, no. 13 (2018): 3100-3116.

[29] Cheng Lian et al., "Is the Renminbi a Global Currency? An Evaluation Based on Offshore Foreign Exchange Market Trading Patterns", *Social Sciences in China* 43, no. 2 (2022): 144-160.

relax capital controls, the influence of the offshore RMB market is likely to expand further.

Since the landmark decision on 19th July 2010, the offshore Chinese renminbi (CNH) market has seen significant growth and development. Notably, the transfer of RMB funds between accounts and banks for any purpose within the offshore market was permitted, fostering greater flexibility and accessibility for individuals and businesses engaging in international transactions. However, it is important to note that the transfer of RMB between the onshore and offshore markets is still subject to regulations and approval by mainland China's authorities, emphasizing the careful approach taken by Chinese authorities in managing the internationalization of their currency.

In the offshore market, CNH has become the widely used currency code to reference offshore RMB traded in various financial centres, with Hong Kong being the primary hub. The CNH market offers a wide range of financial products, catering to the diverse needs of investors and businesses seeking to utilize RMB in their international dealings. Some of the available products include spot FX, deliverable forwards, and FX swaps, providing the necessary tools for managing currency risk and facilitating international trade settlements. Moreover, the CNH market offers an array of financial instruments that go beyond foreign exchange, such as bonds, time deposits, certificates of deposits, currency swaps, and interest rate swaps. This diversified product offering enhances the appeal of CNH as an investment currency and enables market participants to engage in various financial activities using RMB.

Additionally, the market facilitates the trading of structured products, including structured deposits, notes, and swaps, allowing investors to access innovative and tailored investment strategies denominated in RMB. Furthermore, the exchange-traded products available in the CNH market, such as equities, exchange-traded funds (ETFs), real estate investment trusts (REITs), and CNH futures, provide avenues for investors to access different asset classes and achieve portfolio diversification.

Products

The exchange rate mechanism of the offshore Chinese renminbi (CNH) operates in a fully deliverable manner offshore. Unlike the onshore Chinese yuan (CNY), which has a trading band imposed by authorities, the CNH trades freely against the USD. Despite this freedom, market forces typically keep the spread between the CNH and CNY rates minimal. These market forces primarily arise from offshore foreign exchange positions resulting from trade, services, and direct investments, which can be squared with the clearing bank or onshore correspondent banks. Additionally, cross-border portfolio flows have emerged as influential factors in driving the demand and supply of CNH.[30]

To establish a benchmark for USD-CNH rates, the official name of the Spot USD-CNH fixing was changed to the USD-CNH (HK) Spot Rate as of 1 August 2016. This benchmark is calculated based on actual transactions executed within a 30-minute window centred at 1100 HKT. The eligible transactions must be carried out through an Approved Money Broker with a dedicated FX spot business and involve a transacted amount of at least USD 1 million, taking place between 1045 HKT and 1115 HKT. The benchmark is then calculated as the volume-weighted median of these eligible transactions and published on Reuters page CNHFIX at 1130 HKT.

Bank of China (Hong Kong) serves as the designated clearing bank for CNH settlement in the offshore market. The bank provides a robust platform for facilitating smooth and efficient CNH transactions. In this context, the Hong Kong Monetary Authority (HKMA) expects banks in Hong Kong to treat offshore RMB on par with other currencies concerning managing their foreign exchange risks. This approach ensures that banks operating in the offshore CNH market adhere to prudent risk management practices and promote stability in the currency's trading environment.

The offshore Chinese renminbi (CNH) market in Hong Kong offers a range of spot and derivative products, providing participants with multiple options for hedging, investment, and financing purposes. Participating banks in Hong Kong facilitate two types of spot RMB exchange rate transactions. The first type is meant for trade, service, and direct investment purposes and can be offset with the clearing bank or onshore correspondent banks, leading to close alignment with the onshore rate. This type was expanded in 2015 to include direct investments and service trade transactions. The second type caters to general purposes other than trade and requires banks to warehouse the risk or offset the position in the interbank USD-CNH market, causing potential divergence from the onshore spot exchange rate.

The CNH market also offers various derivative products. Deliverable CNH forwards are available for up to five years, and liquidity has surpassed that of the non-deliverable forwards market. Deliverable CNH options are available without restrictions to non-individual counterparties with physical CNH nostro accounts. Cross-currency swaps (CCS) predominantly against the USD are available for up to five years, and the liquidity for CNH CCS has constantly been

---

[30] Guanyu Su and Junhui Qian, "Does the Offshore Market Matter to China's Exchange Rate Policy?", *Applied Economics Letters* 30, no. 13 (2023): 1734-1737.

improving as customers move interest from the non-deliverable cross-currency swap market.[31]

Interest rate products in the offshore market include CNH interest rate swaps (IRS) based on the 3-month HIBOR. The CNH IRS market benefits from the CNH HIBOR fixing, providing an offshore floating interest rate benchmark. Various hedging and investment products in RMB are available, such as vanilla, European barriers, digital options, structured deposits, notes, or swaps. The development of the offshore RMB bond market, including Dim Sum bonds, has been significant, with primary and secondary markets evolving to meet increasing demand. Mainland China's Ministry of Finance (MoF) issues government bonds in Hong Kong to establish an offshore CNH yield curve.

Opening a CNH account is subject to normal procedures in Hong Kong or other jurisdictions. Offshore RMB loans to designated business and personal customers are permitted, allowing banks to borrow funds from mainland China correspondent banks for up to 12 months for trade finance-related loans. The expansion of the RMB Qualified Foreign Institutional Investor (RQFII) and Bond Connect schemes is expected to accelerate the convergence of the onshore-offshore bond markets. With continuous developments and initiatives, the CNH market remains an essential hub for RMB-denominated financial products and liquidity management tools.

Regulations on Cross-Border Flows

The basic principles of the offshore Chinese renminbi (CNH) market allow foreign exchange positions resulting from goods, service trades, and direct investments to be squared with the clearing bank or onshore correspondent banks. Offshore RMB accounts can also be set up in other jurisdictions, and the offshore yuan can be remitted to any foreign centre, subject to local regulations, making the currency fungible in different offshore centres.[32]

Regarding individuals' conversion, the daily conversion limit for Hong Kong residents of RMB20,000 was removed on 17 November 2014. Furthermore, RMB conversions for Hong Kong residents are conducted in the offshore market instead of onshore through the designated RMB clearing bank. However, the daily remittance limit to mainland China remains at RMB80,000, subject to the rules and requirements of mainland China.

---

[31] Von Spreckelsen et al., "Forecasting Renminbi Quotes in The Revised Chinese FX Market–Can We Get Implications for the Onshore/Offshore Spread-Behaviour?", *International Journal of Economic Policy in Emerging Economies* 7, no. 1 (2014): 66-76.

[32] R. Sean Craig et al., *Development of The Renminbi Market in Hong Kong SAR: Assessing Onshore-Offshore Market Integration*. International Monetary Fund, 2013.

In terms of trade settlement, the State Council approved RMB trade settlement on trade between Hong Kong and the Guangdong/Yangtze River Delta in June 2009, and over the following years, this scheme was gradually rolled out nationwide. In March 2012, the People's Bank of China (PBoC) announced that all qualified exporters were eligible to settle trade in RMB for the export of goods without prior approval, fully opening the cross-border RMB trade settlement channel.[33]

For foreign direct investment (FDI), the PBoC initiated a trial program for inward FDI denominated in RMB in April 2011, which was later expanded nationwide in October 2011. As of 1 January 2014, specific RMB FDI rules were replaced by existing FDI rules for foreign currencies, simplifying the approval process. In many economic pilot zones or free trade zones, FDI rules were further simplified, replacing approval by the Ministry of Commerce with a filing with local authorities. However, restrictions on using RMB capital injections for certain investments in the onshore security markets, financial derivatives, or entrusted loans still apply.

In the area of outbound direct investment (ODI), the PBoC allowed mainland Chinese banks and enterprises to make overseas direct investments in RMB for the first time in January 2011. On 6 October 2014, mainland China's Ministry of Commerce simplified the rules on making outbound investments by domestic firms by abolishing approval for most outbound investments and shortening the lead time for the filing process.

To facilitate cross-border investment, mainland China introduced several cross-border investment schemes, starting with the inward Qualified Foreign Institutional Investor (QFII) scheme in 2002 and the outbound Qualified Domestic Institutional Investor (QDII) scheme in 2006. The RMB-denominated investment scheme started in 2010 through the Interbank Bond Market (CIBM) scheme, allowing offshore institutions to reinvest offshore RMB accumulated from cross-border trade settlement into the onshore interbank bond markets. Over time, other important RMB-denominated schemes, including RQFII, Stock Connect, Northbound Bond Connect, Southbound Bond Connect, Wealth Connect, and others, were introduced to further liberalize cross-border portfolio investment.

Offshore RMB Centres and RMB FX Swap Agreements

Offshore Chinese renminbi (CNH) centres have been established in various locations, as shown in Table 4. These offshore centres allow for the trading and

---

[33] Cheung, Yin-Wong, and Matthew S. Yiu. "Offshore renminbi trading: findings from the 2013 Triennial Central Bank Survey." *International Economics* 152 (2017): 9-20.

settlement of CNH, making the currency largely fungible across different locations. However, slight variations in interest rates may occur due to differences in RMB clearance mechanisms, the composition of the RMB liquidity pool, credit ratings of local clearance banks, and the risk appetite of participant banks and investors. Despite these differences, CNH remains freely transferable between offshore accounts in these centres, promoting cross-border trade and financial transactions.[34]

To further facilitate trade and financial activities, the PBoC has entered into bilateral local currency swap agreements with various countries. These agreements aim to enhance currency convertibility and provide additional support for international transactions involving RMB.[35]

The Shanghai Free Trade Zone (SFTZ), established in May 2014, plays a crucial role in the offshore RMB market within mainland China. It allows for the opening of free trade accounts (FTA) that enable RMB transactions for current account business, foreign direct investments, and cross-border lending. Essentially, the SFTZ and potentially other free trade zones function as offshore RMB centres within mainland China, providing a conducive environment for conducting RMB-related activities.

In a significant development, on 30 October 2015, the PBoC and other regulators announced that the Shanghai Free Trade Zone would embark on a capital account convertibility experiment. This move aimed to promote further liberalization and integration of the RMB into the global financial system. In line with offshore RMB markets, the foreign exchange and interest rates within the SFTZ are subject to market forces and fluctuations, offering a more market-driven environment for cross-border financial activities. These initiatives reinforce China's commitment to internationalize the RMB and enhance its role in global trade and investment.[36]

Offshore RMB Centre – Hong Kong

Hong Kong's pioneering role in launching the renminbi (RMB) business in 2004 marked a significant milestone in the internationalization of the Chinese currency. As the first offshore market to embrace RMB, Hong Kong established itself as the global hub for various RMB-related activities, including trade

---

[34] Yin-Wong Cheung et al., "The Evolution of Offshore Renminbi Trading: 2016 To 2019", *Journal of International Money and Finance* 113 (2021): 102369.

[35] Alicia Garcia-Herrero and Le Xia, "China's RMB Bilateral Swap Agreements: What Explains the Choice of Countries?", BBVA 13/18 Working Paper, 2013.

[36] Yin-Wong Cheung, "A Decade of RMB Internationalisation", *Economic and Political Studies* 11, no. 1 (2023): 47-74.

settlement, financing, and asset management. Over the years, Hong Kong has developed a comprehensive ecosystem that caters to the diverse needs of businesses, financial institutions, and investors seeking RMB products and services.[37]

One of the key areas where Hong Kong excels is the renminbi trade settlement. The city has established efficient channels and infrastructure to facilitate the smooth and secure settlement of cross-border trade transactions in RMB. This has greatly facilitated trade between Mainland China and the rest of the world, enabling businesses to transact in their local currency and reducing foreign exchange risks. Hong Kong's expertise in renminbi trade settlement has been instrumental in promoting the use of RMB as an international trade currency.

Moreover, Hong Kong has emerged as a prominent centre for renminbi financing. The city's deep pool of RMB liquidity, coupled with its robust financial system and extensive network of banks, allows businesses and financial institutions to access a wide range of RMB financing options. This includes RMB-denominated loans, bonds, and other debt instruments, providing flexibility and diversification in funding sources. The availability of renminbi financing in Hong Kong has not only supported the growth of businesses operating in Mainland China but has also attracted international companies seeking RMB funding for their operations. In recent months, Hong Kong has faced a period of uncertainty due to various factors, including trade negotiations between the United States and China, social events, and the COVID-19 pandemic. These circumstances have had a significant impact on the city's economy, with GDP contracting by 6.1% in 2019 and projected to shrink further by 4-7% in 2020. However, despite these challenges, Hong Kong has maintained its position as a preeminent provider of financial services in Asia, particularly as a leading offshore renminbi (RMB) financial hub.

Hong Kong plays a crucial role as a gateway between Mainland China and the rest of the world, facilitating a substantial portion of China's inward foreign direct investment (FDI) and outward direct investments. In 2019, 54% of mainland China's inbound FDI and 65% of outbound direct investment flowed through Hong Kong, illustrating the city's importance as a key conduit for China's capital flows. This highlights Hong Kong's enduring strategic role as a trading partner with Mainland China and its ability to facilitate global trade in goods

[37] Jeremy Green and Julian Gruin, "RMB Transnationalization and The Infrastructural Power of International Financial Centres", *Review of International Political Economy* 28, no. 4 (2020): 1028-1054.

and services while promoting the international usage of RMB even amid recent headwinds.[38]

Since the launch of the pilot scheme for cross-border trade settlement in the renminbi in 2009, the volume of RMB trade settlement handled by Hong Kong banks has experienced rapid growth, rising from just 3 billion RMB in 2009 to 5.38 trillion RMB in 2019. This represents a remarkable compound annual growth rate of 71% over the past decade. In 2019, Hong Kong accounted for approximately 89% of total RMB cross-border trade settlement, up from just 13% in 2010. This growth underscores Hong Kong's position as a globally significant player in facilitating trade flows between Mainland China and the rest of the world using the RMB.[39]

Hong Kong has also been instrumental in enabling two-way financial investment flows between the mainland and overseas. Stock connect programs such as the Shanghai-Hong Kong Stock Connect and the Shenzhen-Hong Kong Stock Connect have facilitated cross-boundary investment fund flows through transactions with a total Northbound and Southbound value of over RMB21 trillion as of March 2020. These landmark stock connect initiatives have further strengthened Hong Kong's role as the gateway for foreign investment into mainland Chinese equities and vice versa, providing international investors with unprecedented access to China's stock markets.

Furthermore, Hong Kong has firmly established itself as a crucial hub for offshore RMB settlement, handling a substantial portion of the world's offshore RMB payment, remittance, and settlement transactions. In 2019, the RMB Real Time Gross Settlement system operated by the Hong Kong Monetary Authority recorded an average daily turnover of RMB1,100 billion, a major increase of 55% compared to the 2014 average of RMB710 billion. This underscores the dramatic growth in cross-border RMB settlement flows processed through Hong Kong's financial system infrastructure. Hong Kong now accounts for approximately 75% of global RMB payment activity outside Mainland China, according to data from the Society for Worldwide Interbank Financial Telecommunication (SWIFT), further demonstrating the high degree of trust and reliance placed on its platforms for offshore RMB transactions by international firms.

Hong Kong's ability to efficiently provide RMB trade, investment, and payment services is strongly supported by its deep pool of RMB deposits and liquidity.

---

[38] Hung-Gay Fung and Jot Yau, "Chinese Offshore RMB Currency and Bond Markets: The role of Hong Kong, *China & World Economy* 20, no. 3 (2012): 107-122.

[39] Ke Song and Le Xia, "Bilateral Swap Agreement and Renminbi Settlement in Cross-Border Trade", *Economic and Political Studies* 8, no. 3 (2020): 355-373.

As of the end of 2019, the cumulative value of Hong Kong's RMB customer deposits and certificates of deposits amounted to an impressive RMB658 billion, constituting over 10% of the city's total deposits. This substantial presence of RMB funds within Hong Kong's banking system demonstrates its significance as a hub for RMB-related financial activities.

Moreover, Hong Kong boasts the largest pool of offshore RMB liquidity worldwide. According to data from the People's Bank of China, it holds nearly half of all offshore RMB deposits globally. This substantial reserve of RMB funds positions Hong Kong as an attractive destination for businesses, financial institutions, and investors seeking RMB-related financial services.

The deep pool of RMB deposits and liquidity in Hong Kong offers several advantages. Firstly, it ensures ample availability of RMB funds for various financial transactions, such as trade settlements, cross-border investments, and payment services. The abundant liquidity enables smoother and more efficient execution of RMB-related transactions, supporting the seamless flow of funds between Mainland China and the rest of the world.

Secondly, the presence of a substantial RMB deposit base in Hong Kong strengthens the city's position as a leading offshore RMB trading centre. The availability of a large pool of RMB funds facilitates a vibrant and active market for RMB-denominated financial products and services. This includes RMB foreign exchange transactions, interest rate derivatives, and other investment instruments denominated in RMB. The deep liquidity pool enhances market depth, liquidity, and price stability, attracting market participants and investors looking to access and engage in RMB-related activities. The significant RMB deposit base in Hong Kong contributes to the stability and resilience of the city's financial system. The ample availability of RMB funds strengthens the banking sector's ability to meet the financing needs of businesses and individuals, fostering economic growth and stability. It also provides a solid foundation for the development and expansion of RMB-related financial services, which further enhances Hong Kong's role as a global financial hub.[40]

The presence of a deep RMB liquidity pool in Hong Kong also supports the city's status as a leading offshore RMB clearing centre. Hong Kong's robust infrastructure and expertise in RMB clearing and settlement services enable efficient and secure processing of RMB transactions. This includes the handling of cross-border trade settlements, remittances, and other payment transactions denominated in RMB. The availability of a large pool of RMB funds ensures the smooth functioning and effectiveness of these clearing and settlement activities,

---

[40] Alicia Garcia-Herrero and Le Xia. "RMB Bilateral Swap Agreements: How China Chooses Its Partners?", *Asia-Pacific Journal of Accounting & Economics* 22, no. 4 (2015): 368-383.

contributing to the overall stability and efficiency of Hong Kong's financial system. Moreover, Hong Kong has developed into the largest offshore RMB foreign exchange and interest rates derivatives marketplace. As of April 2019, the average daily turnover of Hong Kong's RMB foreign exchange spot and forwards market hit USD107.6 billion, representing a sizable increase of 39.6% compared to the 2016 average. Hong Kong now accounts for around 41% of global offshore RMB foreign exchange turnover, exceeding the share of other major RMB trading centres like London (22%) and Singapore (16%). Additionally, Hong Kong offers a diverse suite of offshore RMB investment products, including futures and options in foreign exchange, gold, stocks and commodities that are cleared through Hong Kong Exchanges and Clearing. These provide international investors with unique risk management and investment opportunities linked to RMB.[41]

Through supportive policy initiatives, world-class financial infrastructure, and continuing financial innovation, Hong Kong has cultivated a trusted, efficient and stable ecosystem for RMB finance over the past decade. Looking ahead, Hong Kong is poised to maintain its status as the premier global offshore RMB financial centre. Further integration with mainland China's Greater Bay Area and tapping potential growth areas such as investment and risk management services will ensure Hong Kong remains a magnet for offshore RMB activity.

Dim Sum Bonds

Dim Sum bonds are bonds denominated in Chinese yuan (RMB) but issued outside of Mainland China. They are named after the famous Chinese cuisine, symbolizing the deliciousness and uniqueness of these bonds. The issuance of Dim Sum bonds serves several purposes and has been motivated by various factors.[42]

One primary reason for issuing Dim Sum bonds is to tap into the growing pool of offshore RMB liquidity. As the internationalization of the RMB progressed, there was a need to provide investment opportunities for the increasing amount of offshore RMB funds held by investors and financial institutions. Dim Sum bonds enable issuers to attract these funds and utilize them for financing purposes.

---

[41] Steffen Murau et al., "The Future of Offshore Dollar Creation: Four Scenarios for The International Monetary System by 2040", ASS Discussion Paper, doi: 10.2312/iass.2018.008, June 2018.

[42] Hung-Gay et al., *Dim Sum Bonds: The Offshore Renminbi (RMB)-Denominated Bonds*, (John Wiley & Sons, 2014).

Another motivation for issuing Dim Sum bonds is to diversify funding sources. Companies and governments, particularly those with business interests or trade ties to Mainland China, have sought to access the offshore RMB market as an alternative source of funding. By issuing Dim Sum bonds, they can tap into a broader investor base and diversify their funding options beyond traditional currency-denominated bonds.

The methods used for issuing Dim Sum bonds vary. They can be issued by both Chinese and non-Chinese issuers, including multinational corporations, financial institutions, and sovereign entities. Dim Sum bonds can be issued in multiple formats, such as fixed-rate bonds, floating-rate notes, and even green bonds to support environmentally friendly projects. The bonds are typically listed on offshore exchanges, such as the Hong Kong Stock Exchange, and are available for trading by both institutional and retail investors.

Hong Kong has been the primary hub for Dim Sum bond issuances since the market's inception. The city's status as an international financial centre, its deep pool of offshore RMB liquidity, and its proximity to Mainland China have made it an attractive location for issuing Dim Sum bonds. However, Dim Sum bonds have also been issued in other financial centres, including Singapore, London, and Luxembourg, as these cities aim to capture a share of the growing offshore RMB market.

The issuance of Dim Sum bonds has provided issuers with access to a new investor base and diversified funding sources. It has also contributed to the development of offshore RMB markets, promoting the internationalization of the Chinese currency. As the RMB continues to gain prominence globally, the market for Dim Sum bonds is expected to expand further, offering more opportunities for issuers and investors alike.

A common index to track the performance of Dim Sum bonds is the Dim Sum Bond Index, which is a weighted index that tracks the performance of dim sum bonds denominated in Chinese yuan (RMB) and issued and settled outside of Mainland China. It uses a market capitalization methodology to determine the weightings of the bonds included in the index. The index is rebalanced on a monthly basis and is managed by Citigroup.[43]

Among the top ten issuers included in the Dim Sum Bond Index by market weight are the PRC, Bank of China Ltd., Lenovo Group Ltd., China Development Bank Corp., Asian Development Bank, Beijing Enterprises Group, Beijing Enterprises Water Group, Export-Import Bank of China, China Construction Bank Corp., and International Finance Corp. These issuers represent a diverse

[43] https://etfdb.com/index/citigroup-dim-sum-offshore-cny-bond-index/.

range of entities, including government institutions, financial institutions, and corporations.[44]

Citigroup, as the index manager, oversees the administration and maintenance of the Dim Sum Bond Index. They ensure that the index accurately reflects the performance of the RMB-denominated dim sum bond market outside of Mainland China. The index's methodology takes into account the market capitalization of the included bonds, which means that larger issuers have a higher weighting in the index.[45]

The rebalancing of the Dim Sum Bond Index occurs on a monthly basis. During this process, the index manager reviews the constituent bonds and adjusts their weightings based on changes in market capitalization. This ensures that the index remains representative of the current market conditions and provides an accurate measure of the performance of the dim sum bond market.

Conclusion

In conclusion, this chapter has explored the central banking system, monetary policy, and currency markets in China, with a particular focus on the role of the PBoC. The PBoC's decisions and actions have far-reaching consequences for China's economic growth, financial stability, and its position as a major player in the global economy. The PBoC plays a critical role in implementing monetary policies that support growth and stability. By setting interest rates and reserve requirement ratios and utilizing other monetary policy tools, the bank aims to control inflation, stabilize the economy, and promote financial stability. The PBoC's efforts in managing monetary policy are integral to ensuring a healthy economic environment for businesses, investors, and individuals.

The chapter also examined the foreign exchange market in China, including the onshore and offshore Renminbi markets. The PBoC plays a central role in managing and regulating these markets, ensuring their stability and facilitating economic development. The establishment of offshore RMB centres, such as Hong Kong, has expanded the international use of the Renminbi and contributed to China's integration into the global financial system. The issuance of Dim Sum bonds in offshore markets has provided additional investment opportunities and fostered international cooperation.

---

[44] Hung-Gay Fung et al., "Dim Sum Bonds: Do They Whet Your Appetite?", *The Journal of Portfolio Management* 41, no. 5 (2015): 127-135.

[45] Ike Mathur and Soumen De, "The Dim Sum Bond Market in Hong Kong", in *Risk Management Post Financial Crisis: A Period of Monetary Easing,* (Emerald Group Publishing Limited, 2014), . 367-388

Looking ahead, the PBoC's approach to digital currency, fintech, and cryptocurrency will be crucial in shaping the future of money and the financial system. The PBoC's exploration and implementation of digital currency initiatives, such as the digital yuan, have the potential to revolutionize financial transactions, enhance efficiency, and promote financial inclusion. The ongoing efforts to develop digital currency, fintech, and cryptocurrency showcase China's determination to embrace technological advancements and shape the future of the financial landscape.

Understanding the intricacies of China's central banking system, monetary policy, and currency markets is essential for researchers and policymakers to gain insights into China's economic growth trajectory, financial stability, and global economic dynamics. The PBoC's role as a regulator, issuer of currency, and promoter of financial inclusion demonstrates its pivotal position in China's economy. As China continues to exert its presence as a major player in the global economy, the decisions and actions of the PBoC will continue to have far-reaching consequences.

Resources and References consulted

Bloomberg Fixing Page APF
China Banking and Insurance Regulatory Commission www.cbrc.gov.cn
China Banking Regulatory Commission www.cbrc.gov.cn
China Foreign Exchange Trade System www.chinamoney.com.cn Offshore market
China Securities Regulatory Commission www.csrc.gov.cn
HSBC Reuters Page HSBCRMB
Invest Hong Kong www.investhk.gov.hk The People's Bank of China www.pbc.gov.cn
Ministry of Commerce www.mofcom.gov.cn
National Development and Reform Commission www.ndrc.gov.ch
Reuters Fixing Page PBoCA, HSBCNDF, SAEC, CHIBOR, SHIBOR, HSBCCN
State Administration of Foreign Exchange www.safe.gov.cn
The Hong Kong Monetary Authority www.info.gov.hk/hkma
The People's Bank of China www.pbc.gov.cn

Bibliography

Anderson, Jonathan. "The China Monetary Policy Handbook", in *China's Emerging Financial Markets: Challenges and Opportunities* (2009): 167-265.

Bell, Stephen, and Hui Feng. "How Proximate and 'Meta-institutional' Contexts Shape Institutional Change: Explaining The Rise of The People's Bank of China." *Political Studies* 62, no. 1 (2014): 197-215.

Burdekin, Richard CK, and Pierre L. Siklos. "What Has Driven Chinese Monetary Policy Since 1990? Investigating The People's Bank's Policy Rule." *Journal of International Money and Finance* 27, no. 5 (2008): 847-859.

Cheung, Yin-Wong. "A Decade of RMB Internationalisation." *Economic and Political Studies* 11, no. 1 (2023): 47-74.

Cheung, Yin-Wong. "The Role of Offshore Financial Centers in The Process of Renminbi Internationalization." (2014).

Cheung, Yin-Wong, and Dagfinn Rime. "The Offshore Renminbi Exchange Rate: Microstructure and Links to the Onshore Market." *Journal of International Money and Finance* 49 (2014): 170-189.

Cheung, Yin-Wong, Louisa Grimm, and Frank Westermann. "The Evolution of Offshore Renminbi Trading: 2016 to 2019." *Journal of International Money and Finance* 113 (2021): 102369.

Cheung, Yin-Wong, and Matthew S. Yiu. "Offshore Renminbi Trading: Findings From The 2013 Triennial Central Bank Survey." *International Economics* 152 (2017): 9-20.

Cheung, Yin-Wong, "The Role of Offshore Financial Centers in The Process of Renminbi Internationalization." *China Economic Journal* 7, no. 2 (2014): 133-150.

Craig, Mr R. Sean, Mr Changchun Hua, Philip Ng, and Raymond Yuen. Development of the Renminbi Market n Hong Kong SAR: Assessing Onshore-Offshore Market Integration. International Monetary Fund, 2013.

Drysdale, Peter, Adam Triggs, and Jiao Wang. "China's New Role in The International Financial Architecture." *Asian Economic Policy Review* 12, no. 2 (2017): 258-277.

Feng, Yongqi, and Tianshu Zhang. "Interest Rate Linkages Between Offshore and Onshore Renminbi Markets." *Australian Economic Papers* 55, no. 4 (2016): 434-450.

Fernald, John G., Mark M. Spiegel, and Eric T. Swanson. "Monetary Policy Effectiveness in China: Evidence from A FAVAR Model." *Journal of International Money and Finance* 49 (2014): 83-103.

Fung, Hung-Gay, Chuan-Hao Hsu, Wai Lee, and Jot Yau. "Dim Sum Bonds: Do They Whet Your Appetite?." The *Journal of Portfolio Management* 41, no. 5 (2015): 127-135.

Fung, Hung-Gay, Glenn Chi-Wo Ko, and Jot Yau. Dim Sum Bonds: The Offshore Renminbi (RMB)-Denominated Bonds. John Wiley & Sons, 2014.

Garcia-Herrero, Alicia, and Le Xia. "China's RMB Bilateral Swap Agreements: What Explains the Choice of Countries?." (2013).

Garcia-Herrero, Alicia, and Le Xia. "RMB Bilateral Swap Agreements: How China Chooses Its Partners?." *Asia-Pacific Journal of Accounting & Economics* 22, no. 4 (2015): 368-383.

Goldstein, Morris, and Nicholas Lardy. "China's Exchange Rate Policy Dilemma." *American Economic Review* 96, no. 2 (2006): 422-426.

Green, Jeremy, and Julian Gruin. "RMB Transnationalization and the Infrastructural Power of International Financial Centres." *Review of International Political Economy* 28, no. 4 (2020): 1028-1054.

Guijun, Lin, and Ronald M. Schramm. "China's Foreign Exchange Policies Since 1979: A Review of Developments and an Assessment." *China Economic Review* 14, no. 3 (2003): 246-280.

He, Qing, Pak-Ho Leung, and Terence Tai-Leung Chong. "Factor-augmented VAR Analysis of The Monetary Policy in China." *China Economic Review* 25 (2013): 88-104.

Laurens, Bernard and Rodolfo Maino. "China: Strengthening Monetary Policy Implementation." *IMF Working Papers.* Jan. 1, 2007.

Lian, Cheng, Luo Junru, and Liu Lin. "Is the Renminbi a Global Currency? An Evaluation Based on Offshore Foreign Exchange Market Trading Patterns." *Social Sciences in China* 43, no. 2 (2022): 144-160.

Lewis, Greg. "Financial Warfare in Revolutionary China, 1949–1950: Chen Yun, Nan Hanchen, and the People's Bank." *Twentieth-Century China* 29, no. 1 (2003): 105-119.

Li, Wenzhe. "Does Targeted Monetary Policy Matter? A Perspective From China." *Economic Affairs* 38, no. 1 (2018): 106-124.

Lin, Chaoying, and Lerong He. "Targeted Monetary Policy and Agriculture Business Loans." *The North American Journal of Economics and Finance* 54 (2020): 101290.

Lin, Jianhao, Ziwei Mei, Liangyuan Chen, and Chuanqi Zhu. "Is the People's Bank of China Consistent in Words and Deeds?." *China Economic Review* 78 (2023): 101919.

Mathur, Ike, and Soumen De. "The Dim Sum Bond Market in Hong Kong," in *Risk Management Post Financial Crisis: A Period of Monetary Easing*, Emerald Group Publishing Limited, 2014.

Mehrotra, Aaron, and José R. Sánchez-Fung. "China's Monetary Policy and The Exchange Rate." *Comparative Economic Studies* 52 (2010): 497-514.

Murau, Steffen, Joe Rini, and Armin Haas. "The Future of Offshore Dollar Creation: Four Scenarios For The International Monetary System by 2040." (2018).

Pißler, Knut Benjamin. "History and Legal Framework of the People's Bank of China," in *Central Banking and Financial Stability in East Asia*, Cham: Springer International Publishing, 2015.

Qin, Jing. "Relationship Between Onshore and Offshore Renminbi Exchange Markets: Evidence from Multiscale Cross-Correlation and Nonlinear Causal Effect Analyses." *Physica A: Statistical Mechanics and its Applications* 527 (2019): 121183.

PBoC history, http://www.pbc.gov.cn/en/3688066/3688089/index.html, 2023.

PBoC MPC meeting notes, http://www.pbc.gov.cn/en/3688229/3688311/3688329/index.html, 2023.

Ren, Yinghua, Lin Chen, and Ye Liu. "The onshore-offshore exchange rate differential, interest rate spreads, and internationalization: Evidence from the Hong Kong offshore renminbi market." Emerging Markets Finance and Trade 54, no. 13 (2018): 3100-3116.

Shi, Song, and Xunpeng Shi. "The impact of Chinese Regulation of Limitation on Currency Transactions (LCT) on Sydney Housing Prices." *Housing Studies* (2023): 1-22.

Shu, Chang, Dong He, and Xiaoqiang Cheng. "One Currency, Two Markets: The Renminbi's Growing Influence in Asia-Pacific." *China Economic Review* 33 (2015): 163-178.

Song, Ke, and Le Xia. "Bilateral Swap Agreement and Renminbi Settlement in Cross-Border Trade." *Economic and Political Studies* 8, no. 3 (2020): 355-373.

Su, Guanyu, and Junhui Qian. "Does the Offshore Market Matter to China's Exchange Rate Policy?." *Applied Economics Letters* 30, no. 13 (2023): 1734-1737.

Sun, Rongrong. "Does Monetary Policy Matter in China? A Narrative Approach." *China Economic Review* 26 (2013): 56-74.

Von Spreckelsen, Christian, Frederik Kunze, Torsten Windels, and Hans-Jörg Von Mettenheim. "Forecasting Renminbi Quotes in the Revised Chinese FX Market–Can We Get mplications for the Onshore/Offshore Spread-Behaviour?." *International Journal of Economic Policy in Emerging Economies* 7, no. 1 (2014): 66-76.

Wang, Zhaohui, and Zhaohui Wang. "The Faltering RMB Exchange Rate Reform, 2005–2007", in *The International Political Economy of China's Exchange Rate Policy Making* (2021): 81-101.

Xiong, Weibo. "Measuring the Monetary Policy Stance of The People's Bank of China: An Ordered Probit Analysis".

Chapter 11

Determinants of the Political Interest Rate as a Monetary Policy Tool: An Evaluation on BRICS

Gökhan Karhan

Batman University, Turkey

Mücahit Çayın

Batman University, Turkey

M. Ali Seyidoğlu

Financial consultant, Batman, Turkey

Abstract

The concepts of interest rate and inflation which express the increases in the general price level, and the relationship between these two concepts are one of the most discussed topics in the economics literature. The main source of these discussions is that there are many different approaches to the explanation of the concepts of interest and inflation, as well as different approaches to the existence and direction of the relationship between these two concepts. The subject has been discussed in detail within the framework of these theories, as well as in the context of policy rates and bank loan rates. The function of the policy rate in the markets enables decision-makers such as consumers and investors to make rational decisions for the future. Policy interest rates are set by central banks to control the money supply in an economy. When the central bank raises interest rates, borrowing becomes more expensive, which can slow spending and investment and reduce inflationary pressures. Conversely, when interest rates are lowered, borrowing becomes cheaper, which can stimulate spending and investment and increase inflation. High inflation rates can cause serious damage to the economy as they can lead to lower purchasing power, less investment and slower economic growth. Therefore, by adjusting policy interest rates, central banks can affect inflation rates and promote stable economic growth. It will be important to reveal the determinants of the policy rate in light of all these theories. In this study, the determinants of the policy rate will be evaluated for BRICS (Brazil, Russia, India, China, South Africa) countries. This relationship, which we will try to analyze using econometric tests, will be evaluated on indicators such as inflation, unemployment and external debt stock. Although the developing BRICS countries have an important share of the world economy, many of them have a fragile economic structure. For this reason, the effectiveness of monetary policy and the reasonable level of interest and inflation rates in these countries are of great importance in terms of getting rid of their fragile structure. The study was designed in four parts. In the first part of the study, theoretical discussions on the subject and in the second part, an empirical literature review on the subject will be included. In the third part of the study, the relationship between variables such as policy interest, external debt stock, unemployment and inflation will be revealed for the countries in question. The study will conclude with the implementation results and some policy recommendations.

Keywords: Policy Rate, Inflation, Unemployment, Debt, BRICS

***

Introduction

Policy rates determined by central banks are critical tools that summarize a country's economic situation and define its financial stability. This tool is one of the key elements that indirectly affect the daily life of individuals as it has the power to directly affect the costs of interest in the economy, money supply, inflation and unemployment rates. Due to these characteristics, changing the policy rates, which are updated periodically, only by taking certain factors as a reference carries a great risk. This process requires a complex analysis and evaluation because this instrument is used to achieve the main objectives, such as ensuring economic stability and keeping inflation under control.

Inflation, unemployment and interest rates are important indicators that reflect the macroeconomic situation of countries. Inflation is the continuous increase in the general level of prices and occurs when the money supply exceeds the demand. Thus, the value of the local currency decreases, and its purchasing power decreases. In other words, since inflation reduces real income, it causes fewer goods and services to be purchased with the same amount of money compared to the past. This situation causes the companies to make fewer sales, thus reducing the profits of the companies. Therefore, high inflation can slow economic growth and increase unemployment rates.[1] Low inflation rates, on the other hand, accelerate economic growth. However, since high inflation rates can be caused by many factors, they differ in the context of countries. For this reason, there is an inflation threshold specific to countries

[1] Sumera Arshad and Amajd Ali, "Trade-off Between Inflation, Interest and Unemployment Rate of Pakistan: Revisited", *Bulletin of Business and Economics* 5, no.4 (2016): 194.

where the relationship between inflation and growth evolves from positive to negative.[2]

Although unemployment has decreased in some periods, such as during the wars, it has been evaluated as the macroeconomic indicator of countries over time and has become one of the main objectives of economic policies. Especially with the oil crises that affected the world in the 1970s, the problem of unemployment increased throughout the world and thus has become an economic issue that is difficult to deal with. Even at the end of these years, the acceleration of the phenomenon of globalization increased the mobility of labour and thus, unemployment became a problem between countries and regions that became difficult to control.[3]

One of the main discussion topics of macroeconomics is nominal interest rates. As a matter of fact, both the definition of interest and its management have been the subject of debate among macroeconomists. According to Keynesian economics advocates, nominal interest is the opportunity cost of holding money. Interest rate changes affect the demand for money. Therefore, interest rates need to be controlled. In contrast, for monetarists, interest is a fraction of the price in the market for loanable funds. For the stability of this market, interest rates should be allowed to fluctuate on a non-narrow margin.[4]

External debts that countries apply for economic, social or political reasons are also important in terms of macroeconomic variables. Foreign debts, which are due to many reasons such as insufficient domestic capital, financing of economic development, budget deficits, and adverse geographical conditions, can affect the macroeconomic variables of countries.[5]

On the other hand, the relationship of these macroeconomic indicators with each other is among the main issues frequently discussed in the economics literature. For example, both theoretical studies and recently increasing empirical studies have not been able to reveal a clear and precise result regarding the relationship between interest and these macroeconomic

---

[2] Shrikant Krupasindhu Panigrahi et al., "Effects of Inflation, Interest, and Unemployment Rates on Economic Growth: Evidence from ASEAN Countries", *ABAC Journal* 40, no.2 (2020):143-144.

[3] Ahmet Tayfur Akcan and Meliha Ener, "Makroekonomik Değişkenlerin İşsizlik ile İlişkisi: Türkiye Örneği", *Journal of Administrative Sciences* 16, no. 31 (2018): 264.

[4] Nejla Adanur Aklan, Hülya Kanalıcı Akay and Mehmet Çınar, "Türkiye'de Faiz Haddi ve Enflasyon İlişkisi: Gibson Paradoksu'na Yönelik Bir Değerlendirme", *International Conference in Economics*, (EconWorld, 2014), 2.

[5] Eren Sümer, "Türkiye'de Dış Borç Faiz Ödemelerinin Gelir Dağılımına Etkisi: ARDL Sınır Testi Yaklaşımı (1989-2019 Dönemi)", *Siyaset, Ekonomi ve Yönetim Araştırmaları Dergisi* 9, no.1 (2021): 44.

variables, which are cited as examples. In other words, it is seen that there is no complete consensus on the subject.

The relationship between interest and inflation is based on the general theory that high interest rates reduce aggregate demand and, thus, lower the inflation rate. In other words, when interest rates increase, both consumption expenditures and investment expenditures decrease as the cost of borrowing increases. Also, in such a case, savings increase and money in circulation decreases. The decrease in the currency in circulation both prevents inflation and increases the value of the local currency.[6] The rise in interest rates ensures the transfer of foreign capital to the country. This incoming hot money increases the foreign exchange supply and causes the exchange rate to fall. A low exchange rate also reduces exports and increases imports. This means an increase in the current account deficit of countries. However, low exchange rates cause the prices of imported products/inputs to fall, thus reducing inflation. In the opposite case, the costs of imported products/inputs increase and thus inflation increases.[7]

However, the relationship between interest and inflation has been discussed for a long time within the scope of the "*Gibson paradox*". Gibson, found a positive relationship between inflation and bond rates for the British economy in his applied study. However, Keynes emphasized that this was not based on a theoretical basis and, therefore, could be "*a coincidence*" and named the situation in question as the "*Gibson paradox*".[8] The "*Gibson paradox*", first used by Keynes and based on Gibson's research in 1923, has been tested in many empirical studies.[9]

The relationship between inflation and interest has also been frequently discussed within the scope of the hypothesis known as the "*Fisher effect*" in the literature. Fisher states that the nominal interest rate is equal to the sum of the real interest rate and the expected inflation rate. In other words, after high inflation, lenders will want a higher nominal interest rate, taking into account their price expectations. This will require an adjustment in real interest rates,

---

[6] Jón Helgi Egilsson, "How Raising Interest Rates Can Cause Inflation and Currency Depreciation", *Journal of Applied Economics* 23, no.1 (2020): 451.

[7] Hüseyin İşcan and Ayşe Durgun-Kaygısız, "Türkiye'de Döviz Kuru, Enflasyon ve Faiz Oranı İlişkisi: 2009-2017 Uygulaması", *Iğdır Üniversitesi Sosyal Bilimler Dergisi* 17, (2019):583-584.

[8] Metin Özdemir and Salih Yıldırım, "Fiyat Düzeyi ve Faiz Oranı: Gibson Paradoksu Türkiye Ekonomisi için Geçerli (mi)?", *Maliye Dergisi* 174, (2018):28.

[9] Egilsson "How Raising Interest Rates", 451.

so inflation and nominal interest rates will go hand in hand.[10] According to the hypothesis, a change in the expected inflation rate will change the nominal interest rate both in the same direction and at the same rate. However, no consensus has been reached for the "Fisher effect" in empirical studies for reasons such as incorrect measurement of inflation expectations, differences in estimation methods, and handling of long- and short-term rates.

On the contrary, it is seen that the response of interest rates to inflation, in the long run, is not at the same rate, and even there is no relationship at all.[11]

The relationship between interest and unemployment arises from the negative effects of interest rates on investments. Because it is generally accepted that there is an inverse relationship between interest rates and economic growth. However, there is an inverse relationship between the unemployment rate and economic growth. In this respect, sustainable and stable growth is an important issue in terms of reducing unemployment. In other words, high interest rates can increase unemployment by reducing production levels and growth rates.[12] From this point of view, low interest rates in countries with high unemployment are important in terms of combating unemployment.

The relationship between interest and external debt can also be evaluated within the framework of interest cost. Interest cost in foreign borrowing, which can be effective on many macroeconomic variables of countries, is of great importance. In other words, although foreign debts have a positive effect in the period they are obtained, they may cause economic difficulties in the repayment periods. When the borrowed debts are not used in production and productive investments, they may not cover the cost of interest and thus harm the economy.[13] In short, when the interest rates increase, the foreign debts of the countries increase. For this reason, low interest rates are important for sustainable external debt. If it is noticed, the relationship between interest and inflation, unemployment and foreign debts is briefly mentioned here.

---

[10] Maria Chiara Cucciniello et al., "The Cost Channel of Monetary Policy: The Case of The United States in the Period 1959–2018", *Structural Change and Economic Dynamics* 61, (2022):410.

[11] David O. Cushman et al., "Is the Fisher Effect Asymmetric? Cointegration Analysis and Expectations Measurement," *International Journal of Finance & Economics*, https://doi.org/10.1002/ijfe.2616, (2022): 2.

[12] Ceren Pehlivan et al., "İşsizlikle Faizin Türkiye'de Ekonomik Büyümeye Etkisi: 1980-2016", *Global Journal of Economics and Business Studies* 6, no. 12 (2017):16.

[13] Sümer, "Türkiye'de Dış Borç Faiz Ödemelerinin Gelir Dağılımına Etkisi", 44.

In the next part of the study, some studies in the empirical literature will be examined. After evaluating the empirical literature, an application will be made for BRICS (Brazil, Russia, India, China, South Africa) countries in the study. In practice, the relationship between interest and these macroeconomic variables will be examined within the scope of the determinants of interest rates. Therefore, some studies in this context in the empirical literature will be discussed. In the conclusion part of the study, the findings will be summarized, and some policy implications will be presented.

Empirical Literature

As mentioned above, the relationship between interest and inflation is mostly examined within the scope of the "Fisher effect", which is based on the relationship between nominal interest rates and inflation. In the empirical literature, it has been determined that this hypothesis is valid in some studies and not valid in others. In some studies, the results differ according to the short and long term. For example, Mishkin conducted a study in the USA sample to test the validity of the Fisher hypothesis. In the study, monthly data for the 1964-1986 period were tested with time series analysis. As a result of the research, it was revealed that the Fisher hypothesis was not valid in the short term but was valid in the long term.[14] In a similar study, Mishkin and Simon tested the subject in an Australian sample. In the study, the researchers used data from three periods, namely 1962-1993, 1962-1979 and 1979-1993. As a result of the study, it was found that the Fisher hypothesis was valid in the long term but not valid in the short term.[15]

Atkins and Coe conducted a study in the USA and Canada to test the validity of the Fisher hypothesis. In the study, monthly data of these countries in the 1953-1999 period were tested with the ARDL technique. As a result of the study, the researchers found that there is a long-term relationship between nominal interest rates and inflation. Although these findings are evidence for the validity of the Fisher hypothesis in the post-war period for these countries, unclear evidence for the validity of the tax-adjusted Fisher hypothesis for the USA was also found in the study. No evidence was found for Canada.[16]

---

[14] Frederic S. Mishkin, "Is the Fisher Effect for Real? A Reexamination of the Relationship between Inflation and Interest Rates", *Journal of Monetary Economics* 30, no.2 (1992): 195-215.

[15] Frederic S. Mishkin and John Simon, "An Empirical Examination of the Fisher Effect in Australia", *Economic Record* 71, no.3 (1995):217-229.

[16] Frank J. Atkins and Patrick J. Coe, "An ARDL Bounds Test of The Long-Run Fisher Effect in The United States and Canada", *Journal of Macroeconomics* 24, (2002):255-266.

Westerlund investigated the issue in a sample of 20 OECD countries. As a result of the panel data analysis using quarterly data of the countries in the 1980-2004 period, it was found that the Fisher hypothesis is valid.[17] However, in the same year, Uddin et al. found that there is no relationship between inflation and interest rates in their study done for Bangladesh. In other words, it has been determined that the Fisher hypothesis is not valid for the 1996-2003 period in this country.[18] Yılancı tested the validity of the Fisher hypothesis in the sample of Türkiye. In the study, the data from the 1989-2008 period were analyzed with KSS cointegration tests developed by Kapetanios et al. and Engle-Granger.[19] As a result of the study, the researcher concluded that the Fisher hypothesis was not valid.[20]

In another study for Turkey the data for the period 2002-2011 were analyzed with the cointegration test introduced to the literature by Seo, and as a result, it was found that the Fisher hypothesis was not valid.[21]

Sheefani, investigated the validity of the Fisher hypothesis in the sample of Namibia. In the study, the data for the period 1992-2011 were estimated with the Johansen cointegration test. In the study, no relationship was found between inflation and interest rates. Therefore, it turned out that the Fisher hypothesis is not valid for Namibia.[22] One of the studies that analyzed the validity of the Fisher hypothesis with the Johansen cointegration test was conducted by Etuk et al. The autoregressive fractional integrated moving average (ARFIMA) technique was also used in the study. In the study, the long-term relationship between nominal interest and inflation rates for the Nigerian economy in the 1970-2003 period was tested, and it was determined that the Fisher hypothesis was valid.[23]

---

[17] Joakim Westerlund, "Panel Cointegration Tests of the Fisher Effect", *Journal of Applied Econometrics* 23, (2008): 193-233.

[18] Md. Gazi Salah Uddin et al., "An Empirical Evidence of Fisher Effect in Bangladesh: A Time-Series Approach", *ASA University Review* 2, no.1 (2008):1-8.

[19] Robert F., Engle, and C. W. J. Granger. "Co-Integration and Error Correction: Representation, Estimation, and Testing", *Econometrica* 55, no. 2 (1987): 251–76. https://doi.org/10.2307/1913236.

[20] Veli Yılancı, "Fisher Hipotezinin Türkiye için Sınanması: Doğrusal Olmayan Eşbütünleşme Analizi", *Atatürk Üniversitesi İktisadi ve İdari Bilimler Dergisi* 23, no.4 (2009): 205-213.

[21] Tayfur Bayat, "Türkiye'de Fisher Etkisinin Geçerliliği: Doğrusal Olmayan Eşbütünleşme Yaklaşımı", *Erciyes Üniversitesi İktisadi ve İdari Bilimler Fakültesi Dergisi* 38, (2011): 47-60.

[22] Johannes Peyavali Sheefeni Sheefeni, "Testing for the Fisher Hypothesis in Namibia", *Journal of Emerging Issues in Economics, Finance and Banking* 2, no.1 (2013): 571-582.

[23] I.E. Etuk et al., "Fractional Cointegration Analysis of Fisher Hypothesis in Nigeria", *Asian Journal of Applied Sciences* 2, no.1 (2014): 88-94.

To test the validity of the Fisher hypothesis, Edirisinghe et al. conducted a study in the Sri Lanka sample. The data of the country for the period 1959-2011 were analyzed with the Engle-Granger cointegration test. In the study, it was determined that the Fisher hypothesis was valid for the country in the long term, but it was not valid in the short term.[24]

One of the studies examining the subject with the Engle-Granger cointegration test was conducted by Ito. The researcher examined the subject within the framework of inflation targeting in the Swedish sample with the data for the period 1993-2015. As a result of the study, it is seen that the Fisher hypothesis is valid for 2, 3, 4, 5 and 7-year inflation targeting maturities, but not for 10 years.[25]

Abubakar and Sivagnanam examined the issue for India with the ARDL cointegration test. As a result of the study using the data for the period 1990-2015, no long-term relationship was found between interest and inflation. In other words, it was found that the Fisher hypothesis is not valid for India.[26] Researchers tested the validity of the hypothesis in a sample of five fragile countries (Brazil, India, Indonesia, South Africa, and Turkiye). As a result of the analyses made with the data of the 2000-2016 period, it was revealed that the Fisher hypothesis is valid only for Brazil and Indonesia.[27]

Yuliati et al. investigated the subject of Indonesia with the ARDL technique. As a result of the study, in which the data for the 2008-2017 period was used, no relationship was found between inflation and nominal interest rates in both the short term and the long term. In other words, it has been revealed that the Fisher hypothesis is not valid.[28]

Camba and Camba examined the validity of the Fisher hypothesis in the Philippines sample. In the study, the data for the period of 1995-2020 were

---

[24] Navoda Edirisinghe et al., "An Empirical Study of the Fisher Effect and The Dynamic Relationship between Inflation and Interest Rate in Sri Lanka", *International Journal of Business and Social Research* 5, no.1 (2015): 47-62.

[25] Takayasu Ito, "Does the Fisher Hypothesis Hold in Sweden? An Analysis of Long-term Interest Rates under the Regime of Inflation Targeting", *Review of Integrative Business and Economics Research* 5, no.3 (2016): 283-295.

[26] Jamaladeen Abubakar and K. Jothi Sivagnanam, "Fisher's Effect: An Empirical Examination Using India's Time Series Data", *Journal of Quantitative Economics* 15, (2017): 611-628.

[27] Tayfur Bayat et al., "Re-visiting Fisher Effect for Fragile Five Economies", *Journal of Central Banking Theory and Practice* 7, no.2 (2018): 203-218.

[28] Lilis Yuliati et al., "Autoregressive Distributed Lag (ARDL) Approach for Re-testing the Fisher Effect in Indonesia", *Jurnal Perspektif Pembiayaan dan Pembangunan Daerah* 8, no.3 (2020):209-218.

analyzed with Engle-Granger and Johansen cointegration tests. As a result of the study, a long-term relationship was determined between nominal interest rates and inflation rates.[29]

Han tested the validity of the Fisher hypothesis in terms of the Turkish economy. In the study, the data for the period 2003-2021 were estimated with the KSS (2006) nonlinear cointegration test and as a result, it was revealed that the Fisher hypothesis was not valid for this period in Turkiye.[30]

Finally, Ruzima et al. examined the issue in terms of the Rwandan economy. In the study, the data for the period of 2012-2020 were analyzed with the ARDL technique. As a result of the study, it was revealed that the Fisher hypothesis was not valid in the short term, and the hypothesis was partially valid in the long term.[31]

Data, Method and Analysis

This study aims to investigate the effects of inflation (INF), unemployment (UNEMP), external debt stock to national income (EDS), and domestic credit by private sector (DCPS) variables on the policy rate (IR) in the BRICS countries for the 1998-2022 period. Despite the varying variance problem, the natural logarithm of all variables was taken. Thus, the obtained parameters will be interpreted in terms of %. All data were obtained from the World Bank data distribution system. In the application phase of the study, descriptive statistics, homogeneity test, cross-section dependency test, unit root test and finally Auto Regressive Distributed Lag model (ARDL) results were included, respectively. In this context, the following model was established.

$$\ln IR_{it} = \beta_0 + \beta_1 \text{lnENF}_{1t} + \beta_2 \text{lnUNEMP}_{2t} + \beta_3 \text{lnEDS}_{3t} + \beta_4 \text{lnDCPS}_{4t} + \varepsilon_{it} \quad \text{(Eq.1)}$$

The main purpose of this study is to observe the effects of other variables while investigating the effects of inflation and unemployment on the policy rate. In the model, β_0 is a constant term, β_1 parameter shows the effect of inflation on the policy rate, and β_2 coefficient shows the effect of unemployment

---

[29] Abraham C. Camba Jr and Aileen L. Camba, "An Engle-Granger and Johansen Cointegration Approach in Testing the Validity of Fisher Hypothesis in the Philippines", *The Journal of Asian Finance, Economics and Business* 8, no.12 (2021):31-38.

[30] Ayşegül Han, "Türkiye'de Faiz ve Enflasyon Arasındaki İlişkinin Fisher Hipotezi Kapsamında Ampirik Olarak Sınanması", *Birey ve Toplum Sosyal Bilimler Dergisi* 12, no.1 (2022): 5-27.

[31] Martin Ruzima et al., "Does the Fisher Effect Hold in Rwanda?", *Quality & Quantity* 57, no. 3 (2023): 2657-2672.

on the policy rate. The β_3 coefficient represents the external debt stock, the β_4 coefficient represents the effect of domestic credit by the private sector on the policy rate, and the E_{it} error term.

Table 11.1 Descriptive Statistics

	IR	INF	UNEMP	EDS	DCPS
Mean	0.869551	6.677999	0.941711	1.371130	1.807683
Median	0.838149	5.184247	0.908217	1.338913	1.764015
Maximum	1.776338	85.74649	1.474304	1.980777	2.268024
Minimum	0.424609	-1.401473	0.510545	0.922151	1.204153
Std.Dev.	0.285403	8.373303	0.246620	0.198777	0.271601
Skewness	0.588906	7.012258	0.441209	0.281521	-0.241359
Kurtosis	3.433462	65.20225	2.238175	2.641708	2.108676
Jarque-Bera	8.203813	21176.08	7.078325	2.319735	5.351428
Probability	0.016541	0.000000	0.029038	0.313528	0.068858
Sum	108.6939	834.7499	117.7139	171.3912	225.9604
SumSq.Dev.	10.10039	8693.914	7.541868	4.899512	7.013800

Source: Created by the authors.

When descriptive statistics (Table 11.1) are examined, it is seen that the highest standard deviation belongs to inflation. However, the skewness and kurtosis coefficients of all variables except inflation show that the data are in accordance with the normal distribution. The reason for this divergence in the inflation data set is that Russia faced high inflation especially in 1998-1999. For this reason, it should be investigated whether the coefficients of the countries included in the panel are homogeneous.

In the study, the homogeneity test developed by Hsiao was used to understand the status of the coefficients.[32] With the help of this test, it is investigated whether other countries have similar reactions to the economic shocks faced by one of the countries included in the panel. Heterogeneous coefficients mean that the economic structures of the countries included in the panel are different from each other, and homogeneous means that the economic structures of the countries that are the subject of the research are similar.

The Hsiao test tests three sub-hypotheses. The null hypothesis of the H1 and H2 hypotheses states that the coefficients are homogeneous, while the alternative hypothesis states that the coefficients are heterogeneous. In the H3 hypothesis, unlike the H1 and H2 hypotheses, the alternative hypothesis is based on the assumption that the coefficients are partially heterogeneous.

[32] Cheng Hsıao, *Analysis of Panel Data*, Third Edition, (Cambridge: University Press, 1986: Cambridge), ISBN: 1107038693,9781107038691.

Table 11.2 Homogeneity Test Results

Hypotheses	F-Stat	P-Value
H1	4.915478	3.74E-08
H2	2.431010	0.003899
H3	12.40487	1.97E-08

Source: Created by the authors.

As can be seen in Table 11.2, the alternative hypothesis is accepted in all three hypotheses; that is, it is understood that all of the coefficients are heterogeneous. The heterogeneity of the coefficients necessitates that the tests to be used in the next part of the study should especially take into account heterogeneity. In addition, it is necessary to investigate the cross-sectional dependence between the countries in the panel because cross-sectional dependence can affect the results of stationarity tests. In cases where there is cross-section dependency, 1st generation unit root tests are used, and in cases where there is no cross-section dependency, 2nd generation unit root tests are used.

In the study, Breusch-Pagan CD_{LM1}[33] and Peseran CD_{LM2}[34] tests were used to detect cross-sectional dependence.

Null and alternative hypotheses in cross-section dependency tests are as follows:

H_0: No cross-section dependency.
H_1: There is a cross-section dependency.

Table 11.3 Cross-section Dependency Tests

	IR		INF		UNEMP	
	Statistic	p-value	Statistic	p-value	Statistic	p-value
Breusch-Pagan LM	93.08894	0.00***	12.32539	0.2639	39.35214	0.00***
Pesaran scaled LM	18.57925	0.00***	0.519972	0.6031	6.56337	0.00***
	DCPS		EDS			
	Statistic	p-value	Statistic	p-value		
Breusch-Pagan LM	109.7439	0.00***	32.28592	0.00***		
Pesaran scaled LM	22.30342	0.00***	4.983284	0.00***		

Source: Created by the authors.

[33] Trevor Breusch, T. S., and Adrian. R. Pagan. "A Simple Test for Heteroscedasticity and Random Coefficient Variation", *Econometrica* 47, no. 5 (1979): 1287–94. https://doi.org/10.2307/1911963.

[34] Hashem M. Pesaran, "General Diagnostic Test for Cross Section Dependence in Panels", IZA Discussion Paper no. 1240, 2004.

Considering the probability values, it is seen that the alternative hypothesis, which accepts the cross-section dependence in all variables except inflation, is valid (Table 11.3). For this reason, ADF, one of the first-generation unit root tests, was applied to the inflation variable and the CADF test, which takes into account the cross-sectional dependence, was applied to the other variables.

The CADF unit root test is a useful test both for the whole panel and for giving country-based results. This test can be used in the case of T>N and N>T. The null hypothesis and alternative hypothesis regarding the test are as follows.

H0: Series has a unit root, so it is not stationary.
H1: The series does not carry a unit root; that is, it is stationary.

The absolute value of the CADF test statistic is compared with the table values given in Peseran.[35] If the table value is greater than the test statistic, the alternative hypothesis is accepted, and it is concluded that the data set for that country is stationary. The CADF stationarity tests of the series are given below.

Table 11.4 CADF Unit Root Test Results

	IR				EDS			
	Level		First difference		Level		First difference	
	Lags	CADF stat	Lags	CADF stat	Lags	CADF stat	Lags	CADF stat
Brazil	1	-3.689*	1	-2.944	2	0.0206	1	-3.122
Russia	1	-1.974	1	-4.370**	1	-3.42	1	-2.204
India	1	-0.986	1	-2.602	1	-2.39	1	-2.662
China	1	-3.080	1	-3.595*	1	-3.81**	1	-4.282**
South Africa	1	-2.453	1	-3.106	1	-3.96**	1	-3.631*
Panel CIPS		-2.436		-3.323***		-2.71		-3.180***

	DCPS				UNEM		
	Level		First difference		Level		First difference
	Lags	Stat	Lags	Stat	Lag	Stat	Stat
Brazil	3	-2.873	3	-2.139	1	-0.226	-1.304
Russia	1	-3.709*	1	-3.947**	3	-1.848	-1.910
India	1	-0.931	3	-1.548	1	-1.964	-0.785
China	1	-2.746	1	-3.581**	1	-3.537*	-4.249
South Africa	1	-2.597	1	-2.823	2	-0.743	-2.097
Panel CIPS		-2.571		-2.808*		-1.664	-2.069

Source: Created by the authors.

Notes: Maximum lag length is considered as 4 and determined according to Schwarz Information Criteria. CADF test statistics values for constant and trend -4.67 (%1), -3.87 (%5) and -3.49 (%10) (Pesaran 2007, table I(c), p:276). Panel statistics critical values for

[35] Hashem M. Pesaran, "A Simple Panel Unit Root Test in the Presence of Cross-Section Dependence", *Journal of Applied Econometrics* 22 (2), (2007): 265-312.

INFLATION	
Stationary Test	Level
Tests	Stat
LLC	-13.0995***
IPS	-8.86851***
ADF	81.6868***
PP	35.3444***

constant and trend model -3.10 (%1), -2.86 (%5) and -2.73 (%10) (Pesaran 2007, table II (c), p:281). Panel statistics are the average of CADF statistics. The figures which is ***, ** and * show 1 %, 5 % and 10 % levels, respectively

According to the unit root test results (Table 11.4), it is understood that interest, demand for credit by the private sector, external debt stock and unemployment data are not stationary at their level values. It is seen that the unit root problem disappears when the first difference of the same data sets is taken. However, inflation dataset appears to be stationary at the level value.

In the next part of the research, the panel ARDL method was applied to the model established above (Eq.1).

$$\ln IR_{it} = \beta_0 + \sum_{i=1}^{m} \beta_{1i} \ln ENF_{t-i} + \sum_{i=0}^{n} \beta_{2i} \ln UNEMP_{t-i} + \sum_{i=0}^{k} \beta_{3i} \ln EDS_{t-i} + \sum_{i=0}^{p} \beta_{4i} \ln DCPS_{t-i} + \varepsilon_{it} \quad \text{(Eq.2)}$$

Here, m, n, k and p represent delay lengths. The optimum delay length was calculated as 3 with the help of AIC. The method suggested by Kamas and Joyce was used to determine the lag lengths.[36] According to this method, first the dependent variable was regressed with its lagged values and the lag length with the smallest AIC value was found. Then, the lag value calculated for the dependent variable was kept constant, and the lag lengths were calculated for the other independent variables, respectively. According to the calculated lag lengths, the most appropriate short and long-term ARDL model is (3,3, 3,3,3).

When Table 11.5 is examined, the effects of unemployment, inflation, external debt stock and demand for credit by the private sector on the policy rate are significant in the long run. A 1% increase in unemployment causes the policy rate to increase by 0.3%. However, the 1% increase in inflation and external debt stock increases the policy rate by 0.02% and 0.20%, respectively. Again, according to the test results, it is understood that there is an inverse relationship between the volume of demand for credit by the private sector and the policy rate. Because, it is possible to say that a 1% increase in DCPS reduces

[36] Linda Kamas and Joseph Joyce, "Money, Income and Prices Under Fixed Exchange Rates: Evidence from Causality Tests and VARs", *Journal of Macroeconomics* 15, (4) (1993): 747-768.

the policy rate by 0.26%. It is understood that among the variables included in the model, according to the calculated coefficients, the variable that has the most determining power on the policy rate is unemployment. In the short run, the relationship between the variables is insignificant.

Table 11.5. ARDL (3,3,3,3,3) PMG Test Results

Variable	Coefficient	Std. Error	t-Statistic	Prob.*
	Long Run Equation			
UNEMP	0.317193	0.110291	2.875977	0.0064
INF	0.025023	0.001308	19.12608	0.0000
DCPS	-0.267206	0.015078	-17.72215	0.0000
DBS	0.201958	0.021552	9.370846	0.0000

Source: Created by the authors.

Result and Policy Recommendation

BRICS countries (Brazil, Russia, India, China and South Africa) constitute an important part of the world economy. The economic performance of these countries and the determination of their policy rates are of great importance in terms of global economic stability. This study aims to shed more light on the policy rate determination process of central banks by examining the policy rate determinants in BRICS countries.

According to the findings obtained from the study, every 1% increase in the inflation rate in the long run increases the policy rate by 0.02 %. This result shows that the Fisher effect is valid in the long term in BRICS member countries. In this regard, our study supports the results of the research done by Mishkin[37], Mishkin and Simon,[38] Westerlund,[39] Etuk et al.,[40] Edirisinghe et al.,[41] Camba and Camba.[42]

However, in the long run, it is understood that inflation affects the interest policies implemented by central banks, which act to maintain economic stability. Keeping inflation under control is part of efforts to ensure price stability. Especially during the pandemic period, inflation became the main

[37] Mishkin, "Is the Fisher Effect for Real?", 195-215.

[38] Mishkin and john Simon, "An Empirical Examination of the Fisher Effect", 193-233.

[39] Westerlund, "Panel Cointegration Tests", 193-233.

[40] Etuk et al., "Fractional Cointegration Analysis", 88-94.

[41] Edirisinghe et al., "An Empirical Study of the Fisher Effect", 47-62.

[42] Camba and Camba, "An Engle-Granger and Johansen Cointegration Approach", 31-38.

economic problem in BRICS member countries, as well as all over the world. Demand and supply imbalances, supply chain problems, public expenditures, increased energy and raw material prices caused inflation to rise rapidly. For this reason, BRICS member countries have changed their monetary and fiscal policies to combat increasing inflation. Brazil, Russia, India and South Africa, which are members of the union, increased their interest rates, while the Central Bank of China kept interest rates constant (2.90 %). The fact that China is the largest exporting country in the world has a great impact on keeping interest rates constant. Because other countries, which could not meet the increasing demand in this period, increased their imports, thus China's export volume increased rapidly. With increasing exports, investments continued unabated.

However, every 1% increase in the unemployment rate increases the policy rate by approximately 0.30 %. This result shows that unemployment levels play a critical role in the process of determining the policy rate by central banks. High unemployment can negatively impact economic growth and encourage central banks to raise interest rates. One of the reasons why increased unemployment harms the economic system is the decrease in savings of individuals whose income decreases. Insufficient domestic savings increases the external debt stock of BRICS member countries.

According to the research results, every 1% increase in the external debt stock increases the policy rate by approximately 0.20 %. This result highlights the impact of external financial relations on the policy rate. High external debt can threaten a country's economic stability and prompt central banks to raise interest rates.

Finally, according to the findings obtained from the study, it is seen that there is an inverse relationship between the volume of private sector bank loans and the policy rate. Increasing credit demand in BRICS member countries creates inflationary pressure. By increasing the policy interest rate, central banks try to reduce loan demand and neutralize inflationary pressure. This result shows that central banks can use the policy rate to regulate credit activity.

The policy rate determination process may take place differently in each country and may vary depending on the targets set by central banks, economic conditions and policy priorities. Therefore, the factors that determine the policy rate may differ depending on the country and the central bank's approach. In future studies, testing the relationship of different parameters (etc. domestic debt stock, money supply, savings volüme) with interest rates with non-linear methods may contribute to the policy rate determination process of the central banks of the BRICS member countries.

Bibliography

Abubakar, Jamaladeen and K. Jothi Sivagnanam. "Fisher's Effect: An Empirical Examination Using India's Time Series Data." *Journal of Quantitative Economics* 15, (2017): 611-628.

Adanur-Aklan, Nejla, Hülya Kanalıcı Akay, and Mehmet Çınar "Türkiye'de Faiz Haddi ve Enflasyon İlişkisi: Gibson Paradoksu'na Yönelik Bir Değerlendirme." International Conference in Economics (EconWorld2014):1-14.

Akcan, Ahmet Tayfur and Meliha Ener. "Makroekonomik Değişkenlerin İşsizlik ile İlişkisi: Türkiye Örneği." *Journal of Administrative Sciences* 16, no. 31 (2018): 263-285.

Arshad, Sumera and Amajd Ali. "Trade-off between Inflation, Interest and Unemployment Rate of Pakistan: Revisited." *Bulletin of Business and Economics* 5, no.4 (2016): 193-209.

Atkins, Frank J., and Patrick J. Coe. "An ARDL Bounds Test of The Long-Run Fisher Effect in The United States and Canada." *Journal of Macroeconomics* 24, (2002):255-266.

Bayat, Tayfur. "Türkiye'de Fisher Etkisinin Geçerliliği: Doğrusal Olmayan Eşbütünleşme Yaklaşımı." *Erciyes Üniversitesi İktisadi ve İdari Bilimler Fakültesi Dergisi* 38, (2011): 47-60.

Bayat,Tayfur, Selim Kayhan, and İzzet Taşar. "Re-visiting Fisher Effect for Fragile Five Economies." *Journal of Central Banking Theory and Practice* 7, no.2 (2018). 203-218.

Breusch, T. S., and A. R. Pagan. "A Simple Test for Heteroscedasticity and Random Coefficient Variation." *Econometrica* 47, no. 5 (1979): 1287–94. https://doi.org/10.2307/1911963.

Camba Jr, Abraham C, and Aileen L. Camba. "An Engle-Granger and Johansen Cointegration Approach in Testing the Validity of Fisher Hypothesis in the Philippines." *The Journal of Asian Finance, Economics and Business* 8, no.12 (2021):31-38

Cucciniello, Maria Chiara., Matteo Deleidi, and Enrico Sergio Levreroa. "The Cost Channel of Monetary Policy: The Case of The United States in the Period 1959–2018." *Structural Change and Economic Dynamics* 61, (2022): 409-433.

Cushman, David O., Glauco De Vita, and Emmanouil Trachanas. "Is the Fisher Effect Asymmetric? Cointegration Analysis and Expectations Measurement." *International Journal of Finance & Economics*. https://doi.org/10.1002/ijfe.2616, (2022):1-39.

Edirisinghe, Navoda., Selliah Sivarajasingham, and John Nigel. "An Empirical Study of the Fisher Effect and The Dynamic Relationship between Inflation and Interest Rate in Sri Lanka." *International Journal of Business and Social Research* 5, no.1 (2015): 47-62.

Egilsson, Jón Helgi. "How Raising Interest Rates Can Cause Inflation and Currency Depreciation." *Journal of Applied Economics* 23, no.1(2020): 450-468.

Engle, Robert F., and C. W. J. Granger. "Co-Integration and Error Correction: Representation, Estimation, and Testing." *Econometrica* 55, no. 2 (1987): 251–76. https://doi.org/10.2307/1913236.

Etuk, I.E., T. O. James, and B. K. Asare. "Fractional Cointegration Analysis of Fisher Hypothesis in Nigeria." *Asian Journal of Applied Sciences* 2, no.1 (2014): 88-94.

Han, Ayşegül. "Türkiye'de Faiz ve Enflasyon Arasındaki İlişkinin Fisher Hipotezi Kapsamında Ampirik Olarak Sınanması." *Birey ve Toplum Sosyal Bilimler Dergisi* 12, no.1 (2022): 5-27.

Hsıao, Cheng. (1986). Analysis of Panel Data, Cambridge University Press: Cambridge Third Edition. ISBN: 1107038693,9781107038691

Ito, Takayasu. "Does the Fisher Hypothesis Hold in Sweden? An Analysis of Long-term Interest Rates under the Regime of Inflation Targeting." *Review of Integrative Business and Economics Research* 5, no.3 (2016): 283-295.

İşcan, Hüseyin, and Ayşe Durgun Kaygısız. "Türkiye'de Döviz Kuru, Enflasyon ve Faiz Oranı İlişkisi: 2009-2017 Uygulaması." *Iğdır Üniversitesi Sosyal Bilimler Dergisi* 17, (2019): 581-604.

Kamas Linda and Joyce Joseph, (1993). "Money, Income and Prices Under Fixed Exchange Rates: Evidence from Causality Tests and VARs", *Journal of Macroeconomics*, 15(4): 747-768.

Mishkin, Frederic S. "Is the Fisher Effect for Real? A Reexamination of the Relationship between Inflation and Interest Rates." *Journal of Monetary Economics* 30, no. 2 (1992): 195-215.

Mishkin, Frederic S., and John Simon. "An Empirical Examination of the Fisher Effect in Australia." Economic Record 71, no.3 (1995):217-229.

Özdemir, Metin, and Salih Yıldırım. "Fiyat Düzeyi ve Faiz Oranı: Gibson Paradoksu Türkiye Ekonomisi için Geçerli (mi)?." *Maliye Dergisi* 174, (2018): 26-47.

Panigrahi, Shrikant K., Noor A. Azizan, Shahryar Sorooshian, and Prabha Thoudam. "Effects of Inflation, Interest, and Unemployment Rates on Economic Growth: Evidence from ASEAN Countries." *ABAC Journal* 40, no.2 (2020):140-155.

Pehlivan, Ceren., Nergis Bingöl, and Ferhat Özbay. "İşsizlikle Faizin Türkiye'de Ekonomik Büyümeye Etkisi: 1980-2016." *Global Journal of Economics and Business Studies* 6, no.12 (2017): 15-29.

Pesaran, M, Hashem. (2004). *General Diagnostic Test for Cross Section Dependence in Panels.* IZA Discussion Paper No. 1240

Pesaran, M. Hashem. (2007). A Simple Panel Unit Root Test in the Presence of Cross-Section Dependence. *Journal of Applied Econometrics*, 22(2), 265-312.

Ruzima, Martin., Micheal Kof Boachie., Tatjana Põlajeva, and Abdul-Aziz Iddrisu. "Does the Fisher Effect Hold in Rwanda?." *Quality & Quantity* 57, no. 3 (2023): 2657-2672.

Sheefeni, Johannes Peyavali Sheefeni. "Testing for the Fisher Hypothesis in Namibia." *Journal of Emerging Issues in Economics, Finance and Banking* 2, no.1 (2013): 571-582.

Sümer, Eren. "Türkiye'de Dış Borç Faiz Ödemelerinin Gelir Dağılımına Etkisi: ARDL Sınır Testi Yaklaşımı (1989-2019 Dönemi)." *Siyaset, Ekonomi ve Yönetim Araştırmaları Dergisi* 9, no.1 (2021): 42-58.

Uddin, Md. Gazi Salah., Md. Mahmudul Alam, and Kazi Ashraful Alam. "An Empirical Evidence of Fisher Effect in Bangladesh: A Time-Series Approach." *ASA University Review* 2, no.1 (2008):1-8.

Westerlund, Joakim. “Panel Cointegration Tests of the Fisher Effect.” *Journal of Applied Econometrics* 23, (2008): 193-233.

Yılancı, Veli. “Fisher Hipotezinin Türkiye için Sınanması: Doğrusal Olmayan Eşbütünleşme Analizi.” *Atatürk Üniversitesi İktisadi ve İdari Bilimler Dergisi* 23, no.4 (2009): 205-213.

Yuliati, Lilis. Ananda Fauziah Mukti, and Riniati. “Autoregressive Distributed Lag (ARDL) Approach for Re-testing the Fisher Effect in Indonesia.” *Jurnal Perspektif Pembiayaan dan Pembangunan Daerah* 8, no.3 (2020):209-218.

PART IV:
ISLAMIC MONETARY POLICY AND CHALLENGES FOR THE MIDDLE WAY

Chapter 12

Redefining Capital and Monetary Policy in G20 Countries: Lessons from Islamic Political Economy

M. Uzair Zulkifly

Durham University, UK

Abstract

This chapter proposal seeks to investigate the concept of capital within the framework of Islamic political economy and its implications on monetary policy in G20 countries. The emphasis will be placed on the divergence between contemporary Islamic banking practices and the authentic teachings of Islamic political economy. Moreover, the potential for realizing an equitable and ethical financial system as visualized by the authentic teachings of Islamic political economy will be explored. The chapter will commence with an overview of capital, monetary policy, and Islamic political economy, followed by a discussion on the conventional understanding of capital as opposed to its unique conceptualization within Islamic political economy. The key distinctions, such as the prohibition of interest, risk-sharing, and the focus on real economic activities, will be highlighted. Subsequently, the chapter will delve into the current practices and challenges of monetary policy in G20 countries and examine the factors responsible for the divergence of Islamic banking practices from the authentic teachings of Islamic political economy. These factors include the influence of conventional financial systems, regulatory challenges, and market pressures. Illustrative examples will be provided to showcase how contemporary Islamic banks deviate from the fundamental principles of Islamic political economy. The chapter will then propose a vision of an equitable and ethical financial system rooted in the authentic teachings of Islamic political economy. The potential benefits of implementing these principles in G20 countries will be discussed, such as fostering financial inclusion, mitigating income inequality, and promoting sustainable economic growth. Furthermore, the implications of incorporating Islamic political economy principles into monetary policy will be analyzed, including the use of alternative policy instruments, bolstering financial stability, and supporting sustainable development. Finally, the challenges and opportunities in implementing such changes will be investigated, addressing the necessity for regulatory reforms, capacity building, and collaboration between conventional and Islamic financial institutions. The chapter will conclude with a summary of the main findings and policy recommendations for redefining capital and monetary policy in G20 countries based on the lessons gleaned from the Islamic political economy. In essence, this proposed chapter aims to offer a comprehensive understanding of the concept of capital from the perspective of Islamic political economy and its impact on monetary policy, the divergence of Islamic banking from its authentic teachings, and the envisioned equitable and ethical financial system. The chapter will provide valuable insights into how the principles of the Islamic political economy can potentially transform central banking practices and monetary policy in G20 countries, underscoring the challenges and opportunities that such a transformation entails.

Keywords: Islamic Political Economy, Islamic Banking, Authentic Teachings

***

Introduction

The advancement of the financial landscape throughout the years has not only created a sophisticated system but also vast wealth extracted from financial instruments. The latter can be seen through the burgeoning dominance of fictitious capital, where the trend is underscored by the ascent of financial assets, which swelled from 4.4 times the GDP in 2000 to 6.0 times by 2020.[1] Such an expansion is not merely illustrative of the proliferation of financial instruments but also mirrors the underlying, intricate structural complexities. While Merton and Bodie emphasize understanding these changes through functional effectiveness, this might overlook deeper structural nuances, such as politico-legal structure and broader economic influences.[2] Hence, this chapter aims to scrutinise the structures that form the foundation of monetary economics with the objective of exploring the intricate relationship of the structures.

One notable change in this landscape is the emergence of Islamic banking, representing an amalgamation of economic, legal and ethical shifts. Rooted in Shariah compliance and the ethos against interest rate (*riba*), Islamic banking

[1] "The Rapid Growth in Global Wealth Mckinsey", https://www.mckinsey.com/industries/financial-services/our-insights/the-rise-and-rise-of-the-global-balance-sheet-how-productively-are-we-using-our-wealth.

[2] Louis Althusser, *On the Reproduction of Capitalism: Ideology and Ideological State Apparatuse,s* (Verso Books, 2014); Zvi Bodie and Robert C. Merton, "A Conceptual Framework for Analyzing the Financial Environment", SSRN Scholarly Paper (Rochester, NY, 25 August, 1998), https://papers.ssrn.com/abstract=6638.

has gained traction, especially after the 2007-2008 financial crisis.[3] This system, emphasizing risk-sharing and ethical investing, has been embraced by financial hubs like London and Tokyo, indicating its global appeal beyond mere religious connotations.

In the G20 context, nation-states with significant Muslim populations, like Indonesia and Turkey, have adopted Islamic banking, intertwining economic aspirations with socio-religious ideals. Yet, this acceptance is layered, as the G20 both propels Islamic banking's growth and challenges it against global standards. The core distinction of Islamic banking lies not only in its commitment to Shariah principles but also in the moral economy embedded in the system.[4]

This chapter delves into the challenges faced by the Islamic economy, particularly within the operations of G20 central banks, using two pivotal case studies. The first examines the unlimited swap agreement to discern currency power dynamics, notably the dominance of the dollar, influenced by select G20 countries. On the other hand, the second case study inspects the Bank of England's (BoE) 'Alternative Liquidity Facility' to comprehend the impact of contemporary economic structures on realizing a genuine Islamic political economy. Both of the case studies lead to the exploration of the phenomenon of dollar hegemony and subordinate financialisation. Central to this exploration is the overarching question: Does Islamic banking offer a genuine alternative for a more equitable financial landscape, or does it merely reshape religious tenets to suit capitalist objectives?

The chapter progresses by exploring the Islamic Political Economy's (IPE) foundations and their departure from traditional economic ideologies. Subsequent sections delve into Monetary Economics in Islam and provide detailed insights into both case studies. Reflections on these studies are then discussed from an Islamic political economy perspective, followed by suggestions to better align central banking systems with IPE tenets by redefining capital and its impact towards the central bank. The conclusion ties together these discussions, underscoring the need for a holistic perspective on central banking. In sum, this chapter seeks to decode central banking dynamics by harmonizing functional insights with structural perspectives, particularly in the G20 and Islamic banking realms.

---

[3] Muhammad Ayub, *Understanding Islamic Finance,* (John Wiley & Sons, 2009).

[4] Mehmet Asutay, "A Political Economy Approach to Islamic Economics: Systemic Understanding for an Alternative Economic System", SSRN Scholarly Paper (Rochester, NY, 2007), https://papers.ssrn.com/abstract=1735619.

Islamic Political Economy

The ascendance of Islamic banking has piqued intellectual curiosity, leading scholars to probe the epistemological foundations of the discipline. One might indeed query the ontological veracity of Islamic banking, seeking assurance that its current manifestation faithfully mirrors the values as outlined in the Shariah principle. To address this epistemic quandary, I entreat readers to revisit the rudimentary principles upon which such monetary economics are erected.

For Islamic monetary economics, it is apropos to turn our attention to its more encompassing framework, that of the Islamic economic system. The dissection of any economic modality, whether it be Islamic or otherwise, can be elucidated with clarity by systematizing the subject matter. Adopting a political economy lens in analyzing the underlying structures of an economic system offers a holistic vantage point, ensuring that the societal cornerstone of economics—the populace—is never obscured. This analytical avenue aligns harmoniously with the etymological exploration grounded in tangible societal praxis. Hence, the essence of an economic system is discerned through the sociocultural lattice underpinning a civilization.[5] Echoing this, Nomani and Rahnema conceptualise the economic system as an architectural framework delineating the multifaceted interactions individuals engage in to uphold their quotidian existence—spanning production, exchange, consumption, and distribution.[6] In other words, IPE is driven by its ontology to develop the moral and development base in order to ensure the seamless connection between the ontological proposition and the man-made system that governs everyday life.

IPE emerged in the post-colonial period as part of the Muslim identity research of its own social law. The rise of independent Muslim countries has encouraged Muslims to re-institute their social formation in modern times instead of being trapped under the social formation of the colonial powers, which does not represent their identity at all. Thus, IPE arises from the Islamic order relating to the world. The system of Islamic economics explains as to how the political economy of Islam works as the nature of Islamic economics can be considered as a system of political economy.

To understand the system of Islamic economics, one should consider its organization, fundamental principles of rationality, and property rights, among

[5] Raymond Williams, *Marxism and Literature*, (OUP Oxford, 1977).

[6] Farhad Nomani and Ali Rahnema, *Islamic Economic Systems*, (Bloomsbury Academic, 1994).

other aspects.[7] In other words, the framework paradigm, methodological framework, and philosophic foundations of the Islamic economic system (IES) are necessary to understand the nature of its system.[8] Such requirements of IES also help to explain the IPE perspectives on moral and development bases.

The framework paradigm of Islamic economics is related to the system's objective. The main goal is to innovate an immaculate and just economic system aligned with the Shari'ah principle.[9] Thus, the framework paradigm of this system should be based on specific values, norms and rules which comply with Shari'ah. To approach the moral and development base from the IPE perspective, one should be attentive towards the framework paradigm.

As for the methodological framework of IES, it relies on homo- islamicus.[10] Homo-Islamic is argued to derive from a dual-dimensional utility function.[11] This utility function represents the preference of an economic agent in both present and hereafter. As the ontological and epistemological sources state that a believer should have faith in the hereafter life, the utility function of an economic agent under the IES should consider the dual-dimensional utility function. Thus, the methodological framework of IES encapsulates a human-centric worldview. In other words, every development and moral activity should not only focus on oneself but towards the goals of a bigger society or healthy society.

Besides that, the philosophic foundation or the foundational axioms of IES have been dissected by a number of prominent figures in Islamic economics. [12] This chapter follows the eight axioms in IES, which are discussed briefly in relation to development and moral base.[13] The most important foundational

---

[7] Paul R. Gregory and Robert C. Stuart, *Comparing Economic Systems in the Twenty-First Century*, (Houghton Mifflin, 2004).

[8] Asutay, "A Political Economy Approach".

[9] EL Ghazali, *Man Is The Basis of The Islamic Strategy for Economic Development* (Islamic Development Bank, 1994).

[10] Muhammad Arif, "Towards Establishing The Microfoundations of Islamic Economics: The Basis of the Basics", in *Readings in the Concept and Methodology of Islamic Economics*, (Selangor: Pelanduk Publications, 1989).

[11] Asutay, "A Political Economy Approach".

[12] Syed Nawab Haider Naqvi, *Islam, Economics, and Society (RLE Politics of Islam)*, (Routledge, 2013); Ismail Sirageldin, "The Elimination of Poverty: Challenges and Islamic Strategies", in *Islamic Economic Institutions and the Elimination of Poverty*, (Leicester: Islamic Foundation, 2002); M. Umer Chapra, *Islam and the Economic Challenge* (International Institute of Islamic Thought (IIIT), 1992).

[13] Asutay, "A Political Economy Approach".

axiom of IES is tawhid or oneness of God, which axiom shows the freedom of economic agents in doing any action with respect towards the Islamic economic system. Having this axiom embedded in one's action, one should be more rational in making any judgement. Added to that, this axiom ensures the economic agent believes that the hereafter is inevitable and ultimate justice will be served. Any sense of development is filtered morally as the introduction of the extension of the time horizon will encourage the economic agent to do so.

The second axiom is *al-adl wal-ihsan,* also known as socioeconomic justice. The determinant of social equilibrium is when individuals are justice and promote beneficence.[14] The axiom also shows that any development under the IES should consider not only the form but also the substance. In other words, the development must represent the value of justice.

The third axiom is *ikhtiyar,* or free will. Individuals have the freedom of will as this will help them to shape their destiny.[15] In relation to the political economy approach towards development, the economic agent should be responsible for their action as one will certainly face the arena of ultimate justice, which is the hereafter.

The fourth axiom is *fard* or responsibility, where a conscious individual should have a functional responsibility towards the society that one is part of. In the context of development, it is imperative to assume responsibility for the societal implications of the given developmental activities. This suggests that individuals and institutions should be conscientious of the repercussions their developmental endeavours might have, not just on their immediate surroundings but also on distant societies.

The fifth axiom is *rububiyyah,* which, from an etymological perspective, is derived from the word *rabb,* defined as owner or nourisher. Within the framework of the IES, "*rububiyah*" is delineated as the divine orchestration for nourishment, sustenance, and guidance towards ultimate refinement.[16] This definition underscores the pathways of development, emphasizing its role in fostering genuine economic progress and sustainable advancement.

The sixth axiom is *tazkiyah,* or purification. *Tazkiyah* prevailed after calibrating the natural consequences of *tawhid, adl, fard* and *rububiyyah.*[17] Moving towards a development base, one should lead development through the

[14] Naqvi, *Islam, Economics, and Society.*

[15] Naqvi, *Islam, Economics, and Society.*

[16] Khurshid Ahmad, *Economic Development in an Islamic Framework,* (1981).

[17] Asutay, "A Political Economy Approach".

purification of relationships and attitudes.[18] Thus, better social and economic development can be achieved through a purified growth activity.

The seventh foundational principle, referred to as "khilafah" or vicegerency on earth, positions individuals as stewards or trustees of the planet. This role inherently dictates their scope of responsibility and the accountability they bear for their actions and decisions. The implications of the "*khilafah*" principle inherently promote sustainable resource consumption. Consequently, this emphasizes the principle that development initiatives should prioritize sustainability and, importantly, yield tangible benefits for the wider society, akin to the concept of "*fard*".

The final axiom pertains to "*maqasid al-shariah,*" or the objectives of Shari'ah. Shari'ah represents a unified Islamic legal framework derived from ontological and epistemological sources. Economic activities within the Islamic system must adhere to the tenets of Shari'ah and should also embrace a human-centric economic approach. Consequently, development initiatives should adhere not merely to the superficial aspects but also to the deeper essence by incorporating all of the axioms.

The mentioned axioms should bring an idea of such a moral orientation in IPE. Thus, these axioms will drive a society towards a morally functioning society.[19] These axioms should also be embedded in one's inner soul and thus undervalue the temptation of another hegemonic economic system, such as communism and capitalism, due to their exogenous nature of morality.[20] An exemplary axiom that delineates the contours of Islamic finance, determining its alignment with the broader tapestry of IPE, is the axiom of maqasid al-shariah, or the objectives of shariah. Shariah, the canonical jurisprudence intrinsic to Islamic tenets, lays the foundational bedrock upon which Islamic economics is structured. The imperatives of maqasid al-shariah underscore that the culmination of Islamic economic endeavours ought to gravitate towards fostering human well-being. This implies a pivot towards fostering societal interplay rather than an undiluted pursuit of wealth accumulation. Consequently, it can be posited that the analytical lens of IPE accentuates societal interrelations as an intrinsic component of its production paradigm rather than profit maximisation.

---

[18] Ahmad, *Economic Development.*

[19] Bjorn Olav Utvik, *The Pious Road to Development: The Ideology and Practice of Islamist Economics in Egypt,* (London: C Hurst & Co Publishers Ltd, 2006).

[20] Charles Tripp, *Islam and the Moral Economy: The Challenge of Capitalism,* (Cambridge University Press, 2006).

Figure 12.1 Foundational Axioms of Islamic Political Economy

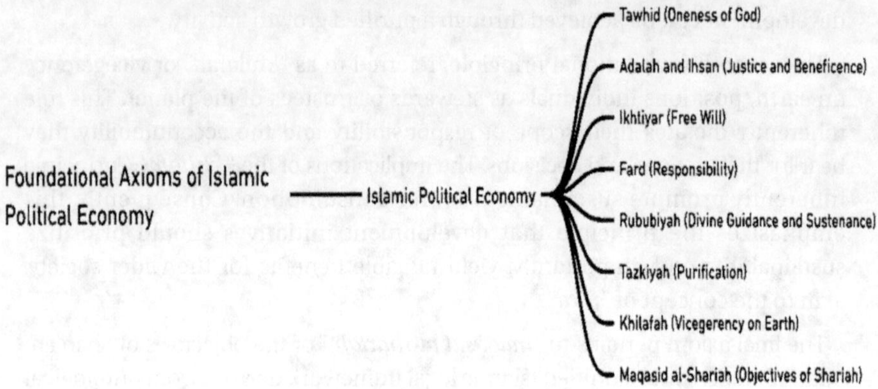

Source: Belongs to the author.

In a nutshell, one can define the IPE as an approach to produce a better society and economic development under the careful surveillance of foundational axioms which also empower the moral base of the society at the same time. However, due to the different historical blocs in the post-colonial world, IPE could not be entertained as a system in the Muslim world; therefore, various institutions of IPE emerged within the available opportunity space to respond to the needs of Muslims in ensuring their identity is sustained.

Foundational Perspectives on Islamic Monetary Economics

In the preceding discourse, the quintessence of Islamic Political Economy (IPE) has been framed as an ontological construct that steers the conduct and institutional rationale of a given system. The primary aim of this segment is to introduce a novel paradigm for interpreting monetary economics by bridging the day-to-day operational aspects—or the horizontal dimension of institutions—with the ontological framework. Figure 12.1 embodies the conceptual verticality or the ordained structure of IPE, which ought to be reflected and ingrained within the behaviours and institutions prevalent within the IPE framework. Prior to delving into this proposition, an extensive review of the pertinent literature has been undertaken to situate conventional monetary economics within the Islamic paradigm. This review reveals a pronounced focus on functionality within the existing scholarship, which, perhaps inadvertently, segregates monetary economics from the broader societal context. Nevertheless, the fundamental Islamic axiom of 'Tawhid' suggests that a holistic, interdisciplinary approach is imperative for scholarly inquiry, as opposed to a fragmented methodology. On the strength of this conceptual groundwork, the current section endeavours to present an alternative perspective on monetary economics. It postulates the principles of IPE, as elucidated previously, as essential reference points for departure. This theoretical framework thus paves the way for the forthcoming detailed case studies that will be explored in the subsequent sections of this analysis.

Literature review

Islamic Monetary Economics presents a unique paradigm, weaving fundamental Islamic tenets into overarching macroeconomic frameworks. Given the ascension of Islamic banking, there exists an augmented necessity for macroeconomic strategies to ensure adherence to Shariah standards in monetary directives. Central to this narrative is the scholarly discourse prominently emphasizing the alignment of monetary guidelines with Islamic doctrines, positioning it as a mechanism to break free from secular or colonial ideologies.[21] Notwithstanding the post-colonial momentum towards Islamisation, the literature indicates a predilection for surface-level assimilation. A more granular examination reveals that scholars categorize Islamic monetary economics into two dominant schools: the equity-centric methodology and the traditional model that abstains from interest rates.[22]

The equity-based perspective, rooted in the theoretical constructs put forth by Al-Jarhi, advocates for a fundamental overhaul in Islamic economics.[23] Al-Jarhi's paradigm champions a comprehensive monetary and fiscal system that deviates from conventional interest-dependent structures. Key to this is an institutional blueprint replacing interest-centric finance with processes for fluid money creation, allocation, and effective monetary and fiscal policies. Money is disseminated via central bank investment deposits, anchored in a Profit and Loss Sharing (PLS) ethos. This setup fosters diverse Islamic finance contracts, permitting banks to engage in both equity investments in firms and commodity trading, addressing challenges such as information disparity. Fiscal structures in this model channel returns from central deposits back to the central bank, forming a cornerstone of government fiscal planning. For endeavors not generating revenue, the government leans on taxation, and for revenue-

---

[21] M. Umer Chapra, *Towards a Just Monetary System,* (International Institute of Islamic Thought (IIIT), 1985).

[22] Md. Akther Uddin, "Islamic Monetary Economics: Insights from the Literature", in *Islamic Monetary Economics and Institutions: Theory and Practice,* ed. Muhamed Zulkhibri et al., (Cham: Springer International Publishing, 2019), 39–53, https://doi.org/10.1007/978-3-030-24005-9_3.

[23] Mabid Al-Jarhi, "A Monetary and Financial Structure for an Interest-Free Economy: Institutions, Mechanism & Policy", MPRA Paper, (University Library of Munich, Germany, 2004), https://econpapers.repec.org/paper/pramprapa/66741.htm.

driven pursuits, it aligns with the private sector for bank finance. Further, public services like education and health are envisioned to be largely funded through awqaf (endowments). A salient feature of Al-Jarhi's model is the transition from fractional to total reserves, underscoring the intrinsic flaws of the former system, particularly in terms of inequitable wealth distribution and compromised central bank autonomy over the money supply. This model's linchpin is the central deposit certificates (CDC), which not only encapsulate the economic performance metrics but also underpin the monetary policy, rooted in genuine market-determined returns.

Central to the equity-based model, as elucidated by Al-Jarhi, is the positioning of depositors akin to bank stakeholders, wherein returns mirror actual bank profits and the nominal deposit value isn't guaranteed, bestowing the system with intrinsic financial resilience. This model's essence, underscored by PLS mechanisms, harmonizes assets and liabilities. Any returns from the financial sector are intrinsically tied to real sector performance, safeguarding against speculative bubbles.[24] Inherently, this ensures the financial edifice remains congruent with tangible economic activities. Noteworthy is the assertion that Islamic monetary tools can seamlessly manoeuvre both resource allocation and overarching macroeconomic objectives. Adjustments in the PLS ratios, for instance, mirror the effects in conventional monetary systems, reflecting the seamless interplay between the economy's financial and real sectors.[25] This exploration of the equity-based approach naturally paves the way for a subsequent discussion on the second school of thought.

In an examination of equity-financed systems, it is underscored that they possess inherent instability. This is primarily attributed to fluctuating investment returns, which bring about unpredictability for investors.[26] To mitigate potential losses, he proposes protective measures like deposit insurance schemes, cautioning that without such mechanisms, the broader economic framework could face significant instability. Moreover, he believes optimal saving and investment in an interest-free context can only be ensured by state intervention. The ban on interest is also argued to be challenging in vast, diverse societies as while equity-based contracts might be viable in the absence of a dynamic stock

---

[24] Adam B. Elhiraika, "On the Design and Effects of Monetary Policy in an Islamic Framework: The Experience of Sudan", Occasional Papers, 2004, https://ideas.repec.org//p/ris/irtiop/0203.html.

[25] International Monetary Fund, *Stabilization and Growth in an Open Islamic Economy,* (International Monetary Fund, 1988).

[26] Syed Nawab Haider Naqvi, *Ethics and Economics: An Islamic Synthesis,* (Islamic Foundation, 1981).

market, they can't fully address the preference of certain individuals for interest-driven ventures or the varying lending and borrowing preferences of banks and firms, respectively.[27]

Moreover, it is crucial to underscore the absence of consensus among Shariah scholars regarding the applicability of PLS mechanisms.[28] Two primary contentions emerge: the imperative for Islamic banking institutions to adhere strictly to their fundamental role as financial intermediaries, and the possible emergence of conflicts of interest. These concerns become particularly salient when applied to the sphere of central banking, where a critical examination of the central bank's essential functions and its fiduciary responsibilities is necessitated.

1. Fundamental Intermediary Function: In essence, the quintessential function of banking institutions, inclusive of Islamic entities, is to serve as financial intermediaries—effectuating the allocation of capital from savers to borrowers. This intermediary role is pivotal in ensuring market liquidity, thereby facilitating business expansion and consumer expenditure. Engaging in PLS mechanisms, however, could potentially deviate Islamic banks from this central role, diminishing their effectiveness as intermediaries and adversely affecting the overall liquidity within the market.
2. Emergent Conflicts of Interest: Islamic financial institutions bear the onus of safeguarding the interests of their depositors and stakeholders. The introduction of PLS mechanisms could precipitate scenarios wherein the bank's interests may become misaligned with those of their clientele. For example, the bank may exhibit a predilection for ventures promising higher returns despite accruing elevated risks, thereby imperiling the security of depositor assets. Such conflicts are deleterious to the bedrock of trust and integrity upon which the edifice of banking is established.

However, a thorough critique of both schools of thought reveals an underlying issue that has often been overlooked: their failure to challenge the hegemony of capital in the form of the market. For the equity-based school, while it ambitiously proposes an equity framework, it inadvertently remains tethered to conventional economic paradigms. For instance, even though Al-Jarhi's

---

[27] Timur Kuran, "The Economic System in Contemporary Islamic Thought: Interpretation and Assessment", *International Journal of Middle East Studies* 18, no. 2 (1986): 135–64.

[28] Islamic Economics and Finance Pedia, "Summary of the Discussions on Profit Loss Sharing (PLS) with Dr. Daud Bakar's Thesis Five Reasons Why Profit and Loss Sharing Financing Does Not Fit Islamic Banks – Islamic Economics & Finance Pedia", *Iefpedia* (blog), 27 March 2010, https://www.iefpedia.com/english/?p=7630&cpage=1#comments.

model introduces equity-based instruments like CDC for monetary policy, its anchoring of the monetary policy to the market-determined rate of return on CDC exemplifies this entrapment. In essence, riba is narrowly conceptualized based solely on its functional role, overlooking broader implications such as the market's unchecked dominance. Thus, the supposed liberation from interest does not equate to liberation from the prevailing market hegemony. Conversely, the second school, while critiquing the viability of the equity-based approach, bases its arguments from a market-centric perspective. Such a standpoint not only subjugates Islamic principles to the whims of the market but also insidiously structures Islamic economic thought from a market-determined viewpoint. Both schools, therefore, inadvertently prioritize the market's dictates, showcasing a latent subservience to market forces rather than truly *emancipating* Islamic monetary economics from such constraints.

Nevertheless, moving beyond the paradigms of the two school of thoughts, recent research aims to delineates the macroeconomics model as whole for Islamic economics system.[29] Figure 12.2 elucidates the intricate fabric of the Islamic Monetary Economics framework. The "Islamic Macro Model" underscores the importance of the Production of Goods & Services, providing a basis for understanding how economic decisions in an Islamic context revolve around societal capacities and needs. This is more than just an economic model; it embodies the essence of the societal fabric where the state doesn't merely oversee but actively facilitates, ensuring alignment with Islamic doctrines.

However, although the model includes the politico-legal structures in the form of state and law, the model only limit itself towards the economic implications of the injunction of *riba*. To elucidate further, within this framework, *'riba'* is predominantly conceptualized as merely an interest rate, thereby neglecting the complex nexus between economic dynamics and politico-legal constructs inherent to Islamic paradigms. In other words, the value system inherited in the system does not prevail as the embedded value throughout all the structures. In light of this circumscription, the present discourse advances a comprehensive model, meticulously interweaving the doctrines of IPE. This model which is explained in the next section emanates vertically from its ontological underpinnings as depicted in Figure 1.0 and is manifested horizontally in the pragmatic structuring of both economic and politico-legal domains.

---

[29] Muhammad Ayub and M. Fahim Khan, "Evolving Monetary Economics in Islamic Perspective", *Journal of Islamic Monetary Economics and Finance* 7, no. 2 (2021): 317–40.

Figure 12.2 Islamic Macro Model

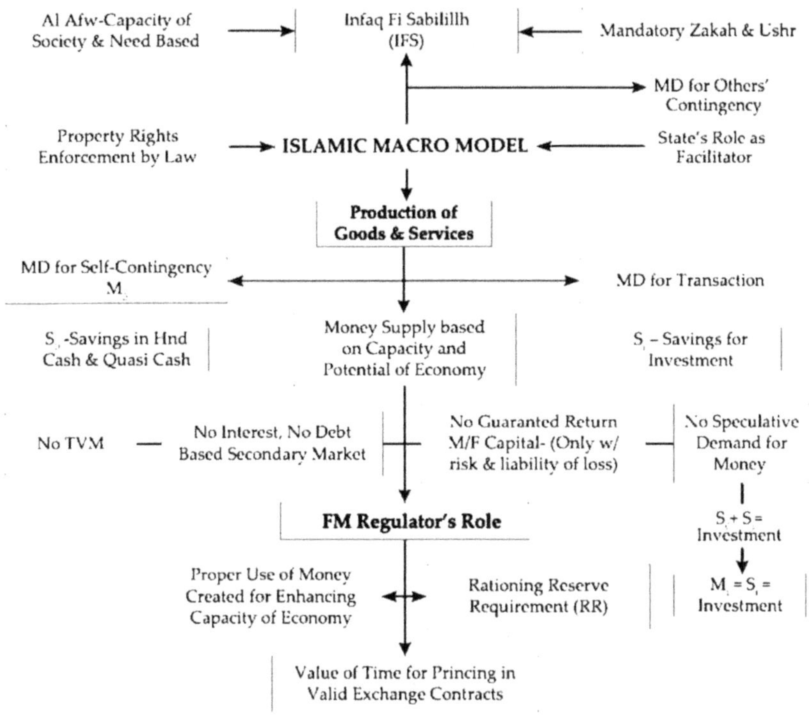

Note: FM = Financial Market; MD = Money Demand; So = Savings in Hand; Si = Savings for Investment; Mo = MD (Money in Hand); Mi = Investment Demand; TVM = Time Value of Money

Source: Belongs to the author.

Relocating the Value of Islamic Political Economy in Monetary Economics

Based on the literature review, one can deduce the disembeddedness of islamic monetary economics (IME) where the vantage point is remained at the hegemon of market. Thus, this chapter with the aim to propose a new model of IME by exploring the bridge that connect the horizontal, which represents the everyday functioning of economic activities such as the monetary economics, and the vertical, which draws from the ontological foundations of Islamic axioms as depicted in Figure 12.1. Nevertheless, Figure 12.3 showcases the IPE system in locating the monetary system.

Figure 12.3 Islamic Political Economy

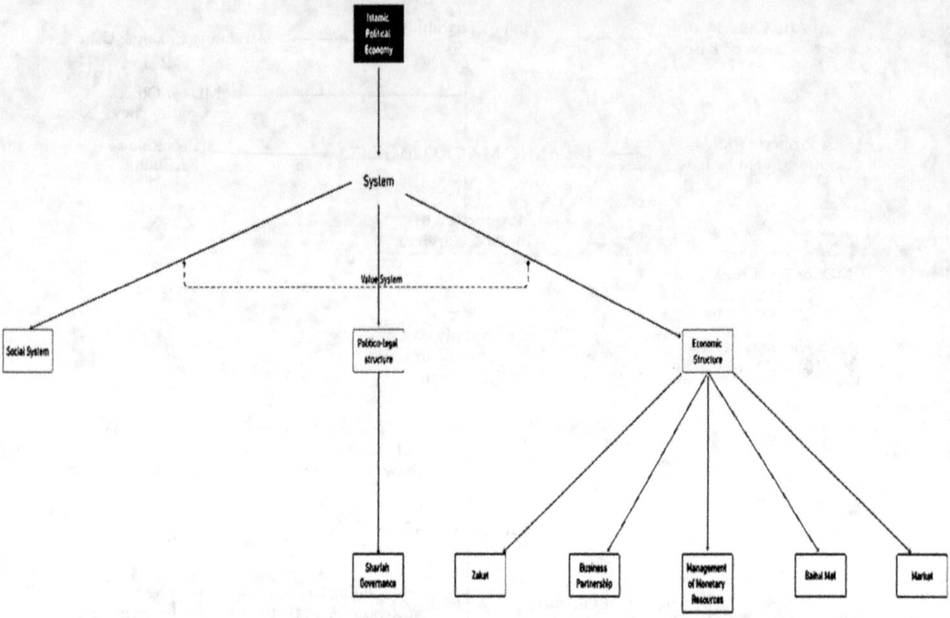

Source: Belongs to the author.

Prior to delving into the formation of monetary economics of IPE, it is pertinent to dissect the horizontal and vertical spectrums. The vertical dimension is where the 'meta-system' of IPE gains its defining character, shaped by the transcendental principles that govern its ethics and laws. It is through this verticality that the profound essence of IPE's value system is understood, rooted in the ontology of Islamic teachings. The foundational axioms are not confined to abstract notions but are made manifest in the socio-economic fabric. In particular, the axiom of *Tawhid*, the concept of the unity and sovereignty of Allah, permeates every layer of IPE, asserting that no currency, nation-state, or temporal power can claim ultimate authority. This concept underscores that economic practices, while serving immediate societal needs, must also align with the divine order and the universal principles of justice, equity, and human dignity.

On the other hand, the horizontal plane encapsulates the dynamic interactions of societal and economic behaviors — the 'system' of daily transactions and governance. The integration of the two different spectrums, produce an ethically anchored system where the meeting point is provided as the dotted line labelled as value system in figure 3.0. the interconnectedness of these dimensions signifies the profound influence the value system exerts upon the politico-legal, social system and economic structures. The embedded ethics of the value system challenge the supremacy of any entity other than Allah, redefining concepts of wealth, ownership, and authority within the economy. It is here that the IPE model offers a radical departure from mainstream economic paradigms, for it refuses to accept the primacy of any entity — be it currency or nation — over the ethical and moral imperatives derived from the Tawhid.

Consequently, the emergence of IPE heralds a paradigm where the economic, politico-legal and social system structures are not segregated entities operating in isolation. These structures are integral components of a composite whole, revealing the multifaceted dimensions of society and refuting the traditional separation seen in conventional economic discourses. This unified framework mandates that the management of monetary resources is not merely a technical endeavour from the economic perspective but one steeply rooted in the integrated principles of Islamic ethics. Thus, from this integration, the study of monetary economics can be located in the realm of IPE. It is pertinent to touch on the key institution, which is the central bank.

In the monetary economics of IPE, while the social system forms an essential backdrop, the emphasis shifts to the politico-legal and economic structures due to their direct influence on monetary economics. Both of these structures, play significant role in shaping the operation of central bank which embodying the fusion of governance, legal directives, and economic strategies. Thus, the central bank should not be focused on its role as a regulator of currency and overseer of financial stability but also as an embodiment of the values and objectives laid out by the politico-legal and economic systems within the IPE.

Central bank, through its organic formation as an institution of IPE, is guided with the parameter frames by politico-legal structure. This parameter reflects the value system which serve as the guiding normative bedrock. In other words, the operation of central bank does not only embedding Shariah-compliant practices into the very core of monetary policy and financial regulation, but also provides the checks and balances necessary to maintain economic justice, prohibit usurious practices, and ensure equitable wealth distribution.

Concurrently, the operational realities of the central bank are determined by the economic structure. Similar to the politico-legal structure, it provides the moral and development base from the vantage point of the economics spectrum. Thus, the policy decisions are made with a heightened awareness of their socio-economic impact, aiming to foster economic resilience and sustainable growth that benefits the entire community.

Thus central bank as the key institution in monetary economics is calibrated to ensure it is align with the IPE system. The calibration does not entail changing the mechanism used in the operation, just like what has been proposed by the traditional literature, but emerge in organically from the IPE system. Thus central bank would not merely focus on traditional metrics of economic success but would be guided by a broader, value-driven approach. In essence, the central bank becomes a facilitator for actualizing the principles of IPE within the economic activities of society.

In general, monetary economics are not merely interconnected but dynamically dependent on the structures reflecting the broader Islamic socio-economic and political fabric. In other words, the management of monetary resources entails the embedding of a value system, upholding the ethical compass that directs all aspects of economic activity. Thus, the true potential of IME is realised when it is examined not only their functional role but also their place within this vertical and horizontal spectrum. As a result, this model challenges the common fallacy of isolated monetary economic models, where it can be understood as devoid of not only ethical but also societal context.

In conclusion, the repositioning of monetary economics within IPE offers a holistic and comprehensive framework, ensuring that the management of monetary resources is deeply embedded within the ethical, politico-legal, and economic infrastructures. This alignment not only critiques but also transforms current monetary practices, advocating for a system where monetary policy is consistent with the ethical and value-driven principles at the core of the IPE. It is within this integrative and ethically anchored system that the true potential of IME can be realized. Such an approach requires a shift from isolated analysis to a recognition of the intertwined nature of economic systems, where each component, from financial transactions to state policies, is guided by the overarching ethical imperatives of justice, equity, and social welfare. By adopting this model, we pave the way to form a monetary economy that is not only sustainable but also reflective of a commitment to the well-being of all members of society, in accordance with the rich heritage of the teaching of IPE.

Dollar Hegemony

In the dynamic evolution of the global financial landscape, a prominent challenge that has emerged is the shifting power dynamics within the financial structure. This dynamism is particularly evident in monetary systems, especially in the dominant role played by certain currencies. Over recent decades, intense debate has emerged around the hegemony of the dollar, marked by its continued ascendancy. However, the intersection of Islamic banking and dollar hegemony remains an underexplored area in existing literature. This chapter seeks to identify the points at which Islamic monetary economics (IME) can coexist with, or even support, the entrenched system of dollar hegemony. A critical inquiry follows: Can a system underpinned by currency hegemony pave the way for the organic emergence of Islamic banking? This section examines the unlimited bilateral swap agreements among key financial institutions – the Federal Reserve (Fed), European Central Bank (ECB), Bank of England (BoE), Bank of Japan (BoJ), Swiss National Bank (SNB), and Bank of Canada (BoC) – as a case study. The goal is to analyze the collective unilateral actions among G20 countries in maintaining dollar hegemony and to compare these actions against the moral and developmental foundations of a central banking system that could naturally arise from an IPE perspective.

Swap Agreements

The evolution of international monetary cooperation is vividly illustrated by the unlimited bilateral swap agreements. These agreements' historical origins date back to the early 1960s, initiated primarily by the Fed and various central banks to support foreign exchange interventions.[30] As the financial landscape underwent transformations, such as the dissolution of the Bretton Woods system in 1973, the purpose and scope of these agreements evolved, evidenced by their increasing nominal value. The establishment of the Euro led to a temporary cessation of these agreements, which were later revitalized in late 2007 with a shifted focus from funding foreign exchange interventions to temporarily providing U.S. dollar liquidity.[31]

The 2007 global financial crisis (GFC) catalyzed a significant expansion of the U.S. dollar liquidity swap agreements by the Federal Reserve. Initially, these agreements, aimed at enhancing international liquidity mechanisms, were limited to partnerships with the ECB and the SNB. By 2008, the number of participating central banks had grown to fourteen. Although there was a brief discontinuation post-GFC, the European sovereign debt crisis in 2010 marked the return of these swaps. In a significant shift, these arrangements transitioned from temporary measures to standing facilities in October 2013, highlighting their role as stabilizers in offshore dollar funding markets. The current case study focuses on a standing facility comprising six central banks, including the Fed, ECB, BoE, BoJ, SNB, and BoC.

Figure 12.4, extracted from the Federal Reserve Bank of New York database, presents a comparative analysis of standing swap line central banks' (SSCBs) utilization amidst two pivotal financial disturbances: the GFC and the COVID-19 pandemic. The institutions under examination include the BoJ, ECB, BoE, and the SNB. Notably, the BoC is the sole SSCB that has not accessed the facility. The data illustrate that swap line usage during the GFC and the pandemic varied significantly. The BoJ's engagement surged during the COVID-19 liquidity turmoil, surpassing its activity during the GFC. Meanwhile, the ECB demonstrated substantial demand across both events, albeit with a slight

[30] Mark Choi et al., "The Fed's Central Bank Swap Lines and Fima Repo Facility", SSRN Scholarly Paper (Rochester, NY, 1 July 2022), https://doi.org/10.2139/ssrn.4155548.

[31] Linda S. Goldberg et al., "Central Bank Dollar Swap Lines and Overseas Dollar Funding Costs", NBER Working Paper, (February 2010), https://doi.org/10.3386/w15763.

reduction during the pandemic. The requisitions by the BoE and SNB in the face of COVID-19 were considerably less than their GFC utilization.

Figure 12.4 Standing Swap Line Central Banks

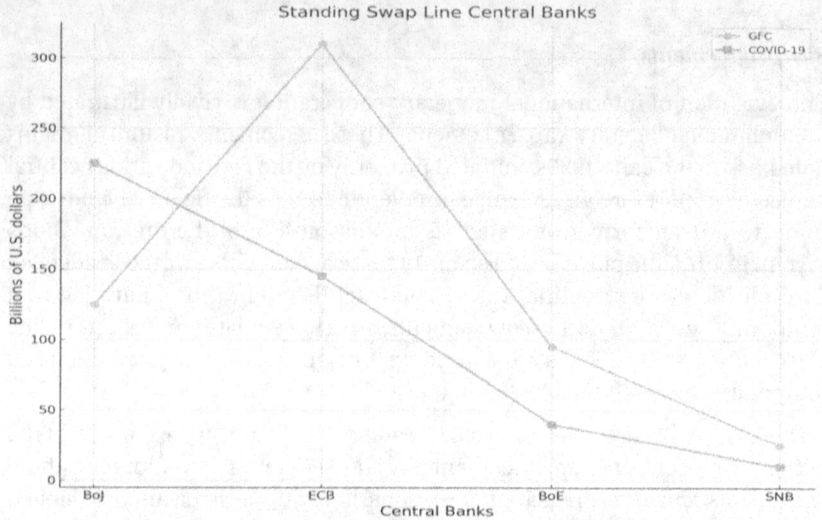

Source: Compiled by the author.

The onset of the COVID-19 crisis in 2020 tested the robustness and flexibility of these swap agreements. Confronted with the pandemic's financial disruptions, SSCBs were propelled into action, enacting crucial modifications to the terms and pricing of the swap lines to mitigate the adverse funding conditions. By late May 2020, the use of swap lines had escalated to $449 billion, underscoring the critical dependency on these liquidity conduits during times of economic stress.

Dollar Hegemony and Islamic Political Economy: An Analysis

The shift in swap arrangements from temporary mechanisms to standing facilities underscores the stark reality of dollar hegemony. While one could argue this transition aims to promote monetary stability, it also suggests a progression towards a hierarchical monetary order. Understanding this dynamic interplay necessitates a broader view of the global market's architecture, where public authorities and private transnational entities maintain distinct, yet interrelated, roles. For example, the International Swaps and Derivatives Association typically functions as a market facilitator during periods of economic normalcy. In times of financial upheaval, however, the Fed steps into this role, reinforcing the essential symbiosis between public and private sectors within the monetary realm.

In crisis scenarios, the established monetary hierarchy becomes more pronounced. The bilateral central bank swap arrangements have proven to be a bulwark for the global economy against potential USD liquidity shortages. From a legal perspective, these swap agreements resemble 'gentlemen's agreements,' where moral commitments are emphasized over stringent legal constraints.[32] Here, the moral imperative aligns with the interests of nation-states situated at the apex of the hierarchy, thereby legitimizing the Fed's position as a de facto global liquidity provider and arbiter of access to dollar liquidity.

Figure 12.5 Currency Hegemony

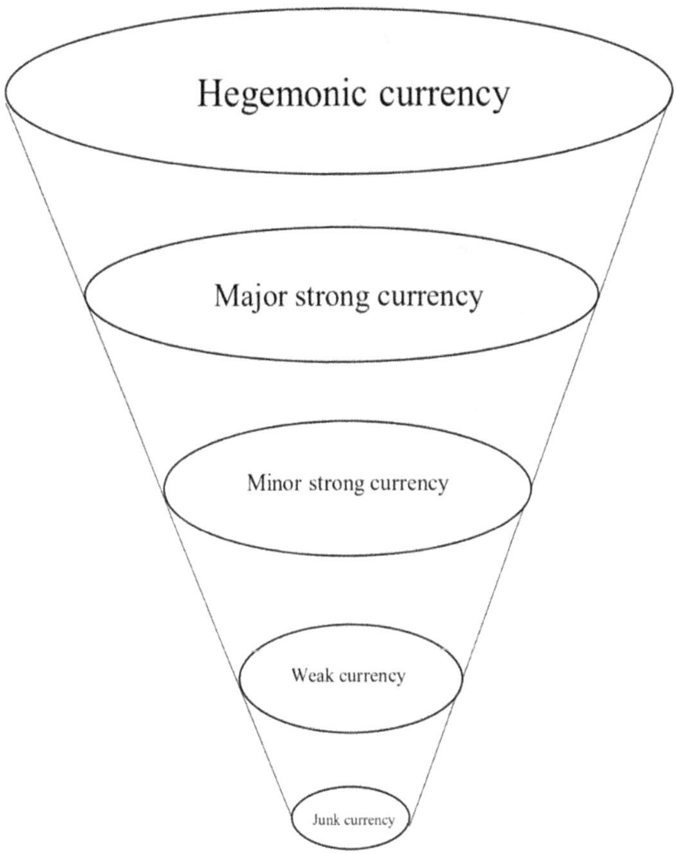

Source: Belongs to the author.

[32] Aliénor Nina Burghartz, "The Credit Suisse Crisis and International Law II: We Live in a Swap Line World", *EJIL: Talk!* (blog), 1 May 2023, https://www.ejiltalk.org/the-credit-suisse-crisis-and-international-law-ii-we-live-in-a-swap-line-world/.

These 'gentlemen's agreements' exemplify the international legal frameworks that regulate the contemporary global monetary system. Within this schema, entities like the International Monetary Fund (IMF) play supportive, albeit secondary, roles. The prevailing structure, marked by its asymmetrical liquidity provisions, cements a hierarchical system that places peripheral central banks at a relative disadvantage. These arrangements are emblematic of dollar hegemony's essence and its perpetuation within the global monetary system.

Figure 12.5 succinctly encapsulates the essence of currency hegemony, depicting it through the metaphor of a "currency cone".[33] This multidimensional cone is emblematic of the monetary hierarchy, with its apex representing currencies that exhibit profound depth, liquidity, and a broad spectrum of assets. The justification for the 'gentlemen's agreements' within this structure stems from the perceived moral obligations of those at the pinnacle of this hierarchy.

Contrasting these agreements with the foundational tenets of IPE, we encounter a paradigmatic divergence. The IPE, deeply rooted in the principle of 'adl wal ihsan' (justice and benevolence), champions socioeconomic justice. A global monetary framework, harmonious with IPE values, would inherently strive for equitable distribution of economic resources and opportunities, circumventing the monopolistic advantages engendered by hegemonic dominance. The currency hierarchy, as perpetuated by such 'gentlemen's agreements', evidences a stark asymmetry of power within monetary economics, allowing the US to gain disproportionate benefits across trade, debt issuance, monetary policy, and international financial negotiations.

Furthermore, the IPE's ethos of 'ikhtiyar' (free will) underlines the imperative for central banks and their respective states to exercise autonomy and self-determination. This concept transcends abstractness, urging central banks to assert their inalienable right to shape their economic destinies, free from external hegemonic pressures. The extant hierarchical system not only favors dominant central entities but also marginalizes peripheral nations, exacerbating their struggle to withstand financial crises. The evolution of swap facilities from temporary mechanisms to established norms constrains the organic development of the Islamic banking industry, impeding its alignment with IPE principles.

The plight of countries that adhere to Islamic banking practices, often situated on the periphery, is further compounded by their central banks' prioritization of market efficiency and economic stability over socio-economic

---

[33] Thomas Palley, "Theorizing Dollar Hegemony, Part 1: The Political Economic Foundations of Exorbitant Privilege", IDEAS Working Papers, (August 2022), https://ideas.repec.org//p/pke/wpaper/pkwp2220.html.

equity, given their limited access to support mechanisms such as those available to the privileged six central banks. The peripheral central banks, in the absence of such facilities, face heightened risks and are consequently less empowered to pursue initiatives centered on social justice and equity. Moreover, economic decisions in these regions tend to be disproportionately influenced by state-centric interests, which may not necessarily align with the collective needs and aspirations of society.

In conclusion, a recalibration toward long-term, value-driven goals that synergize economic efficiency with societal well-being is essential for reflecting the core principles of Islamic economics. Such a strategic realignment would not only uphold the values of 'adl wal ihsan' and 'ikhtiyar' but would also facilitate a more equitable and just global economic landscape, allowing the Islamic banking sector to thrive in alignment with its foundational ethos.

Subordinate Financialisation

Previous case studies have postulated that the Islamic banking industry is predominantly under the jurisdiction of peripheral central banks. Such positioning, alongside the prevailing dollar hegemony contributing to a power imbalance, inhibits the natural progression of Islamic banking institutions. However, when examining the emergence of Islamic banking within the centers of financial influence, such as the United Kingdom (UK) under the aegis of the BoE, a different dynamic may be anticipated. This case study explores the role of central banking facilitation in the rise of Islamic banking within the UK, probing whether Islamic banks, with the support from financial centers, can flourish in accordance with IPE teachings, compared to those originating from peripheral regions.

The establishment of the Islamic banking industry in central financial hubs is a crucial step in challenging existing financial hegemonies. It represents a part of the broader decolonization process, positioning Islamic banking to negotiate its place within the historic bloc of mainstream financial markets. The conventional financial hub in London, with its dominant market presence, necessitates that Islamic banking entities engage in negotiation without significant bargaining power, often resulting in grafting to sustain their presence in the center. The attraction to these centers is driven by the substantial capital flows they command, which hold greater gravitational pull compared to their peripheral counterparts.

In a landmark move, the Bank of England initiated the Alternative Liquidity Facility (ALF), a pioneering measure in Western banking systems. Through this innovative arrangement, the BoE has carved out a space for Islamic banking to flourish, albeit within the confines of mainstream institutional logic. This includes the mandate for Islamic banks to maintain a buffer of High-Quality Liquid Assets (HQLA) to fulfil obligations in a timely manner.

The ALF, which began its operations in December 2021, reported in the fiscal year ending February 2023 the acquisition of two sukuk that qualify as HQLA. This demonstrates the UK's Islamic banking industry's compliance with regulatory requirements for HQLA buffers. Predicated on a Wakalah contract, the ALF incorporates an expected profit rate in place of interest, which is distributed to participants.

Table 12.1 The Bank of England Alternative Liquidity Facility Limited

	2022 (£mn)	2023 (£mn)
Net gains on financial instruments	8.5	2
Income received on financial instruments	1.2	0.3
Net losses from foreign exchange revaluation	-2.3	
Total income	**7.4**	**2.3**
Administrative expenses	-0.9	-0.1
Return on derivative allocated to depositors	-3.2	
Total expenses	**-4.1**	**-0.1**
Profit before taxation	**3.3**	**2.2**
Taxation	-1.1	-0.7
Profit after taxation	**2.2**	**1.5**

Source: Compiled by the author.

The Bank of England Alternative Liquidity Facility Limited (BoE-ALFL) net gains on financial instruments, based on the fiscal year ending February 2023, primarily emanating from the cross-currency swaps, burgeoned from £2mn in 2022 to £8.5mn in 2023, an appreciable augmentation. Concurrently, the net income derived from the sukuk experienced a four-fold ascent, moving from £0.3mn in the previous year to £1.2mn. These upward trajectories, however, were offset by the incursion of net losses from foreign exchange revaluation, which amounted to £2.3mn. The latter had no precedent in the previous year, thus signifying its inaugural appearance in the fiscal ledgers. The amplification in BoE-ALFL financial yield is attributed to strategic acquisitions made during the year, which included a second sukuk and an ancillary cross-currency swap, bolstering its fiscal activities throughout the entirety of the financial year. Such enhancements paved the way for a pre-tax profit of £3.3mn in 2023, a rise by £1.1mn from the preceding year's £2.2mn. Despite the incurrence of a tax obligation amounting to £1.1mn, primarily as deferred tax, BoE-ALFL post-tax profit still manifested a favourable trend, marking an increase of £0.7mn, culminating at £2.2mn for the year, up from 2022's £1.5mn.

Subordinate Financialization and Islamic Political Economy: An Analysis

Table 12.1 elucidates the manner in which the Alternative Liquidity Facility (ALF) mediates liquidity risk and positions the Islamic banking industry to capitalize on profit-making financial activities. As the previous discourse revealed, the surge in total income is chiefly a consequence of net gains on financial instruments, particularly from cross-currency swaps. This prominent profit influx from financial instruments is a reflection of the pervasive economic phenomenon of financialization – a process where the Islamic banking industry is increasingly embedded within market hegemony, characterized by the prioritization of profits derived from financialization over those from the real economy.

Financialization, a term increasingly invoked in contemporary political economy, refers to the escalated role of financial motives, markets, actors, and institutions in the functioning of domestic and international economies.[34] However, within the Islamic banking industry, particularly within peripheral financial systems, this process assumes the form of 'subordinate financialization'. This term encapsulates the dynamic interplay between global core economies and those at the periphery.[35] Much of the current literature on subordinate financialization concentrates on the economic status of nations and geographical considerations, yet this chapter approaches the phenomenon from the purview of IPE. It postulates that Islamic banking, situated at the periphery, is compelled to emulate its conventional counterparts and engage in financialization.

The dominant financial industry, guided by the Basel Accords, epitomizes the priorities of the conventional banking system: risk management, capital adequacy, and liquidity standards. Islamic banking, emerging from a distinct ontological base and espousing a unique ethos, seeks integration within this conventional framework, which inadvertently engenders a dichotomy. Capital requirements as mandated by the Basel framework, practical from the standpoint of mainstream risk management, unwittingly conflict with the Islamic principle of risk-sharing rather than risk-transfer. Consequently, Islamic banks find themselves navigating between their foundational principles and the necessities imposed by global financial norms.

The core argument against the inevitability of financialization, particularly subordinate financialization, in Islamic banking and finance (IBF) is embedded

---

[34] Gerald A. Epstein, *Financialization and the World Economy*, (Edward Elgar Publishing, 2005).

[35] Bruno Bonizzi et al., "Subordinate Financialization in Emerging Capitalist Economies", Greenwich Papers in Political Economy, (25 February 2019), https://ideas.repec.org//p/gpe/wpaper/23044.html.

within its intrinsic normative value system. Central to IPE is the principle of 'tawhid,' denoting the oneness of God but extending conceptually to a holistic economic system that integrates moral and spiritual dimensions. The principle of tawhid inherently challenges the narrow focus of financialization, which is primarily concerned with value extraction through financial avenues, thereby neglecting the broader ethical and societal ramifications of economic endeavours.[36]

Furthermore, the axioms of 'adl wal ihsan' (justice and benevolence) and 'rububiyah' (divine providence) within IPE underscore the dissonance with financialization. Financialization's propensity to amplify socio-economic disparities and underscore shareholder value stands in stark contrast to the IPE's advocacy for socio-economic justice and equitable wealth distribution. The predilection of financialization for prioritizing abstract financial profits over substantive economic contributions is fundamentally at odds with the normative values of IPE.

Moreover, the axioms of 'tazkiyah' (purification and growth) and 'khilafah' (stewardship) are pivotal at the microeconomic level. The micro-foundations of financialization are often driven by speculative gains, such as the credit swaps observed in the ALF operations. Tazkiyah promotes economic activities that are ethically and morally sound, while khilafah emphasizes humanity's role as responsible stewards of the Earth's resources. Given that the nature of sukuk contracts often leans towards asset-based rather than asset-backed securities, there is a potential disconnection between the value of the sukuk and the intrinsic value of the underlying assets. The overarching emphasis of IPE on sustainable and ethical resource utilization, coupled with a focus on long-term societal and environmental welfare, renders financialization a fundamentally incompatible approach within the IPE framework.

Redefining Capital and the Role of Central Banks in Light of Islamic Political Economy

The contemporary landscape of the Islamic banking industry, both within the G20 nations and on a global scale, may be aptly characterized as a 'second-best solution'.[37] Case studies reveal that Islamic banking entities must often

[36] Hulya Dagdeviren et al., "Financialisation, Welfare Retrenchment and Subsistence Debt in Britain", *New Political Economy* 25, no. 2 (23 February 2020): 159–73, https://doi.org/10.1080/13563467.2019.1570102; Emma Dowling, "In the Wake of Austerity: Social Impact Bonds and the Financialisation of the Welfare State in Britain", *New Political Economy* 22, no. 3 (4 May 2017): 294–310, https://doi.org/10.1080/13563467.2017.1232709.

[37] Mehmet Asutay, "Conceptualisation of the Second Best Solution in Overcoming the Social Failure of Islamic Finance: Examining the Overpowering of Homoislamicus by

compromise on their foundational values to integrate into the prevailing conventional financial system. This system not only fosters financialization but also consolidates the hegemony of dominant currencies within an entrenched hierarchical framework. To cultivate the organic growth of the Islamic banking industry, a reversion to its core ontological principles is warranted.

An instructive hadith concerning economic matters recounts how Prophet Muhammad, when consulted by his followers about high market prices, refrained from market intervention, attributing pricing to divine will.[38] This hadith must be interpreted within its political-economic context to avoid misconceptions. The Prophet's approach eschewed the commodification of natural resources, which leads to a disconnection between the value of goods and the labor involved in their production. Prophet Muhammad, an entrepreneur alongside his wife, engaged in the trading of goods rather than commodities. The market system established by the Prophet adhered to the capital circuit of Goods-Money-Goods (G-M-G), where money served merely as a transient medium, thus preventing the accumulation of capital.

This resistance to transforming resources into commodities, as demonstrated by the hadith, is critical to understanding the contemporary issues discussed in previous case studies. A capital circuit dominated by commodities and the process of commodification precipitates both financialization and hierarchical structuring within the monetary system. The conceptualization of capital that fosters commodification creates avenues for shareholders to extract value through financial instruments rather than contribute to the real economy, as these instruments typically promise higher returns. Furthermore, the trend towards commodification prompts nation-states to shift their focus from human development to capital growth, a transition evident in the tendency of developing countries at the periphery to offer cheap labor to maximize profits from commodities, thereby reinforcing global economic hierarchies, including those within the monetary system.

In redefining capital from an IPE perspective, capital must be viewed not solely in terms of transactional processes but more holistically, encompassing the normative values that inform the concept of capital. From the viewpoint of

Homoeconomicus", SSRN Scholarly Paper (Rochester, NY, 18 October 2010), https://papers.ssrn.com/abstract=1693608.

[38] Mustapha Abubakar Halidu Suleiman Dalhatu Sani and Isiaka Ahmed, "Does Islamic Finance Need Benchmarking?", in *Benchmarking Islamic Finance*, (Routledge, 2021).

central banking, the institutional logic must be restructured to align with IPE principles. This realignment can be conceptualized in Figure 7.0.[39]

Figure 12.6 illustrates that the genesis of institutions is rooted in values or normative constructs, which are indicated by the dotted line in Figure 12.3. These values, derived from the ontology of IPE, shape the subsequent norms and cognitive repertoires (cultural capital) that, in turn, inform the structural formation of institutions. In essence, from a field perspective, the emergence of a central bank should reflect the economic, politico-legal, and social environment structured by IPE expectations. Conversely, from a capital perspective, the central bank must operate within an Islamic economic framework, while the habitus—its operational nature—should embody IPE values and expectations.

Figure 12.6 The Genesis of Institutions

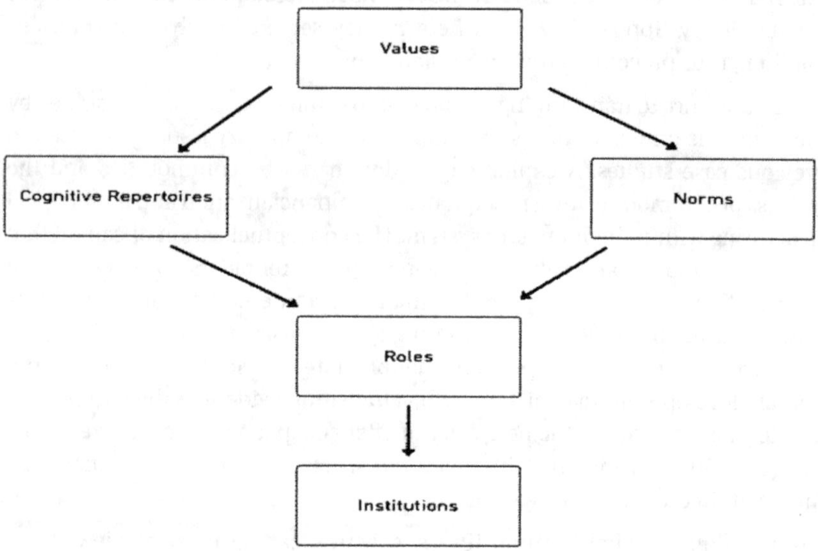

Source: Belongs to the author.

Conclusion

The conclusion drawn from these collective analyses is that Islamic banking, and by extension, Islamic monetary economics, cannot be fully understood nor appreciated without considering the values and norms prescribed by IPE. The current global financial system, with its entrenched structures and practices,

---

[39] Alejandro Portes, *Economic Sociology: A Systematic Inquiry,* (Princeton University Press, 2010).

often stands at odds with the ethical and moral principles central to Islamic finance. The challenge, therefore, is to recalibrate the financial system to embed these values at its core rather than as an afterthought.

Central banks, particularly within G20 countries, are at a crossroads. They can either continue to operate within a framework that perpetuates financial hegemonies and inequalities, or they can embrace a redefined role that resonates with the moral economy of IPE. This would entail not only a shift in policy and practice but a transformation in the philosophical underpinnings that drive economic decision-making.

A redefined approach to capital within central banking would not only address the ethical dimensions of finance but also contribute to a more just and equitable global financial system. It would challenge the dominance of market hegemony and speculative financial practices, paving the way for an economic landscape where real economic activities and human welfare take precedence.

As the previous sections have elucidated, there is a profound need for a system where central banks and financial institutions are not merely guardians of monetary stability but also champions of socio-economic justice. The insight from this chapter beckons a future where the true spirit of Islamic banking is actualized, not as a 'second-best solution' within a flawed system, but as a leading model for ethical and equitable finance, redefining the role of money and capital to serve humanity's broader interests. This conclusion is a clarion call for the reformation of global monetary policy, inspired by the rich teachings of IPE, to create a financial world that is not only economically robust but morally sound and just.

Bibliography

Ahmad, Khurshid. *Economic Development in an Islamic Framework* (1981).

Ahmed, Habib. "Islamic Finance at a Crossroads: The Dominance of the Asset Based Sukuk". *Butterworths Journal of International Banking and Financial Law.* 25, no. 6 (1 June 2010). https://durham-repository.worktribe.com/output/1545162.

Al-Jarhi, Mabid. "A Monetary and Financial Structure for an Interest-Free Economy: Institutions, Mechanism & Policy". *MPRA Paper.* University Library of Munich, Germany, 2004. https://econpapers.repec. org/paper/pramprapa/66741.htm.

Althusser, Louis. *On the Reproduction of Capitalism: Ideology and Ideological State Apparatuses.* Verso Books (2014).

Arif, Muhammad. 'Towards Establishing The Microfoundations Of Islamic Economics: The Basis Of The Basics'. In *Readings in the Concept and Methodology of Islamic Economics.* Selangor: Pelanduk Publications (1989).

Asutay, Mehmet. 'A Political Economy Approach to Islamic Economics: Systemic Understanding for an Alternative Economic System'. SSRN Scholarly Paper. Rochester, NY (2007). https://papers.ssrn.com/abstract=1735619.

Asutay, Mehmet. "Conceptualisation of the Second Best Solution in Overcoming the Social Failure of Islamic Finance: Examining the Overpowering of Homoislamicus by Homoeconomicus". *SSRN Scholarly Paper*. Rochester, NY, 18 October 2010. https://papers.ssrn.com/abstract=1693608.

Ayub, Muhammad. *Understanding Islamic Finance*. John Wiley & Sons (2009).

Ayub, Muhammad, and M. Fahim Khan. "Evolving Monetary Economics in Islamic Perspective". *Journal of Islamic Monetary Economics and Finance* 7, no. 2 (2021): 317–40.

B. Elhiraika, Adam. "On the Design and Effects of Monetary Policy in an Islamic Framework: The Experience of Sudan (Research Paper)". *Occasional Papers*, 2004. https://ideas.repec.org//p/ris/irtiop/0203.html.

Bodie, Zvi, and Robert C. Merton. "A Conceptual Framework for Analyzing the Financial Environment". *SSRN Scholarly Paper*. Rochester, NY (25 August 1998). https://papers.ssrn.com/abstract=6638.

Bonizzi, Bruno, Annina Kaltenbrunner, and Jeffrey Powell. "Subordinate Financialization in Emerging Capitalist Economies". *Greenwich Papers in Political Economy*, (25 February 2019). https://ideas.repec.org//p/gpe/wpaper/23044.html.

Burghartz, Aliénor Nina. "The Credit Suisse Crisis and International Law II: We Live in a Swap Line World". *EJIL: Talk!* (blog), (1 May 2023). https://www.ejiltalk.org/the-credit-suisse-crisis-and-international-law-ii-we-live-in-a-swap-line-world/.

Chapra, M. Umer. *Islam and the Economic Challenge*. International Institute of Islamic Thought (IIIT) (1992).

Chapra, M. Umer. *Towards a Just Monetary System*. International Institute of Islamic Thought (IIIT) (1985).

Choi, Mark, Linda S. Goldberg, Robert I. Lerman, and Fabiola Ravazzolo. "The Fed's Central Bank Swap Lines and Fima Repo Facility". *SSRN Scholarly Paper*. Rochester, NY, (1 July 2022). https://doi.org/10.2139/ssrn.4155548.

Crane, Dwight B. *The Global Financial System: A Functional Perspective*. Harvard Business School Press (1995).

Dagdeviren, Hulya, Jiayi Balasuriya, Sheila Luz, Ali Malik, and Haider Shah. "Financialisation, Welfare Retrenchment and Subsistence Debt in Britain". *New Political Economy* 25, no. 2 (23 February 2020): 159–73. https://doi.org/10.1080/13563467.2019.1570102.

Dowling, Emma. "In the Wake of Austerity: Social Impact Bonds and the Financialisation of the Welfare State in Britain". *New Political Economy* 22, no. 3 (4 May 2017): 294–310. https://doi.org/10.1080/13563467.2017. 1232709.

El-Gamal, Mahmoud A. *Islamic Finance: Law, Economics, and Practice*. Cambridge University Press (2006).

EL-Ghazali. *Man Is The Basis of The Islamic Strategy for Economic Development*. Islamic Development Bank (1994).

Fund, International Monetary. *Stabilization and Growth in an Open Islamic Economy*. International Monetary Fund (1988).

Goldberg, Linda S., Craig Kennedy, and Jason Miu. 'Central Bank Dollar Swap Lines and Overseas Dollar Funding Costs'. Working Paper. Working Paper Series. *National Bureau of Economic Research* (February 2010). https://doi.org/10.3386/w15763.

Gould, Rebecca Ruth. 'Laws, Exceptions, Norms: Kierkegaard, Schmitt, and Benjamin on the Exception'. *SSRN Scholarly Paper.* Rochester, NY, 2 February 2013. https://papers.ssrn.com/abstract=2211016.

Gregory, Paul R., and Robert C. Stuart. *Comparing Economic Systems in the Twenty-First Century.* Houghton Mifflin (2004).

Halidu, Mustapha Abubakar, Suleiman Dalhatu Sani, Isiaka Ahmed. "Does Islamic Finance Need Benchmarking?" In *Benchmarking Islamic Finance.* Routledge (2021).

Iqbal, Munawar. *Islamic Economic Institutions and the Elimination of Poverty.* Islamic Foundation (2002).

Islamic Economics and Finance Pedia. "Summary of the Discussions on Profit Loss Sharing (PLS) with Dr Daud Bakar's Thesis Five Reasons Why Profit and Loss Sharing Financing Does Not Fit Islamic Banks – Islamic Economics & Finance Pedia". *Iefpedia* (blog) (27 March 2010).

Kuran, Timur. "The Economic System in Contemporary Islamic Thought: Interpretation and Assessment". *International Journal of Middle East Studies* 18, no. 2 (1986): 135–64.

Mckinsey. "The Rapid Growth in Global Wealth | McKinsey". Accessed 26 October 2023. https://www.mckinsey.com/industries/financial-services/our-insights/the-rise-and-rise-of-the-global-balance-sheet-how-productively-are-we-using-our-wealth.

Naqvi, Syed Nawab Haider. *Ethics and Economics: An Islamic Synthesis.* Islamic Foundation (1981).

Naqvi, Syed Nawad Haider. *Islam, Economics, and Society (RLE Politics of Islam).* Routledge (2013).

Nomani, Farhad, and Ali Rahnema. *Islamic Economic Systems.* Bloomsbury Academic (1994).

Omar (Syed.). *Readings in the Concept and Methodology of Islamic Economics.* Pelanduk Publications (1989).

Palley, Thomas. "Theorizing Dollar Hegemony, Part 1: The Political Economic Foundations of Exorbitant Privilege". *Working Papers,* Working Papers (August 2022). https://ideas.repec.org//p/pke/wpaper/pkwp 2220.html.

Portes, Alejandro. *Economic Sociology: A Systematic Inquiry.* Princeton University Press, 2010.

Sirageldin, Ismail. "The Elimination of Poverty: Challenges and Islamic Strategies". In *Islamic Economic Institutions and the Elimination of Poverty.* Leicester: Islamic Foundation (2002).

Tripp, Charles. *Islam and the Moral Economy: The Challenge of Capitalism.* Cambridge University Press (2006).

Uddin, Md. Akther. "Islamic Monetary Economics: Insights from the Literature". In *Islamic Monetary Economics and Institutions: Theory and Practice,* edited by Muhamed Zulkhibri, Turkhan Ali Abdul Manap, and Aishath Muneeza, 39–53. Cham: Springer International Publishing (2019).

Utvik, Bjorn Olav. *The Pious Road to Development: The Ideology and Practice of Islamist Economics in Egypt.* London: C Hurst & Co Publishers Ltd (2006).

Williams, Raymond. *Marxism and Literature.* OUP Oxford (1977).

Chapter 13
The Neglected Cause of the Global Financial Crisis: Interest Rate Policies

İsmail Özsoy

Advisory Board Member, EFC Ethical Funding Co., CA, USA

Birol Görmez

Cyber security trainee, Germany

Abstract

The Global Financial Crisis of September 2008 was triggered by a dramatic rise in mortgage delinquencies and foreclosures in the United States. With its destructive consequences for financial markets and institutions around the globe, it has exposed pervasive weaknesses in the current global financial system. The US housing collapse is often cited as having caused the crisis, and the loose U.S. monetary policy is criticized for making the cost of credit negligible, thus encouraging high levels of leverage and causing hypertrophy and bubbles in the financial sector. What is clear from the crisis is that the current global financial system is vulnerable because of intricate and highly leveraged financial contracts and operations mainly based on derivatives and *interest rates.* The effect of interest policy on the crisis, we think has not been sufficiently examined because it is taken for granted within the capitalist system. Therefore, this work first investigates the aspects of interest policy that contradict the market system and produce crises. After rating the reasons for the crisis and dealing with the financialization process of the economy, it argues that the main reason for the crisis is interest-based transactions of derivatives. Mostly being a zero-sum game, rather than being a result of win-win action, these transactions do not produce any economic value. The paper bases its arguments on the concise hadith of Prophet Muhammad called 'the Hadith of Six Things'. Even if it is a saying of two sentences, the hadith defines the term 'interest' with all types, gives the formulas of sales/exchanges cleared of interest, and miraculously states in a short statement that 72 out of 120 transactions among these six items by permutation are subject to interest. It proposes that financial operations be based on real assets, producing real values, not on virtual ones. Finally, suggestions derived from this hadith to avoid financial crises will be expressed.

Keywords: Financial Bubble, Financialization, Global Financial Crisis, Hadith of Six Things, Interest/Riba, Interest of Exchange, Interest policy, Islamic Finance

***

Introduction

The term financial crisis broadly refers to a variety of situations in which some financial institutions or assets suddenly lose a large part of their value. Many financial crises were associated with banking panics, recessions, stock market crashes, the bursting of other financial bubbles, currency crises, and sovereign defaults. The global financial crisis of September 2008 began in July 2007 when a loss of confidence by investors in the value of *securitized mortgages* in the United States resulted in a liquidity crisis. This liquidity crisis prompted a substantial injection of capital into financial markets by the US Fed, the Bank of England, and the European Central Bank. The crisis deepened in September 2008 as stock markets worldwide crashed and entered a period of high volatility, and a considerable number of banks, mortgage lenders, and insurance companies failed in the following weeks. Liquidity problems, harder credit facilities, devaluated assets, increased public debt due to the provision of public funds to the financial services industry and other affected industries, and the devaluated currencies were the outstanding symptoms of the crisis.[1] The Global Financial Crisis of 2008, to summarize simply, was the collapse of the housing bubble—fueled by low-interest rates, easy and available credit, scant regulation, and toxic mortgages— that was the spark that ignited a string of events, which led to a full-blown crisis in the fall of 2008. Trillions of dollars in risky mortgages had become embedded throughout the financial system as mortgage-related securities were packaged, repackaged, and sold to investors around the world. When the bubble burst, hundreds of billions of dollars in losses in mortgages and mortgage-related securities shook markets as well as financial institutions that had significant exposures to those mortgages and had borrowed heavily against them. This happened not just in the United States but around the world. The losses were magnified by derivatives such as synthetic securities.[2]

---

[1] Wikipedia. "Financial Crisis of 2007–2009." Last modified September 13, 2008. http://en.wikipedia.org/w/index.php?title=Financial_crisis_of_2007%E2%80%932009&oldid=289330105. (Accessed May 12, 2009).

[2] The Financial Crisis Inquiry Commission. *The Financial Crisis Inquiry Report*, Official Government Edition, January 2011, https://www.govinfo.gov/content/pkg/GPO-FCIC/pdf/GPO-FCIC.pdf, pp. XVI, October 21, 2023.

Almost everybody agrees that this crisis was the biggest in scale that the world has experienced since the Great Depression of 1929. Unlike at the time of the Great Depression, when governments were slow to take countermeasures, the financial authorities of Japan, the United States, and Europe have been coordinating their response to provide financial institutions with infusions of public funds. This seems to have worked for now, causing the situation to become somewhat calmer.[3]

It is generally admitted that capitalism, as a whole, is speculative and inherently unstable. John Maynard Keynes believed that the market economy was unstable and that it was necessary to use monetary and fiscal policy to tame its instability.[4] The current financial system seems to be inherently plagued by persistent crises. According to one estimate, over the last four decades, more than 100 crises occurred.[5] Not a single geographical area or major country has been spared the effect of these crises. Even some countries that have generally followed sound fiscal and monetary policies have become engulfed in these crises.[6] Kalaycı likens the relationship between crises and economies to the one between diseases and human beings. Just like diseases in people, crises arise, grow, and disappear in economies. Therefore, a crisis that ends is a harbinger of another new crisis.[7]

Taking financialism as a recent phase of capitalism, this paper first deals with the most discussed causes of the 2008 Global Financial Crisis. Since the effect of interest policy on the Crisis, we think, has not been examined sufficiently because it is taken for granted within the capitalist system, this work first investigates the aspects of interest policy that contradict the market system and produce crises. The impact of interest policy was taken into account in most studies only at the house-purchasing stage, and it was evaluated that the low-

---

[3] Katsuhito Iwai, "Global Financial Crisis Shows Inherent Instability of Capitalism," December 08, 2008. Available at http://www.tokyofoundation.org/en/articles/2008/global-financial-crisis-shows-inherent-instability-of-capitalism, (accessed May 20, 2009).

[4] Katsuhito Iwai, "Global Financial Crisis".

[5] Joseph Stiglitz, "Dealing with Debt: How to Reform the Global Financial System", *Harvard International Review*, (Spring 2003): 54- 59.

[6] M. Umer Chapra, "The Global Financial Crisis: Can Islamic Finance Help Minimize the Severity and Frequency of Such a Crisis in the Future?", the Forum on the Global Financial Crisis, *Islamic Development Bank*, October 25, 2008. https://www.researchgate.net/publication/237255008_The_Global_Financial_Crisis_Can_Islamic_Finance_Help_Minimize_the_Severity_and_Frequency_of_Such_A_Crisis_in_the_Future, October 19 2023.

[7] İrfan Kalaycı, "Finansal Enfeksiyon ve "Aşı" Kuramı: Bir Genel Kriz Eleştirisi (Financial Infection and "Vaccine" Theory: A General Critique of Crisis)", *Maliye Dergisi* sayı. 160 (Ocak-Haziran 2011): 52, https://ms. hmb.gov.tr/uploads/2019/09/002-1.pdf, October, 2023.

interest rates encouraged low-income clients to buy houses in the US. However, interest-bearing transactions during the packaging, repackaging, and selling of mortgage certificates to investors have not been subjected to sufficient searches. Thus, this study aims to discuss interest-bearing transactions and the ballooning they cause at these stages. It argues that the main reason for the crisis is interest-based transactions of derivatives. These instruments are mostly a zero-sum game,[8] thus not producing any economic value, rather than being a result of win-win action, yet paying interest to investors. The paper sets out to answer why the Vatican recommended Islamic finance to Western banks after this crisis. For this purpose, it examines the Islamic understanding of interest based on a concise hadith of the Prophet Muhammad, which is called "The Hadith of Six Things", and tries to understand financial crises from the perspective of this hadith. In this concise hadith, Prophet Muhammad interestingly adds great depth to the concept of interest and explains that 72 transactions out of 120 transactions fall within the concept of interest. This study ends with the financial crisis preventive suggestions derived from this hadith.

The Most Talked Causes of the Current Global Financial Crisis

The 2008 Global Financial Crisis did not take anybody by surprise. Few now doubt that the housing bubble in the US was bound to burst or that a general financial crisis and a global economic slowdown were to be the unavoidable results. Warning signs were evident for years to all of those not taken in by the new financial alchemy of high-risk debt management and not blinded, as was much of the corporate world, by huge speculative profits.[9] Years ago, in August 2002, the analyst Dean Baker identified a housing bubble and wrote that from 1953 to 1995, house prices had simply tracked inflation, but that when house prices from 1995 onwards were adjusted for inflation, they showed a marked increase over and above inflation-based increases. Baker concluded that a bubble in the United States (US) housing market existed and predicted an ensuing crisis.[10] Baker's argument was confirmed with the construction of a data series from 1895 to 1995 by the influential economist Robert Shiller, which showed that real house prices had been essentially unchanged over that a

---

[8] Zero-sum game is the result of a transaction in which one party's gain is offset by the other party's loss.

[9] John Bellamy Foster, "The Financialization of Capital and the Crisis", April 2008. http://www. monthlyreview.org/080401foster.php, 16 May 2009.

[10] Dean Baker, "The Run-up in Home Prices: Is it Real or is it Another Bubble?", http://www.cepr.net/documents/publications/housing_2002_08.pdf, 12 May 2009.

hundred years.[11] It later proved impossible to convince responsible parties, such as the Board of Governors of the Federal Reserve, of the need for action.

A common claim during the first weeks of the financial crisis was that the problem was simply caused by reckless, sub-prime lending. However, the sub-prime mortgages were only part of a far more extensive problem affecting the entire $20 trillion US housing market: the sub-prime sector was simply the first place that the collapse of the bubble affecting the housing market showed up.

The ultimate point of origin of the great financial crisis of 2007-2009 can be traced back to an *extremely indebted* US economy. The collapse of the real estate market in 2006 was the close point of origin of the crisis. The failure rates of subprime mortgages were the first symptom of a credit boom that turned into a bust and a real estate shock. However, large default rates on subprime mortgages cannot account for the severity of the crisis. Rather, low-quality mortgages acted as an accelerant to the fire that spread through the entire financial system. The latter had become fragile as a result of several factors that are unique to this crisis: the transfer of assets from the balance sheets of banks to the markets, the creation of complex and opaque (unclear) assets, the failure of rating agencies to assess the risk of such assets properly, and the application of fair value accounting. To these novel factors, one must add the now standard failure of regulators and supervisors in spotting and correcting emerging weaknesses.[12]

Subprime lending is listed among the outstanding reasons. Subprime lending refers to financial institutions lending in ways that do not meet prime standards to an extent, which puts the loans into the riskiest category of consumer loans typically sold in the secondary market. Proponents of subprime lending maintain that the practice extends credit to people who would otherwise not have access to the credit market. Some, like American Enterprise Institute fellow Peter J. Wallison, believe the roots of the crisis can be traced directly to sub-prime lending by Fannie Mae and Freddie Mac, which are government-sponsored entities. On 30 September 1999, The New York Times reported that the Clinton Administration expanded mortgage loans among low- and moderate-income people.

Deregulation is cited as another reason for the crisis. In 1992, the US Congress weakened regulation of government-sponsored enterprises Fannie Mae and

[11] R. Shiller, *Irrational Exuberance* (Princeton, NJ: Princeton University Press, 2006).

[12] Michele Fratianni and Francesco Marchionne, "The Role of Banks in the Subprime Financial Crisis", (April 10, 2009) Review of Economic Conditions in Italy, (2009/1): 21, Available at SSRN: https://ssrn.com/abstract=1383473 or http://dx.doi.org/10.2139/ssrn.1383473, October 12, 2023.

Freddie Mac to make available more money for the issuance of home loans. More importantly, in 1999, Congress passed the Gramm-Leach-Bliley Act, paving the way for the increase in the complex and opaque financial instruments that are at the heart of the crisis.

The *housing bubble* grew up alongside the stock bubble of the mid-1990s. People who had increased their wealth substantially with the extraordinary run-up of stock prices were spending based on this increased wealth. This led to the consumption boom of the late 1990s, with the savings rate out of disposable income falling from five percent in the mid-90s to two percent by 2000. The stock-wealth-induced consumption boom led people to buy bigger and/or better homes since they sought to spend some of their new stock wealth on housing.[13]

The next phase of the housing bubble was the supply-side effect of the dramatic increase in house prices, as housing starts rose substantially from the mid-1990s onwards. The collapse of the stock bubble helped to feed the US housing bubble. After collectively losing faith in the stock market, millions of people turned to investments in housing as a safe alternative. In addition, the 2001 recession led the Federal Reserve to continue to cut *interest rates*. Fixed-rate mortgages and other *interest rates* hit 50-year lows. To further fuel the housing market, Federal Reserve Board Chairman Alan Greenspan suggested that homebuyers were wasting money by buying fixed-rate mortgages instead of Adjustable-Rate Mortgages (ARMs). This was peculiar advice at a time when fixed-rate mortgages were near 50-year lows, but even at the low rates of 2003, homebuyers could still afford larger mortgages with the adjustable rates available at the time.

The bubble began to burst in 2007, as the building boom led to so much over-supply that prices could no longer be supported. Prices nationwide began to head downward, with this process accelerating through the fall of 2007 and into 2008. As prices declined, more homeowners faced foreclosure. In cases where a home is valued far lower than the amount of the outstanding mortgage, homeowners may be able to simply walk away from their mortgage.

Another cause of the crisis was *miscalculation* of the level of risk inherent in the unregulated Collateralized Debt Obligation (CDO) and Credit Default Swap (CDS) markets. Under this theory, banks and investors systematized the risk by taking advantage of low *interest rates* to borrow tremendous sums of money that they could only pay back if the housing market continued to increase in value.

---

[13] John Bellamy Foster, "The Financialization of Capital and the Crisis", April 2008. http://www.monthlyreview. org/080401foster.php, accessed 16 May 2009.

The risk was further systematized by the use of the false pricing model, the Gaussian copula model, which will go down in history as instrumental in causing the unfathomable losses that brought the world's financial system to its knees.

Different from the mainstream explanation, another analysis is that the financial crisis is merely a symptom of another, deeper crisis, which is a systemic crisis of capitalism itself. According to Samir Amin, an Egyptian economist, the constant decrease in GDP growth rates in Western countries since the early 1970s created a growing surplus of capital, which did not have sufficient profitable investment outlets in the real economy. The alternative was to place this surplus into the financial market, which became more profitable than productive capital investment, especially with subsequent deregulation. According to Samir Amin, this phenomenon has led to recurrent financial bubbles.[14]

A Less Talked Cause: Financialization of the Economy

Although the US mortgage crisis is often cited as having caused the crisis, the financial system itself was vulnerable due to intricate and highly leveraged financial contracts and operations because the U.S. monetary policy made the cost of credit negligible and encouraged such high levels of leverage and hypertrophy of the financial sector.

Foster argues that this crisis is not just another massive credit crunch but signals a new phase in the development of the capitalistic system, which is labelled 'monopoly-finance capital'. The bursting of two major financial bubbles in seven years points to a crisis of financialization, a progressive shift from production to finance that has characterized the economy over the last four decades.[15] Paul Sweezy called it "the financialization of the capital accumulation process" just over a decade ago. It has been the main force lifting economic growth since the 1970s.[16]

The financial system is supposed to serve a range of functions in the broader economy. Banks and other financial institutions mop up savings and then allocate that capital, according to mainstream theory, to where it can most productively be used. For households and corporations, the credit markets

---

[14] Samir Amin, "Economic, Social and Political Distortions in the Modern World", 1996, http://www.ismea.org/INESDEV/AMIN.eng.html, May 20, 2009.

[15] John Bellamy Foster, "The Financialization of Capital and the Crisis," April 2008, Http://www.monthlyreview.org/080401foster.php, accessed 16 May 2009.

[16] Paul M. Sweezy, "More (or Less) on Globalization," *Monthly Review* 49, no. 4 (September 1997): 3.

facilitate greatly increased borrowing, which should foster investment in capital goods like buildings and machinery, in turn leading to expanded production. Finance, in other words, is supposed to facilitate the growth of the 'real' economy—the part that produces useful goods (like bicycles) and services (like medical care). In recent decades, finance has undergone massive changes in both size and shape.[17]

Financialization is a process whereby financial markets, financial institutions, and financial elites gain greater influence over economic policy and economic outcomes. Financialization transforms the functioning of the economic system at both the macro and micro levels. Its principal impacts are to (1) elevate the significance of the financial sector relative to the real sector, (2) transfer income from the real sector to the financial sector, and (3) increase income inequality and contribute to wage stagnation. Additionally, there are reasons to believe that financialization may render the economy prone to the risk of debt deflation and prolonged recession.[18] The transformation in the system is reflected in the rapid growth since the 1970s of financial profits as a percent of total profits (see Figure 13.1). The fact that such financialization of capital appears to be taking the form of bigger and bigger bubbles that burst more frequently and with more devastating effects, threatening each time a deepening of stagnation and rising excess capacity and unemployment/underemployment, is thus a development of major significance.

The term financialization is sometimes used in discussions of financial capitalism. "Financial capital (also simply known as capital or equity in finance, accounting, and economics) is any economic resource measured in terms of money used by entrepreneurs and businesses to buy what they need to make their products or to provide their services to the sector of the economy upon which their operation is based, e.g., retail, corporate, investment banking, etc. In other words, financial capital is internal retained earnings generated by the entity or funds provided by lenders (and investors) to businesses to purchase real capital equipment or services for producing new goods and/or services. In contrast, real capital (or economic capital) comprises physical goods that assist

---

[17] Ramaa Vasudevan, "Financialization: A Primer", 2008, http://www.dollarsandsense.org/archives/2008/1108vasudevan.html, 16 May 2009.

[18] Thomas I. Palley. "Financialization: What it is and Why it Matters," in TUAC Labour/Management Seminar on "Financialisation of the Economy: Regulating Private Equity", OECD, November 2007, 3, https://scholarworks.umass.edu/cgi/viewcontent.cgi?article=1124&context=peri_workingpapers, October 23, 2023.

in the production of other goods and services, e.g., shovels for gravediggers, sewing machines for tailors, or machinery and tooling for factories."[19]

Figure 13.1 Financial Profits as a Percent of Total Profits (five-year moving average)

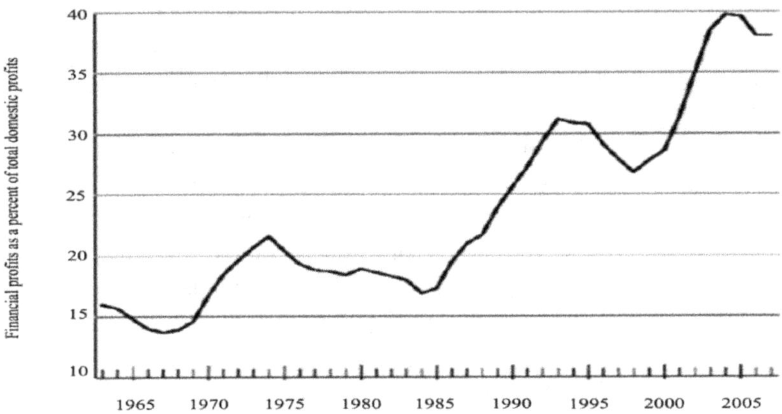

Source: Table B-91. Corporate Profits by Industry, 1959–2007, Economic Report of the President, 2008.

Financial capital developed over several decades leading up to the 2007-2009 financial crisis, in which financial leverage tended to override capital (equity) and financial markets tended to dominate over the traditional industrial economy.

Greta Krippner defines financialization as a phase in capitalist development in which profits are accumulated primarily (or at least increasingly) through financial channels.[20] Another definition by Dore is: "the increasing dominance of the finance industry in the total of economic activity, of financial controllers in the management of corporations, of financial assets among total assets, of marketized securities and particularly equities among financial assets, of the stock market as a market for corporate control in determining corporate

[19] Wikipedia Contributors, "Financial Capital," Wikipedia, The Free Encyclopedia, https://en.wikipedia.org/w/index.php?title=Financial_capital&oldid=1177254644, (accessed October 4, 2023).

[20] Benjamin Lemoine, "The Politics of Financialization. An Interview with Greta Krippner," Revue de la Régulation, 2017, https://www.academia.edu/37856151/The_Politics_of_Financialization_An_Interview_with_Greta_Krippner and https://journals.openedition.org/regulation/12637, October 23, 2023.

strategies, and of fluctuations in the stock market as a determinant of business cycles."[21]

The basic mechanism of financialization is the transformation of future streams of income (from profits, dividends, or interest payments) into a tradable asset like a stock or a bond. For example, the future earnings of corporations are transmuted into equity stocks that are bought and sold in the capital market. Likewise, a loan, which involves certain fixed interest payments over its duration, gets a new life when it is converted into marketable bonds. Multiple loans, bundled together and then "sliced and diced" into novel kinds of bonds ("collateralized debt obligations"), take on a new existence as investment vehicles that bear an extremely complex and opaque relationship to the original loans.[22]

Kevin Phillips, an American writer, presents financialization as a process whereby financial services take over the dominant economic, cultural, and political role in a national economy."[23] Philips considers that the financialization of the U.S. economy follows the same pattern that marked the beginning of the decline of the American economy as Habsburg Spain in the sixteenth century, the Dutch trading empire in the eighteenth century, and the British Empire in the nineteenth century.

The roots of financialization are traced to the rise of Neoliberalism and the free-market doctrines of Milton Friedman and the Chicago School of Economics, of which the politico-economic philosophy has been summarized as one in which "markets, private property and minimal government will achieve maximum welfare." One of the most important impetuses to the rise of financialization was the end of the post-World War Two Bretton Woods system of fixed international exchange rates and the dollar peg to gold in August 1971. The demise of fixed exchange rates initiated a rapid rise in the level of foreign exchange trading (forex), leaping in the United States from $110.8 billion in 1970, 10.7 percent of U.S. GDP, to $5.449 trillion in 1980, 195.3 percent of U.S. GDP, meaning five times increase. An April 1977 study found there was $4.8 billion in daily forex trading, or around $1.2 trillion a year. However, this study did not include all the trading in futures trading for various currencies. Currency futures were first created at the Chicago Mercantile Exchange (CME) in 1972, the year after fixed exchange rates were abandoned.

---

[21] R. Dore, *Stock Market Capitalism: Welfare Capitalism: Japan and Germany vs. the Anglo-Saxons*, (Oxford: Oxford University Press, 2000).

[22] Ramaa Vasudevan, "Financialization: A Primer", 2008, http://www.dollarsandsense.org/archives/2008/1108vasudevan.html, 16 May 2009

[23] Kevin Phillips, *American Theocracy: The Peril and Politics of Radical Religion, Oil, and Borrowed Money in the 21st Century*, (Viking, 2006), 268.

Figure 13.2 Share in GDP of US Financial Sector Since 1860

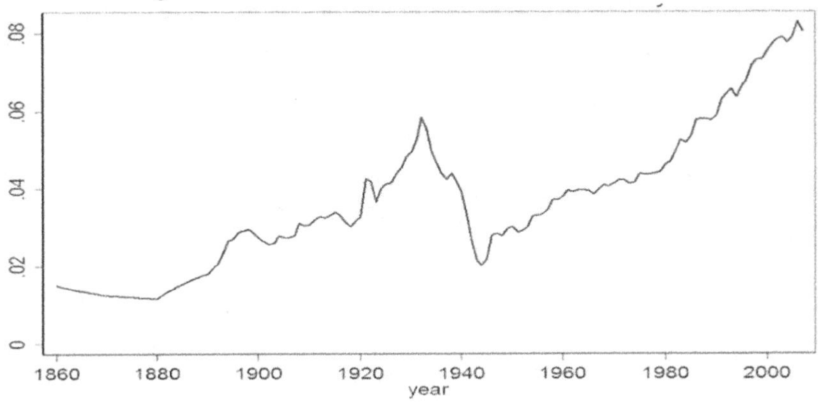

Source: Wikipedia contributors, "Financialization," Wikipedia, The Free Encyclopedia, https://en.wikipedia.org/w/index.php?title=Financialization&oldid=1153448096 (accessed October 4, 2023).

Other financial markets exhibited similarly explosive growth. While the volume of trade in US equity (stock) markets was 13.1 percent of the US GDP in 1970, it rose to 28.8 percent of U.S. GDP in 1990, and 144.9 percent of GDP.

Thus, derivatives trading -mostly futures contracts on *interest rates*, foreign currencies, treasury bonds, etc. had reached a level of $1,200 trillion, $1.2 quadrillion, a year. By comparison, U.S. GDP in 2006 was $12.456 trillion. Table 13.1 provides data for the annual amount of financial trading in U.S. financial markets, compared to GDP.

A dramatic shift is observed in the types of futures contracts traded from 1970 to 2004. For a century after organized futures exchanges were founded in the mid-1800s, all futures trading was solely based on agricultural commodities. But after the end of the dollar gold-backed fixed-exchange-rate system in 1971, contracts based on foreign currencies began to be traded. After the deregulation of *interest rates* by the Bank of England and then the U.S. Federal Reserve in the late 1970s, futures contracts based on various bonds/*interest rates* began to be traded. The result was that financial futures contracts -based on such things as interest rates, currencies, or equity indices- came to dominate the futures markets.

The average value for *interest rate* contracts is around ten times that of agricultural and other commodities, while the average value of currency contracts is twice that of agricultural and other commodities.

Table 13.1 The Dollar Value of Trading in U.S. Financial Markets Compared to GDP (Annual, in billions of dollars. Italics indicate estimates)

	1956	1960	1963	1966	1970	1980	1990	2000	2001
Equity Markets Trading	36	47	61	128	135	522	1,671	14,22	
U.S. government securities trading	276	*473*	722	*1,091*	*1,391*	*4,840*	26,688	67,05	
Futures Trading	*150*	*165*	203	*250*	330	5,584	152,717	343,13	
Foreign Exchange Trading	41	47	55	74	111	5,449	*36,000*		60,960
Corporate Debt Trading	*19*	35	56	*90*	*na*	*821*	3,972	3,96	
State and Municipal Bonds	*12*	*23*	37	*60*	*112*	*542*	*2,622*	2,11	
Options trading, on exchange	na	na	na	na	na	46	81	330	
Mortgage Derivatives	na	na	na	na	na	na	3,697	16,68	
OTC swaps, forwards, options	na	na	na	na	na				
TOTAL FINANCIAL TURNOVER	534	795	1,134	1,692	2,749	17,804	227,448	508,45	
U.S. Gross Domestic Product	425	526	603	770	1,039	2,790	5,803	9,817	
Turnover divided by GDP	1.256	1.511	1.331	2.198	2.647	6.383	39.194	51.79	
GDP as % of financial turnover	79.6	66.2	53.2	45.5	37.8	15.7	2.6	1.9	

Source: http://en.wikipedia.org/wiki/Financialization, May 19, 2009.

As a result of the process of financialization, financial services have become a key industry in developed economies which represents a sizeable share of the GDP and an important source of employment. Those activities also played a key facilitator role in fostering economic globalization: "The Reagan-Thatcher model, which favoured finance over domestic manufacturing, has collapsed".[24]

One of the most notable features of financialization has been the development of over-leverage (more borrowed capital and less own capital) and, as a related tool, financial derivatives. Financial derivatives are the financial instruments, the price or value of which is derived from the price or value of another underlying financial instrument. Those instruments, the initial purpose of which was hedging and risk management, have become widely traded financial assets on their own. The most common types of derivatives are futures contracts,

[24] Harold Meyerson, "Building a Better Capitalism," *The Washington Post*, March 12, 2009, http://www.washingtonpost.com/wp-dyn/content/article/2009/03/11/AR2009031103218.html?wpisrc=newsletter, May 19, 2009.

swaps, and options. In the past few years, the number and types of financial derivatives have grown enormously. In November 2007, commenting on the financial crisis sparked by the sub-prime mortgage collapse in the United States, Doug Noland writes that according to the Bank of International Settlements, the Over-the-counter[25] (OTC) market for Credit Default Swaps (CDS) jumped from $4.7 trillion (TN) at the end of 2006 to $22.6 TN at to end of 2006. From the International Swaps and Derivatives Association, we know that the total notional volume of credit derivatives jumped about 30% during the first half to $45.5 TN. And to the Comptroller of the Currency, total U.S. commercial bank Credit derivative positions ballooned from $492bn to begin 2003 to $11.8 TN as of this past June.[26]

A major unknown regarding derivatives is the actual amount of cash behind a transaction. A derivatives contract with a notional value of millions of dollars may only cost a few thousand dollars. For example, an interest rate swap might be based on exchanging the interest payments on $100 million in U.S. Treasury bonds at a fixed interest of 4.5 percent for the floating interest rate of $100 million in credit card receivables. This contract would involve at least $4.5 million in interest payments, though the notional value may be reported as $100 million. However, the actual "cost" of the swap contract would be some small fraction of the minimal $4.5 million in interest payments. The difficulty of determining exactly how much this swap contract is worth when accounted for on a financial institution's books is typical of the worries many experts and regulators have over the explosive growth of these types of instruments.

The root causes of the US financial crisis are now well known, but excessive leverage and derivative trade featured prominently as one of the explanations. As Figure 13.3 shows, the global per capita derivative in 2008 outstripped global per capita GDP by a factor of 10, as opposed to a factor of less than 2 a decade

---

[25] Over-the-counter (OTC) off-exchange trading or pink sheet trading is done directly between two parties, without the supervision of an exchange It is contrasted with exchange trading, which occurs via exchanges. A stock exchange has the benefit of facilitating liquidity, providing transparency, and maintaining the current market price. In an OTC trade, the price is not necessarily publicly disclosed. OTC trading, as well as exchange trading, occurs with commodities, financial instruments (including stocks), and derivatives of such products. Products traded on traditional stock exchanges, and other regulated bourse platforms, must be well-standardized. The OTC market does not have this limitation. The OTC derivative market is significant in some asset classes: interest rate, foreign exchange, stocks, and commodities. (Wikipedia contributors, "Over-the-counter (finance)," Wikipedia, The Free Encyclopedia, https://en.wikipedia.org/w/index.php?title=Over-the-counter_(finance)&oldid=1170203891, accessed October 12, 2023.)

[26] Doug Noland, "Credit Bubble Bulletin: Road to Ruin," Asia Times Online, (6 November 2007). http://www.atimes.com/atimes/Global_Economy/IK06Dj01.html, May 14, 2009.

ago. This trend highlights not only the rapidity with which derivative trade grew over the years but also the dangers of undertaking such colossal transactions without adequate underlying assets to back them.[27]

Figure 13.3 World Per Capita Derivative and Per Capita GDP 1000

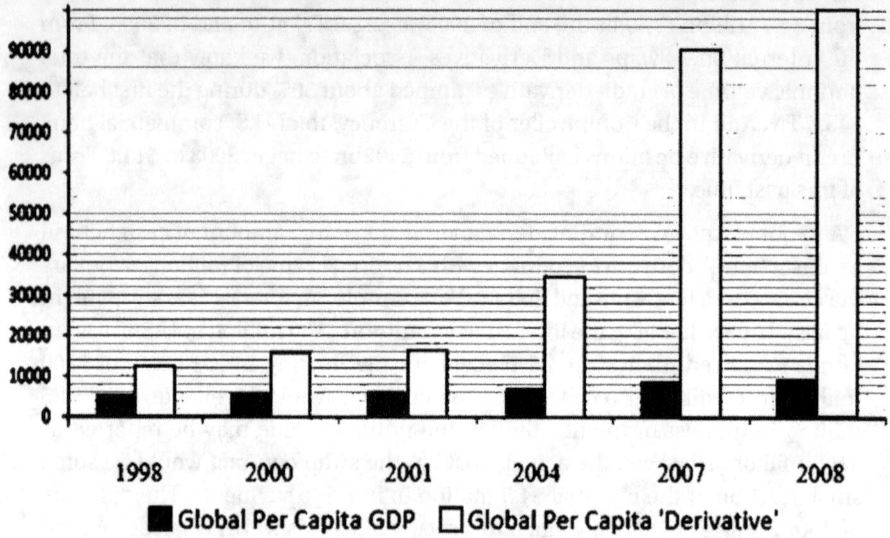

Source: BIS, IMF, World Bank.

The Neglected Cause: Interest Rate Policies

a. Interest policy and market system

Interest policy is the backbone of capitalism, and capitalism is claimed to be based on the market system. Contrary to this popular belief, the interest mechanism is in no way compatible with the market system. Because, even if any interest rate is determined according to the supply and demand conditions of the day, today's interest rate is determined to be valid for future maturity. However, tomorrow's supply and demand conditions may change, and the previously determined interest rate may no longer be valid for the new conditions. Despite this, the initially determined interest rate remains valid for the stated maturity, and the already changed supply and demand conditions can be taken into account only in the *interest rates* to be determined for the next maturity. However, this new interest rate also experiences the contradictions of the previous one, and this process continues likewise in zigzags. In short, full harmony can never be achieved between *interest rates* and the supply and

[27] *Gulf One Investment Bank Research Bulletin*, vol. 2, no.1, January 2009.

demand conditions of the market system and *interest rates* always lag behind the supply and demand conditions. *No interest rate is exactly compatible with today's supply and demand conditions because each interest rate is under the influence of changing market conditions, both past and up to maturity. Despite the variability of the market conditions, interest rates are always the same until maturity.*

In other words, in the capitalistic system, *interest rates* are not determined by supply and demand conditions, but rather, it is expected that future supply and demand conditions will match the *interest rates* that have already been determined. It is as if *interest rates* are not expected to follow the divine/natural order. On the contrary, the divine/natural order is expected to follow *interest rates.* With the *interest rates* determined to be valid in the future, mortgages are placed on the divine will/natural order, and the divine will is asked to be shaped according to the interest rate. In short, interest rate policy is no different than grappling with the natural order and the forces of supply and demand. This must probably be why Allah states in the Holy Qur'an that interest is a war waged against Him.[28] Because interest, whose rate is determined today for tomorrow, is nothing but the audacity of helpless humans to rule over the future, which no one other than God knows and can control. Indeed, one of the most important reasons for the collapse of the Soviet system was that it did not recognize the universal rules of the economy and resisted the forces of supply and demand of the market that were impossible to resist for a long time. The price for fighting the irresistible forces of the economy was to succumb to those forces.[29]

So, the most important impasse and paradox of the interest mechanism is here: because life is full of surprises, human beings cannot make definitive judgments on any issue regarding the future and always make evaluations within the framework of flexibility and possibility. The only exception to this is *the interest mechanism, which is a definite and fixed income applied to monetary/financial capital whose productivity is uncertain. Therefore, the interest system and market conditions are in constant conflict, and this causes economies to experience constant shocks.* That's why the Austrian School

---

[28] "*O believers! Fear Allah, and give up from now on what remains of interest if you are true believers. If you do not, then beware of a war with Allah and His Messenger! But if you repent, you may retain your principal—neither wronging nor being wronged.*", (The Holy Qur'an, Baqarah, II/278-279).

[29] İsmail Özsoy, "Sovyet Sisteminin Çöküşünden Tarihî ve Evrensel Dersler (Historical and Universal Lessons from Collapse of the Soviet System", *Bilig-Türk Dünyası Sosyal Bilimler Dergisi* 39 (Sep.2 006): 164, 172, 187. https://bilig.yesevi.edu.tr/yonetim/icerik/makaleler/2928-published.pdf, also available at https://bilig.yesevi.edu. tr/shw_artcl-1231.html

economists rejected the intervention of central banks in the financial markets with arbitrary determination of *interest rates*. They have asserted that the crisis is an excellent example of the Austrian Business Cycle Theory, in which credit created through the policies of central banking gives rise to an artificial boom, which is inevitably followed by a bust. Proponents of this theory have predicted the current financial crises and argue that central banks should not be involved in debt markets.[30]

b. Interest Policy Is an "Economic Engineering"

In the interest system, the future of the economy is determined by mathematical calculations, the main lines of the economy are determined like drawing a project to construct a building. However, the real economy rarely submits to that kind of intervention. Because, as well as the material elements of the real economy that can be controlled and be almost accurately predicted, there are also psychological elements that cannot be controlled, cannot be predicted, and are affected by the spiritual world of the human being, who is the most basic actor of the economy. For example, expectations are among the most important determinants of both supply and demand.

The productivity of monetary/financial capital is uncertain and dependent on labor. Its contribution to production cannot be predicted with certainty from the beginning. However, in the interest system, the return on monetary capital is fixed by the interest rate at the beginning of the production process and independently of its outcome. Thus, the return on monetary capital increases steadily and in fixed amounts at the end of each maturity. This increase, which is guaranteed by the interest rate and has no direct connection with the real economy, may not be real but a bubble. In other words, interest may be an income paid without any real production or it may be an income that the debtor has to pay even when he does not earn enough to pay for it.

c. Angular Wheel of Financial Sector versus Reel Sector Wheel in the Economy Cart

If we think of the economy as a two-wheeled car; one of these wheels is the financial sector and the other is the real one. The financial sector is like an angular wheel without shock absorbers and does not take into account the ups, downs, and bends of the road. Since each fixed interest rate is valid until its maturity, this wheel is conditioned to move forward at a constant speed and determinedly, but with shakes because of changing market conditions, until

---

30 Wikipedia, "Business Cycle", The Free Encyclopedia, https://en.wikipedia.org/w/index.php?title=Business_cycle&oldid=1175987738, (accessed October 7, 2023).

the maturity date. Because, although economic conditions are very variable, every interest rate determined does not change until the end of maturity.

In contrast to this angular wheel of the financial sector, the real sector pillar to which it is connected is like a normal round wheel with shock absorbers, traveling sometimes slowly, sometimes fast, on a bumpy road with ups and downs, at an unpredictable, so continuously changing speed due to changeable conditions of the road. This is because economic activities sometimes accelerate, sometimes slow down, sometimes stop, or even decline. Except for extraordinary situations such as war or natural disasters, economic ups and downs in the real sector can be compensated smoothly or with little damage. Sudden shocks rarely occur.

However, in the financial sector, *interest rates* are always positive and since they are always determined at the beginning of the process, they are sometimes determined higher than they should be and sometimes lower, as the Austrian school emphasizes.[31] Because it is not possible to predict the future of the economy without error, deviations are inevitable. Therefore, in this process, sometimes the angular wheel and sometimes the round wheel take the lead, and this economy cart constantly lurches left and right. Speculations and manipulations that the financial sector is exposed to[32] also contribute to these shakes. Periods of stability are very limited and temporary, as every wrong clock shows the correct time twice a day.

Whenever *interest rates* are determined, whether on micro or macro basis and whenever interest-bearing contracts mature, payments are to be made, or defaults occur, there are shocks in the interest-based markets, like the shaking of the angular wheel. These shocks either lead to new investments in positive market conditions or to bankruptcies and crises in negative ones. Because, not every payment in the finance sector may have a real, matching equivalent in terms of goods or services due to the bubbles that have formed in the economy. The *interest rates* and the length of maturities determine the magnitude of these positive or negative consequences. In addition to the shocks caused by the angular wheel, the incompatibility of the two wheels also shakes the economy, resulting in crises. That is why the Holy Qur'an likens the interest system to the staggering of a person struck by a devil.[33]

---

[31] Wikipedia, "Business Cycle", The Free Encyclopedia, https://en.wikipedia.org/w/index.php?title=Business_cycle&oldid=1175987738, (accessed October 7, 2023).

[32] İrfan Kalaycı, "Finansal Enfeksiyon ve "Aşı" Kuramı", 34.

[33] "*Those who devour interest become like the one whom Devil has bewitched and maddened by his touch. They have been condemned to this condition because they say, "Trade is just like interest", whereas Allah has made trade lawful and interest unlawful. Henceforth, if one abstains from taking interest after receiving this admonition from his*

d. Fixing the Steering Wheel of a Truck on a Winding Road?

It is also possible to understand the following meaning from being hit by the devil: It is not possible to predict the future of the economy exactly from today, we can liken it to traveling on a winding road. Accordingly, each interest rate determined for a future maturity, regardless of its duration, is no different from fixing both the steering and the speed of a vehicle traveling on a winding road.

There is no difference between determining a new direction for the steering wheel and a new speed for the vehicle at each new turn fixing both the steering wheel and the speed again, and determining a new interest rate for each new maturity in the interest system. Just as this vehicle drifts from side to side, an interest-based economy is subject to constant fluctuations and instabilities.

Whereas, in the real sector, such situations may be overcome with smooth transitions. Because in the real economy, every economic decision is made based on a good or service. So, each debt has a reel equivalent.

e. The Yield Curve

The Yield Curve is a graphical representation of the *interest rates* on debt for a range of maturities. It shows the yield an investor expects to earn if he lends his money for a given period. The graph displays a bond's yield on the vertical axis and the time to maturity across the horizontal axis. The curve may take different shapes at different points in the economic cycle, but it is typically upward-sloping.[34]

Treasury yield is one tool of monetary policy. The history of the yield curve from 2000 through 2007 illustrates the role that credit creation through interest rate policies by the Federal Reserve may have played in the onset of the financial crisis in 2007 and 2008.

The *yield curve* (also known as the term structure of *interest rates*) is the shape formed by a graph showing US Treasury Bill or Bond *interest rates* on the vertical axis and time to maturity on the horizontal axis (Figure 13.4). When short-term *interest rates* are lower than long-term *interest rates* the yield curve is said to be "positively sloped". This in turn encourages an expansion in money supply and in turn, favors debt-induced bubbles. When long-term *interest rates* are lower than short-term *interest rates* the yield curve is said to be "inverted".

Lord, no legal action will be taken against him regarding the interest he had devoured before; his case shall ultimately go to Allah. But if one repeats the same crime after this, he shall go to Hell, where he shall abide forever." (The Holy Qur'an, Baqara, II/275, interpreted by Abul Ala Maududi. https://myislam.org/surah-baqarah/ayat-275/, October 7, 2023).

[34] Corporate Finance Institute Team, "What is the Yield Curve?", https://corporatefinanceinstitute.com/resources/fixed-income/yield-curve, accessed October 9, 2023.

This favors a contraction in the money supply. When long-term and short-term *interest rates* are equal the yield curve is said to be "flat". The yield curve is believed by some to be a strong predictor of recession (when inverted) and inflation (when positively sloped).

A positively sloped yield curve allows primary dealers (such as large investment banks) in the Federal Reserve System to fund themselves with cheap short-term money while lending out at higher long-term *interest rates.* This strategy is profitable so long as the yield curve remains positively sloped. However, it creates a liquidity risk if the yield curve were to become inverted and banks would have to refund themselves at expensive short-term *interest rates* while losing money on longer-term loans.

Following the bursting of the Dot-com bubble in 2000 and the Stock market downturn of 2002, the US Federal Reserve reacted by sharply lowering short-term *interest rates.* The Fed lowered the Fed Funds target rate beginning in January 2001 at 6.5% to a nadir of 1% in June 2003.[35] The Fed also held rates at this low level for an unusually long period (1 year) until June 2004. This prolonged period of stimulative Fed monetary policy created a very positively sloped yield curve. The yield on the 3-month T-bill reached its lowest point (0.88%) for the cycle in the late fall of 2003, while at the same time, 30-year T-bond rates were over 5%.

In June 2004 the Fed began to slowly increase Fed Funds rates and the yield curve slowly narrowed. Fed Chairman Alan Greenspan notably described this narrowing of spreads between short-term and long-term rates as a "conundrum" during testimony in February 2005. The chairman expected long-term rates to rise in line with short-term rates. However, the tightening of monetary policy caused by rising short-term rates was slowing the economy and reducing demand for long-term borrowing.

The Fed raised Fed Funds target rates to a peak of 5.25% in June 2006. By October 2006 the yield curve on 90-day T-bills vs 30-year T-bonds was essentially flat indicating a neutral monetary policy (neither stimulative nor contractionary). While the Fed maintained Fed Funds rates at these high levels, long-term rates began to fall causing the yield curve to become more and more inverted. The yield curve was most strongly inverted in March 2007 when concern about current inflation was reaching its peak.

The narrowing of the yield curve from 2004 and the inversion of the yield curve during 2007 indicated a bursting of the housing bubble and a wild gyration of commodities prices as money flowed out of assets like housing or

---

[35] Heleen Mees, "US Monetary Policy and The Saving Glut", March 24, 2011, https://cepr.org/voxeu/columns/us-monetary-policy-and-saving-glut, October 22, 2023.

stocks. A commodity bubble was created following the collapse of the housing bubble. The price of oil rose to over 140 dollars per barrel in 2008 before plunging as the financial crisis began to take hold in late 2008. A similar bubble in oil prices has preceded other historical economic contractions.

Figure 13.4 Yield Curve

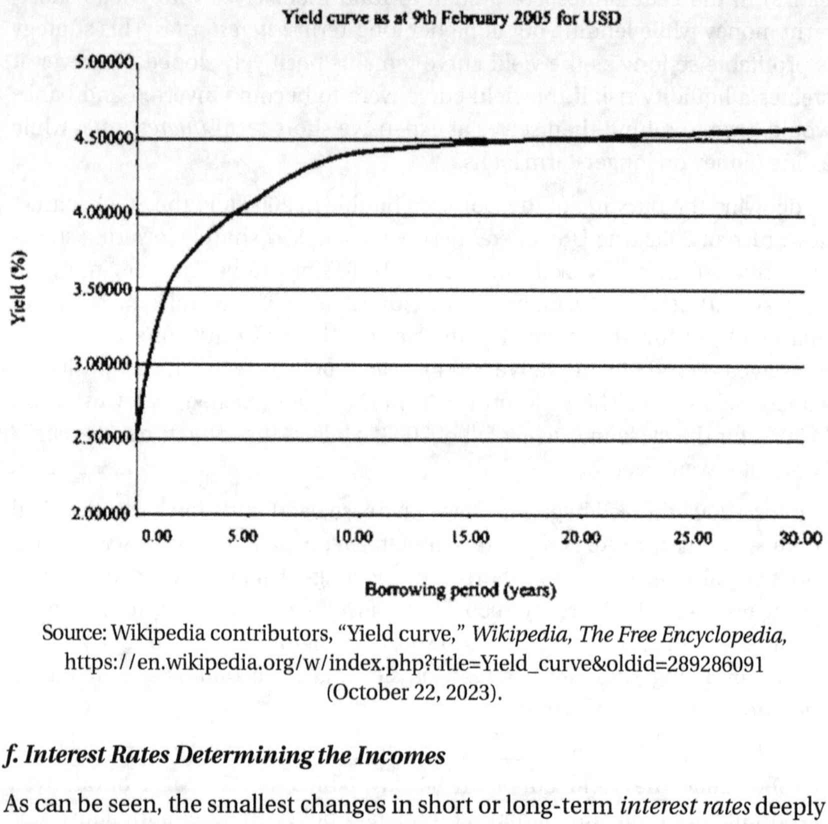

Source: Wikipedia contributors, "Yield curve," *Wikipedia, The Free Encyclopedia,* https://en.wikipedia.org/w/index.php?title=Yield_curve&oldid=289286091 (October 22, 2023).

f. Interest Rates Determining the Incomes

As can be seen, the smallest changes in short or long-term *interest rates* deeply affect the economy and incomes. Although the term 'interest' is the most condemned notion throughout history, it has been the factor that most affected the individual and social life of humankind. Yet, it has been the foundation stone of a capitalist liberal economy. The financial crisis of 2008 was the result of the bursting of financial bubbles that grew in recent decades, and the most effective factor that generated the bubbles was interest, which is the backbone of modern finance. Interest-bearing negotiable instruments and securities change hands without any limit. Markets of trillion dollars' bonds fluctuate upon any interest rate change and some earn billions of dollars in a few hours while others lose. A point hike in the *interest rates* pulls upward the debt stocks of a state, while an opposite move causes losses to the creditors. Interest has become an indispensable element of modern economies, penetrating their cells. Even the financial transactions seemingly irrelevant to interest are somehow hand in hand with it. For example, in futures contracts, what determines the spread, the difference between spot and future prices, is nothing other than the interest. In short, interest makes the financial world, for some, a door to happiness and, for some, a door to misfortune.[36]

Doesn't that mean that in the interest-based capitalist system, a very small minority group at the helm of the economy determines who will be rich, who will be poor, and who will get the great fortunes? So, isn't interest a policy tool that should be used very, very carefully and should not be used unless necessary? Or, if there is an alternative to the interest rate system as a safer alternative, shouldn't we try it?

g. Vatican Offering Islamic Finance System to Western Banks

The most meaningful answer to the question we asked in the last sentence of the previous paragraph came from the Vatican. It should not take anybody by surprise that the Vatican offered Islamic finance principles to Western banks as an alternative to capitalism to solve the worldwide economic crisis, with the Daily Vatican newspaper, 'L'Osservatore Romano, reporting that the Islamic banking system may help to overcome the global crisis. Undoubtedly, this is because Islamic finance refuses to use interest as a policy tool.

Having resisted the interest for 1,500 years in its 2000 years history, the Vatican suggested that the banks look at the ethical rules of Islamic finance to restore confidence amongst their clients at a time of global economic crisis. The newspaper drew the attention of the banks to the ethical principles on which Islamic finance is based to bring them closer to their clients and to the true spirit which should mark every financial service. Author Loretta Napoleoni and Abaxbank Spa fixed income strategist Claudia Segre said in the article that Western banks could use tools such as Islamic bonds, known as sukuk, as collateral. They also said that the profit share, gained from sukuk,[37] may

---

[36] Sami Uslu, "Küresel Krizin Derin Sebepleri (Deep Causes of the Global Crisis)", 2008. http://www. zaman.com.tr/haber.do?haberno=762286, May 10, 2009. (Since this newspaper was closed by the political government in 27 July 2016 for political reasons, this source is currently unavailable. See, Wikipedia, "Zaman (gazete)", https://tr.wikipedia.org/w/index.php?title=Zaman_(gazete)&oldid=30061154 (accessed October 22, 2023).

[37] Sukuk is popularly known as an Islamic or Sharia-compliant 'Bond' whilst it is an asset-backed trust certificate. In its simplest form, Sukuk is a certificate evidencing ownership of an asset or its usufruct and was developed by Sharia experts for the express purpose of answering the financial world's demand for a Sharia-compliant debt instrument. A more accurate translation of the Arabic word would be an "Islamic investment certificate."

become an alternative to the interest. They underlined that the sukuk system could help the automotive sector and support investments in the infrastructure area. The Islamic sukuk system is similar to the bonds of the capitalist system. But in sukuk, money is invested in concrete projects, and the profit share is distributed to clients instead of interest earned.[38]

Of course, Islamic finance does not consist only of sukuk. Then, it is useful to look closely and in detail at what Islamic finance, which is proposed by the Vatican, suggests. While the traditional finance and banking system takes the interest as an anchor, the Islamic system of finance and banking is based on the *'anchor of interest ban.*[39] Islamic finance and banking rejects interest policy as an instrument for any business or finance activity. It is based on the non-interest substitutions that are profit, rental, commission, and wage. These are regarded as legitimate earnings of trade, its kinds, leasing, joint venture and partnership, and other lawful and real productive economic activities.

h. Islamic Perspective of 'Interest'

The definition of interest in Islamic finance is also quite broad. From the Islamic perspective, interest is a value that is transferred from one party to another in any transaction without any matching value given back, resulting in an unequal distribution of income between individuals or groups. It takes place not only in loans but also in the sales of goods for each other or in the

Accounting and Auditing Organization for Islamic Financial Institutions (AAOIFI) Standard 17 defines Investment Sukuk as being: "Certificates of equal value representing after closing subscription, receipt of the value of the certificates and putting it to use as planned, common title to shares and rights in tangible assets, usufructs, and services, or equity of a given project or equity of a special investment activity". Dar Al Istithmar, "Sukuk-An Introduction to the Underlying Principles and Structure", (June 2006): 5,7. https://www.sukuk.com/wp-content/uploads/2014/03/Sukuk-Structures.pdf, October 20, 2023).

See, Wikipedia contributors, "Sukuk," Wikipedia, The Free Encyclopedia, https://en.wikipedia.org/w/index.php?title=Sukuk&oldid=1172631303 (accessed October 10, 2023).

[38] "Vatican Paper Supports Islamic Finance. France Wants Its Share of Sharia Banking", available at http://www.brusselsjournal.com/node/3819, May 20, 2009; "Vatican Backs Islamic Finance". http://www. newhorizon-islamicbanking.com/index.cfm?section=news &action=view&id=10751, May 20, 2009; "Vatican Offers Islamic Finance System to Western Banks", March 6, 2009, available at http://www. worldbulletin.net/news_detail.php?id=37814, May 20, 2009.

[39] İrfan Kalaycı, "Participation Banking: How is It an Alternative in Financial Sector?", *International Journal of Management Economics and Business* 9, no. 19 (2013): 67, https://dergipark.org.tr/tr/download/article-file/1142639, October 10, 2023.

exchanges[40] of currencies as well. The saying of the prophet Muhammed called "The Hadith of Six Things" concisely expresses 72 sales/exchanges that bear interest out of 120 transactions included in that hadith.[41]

At first glance, the Prophet Muhammad's words seem to be very simple and it may be possible to think that these words are told to regulate the small market of his own time. However, when this saying is examined closely, it is seen that it looks more at today than at that day and offers suggestions even for global financial crises. The hadith of the Prophet Muhammad is as follows:

> *Gold is to be paid for by gold, silver by silver, wheat by wheat, barley by barley, dates by dates, and salt by salt, like for like and equal for equal, payment to be made hand to hand. If these classes differ, then sell as you wish if payment is made hand to hand.*[42]

In this hadith, gold and silver represent all currencies and all financial instruments, and four other commodities stand for all *fungible (standard) goods.*[43]

---

[40] The concept of *'exchange'*, which is used in every sentence where we discuss the subject of *'interest'*, means the *'exchange of two items for each other', a sale,* not the *'foreign exchange'*.

[41] Some call this hadith 'the Hadith of Six Commodities'. We object to this naming because two of the six items in the hadith are gold and silver, representing money. Accepting money as a commodity is fundamentally contrary to the Islamic understanding of interest.

[42] Muslim b. Al-Hajjaj al-Qushayri (D. 261/875), *Translation of Sahih Muslim, Kitab Al-Buyu' (The Book of Transactions), Book 10, Number 3853,* https://www.iium.edu.my/deed/hadith/muslim/010_smt.html, *October 9, 2023.*

[43] In the Islamic approach, the separation between *fungible* and *non-fungible goods* is crucially important in terms of interest to occur or not.

Fungible (standard) goods are goods of the same type that are similar in the market, where there is no separation between their parts and units, or this difference is neglectable. They are exactly interchangeable and each unit of their parts is indistinguishable from any other part. Fungible goods are normally valued by weight, volume measure, or number. Gold, silver, iron, copper, company shares, bonds, other precious metals, and currencies; liquid products such as petroleum, oil, olives, and grains; pots, plates, spoons, books, and the like; eggs, melons of the same size, and watermelons are examples. Today, goods produced in the same series in factories or with the same qualities are considered fungible goods. Therefore, the same brand and model of television, computer, refrigerator, etc. technological products are included in the fungible goods.

Non-fungible (non-standard) goods are things that are not similar in the market or that are similar but have significant differences between them and cannot normally be found similar. Real estate assets such as houses, flats -even if in the same apartment-, workplaces, and land; horses, camels, sheep, and similar live animals, precious stones, manuscripts,

This hadith constitutes the backbone of a commercial life cleared of interest and contains the sound fundamentals of finance, money, and banking transactions. In this hadith, instead of listing 72 interest-bearing transactions one by one, Prophet Muhammad gave a few formulas of the entire interest-free system and avoided so many repetitions.

With this concise saying, Prophet Muhammad expresses exactly 120 kinds of exchanges, which are,

(1) the exchange of a commodity for another commodity or
(2) a currency for another currency
(3) on credit or the spot, and
(4) for matching or different quantities.

According to this Prophetic saying, 72 kinds of sales/exchanges out of these 120 bear a forbidden "interest."[44] This hadith is so comprehensive that it even includes the *'Interest of Debt'* that occurs on loans in addition to the *'Interest of Exchange'*.

From the Islamic perspective, being exactly interchangeable with riba or usury, interest is an actual or potential excess or surplus without a returning equivalent. Based on this hadith, it can be defined as follows:

---

antique items, etc. are non-fungible goods. Fungible goods that have fallen into secondhand also become non-fungible. For example, a car that has never been used and a new edition book is considered fungible while the ones that have been used are considered non-fungible. *All the things that are subject to interest are fungible. Non-fungible goods are rarely subject to interest when the exchange is on credit.* For example, gold is fungible because its value does not depend on any specific form, whether of coins, lingots, or other states. However, a unique item such as a gold statue by a famous artist would not be considered fungible. In short, a thing is fungible when all equivalent amounts of that thing are interchangeable. Fungible tokens can be exchanged or replaced; for example, a $100 bill (note) can easily be exchanged for twenty $5 bills (notes). In contrast, non-fungible tokens cannot be exchanged in the same manner. See, Hasan Hacak, "Mislî", *TDV İslâm Ansiklopedisi,* https://Islamansiklopedisi.org.tr/Misli (16.10.2023); Beşir Gözübenli, "Kiyemî", *TDV İslâm Ansiklopedisi,* https://Islamansiklopedisi.org.tr/Kiyemi (16.10.2023); Wikipedia, "Fungibility", The Free Encyclopedia, https://en.wikipedia.org/w/index.php?title=Fungibility&oldid=1177280204 (accessed October 12, 2023).

[44] İsmail Özsoy, "An Islamic Suggestion of Solution to the Financial Crises", *Procedia Economics and Finance* 38, (2016): 174-184, http://www.sciencedirect.com/science/article/pii/S2212567116301885 or https://doi.org/10.1016/S2212-5671(16)30188-5, 23 October 2023. *Please, see the Attachment at the end of the chapter (see, p. 407) showing all these 120 exchanges, and the cases of interest and non-interest thereof.*

> *Interest is a value that is transferred from one party to another without a matching value given back. It occurs not only in loans—whatever the interest rate is—but also in the exchanges of commodities and currencies. It is sometimes 'unearned income' in a zero-sum or minus-sum game and sometimes 'unequally distributed income' in a positive-sum game. So, interest is, in any case, an injustice done to one of the two parties in loans or exchange transactions.*

Thus, there are two kinds of interest: (1) Interest of Debt or loan, and (2) Interest of Exchange.

i. Interest of Debt or Loan (Riba al-Dain)

Interest of debt or loan appears in loans as a percentage or as a fixed payment added to the principal. It is the most widespread kind of interest. The interest of debt unavoidably causes an injustice either to the borrower or to the lender since it is based on an uncertain outcome.

When a borrower does not earn enough to pay the fixed rate, interest of debt causes harm to the borrower; then, it can be described as an 'unearned income.' When a borrower earns unexpectedly a high income thanks to the loan, interest on debt causes harm this time to the lender; then, that earning turns into 'unequally distributed income' between lender and borrower.

Hence, there is no difference between an interest rate of 1% and an interest rate of 100% regarding the unfairness it causes. This is because any high interest rate may be an injustice to the borrower in unfavourable economic conditions, and any low rate may be an injustice to the lenders in favourable ones. However, the low rate is mostly favoured.

j. Interest of Exchange (Riba al-Bay')

As for the interest of exchange, it occurs on the exchange of goods for goods and the exchange of currencies for currencies on the spot or credit. The interest of exchange is also divided into two kinds; one is called *Interest of Surplus (Riba al-Fadl)*, which appears as a quantitative surplus in one of the exchanged goods of the same kind -as in the case when a corn of two measures is exchanged for another corn of three measures, even if it is due to the difference of quality. The interest of exchange occurs only on fungible goods.

The other is called *Interest of Delay or Deferral (Riba al-Nasia)*, which appears in exchanges as a quantitative or potential surplus (value differentiation) when the delivery of one of the things (goods or currencies) exchanged is delayed, as in the case when a ton of iron is sold for the same amount of iron on a deferral/credit basis; let alone for a larger amount of delayed/credit iron. Or, when €100 is sold/exchanged for $110 on credit is also the interest of delay.

Here, interest arises as a *potential value differentiation* between two goods - iron for iron- or two currencies -dollar for euro- due to the delayed delivery of one of the items. Time, or term, is pointed to by Prophet Muhammad as a primary reason for the 'value differentiation' between the present and future goods or currencies that are exchanged; hence, it causes a potential excess in one of the items when compared to the other. Since nobody knows in advance for whom and how much this potential surplus proves to be realized, Islam prohibited all delayed sales or futures.

Thus, Islam does not accept basing the legitimacy of interest on the time preference theory as suggested by the economists of the Austrian School.[45] Because there is no guarantee that present goods are more valuable than future goods, nor is it possible to determine the amount of this value difference even if today's goods are more valuable than future goods.

There is only one permissible exception to on-credit-exchanges: It is the exchange of 'goods for money' or 'money for goods', just as we buy some goods on credit for delayed monetary payment or sometimes, we pay money today and the delivery of goods is made at a future date. This permission meets the needs of people without ready purchasing power for pressing daily needs. Otherwise, life would be very difficult for those who do not have the purchasing power to pay in cash for urgent needs.

k. Financial Sector Versus Real Sector

Money and other financial instruments are of no use on their own for human life. Their circulation in the market, disconnected from the goods, does not produce any value. For example, 100 dollars is 100 dollars in everyone's possession and everywhere. The circulation of this money from one hand to another without purchasing any goods contributes nothing to the economy.

On the other hand, if there were no money and financial instruments but there were goods needed everywhere, life would normally continue. The basic function of money is to facilitate the exchange of goods by serving as a measure and that of other financial instruments is to canalize savings to the economy.

For this reason, Prophet Muhammad never allowed forward transactions of money and financial instruments disconnected from the real market, only

---

[45] Wikipedia, "Time Preference", The Free Encyclopedia, https://en.wikipedia.org/w/index.php?title=Time_preference&oldid=1178876707 (accessed October 12, 2023).

permitting spot exchanges on the condition that their transactions were made at their nominal values.

Thus, the Hadith of Six Things suggests that *all the futures, such as forward rate agreements and exchanges of financial derivatives with each other without corresponding to any real value increase in the underlying real assets on which derivatives are based, are also included in interest.* For example, selling €100 for a delayed $110 includes interest since there may be a difference between the current and future exchange rates of the two currencies, resulting in a transfer of value not derived from the production of any good or service from one party to another, making it a zero-sum game.

Another example is the exchange of a certain amount of oil for a certain amount of cotton on credit. Similarly, the exchange of *loan-for-loan* with different quantities or with different *interest rates* gives way to interest as with the derivatives so widespread in developed countries, in the US particularly. The exception to this is *'swap'* wherein two loans of the same quantity and the same term are exchanged. Or, two in-kind (non-fungible) debts can be settled at the exchange rate of the transaction day.[46]

Shortly, *interest is a measurable or noticeable imbalance or disproportionate in exchanges or loans for one party to the loss of the other.* With this nature, interest causes economic disparities between individuals, factors of production, and even nations, resulting in considerable social and economic problems. These imbalances appear as bubbles and crises eventually in the financial markets when they cannot be sustained.

Though not expressed so far so clearly, interest-based transactions are the most effectual reasons for the economic bubbles[47] and their consequences in the form of crises. This is a reason for interest to be banned by all religions and for its being criticized by most of the philosophers and scholars throughout history.

As seen, based on the Hadith of Six Things, Prophet Muhammad introduced to mankind the 'Interest of Exchange' that occurs in all on-credit exchanges of goods for goods and currencies for currencies, besides the interest of debt or loan known to all. The interest of exchange seems to make the Islamic approach to interest original and distinctive.

---

[46] See, Footnote no. 43, where *fungible* and *non-fungible goods* are defined.

[47] Wikipedia, "Economic Bubble", The Free Encyclopedia, https://en.wikipedia.org/w/index.php?title=Economic_bubble&oldid=1235665734 (accessed October 12, 2023).

I. The 2008 Financial Crisis from the Islamic View

A more concrete example of the burst of the financial bubble that resulted in the 2008 financial crisis is the sale of financial certificates with different *interest rates* and different terms for each other. For example, the sale of a financial certificate of $100—with a 5 percent rate of interest and for one year period—in return for another certificate of $100—but this time with a 10 per cent rate of interest and for two years—bears a value transfer from one party to another by the size of the interest rate. Thus, *a financial bubble begins to arise if the nominal increase in the value of the financial certificate due to interest payment is not balanced with a real value increase in the underlying assets, such as houses.*[48]

If the nominal value of mortgage-related securities contained in a package is sold at a higher price in a new package without adding new securities to this package, this increase is nothing more than a bubble if it does not correspond to an increase in the market value of the underlying asset. This was what happened in the 2008 crisis, as *mortgage-related securities were packaged, repackaged, and sold to investors* around the world. When the bubble burst, hundreds of billions of dollars in losses in mortgages and mortgage-related securities shook markets as well as financial institutions.[49]

There are two stages in a mortgage transaction. The first one is a trade which is the sale of a house to a client. The second and consequent stages are exactly interest-bearing transactions and bubble-building processes.

As a basic real economic activity, *trade is the process of purchase and sale that increases the 'location value'" or 'ownership value'" of a commodity to make a profit.* When you buy a commodity from its producer and sell it to consumers it is the increasing of the ownership value. When you buy an orange for TL 1 per kilo in Antalya and sell it for TL 1.5 in Istanbul it is the increasing of the location value because it is more valuable in Istanbul.

So, trade is "the increasing of the time value of a commodity" when a house is bought by the bank on the spot, say for $100,000, and it is sold on credit to a client, say for $110,000, who otherwise could only obtain it months or years later with his regular savings. Thanks to this transaction, the client begins to

---

[48] Houses have been the most frequently used as underlying assets upon which the financial certificates or derivatives are based in the US and other countries. Underlying asset is an investment term that refers to an asset a financial derivative is based on. Real underlying assets include real estate and commodities that are of direct use. Financial underlying assets are not of any direct use. Examples include stocks, bonds, interest rates, market indexes, and currencies.

[49] The Financial Crisis Inquiry Commission, *The Financial Crisis Inquiry Report, XVI.*, 2010.

benefit from the house immediately. The client's additional payment, which makes up bank profits, say 10 percent, is in return for the real increase in the time value of the home, and the client benefits from the time value of the home due to being able to utilize it right away thanks to the bank's trade.

But when receivables – in our example, the receivable of $110,000 – are not kept in the safe of the bank, and when they are sold to a mortgage firm at a discount, there begins the process of interest and bubble building because mortgage firms sell these receivables in derivatives markets at higher prices for longer terms and interest rates by slicing them into small pieces as was in the Financial Crisis of 2008.

The interest and ballooning process operates in the most obvious and risky way on financial assets-based derivatives because, while that process begins with the sale of mortgage receivables in real-assets-based derivatives, it begins at the first stage in financial-assets-based derivatives. From the mortgage originator to the loan servicer to the mortgage-backed security issuer to the CDO issuer, to the CDS protection seller, to the credit rating agencies, and to the holders of all those securities, no institution put an end to that process.[50]

Thus, to prevent the process of creating financial bubbles, it is necessary:

- to avoid all delayed sales of the financial instruments
- and keep them in the vaults of the bank until they are paid by the clients,[51] If financial instruments of the same kind but with different

[50] Martin N. Baily, Robert E. Litan, Matthew S. Johnson, *The Origins of the Financial Crisis*, The Initiative on Business and Public Policy, (November 2008), 8, https://www.brookings.edu/wp-content/uploads/2016/06/11_origins_crisis_baily_litan.pdf, October 21, 2023.

[51] As in Turkiye during the 2008 financial crisis, which left the country very far from the damage of the crisis. Yet Turkey was subjected to downgrading first by Standard and Poor's and Moody's for not having a local derivatives market before the crisis, but later being admired for being the least affected by the crisis.

This was the case also in the US before 1968. Before 1968 Fannie Mae generally held the mortgages it purchased, profiting from the difference—or spread—between its cost of funds and the interest paid on these mortgages. The 1968 and 1970 laws gave the option of securitization. A lender would assemble a pool of mortgages and issue securities backed by the mortgage pool. Those securities would be sold to investors, with Ginnie Mae (officially, the Government National Mortgage Association) guaranteeing timely payment of principal and interest. Ginnie charged a fee to issuers for this guarantee. In 1971 Freddie got into the business of buying mortgages, pooling them, and then selling mortgage-backed securities. Freddie collected fees from lenders to guarantee timely payment of principal and interest (The Financial Crisis Inquiry Commission, *The Financial Crisis Inquiry Report*, (January 2011)), 39, https://www.govinfo.gov/content/pkg/GPO-FCIC/pdf/GPO-FCIC.pdf, October 21, 2023.

interest rates and times are to be exchanged for each other, the transaction must be done at face value and on the spot.

- Different kinds of financial instruments can be exchanged for each other at any price if the transaction is done on the spot. That applies to the sale of financial instruments for money provided it is done on the spot, as in the exchange of foreign currencies for each other, or the sale of stocks for currencies on the spot.

These are suggestions that can be derived from the hadiths of the Prophet to protect against financial crises.

m. Interest-Free Banking versus Traditional Banking

While loans from traditional banks do not necessarily enter the real economy, each monetary or financial transaction in the Islamic finance and banking system inevitably corresponds to a real economic activity, In Islamic economics, interest income is substituted with profit, rental, commission, and wage, all of which are regarded as legitimate earnings of trade, its kinds, joint venture and partnerships, leasing, and other lawful and real economic activities. What makes profit legitimate is that it accrues to monetary capital in real economic activity on the condition that it contributes to national revenue. As for rental, it accrues to durable capital as an initially determined income since the productivity of capital goods is direct and certain. Thus, rental is a fixed income that is based on certain and fixed productivity. In profit and rental, there is a balance between income and productivity, hence a balance between income received and contribution to national revenue.

On the other hand, interest accrues on loanable funds even when there is no contribution to national revenue thereby; and when there is a contribution it is not necessarily as much as is earned. It is almost impossible to balance between interest income and the productivity of monetary capital. This is because interest is an initially fixed income based on uncertainties, eventually resulting in unequal distribution of income and macroeconomic instabilities. While there is no "give and take" balance in interest income, there is an established "give and take" balance in the general sense of profit and rental, including wage and commission.

The alternatives to interest-bearing transactions are many kinds of trade, partnership, and leasing, each yielding income of profit or rental fee instead of interest. These are mainly, mudaraba, musharaka, murabaha, bai muajjal (deferred sale), salam, istisna' and ijara (leasing).

Islamic finance mainly aims to significantly increase the share of equity in enterprises and profit and loss sharing in projects and initiatives through mudaraba and musharaka financing methods. However, greater reliance on equity does not necessarily mean that debt financing is ruled out. Islamic finance requires the creation of debt through the sale or lease of real assets through its sales- and lease-based modes of financing mentioned above. The purpose is to enable an individual or firm to buy urgently needed real goods and services in conformity with his ability to make the payment later. Islam has, however, laid down certain conditions that would help prevent excessive expansion of debt. Some of these are: 1) The asset that is being sold or leased must be real, and not imaginary/virtual or notional; 2) The seller must own and possess the goods being sold or leased; 3) The transaction must be a genuine trade transaction with full intention of giving and taking delivery; and 4) The debt cannot be sold and thus the risk associate with it cannot be transferred to someone else. It must be borne by the creditor himself.[52] These basic principles no doubt need a detailed explanation, not possible for the time being due to lack of space, since it has already exceeded its limits.

Conclusion and Suggestions

Though it is inherently the primary reason for business cycles, *interest rates* have not been criticized by mainstream economics since it is taken for granted although it is a problematic policy tool. However, the truth is clear that the global financial system is quite volatile due to its being dependent on mostly questionable *interest rates* and interest-based transactions. Since mankind can't foresee the future, any interest rate that is fixed according to the current supply and demand conditions should not be expected to be valid in the coming days since these days will have their own supply and demand conditions that determine another interest rate, which may be highly different than the already fixed one, thus arising a deviation between the two, and causing the shakes. The succession of these deviations and shakes all in micro and macro levels is one of the reasons for financial instabilities and distress.

Restructuring and selling all kinds of derivative instruments with new maturities and new *interest rates* is called *'interest of exchange'* in Islamic finance and is the most important reason for the ballooning process. If an increase in the sum of the nominal value of these financial instruments as a result of these purchases and sales does not correspond to an increase in the market value of the underlying asset, i.e., the house, this difference between the nominal value and the real value is nothing but a bubble. We should note that the equivalent of the term interest in Islamic literature is *'riba',* which means

---

[52] Chapra, "The Global Financial Crisis".

'growth' and *'bubble'*. Since all financial transactions, including futures trading and currency futures, are carried out based on interest rates, these transactions cause a series of deviations, leading to a bubble that grows over time.

We can surely answer "Yes" to the question "Is the interest policy the basic responsible for the 2008 global financial crisis?" if we look at the matter from the Islamic perspective since the Islamic perspective has a very precise definition of interest and its kinds, particularly the kind of interest of exchange. While the *interest of debt* is one of the main reasons for unequal income sharing between the lender and the borrower, the *interest of exchange* is a primary reason for ballooning in the finance sector. This is because not only interest but also principal is paid by the borrower even though he cannot earn enough to pay for them in the case of interest of the loan and because interest is paid on derivative instruments even though the underlying asset on which these instruments are based does not gain real value in the case of interest of exchange. Consequently, since interest, whatever its kind is, is a process of a value or income transfer from one party to another without any comparable matching, all interest-bearing transactions result in financial and economic imbalances between individuals, social groups, factors of production as well as nations in the process of lending or exchanges. For instance, trillions of US dollars changed hands in the Financial Crisis of 2008 in the US.[53] While some won, others lost, ending with a zero-sum game.[54]

These imbalances appear eventually as economic and social shocks, bubbles, and crises in the financial markets when they cannot be sustained.

To prevent the process of creating financial bubbles, it is necessary to take into consideration the following suggestions, which are derived from the Hadith of Six Things of Prophet Muhammad:

1. *avoiding all delayed sale/trade/exchange of the financial instruments*
2. *and keeping them in the vaults of the bank until they are paid by the clients,*

---

[53] Deborah Lucas and Laurence B. Siegel, "Measuring The Cost of Bailouts", in *Ten Years After-Reflections on The Global Financial Crisis,* Laurence B. Siegel and Luis Garcia-Feijóo, (CFA Institute Research Foundation, May 24 2019): 14, https://rpc.cfainstitute.org/-/media/documents/article/rf-brief/10-years-after-global-financial-crisis.pdf, October 11, 2023.

[54] İrfan Kalaycı, "Finansal Kriz Konjonktürü (2007–2009) ve Küresel Ticaretin Anatomisi (Financial Crisis Conjuncture (2007-2009) and Anatomy of Global Trade)", *Avrasya Etüdleri* 41/1, (2012-1): 152, https://dergipark.org.tr/tr/download/article-file/421976, October 11, 2023.

3. *conducting the transactions at face value and on the spot, if financial instruments of the same kind but with different interest rates and terms are to be exchanged for each other*
4. *exchanging different kinds of financial instruments for each other at any market price if the transaction is done on the spot. That applies to the sale of financial instruments for money provided it is done on the spot, as in the exchange of foreign currencies for each other, or the sale of stocks for currencies on the spot.*

The crisis-preventive nature of interest-free modes of finance contributes to economic stability and common welfare. Western communities and Muslim societies can collaborate for world peace and the common good, as the roots of cooperation trace back to the shared origins of Jewish, Christian, and Islamic traditions—all of which prohibit interest policies. The Vatican played a historic role by suggesting the Islamic finance and banking system to the present Western financial world. A better future, characterized by peace and socio-economic well-being for all humanity, awaits if Western economists and finance authorities do not wait for a second call from the Vatican to explore and embrace proactively Islamic finance and banking.

Bibliography

Amin, Samir. "Economic, Social and Political Distortions in the Modern World". 1996. http://www.ismea.org/I NESDEV/AMIN.eng.html, May 20, 2009.

Baily, Martin N., Robert E. Litan and Matthew S Johnson. "The Origins of the Financial Crisis". *The Initiative on Business and Public Policy,* (November 2008). https://www.brookings.edu/wp-content/uploads/2016/06/11_origins_crisis_baily_litan.pdf, October 21, 2023.

Baker, Dean. "The Run-up in Home Prices: Is It Real or Is It Another Bubble?". 2002. http://www.cepr.net/documents/publications/housing_2002_08.pdf, 12 May 2009.

Chapra, M. Umer. "The Global Financial Crisis: Can Islamic Finance Help Minimize the Severity and Frequency of Such a Crisis in the Future?" Paper presented at the *Forum on the Global Financial Crisis, Islamic Development Bank,* October 25, 2008. https://www.researchgate.net/publication/237255008_The_Global_Financial_Crisis_Can_Islamic_Finance_Help_Minimize_the_Severity_and_Frequency_of_Such_A_Crisis_in_the_Future, October 19 2023.

Corporate Finance Institute Team. "What is the Yield Curve?". https://corporatefinanceinstitute.com/resources/fixed-income/yield-curve, accessed October 9, 2023.

Dar Al Istithmar. June 2006. "Sukuk-An Introduction to the Underlying Principles and Structure", https://www.sukuk.com/wp-content/uploads/2014/03/Sukuk-Structures.pdf, October 20, 2023.

Dore, R. *Stock Market Capitalism: Welfare Capitalism: Japan and Germany vs. the Anglo-Saxons.* Oxford: Oxford University Press, 2000. ISBN 0-19-924061-2.

The Financial Crisis Inquiry Commission. *The Financial Crisis Inquiry Report.* Official Government Edition, January 2011, https://www.govinfo.gov/content/pkg/GPO-FCIC/pdf/GPO-FCIC.pdf, October 21, 2023.

Foster, John Bellamy. "The Financialization of Capital and the Crisis". April 2008. http://www.monthlyreview .org/080401foster.php, accessed 16 May 2009.

Fratianni, M. and F. Marchionne. "The Role of Banks in the Subprime Financial Crisis", 2009, 1-37, http://papers.ssrn.com/sol3/papers.cfm?abstract_id=1383473; https://papers.ssrn.com/sol3/papers.cfm?abstract_id=1383473

Gözübenli, Beşir. "Kiyemî", *TDV İslâm Ansiklopedisi.* https://Islamansiklopedisi.Org.Tr/Kiyemi (16.10.2023).

Gulf One Investment Bank Research Bulletin. vol.2, no.1, January 2009.

Hacak, Hasan. "Mislî", *TDV İslâm Ansiklopedisi.* https://Islamansiklopedisi.Org.Tr/Misli (16.10.2023).

Iwai, Katsuhito "Global Financial Crisis Shows Inherent Instability of Capitalism," December 08, 2008. http://www.tokyofoundation.org/en/articles/2008/global-financial-crisis-shows-inherent-instability-of-capitalism, May 20, 2009.

Kalaycı, İrfan. "Finansal Enfeksiyon ve "Aşı" Kuramı: Bir Genel Kriz Eleştirisi (Financial Infection and "Vaccine" Theory: A General Critique of Crisis)". *Maliye Dergisi,* Sayı: 160 (Ocak-Haziran 2011): 28-56. https://ms.hmb.gov.tr/uploads/2019/09/002-1.pdf, October 2023.

Kalaycı, İrfan. "Finansal Kriz Konjonktürü (2007–2009) ve Küresel Ticaretin Anatomisi (Financial Crisis Conjuncture (2007-2009) and Anatomy of Global Trade)." *Avrasya Etüdleri* 41/1 (2012-1):145-182, https://dergipark.org.tr/tr/download/article-file/421976, October 11, 2023

Kalaycı, İrfan. "Participation Banking: How is It an Alternative in Financial Sector?". *International Journal of Management Economics and Business* vol. 9, no. 19 (2013): 51-74, https://dergipark.org.tr/tr/download/article-file/1142639, October 10, 2023.

Lemoine Benjamin, "The Politics of Financialization. An Interview with Greta Krippner," *Revue de la Régulation* 2017, https://www.academia.edu/37856151/The_Politics_of_Financialization_An_Interview_with_Greta_Krippner and https://journals.openedition.org/regulation/12637, October 23, 2023.

Lucas, Deborah and Laurence B Siegel. "Measuring The Cost of Bailouts", *in Ten Years After-Reflections on The Global Financial Crisis.* Laurence B. Siegel and Luis Garcia-Feijóo, CFA Institute Research Foundation, May 24, 2019. https://rpc.cfainstitute.org/-/media/documents/article/rf-brief/10-years-after-global-financial-crisis.pdf, October 11, 2023.

Mees, Heleen. "US Monetary Policy and the Saving Glut", 24 Mar 2011. https://cepr.org/voxeu/columns/us-monetary-policy-and-saving-glut, October 22, 2023.

Meyerson, Harold. "Building a Better Capitalism". *The Washington Post,* March 12, 2009. http://www.washington post.com/wp-dyn/content/article/2009/03/11/AR2009031103218.html?wpisrc=news let te r, May 19, 2009.

Muslim b. Al-Hajjaj al-Qushayri. *Translation of Sahih Muslim, Kitab Al-Buyu' (The Book of Transactions) Book 10,* Number 3853. https://www.iium.edu.my/deed/hadith/muslim/010_smt.html, October 9, 2023

Noland, Doug. "Credit Bubble Bulletin: Road to Ruin." *Asia Times Online*, 6 November. http://www.atimes.com/atimes/Global_Economy/IK06Dj01.html, May 14, 2009.

Özsoy, İsmail. "An Islamic Suggestion of Solution to the Financial Crises". *Procedia Economics and Finance* 38 (2016): 174-184. Istanbul Conference of Economics and Finance, ICEF 2015, Istanbul, Turkiye, May 22-23, 2015. http://www.sciencedirect.com/science/article/pii/S2212567116301885, https://doi.org/10.1016/S2212-5671(16)30188-5.

Özsoy, İsmail. "Sovyet Sisteminin Çöküşünden Tarihî ve Evrensel Dersler (Historical and Universal Lessons from Collapse of the Soviet System". *Bilig-Türk Dünyası Sosyal Bilimler Dergisi* 39 (Sep. 2006): 163-194. https://bilig.yesevi.edu.tr/yonetim/icerik/makaleler/2928-published.pdf, also https://bilig.yesevi.edu.tr/shw_artcl-1231.html, October 23, 2023.

Palley, Thomas I. "Financialization: What it is and Why it Matters". in *TUAC Labour/Management Seminar on "Financialisation of the Economy: Regulating Private Equity"*. OECD, November 2007. https://scholarworks. umass.edu/cgi/viewcontent.cgi?article=1124&context=peri_workingpapers, October 23, 2023.

Phillips, Kevin. *American Theocracy: The Peril and Politics of Radical Religion, Oil, and Borrowed Money in the 21st Century.* Viking, 2006.

Qur'an, the Holy. Baqara, II/275, interpreted by Abul Ala Maududi. https://myislam.org/surah-baqarah/ayat-275/, October 7, 2023.

Shiller, R. *Irrational Exuberance.* Princeton, NJ: Princeton University Press, 2006.

Stiglitz, Joseph. "Dealing with Debt: How to Reform the Global Financial System". *Harvard International Review* (Spring 2003): 54- 59.

Sweezy, Paul M. "More (or Less) on Globalization". *Monthly Review* 49, no. 4 (September 1997): 3.

Uslu, Sami. "Küresel Krizin Derin Sebepleri (Deep Causes of the Global Crisis)". 2008. http://www.zaman.com.tr/haber.do?haberno=762286, May 10, 2009.

Vasudevan, Ramaa. "Financialization: A Primer". 2008. http://www.dollarsandsense.org/archives/2008/1108vasudevan.html, 16 May 2009.

"Vatican Backs Islamic Finance". http://www.newhorizon-islamicbanking.com/index.cfm?section=news& action=view&id=10751, May 20, 2009.

"Vatican Offers Islamic Finance System to Western Banks". March 6, 2009. http://www.worldbulletin.net /news_detail.php?id=37814, May 20, 2009.

"Vatican Paper Supports Islamic Finance. France Wants Its Share of Sharia Banking". 2009. http://www. brusselsjournal.com/node/3819, May 20, 2009.

Wikipedia Contributors. "Business Cycle." Wikipedia, The Free Encyclopedia. Accessed October 7, 2023. https://en.wikipedia.org/w/index.php?title=Business_cycle&oldid=1175987738.

Wikipedia Contributors. "Economic Bubble," Wikipedia, *The Free Encyclopedia.* Accessed October 12, 2023. https://en.wikipedia.org/w/index.php?title=Economic_bubble&oldid=1178479351.

Wikipedia Contributors. "Financial Capital," Wikipedia, The Free Encyclopedia. Accessed May 19, 2009. https://en.wikipedia.org/w/index.php?title=Financial_capital&oldid=1177254644.

Wikipedia Contributors. "Financial Crisis of 2007–2009." Wikipedia, The Free Encyclopedia. Accessed May 12, 2009. https://en.wikipedia.org/w/index.php?title=Financial_crisis_of_2007%E2%80%932009&oldid= 289330 105.

Wikipedia Contributors. "Financialization." Wikipedia, The Free Encyclopedia. Accessed October 4, 2023. https://en.wikipedia.org/w/index.php?title=Financialization&oldid=1153448096.

Wikipedia Contributors. "Fungibility." Wikipedia, The Free Encyclopedia. Accessed October 12, 2023. https://en.wikipedia.org/w/index.php?title=Fungibility&oldid=1177280204.

Wikipedia Contributors. "Over-the-counter (finance)." Wikipedia, The Free Encyclopedia. Accessed October 12, 2023. https://en.wikipedia.org/w/index.php?title=Over-the-counter_(finance)&oldid=1170203891.

Wikipedia Contributors. "Sukuk." Wikipedia, The Free Encyclopedia. Accessed October 10, 2023. https://en.wikipedia.org/w/index.php?title=Sukuk&oldid=1172631303.

Wikipedia contributors. "Time preference." Wikipedia, The Free Encyclopedia. Accessed October 12, 2023. https://en.wikipedia.org/w/index.php?title=Time_preference&oldid=1178876707.

APPENDIX

The Scenarios of Interest and Non-Interest in the Exchanges of Currencies and Goods according to the Saying of Prophet Muhammad[55]

Table 13.2 Monetary Category
(All the quantities are hypothetical)

		GOLD for GOLD			
1.	100 gr	for	100 gr	on spot	non-interest
2.	100 gr	for	100 gr	deferred	*nterest of term*
3.	100 gr	for	101gr	on spot	*nterest of surplus*
4.	100 gr	for	101gr	deferred	*nterest of term*
5.	100 gr	for	99 gr	on spot	*nterest of surplus*
6.	100 gr	for	99 gr	deferred	*nterest of term*
		SILVER for SILVER			
7.	100 gr	for	100 gr	on spot	non-interest
8.	100 gr	for	100 gr	deferred	*nterest of term*
9.	100 gr	for	101gr	on spot	*nterest of surplus*
10.	100 gr	for	101gr	deferred	*nterest of term*
11.	100 gr	for	99 gr	on spot	*nterest of surplus*
12.	100 gr	for	99 gr	deferred	*nterest if term*
		GOLD for SILVER			
13.	10 gr	for	500 gr	on spot	non-interest
14.	10 gr	for	500 gr	deferred	*nterest of term*
15.	10 gr	for	550 gr	on spot	*non-interest*
16.	10 gr	for	550 gr	deferred	*nterest of term*
17.	10 gr	for	450 gr	on spot	*non-interest*
18.	10 gr	for	450 gr	deferred	*nterest of term*
		SILVER for GOLD			
19.	500 gr	for	10 gr	on spot	non-interest
20.	500 gr	for	10 gr	deferred	*nterest of term*
21.	500 gr	for	11 gr	on spot	non-interest
22.	500 gr	for	11 gr	deferred	*nterestof term*
23.	500 gr	for	9 gr	on spot	non-interest
24.	500 gr	for	9 gr	deferred	*nterest of term*

[55] To understand what these tables say, see the topic '*Hadith of Six Things*', dealt with under the title "*Islamic Perspective of "Interest*" on page 390 and onwards of this chapter.

Table 13.3 Category of Goods

			WHEAT for WHEAT		
25.	100 kg	for	100 kg	on spot	non-interest
26.	100 kg	for	100 kg	deferred	*nterest of term*
27.	100 kg	for	101 kg	on spot	*nterest of surplus*
28.	100 kg	for	101 kg	deferred	*nterest of term*
29.	100 kg	for	99 kg	on spot	*nterest of surplus*
30.	10 kg	for	99kg	deferred	*nterest of term*
			BARLEY for BARLEY		
31.	100 kg	for	100 kg	on spot	non-interest
32.	100 kg	for	100 kg	deferred	*nterest of term*
33.	100 kg	for	101 kg	on spot	*nterest of surplus*
34.	100 kg	for	101 kg	deferred	*nterest of term*
35.	100 kg	for	99 kg	on spot	*nterest of surplus*
36.	100 kg	for	99 kg	deferred	*nterest of term*
			DATES for DATES		
37.	100 kg	for	100 kg	on spot	non-interest
38.	100 kg	for	100 kg	deferred	*nterest of term*
39.	100 kg	for	101 kg	on spot	*nterest of surplus*
40.	100 kg	for	101 kg	deferred	*nterest of term*
41.	100 kg	for	99 kg	on spot	*nterest of surplus*
42.	10 kg	for	99 kg	deferred	*nterest of term*
			SALT for SALT		
43.	100 kg	for	100 kg	on spot	non-interest
44.	100 kg	for	100 kg	deferred	*nterest of term*
45.	100 kg	for	101 kg	on spot	*nterestof surplus*
46.	100 kg	for	101 kg	deferred	*nterest of term*
47.	100 kg	for	99 kg	on spot	*nterest of surplus*
48.	100 kg	for	99 kg	deferred	*nterest of term*
			WHEAT for BARLEY		
49.	100 kg	for	100 kg	on spot	non-interest
50.	100 kg	for	100 kg	deferred	*nterest of term*
51.	100 kg	for	101 kg	on spot	non-interest
52.	100 kg	for	101 kg	deferred	*nterest of term*
53.	100 kg	for	99 kg	on spot	non-interest
54.	100 kg	for	99 kg	deferred	*nterest of term*
			WHEAT for DATES		
55.	100 kg	for	100 kg	on spot	non-interest
56.	100 kg	for	100 kg	deferred	*nterest of term*
57.	100 kg	for	101 kg	on spot	non-interest
58.	100 kg	for	101 kg	deferred	*nterest of term*
59.	100 kg	for	99 kg	on spot	non-interest
60.	100 kg	for	99 kg	deferred	*nterest of term*
			WHEAT for SALT		
61.	100 kg	for	100 kg	on spot	non-interest
62.	100 kg	for	100 kg	deferred	*nterest of term*

63.	100 kg	for	101 kg	on spot	non-interest
64.	100 kg	for	101 kg	deferred	*nterest of term*
65.	100 kg	for	99 kg	on spot	non-interest
66.	100 kg	for	99 kg	deferred	*nterest of term*
			BARLEY for WHEAT		
67.	100 kg	for	100 kg	on spot	non-interest
68.	100 kg	for	100 kg	deferred	*nterest of term*
69.	100 kg	for	101 kg	on spot	non-interest
70.	100 kg	for	101 kg	deferred	*nterest of term*
71.	100 kg	for	99 kg	on spot	non-interest
72.	100 kg	for	99 kg	deferred	*nterest of term*
			BARLEY for DATES		
73.	100 kg	for	100 kg	on spot	non-interest
74.	100 kg	for	100 kg	deferred	*nterest of term*
75.	100 kg	for	101 kg	on spot	non-interest
76.	100 kg	for	101 kg	deferred	*nterest of term*
77.	100 kg	for	99 kg	on spot	non-interest
78.	100 kg	for	99 kg	deferred	*nterest of term*
			BARLEY for SALT		
79.	100 kg	for	100 kg	on spot	non-interest
80.	100 kg	for	100 kg	deferred	*nterest of term*
81.	100 kg	for	101 kg	on spot	non-interest
82.	100 kg	for	101 kg	deferred	*nterest of term*
83.	100 kg	for	99 kg	on spot	non-interest
84.	100 kg	for	99 kg	deferred	*nterest of term*
			DATES for WHEAT		
85.	100 kg	for	100 kg	on spot	non-interest
86.	100 kg	for	100 kg	deferred	*nterest of term*
87.	100 kg	for	101 kg	on spot	non-interest
88.	100 kg	for	101 kg	deferred	*nterest of term*
89.	100 kg	for	99 kg	on spot	non-interest
90.	100 kg	for	99 kg	deferred	*nterest of term*
			DATES for BARLEY		
91.	100 kg	for	100 kg	on spot	non-interest
92.	100 kg	for	100 kg	deferred	*nterest of term*
93.	100 kg	for	101 kg	on spot	non-interest
94.	100 kg	for	101 kg	deferred	*nterest of term*
95.	100 kg	for	99 kg	on spot	non-interest
96.	100 kg	for	99 kg	deferred	*nterest of term*
			DATES for SALT		
97.	100 kg	for	100 kg	on spot	non-interest
98.	100 kg	for	100 kg	deferred	*nterest of term*
99.	100 kg	for	101 kg	on spot	non-interest
100.	100 kg	for	101 kg	deferred	*nterest of term*
101.	100 kg	for	99 kg	on spot	non-interest
102.	100 kg	for	99 kg	deferred	*nterest of term*

			SALT for WHEAT		
103.	100 kg	for	100 kg	on spot	non-interest
104.	100 kg	for	100 kg	deferred	*nterest of term*
105.	100 kg	for	101 kg	on spot	non-interest
106.	100 kg	for	101 kg	deferred	*nterest of term*
107.	100 kg	for	99 kg	on spot	non-interest
108.	100 kg	for	99 kg	deferred	*nterest of term*
			SALT for DATES		
109.	100 kg	for	100 kg	on spot	non-interest
110.	100 kg	for	100 kg	deferred	*nterest of term*
111.	100 kg	for	101 kg	on spot	non-interest
112.	100 kg	for	101 kg	deferred	*nterest of term*
113.	100 kg	for	99 kg	on spot	non-interest
114.	100 kg	for	99 kg	deferred	*nterest of term*
			SALT for BARLEY		
115.	100 kg	for	100 kg	on spot	non-interest
116.	100 kg	for	100 kg	deferred	*nterest of term*
117.	100 kg	for	101 kg	on spot	non-interest
118.	100 kg	for	101 kg	deferred	*nterest of term*
119.	100 kg	for	99 kg	on spot	non-interest
120.	100 kg	for	99 kg	deferred	*nterest of term*

Total Transactions: 120=Transactions bearing interest 72 + Non-interest 48

Table 13.4 Monetary Category in Today's Currencies

TURKISH LIRA for TURKISH LIRA				
100 TL	for	100 TL	on spot	non-interest
100 TL	for	100 TL	deferred	*nterest of term*
100 TL	for	101 TL	on spot	*nterest of surplus*
100 TL	for	101 TL	deferred	*nterest of term*
100 TL	for	99 TL	on spot	*nterest of surplus*
100 TL	for	99 TL	deferred	*nterest of term*
US DOLLAR for US DOLLAR				
100 $	for	100 $	on spot	non-interest
100 $	for	100 $	deferred	*nterest of term*
100 $	for	101 $	on spot	*nterest of surplus*
100 $	for	101 $	deferred	*nterest of term*
100 $	for	99 $	on spot	*nterest of surplus*
100 $	for	99 $	deferred	*nterest of term*
EURO for EURO				
100	for	100	on spot	non-interest
100	for	100	deferred	*nterest of term*
100	for	101	on spot	*nterest of surplus*
100	for	101	deferred	*nterest of term*
100	for	99	on spot	*nterest of surplus*
100	for	99	deferred	*nterest of term*
TL for US DOLLAR				
300 TL	for	100 $	on spot	non-interest
300 TL	for	100 $	deferred	*nterest of term*
300 TL	for	101 $	on spot	non-interest
300 TL	for	101 $	deferred	*nterest of term*
300 TL	for	99 $	on spot	non-interest
300 TL	for	99 $	deferred	*nterest of term*
US DOLLAR for EURO				
130 $	for	100	on spot	non-interest
130 $	for	100	deferred	*nterest of term*
130 $	for	101	on spot	non-interest
130 $	for	101	deferred	*nterest of term*
130 $	for	99	on spot	non-interest
130 $	for	99	deferred	*nterest of term*

Table 13.5 "Category of Currencies" for "Category of Goods"

GOLD for WHEAT				
10 gr	for	100 kg	on spot	Non-interest
10 gr	for	100 kg	deferred	Non-interest
10 gr	for	99 kg	on spot	Non-interest
10 gr	for	99 kg	deferred	Non-interest
10 gr	for	101 kg	on spot	Non-interest
10 gr	for	101 kg	deferred	Non-interest
WHEAT for GOLD				
100 kg	for	10 gr	on spot	Non-interest
100 kg	for	10 gr	deferred	Non-interest
100 kg	for	11 gr	on spot	Non-interest
100 kg	for	11 gr	deferred	Non-interest
100 kg	for	9 gr	on spot	Non-interest
100 kg	for	9 gr	deferred	Non-interest

Table 13.6 "Category of Currencies" for "Category of Goods"

SILVER for WHEAT				
500 gr	for	100 kg	on spot	Non-interest
500 gr	for	100 kg	deferred	Non-interest
500 gr	for	99 kg	on spot	Non-interest
500 gr	for	99 kg	deferred	Non-interest
500 gr	for	101 kg	on spot	Non-interest
500 gr	for	101 kg	deferred	Non-interest
WHEAT for SILVER				
100 kg	for	500 gr	on spot	Non-interest
100 kg	for	500 gr	deferred	Non-interest
100 kg	for	550 gr	on spot	Non-interest
100 kg	for	550 gr	deferred	Non-interest
100 kg	for	450 gr	on spot	Non-interest
100 kg	for	450 gr	deferred	Non-interest

Gold for Wheat & Wheat for Gold=12

Gold for Barley & Barley for Gold=12

Gold for Dates & Dates for Gold=12

Gold for Salt & Salt for Gold=12

Silver for Wheat & Wheat for Siver=12

Silver for Barley & Barley for Silver=12

Silver for Dates & Dates for Silver=12

Silver for Salt & Salt for Silver=12

In sum, 96 transactions take place between "the category of currencies" and "the category of goods"

Grand Total=120+96=216

Chapter 14

Intersecting Solutions to the Two Major Crisis of Capitalism: State Capitalism

Mehmet Kaya

Dice University, Diyarbakır, Turkey

Hatice Özkurt Çokgüngör

İstanbul University-Cerrahpaşa, Turkey

Abstract

In its adventure of nearly five hundred years, capitalism has gone through different stages according to the dominant sector in the economic structure and the form of capital. As a matter of fact, the economy in mercantilism, trade and commercial capital, in industrial capitalism, the real sector/capital, and finally in the neo-liberalism-globalization or financial capitalism that has continued since the 1970s, the financial sector and financial capital have been dominant. Although the first name of capitalism has changed, its operation focused on the benefit of capital has been accompanied by the predictions of the (neo) Classical school (market mechanism, etc.) except for extraordinary times (crisis, depression, etc.), especially starting from the first industrial revolution. An interesting aspect of the history of capitalism is that these extraordinary times have often occurred. As a matter of fact, throughout the nineteenth century, there were many crises for almost 8-10 years, the effects of which were mostly limited to that country (England, USA, etc.), but these were described as temporary deviations from the equilibrium state. However, capitalism experienced its deepest and longest crisis (World Depression I) in 1929. Against the economic destruction and systemic risks created by the crisis in the whole world, especially in the USA, every country has embraced the visible and powerful hands of the state instead of the "invisible hand". Thus, in this crisis; The classical school is that the economy is constantly in equilibrium at full employment and so on. The Keynesian school, which criticizes the theses and argues that capitalism can experience such crises but that the intervention of the state is necessary to get rid of it, has brought it to the economic stage. With the effect of this school, the role of the state in the economy increased, and in many countries, an economic model (mixed economic system) operating with the coordination of the market system and the state has also been implemented. This model, during the period it was implemented (1950-1970), not only helped to mitigate crises but also ushered in the golden age of capitalism, marked by significant success in production, employment, and welfare. So much so that even the liberals of the period (J. Schumpeter and M. Friedman) feared that the economic system would evolve into socialism. When we came to the 1970s, what they feared did not happen to them; on the contrary, the simultaneous occurrence of two bad things (inflation and recession, that is, stagflation) in the economy with two big artificial oil crises, and the failure of Keynesian policies to solve the problem caused the Monetarist Theory to take over the stage in the economy. Under the leadership of this theory, capitalism returned to its factory settings with the elimination of the social state and the minimization of its role in the economy, as well as the removal of practices contrary to the free market mechanism. However, capitalism, which lost its reputation with each crisis, needed a fresh image with a new story to excite the market. This new story has become globalization or the neoliberal order. Despite its commercial, technological and production dimensions, globalization has become widespread with financial liberalization. Although it is claimed that the period of 1990-2008, when globalization was effective, was the most spectacular, even its own "golden age", the many crises that developed countries shared cannot be ignored. Especially, as if saying, "the biggest radish/crisis is hidden in the saddlebag/ Atlantic", many segments confess that with the 2008 Global Financial Crisis/Crash, many people confessed that the standards were missed in deregulation-liberalization and securitization of the markets. Has given rise to controversy. Just as the homeowner who was stuck at the door called a locksmith, Keynes was immediately called to duty when the business/markets got stuck in this crisis. However, on the occasion of this crisis, shouldn't the free market advocates have to make a decision about their resentful relations with Keynes and his policies for economic/financial stability? At this point, in terms of the well-being of the neo-liberal order, will the convictions that the state is no longer a saviour but a preventer in crises and that it should be more actively involved in the financial sector, open the door to an "eternal peace" with Keynes?

Keywords: Two crisis, Keynesian, Monetarism, State Capitalism

***

Introduction

Capitalism is one of the economic systems used to achieve political-economic goals which are growth, economic efficiency and stability, income distribution, etc. and to organize all economic activities of humanity, especially production, and in this way to solve economic problems. This system has been integrated into the long history of humanity with mercantilism since the fifteenth century and has taken its place in history with industrial, financial and digital transformation. In this relatively short journey, capitalism's economic life structure has been guided by neo/liberal economic theory. Accordingly, the main purpose of this fiction is to create suitable conditions for capital to increase its profits and for individuals to increase their interests. This aim has been tried to be achieved through private property, free entrepreneurship and market mechanisms. The world of value consists of these, capitalism, as Amin states, can be considered a successful system for some in terms of economic performance and potentially being a source of 'social' and even democratic progress. Moreover, they say, it has proven itself or can prove itself in the globalized context that is now.

The theses of those who think in this way are based on the production level that humanity and capitalism have roughly reached with the industrial/technology revolutions in a period of approximately two hundred and fifty years, and the level of welfare that is a reflection of this. However, due to the polarizing characteristics of the system, not every society had the same chance to access production opportunities and societies were categorized as developed/ developing. In addition, the difference in access to the values created by production for all segments of society in each country has led to the distinction between rich and poor. In this respect, when accounting for capitalism in terms of humanity, *winners/losers*, as well as *gains/losses*, should be taken into consideration. The inequality in its distribution is one of the main problems that make society's opinion about it negative, as well as the criticism of capitalism itself and the opposition front. In addition, the economic crises that the economy has experienced since its beginning and which has become more frequent especially with globalization, not only feed this negative judgment but also undermine the reliability of the system.

Here is the process of globalization/neoliberalism, the 'new face' of capitalism since the 1970s. It was realized with dynamics such as the crisis based on overproduction created by the high pace of accumulation during the golden age, ii-the profit crisis fed by Fordist industrial relations, iii-the intensification of international capitalist competition, and iv-the increasing financial capital and speculative accumulation preferences preceded industrial investments with the liberalization of the financial system.1 Undoubtedly, another important feature of this process that attracts attention is the weakening of the state's power in the economy over time with neo-liberal policies and privatization.

Although it was aimed to evolve into a new era with this process, also referred to as financialization, capitalism's 'crisis age' began with national, regional and

---

[1] Erinç Yeldan, "Neoliberal Küreselleşme Sürecinin Kalkınma Söylemi Üzerine Değerlendirmeler", *Praksis Dergisi*, yaz, sayı.7, 19 (2011): 34,21.

eventually global crises, especially as a result of the liberalization of capital movements and the easy transmission of financial diseases.[2]

While the global capitalist system was living its 'neoliberal' golden age and reaping the fruits of the social-welfare state, it came across with a crisis. The effects of the financial crisis which broke out in the USA in 2008 and spread to the world through 'combined vessels' are yet to be over. This latest crisis, which is considered a kind of repetition or equivalent of the crisis of 1929, reminds us of a 'deja-vu' or 'we have already seen this movie' situation.

Although the story of both crises is similar, the analysis of these and all crises differs on a theoretical basis. As a matter of fact, regarding the causes of the crisis, the theory of capitalism and mainstream economics emphasized external factors and even blamed the state for not creating the conditions for competition and intervening in the market from time to time. She also described crises as temporary imbalances in the market and argued that the market could automatically eliminate these imbalances. Contrary to mainstream economics, as Yeldan states, the main fiction of Keynesian economic thought is the necessity of "intervention against lack of demand".According to Keynesian thought, a capitalist market economy may not be able to create full employment equilibrium when left on its own. More precisely, the equilibrium maintained by the market may involve disequilibrium due to unemployment and/or high inflation and insufficiency of aggregate demand. The policy proposal is clear; Market intervention is necessary.[3] Marxist theory, on the other hand, emphasizes that the crisis analysis of both theories focuses on environmental factors and rituals in its functioning without touching the essence of capitalism, whereas the structure of the system, which is based on access to profit under all circumstances for capital accumulation, paves the way for the crisis. So much so that, as Akıncılar stated, the crisis occurs when the rate of increase in the organic composition of capital cannot be met by the rate of increase in surplus value. This law is valid for all accumulation processes of capitalism. Free competition, monopolistic competition, Fordist accumulation and global capital cannot prevent the operation of this law; however, they can affect the momentum and the experience of the crisis with the social conditions they create.[4]

The same differentiation regarding the causes of the crisis was also experienced in the implementation of solution strategies. However, according to Durusoy,

---

[2] Mahfi Eğilmez, *Tarihsel Süreç İçinde Dünya Ekonomisi,* (Remzi Kitabevi, 2018), 150.

[3] Erinç Yeldan, "Makroekonominin Keynes ile Sınavı", *İktisat ve Toplum Dergisi* s.74 (2016): 28-31,28.

[4] Murad Akıncılar, "Krize Teorik ve Siyasal Yaklaşım Sorunları", Özgür Üniversite Forumu, 01,1999,52-61,53-54.

although the capitalist system has faced many crises, it has been able to continue until today by ensuring the oscillation between state capitalism (state-interventionist capitalism) and private capitalism. When the crisis in its current form became extreme (increased unemployment, bankrupt businesses, etc.), capitalism immediately tried to prevent questions with reform-oriented programs.[5]

Conceptual and Theoretical Framework

Concept of Crisis and Its Evolution

The word crisis is derived from the Greek words "krisis",[6], which means "to decide" and "turning point", that is, the moment of decision that determines the positive or negative development of something or a situation. The essence of the crisis is that someone needs to make a decision but has not made one yet. Additionally, the word "krisis" means "separation, discernment, choice, judgment, disagreement." There is a long list[7] of different meanings, such as.[8] The modern concept of crisis is generally defined as 'a symptom of a disease that suddenly appears', 'a disease has reached an advanced stage', or an organism cannot recover without permanent damage, external intervention or fundamental restructuring because its defence mechanisms are insufficient to bring it out of crisis. It comes from the medical literature that it is defined as a dangerous situation. Social scientists have also borrowed this basic medical metaphor to describe crises in economic, political, social and cultural systems.[9] As a matter of fact, in social sciences, it is generally defined as 'a sudden deterioration in development' and is used synonymously with words such as

---

[5] Serap Durusoy, "Kriz Sonrası Küresel Kapitalizmin Geleceği", *Alternatif Politika*, cilt. 1, sayı. 3 (Aralık 2009): 363-389.

[6] This word, which we use as crisis in Turkish, is translated into English as; *crisis*, In German; *krise*, French; *crise*, Italian; *crisi*, Spanish; *crisis*, Albanian; *krizë*, Czechoslovakian; *krize*, Finnish; *kriisi*, Croatian; *kriza*, Swedish; *kris*, Catalan; *crisi*, Hungarian; *krizis*, Portuguese; *crise*, Slovenian; *kriza*It is settled in European languages see. Ahmet Arif Eren ve Metin Sarçoğlu," Kapitalizmin Tarihinde Finansal Krizler: Tarih Tekerrür Mü Ediyor?", *Ömer Halisdemir Üniversitesi İktisadi ve İdari Bilimler Fakültesi Dergisi* cilt-sayı 10 (Ocak 2017): 87-97, 89.

[7] According to the Merriam-Webster Dictionary, there are 44 synonyms for the word crisis https://www.merriam-webster.com/thesaurus/crises

[8] Srdan Milasinovic and Zelimir Kesetovic, "Crisis and Crisis Management – A Contrıbutıon to a Conceptual&Terminological Delimitatıon", *Megatrend Review*, 5 (1) 2008, 167-185,185

[9] I wonder if this medical metaphor is the source of inspiration for the expressions "correct diagnosis for the right treatment" or "anatomy of the crisis", which are often voiced especially in solution discussions regarding economic crises.

'great distress', 'crisis' and 'depression'.It is not easy to give a general definition of the concept of crisis in terms of social sciences due to its visibility for different reasons and faces in every aspect of modern life. Moreover, judgments about the extent to which the current situation or the events encountered are a 'crisis' may vary from person to person.[10]

So much so that Eastham et al. According to and Dayton, "crisis" is one of the commonly used and talked about but difficult concepts in social sciences. Because of its immediate appeal, it is used frequently and in a variety of contexts for virtually any problem or event in any field. However, due to its wide-ranging use, definitions lack a common interpretation, precision and specificity; So much so that even those working in crisis intervention and research are reluctant to bind themselves to any single definition.[11] In fact, definitions vary depending on the scope of what is included and the components considered important. These differ in terms of different disciplines and fields that use the concept of crisis or an equivalent or similar concept. There may be a potential conflict between a simple, short definition that might describe the crisis and a longer, more comprehensive definition that refers to a wide range of overarching elements.[12] It is possible to see these issues in some definitions chosen by chance.

As a matter of fact, a crisis can be briefly defined as "the collapse of the usual structures that sustain and legitimize the current socio-political order" or as "chaotic situations that can be experienced by people, states, governments, organizations, etc. in social relations".[13]

More broadly, "Crises include disasters and complex emergencies that seriously disrupt the functioning of society and cause widespread human, material, environmental or institutional losses, often exceeding the ability of the affected society to cope using its own resources".[14]

---

[10] Coşkun Can Aktan ve Hüseyin Şen, "Ekonomik Kriz: Nedenler ve Çözüm Önerileri", *Yeni Türkiye, Ekonomik Kriz Özel Sayısı* 42 (Kasım-Aralık 2001): 1225-1230,1225.

[11] Katherine Eastham et al., "The Concept of Crisis", *Canad. Psychiat Ass. J* 15 (1970): 463; Bruce W. Dayton, "Managing Crises in theTwenty-First Century", *International Studies Review* 6 (2004): 165–194,166-167.

[12] Sylvia Walby, "Crisis and Society: Developing The Theory of Crisis in The Context of COVID-19", Global Discourse, 12, (3-4) (2022): 498–516, 499.

[13] Ömer Göksel İşyar, "Definition and Management of International Crises", *Perceptıons* (winter 2008): 1-49,1

[14] ILO, *Crisis Response, Recovery and Reconstruction Department,* Geneva, October 2001, 1-92.

In the final analysis, in general, a crisis is a significant event that has the potential to negatively affect (a country's) institutions, companies or sectors, its people, its products and services (such as production, supply, etc.) and its reputation.[15]

As can be seen, there is a wide literature on crisis and many definitions that partially overlap or differ from each other. In our efforts to harmonize various perspectives, the term crisis is often used as a "universal box", that is, as a concept that covers all types of negative events. In an even broader perspective, the term crisis is used for unwanted, unexpected, unpredictable and almost unthinkable events that cause insecurity and uncertainty.[16]

But although crisis typically refers to various political events, conflicts and extraordinary situations, its emphasis in contemporary life is mainly on economic problems and, in recent years, on natural disasters and disasters (such as the Covid 19 pandemic). Although crises are abnormal or extraordinary situations by definition and nature, they also seem to be embedded in the routine conditions of life.

Although crisis is an inherent phenomenon in every aspect of our individual and social life, over time the balance between all layers of life is disrupted in favor of the economy, that is, almost everything in life is under the influence of economic elements and events, as well as the transformation of the economic system and the indicators of global financial markets that are on a knife edge. The existence of the possibility that the course of our economic life may deteriorate at any time for any reason has made economic crises more current. Undoubtedly, rather than individual and corporate economic crises, many national crises in the surrounding economies, which are the weak links of the global economy, but most importantly, the global economic/financial crisis due to its impact and speed of spread, have become more prominent.

As a matter of fact, when the crisis is mentioned in daily conversations, it mostly refers to different and more visible aspects or mechanisms/functioning of the economy. It is understood that problems/difficulties such as inflationary crisis, stock market-banking-foreign payments-public finance crisis, sales and payment difficulties, and lack of supply may arise.[17]

However, the problem encountered in defining the crisis, in general, is also valid for the economic crisis in particular because there is no consensus on what should be understood when it comes to an economic crisis. So much so

---

[15] Kathleen Fearn-Banks, *Crisis Communications: A Casebook Approach*, (Mahwah NJ: Lawrence Erlbaum Associates Publishers, 1966), 6.

[16] Milasinovic and Kesetovic, "Crısıs and Crısıs", 169-170.

[17] Ahmet Emin Kotil, *Kriz ve Gelişme*, (İstanbul: Derin Yayınları, 2015), 2.

that among the representatives of the economic environment, recession, as well as inflation and deflation, are defined as economic crises. In addition, the definition of each crisis in the financial sector as an economic crisis has made the situation more complicated. There is no consensus on which of these is an economic crisis, as well as what exactly each of them means.[18]

To clarify this situation and determine the framework of the economic crisis, according to Dura, the concepts of recession and depression, which are used together in case of economic crisis and have a transitivity and hierarchical (priority and posteriority) relationship between them, need to be explained.[19] According to one understanding, recession means a slowdown/decline in economic activities. A contraction is a decrease in the level of the conjuncture in relation to a previously attained position; The fall may be shallow or deep. Recession is sometimes used synonymously with "crisis".[20] According to Claessens and Köse, there is no official definition of recession, but it is generally accepted that this concept refers to a period of decline in economic activities. Very short-term declines in economic activities are not considered recessions. Many experts and analysts accept the practical/technical definition of a recession as a decline in a country's real GDP for two consecutive quarters. Although this definition is generally accepted (canonical), it also has some shortcomings. Focusing solely on GDP is a narrow perspective, and to determine whether a country is truly experiencing a recession, it is often better to consider a broader set of measures of economic activity. Because the use of other indicators can provide a more accurate assessment of the state of the economy.[21]

As a matter of fact, Moore, as if to complete the deficiencies in this conventional definition, stated that a recession is "a period of decline in total output, income, employment and trade, usually lasting from six months to a year, during which widespread contractions occur in many sectors of the

---

[18] Mahfi Eğilmez, *Küresel Finans Krizi,* (İstanbul: Remzi Kitabevi, 2020), 48.

[19] The concept of crisis was examined with different concepts in the economic literature after the 1929 World Economic Depression. However, the transformation of the concept into a crisis is a phenomenon that occurred in the following years. Its common usage is "depression", which corresponds to the contraction of the business cycle. For this reason, the general expression of the crisis in 1929 is not "World Crisis" but "1929 World Economic Depression". See. Ömer Eroğlu ve Mesut Albeni, *Küreselleşme, Ekonomik Krizler ve Türkiye,* (Isparta: Bilim Kitabevi, 2002), 90.

[20] Cihan Dura, "Ekonomik Kriz Nedir, Özellikleri Nelerdir, Nasıl Gelişir?", 2009, http://www.cihandura.com/index.php?option=com_content&task=view&id=326&Itemid=49

[21] Stijn Claessens and M. Ayhan Köse, "What is a Recession?", *Finance & Development* (March 2009): 52-53.

economy".[22] NBER similarly defines a recession as a significant decline in economic activity that is reflected in the economy as a whole and lasts for more than a few months.[23] However, concepts such as crisis, depression, collapse and depression, which are often confused, are used to express the relatively worse economic situation that emerges due to the prolongation of the recession and the severity of its impact and speed of spread.

Accordingly, if economic activities, especially GDP, remain at a low level for a long time compared to the level they reached before, this situation is defined as depression (or, as it was more commonly used in the past, "depression"). Depression is an expression used for economic crises that last for many years and create great shocks in the economy and people's lives, unlike temporary, one- or two-year or even shorter stagnation and recessions.[24] So much so that depression is defined as an economic disaster/earthquake accompanied by great destruction, especially in the banking, trade and manufacturing sectors, accompanied by rising prices, shrinking loans, low investments, increasing bankruptcies and high unemployment.[25]

Although it is now possible to diagnose the economic crisis relatively unequivocally and easily based on these explanations,[26] which of these will be considered a crisis depends on the duration, size and impact it creates. While sometimes a long period of stagnation does not lead to a full-blown crisis, as in the recession experienced by Japan, sometimes a short recession can create a crisis.[27] In this context, if recession is foreseen as a relatively mild form or the first phase of the crisis in the economy, and depression as a rather harsh form or the second phase, then economic crisis means 'the events that occur suddenly and unexpectedly in the economy that affect the country's economy in macro terms and companies (*of course, in micro terms*) It means that it will produce results that will seriously shake the consumers.[28]

---

[22] G.H. Moore,"Recession or Depression?", in *Busıness Cycles, Inflatıon, And Forecastıng*, 2nd edition, H. Geoffrey and Ballınger Moore, (1983), 19-22.

[23] NBER, "Business Cycle Dating", https://www.nber.org/research/business-cycle-dating, access 12.08.2023. 12.08.2023.

[24] Sungur Savran, *Üçüncü Büyük Depresyon Kapitalizmin Alacakaranlığı*, (Yordam Kitabevi, 2013),18.

[25] Chris Seabury, "Recession and Depression: They Aren't So Bad", https://www.scribd.com/document/281120463/Recession-and-Depression

[26] Savran, *Üçüncü Büyük Depresyon*, 18.

[27] Eğilmez, *Küresel Finans Krizi*, 50.

[28] Aktan ve Şen, "Ekonomik Kriz: Nedenler ve Çözüm Önerileri", 1225-1230.

Following a similar logic, an economic crisis, first and foremost, is a crisis, that is, a breakdown of established social relations, manifested in dry economic indicators of employment, growth, and inflation. This suggests a connection between economic and financial disruptions to internal processes specific to a given society at a given development stage.[29]

In addition, relatively deep recessions can also be considered crises. In some cases, sharp movements in parameters such as unemployment, inflation, interest rates and exchange rates can also be used to identify crisis periods.[30]

As seen in the light of all these definitions, an economic crisis can be defined as severe fluctuations in prices and/or quantities of goods, services, production factors (*real economy/market*) or foreign exchange market (*financial economy/ market*), beyond the acceptable or normal change limit. From this dual division of the economic structure, the economic crisis is divided into real and financial crises. Real sector crises occur in the form of inflation-recession and serious contractions in employment in the goods-services and labour markets. Although financial crisis is defined in many different ways, it is generally used for situations where some financial assets and institutions suddenly lose a significant portion of their market value.[31] Although economic crises are separated in this way, there is a transitivity between them as the financial crisis turns into a real crisis and the real crisis turns into a financial crisis.[32]

Economic crisis with globalization: On the one hand, it has gained a global dimension and quality with the merging economies. On the other hand, it has declared its independence from the economy (!), especially with the financial globalization that has accelerated since the 1980s and attracts economic actors with its rapidly increasing products and techniques. Therefore, it has changed its type with the unregulated and uncontrolled structure of the financial sector, which pushes the real economy to the background and the occurrence of many financial crises, especially in developing countries.

Here is the twentieth century of developing and slightly underdeveloped countries that wanted to be included in the developed world by overcoming

---

[29] Aleksandr V. Gevorkyan, "Economic Crisis", *Weom 060061* 6 V1 (2015): 1.

[30] Hasan Cömert and Erinç Yeldan, "A Tale of Three Crises in Turkey: 1994, 2001 and 2008–09", *ERC Working Papers in Economics* June, 2018, 1-24, 3.

[31] Aykut Kibritçioğlu, "2008 Küresel Finans Krizi Öncesi Krizler ve Türkiye Ekonomisi", in *İktisadi Krizler ve Türkiye Ekonomisi*, haz. Nadir Eroğlu, İlhan Eroğlu ve İbrahim Aydın, (Ankara: Orion, 2015), 503-519-504.

[32] Can we think of the transitivity between crises, again based on the medical metaphor of the concept of crisis, as physiological disorders in humans causing psychological disorders, and psychological disorders causing physiological disorders?

their various economic limitations, especially capital, thanks to globalization. Especially in the last quarter of financial globalization, where it took place rapidly and uncontrollably, there were many economic (*financial*) crises.[33] The 1994 Mexico and Turkey, 1997-1998 Asian Crises, 1998 Brazil and Russia, and 2001 Turkey and Argentina crises were among the most notable ones. Although the crises in this period are different in terms of their depth and consequences, they have commonalities in that they originate from the banking and financial fields because money and capital markets can react immediately to all kinds of developments. The extent of this reaction has become even more damaging because the financial markets of developing countries are open to speculative movements. Moreover, the sudden entry of mobilized funds, which reach trillions of dollars between countries due to financial globalization, into the developing markets creates a positive spring atmosphere (false spring), while their sudden exits create a shock effect (*the frost of the ground*). This turns into an economic crisis that results in the depreciation of the domestic currency, balance sheets being turned upside down, distrust becoming widespread, and production being unable to be financed. It is possible that developing countries, which have experienced this many times, will wake up to a (financial) crisis every morning due to their unique economic fragilities (savings, current account and budget deficits, etc.).[34]

For this reason, although economists generally understand real crises when they say crisis, that is, crises on the production front, and crisis theories generally explain real crises, since the crises we mentioned above in the 1990s and 2000s started with the frightened and displaced of short-term capital, they call these crises financial crises and It is a tradition to emphasize that the real effects of these crises are temporary.[35] However, the "mega crisis" originating from the financial sector, which started in the USA in 2007-2008, not only destroyed this tradition with its global nature, speed of spread and effects, but also shifted the axis of crises to developed countries. In addition to being the biggest crisis of capitalism, it is thought to be the gravest crisis since the 1929 crisis, which is etched in memory with its devastating social effects. In this

---

[33] Ömer Yılmaz, Alaattin Kızıltan ve Vedat Kaya, "İktisadi Kriz Kuramları, Finansal Küreselleşme ve Para Krizleri", *Erciyes Üniversitesi İktisadi ve İdari Bilimler Fakültesi Dergisi* 24 (Ocak - Haziran 2005): 77-96, 88.

[34] Fikret Şenses, *İktisada (Farklı Bir) Giriş*, (İstanbul: İletişim Yayınları, 2017), 121; Eroğlu ve Albeni, *Küreselleşme, Ekonomik Krizler*, .94-95; Merih Celasun, "Gelişen Ekonomilerin Dış Kaynak Kullanımı, Finansal Krizler ve Türkiye Örneği", *Doğu Batı Düşünce Dergisi* 17 (2001): 161-181,165.

[35] Şiir Yılmaz, "Dünya Ekonomisi ve Türkiye: Globalleşme, Liberalizasyon ve Kriz", in *Yerel Ekonomilerin Sürdürülebilir Kalkınması ve Çanakkale Örneği*, ed.Serdar Sayan, (2002), 3.

respect, although an attempt is made to create the perception that the economic crisis in question is limited to financial markets by calling it a "global financial crisis", it is clearly obvious that the so-called "financial" crisis has turned into a crisis that creates destruction in the production-real sphere. This crisis, which we will discuss later, has also always kept hot debates on seriously criticizing and questioning the future of capitalism and the market economy.[36] Discourses about the fact that crises cannot be considered independently of the structure and functioning of capitalism have begun to be voiced loudly both in their own neighborhood and in the neighborhood opposite.

Economic Crisis Theories

Although the history of economic crises dates back to ancient times, dealing with crises at a theoretical level is recent. Moreover, the perfect structure of the classical economic doctrine, which is considered equivalent to the history of modern economics, in the design of economic life does not allow for crises, and the belief that possible problems related to this will be solved with the magic formula "the boss/market mechanism wants a happy ending" has eliminated all concerns. However, the 1929 World Economic Depression painfully showed that "the calculation/theory at home does not suit the market" and also revealed the inadequacy of the existing theory and, therefore, the discipline of economics regarding the crisis. With the process that started from here, while the phenomenon of crisis took place in the economics literature, as Mumyakmaz stated, the understanding and interpretation of economic crises in their real dimensions, apart from being explained within the theoretical framework of the economics discipline, opened the ontological foundations of the economics discipline to discussion. Schools with different perspectives have shed light on the questions regarding why and how crises emerged and on what basis they were shaped.[37]

In this context, three different approaches can be mentioned in looking at economic crises: i- Mainstream economics, ii- Keynes and her successors, iii- Marxist economists' approaches.

Mainstream Economic Approach: The (neo)classical economic school, in which capitalism grew, accepts crises (the first observed industrial crises) as temporary, short-term deviations from balance that occur by chance during

---

[36] Alaine Touraıne, *Krizden Anlamak,* (YKY Yayınları, 2016),16; Sungur Savran, "Kapitalizmde Kriz: İktisat Teorisinde Bir Ufuk Taraması", *in Kriz ve Türkiye: Aşınan Teoriler,* eds. Hale Balseven ve Fuat Ercan, (Ankara: Siyasal Kitabevi, 2013), 39.

[37] Alper Mumyakmaz," İktisadi Kriz mi, İktisadın Krizi mi Metodolojik Bir Tartışma", in *Sosyal, Siyasal ve Kuramsal Yönleriyle İktisadi Krizler,* ed. Semra Buğra, (Gazi Kitabevi, 2020), 5-35, 20-21.

the development of capital accumulation or as an accident in the natural flow of economic life, without leaving capitalism in the dust. This is also valid for the neo-classical school established at the end of the nineteenth century as a result of the work of W.S.Jewons (1871), C.Menger (1871) and especially L.Walras (1874), the founder of the general equilibrium theory. Since balance is theoretically automatic in the construction of the neo-classical model, it is logically impossible to conceptualize crisis and, thus, the object/event since it does not exist. Imbalances encountered in practice, especially crises, have been attributed to external factors, especially state interventions, which are assumed to have a protective role in balance but actually hinder the functioning of the free market economy. They argued and tried to prove that as long as the natural rules of the economy were followed and there was no intervention in them, capitalist production relations would grow and develop in a balanced and trouble-free manner. In this respect, for them, crisis is a demonic force (what the Latins call *deuxexmachina*). Due to this understanding, they searched for the causes of the economic crisis outside capitalism. However, when the historical importance and periodic structures of classical crises are known, the "denying of the existence" of crises is an important gap that should be underlined in terms of the neo-classical model.[38]

Moreover, as a continuation of this trend that has emerged since the 1980s, specific new schools such as "monetarism," named after Milton Friedman, "supply-side economics," which rose to prominence in the USA during the Ronald Reagan period, and "rational expectations," which made a significant breakthrough in academic circles, have also become branches of the same river. The most common aspect that brings this together is the view that the crisis is a result of the obstacles that prevented the functioning of the market mechanism in the Long Expansion Period (LGD). Behind this view lies the judgment of bourgeois economics that capitalism, which dates back to Adam Smith, is generally a rational and harmonious social system. Accordingly, as long as there are no interventions in the market operating through the price system, possible problems/imbalances/crises in economic life will disappear.[39]

So much so that A.Smith was optimistic about the future of capitalism due to the increasing productivity in the industrial and agricultural sectors of the economy, and Say was optimistic about the future of capitalism due to the fact that even if the wrong decisions of some investors led to excess supply, it was possible to correct this with the explanation of the interest theory. Although D. Ricardo, who was pessimistic, accepted that productivity increased in industry,

[38] Yılmaz Kızıltan ve Kaya, "İktisadi, 80, Orhan Dilber, Herkesin Krizi Kendine", Özgür Üniversite Forumu 01, 1999, 28-39,29.

[39] Savran, *Üçüncü Büyük Depresyon*, 61-62.

she predicted that its decrease in agriculture would reduce total productivity and that capitalism would enter stagnation in the long run. It can be said that classical economists, who focused on long-term growth problems, did not take into account business cycle fluctuations due to Say's Law.[40]

Because of this eternal law or prescription of capitalism, the crisis is not attributed to it, and according to Önder, in the capitalist world, the central capitalist economies transfer potential crises to the peripheral economies, first through colonial practices and later through intense imperialist pressures through the processes of commercial imperialism and foreign-dependent assembly industry imperialism. They solved it by applying it. Therefore, in this process, mainstream economics literature did not focus on the crisis problem as a systemic phenomenon.[41]

However, in the new financial system, which was built step by step through the financial globalization process in order to overcome a crisis after 1970, the functioning of national/international financial markets was also referred to the relevant prescription, but it did not work. The financial infection[42]/crisis occurred first in the emerging economies and lastly in the USA, the centre of finance capital. Mainstream economic theories have generally remained distant from evaluating these developments and their consequences. In these theories, the financial system is assigned a role that increases the efficiency and growth of the economy by simply meeting the resource needs of the economy. In the system, financial markets and institutions collect savings in a pool and transfer them as capital to entrepreneurs in order to be directed to investment and direct investments in this process. In financial markets, the balance between savings and capital amounts is ensured by the laws of supply and demand of the market economy. It is claimed that indicators such as interest rates and stock prices determined at this balance point also direct the effective functioning of the economy. In short, it is accepted that the efficient and profitable operation of financial markets will increase the efficiency of the

---

[40] Ercan Bocutoğlu, "Krizin Makro İktisadından Makro İktisadın Krizine: Eleştirel Bir Değerlendirme", in *Küresel Bunalım ve İktisat Eğitimi*, ed. Ercan Uygur, (Ankara: İmaj, 2011), 201, 221, 206.

[41] İzettin Önder, *Ekonomik Kriz, İktisat Üzerine Düşünceler*, (İstanbul: Yordam Kitap, 2016), 245-260, 246.

[42] Again, with reference to the medical origin of the concept of crisis, this term can be considered a "cosmetic" term used to reinforce or make visible an expression such as the financial crisis changing hands and/or spreading globally. (For details see İrfan Kalaycı, "Finansal Enfeksiyon ve "Aşı" Kuramı", 28-56,31.

economy.[43] While there are those who want to purify capitalism by attributing the cause of the crisis in the system, which they idealize to such an extent and think that it will function almost perfectly, to the excessive profit desire of fund managers or the lack of liberalization, those who want to see it as "financial irregularity and lack of control" blame the "lack of rules" on the "masters". It is an important contradiction that they see it not as the market order itself that produces but as the state that does not prevent them. These contradictions/ mistakes of those who are blindly committed to the emergence of the market and who aim to integrate into the global economy, in any case, will probably always exist as long as they cannot read capitalism correctly and their predictions that the crisis can be postponed permanently with temporary regulations continue.[44]

Therefore, it is undeniable that this mindset focuses only on bad management or other non-economic factors in the analysis of the causes of crises, and especially ignores the historical dimension and the organic consequences of the functioning of the system[45].n short, mainstream economic theories that are far from seeing the whole picture and close the doors to self-criticism of the current economic system, Stiglitz[46] argued, as before, that nothing should be done for the last global financial crisis, as government intervention would make things worse. As the Depression became a distant memory, economics lost sight of these lessons. Dogmas and doctrines that markets function well and are self-correcting once again became dominant. This time the theories were more sophisticated, but the basic assumptions were equally invalid. These ideas, in turn, helped shape the intellectual environment that gave rise to the flawed policies that led to the crisis and, to some extent, the policies aimed at finding a solution to the crisis today.

Keynesian Approaches: Fortunately, economics was saved from this shame by considering the phenomenon of crisis as a more systemic phenomenon within the movement that developed with Keynes and by proposing social policies as the only way to overcome crises, which we will focus on later. In this context, contrary to economic liberalism, expanding the fields of activity of the

---

[43] Özgür Orhangazi, "Günümüz Kapitalizminde Finansın Rolü Üzerine Birkaç Not", *İktisat ve Toplum Dergisi* (Aralık 2017): 32-39,.33-34.

[44] Sinan Sönmez, "Liberal Paradigma ve Küresel Kriz", in *Kriz ve Türkiye Aşınan Teoriler,* 53-71; İrfan Kalaycı, Barış Aytekin ve Berna Balcı Izgi, "Krizin İktisadı – İktisadın Krizi", in Politik *İktisat, Kriz ve Kalkınma, eds.* İsmail Şiriner et al., (İstanbul: IJOPEC Publication, 2011), 49-71, 51-52.

[45] Önder, *Ekonomik Kriz,* 245.

[46] Joseph E. Stiglitz, "The Current Economic Crisis and Lessons for Economic Theory", *Eastern Economic Journal* 35 (2009): 281–296, 293.

state, providing flexibility in the transition to open budget policies, etc. Policies such as these that will make future expectations positive have been put on the agenda and implemented.[47]

In fact, Keynes stated in the lectures and conferences she had given since 1924 that the end of economic liberalism was approaching and that the state must be more active. So much so that, in 1926, he broke away from the classical and neoclassical mainstream with his work "The end of Laissez Faire", which consisted of conference texts, and in the following period, he tried to show that deep crises could occur in the economy due to lack of demand, by observing the conditions of the age in which he lived, the world and especially England. His subsequent works are, respectively: In A Tract on Monetary (1924), he discussed purchasing power and the latest economic developments, and in A Treatise on Money (1930), he discussed the dynamics of prices and income, as well as monetary institutions and their modes of operation. With the Great Depression of 1929, which started in this very period, unemployment rose rapidly in a short time. In contrast, the orthodox policy of cutting wages and government spending has not solved the problem but worsened it. A new approach was urgently needed to solve the unemployment problem, and Keynes was about to produce it.[48]

As a matter of fact, on the occasion of the Great Depression, Keynes matured his studies on money, prices and employment and published the book The General Theory of Employment, Interest and Money (1936), which would create a revolution in economic thought and world economic history (the Keynesian Revolution). In her book, Keynes became the founder and representative of the macroeconomic movement by gathering together many concepts and intellectual tools that were ignored by the classical-neoclassical approach and would later be developed as the building blocks of macroeconomics. Moreover, Keynes challenged both the classical and neoclassical defence of free-market capitalism.[49] The Keynesian revolution is essentially an intellectual framework that shows that capitalism can experience deep and long-lasting crises but that capitalism needs the intervention of the state in order to survive, as the Great Depression clearly showed. However, the Keynesian revolution proposes that the state manage total demand and leave the supply side to

---

[47] Önder, *Ekonomik Kriz*, 245; Bocutoğlu, *Krizin Makroiktisadından*, 201.

[48] Şenses, *İktisada (Farklı Bir) Giriş*, 98; Meghnad Desal, "Keynes ve Seksen Yıl Sonra Onun Genel Teorisi", *İktisat ve Toplum Dergisi* 74 (Aralık 2016): 0-13,11.

[49] Although it is difficult to assign a left/socialist identity to Keynes based on this approach, we can at least say that he was the "tamer of capitalism" (For details, see. Ömer Faruk Çolak, P"olitik İktisatçı Kimliğiyle Keynes ve Barışın Ekonomik Sonuçları", *İktisat ve Toplum Dergisi* sayı 125 (2021): 32-35, 32.

market forces.[50] In this regard, the main claims of Keynesianism, which has found a wide application area, especially after the Great Depression, are as follows:[51]

i- In capitalist market economies, there is no natural mechanism that will automatically eliminate external shocks and maintain balance at full employment.

ii- Capitalist economies may encounter a general unemployment problem from time to time, but there is no mechanism that will solve this problem spontaneously, as claimed. The main reason why full employment of the workforce cannot be achieved is the insufficiency of total demand expenditures.

iii- The most obvious reason for the inadequacy in total expenditures is the decrease in investment expenditures. The fluctuation in investment amounts due to the fluctuation in the profitability expectations of private investors will reduce consumers' incomes and therefore private consumption expenditures. Thus, effective demand remains below the desired level.

iv- Saving is a bad habit of investors. In periods when private savings exceed investments and expenditures are reduced - that is, demand decreases - the economy contracts, and unemployment rises to high levels. In this situation, which indicates economic stagnation, if measures are not taken to stimulate demand, unemployment may spread over the long term, and stagnation may turn into depression.[52]

v- Finally, the course of economic development can be determined through trade/business cyclical movements. Although fluctuations in consumption tendency and liquidity preference are especially effective in this, fluctuations in the marginal efficiency of capital are decisive. So much so that although it is a dominant and typical tendency to explain crises by the tendency for interest rates to increase in cases where the demand for money increases for both trade and speculative purposes, the main

---

[50] Şenses, *İktisada (Farklı Bir) Giriş*, 98-99.

[51] Ferda Dönmez, "Keynes ve Keynesçilik", in *Ekonomik Kurumlar ve Kavramlar Sözlüğü Eleştirel Bir Bakış*, eds. Fikret Başkaya ve Aydı Ördek, (İstanbul: Özgür Üniversite, 2008), 675-685, 680.

[52] Bayram Eşiyok, "Keynesyen "Altın Çağ"dan Neoliberal Orta Çağ"a: Geriye Ne Kaldı?", *İktisat ve Toplum Dergisi* 74 (2016): 60-65, 65; Şenses, *İktisada (Farklı Bir) Bakış*, 100.

cause of crises is the sudden decrease in the marginal efficiency of capital.[53]

The accuracy of Keynesianism's claims has been relatively proven by the findings regarding what happened in the period leading up to the Great Depression. Namely:[54] i-The Great Depression emerged as a contraction in demand after a revival that started in 1924 when financial markets transferred resources to the real sector and lasted until the crisis. ii-Crisis; Not only did it show the consequences of the insufficiency of effective demand, it invalidated J.B. Say's famous thesis that "every supply creates its own demand" and, more precisely, it put supply-side economics aside. iii- Finally, the New Deal policies implemented to end the crisis are based on creating effective demand through state intervention, which is denied by classical economics and which we mentioned above.

The approximately thirty-year period in which developed countries on both sides of the Atlantic Ocean implemented the economic policies[55] designed by Keynes to overcome crises in particular and to ensure the stable functioning of a capitalist economy in general, from the end of the Second World War until the 1970s, reached their highest growth rate. It is known as the golden age of capitalism. There were no crises in this process, and no trace of economic crisis theories was found in the economic literature.[56]

However, it must be a strange irony in economic history that, just as the Great Depression brought about the end of liberal economic theory, Keynesian theory experienced a similar end with the systemic crisis that capitalism faced in the mid-1970s. Capitalism since 1980 While the new story, which started with the feeling of "where were we?", again under the free market discourse, with the aim of realizing the profitability of capital, but on the world level and with neoliberal restructuring policies[57] based on the financial capital regime, ended with a financial crisis/dissolution, history repeated itself, and again it was necessary to understand and understand the crisis. The General Theory book has been taken down from the dusty shelves because the "invisible hand" has

---

[53] John Maynard Keynes, *Genel Teori İstihdam, Faiz ve Paranın Genel Teorisi*, çev. Uğur Selçuk Akalın, (İstanbul: Kalkeden, 2010), 267-269.

[54] Ömer Faruk Çolak, "1929 ve 2008 Krizinin Dinamikleri", in *Zor Zamanlarda İktisat*, eds. Gökçer Özgür ve Hakan Yetkiner, (Ankara: Efil Yayınevi, 2011), 17-30, 22.

[55] Dönmez, "Keynes ve Keynesçilik", 680

[56] Şevket Pamuk, "Keynes'in Son 100 Yılda Gelişmiş Ekonomiler Üzerindeki Etkisi", *İktisat ve Toplum Dergisi* sayı 74 (2016): 15-16, 15; Şenses, *İktisada (Farklı Bir) Giriş*, 100.

[57] Eşiyok, "Keynesyen Altın Çağ"dan Neoliberal Orta Çağ"a", 61-64.

disappeared to solve the problem.[58] So, although Keynes died more than half a century ago, his diagnoses of recessions and depressions continue to form the basis of modern macroeconomics. Keynes wrote: "Practical men who exempt themselves from all intellectual influence often become the slaves of an economist. In 2008, no ancient economist was more prominent than Keynes.[59]

Despite this, although there is a general opinion that the General Theory has a suprahistorical place for the discipline of economics, there are doubts about its guidance to this new crisis. As a matter of fact, Eğilmez expressed this as follows:[60]"... However, this time we realized that the book cannot be as useful in this crisis as it was in the past. Because the Keynesian model was not designed for a system in which capital movements are so free."

Atbaşı, on the other hand, drew attention to the difference in the time and ground conditions when the crisis occurred with his General Theory analyses. Namely:[61]... Moreover, all these/events took place within a capitalism that was very different from the capitalism that Keynes analyzed in his Treatise or General Theory. Of course, the fundamental contradictions of the capitalist production and distribution system have been preserved, but world capitalism has undergone significant transformations in the last twenty years, called neoliberalism."

Finally, Desal this etc. To resolve doubts, he made the following appeal to Keynes' heirs:[62] "An environment of trust has been created for the revival of Keynesian ideas. However, these ideas need to be renewed and adapted to today. There are many economists seeking a new synthesis of Keynes' theory with recent developments in financial markets and technology. "Perhaps there will be another Keynes who can restore hope in the functioning of economists and economies."

In fact, as we can see from the clues above in his post-Great Depression theses, Keynes also drew a perspective on the financial market and its basic

---

[58] As the global recession was unfurling in late 2008, Harvard professor N. Gregory Mankiw wrote in the New York Times, "If you were going to turn to only one economist to understand the problems facing the economy, there is little doubt that the economist would be John Maynard Keynes (Jahan Sarwat, Ahmed Saber Mahmud, and Chris Papageorgiou, "What is Keynesian Economics?", *Finance & Development,* (2014): 53-54, 54.

[59] Sarwat vd., "What is Keynesian", 54.

[60] Mahfi Eğilmez, "Kriz Halinde Camı Kırınız", Ağustos 02, 2012, https://www.mahfiegilmez.com/2012/08/kriz-halinde-cam-krnz.html.

[61] Ferda Dönmez Atbaşı,"Kriz, Kapitalizm ve Keynes", *Toplum ve Demokrasi* 3 (6-7) (Mayıs-Aralık, 2009): 67-74,73.

[62] Desal, "Keynes ve Seksen Yıl", 13.

issues in his works. As a matter of fact, according to Keynes: ***i***-the primary task of the financial market is to "provide liquidity" to the economy because when the necessary liquidity is not provided, unemployment will increase in the economy, spare capacity will occur, economic growth will slow down and the economy will be dragged into depression. ***ii***-"Finance motive/reason" can be considered as the fourth reason for the demand for Money. An important consequence of this is that it has proven the relationship between the real and monetary sectors. The demand for money is not independent of demand in the real sector. This dependence between the demand functions of the real and monetary sectors also rejects the "classical dichotomy" approach that treats the sectors in question independently of each other. ***iii***- The development of the financial market has separated the investment owner and the investor. Such a separation further increased the instability of financial markets, and decisions regarding employment and production were left to expectations,[63] just like in a casino.[64]

Although Keynes partially explained the functioning of financial markets, he did not write specifically about financial crises and kept indebtedness analysis in the background. Although Keynes's finance motif presents elements of the endogenous money supply, Keynes's approach is inadequate.[65] Here, H.Minsky, one of Keynes' heirs, describes the "Financial Instability Theory (FIT)", which he describes as an interpretation of the basis of the General Theory and includes the analysis of the effect of borrowing on the system, which Keynes neglected, and provides the most obvious explanation for financial instabilities and crises in an economy. As a matter of fact, according to the basic understanding of FİT, the most typical feature of a capitalist economy is the existence of complex capital assets and a complex and developed financial system. The main problem of this type of economy is not the efficient use of resources, as suggested by traditional theory, but the development of capital in the economy, as Keynes stated. In short, the focus is on the economy of capitalist accumulation progressing in real calendar time.[66]

---

[63] According to Kazgan, Keynes was absolutely right when he called finance capitalism "casino capitalism".Casino capitalism operates in international finance in the neoliberal age, thanks to the computer; no longer millions, but billions, trillions of dollars change hands (For details, see Gülten Kazgan, "2008 Küresel Krizi: Nedenleri, Etik İlkeleri ve İktisat Eğitimi", *Küresel Bunalım ve İktisat Eğitimi,* 1-35,7.

[64] Vural Fuat Savaş, *Küresel Finans ve Makro iktisat,* (İstanbul: Efil Yayınevi, 2012).

[65] Nina Dodig and Hansjörg Herr, "Theories of Finance and Financial Crisis – Lessons for the Great Recession", *Institute for International Political Economy Berlin,* Working Paper, no. 48/2015 2015, 12.

[66] Hyman P. Minsky, "The Financial Instability Hypothesis", Working Paper, no. 74, 1992, 1-2.

According to the Keynesian Approach, the capital accumulation process, that is, investments, is at the centre of economic growth. Post-Keynesian economists also argue in their models that financial stability will support higher investment levels. Because in periods of financial stability, interest rates and debt rates are at low levels and both households and businesses have high liquidity. In addition to these positive conditions, there are also financing options for investment expenditures with new financial techniques. All of this means creating more demand than the current steady state predicts. The increase in investment expenditures leads to an increase in growth and profits, which, through feedback, increases the price of capital assets and, therefore, the price of investment demand. Thus, any full employment equilibrium leads to an expansion of debt financing that drives the economy to move beyond full employment. However, full employment is a temporary situation because financial liability structures and speculation and operations on new financial assets will drive the economy into an investment boom. This investment boom causes inflation, and with subsequent processes, the inflationary boom causes a financial structure suitable for financial crises.[67]

In short, financial stability allows investments and growth to increase in the first stage. However, in a capitalist economy open to financial innovation, it is not easy to make this sustainable because internal destabilizing forces are constantly at work that will lead to destabilization. Thus, in Minsky's words, stability can/will create instability.[68]

Finally, it can be said that the analyses of both Keynes and his successors regarding the financial crisis are in common in explaining the crisis mostly through market dynamics, the transforming structure of capitalism and external shocks or factors, without touching or questioning the fiction of capitalism. In this respect, according to Savran, Keynes' breakthrough in the thirties can be summarized as deepening the views of the realistic school (*underemployment*) and bringing them together with the views of the dogmatic school (*full employment*) (*neo-classical synthesis*).In the real world, both can exist. That's why Keynes calls his theory the general theory. However, Keynes's approach is a polished and improved realistic approach, and its limits become clear at this point. Because Keynes's "underemployment balance" deals with the most superficial characteristics of the crisis through some total economic quantities (investment, consumption, income, etc.). But in Keynes, the dynamic process behind these, the dialectical transition between "incomplete" and "full" employment situations, is not there, nor is the internal connection

[67] Orhangazi, "Günümüz Kapitalizminde Finansın Rolü", 35.

[68] Orhangazi, "Günümüz Kapitalizminde Finansın Rolü", 35.

established. In short, the place of crisis in the accumulation process was not theorized in Keynes either.[69]

Marxian Approaches: Although the nature of capitalism and its basic relations of production have not changed in the process of historical development, the conditions of capital accumulation, its technological foundations, the nature of the international division of labour and certain aspects of the relationship between the working class and capital have undergone significant changes. This is a consequence of the dynamic structure of capitalism: capital constantly changes the conditions of its own production.[70] Especially when the growth or profit opportunities of capital decrease, not only the accumulation model but also the social formation can be changed. As a matter of fact, although many meanings are attributed to the new historical phase of capitalism after 1980, neo-liberalism or globalization, its main purpose can be described as "*an attempt to establish and establish the domination of capital*", as Boratav puts it, rather than finding new/virgin markets where capital can flourish more. In this context, the brain centres of capitalism and the collective will that directs the system, inspired by the past, have initiated a program to realize the longing for "another golden age" that existed in the initial stages of the system. In a way, this can be considered as the return program of capitalism. In short, the golden age of labour and people is gradually transforming into wild capitalism, the golden age of capital.[71]

Moreover, since the rival team (socialist bloc) was dissolved and the "end of history" had come, it was not very difficult to get the surrounding capital to open its doors forever and to include it in this process. In this way, even though things seem to be going smoothly for the capital and the program seems to be working, over time, the capital, which dives into the markets "like an elephant entering a glassware shop", probably due to many other factors, the intoxication of uncontrolled power and the never-ending desire for profit, firstly to the environment and finally to its owner with the 2008 global financial crisis. It has also started to damage the centre. We can say that this crisis was "the last straw" for the defenders of capitalism as well as for all opposition circles. So much so that, in all circles, the feeling that it is time to question the system/house owner, who has remained a spectator to all the crises/criminal events in the system/house until today and evaded responsibility by placing the blame on others (the state), has begun to dominate.

---

[69] Savran, *Üçüncü Büyük Depresyon*, 29.

[70] Sungur Savran, "Bunalım, Sermayenin-Yeniden Yapılanması", in *Yeni Liberalizm, Dünya Kapitalizminin Krizi*, haz. Sungur Savran ve Nail Atılgan, (Belge Yayınları, 2009), 19-65,43.

[71] Korkut Boratav, *Dünyadan Türkiye'ye İktisattan Siyasete*, (Yordam Kitap, 2015) ,188-189.

Whether it is economic processes, problems related to blockages in the political plan, natural disasters, etc, there has never been a lack of crises affecting a wide segment of society, regardless of the reasons. Therefore, the problem of crisis should be approached in terms of what kind of social order it occurs in and what kind of consequences it will have according to the rules of the order, rather than what kind of crisis it is and what factors cause it.[72] However, one of the most important features of the dominant theories regarding the crisis is that the crisis is analyzed as an "event" that occurs only at certain intervals (*periodic*) and rather at a "certain moment" due to sudden external shocks or some wrong decision processes. Of course, crisis moment(s) are important because they are the moments when the expanding reproduction of the system does not continue and the rule does not work. But in order to explain and overcome the crisis, if we look behind the scenes[73] at the moment of crisis, the share/responsibility of the big picture/capitalist system in the crisis, rather than the actors (economic actors), can be revealed.

For this purpose, in Marxist doctrine, the phenomenon of crisis is explained by the organic transformations inherent in the system, which occur in different ways, such as excessive accumulation, decline in profit rates, profit squeeze and imbalances between sectors, in the context of the operating dynamics of the system and the organic composition of capital. In other words, crises arise from the functioning of capitalism and emerge in some periods to overcome the congestion.[74] As a matter of fact, according to Marx, crisis, "as a sudden and forceful solution" and "imposing itself with violent explosions", is the condition for stable capitalist development, but every stable development is also pregnant with a crisis. He explained this claim at two levels: the possibility and causality of the nature of capitalism for the crisis:[75]

i- It has shown that capitalist production relations may periodically encounter crises of overproduction or underconsumption due to their

---

[72] Dilber, "Herkesin Krizi Kendine", 34.

[73] Fuat Ercan, "Kriz: Tekrar ve Fark, Liberal Paradigma ve Küresel Kriz", in *Kriz ve Türkiye Aşınan Teoriler*, 109-133, 128; İzzettin Önder, "Küresel Kriz ve Türkiye Ekonomisi", *Muhasebe ve Finansman Dergisi* 42, (2009): 12 – 25, 15.

[74] Önder, "Küresel Kriz ve Türkiye Ekonomisi", 15.

[75] The existence of a close connection between growth and economic fluctuations in Marx can be verified. Although Marx showed that economic life would go through phases of "....average activity, prosperity, overproduction, depressions and stagnation" with ten-year crises, nowhere in Das Kapital did he say that capitalism would collapse with economic fluctuations and a general depression, (Sencer Divitçioğlu, *Karl Marx'da İktisadi Büyüme Marx'ın Görüşleri ve Harrod'la Karşılaştırma*, (Ankara: Efil Yayınevi, 2016)), 6.

internal contradictions. ii-The fact that profitability tends to decrease in parallel with the increase in the organic composition of capital and the belief that it will continue to decrease is in itself a harbinger of crisis.[76]

In parallel with the development of capitalism, production has become highly socialized, and all production and distribution activities have become interdependent. Especially with globalization, the division of labour in production has moved to an international dimension, and each part of the production has been carried out in different places and, moreover, by workers whose languages, cultures, etc., are different and who do not know each other. This can be called the international collectivity of labour. However, the (*new*) sociality that emerged with the significant development in all productive forces in this process, with the help of technology, experienced serious contradiction with the existing production relations. Because all decisions regarding the production process are made independently of each other and focused on profit rather than human needs by the owners of the means of production, each looking out for their own interests, that is the ever-growing capital. That's why underconsumption and overproduction situations occur both opposite and together. As a result of these two opposing features, the very complex production mechanism is completely unplanned or "anarchic".It is this contradiction that makes crises possible in capitalism.[77]

For this reason, according to Durmuş, the phenomenon called financial crisis is actually a symptom, but it is a symptom of capitalism, an irregular, diseased or problematic mode of production that is disconnected from human needs because capitalism is an economic system that creates permanent and destructive conflicts regarding the production and distribution of goods and services. In addition, capitalism not only leads to conflict between workers and capitalists but also to endless struggles, that is, competition between capitalists seeking profit. Competition also causes conflicts and crises.[78]

In addition, according to Marx, the rate of profit decreases due to the law of downward trend (KODE). The capital itself, on which capitalism is based and which it tries to expand through its functioning and development, becomes an obstacle to capitalist production, that is, capital accumulation, over time. What is meant by this is that capital accumulation reduces profitability, making reproduction impossible, and the tendency for profitability to decrease gives rise to capitalist crises. Although it may seem incomprehensible at first, an

[76] Dilber, "Herkesin Krizi Kendine", 30.

[77] Gencer Çakır, "Krizler Kapitalizmin Doğasında Vardır", *DİSKAR* 3 (2014): 6-19, 8; Savran, *Üçüncü Büyük Depresyon*, 33.

[78] Mustafa Durmuş, "Kapitalizmin Krizi ve Türkiye'ye Yansımaları", *Mülkiye* 33, 263 (2008): 9-27,13.

economic structure in which profitability is the main source of motivation also contains dynamics that will reduce profitability. The starting point for creating dynamics that reduce the profitability of capital accumulation, as if it puts a shackle on its feet, is the logic of capitalist competition.[79]

So much so that while competition between capitalists forces them to use effective technology, fixed capital investments made for this may increase profitability in the short term but decrease it later because, under all circumstances, the level and composition of total demand is the most important determinant in achieving the sales and therefore profit targets of all companies. As a matter of fact, while the new technology applied in a company provides extra profit with its competitive advantage and labour efficiency advantages, it can also cause unemployment rates to increase. Although high unemployment rates and low average wages increase profitability in the first stage, it may pose an obstacle to realizing profits if the total effective demand remains low. In addition, imbalances in the production of different sectors may negatively affect sales and profit performance in some sectors. Thus, although the process seems to be in favour of capital at the beginning, at the last stage, it drags the system into a deadlock/vicious circle, which is essentially a crisis, *a profit/accumulation crisis of capital.*[80] Capitalists, in accordance with their nature, withdraw from production and move to non-production areas because profit returns are not available or are decreasing. This fact lies behind the fact that they have been turning to the field of finance for nearly forty years and embarked on the path of "making money from money", and why the field of finance is more attractive than ever.[81]

Moreover, with the expansion of the financial sector, capitalists have access to capital through borrowing, and workers or other low-income earners have access to credit. In this way, capitalists provide both interest income and a lively demand in the goods and services market by transferring the resources they obtain through labour exploitation as a loan to the workers. In addition, the banking system and capital markets also increase their scale by accelerating the capital accumulation process by enabling investments that are much larger than those that capitalists can make with their profits. However, the financial sector, in the context of its operating dynamics, has the potential to block the system, just like the real sector. As a matter of fact, the slightest problem in profitability or, as in the 2008 crisis, reasons such as disruption of payments to the financial markets may disrupt the capital's pyramid scheme and, at the

---

[79] Ahmet Tonak, "Krizi Anlarken", *Çalışma ve Toplum Dergisi* (2009/01): 9-44, 33.

[80] Orhangazi, "Günümüz Kapitalizminde Finansın Rolü", 35; Önder, "Küresel Kriz ve Türkiye Ekonomisi", 16.

[81] Gencer Çakır, "Kriz, Finansallaşma ve "Çöküş"", *Bilim ve Gelecek* 141 (2015): 1-11,7.

same time, directly pave the way for a financial crisis. In addition, any problem or instability in the financial markets may disrupt investments and, thus, capital accumulation. In short, while the financial system accelerates capital accumulation and expands its scale, it will also increase the likelihood of potential problems, instability and crises.[82]

In fact, the financial system was developed to provide the necessary resources for the continuity of production and investment. However, the contribution that financial capital can make to production capital may often face some restrictions due to the economy's production power and resource creation capacity. However, the financial world, with its own dynamics and although it is controlled to some extent by various mechanisms, has an autonomous structure that can create resources through the expansion of bank loans and the policies of central banks. So much so that, while the banking system is moving away from control with a shift towards off-balance sheet activities, stock exchanges, although controlled by institutions that supervise and regulate the capital market, have produced unlimited mechanisms for value expansion. These may, at some stage of capital accumulation, lead to a tendency for the financial transactions production system to expand beyond what the capital accumulation, which has its basis in production, can handle. Marx defined this as over-credit, that is, the expansion of the financial system beyond the means of production. Thus, a boom period lasts longer than the conditions of production allow but usually ends with a collapse in the financial system.[83] With this bad ending, while huge financial capital stocks were separated from productive investment and dragged into dangerous adventures, capitalism was caught in hail/depression while trying to escape from rain/recession.

Crises Experienced/Caused by Capitalism

According to Wallerstein, capitalism, which has accompanied the last six hundred years of humanity's long journey of civilization, can be considered short but important, and it is possible to take part in this process and discuss the balance sheet of its virtues and sins, is probably unique to capitalism and one of its complementary features. Another feature that has not received much attention is that this system was celebrated by some but harshly condemned by others from the very beginning.[84]

---

[82] Önder, "Küresel Kriz ve Türkiye Ekonomisi", 15-16; Orhangazi, "Günümüz Kapitalizminde Finansın Rolü", 35.

[83] Savran, *Üçüncü Büyük Depresyon*, 39-40.

[84] Immanuel Wallerstein, *Tarihsel Kapitalizm ve Kapitalist Uygarlık*, çev. Necmiye Alpay, (İstanbul: Metis, 2021).

In this historical and long discussion, Başkaya's point that most of us will be sensitive to is "...so there will be two different views of the human condition depending on where it is viewed from." Are you looking at it from the side of those who confiscated the wealth of the world, are the main ones responsible for ecological destruction and say, 'After me, there will be a flood', or are you looking at it from the side of those who produce the wealth of the world but still cannot avoid being 'the cursed of the earth'? Answering the questions "will probably be decisive in clarifying the theses of the parties.[85] "However, recent discussions on the accounting of capitalism, which has been a world system for more than a century and covers the entire globe, from the perspective of humanity, is centred around national crises that threaten the gains achieved as a result of chance and become more frequent with the neoliberal model, and finally the global crisis. In this context, according to Cespedes and Quintana, humanity has reached a significant level of production and consumption (the world's average GDP per capita has constantly increased until 2008) despite such a crowded population (the world's population has now exceeded seven billion), as well as its distances. It also has the most advanced technologies. However, during this process, we also experienced one of the biggest crises of modern times in 2008. So much so that the economic and financial crisis: ***i***-reduced production and trade, ***ii***-unemployed millions of people worldwide, ***iii***-increased inequalities both domestically and internationally, ***iv***-escalated conflicts and violence, and ***v***-intensified the exploitation of natural resources. Due to all these negative effects, the current crisis has gone beyond economic decline.[86]

Such a global "expansion and crisis (*boom-bust*)" process has undoubtedly not been experienced for the first time in human history but has been experienced many times throughout the long history of capitalism. Because there is a line of development that occurs with an interesting regularity in the history of capitalism, and periods of vibrant capital accumulation are always followed by periods of stagnation. These are generally crisis periods when production and investment slow down; there is a surplus of commodities that cannot be sold, capacity utilization decreases, unemployment increases and

[85] Fikret Başkaya, "Finansal Kriz mi? Piyasacı Fundamentalizmin Çöküşü mü?", Özgür Üniversite Forumu, 01,1999,5-18,5-6.

[86] Gemma Cairo-i-Cespedes ve David Castells-Quintana, "Dimensions of The Current Systemic Crisis: Capitalism in Short Circuit?", *Progress in Development Studies* 16, 1 (2016): 1–23,1-2.

financial collapses occur.[87] In this context, it is possible to talk about three types of boom-bust cycles under one hundred and fifty years of capitalism.[88]

i- These are national or regional cycles that occur in periods of approximately 8-10 years (such as the 1974/1975, 1981/1982 and 2001/2002 crises)

ii- Also called Kondratieff Cycles, they are long-term cycles that occur globally every 50-60 years on average. The cycle ends with approximately 25-30 years of boom, followed by 25-30 years of stagnation and crisis. In this respect, it can be said that the global cycle we are in started in 1945, and after it first rose and reversed in 1970-1973, a downward process that lasted longer than normal began.

iii- Finally, much longer-term cycles resulting from geographical changes in imperialist hegemony can also be mentioned. So much so that while the hegemonic center of capitalist accumulation was Great Britain since the eighteenth century, the USA rivalled the British hegemonic power at the end of the nineteenth century and has remained unrivalled since 1945. The hegemonic power, on the other hand, is embodied with greater productivity and technological dynamism than its rivals. Against the possibility of the decline of the hegemonic power in the late 1970s, the solution of the centre was globalization and, accordingly, financialization.

Although there are many crises that can be associated with all three cycles in the history of capitalism, the Great World Depression of 1929 and the Global Financial Crisis of 2008 caused significant breaks in both its own history and the history of the economics discipline and occurred worldwide, should be particularly scrutinized.

1929 Great World Depression

In addition to being seen as the most important and deepest crisis in the history of economics, the 1929 Crisis[89], which has always been labelled as the "Great Depression/Depression/Collapse", is also the "biggest crisis" of the Great Recession, the crisis of the 2007-2009 period, especially with the contraction it caused in production and trade. It is accepted as an "ancestor". At this point, Özel says, "How did it happen that the crisis that triggered introversion and fascism (according to some experts, the Second World War) in some countries led to social democracy and dialogue, the organization and rights of labour, the state's control over the market in some other countries?"

---

[87] Savran, "Bunalım, Sermayenin-Yeniden Yapılanması", 19.

[88] Durmuş, "Kapitalizmin Krizi", 14-15.

[89] İrfan Kalaycı, "Finansal Kriz Konjonktürü (2007-2009) ve Küresel Ticaretin Anatomisi", *Avrasya Etüdleri TİKA* (2012): 157.

institutionalized its regulatory role? Good things came out of the Great Burhan; different tones of the social state emerged, or existing tones sharpened, and became the cornerstones of socioeconomic and political life in many countries."[90] He stated that political consequences were as effective as economic consequences *in the frame* of this crisis.

In order to understand how the milestones of the crisis were laid, when we rewind the reel of history and go to the nineteenth century, we encounter a shower of crisis. However, the most striking among these is the first major crisis of capitalism, also known as the "Long Depression", which lasted long enough to cause the First World War, covering the years 1873-1896. It is claimed that, in addition to the decline in the Vienna Stock Exchange, the large war reparations that France had to pay to Germany after the Franco-Prussian War also played a role in the crisis.[91]

When we come to the twentieth century, we encounter the first major crisis in the USA in 1907. The beginning of the crisis dates back to Italy. Namely, the Italian stock market, which is still in its development period, expanded with speculative movements fueled by loans, but many countries, especially Italy, entered into crisis when the Paris, London and New York stock exchanges, which are connected to each other, stopped lending, especially Paris and London. The factors that prepared the panic of 1907 in New York were large amounts of loans given by banks outside New York and loans taken from England. The speculations made with these loans and the failure to repay the debts inevitably brought about the great crisis.[92]

Although some national regulations were envisaged in the USA and Europe to prevent crises, especially after the 1907 crisis, the dominant liberal economic thought structure did not allow this, and the outbreak of World War I prevented the implementation of economic policies that could prevent crises. After the war, as developed countries, especially the USA, and the accompanying new world countries entered a rapid growth and development process, concerns about financial crises and the search for solutions remained in the background. This has led to the continued existence of an immature international monetary system that does not fully accompany the global financial system.[93] As a matter of fact, at the beginning of World War I, the gold standard was valid in many

[90] Işık Özel, "Peki Neymiş Bu Büyük Buhran", 2022, https://t24.com.tr/yazarlar/isik-ozel/peki-neymis-bu-buyuk-buhran,26384

[91] Eğilmez, *Tarihsel Süreç İçinde*, 117.

[92] Melih Gürsoy, *Dünyada Büyük Ekonomik Krizler ve Türkiye Ekonomisine Etkileri*, (Metis Yayınları, 1989), 39.

[93] Mustafa Emre Akbaş, "1800'lerin Küresel Krizleri, Büyük Depresyon ve 2008 Krizi", *İGÜ Sosyal Biimler. Dergisi* 4 (2017): 77-127, 89.

countries. However, after the war broke out, due to the severe need for financing, European countries abandoned the gold standard and started printing money without any return. This caused inflation to rise in these countries and investors to transfer their savings to US banks that still maintain the gold standard. As a result, approximately 40% of the world's gold wealth was concentrated in the USA, and the title of financial centre passed from London to New York.

In this context, the war only strengthened the position of the USA as the world's largest industrial power, but the fact that many countries trying to heal the wounds of the war met their financing needs by borrowing from the USA also made it the world's largest creditor.[94] While these debts deepened the depression in the economies of these countries, they both made the USA the superior power of the world and started the golden age of the American economy. In this period, referred to as the Roaring or "fun" 20s, new investment areas, industries and new products (automobiles, white goods, etc.) led to an expansion of production volume, thanks to the new technologies developed.[95] With this momentum, the USA, which expanded its market at the expense of European producers in the domestic and foreign markets and achieved a very good foreign trade balance, made progress on the path of continuous prosperity with the expanding market, increasing population and developing technology.[96] So much so that, especially during the presidency of J. Calvin Coolidge (1924-1929), the total real income of Americans increased by an average of 3.4% every year. Although the richest earned more, as predicted, most of the country shared the benefits of economic growth.[97]

This spring mood in the economy was also reflected in the capital markets, and the New York Stock Exchange was at the centre of the boom in the world and US capital markets. In fact, the stock market led a rise in prosperity during this period, and dividends paid to investors increased by nearly 100 per cent, especially during the Coolidge presidency. Therefore, market participants had no reason not to be optimistic. They had already prospered, albeit in less than ethical ways.[98]

---

[94] During this period, the total receivables of the USA from 15 countries, including interest, reached 11,563 million dollars, bkz. Hakan Ay ve Öznur Uçar, "Üç Küresel Ekonomik Krizin Analizi", *Dokuz Eylül Üniversitesi Sosyal Bilimler Enstitüsü Dergisi* 17, 1 (2015): 1-32,12.

[95] Eric Hobsbwan, *Kısa 20. Yüzyıl: 1914-1991 Aşırılıklar Çağı*, trans. Yavuz Alogan, (İstanbul: Sarmal, 2001), 125; Ay ve Uçar, "Üç Küresel Ekonomik Krizin Analizi, 12; Oya Köymen, *Sermaye Birikirken, Osmanlı, Türkiye, Dünya*, (İstanbul: Yordam Kitap, 2007), 43.

[96] Tevfik Gürkan, *İktisat Tarihi*, (İstanbul: Der Yayınları, 2011), 203

[97] Selwyn Parker, *Büyük Çöküş*, çev. Burcu Çekmece, (Ankara: Arkadaş Yayınevi, 2008), 10.

[98] Parker, *Büyük Çöküş*, 3-4-9.

This situation reinforces the idea (or is it the feeling) in investors that they will win under all circumstances and, eventually, in financing investments. In addition to savings, it has triggered them to resort to irrational methods such as mortgages of houses, using advances and borrowing by using the purchased securities as collateral to stockbrokers.[99] Moreover, in this period, just as capital exports from the USA accelerated, private borrowing also gained momentum as credit taps were opened within the country. So much so that before the crisis, the ratio of private debts to national income reached 184%.In this environment, speculative placements increased in the stock market, and while the value of stocks increased artificially, new debts were taken for speculation purposes.[100] Although many people in the financial environment draw attention to the danger of this speculation-credit-speculation spiral that is spreading uncontrollably and growing like a snowball, those responsible are primarily President Coolidge. In his speeches on different platforms, he explained that "it has reached the highest level of prosperity in years, and there is no situation more satisfactory than what seems now."In short, "What could be better and what could go worse than this?" He meant to say.[101]

However, his successor Hoover began to see clearly where the economy was heading and warned especially the business world against the dangers of an infectious disease such as speculation. To prevent this situation, in addition to the threat that regulations would be made to monitor the functioning of the stock market and stop excessive speculation, the attempts of the Bank of England and the equivalent Federal Reserve Bank to alleviate the heat in the credit market by increasing the rediscount rate (from 5% to 6%) were not very effective.[102] He explained the reason for this in his memoirs as follows:[103] "It was difficult for an already optimistic public to believe that great suffering and tragedies were hidden in a dark process such as credit inflation. This, of course, paved the way for bad manipulations and promotions of stocks."

Apart from a few magazines and newspapers, the economic press, in general, contributed directly or indirectly to the creation of this exaggerated optimism with its interesting and uncritical news about the rise in the capital markets, as well as the encouraging reports of the banks and finally the academic world

---

[99] Ay ve Uçar, "Üç Küresel Ekonomik Krizin Analizi", 12.

[100] Sinan Sönmez, *Dünya Ekonomisinde Dönüşüm: Sömürgecilikten Küreselleşmeye*, (Ankara: İmge Yayınevi, 1998), 75.

[101] Parker, *Büyük Çöküş*, 10.

[102] Parker, *Büyük Çöküş*, 24-26.

[103] Herbert Hoover, *The Memoirs of Herbert Hoover The Great Depression 1929-1941*, (New York: The Macmillan Company, 1952), 14.

with its evaluations.[104] Moreover, the chorus of "let them do it, let them pass" was immediately rising against possible state interventions in the market.

According to Galbraith, there was no need for anyone, especially wise people, to predict the 1929 crisis; no one, wise or not, could have known whether the time of the crisis had come or gone. He can't know now. This is mostly because the fervent rise in the stock market must eventually come to an end as all rises. On January 1, 1929, with a simple calculation of probability, there was a high probability that this rise would end before the end of the year. Because when prices stop rising, everyone will want to sell what they have, as owning goods on credit will become meaningless. As a result, the market will not stabilize but will decline rapidly.[105]

Again, according to Galbraith, the premiere of the 1929 Depression was staged with the declines seen in the market in February and March, but the inevitable finale was postponed with the repeated rises. However, with the collapse of the New York Stock Exchange on October 24 (Black Thursday) and then on October 29 (Black Tuesday) in 1929, *the Pollyanna Tale or Pollyannaism* in the financial markets came to an end. The crisis, which started with the stock market and soon included banks, also affected the sector. During this period, the USA lost 30% of its national income, the unemployment rate increased from 3% to 25%, and consumer prices fell by 27%. As a result, revenues, profits, prices and wages in all sectors have decreased significantly. This period, in which international trade contracted, caused all capitalist countries to enter a spiral of crisis through globalization mechanisms.[106]

Although there is a general opinion that the crisis started in the financial markets and spread to the real sector, Kindleberger and Aliber draw attention to the slowdown in industrial production that started before the collapse of stock markets in 1929. The industrial production index decreased from 127 in June to 122 in September, 117 in October, 106 in November and 99 in December. Likewise, automobile production, which was 660000 in March 1929, decreased during the months of August (440000), October (319000) and December (92000). These declines in output were too large-scale to be explained simply by changes in the money supply.[107] In this context, as stated

---

[104] Gürsoy, *Dünyada Büyük Ekonomik Krizler*, 83-84.

[105] John Kenneth Galbraith, *Büyük Kriz 1929*, çev. Özkan Özdem ve Elif Nihan Akbaş, (İstanbul: Pegasus, 2013), 37.

[106] Galbraith, *Büyük Kriz*, 37; Özel, "Peki,"Büyük Buhran""; Ay ve Uçar, "Üç Küresel Ekonomik Krizin Analizi", 13; Mustafa Durmuş, *Kapitalizmin Krizi: Küresel Krizin Eleştirel Bir Çözümlemesi*, (Ankara: Gazi Kitabevi, 2013), 94-95.

[107] Charles P. Kindleberger ve Robert Z.Aliber, *Çılgınlık, Panik, Çöküş: Finansal Krizler Tarihi*, çev.Ümit Şensoy, (Ankara, Türkiye İş Bankası Kültür Yay.,2014), 124.

by Gürsoy (1989.87), the depression actually occurred when the depression that started in the economy affected the stock market and caused its collapse.[108] According to Galbreath, the stock market was a mirror that reflected the underlying or main economic situation, albeit with a delay this time. The cause-effect relationship operated between the economy and the stock market, never in the opposite direction. In 1929, the economy was heading towards a disaster. In fact, that disaster manifested itself with all its intensity on Wall Street.[109]

In the final analysis, although opinions diverged on how and at the end of what process the crisis emerged, many people agreed on one point, as Özel stated: The belief in the "invisible hand" of the markets and that the imaginary hand could save the markets from the crisis was greatly shaken. The Keynesian welfare state approach, in which the state set rules for market players, created jobs if necessary to keep demand alive, and implemented active social policy, came to the fore in many countries.[110]

2007-2009 Global Financial Crisis

With Keynesian demand management policies, the crisis was overcome and the Great Depression-sized crises were prevented for approximately 30-35 years following 1945, and the capitalist world experienced dizzying growth rates, especially in the period 1950-1973. During the said period, the growth rate of the world economy reached 2.9%.[111] Moreover, it was not limited to economic geography; the economic growth rate was between 4-5% in Europe, 3% in the USA and 10% in Japan. New nation-states formed after the liquidation of former colonies also reached high growth rates with their development plans in this period.[112]

It was thought that crises remained an unpleasant memory of the nineteenth century, if not the 1930s, when a recession (crisis) broke out in 1974-1975, affecting many countries.[113] The story of the crisis can be explained in a way that most people would agree with, as follows: By the end of the 1960s, the US

---

[108] Gürsoy, *Dünyada Büyük Ekonomik Krizler,* 87

[109] Galbraith, *Büyük Kriz 1929,* 103.

[110] Özel, "Peki "Büyük Buhran"".

[111] Fikret Başkaya, *Küreselleşme mi Emperyalizm mi? Piyasacı Efsanenin Çöküşü,* (Ankara: Ütopya, 1990), 12-13; Erinç Yeldan, "Kapitalizmin Yeniden Finansallaşması ve 2007-2008 Krizi", *Çalışma ve Toplum* 1, (2009): 13.

[112] Ümit Akçay, "Kriz ve Alternatifler", 17/10/2023 https://www.gazeteduvar.com.tr/yazarlar/2017/07/17 kriz-ve-alternatifler,erişim

[113] Başkaya, *Küreselleşme mi Emperyalizm mi?,* 13.

economy could no longer finance the Vietnam War with standard fiscal policies because the budget deficits caused by the costs of the war necessitated extraordinary monetary expansion, which intensified the inflationary pressures in the American economy. As the rapid increase in the dollar amount in international markets brought the value of the dollar against gold to an unsustainable point, the USA ended the dollar gold standard and fixed exchange rate system in 1971. The Bretton Woods system has also technically collapsed.[114] Monetary authorities, freed from the constraints of the fixed exchange rate regime, were able to print as much money as they wanted, which led to an increase in inflation and commodity prices even before the oil embargo of the Yom Kippur War (*1973 Arab-Israeli War*) and the quadrupling of oil prices. The oil crises of 1973 and 1979 (the latter triggered by the Iranian Revolution) were followed by stagflation, a deadly combination of high inflation and recession, and incompetent monetary policies in response to these shocks.

According to Savran, linking the story of the crisis directly and only to oil is ideologically motivated. The responsibility of the crisis, which left millions of workers unemployed and created deep unrest in society, was placed on an "evil" will that remained outside the society. Behind all the troubles are the "Arab sheikhs".There is neither questioning capitalism as a system nor holding bourgeois states responsible.[115]

According to Yeldan, the immutable laws of capitalism were already operating with increasing global competition. As production became globalized and capital accumulation intensified, there was an inevitable decline in profit rates. The decline in industrial profits in almost the entire capitalist world, starting from the mid-1960s, was a sign that the end of the golden age was approaching. The pace of capital accumulation within national markets now required higher profits for new investments. However, the profitability possibilities of capital were limited by the size of the existing national market.[116]

Moreover, when capital accumulation hit the skids, when the sale of produced goods became difficult, and to put it in a Marxist concept, when a realization problem arose,[117] the way out could be to stimulate domestic demand and accelerate capital accumulation in this way. However, this method was not suitable for the profitability of capital as it would allow the income shares of labour to be directly increased. Therefore, there was only one option left: *rapid*

---

[114] Yeldan, "Kapitalizmin Yeniden Finansallaşması", 14.

[115] Savran, *Üçüncü Büyük Depresyon*, 57.

[116] Yeldan, "Kapitalizmin Yeniden Finansallaşması", 13.

[117] Fikret Başkaya, *Çöküş: Kapitalizmin Nihai Krizi Üzerine Bir Deneme*, (İstanbul: Yordam Kitap, 2018), 59.

transition of capital to financial investment areas (financialization) and internationalization.[118] The paradigm that will provide this opportunity to capital is new liberalism, which is one of the main reasons for the integration of the world as a state policy today[119]. After 1980, a new era entered, and the elements of control and audit mechanisms related to finance capital were released. In this context, finance capital, which has had its political program accepted by political powers, has largely eliminated the obstacles that limited it, especially in the process starting from the USA and continuing within the EU.[120] Thus, a period began in which the structure and functioning of capitalism evolved into financialization.

In this way, with liberalization, the "visa" problem was solved, the way for the capital was wide open, and a wave of financialization took over. So much so that the financial system, whose main function and reason for existence is to support international trade and balance of payments, has become independent from production and trade, that is, from the real economy, and has progressed in its own course. Financial transactions are generally oriented towards speculation.[121] So much so that "money games" have become the rule, not the exception, in the world's major financial centres. Moreover, the financial sector does not create new value; It re-evaluates the value created in agriculture, industry and services sectors. Of course, there is financial profit in this process, but this profit does not *correspond to any value,* which is what is meant by the concept of a financial bubble/ *bubble.*[122]

With the rapid financialization of the economy in most countries, especially in advanced Anglo-Saxon countries, financial institutions, in order to expand their customer portfolio, provide loans to all segments of the society, including workers who lack financial means, through various means (overdraft, credit cards, mortgages, etc.) According to Kindleberger and Aliber, *speculation frenzies* gain momentum with the expansion of credit.[123] Increases in the supply of credit do not often lead to a craze—but every craze is associated with

---

[118] Erinç Yeldan, "Kapitalizmin Yeniden Finansallaşması ve Kriz: Öğrenilenler, Unutturulmak İstenenler", in *Kriz ve Türkiye Aşınan Teoriler,* 95-109,99.

[119] Sungur Savran, *Kod Adı Küreselleşme 21. Yüzyılda Emperyalizm,* (İstanbul: Yordam Kitap, 2008), 108.

[120] Korkut Boratav, "Kriz, Direnişler ve Gelecek", *Mülkiye* 36, 274 (2015): 7-12, 7.

[121] Başkaya, *Çöküş,* 62.

[122] Erinç Yeldan, "Büyük Durgunluğun Öğrettikleri", *İktisat ve Toplum* 1 (Ekim 2010): 16-24, 17.

[123] Alfredo Saad-Filho, *Kriz Çağı Neoliberalizm, Demokrasinin Çöküşü ve Pandemi,* çev. Şükrü Alpagut, (İstanbul: Yordam Kitap, 2022), 36.

a rapid growth in the supply of credit to a certain segment of borrowers.[124] In this way, households were drawn into the speculation spiral of asset price inflation, with even spending often financed through "easy" loans or by remortgaging their homes in booming housing markets. In each case, institutions have expanded their opportunities to sell services to households and trade new financial products. This was particularly prevalent in the macroeconomic context between the early 1990s and the mid-2000s when interest rates were low.[125]

When we move in this direction, it is possible to clarify the mechanism of the current financial crisis, which seems quite complex. Our starting point is that there is already a significant amount of "*free*" capital in the countries at the centre of capitalism in search of maximum profitability because periodically, these capitals discover new sources of profit and start a craze fed by "*self-fulfilling prophecies*"; It flocks to the asset that seems to provide the highest return and raises its price, thus confirming the initial optimism. Warnings that the market in question (such as the stock market and the mortgage market) will not rise indefinitely are not taken seriously because the game has worked.[126]

The game, which was constructed in this way and ended in disappointment, caused many financial crises to be recorded both in the periphery (such as Southeast Asian and Russian crises) and in the centre since 1980. As a matter of fact, financial troubles shook Wall Street in 1987, 1990, 1998 and 2001, and a contraction followed especially the 1990 and 2001 crises. Yet, compared to the crises that have shaken every other corner of the world since the rise of neoliberalism, the United States and Canada, as well as their friends in Europe, enjoyed periods of relative tranquillity until the subprime mortgage crisis of 2007.[127]

In fact, the way the last global financial crisis occurred is similar in many respects to the mechanism/structure specific to the financial crisis above. Namely, due to the successive problems seen in the financial markets in the USA and, finally, the fear of recession in 2001, the FED reduced the interest rate to 1% as of 2002, making low-interest borrowing possible and paving the way for the explosion in consumer loans. In other words, US capitalism through debt aimed to: i- postpone the recession due to the increase in total demand by

---

[124] Kindleberger ve Aliber, *Çılgınlık, Panik, Çöküş*, 97.

[125] Filho, *Kriz Çağı*, 36.

[126] Michel Husson, *Toksik Kapitalizm*, çev. Osman S. Binatlı, Inprecor, 541/542, (Eylül-Ekim 2008). http://gesd.free.fr/toksik.pdfI

[127] Ingo Schmidt, *Krizleri Kıyaslamak, Neoliberalizm ve Kriz*, haz. Hakan Tanıttıran, çev. Barış Baysal vd., (İstanbul: Kalkedon Yay.,2008), 65-79, 68.

increasing consumption and investment expenditures (especially housing and automobiles), ii- overcome the profit squeeze in the real sector and revaluate the capital in the financial sector, iii- satisfy the profit hunger of the huge amount of autonomous financial capital.[128]

In this process, the housing need of low-income segments in the USA was seen as an important potential for the financial system. However, crediting this segment; There is also risk due to negative situations regarding savings, income, credit card, etc. Despite this, financial institutions, dazzled by the appetite for profit fueled by this potential, provided mortgage loans to this segment under special conditions and with very relaxed rules. In addition, not only those who wanted to own a house but also investors and speculators turned to the real estate market because they saw it as profitable and also funded their investments with loans. Financial institutions that gave real estate loans against mortgages either sold their loans or created a financing/*ponzi chain* by issuing asset-backed securities (*securitization*) and thus tried to spread the potential risk.[129]

However, interest rates increased after 2004, reaching 4.25% at the end of 2005 and 5.25% in mid-2006. As a matter of fact, the first signs of the crisis began in the spring of 2006 with the disruption of these loans.[130] In this case, banks attempted to seize and sell the houses. This caused both the price and mortgage value of houses to decrease so that when house prices fell, debtors could not borrow again. Thus, when first the house owners, then those who produced and sold securities based on the value of these houses, those who traded them, the banks that held their assets, and those who insured their risks were unable to pay their debts to each other, credit dried up. As the demand for liquidity increased, interest rates rose even more. In the financing chain, which became quite complicated, when financial intermediaries stopped making transactions because the source of the risk could not be fully determined, the financial system was locked and collapsed with a domino effect. The financial crisis spread all over the world in a very short time and also quickly spread to the real sector and deepened.[131]

So much so that the US economy shrank by an average of 3.5% during the contraction period from the fourth quarter of 2007 to the second quarter of

---

[128] Durmuş, *Kapitalizmin Krizi,* 11.

[129] Durmuş, *Kapitalizmin Krizi,* 11; Öztin Akgüç, "Kriz Nedeni ve Çıkış Yolları", *Muhasebe ve Finansman Dergisi* 42 (2009): 6-11,7; İzzettin Önder, *Dünya Ekonomisinde Krizlere Bakış, İktisat Üzerine Düşünceler,* (İstanbul: Yordam Kitap, 2016), 18.

[130] Kazgan, "2008 Küresel Krizi", 4-5; Durmuş, *Kapitalizmin Krizi,* 12.

[131] Durmuş, *Kapitalizmin Krizi,* 12.

2009. While unemployment was 5% in 2007, it reached 7.3% in 2008, double digits in 2009 (10% in October) and 9.9% at the end of the year. EU countries were among the countries most affected by the crisis due to their close economic and commercial relations with the USA. While the three-year average growth rate in the EU was positive (2.7%) before 2008, it turned negative (-0.6%) after the crisis (2008-10). The EU unemployment rate, which was around 8% in the same period, increased by 0.5% points. This meant hundreds of thousands of people lost their jobs.[132]

In short, while the "financial expansion" bubble that the USA inflated in its own economy to overcome the 2000-2001 crisis created a bubble on a global scale, this was followed by a global bubble burst in 2008 (*both those who inflated and burst the bubble were deep capitalists*).[133] However, as in all other crises, the source of this crisis, beyond what appears at first glance, is also systemically based on the internal dynamics and functioning of capitalism, but also on issues specific to its neoliberal form, whose locomotive is financialization. In this way, one dimension of the crisis was created by policies that rejected public control, especially in the financial sector, and liberalized and globalized all kinds of capital, goods and service movements. Secondly, the instability of the world's main reserve currency, the dollar, whose amount and value can change around the world depending on the domestic/foreign policies of the USA. The third is the power of the US financial sector to create liquidity through innovations, through derivatives and without any national/international control.[134]

In addition, on the universal dimension of the crisis, the existence of large current, budget and savings-investment deficits ('triple deficits' or 'black holes') due to excessive domestic consumption in the US economy, financialization and the expansion of the dominant power of "finance capital" is taken into consideration. It should not be ignored. Whichever country is economically dependent or dependent on the USA has been drawn into the vortex of crisis.[135]

Although this panorama of the crisis evokes the feeling of "we have seen this movie before", Yeldan stated the difference between this wave of crisis from the previous ones as follows:[136]: "The current global crisis has coincided with a

---

[132] İrfan Kalaycı, "Euro Bölgesinde Mali Kriz ve Yeni Makro İktisadi Yönetişim", *Akdeniz İ.İ.B.F. Dergisi* (25) (2013): 123–149, 128.

[133] Kalaycı, "Finansal Kriz Kriz Konjonktürü", 151.

[134] Kazgan, "2008 Küresel Krizi", 1-2.

[135] Kalaycı, "Finansal Kriz Konjonktürü", 150.

[136] Yeldan, "Kapitalizmin Yeniden Finansallaşması", 12.

financialization process in human history where money is not tied to any gold or precious metal standards and fictitious values prevail."

Piketty asks: Could the increase in inequalities in the USA have an impact on the emergence of the financial crisis in 2008? He stated that this problem cannot be ignored, considering that the share of the top 10% of the US national income reached two record levels, first in 1928 (before the 1929 crisis) and then in 2007 (before the 2008 crisis). Because, above all, there is no doubt that the increase in inequalities makes America's financial system fragile. There is a simple reason for this: The increase in inequalities has created stagnation in the purchasing power of the public and the middle class, which has increased the tendency for households living in modest conditions to borrow. On the other hand, in parallel with this, banks and intermediary institutions, which were not very meticulous, gave loans to households, as stated above, in order to provide high returns to the huge financial savings of the increasingly wealthy segments offered to the system.[137] It is observed that when the middle and lower income groups, which have a high tendency to spend, borrow rapidly, the demand also increases rapidly. However, this increases/has increased the possibility that the process will result in a debt crisis, as in the US real estate bubble.[138]

To summarize, as Saad-Filho points out, as accumulation and social reproduction become financialized in neoliberalism, economic crises, above all, have now acquired a financial character. Crises today typically arise from *the overproduction of fictitious capital* and are often triggered by the collapse of complex structures of paper-based demands for earnings and wealth. These crises, which centre on the overaccumulation of fictitious capital, are completely different from the crises of disproportionate and overproduction that are typical of earlier stages of capitalism.[139]

Finally, it can be inferred that similar conditions led to similar outcomes in both crises, i.e. a deterministic situation. In this context, the periods in question were characterized by the following factors in order of importance in the outbreak of the crises: ***i***- developments in finance that modified the role of commercial banks; ***ii***- an increase in liquidity at the global level that did not lead to inflation but caused risk premiums to decrease; ***iii***- a banking sector that became concentrated in number and size of banks; and ***iv***-a strong belief

---

[137] Thomas Piketty, *Yirmi Birinci Yüzyılda Kapital,* haz. Hande Koçak, (İstanbul: Kültür Yayınları, 2015), 316-317.

[138] Yılmaz Akyüz, Kriz, "Marx ve Keynes, Bölüşüm, Finansallaşma ve Ekonomik Durgunluk", *İktisat ve Toplum Dergisi* 74 (2016): 18-26, 22.

[139] Filho, *Kriz Çağı,* 46.

in the capacity of central banks to promote economic stability and to prevent financial crises in the long run.[140]

Policies Against Crises and State Intervention Capitalism

The development line of capitalism, which was interrupted by crises, continued on its way with a new strategy, provided that it remained true to its essence after overcoming or completing the improvement process with Keynesian policies after each crisis. As a matter of fact, he regained his throne, which he unintentionally lost to Keynes after the 1929 crisis, with the neoliberal strategy after 1980. However, according to Başkaya, the new strategy envisaged as a solution to capitalism's "inability to create value" also disappointed expectations. In fact, the medication recommended as a treatment for the disease deepened the disease even further. Because it was inevitable that neoliberal policies that encouraged financialization would further exacerbate this disease. In other words, the last financial crisis only revealed the incurable structural disease of the system again. However, this time, the crisis is considered a 'civilization crisis' as it affects the entire system and covers all dimensions of society's life.[141]

Despite this, as Savran points out, establishment/mainstream economists even tried to create the perception that there was a crisis only in the financial world by calling the crisis the 'global financial crisis'.Moreover, as usual, they asserted with great confidence that the crisis was a "temporary fix", that it would be overcome in a short time, and that a long and major crisis should not be expected. However, considering that the financial collapse experienced in 2008 was the product of the contradictions that have been accumulating since the mid-1970s and a significant uneven development between the financial world and the real economy, this crisis may turn into a depression that will last for years. By using the term "Great Recession" for the crisis, the IMF provided a third alternative and at the same time achieved a consensus, albeit partially.[142]

Rather than discussing the differences in the name and diagnosis of current or previous crises, when the main issue is a crisis, it is undoubtedly more indispensable to focus on policies that can be implemented to prevent the destruction it will cause, heal the wounds it has caused in society, and normalize economic life. All of the various 'crisis prescriptions' that can be produced from perspectives that are based on capitalist production relations

---

[140] Cristina Peicuti, "The Great Depression and the Great Recession: A Comparative Analysis of Their Analogies", *The European Journal of Comparative Economics* 1, no.1 (2014): 55-78.

[141] Başkaya, *Çöküş*, 72.

[142] Savran, *Üçüncü Büyük Depresyon*, 17-19.

and accept that there are natural (objective) laws of the economy can be grouped into three main groups.[143]

i- The first of these will consist of approaches based on and derived from the main idea of relegating the solution and prevention of crises to the internal dynamics of the system and avoiding intervention in them. Adherents of the neo-classical school are in this category.

ii- The second group, which also believes that the crisis is caused by an extraordinary and extra-systemic factor, will consist of those who highlight the need to intervene in the crisis with extra-systemic and extraordinary tools and methods. Current suggestions emerging as alternatives to this through Keynesian approaches are also included in this category.

iii- Thirdly, various hybrids or intermediate formulas formed between the first two are ultimate solutions that can be included in one or the other of these groups.

Durmuş, on the other hand, lists direct state interventions in the form of nationalization, Keynesian monetary and fiscal policies, and IMF-supported neo-liberal policies, which are largely identified with the above distinctions, as methods of capitalism's exit from the crisis, as well as corrective wars and oppressive authoritarian regime practices, which can be considered relatively contradictory, as solution alternatives.[144]

As Roubini points out, although crises are the standard rather than the exception in the history of modern capitalism, this does not mean that all crises are the same. On the contrary, the details may vary from disaster to disaster, and crises may have their roots in different problems in different areas of the economy. So much so that the crisis may arise from excessive borrowing, or financial institutions, companies, or even governments may be to blame. Moreover, the damages caused by crises can vary greatly; This often depends on the extent and appropriateness of government intervention. When crises have a global dimension - as has been the case in the worst crises - in addition to numerous economic effects (complete destruction of business lines, large-scale unemployment, etc.), they have even overthrown governments, bankrupted nations, and dragged countries into trade wars. Beyond that, crises even led to wars, just like the Great Burhan II. Just as it prepared the environment for World War II, for these reasons, ignoring crises is not an option.[145]

---

[143] Dilber, "Herkesin Krizi Kendine", 29.

[144] Wallerstein, *Tarihsel Kapitalizm*, 97.

[145] Roubini ve Mihm, *Kriz Ekonomisi*, 23.

In this context, the rush to prevent the economic effects of crises from causing social and political consequences and to save capitalism, which loses credibility in the eyes of societies, the business world and even its defenders around the world with each crisis, necessitated taking steps for a solution. Undoubtedly, in order to decide on the solution strategy that can be applied to the current global financial crisis, one of the first solutions that comes to mind is to look at the dusty pages of history and investigate what the solutions were for similar crises experienced in the past. The same thing happened this time. The most important case study was the First World Crisis between 1929 and 1933. One of the things remembered about this crisis was D. Roosevelt's growth policies, called the 'New Deal', which envisaged the rapid increase in state investments.[146] On the other hand, the Keynesian thought we mentioned above - which is a product of the 1929 crisis - argues that the crises experienced by capitalism are mostly caused by uncontrollable factors (such as consumption tendency, psychological factors that cause interest and investments to fluctuate) and can be eliminated by the state that acts rationally and intervenes adequately in the economy. In other words, it is possible to give capitalism a rational and harmonious character through state intervention.[147] Keynes' analyses and suggestions in this context left their mark on the 'Golden Age' of capitalism.[148]

Here is F.D. to get out of the crisis. The New *Order*, implemented by the Roosevelt Government in two stages between 1933 and 1939, brought about the active intervention of the state in the market and market players, with many new institutions and regulations in line with a new perspective on capitalism (*New Order Capitalism*) in the USA.[149] In short, the order is symbolized by '3R'; It is based on three headings: Relief, Recovery and Reform. The aim was to support the unemployed and the poor with aid, to stabilize the US economy through recovery, and to protect the financial system against possible aftershocks of deflation through reform.[150] Measures passed to this end included banking and monetary reform, the Federal Emergency Relief Act

---

146 Savaş, *Küresel Finans*, 230.

147 Savran, *Üçüncü Büyük Depresyon*, 63; Hüseyin Özel, "Genel Teori'nin 'Kararsızlığı' Üzerine", *İktisat ve Toplum Dergisi* 74 (2016): ,42-52,43. 861

148 Eşiyok," Keynesyen "Altın Çağ'dan Neoliberal Orta Çağ"a", 61.

149 Işık Özel, "Büyük Burhan'da Tango ve "Çivisi Çıkan Dünya"", 9/9/2023 https://t24.com.tr/yazarlar/isik-ozel/buyuk-buhran-da-tango-ve-civisi-cikan-dunya,26478

150 Hüseyin Şen ve Ayşe Kaya, "Ekonomik Krizlerin Değişmeyen İmdatçısı Maliye Politikası", *Sosyoekonomi* (2015): 56-86,62.

(FERA) to support states, the National Industrial Recovery Act (NIRA), and the Agricultural Adjustment Act (AAA) to support farms and farm prices.[151]

However, F.D. The Roosevelt administration did not accept that the measures taken were anti-capitalist and argued that these measures were necessary to prevent the collapse of capitalism. Some business people and conservatives who opposed the *"New Deal"* described it as a *"cautious socialism"*.While the wage earners and unions supported the relevant measures, the American public did not accept the criticism of socialism directed at Roosevelt.[152]

According to Şen and Kaya, although the name was not mentioned clearly, these Keynesian practices, which were initiated with "pump priming"[153] within the scope of the New Deal, had a positive effect on the US economy in a short time and the impact of the crisis began to gradually decrease from the first quarter of 1933. Unemployment fell from a peak of 25% in 1933 to 10% in 1937 but rose again in 1938. Despite this, there was still success. There was also a very rapid growth in GNP, except for 1938. In this way, the US economy had returned to normal before the start of World War II.[154]

In this context, the liberal economic model's flirtation with the New Order, which was the recipe for salvation from the depression, and Keynes' policies, especially when the unemployment rate started to rise again, continued with the same policy step of the US Federal Government's attempt to ensure full employment after the Second World War. It is clear that all the policies implemented are the result of Keynes' views. The fact that capitalism overcame the most important crisis in its history by benefiting from the views of a capitalist economist also shows the flexibility of the system and its suitability for different applications.

Can the policies that were tried and achieved during the Great Depression be a role model for getting out of the 2008 crisis that capitalism recently experienced? In this regard, FED Chairman Ben S. Bernanke said the fourth

---

[151] Richard Walker, "The New Deal in Brief", ,https://livingnewdeal.org/wp-content/uploads/2012/01/New-Deal-in-Brief.pdf 09.11.2023.

[152] Adnan Güriz, *Kapitalist İdeoloji,* (Ankara: Phoenix Yay.,2010), 165.

[153] It is a term that refers to increasing purchasing power to the market and increasing public expenditures in order to stimulate economic life in periods of recession.It is sometimes the case that water is poured from above to operate a pump whose water has been drained from its pipes.The way this water eliminates the air in the pump and pipes and establishes a connection between the well and the tap is called "pump priming" https://www.iktisatsozlugu.com/tr/nedir/pump-priming/4067

[154] Şen ve Kaya, "Ekonomik Krizlerin Değişmeyen İmdatçısı", 64; Walker, "The New Deal", 5.

lesson[155] he learned from the financial crash of the 1930s: "*unfortunately, history is never a perfect guide.*" stated as.[156] Because, as BSB stated, the conjuncture in which each crisis occurs is different from the other. We need to take particular account when evaluating the two areas where this difference manifests, namely the effects of the crisis and the possibilities of overcoming capitalism. The first, and relatively less touched upon, area is the way capital and the state respond to the crisis. This answer is determined by both the political culture of the current geography and the way the crisis emerged.[157] In fact, Aiginger states that all crises have different causes and consequences and that the effects of the crisis should not be exaggerated due to the different development and indebtedness of countries. Moreover, the current crisis is, above all, not regional but worldwide.[158] On the other hand, each country that entered the crisis or was indirectly affected by it tried to manage the crisis in its own way. 'Crisis management' is the first and main method of challenging the crisis. The second challenge is the restructuring of the global financial architecture.[159]

Another important problem at this stage is who will manage the crisis. Since the last crisis shows that uncontrolled market freedom can be the trigger of economic crises, markets that are dragged into crisis can be brought back on track, at least to some extent, not by active market players (*private administration*) but only by public intervention (*public administration*).[160]

In addition, according to Stiglitz, crisis management should be on a global basis, and he expressed some possible negative effects of remaining on a local/national basis as follows:[161]

> "A global crisis requires a global response, but the responses so far have been national. Each country focuses on its own balances; for example,

---

[155] First, economic prosperity depends on financial stability; second, policymakers must respond forcefully, creatively and decisively to serious financial crises; Third, crises that are international in scope require an international response.

[156] Ben Bernanke, "Economic Policy: Lessons from History, 2010", https://www.federal reserve.gov /newsevents/speech/bernanke20100408a.htm,erişim 20.10.2023.

[157] Bağımsız Sosyal Bilimciler, *Türkiye'de ve Dünyada Ekonomik Bunalım 2008-2009,* (İstanbul: Yordam Kitap, 2009), 73.

[158] Karl Aiginger, "The Current Economic Crisis: Causes, Curesand Consequences", *WIFO Working Papers,* no. 341, (Vienna, Austrian Institute of Economic Research (WIFO), 2009): 11.

[159] Kalaycı, "Finansal Kriz Konjonktürü", 153-154.

[160] Önder, "Küresel Kriz ve Türkiye Ekonomisi" , 14.

[161] Stiglitz, "The Current Economic Crisis", 35.

> the cost of increasing national debt with the incentive it will get from spending. Increased expenditures are externalities that will not be taken into account for other countries unless coordinated action is taken. Worse, each country will tend to maximize its multiplier through beg-thy-neighbour policies, such as the "Buy America" clause in the stimulus package... If every country focused only on its own interests, some countries would be free riders. So the size of the global stimulus will be less than necessary, and the global impact will be smaller as each tries to find expenditures with the largest domestic multipliers, regardless of the global multipliers. There is a big difference between local and global multipliers, and an effective global response needs to focus on global multipliers."

However, in the following, Stiglitz calculates that since the fire/crisis started in the USA and spread to the surrounding areas, the fire must be extinguished in the centre first. He says:[162]

> "The United States has a special responsibility to act responsibly. Because this crisis clearly has a "Made in the USA" label on it. We created and then exported toxic mortgages – about half of them, in fact. Once again, we benefited from globalization: if we had not exported so much, we would have had an even deeper crisis here. Our banks would be in even bigger trouble. We exported the philosophy of deregulation, which meant that many people elsewhere did not take precautions to prevent them from purchasing these toxic products. Now we have exported our recession."

To overcome the financial crisis, two models that can be called the *Japanese and Swedish models* stand out. These:[163]

i- How the Japanese coped with the banking crisis of the 1990s. The government initially did not accept the extent of the problem and created a speculative bubble by financially supporting financial institutions. The result is a decade of slow or no growth. In addition, today, significant amounts of public resources have been used to recapitalize a concentrated banking system. It cannot be said that the broader economy is still on track.

ii- The second is the *Swedish* model, where the government reorganizes banks into state ownership. In 1985, when Sweden's credit markets

---

[162] Stiglitz, "The Current Economic Crisis", 35-36.

[163] William K. Tabb, *ABD Kapitalizminin Finansal Kriz, Neoliberalizm ve Kriz,* haz. Barış Baysal vd.,(İstanbul, Kalkedon, 2008), 7-25,18.

became unstable, a real estate speculation and bubble similar to that in the USA broke out. For this reason, the banking sector suffered serious damage between 1990 and 1994, but the government allowed most of the banks to go bankrupt and confiscated their assets. Over time, she disposed of her assets and then sold the banks to the private sector. In this way, taxpayers got their money back and economic growth was achieved.

In the USA, the crisis was underestimated at the first stage, and it was predicted that the crisis could be overcome with interest rate cuts. The FED reduced the interest rate from 5.25% to 0.25% in a few months in 2007-2008, thus trying to alleviate the problems arising from mortgage loans by reducing the borrowing cost of the banking sector. However, since low interest alone would not be sufficient due to the liquidity trap, all countries switched to the policy called *'Quantity Expansion'* with reference to *the Japanese model.* The FED began purchasing $85 billion worth of treasury bonds every month. This meant flooding the market with liquidity.[164] But while this move lacked a farsighted program and was implemented as a wild series of improvised interventions that attempted to cover up the crisis with more money than the previous one, the authorities had no intention of stopping until the bank failures were over.[165]

However, a first occurred in the 2008 crisis, as the efforts made in the field of monetary policy were not successful. Large companies were not allowed to fail under the excuse of "*too big to die*".[166] So much so that this time, with reference to the *Swedish model,* investment banks such as *Fannie Mae and Freddie Mac* in the USA, the world's largest insurance company such as *AIG,* and *NorthernRock Bank* in the UK were nationalized. However, (neo)liberal discourse is strongly against the "rescue" of loss-making or bankrupt companies. But giant companies were "saved" with state support, because even the bankruptcy of one of them could lead to the collapse of the entire system. Thus, by not allowing the corrective effect of crises, it has been accepted that capitalism has crossed the unsustainable threshold. In other words, although they seem to be managing the situation for now by financial speculation, by exploiting accumulated state institution funds, public resources, etc., there is no end to this.[167]

---

[164] Akgüç, "Kriz Nedeni", 8; Savran, *Üçüncü Büyük Depresyon,* 15.

[165] David MCnally, *Çöküş, Kemer Sıkma ve Direniş, Ekonomik Kriz ve Sol,* haz. Leo Panitch, Greg Albo and Vivek Chibber, tarns. Umut Haskan, (İstanbul: Yordam Kitap, 2011), 52-79,54.

[166] Savran, Üçüncü Büyük Depresyon, 15; Başkaya, *Çöküş,* 73.

[167] Durmuş, "Kapitalizmin Krizi", 98 ve Başkaya, *Çöküş,*73.

As a matter of fact, bank rescue operations were not sufficient, as was the radical change in monetary policy. Although the international financial system had overcome the deadlock with these two measures, the world economy was experiencing a major shock. So much so that global production was contracting for the first time since World War II, including a contraction in China. Even in China and India, growth fell to single digits, while in advanced capitalist countries, the decline was much higher. Therefore, in addition to monetary and financial rescue, Keynesian policies, which have been despised for more than thirty years, have begun to be implemented in fiscal policy. One of the first tasks of the Obama administration, which came to power in January 2009, was an 860 billion dollar project. In addition to increasing public expenditures, the aim was to pass a financial support package through Congress that included widespread tax cuts to stop the decline in private demand.[168]

In parallel with this package, the FED, between 2010 and 2013, respectively, Under the names of QE2, OperationTwist, QE3 and finally QE4, continued to implement monetary expansion programs by purchasing long-term treasury and bonds and mortgage-based products from banks.[169]

With the support provided to the economy from two branches through expansionary monetary and fiscal policies, efforts were made to limit the effects on the real sector, primarily by improving the functioning of the financial sector and, at the same time, activating the dynamics of growth and employment under the leadership of the public. According to Köse et al., of the four global recessions experienced since 1950 (1975, 1982, 1991 and 2009), 2009 was the second strongest period after 1975, in which the recovery was experienced thanks to large, rapid and globally coordinated policy support.[170] As a matter of fact, growth rates in the USA reached their normal level, being 2.6% in 2014 and 2.9% in 2015, while the unemployment rate was 9.3% in 2009 and 6.2% in 2014 and 2015. It decreased to 5.3% in 2017. In short, the Keynesian economic model once again came to the rescue of the US economy, the UK, the EU, Japan and finally, the developing economies and saved the system.[171]

Thus, the state once again saved the economy from the brink of the cliff in 2008, as it did in 1929. On this occasion, the increasing role of the state in every country to stabilize the economy and its welfare/social aspect, which is actually

---

[168] Savran, *Üçüncü Büyük Depresyon*, 16

[169] Mahfi Eğilmez, *Değişim Sürecinde Türkiye: Osmanlı'dan Cumhuriyet'e Sosyo-Ekonomik Bir Değerlendirme*, (İstanbul, Remzi Kitabevi, 2018), 79-80.

[170] M. Ayhan Kose, Naotaka Sugawara and Marco E. Terrone, “Global Recessions”, *Policy Research Working Paper* 9172, (WBG, 2020), 3.

[171] Eğilmez, *Değişim Sürecinde Türkiye*, 80.

a requirement of its historical and traditional mission but has been wrathful of neoliberalism in recent years, has become visible again. However, will this situation be cyclical or permanent, depending on the economic crisis-welfare state relationship mentioned by Kalaycı? In short, should the state only be a "bad day friend"? Undoubtedly, on this issue, the decision-making units of the society (families, businesses and the social sector) and the decision-making units that manage the society and influence it from outside (the state, international organizations and foreign states) can defend or oppose the welfare state in line with their interests. Segments of the society with different economic positions and identities, as well as those who are in or affected by the economic crisis, can defend the welfare state for specific reasons. Moreover, the welfare state claims to be at an equal distance to everyone in terms of rights and truth. At this point, the argument that "Man should not exist for the state, but the state should exist for man" becomes important again.[172]

In addition, the economic destruction caused by the economic crises that have become more frequent in recent years has irritated all segments of the society that are directly or indirectly affected, and the possibility of a constant crisis has caused almost trauma in the society. In addition, after each crisis, the continuity/sustainability of the welfare state's existence in the economy should be reconsidered, considering the costs that the repair process of the economy imposes on society, especially on the narrow and fixed-wage segment.

Conclusion and Evaluation

Referring to the neo-classical/mainstream economic theory that capitalism was fed after the industrial revolution, it argued that in addition to the basic problems such as full and effective use of resources and economic growth and development in every economy, all other economic problems can be solved within the market/price mechanism. Within this mechanism, it is emphasized that individuals who are considered rational can make the right decisions with the guidance of prices and that balance can be achieved in the economy as well as harmony in the relations between themselves. In this process, the state has been assigned the task of creating the conditions of competition and guaranteeing the economic freedom of individuals so that the market can fulfill its functions. In addition, in order for the reins of the economy to be taken over by market forces, it was envisaged that the economic power of the state would be minimized and that it would be relegated to its primary functions and assume the guardianship of the market. In this way, although there may be imbalances

---

[172] İrfan Kalaycı, "İktisadi Kriz Karşısında 'Sürdürülebilir' Refah Devleti", *Sosyal Güvenlik Dergisi* 4, 2 (2014): 89-119, 89,93.

in the economy from time to time, there will be no need for the power of the state, as market forces can automatically maintain balance.

This set of values of capitalism, which can be considered pure or theoretical, is not implemented perfectly in any country, and its application differs in each country. The presence of the state in economic life has also varied depending on the developments in the economic history of each country. However, although the state is tried to be pushed out of the system with neo/liberal philosophy, the existence of a mixed economic model in many countries is not surprising, considering that the economic activities of the state structured within this system mostly serve the interests of capital. In this respect, we can say that capitalism, which is already built on the accumulation of capital, has the power of the state behind it at every stage of the historical development process.

In addition, in hundreds of crises in its nearly three-hundred-year history, capitalism has only been able to continue its adventure, which was interrupted by crises, because the market mechanism, which was presented as multi-functional like a wrench, did not have the ability to solve crises, as claimed. As a matter of fact, capitalism emerged from the 2008 crisis, albeit with a delay, not with the "*invisible hand*" as it did in 1929, but ironically, with the "*visible hand*" of the state, which it had been trying to weaken since 1980. In short, we must give *Caesar what is due to Caesar*; history has proven Keynes right for the second time. As Köymen stated, according to Keynes, the state should have a policy that would prevent economic crises. During periods of depression and massive unemployment, the government had to increase spending to reduce unemployment and increase demand.[173]As a matter of fact, in Krugman, free-market believers tend to see Keynesian policies in the broadest definition - the government's intense efforts to mobilize demand - as the enemy of the ground on which they stand. But they are wrong because, in a world where there is not enough demand to act, the cause of free markets will be a difficult one to implement.[174]

However, the return of the state to the economic scene in the 2010s is a different problem than in the 1930s for a simple reason: The state has never had such influence and weight as it does today. In fact, both markets were blamed for the crisis, and the weight and power of the state in the economy were questioned. In fact, the role of the state has been questioned since 1970-1980, and it seems that this will continue in the future. Its increasingly central role in economic and social life after the war initiated this questioning and debate.

---

173 Köymen, *Sermaye Birikirken*, 46

174 Paul Krugman, *Bunalım Ekonomisinin Geri Dönüşü*, haz. Neşenur Domaniç, (İstanbul: Literatür Yay., 2008), 168.

However, there is both confusion and serious disagreement between seemingly irreconcilable attitudes on this issue. So much so that some want the state to return to economic life in every form - as if it did not exist - while others want it to be liquidated, even in the place where it is least present, in the USA.[175]

On the other hand, Kindleberger and Aliber, regarding this discussion:

> "The emergence of yet another frenzy or bubble, "Should governments look for ways to restrain the climb in asset prices in order to reduce the likelihood of the upcoming financial crisis breaking out or reducing its severity?" It raises a policy question. In almost every country, a national central bank has been established as the "credit authority of last resort" to reduce the possibility of the liquidity wrinkle turning into a cash crisis..."[176]

With their evaluations, they draw attention to the experiences that necessitate the existence of the state in the economy. On this occasion, we can say that for those who believe in the correctness of completely eliminating the state from the economy, *the market, like life, does not accept* a vacuum.

In the financialization process, where financialization is already the main actor, the weight of central banks, which are directly aimed at financial markets, has increased in the economy as a whole. Especially after the 2008 crisis, another task of central banks was to ensure price stability in order to stimulate economic activities. However, as long as financial instability hangs over economies like the Sword of Damocles, central banks will be constantly on guard.[177]

In addition, it is debatable whether there are serious differences between interventionist state policies and neoliberal policies. Bu açıdan Keynesyen devletçilikle neoliberalizmin birbirlerine alternatif oluşturduklarını ileri sürmek de yanıltıcı olabilir. Moreover, capitalism could not survive without the usual support of the state as we transitioned from the twentieth century to the twenty-first century.[178]

According to Piketty, there is actually a grain of truth in both anti-market and anti-state perspectives. But in order to bring capitalism back under control, the modern state needs new tools that will ensure its deep and permanent modernization by renewing the public taxation and expenditure systems

---

[175] Piketty, Yirmibirinci Yüzyılda Kapital, 510.

[176] Kindleberger ve Aliber, *Çılgınlık, Panik, Çöküş*, 23.

[177] Arda Tunca, Dünya ekonomilerinin tepesinde Demokles'in Kılıcı: Finansal istikrarsızlık, 2023, https://www.politikyol.com/dunya-ekonomilerinin-tepesinde-demoklesin-kilici-finansal-istikrarsizlik/

[178] Wallerstein, *Tarihsel Kapitalizm*, 98-99.

because these systems have become so complex that they are difficult to understand and reduce their social and economic effectiveness.[179]

Bibliography

Aiginger, Karl. *The Current Economic Crisis:*. Working Papers, Nn. 341, Vienna: WIFO, 2009.

Akbaş, Mustafa Emre. "1800'lerin Küresel Krizleri, Büyük Depresyon ve 2008 Krizi". *İGÜ Sosyal Bilimler Dergisi,* (2017): 77-127.

Akçay, Ümit. Kriz ve Alternatifler, Son Güncelleme". *Kriz ve Alternatifler* (17 Oct. 2107), https://www.gazeteduvar.com.tr/yazarlar/2017/07/17/kriz-ve-alternatifler

Akgüç, Öztin. "Kriz,Nedeni ve Çıkış Yolları". *Muhasebe ve Finansman Dergisi,* (2009): 6-11.

Akıncılar, Murad. "Krize Teorik ve Siyasal Yaklaşım Sorunları". *Özgür Üniversite Forumu,* 1999: 52-61.

Aktan Can Coşkun ve Hüseyin Şen. "Ekonomik Kriz:Nedenler ve Çözüm Çnerileri". *Yeni Türkiye,* (2001): 1225-1230.

Alper Mumyakmaz, İ. "İktisadi Kriz mi, İktisadın Krizi mi Metodolojik Bir Tartışma". In *Sosyal,Siyasal ve Kuramsal Yönleriyle İktisadi Krizler.* Haz. Semra Buğra, Ankara: Gazi Kitabevi (2020): 5-35.

Amin, Samir. *Kapitalizmden Uygarlığa. Çev. Yağmur Dönmez ve Naim Atabağsoy* . İstanbul: Yordam Kitap, 2014.

Atbaşı, Ferda Dönmez. "Kriz, Kapitalizm ve Keynes". *Toplum ve Demokrasi.* (2009): 67-74.

Ay Hakan ve Öznur Uçar. "Üç Küresel Ekonomik Krizin Analizi". *Dokuz Eylül Üniversitesi Sosyal Bilimler Enstitüsü Dergisi,* (2015): 11-32.

Bağımsız Sosyal Bilimciler. *Türkiye'de ve Dünyada Ekonomik Bunalım 2008-2009.* İstanbul: Yordam Kitap, 2009.

Başkaya, Fikret. *Çöküş Kapitalizmin Nihai Krizi Üzerine Bir Deneme.* İstanbul: Yordam Kitabevi, 2018.

Başkaya, Fikret. "Finansal Kriz mi? Piyasacı Fundamentalizmin Çöküşü mü?". *Özgür Üniversite Forumu,* 1999: 5-18.

Başkaya, Fikret. *Küreselleşme mi Emperyalizm mi? Piyasacı Efsanenin Çöküşü.* Ankara: Ütopya, 1990.

BEA. *https://www.bea.gov/help/faq/1004.* 10 Kasım 2023.

Bernanke, Ben. "Economic Policy: Lessons from History". *https://www.federal reserve.gov /newsevents/speech/bernanke20100408a.* 2010. (erişildi: Ekim 20, 2023).

BLS. *https://data.bls.gov/pdq/SurveyOutputServlet.* 10 Kasım 2023.

Bocutoğlu, Ercan. "Krizin Makro İktisadından Makro İktisadın Krizine: Eleştirel Bir Değerlendirme". In *Küresel Bunalım ve İktisat Eğitimi.* Haz. Ercan Uygur. Ankara: İmaj, 2011, 201-221.

---

179 Piketty, *Yirmibirinci Yüzyılda Kapital,* 511.

Boratav, Korkut. *Dünyadan Türkiye'ye İktisattan Siyasete.* İstanbul: Yordam Kitap, 2015.

Boratav, Korkut. "Kriz, Direnişler ve Gelecek". *Mülkiye,* (2015): 7-12.

Çakır, Gencer. "Kriz, Finansallaşma ve "Çöküş". *Bilim ve Gelecek,* (2015): 1-11.

Çakır, Gencer. "Krizler Kapitalizmin Doğasında Vardır". *DİSKAR,* (2014): 6-19.

Celasun, Merih. "Gelişen Ekonomilerin Dış Kaynak Kullanımı, Finansal Krizler ve Türkiye Örneği,2001". *Doğu Bat Düşünce Dergisi,* (2001): 161-181.

Céspedes Gemma Cairó-İ-, Quintana David Castells. "Dimensions of the current Systemic Crisis: Capitalism in Short Circuit?". *Progress in Development Studies,* (2016): 1-23.

Çolak, Faruk Ömer. "Politik İktisatçı Kimliğiyle Keynes ve Barışın Ekonomik Sonuçları". *İktisat ve Toplum Dergis,* (2021): 32-35.

Çolak, Ömer Faruk. "1929 ve 2008 Krizinin Dinamikleri". In *Zor Zamanlarda İktisat.* Yaz. Hakan Yetkiner& Gökçer Özgür, Ankara: Efil Yayınevi, 2011, 7-30.

Cömert Hasan, ve Erinç Yeldan. "A Tale of Three Crises in Turkey: 1994, 2001 and 2008–09". *ERC Working Papers in Economics,* (2018): 1-24.

Dayton, Bruce W. "Managing Crises in the Twenty-First Century". *International Studies Review,* (2004): 165-194.

Desal, Meghnad. "Keynes ve Seksen Yıl Sonra Onun Genel Teorisi". *İktisat ve Toplum Dergisi,* (2016): 10-13.

Divitçioğlu, Sencer. *Karl Marx'da İktisadi Büyüme Marx'ın Görüşleri ve Harrod'la Karşılaştırma.* Ankara: Efil Yayınevi, 2016.

Dodig Nina and Hansjörg.Herr. "Theories of Finance and Financial Crisis - Lessons for the Great Recession". Working Paper, Berlin: Institute for International Political Economy, (2015).

Dönmez, Ferda. "Keynes ve Keynesçilik". In *Ekonomik Kurumlar ve Kavramlar Sözlüğü Eleştirel Bir Bakış.* Yaz. Aydın Ördek ve Fikret Başkaya, İstanbul: Özgür Üniversite, 2008, 675-685.

Dura, Cihan. "Ekonomik Kriz Nedir, Özellikleri Nelerdir, Nasıl Gelişir?". *www.cihandura.com/tr/makale/-EKONOMIK-KRIZ-NEDIR-OZELLIKLERINELERDIR-NASIL-GELISIR-496.* 2009. (Erişildi: Temmuz 15, 2023).

Durmuş, Mustafa. "Kapitalizmin Krizi ve Türkiye'ye Yansımaları". *Mülkiye,* (2008): 9-27.

Durmuş, Mustafa. *Kapitalizmin Krizi: Küresel Krizin Eleştirel Bir Çözümlemesi.* Ankara: Gazi Kitabevi, 2013.

Durusoy, Serap. "Kriz Sonrası Küresel Kapitalizmin Geleceği". *Alternatif Politika,* (2009): 363-389.

Eastham, Katherine, Donald Coates and Federico Allodi. "The Concept of Crisis". *Canad. Psychiat Ass. J,* (1970): 463-472.

Eğilmez, Mahfi. *Değişim Sürecinde Türkiye Osmanlı'dan Cumhuriye'e Sosyo-Ekonomik Bir Değerlendirme.* İstanbul: Remzi Kitabevi, 2018.

Eğilmez, "Mahfi. Kriz Halinde Camı Kırınız". *https://www.mahfiegilmez.com/2012/08/kriz-halinde-cam-krnz.html.* Ağustos 2012. (Erişildi: Ekim 1, 2023).

Eğilmez, Mahfi. *Küresel Finans Krizi.* İstanbul: Remzi Kitabevi, 2020.

Eğilmez, Mahfi. *Tarihsel Süreç İçinde Dünya Ekonomisi.* İstanbul: Remzi Kitabevi, 2018.

Ercan, Fuat. "Kriz: Tekrar ve Fark". In *Kriz ve Türkiye Aşınan Teoriler.* Yaz. Hale Balseven ve Fuat Ercan. İstanbul: Siyasal Kitabevi, 2013, 109-133.

Eren Ahmet Arif ve Metin Sarçoğlu. "Kapitalizmin Tarihinde Finansal Krizler: Tarih Tekerrür mü Ediyor?". *Ömer Halis Demir Üniversitesi İktisadi ve İdari Bilimler Fakültesi Dergisi,* (2017): 87-97.

Eroğlu, Ömer ve Mesut.Albeni. *Küreselleşme, Ekonomik Krizler ve Türkiye.* Isparta: Bilim Kitabevi, 2002.

Eşiyok, Bayram. "Keynesyen "Altın Çağ"dan Neoliberal Orta Çağ"a:Geriye Ne Kaldı?". *İktisat ve Toplum Dergisi,* (2016): 60-65.

Fearn-Banks, Kathleen. *Crisis Communications A Casebook Approach.* New Jersey: Lawrence Erlbaum Assocıates, Publıshers, 1966.

Galbraith, John Kenneth. *Büyük Kriz 1929.* Çev.Özkan Özdem&Elif Nihan Akbaş. İstanbul: Pegasus, 2013.

Gevorkyan, Aleksandr V. "Economic Crisis". *Weom060061,* (2015): 1-8.

Güriz, Adnan. *Kapitalist İdeoloji.* Ankara: Phoenix, 2010.

Gürkan, Tevfik. *İktisat Tarihi.* İstanbul: Der Yayınları, 2011.

Gürsoy, Melih. *Dünyada Büyük Ekonomik Krizler ve Türkiye Ekonomisine Etkileri.* İstanbul: Metis, 1989.

Hobsbwan, Eric. *Kısa 20. Yüzyıl 1914-1991 Aşırılıklar Çağı.* Çev. Yavuz Alogan. İstanbul: Sarmal, 2001.

Hoover, Herbert. *The Memoirs Of Herbert Hoover The Great Depression 1929-1941.* New York: The Macmillan Company, 1952.

Husson, Michel. *Toksik Kapitalizm.* Çev. Osman S. Binatlı. *http://gesd.free.fr/toksik.pdf.* 2008. (Erişildi: Ekim 12, 2023).

İktisat Sözlüğü. 10 Kasım 2023.

ILO. *ILO, Crisis Response, Recovery and Reconstruction Department, Geneva.* Genova: International Labour Organization, October 2001, 9.

Ingo, Schmidt, "Krizleri Kıyaslamak 1930'lar,1970'ler ve Bugün". In *Neoliberalizm ve Kriz.* Neoliberalizm ve Haz. Hakan Tanıttıran. Çev. Barış Baysal vd. İstanbul: Kalkedon, 2008, 65-79.

İşyar, Ömer Göksel. "Definition and Management of International Crises". *Perceptions,* (2008): 1-49.

Kalaycı, İrfan, Barış Aytekin ve Berna İzgi Balcı. "Krizin İktisadı – İktisadın Krizi". In *Politik İktisat, Kriz ve Kalkınma.* Yaz. İsmail Şiriner vd. İstanbul: IJOPEC Publication, 2011, 49-71.

Kalaycı, İrfan. "Euro Bölgesinde Mali Kriz ve Yeni Makro İktisadi Yönetişim". *Akdeniz İ.İ.B.F. Dergisi,* (2013): 123-149.

Kalaycı, İrfan. "Finansal Enfeksiyon ve "Aşı" Kuramı: Bir Genel Kriz Eleştirisi". *Maliye Dergisi,* (2011): 28-56.

Kalaycı, İrfan. "İktisadi Kriz Karşısında 'Sürdürülebilir' Refah Devleti". *Sosyal Güvenlik Dergisi,* (2014): 89-119.

Kalaycı, İrfan. "Finansal Kriz Konjonktürü (2007-2009) ve Küresel Ticaretin Anatomisi". *Avrasya Etüdleri.* TİKA, (2012).

Kazgan, Gülten. "2008 Küresel Krizi: Nedenleri, Etik İlkeleri ve İktisat Eğitimi". In *Küresel Bunalım ve İktisat Eğitimi.* Yaz.Ercan Uygur. Ankara: İmaj Yayınevi,, 2011, 1-35.

Keynes, John Maynard. *Genel Teori İstihdam, Faiz ve Paranın Genel Teorisi.* Çev. Uğur Selçuk Akalın. İstanbul: Kalkeden, 2010.

Kibritçioğlu, Aykut. "2008 Küresel Finans Krizi Öncesi Krizler ve Türkiye Ekonomisi". In *İktisadi Krizler ve Türkiye Ekonomisi.* Yaz. İlhan Eroğlu ve İbrahim Aydın Nadir Eroğlu. Ankara: Orion, 2015, 503-519.

Kindleberger, P. Charles and A. Robert Aliber. *Çılgınlık, Panik, Çökü:ş Finansal Krizler Tarihi.* Çev. Ümit Şensoy. Ankara: Kültür Yay., 2014.

Köse, Ayhan M., Notaka Sugawara and E.Marco Terrone. "Global Recessions". Policy Research Working Paper 9172, World Bank Group, (2020).

Köse, M. Ayhan and "Claessens. «What is a Recession?". *Finance & Development,* (2009): 52-53.

Kotil, Ahmet Emin. *Kriz ve Gelişme.* İstanbul: Derin Yayınları, 2015.

Köymen, Oya. *Sermaye Birikirken, Osmanlı, Türkiye, Dünya.* İstanbul: Yordam Kitap, 2007.

Krugman, Paul. *Bunalım Ekonomisinin Geri Dönüşü.* Çev. Neşenur Domaniç. İstanbul: Literatür, 2008.

McNally, David. "Çöküş, Kemer Sıkma ve Direniş". In *Ekonomik Kriz ve Sol.* Yaz. Greg Albo, Vivek Chibber. Çev. Umut Haskan. Haz. Leo Panich. İstanbul: Yordam Kitap, 2011, 52-79.

Milasinovic, Srdan. "Crisis and Crisis Management: A Contribution to a Conceptual & Terminological Delimination". *Megaternd Review,* (2008): 167-185.

Minsky, Hyman P. "The Financial Instability Hypothesis". Working Paper no. 74, New York: Levy Economics Institute, (1992).

Moore, G.H. "Recession or Depression?". In Business *Cycles, Inflation, and Forecasting.* Yaz. G.H. Moore. Ballınger, 1983, 19-22

NBER. "Business Cycle Dating". https://www.nber.org/research/business-cycle-dating (Erişildi: Ağustos 12, 2023).

Önder, İzzettin. "Ekonomik Kriz". In *İktisat Üzerine Düşünceler.* Yaz. İzzettin Önder. İstanbul: Yordam Kitap, 2016, 245-260.

Önder, İzzettin. "Küresel Kriz ve Türkiye Ekonomisi". *Muhasebe ve Finansman Dergisi,* (2009): 12-25.

Önder, İzzettin. "Dünya Ekonomisinde Krizlere Bakış". In *İktisat Üzerine Düşünceler.*Yaz. İzzettin Önder. İstanbul: Yordam Kitap, 2016.

Orhangazi, Özgür. "Günümüz Kapitalizminde Finansın Rolü Üzerine Birkaç Not". *İktisat ve Toplum Dergisi,* (2017): 32-39.

Özel, Hüseyin. "Genel Teori'nin 'Kararsızlığı' Üzerine". *İktisat ve Toplum Dergisi,* (2016): 42-52.

Özel, Işık. "Peki Neymiş Bu Büyük Buhran". *https://t24.com.tr/yazarlar/isik-ozel/peki-neymis-bu-buyuk-buhran,26384.* 2022. (Erişildi: Eylül 12, 2023).

Özel, Işık. "Büyük Buhranda Tango ve Çivisi Çıkan Dünya". *https://t24.com.tr/yazarlar/isik-ozel/buyuk-buhran-da-tango-ve-civisi-cikan-dunya,26478.* 3 Mayıs 2020. (Erişildi: Eylül 9, 2023).

Pamuk, Şevket. "Keynes'in Son 100 Yılda Gelişmiş Ekonomiler Üzerindeki Etkisi". *İktisat ve Toplum Dergisi,* (2016): 15-16.

Parker, Selwyn. *Büyük Çöküş.* Çev. Burcu Çekmece. Ankara: Arkadaş Yayınları, 2008.

Peicuti, Cristina. "The Great Depression and the Great Recession: A Comparative Analysis of their Analogies". *The European Journal of Comparative Economics,* (2014): 55-78.

Piketty, Thomas. *Yirmi Birinci Yüzyılda Kapital.* Çev. Hande Koça. İstanbul: Kültür Yayınları, 2015.

Roubini, Nouriel and Stephen Mihm. *Kriz Ekonomisi Dünya Ekonomisinin Çöküşü ve Geleceği.* Çev. Işıl Tezcan. İstanbul: Pegasus Yayınları, 2011.

Saad-Filho, Alfredo. *Kriz Çağı Neoliberalizm, Demokrasinin Çöküşü ve Pandemi.* Çev.Şükrü Alpagut. İstanbul: Yordam Kitap, 2022.

Sarwat, Jahan, Ahmed Saber Mahmud and Chris Papageorgiou. "What is Keynesian Economics?". *Finance & Developments.* (2014): 53-54.

Savaş, Vural Fuat. *Küresel Finans ve Makroiktisat.* İstanbul: Efil Yayınevi, 2012.

Savran, Sungur. "Bunalım, Sermayenin-Yeniden Yapılanması, Yeni Liberalizm". In *Dünya Kapitalizminin Krizi* Yaz. Sungur Savran ve Nail Atılgan. İstanbul: Belge Yay., 2009, 19-65.

Savran, Sungur. "Kapitalizmde Kriz: İktisat Teorisinde Bir Ufuk Taraması". In *Kriz ve Türkiye: Aşınan Teoriler.* Yaz. Fuat Ercan & Hale Balseven. Ankara: Siyasal Kitabevi, 2013, 39-53.

Savran, Sungur. *Kod Adı Küreselleşme: 21. Yüzyılda Emperyalizm.* İstanbul: Yordam Kitap, 2008.

Savran, Sungur. *Üçüncü Büyük Depresyon Kapitalizmin Alacakaranlığı.* İstanbul: Yordam Kitabevi, 2013.

Seabury, Chris. "Recession and Depression". *https://www.scribd.com/document/281120463/Recession-and-Depression.* (Erişildi: Ağustos 10, 2023).

Şenses, Fikret. *İktisada (Farklı Bir) Giriş.* İstanbul: İletişim Yayınları,, 2017.

Sönmez, Sinan. *Dünya Ekonomisinde Dönüşüm Sömürgecilikten Küreselleşmeye.* Ankara: İmge Yayınevi, 1998.

Sönmez, Sinan. "Liberal Paradigma ve Küresel Kriz". In *Kriz ve Türkiye Aşınan Teoriler.* Yaz. Hale Balseven ve Fuat Ercan. Ankara: Siyasal Kitabevi, 2013, 53-71.

Stiglitz, Joseph E. "The Current Economic Crisis and Lessons for Economic Theory". *Eastern Economic Journal,* (2009): 281-293.

Tabb, William K. "ABD Kapitalizminin Finansal Kriz". In *Neoliberalizm ve Kriz.* Çev. Barış Baysal vd. İstanbul: Kalkedon, 2008, 7-25.

Tonak, Ahmet. "Krizi Anlarken" *Çalışma ve Toplum Dergisi,* (2009): 29-44.

Touraıne, Alaine. *Krizden Anlamak.* Çev.Olcay Kunal. İstanbul: YKY Yayınları, 2016.

Tunca, Arda. "Dünya Ekonomilerinin Tepesinde Demokles'in Kılıcı: Finansal İstikrarsızlık". *https://www.politikyol.com/dunya-ekonomilerinin-tepesinde-demoklesin-kilici-finansal-istikrarsizlik/*. 2023. (Erişildi: Kasım 5, 2023).

Walby, Sylvia. "Crisis and Society: Developing The Theory of Crisis in the Context of COVID-19". *Global Discourse*, (2022): 498-516.

Walker, Richard. "The New Deal in Brie". *https://livingnewdeal.org/wp-content/uploads/2012/01/New-Deal-in-Brief.pdf*. 2012. (Erişildi: Kasım 11, 2023).

Wallerstein, Immanuel. *Tarihsel Kapitalizm ve Kapitalist Uygarlık*. Çev. Necmiye Alpay. İstanbul: Metis, 2021.

Yeldan, Erinç. "Büyük Durgunluğun Öğrettikleri". *İktisat ve Toplum*, (2010): 16-24.

Yeldan, Erinç. "Kapitalizmin Yeniden Finansallaşması ve Kriz: Öğrenilenler, Unutturulmak İstenenler". In *Kriz ve Türkiye Aşınan Teoriler*. Yaz. Hale Balseven ve Fuat Ercan. İstanbul: Siyasal Yay., 2013, 95-109.

Yeldan, Erinç. "Kapitalizmin Yeniden Finansallaşması ve 2007-2008 Krizi". *Çalışma ve Toplum*, (2009): 11-28.

Yeldan, Erinç. "Makroekonominin Keynes ile Sınavı". *İktisat ve Toplum Dergisi*, (2016): 28-31.

Yeldan, Erinç. "Neoliberal Küreselleşme Sürecinin Kalkınma Söylemi Üzerine Değerlendirmeler". *Praksis Dergisi*, (2011): 7.

Yılmaz, Akyüz. "Kriz, Max ve Keynes, Bölüşüm, Finansallaşma ve Ekonomik Durgunluk". *İktisat ve Toplum Dergisi*, (2016): 18-26.

Yılmaz, Ömer, Alattin Kızıltan ve Vedat Kaya. "Finansal Küreselleşme ve Para Krizleri". *Erciyes Üniversitesi İktisadi ve İdari Bilimler Fakültesi Dergisi*, (2005): 77-96.

Yılmaz, Şiir. "Dünya Ekonomisi ve Türkiye: Globalleşme, Liberalizasyon ve Kriz". In *Yerel Ekonomilerin Südürülebilir Kalkınması ve Çanakkale Örneği*. Yaz. Serdar Sayan. Ankara: TEK, 2002.

Index

A

B

C

D

E

F

G

H

I

N

O

P

Q

R

S

T

U

V

W

Y

Z

www.ingramcontent.com/pod-product-compliance
Lightning Source LLC
LaVergne TN
LVHW011629200926
848484LV00011B/2539/J
* 9 7 9 8 8 8 1 9 0 0 8 2 3 *